P9-DWI-834

35.⁰⁸
₁

RMD   21.⁰⁶

              10 —
T

ALSO BY DAVID McCULLOUGH

Truman

Brave Companions

Mornings on Horseback

The Path Between the Seas

The Great Bridge

The Johnstown Flood

David McCullough

John Adams

Simon & Schuster

NEW YORK LONDON TORONTO

SYDNEY SINGAPORE

SIMON & SCHUSTER
Rockefeller Center
1230 Avenue of the Americas, New York, NY 10020

Copyright © 2001 by David McCullough
Map on pages 184–185 copyright © 2001 by David Cain

All rights reserved, including the right of
reproduction in whole or in part in any form.

SIMON & SCHUSTER and colophon are registered
trademarks of Simon & Schuster, Inc.

Designed by Amy Hill

Manufactured in the United States of America

27   29   30   28

Library of Congress Cataloging-in-Publication Data
McCullough, David G.
John Adams / David McCullough.
p.   cm.
Includes bibliographical references (p.) and index.
1. Adams, John, 1735–1826.   2. Presidents—United States—Biography.
3. United States—Politics and government—1775–1783.
4. United States—Politics and government—1783–1809.   I. Title.
E322.M38   2001   973.4'4'092—dc21   [B]   2001027010
ISBN 0-684-81363-7

ILLUSTRATIONS. Front endpaper: Birthplaces of John Adams and
John Quincy Adams, by Eliza Susan Quincy, 1822. Back endpaper:
View of the Village of Quincy with First Church, by Eliza Susan Quincy,
1822. Frontispiece: Study sketch of John Adams by John Singleton
Copley. Page 15: Independence Square, looking east from Sixth Street.
Page 165: Keizersgracht No. 529 (center), Amsterdam. Page 387:
President's House, Washington, ca. 1800. Credits for these illustrations
and those in the inserts will be found on page 701.

For our sons
David, William, and Geoffrey

Contents

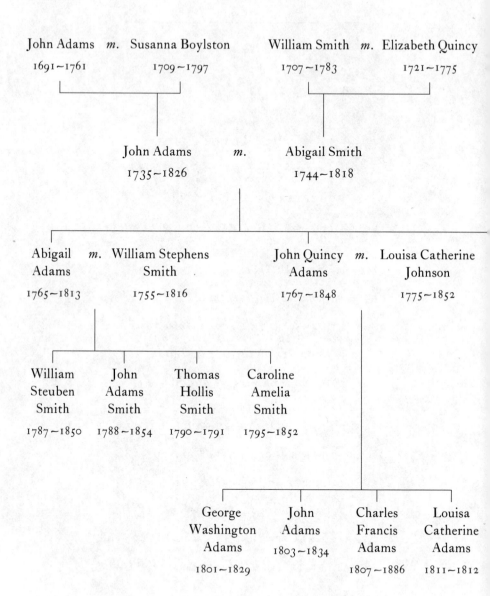

John Adams   *m.*   Susanna Boylston
1691~1761   1709~1797

William Smith   *m.*   Elizabeth Quincy
1707~1783   1721~1775

John Adams   *m.*   Abigail Smith
1735~1826   1744~1818

Abigail Adams   *m.*   William Stephens Smith
1765~1813   1755~1816

John Quincy Adams   *m.*   Louisa Catherine Johnson
1767~1848   1775~1852

William Steuben Smith
1787~1850

John Adams Smith
1788~1854

Thomas Hollis Smith
1790~1791

Caroline Amelia Smith
1795~1852

George Washington Adams
1801~1829

John Adams
1803~1834

Charles Francis Adams
1807~1886

Louisa Catherine Adams
1811~1812

Adams Family Tree

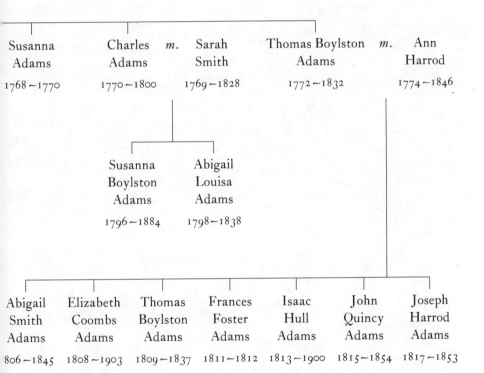

Susanna Adams	Charles Adams	m.	Sarah Smith	Thomas Boylston Adams	m.	Ann Harrod
1768~1770	1770~1800		1769~1828	1772~1832		1774~1846

Susanna Boylston Adams	Abigail Louisa Adams
1796~1884	1798~1838

Abigail Smith Adams	Elizabeth Coombs Adams	Thomas Boylston Adams	Frances Foster Adams	Isaac Hull Adams	John Quincy Adams	Joseph Harrod Adams
806~1845	1808~1903	1809~1837	1811~1812	1813~1900	1815~1854	1817~1853

We live, my dear soul, in an age of trial. What will be the consequence, I know not.

~John Adams to Abigail Adams, 1774

PART I

Revolution

But what do we mean by the American Revolution? Do we mean the American war? The Revolution was effected before the war commenced. The Revolution was in the minds and hearts of the people.

—John Adams

I have heard of one Mr. Adams but who is the other?

—King George III

CHAPTER ONE

THE ROAD TO PHILADELPHIA

*You cannot be, I know, nor do I wish to see you, an
inactive spectator.... We have too many high
sounding words, and too few actions that correspond
with them.*

—Abigail Adams

I

In the cold, nearly colorless light of a New England winter, two men on horseback traveled the coast road below Boston, heading north. A foot or more of snow covered the landscape, the remnants of a Christmas storm that had blanketed Massachusetts from one end of the province to the other. Beneath the snow, after weeks of severe cold, the ground was frozen solid to a depth of two feet. Packed ice in the road, ruts as hard as iron, made the going hazardous, and the riders, mindful of the horses, kept at a walk.

Nothing about the harsh landscape differed from other winters. Nor was there anything to distinguish the two riders, no signs of rank or title, no liveried retinue bringing up the rear. It might have been any year and they could have been anybody braving the weather for any number of reasons. Dressed as they were in heavy cloaks, their hats pulled low against the wind, they were barely distinguishable even from each other, except that the older, stouter of the two did most of the talking.

He was John Adams of Braintree and he loved to talk. He was a known talker. There were some, even among his admirers, who wished he talked less. He himself wished he talked less, and he had particular regard for those, like General Washington, who somehow managed great reserve under almost any circumstance.

John Adams was a lawyer and a farmer, a graduate of Harvard College, the husband of Abigail Smith Adams, the father of four children. He was forty years old and he was a revolutionary.

Dismounted, he stood five feet seven or eight inches tall—about "middle size" in that day—and though verging on portly, he had a straight-up, square-shouldered stance and was, in fact, surprisingly fit and solid. His hands were the hands of a man accustomed to pruning his own trees, cutting his own hay, and splitting his own firewood.

In such bitter cold of winter, the pink of his round, clean-shaven, very English face would all but glow, and if he were hatless or without a wig, his high forehead and thinning hairline made the whole of the face look rounder still. The hair, light brown in color, was full about the ears. The chin was firm, the nose sharp, almost birdlike. But it was the dark, perfectly arched brows and keen blue eyes that gave the face its vitality. Years afterward, recalling this juncture in his life, he would describe himself as looking rather like a short, thick Archbishop of Canterbury.

As befitting a studious lawyer from Braintree, Adams was a "plain dressing" man. His oft-stated pleasures were his family, his farm, his books and writing table, a convivial pipe and cup of coffee (now that tea was no longer acceptable), or preferably a glass of good Madeira.

In the warm seasons he relished long walks and time alone on horseback. Such exercise, he believed, roused "the animal spirits" and "dispersed melancholy." He loved the open meadows of home, the "old acquaintances" of rock ledges and breezes from the sea. From his doorstep to the water's edge was approximately a mile.

He was a man who cared deeply for his friends, who, with few exceptions, were to be his friends for life, and in some instances despite severe strains. And to no one was he more devoted than to his wife, Abigail. She was his "Dearest Friend," as he addressed her in letters—his "best, dearest, worthiest, wisest friend in the world"—while to her he was "the tenderest of husbands," her "good man."

John Adams was also, as many could attest, a great-hearted, persevering man of uncommon ability and force. He had a brilliant mind. He was honest and everyone knew it. Emphatically independent by nature, hardworking, frugal—all traits in the New England tradition—he was anything but cold or laconic as supposedly New Englanders were. He could be high-spirited and affectionate, vain, cranky, impetuous, self-absorbed, and fiercely stubborn; passionate, quick to anger, and all-forgiving; generous and entertaining. He was blessed with great courage and good humor, yet subject to spells of despair, and especially when separated from his family or during periods of prolonged inactivity.

Ambitious to excel—to make himself known—he had nonetheless recognized at an early stage that happiness came not from fame and fortune, "and all such things," but from "an habitual contempt of them," as he wrote. He prized the Roman ideal of honor, and in this, as in much else, he and Abigail were in perfect accord. Fame without honor, in her view, would be "like a faint meteor gliding through the sky, shedding only transient light."

As his family and friends knew, Adams was both a devout Christian and an independent thinker, and he saw no conflict in that. He was hard-headed and a man of "sensibility," a close observer of human folly as displayed in everyday life and fired by an inexhaustible love of books and scholarly reflection. He read Cicero, Tacitus, and others of his Roman heroes in Latin, and Plato and Thucydides in the original Greek, which he considered the supreme language. But in his need to fathom the "labyrinth" of human nature, as he said, he was drawn to Shakespeare and Swift, and likely to carry Cervantes or a volume of English poetry with him on his journeys. "You will never be alone with a poet in your pocket," he would tell his son Johnny.

John Adams was not a man of the world. He enjoyed no social standing. He was an awkward dancer and poor at cards. He never learned to flatter. He owned no ships or glass factory as did Colonel Josiah Quincy, Braintree's leading citizen. There was no money in his background, no Adams fortune or elegant Adams homestead like the Boston mansion of John Hancock.

It was in the courtrooms of Massachusetts and on the printed page, principally in the newspapers of Boston, that Adams had distinguished himself. Years of riding the court circuit and his brilliance before the bar had brought him wide recognition and respect. And of greater consequence in recent years had been his spirited determination and eloquence in the cause of American rights and liberties.

That he relished the sharp conflict and theater of the courtroom, that he loved the esteem that came with public life, no less than he loved "my farm, my family and goose quill," there is no doubt, however frequently he protested to the contrary. His desire for "distinction" was too great. Patriotism burned in him like a blue flame. "I have a zeal at my heart for my country and her friends which I cannot smother or conceal," he told Abigail, warning that it could mean privation and unhappiness for his family unless regulated by cooler judgment than his own.

In less than a year's time, as a delegate to the Continental Congress at Philadelphia, he had emerged as one of the most "sensible and forcible" figures in the whole patriot cause, the "Great and Common Cause," his influence exceeding even that of his better-known kinsman, the ardent Boston patriot Samuel Adams.

He was a second cousin of Samuel Adams, but "possessed of another species of character," as his Philadelphia friend Benjamin Rush would explain. "He saw the whole of a subject at a glance, and . . . was equally fearless of men and of the consequences of a bold assertion of his opinion. . . . He was a stranger to dissimulation."

It had been John Adams, in the aftermath of Lexington and Concord, who rose in the Congress to speak of the urgent need to save the New England army facing the British at Boston and in the same speech called on Congress to put the Virginian George Washington at the head of the army. That was now six months past. The general had since established a command at Cambridge, and it was there that Adams was headed. It was his third trip in a week to Cambridge, and the beginning of a much longer undertaking by horseback. He would ride on to Philadelphia, a journey of nearly 400 miles that he had made before, though never in such punishing weather or at so perilous an hour for his country.

The man riding with him was Joseph Bass, a young shoemaker and Braintree neighbor hired temporarily as servant and traveling companion.

The day was Wednesday, January 24, 1776. The temperature, according to records kept by Adams's former professor of science at Harvard, John Winthrop, was in the low twenties. At the least, the trip would take two weeks, given the condition of the roads and Adams's reluctance to travel on the Sabbath.

TO ABIGAIL ADAMS, who had never been out of Massachusetts, the province of Pennsylvania was "that far country," unimaginably distant, and their separations, lasting months at a time, had become extremely difficult for her.

"Winter makes its approaches fast," she had written to John in November. "I hope I shall not be obliged to spend it without my dearest friend. . . . I have been like a nun in a cloister ever since you went away."

He would never return to Philadelphia without her, he had vowed in a letter from his lodgings there. But they each knew better, just as each understood the importance of having Joseph Bass go with him. The young man was a tie with home, a familiar home-face. Once Adams had resettled in Philadelphia, Bass would return home with the horses, and bring also whatever could be found of the "common small" necessities impossible to obtain now, with war at the doorstep.

Could Bass bring her a bundle of pins? Abigail had requested earlier, in the bloody spring of 1775. She was entirely understanding of John's "arduous task." Her determination that he play his part was quite as strong as his own. They were of one and the same spirit. "You cannot be, I know, nor do I wish to see you, an inactive spectator," she wrote at her kitchen table. "We have too many high sounding words, and too few actions that correspond with them." Unlike the delegates at Philadelphia, she and the children were confronted with the reality of war every waking hour. For though British troops were bottled up in Boston, the British fleet commanded the harbor and the sea and thus no town by the shore was safe from attack. Those Braintree families who were able to leave had already packed and moved inland, out of harm's way. Meanwhile, shortages of sugar, coffee, pepper, shoes, and ordinary pins were worse than he had any idea.

"The cry for pins is so great that what we used to buy for 7 shillings and six pence are now 20 shillings and not to be had for that." A bundle of pins contained six thousand, she explained. These she could sell for hard money or use for barter.

There had been a rush of excitement when the British sent an expedition to seize hay and livestock on one of the islands offshore. "The alarm flew [like] lightning," Abigail reported, "men from all parts came flocking down till 2,000 were collected." The crisis had passed, but not her state of nerves, with the house so close to the road and the comings and goings of soldiers. They stopped at her door for food and slept on her kitchen floor. Pewter spoons were melted for bullets in her fireplace.

"Sometimes refugees from Boston tired and fatigued, seek an asylum for a day or night, a week," she wrote to John. "You can hardly imagine how we live."

"Pray don't let Bass forget my pins," she reminded him again. "I endeavor to live in the most frugal manner possible, but I am many times distressed."

The day of the battle of Bunker Hill, June 17, 1775, the thunder of the bombardment had been terrifying, even at the distance of Braintree. Earlier, in April, when news came of Lexington and Concord, John, who was at home at the time, had saddled his horse and gone to see for himself, riding for miles along the route of the British march, past burned-out houses and scenes of extreme distress. He knew then what war meant, what the British meant, and warned Abigail that in case of danger she and the children must "fly to the woods." But she was as intent to see for herself as he, and with the bombardment at Bunker Hill ringing in her ears, she had taken seven-year-old Johnny by the hand and hurried up the road to the top of nearby Penn's Hill. From a granite outcropping that breached the summit like the hump of a whale, they could see the smoke of battle rising beyond Boston, ten miles up the bay.

It was the first all-out battle of the war. "How many have fallen we know not," she wrote that night. "The constant roar of the cannon is so distressing that we cannot eat, drink, or sleep."

Their friend Joseph Warren had been killed at Bunker Hill, Abigail reported in another letter. A handsome young physician and leading patriot allied with Samuel Adams and Paul Revere, Warren had been one of the worthiest men of the province. John had known him since the smallpox epidemic of 1764, when John had gone to Boston to be inoculated. Now Joseph Warren was dead at age thirty-four, shot through the face, his body horribly mutilated by British bayonets.

"My bursting heart must find vent at my pen," Abigail told her absent husband.

THE ROUTE JOHN ADAMS and his young companion would take to Philadelphia that January of 1776 was the same as he had traveled to the First Continental Congress in the summer of 1774. They would travel the

Post Road west across Massachusetts as far as Springfield on the Connecticut River, there cross by ferry and swing south along the west bank, down the valley into Connecticut. At Wethersfield they would leave the river for the road to New Haven, and from New Haven on, along the Connecticut shore—through Fairfield, Norwalk, Stamford, Greenwich—they would be riding the New York Post Road. At New York, horses and riders would be ferried over the Hudson River to New Jersey, where they would travel "as fine a road as ever trod," in the opinion of John Adams, whose first official position in Braintree had been surveyor of roads. Three more ferry crossings, at Hackensack, Newark, and New Brunswick, would put them on a straightaway ride to the little college town of Princeton. Then came Trenton and a final ferry crossing over the Delaware to Pennsylvania. In another twenty miles they would be in sight of Philadelphia.

All told, they would pass through more than fifty towns in five provinces—some twenty towns in Massachusetts alone—stopping several times a day to eat, sleep, or tend the horses. With ice clogging the rivers, there was no estimating how long delays might be at ferry crossings.

Making the journey in 1774, Adams had traveled in style, with the full Massachusetts delegation, everyone in a state of high expectation. He had been a different man then, torn between elation and despair over what might be expected of him. It had been his first chance to see something of the world. His father had lived his entire life in Braintree, and no Adams had ever taken part in public life beyond Braintree. He himself had never set foot out of New England, and many days he suffered intense torment over his ability to meet the demands of the new role to be played. Politics did not come easily to him. He was too independent by nature and his political experience amounted to less than a year's service in the Massachusetts legislature. But was there anyone of sufficient experience or ability to meet the demands of the moment?

"I wander alone, and ponder. I muse, I mope, I ruminate," he wrote in the seclusion of his diary. "We have not men fit for the times. We are deficient in genius, education, in travel, fortune—in everything. I feel unutterable anxiety."

He must prepare for "a long journey indeed," he had told Abigail.

"But if the length of the journey was all, it would be no burden. . . . Great things are wanted to be done."

He had worried over how he might look in such company and what clothes to take.

> I think it will be necessary to make me up a couple of pieces of new linen. I am told they wash miserably at N[ew] York, the Jerseys, and Philadelphia, too, in comparison of Boston, and am advised to carry a great deal of linen.
>
> Whether to make me a suit of new clothes at Boston or to make them at Philadelphia, and what to make I know not.

Still, the prospect of a gathering of such historic portent stirred him as nothing ever had. "It is to be a school of political prophets I suppose—a nursery of American statesmen," he wrote to a friend, James Warren of Plymouth. "May it thrive and prosper and flourish and from this fountain may there issue streams, which shall gladden all the cities and towns in North America, forever."

There had been a rousing send-off in Boston, on August 10, 1774, and in full view of British troops. Samuel Adams, never a fancy dresser, had appeared in a stunning new red coat, new wig, silver-buckled shoes, gold knee buckles, the best silk hose, a spotless new cocked hat on his massive head, and carrying a gold-headed cane, all gifts from the Sons of Liberty. It was thought that as leader of the delegation he should look the part. In addition, they had provided "a little purse" for expenses.

It had been a triumphal, leisurely journey of nearly three weeks, with welcoming parties riding out to greet them at town after town. They were feted and toasted, prayers were said, church bells rang. Silas Deane, a Connecticut delegate who joined the procession, assured John Adams that the Congress was to be the grandest, most important assembly ever held in America. At New Haven "every bell was clanging," people were crowding at doors and windows "as if to see a coronation."

In New York they were shown the sights—City Hall, the college, and at Bowling Green, at the foot of Broadway, the gilded equestrian statue of King George III, which had yet to be pulled from its pedestal by an angry mob. The grand houses and hospitality were such as Adams had never known, even if, as a self-respecting New Englander, he thought

New Yorkers lacking in decorum. "They talk very loud, very fast, and altogether," he observed. "If they ask you a question, before you can utter three words of your answer, they will break out upon you again—and talk away."

Truly he was seeing the large world, he assured Abigail in a letter from the tavern at Princeton, a day's ride from Philadelphia. "Tomorrow we reach the theater of action. God Almighty grant us wisdom and virtue sufficient for the high trust that is devolved upon us."

But that had been nearly two years past. It had been high summer, green and baking hot under summer skies, an entirely different time that now seemed far past, so much had happened since. There had been no war then, no blood had been spilled at Lexington, Concord, and Bunker Hill. Now fully twenty regiments of red-coated British regulars occupied Boston under General William Howe. British warships, some of 50 guns, lay at anchor in Boston Harbor, while American forces outside the city had become perilously thin.

In the late summer and fall of 1775, the "bloody flux," epidemic dysentery, had ripped through their ranks. Adams's youngest brother, Elihu, a captain of militia, camped beside the Charles River at Cambridge, was stricken and died, leaving a wife and three children. Nor was Braintree spared the violent epidemic. For Abigail, then thirty years old, it had been the worst ordeal of her life.

"Such is the distress of the neighborhood that I can scarcely find a well person to assist me in looking after the sick . . . so mortal a time the oldest man does not remember," she had lamented in a letter to John. "As to politics I know nothing about them. I have wrote as much as I am able to, being very weak."

"Mrs. Randall has lost her daughter, Mrs. Bracket hers, Mr. Thomas Thayer his wife," she reported. "I know of eight this week who have been buried in this town." Parson Wibird was so ill he could scarcely take a step. "We have been four sabbaths without any meeting." Their three-year-old Tommy was so wretchedly sick that "[were] you to look upon him you would not know him." She was constantly scrubbing the house with hot vinegar.

"Woe follows woe, one affliction treads upon the heel of another," she wrote. Some families had lost three, four, and five children. Some families were entirely gone.

The strong clarity of her handwriting, the unhesitating flow of her pen across the paper, line after line, seemed at odds with her circumstances. Rarely was a word crossed out or changed. It was as if she knew exactly what was in her heart and how she wished to express it—as if the very act of writing, of forming letters, in her distinctive angular fashion, keeping every line straight, would somehow help maintain her balance, validate her own being in such times.

She had begun signing herself "Portia," after the long-suffering, virtuous wife of the Roman statesman Brutus. If her "dearest friend" was to play the part of a Roman hero, so would she.

Her mother lay mortally ill in neighboring Weymouth. When, on October 1, 1775, her mother died, Abigail wrote to John, "You often expressed your anxiety over me when you left me before, surrounded with terrors, but my trouble then was as the small dust in the balance compared to what I have since endured."

In addition to tending her children, she was nursing a desperately ill servant named Patty. The girl had become "the most shocking object my eyes ever beheld . . . [and] continuously desirous of my being with her the little while she expects to live." It was all Abigail could do to remain in the same house. When Patty died on October 9, she "made the fourth corpse that was this day committed to the ground."

Correspondence was maddeningly slow and unreliable. In late October she wrote to say she had not had a line from John in a month and that in his last letter he had made no mention of the six she had written to him. "'Tis only in my night visions that I know anything about you." Yet in that time he had written seven letters to her, including one mourning the loss of her mother and asking for news of "poor, distressed" Patty.

Heartsick, searching for an answer to why such evil should "befall a city and a people," Abigail had pondered whether it could be God's punishment for the sin of slavery.

AT CAMBRIDGE THE MORNING of the bitterly cold first day of the new year, 1776, George Washington had raised the new Continental flag with thirteen stripes before his headquarters and announced that the new army was now "entirely continental." But for days afterward, their enlistments up, hundreds, thousands of troops, New England militia, started for home. Replacements had to be found, an immensely difficult and potentially perilous changing of the guard had to be carried off, one army moving out, another moving in, all in the bitter winds and snow of winter and in such fashion as the enemy would never know.

"It is not in the pages of history, perhaps, to furnish a case like ours," Washington informed John Hancock, president of the Continental Congress. Hardly 5,000 colonial troops were fit for duty. Promises of men, muskets, powder, and urgently needed supplies never materialized. Blankets and linen for bandages were "greatly wanted." Firewood was in short supply. With smallpox spreading in Boston, the British command had allowed pathetic columns of the ill-clad, starving poor of Boston to come pouring out of town and into the American lines, many of them sick, and all in desperate need of food and shelter.

"The reflection on my situation and that of this army produces many an unhappy hour when all around me are wrapped in sleep," wrote Washington, who had never before commanded anything larger than a regiment.

The night of January 8, Washington had ordered a brief American assault on Charlestown, largely to keep the British guessing. Adams, at home at his desk writing a letter, was brought to his feet by the sudden crash of the guns, "a very hot fire" of artillery that lasted half an hour and lit the sky over Braintree's north common. Whether American forces were on the attack or defense, he could not tell. "But in either case, I rejoice," he wrote, taking up his pen again, "for defeat appears to me preferable to total inaction."

As it was, Washington saw his situation to be so precarious that the only choice was an all-out attack on Boston, and he wrote to tell Adams, "I am exceedingly desirous of consulting you." As a former delegate to Philadelphia, Washington understood the need to keep Congress informed. Earlier, concerned whether his authority reached beyond Boston to the defense of New York, he had asked Adams for an opinion, and Adams's reply had been characteristically unhesitating and unambiguous: "Your commission constitutes you commander of all the forces . . . and you are vested with full power and authority to act as you shall think for the good and welfare of the service."

No one in Congress had impressed Adams more. On the day he had called on his fellow delegates to put their colleague, "the gentleman from

Virginia," in command at Boston, Washington, out of modesty, had left the chamber, while a look of mortification, as Adams would tell the story, filled the face of John Hancock, who had hoped he would be chosen. Washington was virtuous, brave, and in his new responsibilities, "one of the most important characters in the world," Adams had informed Abigail. "The liberties of America depend upon him in great degree." Later, when she met Washington at a Cambridge reception, Abigail thought John had not said half enough in praise of him.

A council of war with the commander and his generals convened January 16 in the parlor of the large house on Brattle Street, Cambridge, that served as Washington's headquarters. With others of the Massachusetts congressional delegation still at Philadelphia, Adams was the only member of Congress present as Washington made the case for an attack on Boston, by sending his troops across the frozen bay. But the generals flatly rejected the plan and it was put aside.

Two days later, Adams was summoned again. Devastating news had arrived by dispatch rider. An American assault on Quebec led by Colonels Richard Montgomery and Benedict Arnold had failed. The "gallant Montgomery" was dead, "brave Arnold" was wounded. It was a crushing moment for Washington and for John Adams. Congress had ordered the invasion of Canada, the plan was Washington's own, and the troops were mostly New Englanders.

As a young man, struggling over what to make of his life, Adams had often pictured himself as a soldier. Only the previous spring, when Washington appeared in Congress resplendent in the blue-and-buff uniform of a Virginia militia officer, Adams had written to Abigail, "Oh that I was a soldier!" He was reading military books. "Everybody must and will be a soldier," he told her. On the morning Washington departed Philadelphia to assume command at Boston, he and others of the Massachusetts delegation had traveled a short way with the general and his entourage, to a rousing accompaniment of fifes and drums, Adams feeling extremely sorry for himself for having to stay behind to tend what had become the unglamorous labors of Congress. "I, poor creature, worn out with scribbling for my bread and my liberty, low in spirits and weak in health, must leave others to wear the laurels."

But such waves of self-pity came and went, as Abigail knew, and when in need of sympathy, it was to her alone that he would appeal. He was not a man to back down or give up, not one to do anything other than what he saw to be his duty. What in another time and society might be taken as platitudes about public service were to both John and Abigail Adams a lifelong creed. And in this bleakest of hours, heading for Cambridge, and on to Philadelphia, Adams saw his way clearer and with greater resolve than ever in his life. It was a road he had been traveling for a long time.

I I

AT THE CENTER OF BRAINTREE, Massachusetts, and central to the town's way of life, was the meetinghouse, the First Church, with its bell tower and graveyard on the opposite side of the road. From the door of the house where John Adams had said goodbye to wife and children that morning, to the church, was less than a mile. Riding north out of town, he passed the snow-covered graveyard on the left, the church on the right.

He had been born in the house immediately adjacent to his own, a nearly duplicate farmer's cottage belonging to his father. He had been baptized in the church where his father was a deacon, and he had every expectation that when his time came he would go to his final rest in the same ground where his father and mother lay, indeed where leaning headstones marked the graves of the Adams line going back four generations. When he referred to himself as John Adams of Braintree, it was not in a manner of speaking.

The first of the line, Henry Adams of Barton St. David in Somersetshire, England, with his wife Edith Squire and nine children—eight sons and a daughter—had arrived in Braintree in the year 1638, in the reign of King Charles I, nearly a century before John Adams was born. They were part of the great Puritan migration, Dissenters from the Church of England who, in the decade following the founding of the Massachusetts Bay Colony in 1630, crossed the North Atlantic intent on making a new City of God, some twenty thousand people, most of whom came as families. Only one, the seventh and youngest of Henry Adams's eight sons remained in Braintree. He was Joseph, and he was succeeded by a second Joseph—one of Henry's eighty-nine grandchildren!—who married Hannah Bass, a granddaughter of John and Priscilla Alden, and they had eleven children, of whom one was another John, born in 1691.

They were people who earned their daily bread by the work of their hands. The men were all farmers who, through the long winters, in New England fashion, worked at other trades for "hard money," which was always scarce. The first Henry Adams and several of his descendants were maltsters, makers of malt from barley for use in baking or brewing beer, a trade carried over from England. The first John Adams, remembered as Deacon John, was a farmer and shoemaker, a man of "sturdy, unostentatious demeanor," who, like his father, "played the part of a solid citizen," as tithing man, constable, lieutenant in the militia, selectman, and ultimately church deacon, taking his place on the deacon's bench before the pulpit.

In 1734, in October, the golden time of year on the Massachusetts shore, Deacon John Adams, at age forty-three, married Susanna Boylston of Brookline. She was twenty-five, and from a family considered of higher social standing than that of her husband. Nothing written in her own hand would survive—no letters, diaries, or legal papers with her signature—nor any correspondence addressed to her by any of her family, and so, since it is also known that letters were frequently read aloud to her, there is reason to believe that Susanna Boylston Adams was illiterate.

One year later, on October 19, 1735, by the Old Style calendar, their first child, a son, was born and given his father's name. When England adopted the Gregorian calendar in 1752, October 19 became October 30.

"What has preserved this race of Adamses in all their ramifications in such numbers, health, peace, comfort, and mediocrity?" this firstborn son of Deacon John would one day write to Benjamin Rush. "I believe it is religion, without which they would have been rakes, fops, sots, gamblers, starved with hunger, or frozen with cold, scalped by Indians, etc., etc., etc., been melted away and disappeared. . . ." In truth, he was extremely proud of his descent from "a line of virtuous, independent New England farmers." That virtue and independence were among the highest of mortal attainments, John Adams never doubted. The New England farmer was his own man who owned his own land, a freeholder, and thus the equal of anyone.

The Braintree of Adams's boyhood was a quiet village of scattered houses and small neighboring farmsteads strung along the old coast road, the winding main thoroughfare from Boston to Plymouth, just back from the very irregular south shore of Massachusetts Bay. The setting was particularly picturesque, with orchards, stone walls, meadows of salt hay, and broad marshlands through which meandered numerous brooks and the Neponset River. From the shoreline the land sloped gently upward to granite outcroppings and hills, including Penn's Hill, the highest promontory, close by the Adams farm. Offshore the bay was dotted with small islands, some wooded, some used for grazing sheep. Recalling his childhood in later life, Adams wrote of the unparalleled bliss of roaming the open fields and woodlands of the town, of exploring the creeks, hiking the beaches, "of making and sailing boats . . . swimming, skating, flying kites and shooting marbles, bat and ball, football . . . wrestling and sometimes boxing," shooting at crows and ducks, and "running about to quiltings and frolics and dances among the boys and girls." The first fifteen years of his life, he said, "went off like a fairytale."

The community numbered perhaps 2,000 people. There was one other meetinghouse—a much smaller, more recent Anglican church—a schoolhouse, gristmill, village store, blacksmith shop, granite quarry, a half dozen or more taverns and, in a section called Germantown, Colonel Quincy's glass factory. With no newspaper in town, news from Boston and the world beyond came from travelers on the coast road, no communication moving faster than a horse and rider. But within the community itself, news of nearly any kind, good or bad, traveled rapidly. People saw each other at church, town meeting, in the mill, or at the taverns. Independent as a Braintree farmer and his family may have been, they were not isolated.

The Adams homestead, the farmhouse at the foot of Penn's Hill where young John was born and raised, was a five-room New England saltbox, the simplest, most commonplace kind of dwelling. It had been built in 1681, and built strongly around a massive brick chimney. Its timbers were of hand-hewn oak, its inner walls of brick, these finished on the inside with lath and plaster and faced on the exterior with pine clapboard. There were three rooms and two great fireplaces at ground level, and two rooms above. A narrow stairway tucked against the chimney,

immediately inside the front door, led to the second floor. The windows
had twenty-four panes ("12-over-12") and wooden shutters. There were
outbuildings and a good-sized barn to the rear, fields and orchard, and
through a broad meadow flowed "beautiful, winding" Fresh Brook, as
Adams affectionately described it. The well, for household use, was just
out the front door. And though situated "as near as might be" to the
road, the house was "fenced" by a stone wall, as was the somewhat older
companion house that stood forty paces apart on the property, the house
John and Abigail moved into after they were married and from which he
departed on the winter morning in 1776. The one major difference
between the two buildings was that the house of Adams's boyhood sat at
an angle to the road, while the other faced it squarely. Across the road, in
the direction of the sea, lay open fields.

In the dry spells of summer, dust from the road blew in the open windows of both houses with every passing horse or wagon. From June to
September, the heat in the upstairs bedrooms could be murderous. In
winter, even with logs blazing in huge kitchen fireplaces, women wore
heavy shawls and men sat in overcoats, while upstairs any water left in
the unheated rooms turned to ice.

In most of the essentials of daily life, as in their way of life, Adams's
father and mother lived no differently than had their fathers and mothers, or those who preceded them. The furnishings Adams grew up with
were of the plainest kind—a half dozen ordinary wooden chairs, a table,
several beds, a looking glass or two. There was a Bible, possibly a few
other books on religious subjects. Three silver spoons—one large, two
small—counted prominently as family valuables. Clothes and other personal possessions were modest and time-worn. As one of the Adams line
would write, "A hat would descend from father to son, and for fifty years
make its regular appearance at meeting."

Small as the house was, its occupancy was seldom limited to the immediate family. Besides father and mother, three sons, and a hired girl, there
was nearly always an Adams or Boylston cousin, aunt, uncle, grandpar-
ent, or friend staying the night. Men from town would stop in after dark
to talk town business or church matters with Deacon John.

With the short growing season, the severe winters and stony fields, the
immemorial uncertainties of farming, life was not easy and survival
never taken for granted. One learned early in New England about the

battle of life. Father and mother were hardworking and frugal of necessity, as well as by principle. "Let frugality and industry be our virtues,"
John Adams advised Abigail concerning the raising of their own children.
"Fire them with ambition to be useful," he wrote, echoing what had been
learned at home.

About his mother, Adams would have comparatively little to say,
beyond that he loved her deeply—she was his "honored and beloved
mother"—and that she was a highly principled woman of strong will,
strong temper, and exceptional energy, all traits he shared though this he
did not say. Of his father, however, he could hardly say enough. There
were scarcely words to express the depth of his gratitude for the kindnesses his father had shown him, the admiration he felt for his father's
integrity. His father was "the honestest man" John Adams ever knew.
"In wisdom, piety, benevolence and charity in proportion to his education and sphere of life, I have never known his superior," Adams would
write long afterward, by which time he had come to know the most
prominent men of the age on two sides of the Atlantic. His father was his
idol. It was his father's honesty, his father's independent spirit and love
of country, Adams said, that were his lifelong inspiration.

A good-looking, active boy, if small for his age, he was unusually sensitive to criticism but also quickly responsive to praise, as well as being
extremely bright, which his father saw early, and decided he must go to
Harvard to become a minister. An elder brother of Deacon John, Joseph
Adams, who graduated from Harvard in 1710, had become a minister
with a church in New Hampshire. Further, Deacon John himself, for as
little education as he had had, wrote in a clear hand and had, as he said,
"an admiration of learning."

Taught to read at home, the boy went first and happily to a dame
school—lessons for a handful of children in the kitchen of a neighbor,
with heavy reliance on *The New England Primer*. ("He who ne'er learns
his ABC, forever will a blockhead be.") But later at the tiny local schoolhouse, subjected to a lackluster "churl" of a teacher who paid him no
attention, he lost all interest. He cared not for books or study, and saw no
sense in talk of college. He wished only to be a farmer, he informed his
father.

That being so, said Deacon John not unkindly, the boy could come
along to the creek with him and help cut thatch. Accordingly, as Adams

would tell the story, father and son set off the next morning and "with great humor" his father kept him working through the day.

> At night at home, he said, "Well, John, are you satisfied with being a farmer?" Though the labor had been very hard and very muddy, I answered, "I like it very well, sir."
> "Aya, but I don't like it so well: so you will go back to school today." I went but was not so happy as among the creek thatch.

Later, when he told his father it was his teacher he disliked, not the books, and that he wished to go to another school, his father immediately took his side and wasted no time with further talk. John was enrolled the next day in a private school down the road where, kindly treated by a schoolmaster named Joseph Marsh, he made a dramatic turn and began studying in earnest.

A small textbook edition of Cicero's *Orations* became one of his earliest, proudest possessions, as he affirmed with the note "John Adams Book 1749/50" written a half dozen times on the title page.

In little more than a year, at age fifteen, he was pronounced "fitted for college," which meant Harvard, it being the only choice. Marsh, himself a Harvard graduate, agreed to accompany John to Cambridge to appear for the usual examination before the president and masters of the college. But on the appointed morning Marsh pleaded ill and told John he must go alone. The boy was thunderstruck, terrified; but picturing his father's grief and the disappointment of both father and teacher, he "collected resolution enough to proceed," and on his father's horse rode off down the road alone, suffering "a very melancholy journey."

Writing years later, he remembered the day as grey and somber. Threatening clouds hung over Cambridge, and for a fifteen-year-old farm boy to stand before the grand monarchs of learning in their wigs and robes, with so much riding on the outcome, was itself as severe a test as could be imagined. His tutor, however, had assured him he was ready, which turned out to be so. He was admitted to Harvard and granted a partial scholarship.

"I was as light when I came home, as I had been heavy when I went," Adams wrote.

It had long been an article of faith among the Adamses that land was the only sound investment and, once purchased, was never to be sold. Only once is Deacon John known to have made an exception to the rule, when he sold ten acres to help send his son John to college.

THE HARVARD OF JOHN ADAMS'S undergraduate days was an institution of four red-brick buildings, a small chapel, a faculty of seven, and an enrollment of approximately one hundred scholars. His own class of 1755, numbering twenty-seven, was put under the tutorship of Joseph Mayhew, who taught Latin, and for Adams the four years were a time out of time that passed all too swiftly. When it was over and he abruptly found himself playing the part of village schoolmaster in remote Worcester, he would write woefully to a college friend, "Total and complete misery has succeeded so suddenly to total and complete happiness, that all the philosophy I can muster can scarce support me under the amazing shock."

He worked hard and did well at Harvard, and was attracted particularly to mathematics and science, as taught by his favorite professor, John Winthrop, the most distinguished member of the faculty and the leading American astronomer of the time. Among Adams's cherished Harvard memories was of a crystal night when, from the roof of Old Harvard Hall, he gazed through Professor Winthrop's telescope at the satellites of Jupiter.

He enjoyed his classmates and made several close friends. To his surprise, he also discovered a love of study and books such as he had never imagined. "I read forever," he would remember happily, and as years passed, in an age when educated men took particular pride in the breadth of their reading, he became one of the most voracious readers of any. Having discovered books at Harvard, he was seldom ever to be without one for the rest of his days.

He lived in the "lowermost northwest chamber" of Massachusetts Hall, sharing quarters with Thomas Sparhawk, whose chief distinction at college appears to have come from breaking windows, and Joseph Stockbridge, notable for his wealth and his refusal to eat meat.

The regimen was strict and demanding, the day starting with morning prayers in Holden Chapel at six and ending with evening prayers at five. The entire college dined at Commons, on the ground floor of Old

Harvard, each scholar bringing his own knife and fork which, when the meal ended, would be wiped clean on the table cloth. By most accounts, the food was wretched. Adams not only never complained, but attributed his own and the overall good health of the others to the daily fare— beef, mutton, Indian pudding, salt fish on Saturday—and an ever abundant supply of hard cider. "I shall never forget, how refreshing and salubrious we found it, hard as it often was." Indeed, for the rest of his life, a morning "gill" of hard cider was to be John Adams's preferred drink before breakfast.

"All scholars," it was stated in the college rules, were to "behave themselves blamelessly, leading sober, righteous, and godly lives." There was to be no "leaning" at prayers, no lying, blasphemy, fornication, drunkenness, or picking locks. Once, the records show, Adams was fined three shillings, nine pence for absence from college longer than the time allowed for vacation or by permission. Otherwise, he had not a mark against him. As the dutiful son of Deacon John, he appears neither to have succumbed to gambling, "riotous living," nor to "wenching" in taverns on the road to Charlestown.

But the appeal of young women was exceedingly strong, for as an elderly John Adams would one day write, he was "of an amorous disposition" and from as early as ten or eleven years of age had been "very fond of the society of females." Yet he kept himself in rein, he later insisted.

I had my favorites among the young women and spent many of my evenings in their company and this disposition although controlled for seven years after my entrance into college, returned and engaged me too much 'til I was married. I shall draw no characters nor give any enumeration of my youthful flames. It would be considered as no compliment to the dead or the living. This I will say—they were all modest and virtuous girls and always maintained that character through life. No virgin or matron ever had cause to blush at the sight of me, or to regret her acquaintance with me. No father, brother, son, or friend ever had cause of grief or resentment for any intercourse between me and any daughter, sister, mother or any other relation of the female sex. My children may be assured that no illegitimate brother or sister exists or ever existed.

A student's place in his class being determined on entrance to Harvard by the "dignity of family," rather than alphabetically or by academic performance, Adams was listed fourteenth of the twenty-five who received degrees, his placement due to the fact that his mother was a Boylston and his father a deacon. Otherwise, he would have been among the last on the list. At commencement ceremonies, as one of the first three academically, he argued the affirmative to the question "Is civil government absolutely necessary for men?" It was to be a lifelong theme.

How close Adams came to becoming a minister he never exactly said, but most likely it was not close at all. His mother, though a pious woman, thought him unsuited for the life, for all that Deacon John wished it for him. Adams would recall only that in his last years at Harvard, having joined a debating and discussion club, he was told he had "some faculty" for public speaking and would make a better lawyer than preacher, a prospect, he said, that he readily understood and embraced. He knew from experience under his father's roof, when "ecclesiastical councils" gathered there, the kind of contention that could surround a preacher, whatever he might or might not say from the pulpit. "I saw such a spirit of dogmatism and bigotry in clergy and laity, that if I should be a priest I must take my side, and pronounce as positively as any of them, or never get a parish, or getting it must soon leave it." He had no heart for such a life and his father, he felt certain, would understand, his father being "a man of so thoughtful and considerate a turn of mind," even if the profession of law was not one generally held in high esteem.

He judged his father correctly, it seems, but to become a lawyer required that he be taken into the office of a practicing attorney who would charge a fee, which the young man himself would have to earn, and it was this necessity, with his Harvard years ended, that led to the schoolmaster's desk at Worcester late in the summer of 1755.

He made the sixty-mile journey from Braintree to Worcester by horseback in a single day and, though untried and untrained as a teacher, immediately assumed his new role in a one-room schoolhouse at the center of town. To compensate for his obvious youth, he would explain to a friend, he had to maintain a stiff, frowning attitude.

His small charges, both boys and girls numbering about a dozen, responded, he found, as he had at their age, more to encouragement and praise than to scolding or "thwacking." A teacher ought to be an encourager, Adams decided. "But we must be cautious and sparing of our praise, lest it become too familiar." Yet for the day-to-day routine of the classroom, he thought himself poorly suited and dreamed of more glorious pursuits, almost anything other than what he was doing. One student remembered Master Adams spending most of the day at his desk absorbed in his own thoughts or busily writing—sermons presumably. But Adams did like the children and hugely enjoyed observing them:

> I sometimes, in my sprightly moments, consider myself, in my great chair at school, as some dictator at the head of a commonwealth. In this little state I can discover all the great geniuses, all the surprising actions and revolutions of the great world in miniature. I have several renowned generals but three feet high, and several deep-projecting politicians in petticoats. I have others catching and dissecting flies, accumulating remarkable pebbles, cockleshells, etc., with as ardent curiosity as any virtuoso in the Royal Society. . . . At one table sits Mr. Insipid foppling and fluttering, spinning his whirligig, or playing with his fingers as gaily and wittily as any Frenchified coxcomb brandishes his cane and rattles his snuff box. At another sits the polemical divine, plodding and wrangling in his mind about Adam's fall in which we sinned, all as his primer has it.

He perceived life as a stirring drama like that of the theater, but with significant differences, as he wrote to a classmate, Charles Cushing:

> Upon common theaters, indeed, the applause of the audience is of more importance to the actors than their own approbation. But upon the stage of life, while conscience claps, let the world hiss! On the contrary if conscience disapproves, the loudest applauses of the world are of little value.

He boarded with a local physician whose collection of medical books helped satisfy his insatiable appetite for reading. For a time, interest in the law seemed to fade and Adams thought of becoming a doctor. But after attending several sessions of the local court, he felt himself "irresistibly impelled" to the law. In the meantime, he was reading Milton, Virgil, Voltaire, Viscount Bolingbroke's *Letters on the Study and Use of History*, and copying long extracts in a literary commonplace book.

From his reading and from all he heard of the common talk in town, he found himself meditating more and more about politics and history. It was the time of the French and Indian War, when Americans had begun calling themselves Americans rather than colonists. Excitement was high, animosity toward the French intense. In one of his solitary "reveries," Adams poured out his thoughts in an amazing letter for anyone so young to have written, and for all it foresaw and said about him. Dated October 12, 1755, the letter was to another of his classmates and his cousin Nathan Webb.

"All that part of Creation that lies within our observation is liable to change," Adams began.

> Even mighty states and kingdoms are not exempted. If we look into history, we shall find some nations rising from contemptible beginnings and spreading their influence, until the whole globe is subjected to their ways. When they have reached the summit of grandeur, some minute and unsuspected cause commonly affects their ruin, and the empire of the world is transferred to some other place. Immortal Rome was at first but an insignificant village, inhabited only by a few abandoned ruffians, but by degrees it rose to a stupendous height, and excelled in arts and arms all the nations that preceded it. But the demolition of Carthage (what one should think should have established it in supreme dominion) by removing all danger, suffered it to sink into debauchery, and made it at length an easy prey to Barbarians.
>
> England immediately upon this began to increase (the particular and minute cause of which I am not historian enough to trace) in power and magnificence, and is now the greatest nation upon the globe.
>
> Soon after the Reformation a few people came over into the new world for conscience sake. Perhaps this (apparently) trivial incident may transfer the great seat of empire into America. It looks likely to

me. For if we can remove the turbulent Gallics, our people according to exactest computations, will in another century, become more numerous than England itself. Should this be the case, since we have (I may say) all the naval stores of the nation in our hands, it will be easy to obtain the mastery of the seas, and then the united force of all Europe, will not be able to subdue us. The only way to keep us from setting up for ourselves is to disunite us. *Divide et impera.* Keep us in distinct colonies, and then, some great men in each colony, desiring the monarchy of the whole, they will destroy each others' influence and keep the country in *equilibrio.*

Be not surprised that I am turned politician. The whole town is immersed in politics.

At Harvard he had tried keeping a journal. In Worcester he began again in a paper booklet no bigger than the palm of his hand, writing in a minute, almost microscopic script, numbering the days down the left hand margin, his entries at first given to spare, matter-of-fact notations on the weather and what little passed for social events in his new life:

January 23 [1756]. Friday.
A fair and agreeable day. Kept school. Drank tea at Col. Chandler's, and spent the evening at Major Gardiner's.

January 24. Saturday.
A very high west wind. Warm and cloudy. P.M. Warm and fair.

January 25. Sunday.
A cold weather. Heard friend Thayer preach two ingenious discourses from Jeremy [Jeremiah] 10th, 6, and 7. Supped at Col. Chandler's.

Soon he was filling pages with observations like those on his small scholars and on the arrival of spring, with frequently sensuous responses to nature—to "soft vernal showers," atmosphere full of "ravishing fragrance," air "soft and yielding."

Increasingly, however, the subject uppermost in mind was himself, as waves of loneliness, feelings of abject discontent over his circumstances, dissatisfaction with his own nature, seemed at times nearly to overwhelm him. Something of the spirit of the old Puritan diarists took hold. By writing only to himself, for himself, by dutifully reckoning day by day his moral assets and liabilities, and particularly the liabilities, he could thus improve himself.

"Oh! that I could wear out of my mind every mean and base affection, conquer my natural pride and conceit."

Why was he constantly forming yet never executing good resolutions? Why was he so absent-minded, so lazy, so prone to daydreaming his life away? He vowed to read more seriously. He vowed to quit chewing tobacco.

On July 21, 1756, he wrote:

I am resolved to rise with the sun and to study Scriptures on Thursday, Friday, Saturday, and Sunday mornings, and to study some Latin author the other three mornings. Noons and nights I intend to read English authors. . . . I will rouse up my mind and fix my attention. I will stand collected within myself and think upon what I read and what I see. I will strive with all my soul to be something more than persons who have had less advantages than myself.

But the next morning he slept until seven and a one-line entry the following week read, "A very rainy day. Dreamed away the time."

There was so much he wanted to know and do, but life was passing him by. He was twenty years old. "I have no books, no time, no friends. I must therefore be contented to live and die an ignorant, obscure fellow."

That such spells of gloom were failings in themselves, he was painfully aware, yet he was at a loss to know what to do about it. "I can as easily still the fierce tempests or stop the rapid thunderbolt, as command the motions and operations of my own mind," he lamented. Actual thunderstorms left him feeling nervous and unstrung.

By turns he worried over never having any bright or original ideas, or being too bright for his own good, too ready to show off and especially in the company of the older men in the community who befriended him.

"Honesty, sincerity, and openness, I esteem essential marks of a good mind," he concluded after one evening's gathering. He was therefore of the opinion that men ought "to avow their opinions and defend them with boldness."

Vanity, he saw, was his chief failing. "Vanity, I am sensible, is my cardinal vice and cardinal folly," he wrote, vowing to reform himself.

By "vanity" he did not mean he had an excessive pride in appearance. Adams was never one to spend much time in front of a mirror. Rather, in the eighteenth-century use of the word, he was berating himself for being overly proud, conceited.

"A puffy, vain, conceited conversation never fails to bring a man into contempt, although his natural endowments be ever so great, and his application and industry ever so intense. . . . [And] I must own myself to have been, to a very heinous degree, guilty in this respect."

By late summer of 1756 Adams had made up his mind about the future. On August 21, he signed a contract with a young Worcester attorney, James Putnam, to study "under his inspection" for two years. The day after, a Sunday, inspired by a sermon he had heard—and also, it would seem, by a feeling of relief that his decision not to become a minister was at last resolved—he wrote of the "glorious shows" of nature and the intense sensation of pleasure they evoked. Beholding the night sky, "the amazing concave of Heaven sprinkled and glittering with stars," he was "thrown into a kind of transport" and knew such wonders to be the gifts of God, expressions of God's love. But greatest of all, he wrote, was the gift of an inquiring mind.

> But all the provisions that He has [made] for the gratification of our senses . . . are much inferior to the provision, the wonderful provision that He has made for the gratification of our nobler powers of intelligence and reason. He has given us reason to find out the truth, and the real design and true end of our existence.

To a friend Adams wrote, "It will be hard work, but the more difficult and dangerous the enterprise, a higher crown of laurel is bestowed on the conqueror. . . . But the point is now determined, and I shall have the liberty to think for myself."

He changed lodgings, moving in with lawyer Putnam, and while continuing his daytime duties at the Worcester schoolhouse, he read law at night moving fast (too fast, he later thought) through Wood's four-volume *Institute of the Laws of England*, Hawkins's *Abridgment of Coke's Institutes*, Salkeld's hefty *Reports*, Coke's *Entries*, and Hawkins's massive two-volume *Pleas of the Crown* in a single volume that weighed fully eight pounds. *"Can you imagine any drier reading?"* he would one day write to Benjamin Rush, heavily underscoring the question.

Putnam's fee was $100, when Adams could "find it convenient."

With the war continuing, much the greatest excitement in Worcester was the arrival of Lord Jeffrey Amherst and 4,000 of the King's troops on their way west to Fort William Henry on Lake George. They camped on a nearby hill and for several days and nights life in the town was transformed. Writing more than half a century later, Adams could still warm to the memory.

> The officers were very social, spent their evenings and took their suppers with such of the inhabitants as were able to invite, and entertained us with their music and their dances. Many of them were Scotchmen in their plaids and their music was delightful. Even the bagpipe was not disagreeable.

"I then rejoiced that I was an Englishman, and gloried in the name of Britain," he would recall to a friend. How he might fare in the law was another matter. As he wrote at the time, "I am not without apprehensions."

IN THE FALL OF 1758, his studies with Putnam completed, Adams returned to Braintree to move in with his father and mother again after an absence of eight years. "I am beginning life anew," he jubilantly informed a Harvard classmate.

He was busy catching up with old friends, busy with his share of the farm work and preparing for admittance to the bar. For the first time, he was on his own with his studies, and he bent to them with the spirit of independence and intense determination that were to characterize much of his whole approach to life. In his diary he wrote of chopping wood and translating Justinian, with equal resolution.

"I have read Gilbert's first section, of feuds, this evening but I am not a master of it," he recorded October 5, referring to Sir Geoffrey Gilbert's *Treatise of Feudal Tenures*. "Rose about sun rise. Unpitched a load of hay. Translated two leaves more of Justinian . . . and am now reading over again Gilbert's section of feudal tenures," he wrote the day following, October 6. October 7: "Read in Gilbert. . . ." October 9: "I must and will make that book familiar to me." October 10: "Read in Gilbert. I read him slowly, but I gain ideas and knowledge as I go along." October 12: "This small volume will take me a fortnight, but I will be master of it."

Though full of opinions, he often found himself reluctant to express them. "I was young, and then very bashful, however saucy I may have sometimes been since," he would recall long afterward to Thomas Jefferson.

Feeling miserably unsure of himself, he attended court in Boston, where, awestruck, he listened to the leading attorneys of the day, Jeremiah Gridley and James Otis, argue cases. But, as he explained to a friend in Worcester, the appeal of Boston was threefold.

> I had the pleasure to sit and hear the greatest lawyers, orators, in short the greatest men in America, haranguing at the bar, and on the bench. I had the pleasure of spending my evenings with my Harvard friends in the joys of serene, sedate conversation, and perhaps it is worth my while to add, I had the pleasure of seeing a great many and of feeling some very [pretty] girls.

On the morning he found his way through the crooked streets of Boston to Jeremiah Gridley's office for the requisite interview for admission to the bar, Gridley, much to Adams's surprise, gave him not a few cursory minutes but several hours, questioning him closely on his reading. With a kindly, paternal air, Gridley also counseled him to "pursue the study of the law itself, rather than the gain of it," and not to marry early.

Adams was admitted to the bar in a ceremony before the Superior Court at Boston on November 6, 1759, and in a matter of weeks, at age twenty-four, he had taken his first case, which he lost.

In Braintree, as elsewhere in New England, much of town business was taken up with the commonplace problem of keeping one man's live-stock out of another man's fields, and by long-standing custom most legal matters were handled by town clerks and officials who, though without legal training, were thoroughly schooled in procedure, knowing to the last detail all that was required for writs and warrants, matters about which, for all his reading, Adams knew little. The case *Lambert v. Field* involved two horses belonging to Luke Lambert, a coarse, cocksure man whom Adams did not like. Lambert's horses had broken into the enclosure of a neighbor, Joseph Field, and trampled some crops. When Lambert crossed onto Field's land to retrieve them, Field called for him to stop, but Lambert, as Adams noted, "waved his hat and screamed at the horses and drove away, without tendering Field his damages."

As counsel for Field, the plaintiff, Adams felt confident in his understanding of the principles of law involved, but worried that the writ he prepared was "unclerklike" and thus he would fail. He had had no experience in preparing such a document. His anguish was acute. He blamed Putnam for insufficient training. He blamed his mother for insisting he take the case lest it be thought he was incapable of drawing a writ. Nothing, he decided, would ever come easily to him. "But it is my destiny to dig treasures with my own fingers," he wrote woefully.

To gather strength, he read aloud from Cicero's *Orations*. The "sweetness and grandeur" of just the sounds of Cicero were sufficient reward, even if one understood none of the meaning. "Besides . . . it exercises my lungs, raises my spirits, opens my pores, quickens the circulation, and so contributes much to health."

The case was the talk of the village. Everybody knew everybody involved. The justice of the peace, before whom Adams would appear, and the lawyer for Lambert were father and son—Colonel Josiah Quincy and young Samuel Quincy—a circumstance that obviously did not bode well for Adams and his client.

Just as he feared, Adams lost on a technicality. He had neglected to include the words "the county in the direction to the constables of Braintree."

"Field's wrath waxed hot," he recorded, and his own misery was extreme. In his first appearance as a lawyer he had been bested by a crude countryman like Lambert. He had been made to look a fool in the eyes of the whole town, and the humiliation and anger he felt appear to have affected the atmosphere at home. The night following, a terrible family row broke out. Susanna Adams flew into a rage over the fact that Deacon John, in answer to his own conscience and feelings of responsibility as selectman, had brought a destitute young woman to live in the crowded household, the town having no means to provide for her. How was the girl to pay for her board, Susanna demanded of her husband, who responded by asserting his right to govern in his own home. "I won't have the town's poor brought here, stark naked for me to clothe for nothing," she stormed. He should resign as selectman.

When the young woman, whose name was Judah, burst into tears and John's brother Peter pointed this out, Adams told him to hold his tongue, which touched Peter off and "all was breaking into flame." Adams was so shaken, he had to leave the room and take up his Cicero again in order to compose himself.

His mother's uncontrolled responses, her "scolds, rages," were a grievous flaw, he felt. He knew the sudden, uncontrollable rush of his own anger, almost to the point of bursting. He must observe more closely the effects of reason and rage, just as he must never again undertake a case without command of the details. "Let me never undertake to draw a writ without sufficient time to examine and digest in my mind all the doubts, queries, objections that may arise," he wrote. And he never did. The painful lesson had been learned.

Henceforth, he vowed, he would bend his whole soul to the law. He would let nothing distract him. He drew inspiration from his Roman heroes. *"The first way for a young man to set himself on the road towards glorious reputation,"* he read in Cicero, *"is to win renown."* "Reputation," wrote Adams, "ought to be the perpetual subject of my thoughts, and aim of my behavior."

Should he confine himself to the small stage of Braintree? Or would he be better off in Boston? But how possibly could anyone with an interest in life keep a clear head in Boston?

> My eyes are so diverted with chimney sweeps, carriers of wood, merchants, ladies, priests, carts, horses, oxen, coaches, market men and women, soldiers, sailors, and my ears with the rattle gabble of them all that I can't think long enough in the street upon any one thing to start and pursue a thought.

He felt "anxious, eager after something," but what it was he did not know. "I feel my own ignorance. I feel concern for knowledge. I have . . . a strong desire for distinction."

"I never shall shine, 'til some animating occasion calls forth all my powers." It was 1760, the year twenty-two-year-old George III was crowned king and Adams turned twenty-five.

But if self-absorbed and ambitious, he was hardly more so than a number of other young men of ability of his time. The difference was that Adams wrote about it and was perfectly honest with himself.

"Why have I not genius to start some new thought?" he asked at another point in his diary. "Some thing that will surprise the world?" Why could he not bring order to his life? Why could he not clear his table of its clutter of books and papers and concentrate on just one book, one subject? Why did imagination so often intervene? Why did thoughts of girls keep intruding?

"Ballast is what I want. I totter with every breeze."

Chide himself as he would about time spent to little purpose, his appetite for life, for the pleasures of society was too central to his nature to be denied. Further, he had a talent for friendship. To many he seemed prickly, intractable, and often he was, but as his friend Jonathan Sewall would write, Adams had "a heart formed for friendship, and susceptible to the finest feelings." He needed friends, prized old friendships. He kept in touch with his Harvard classmates, and for several in particular maintained boundless admiration. Moses Hemmenway, who had become a Congregational minister known for his interminable sermons, would remain, in Adams's estimate, one of the first scholars of their generation. Samuel Locke, another from the class, was not only the youngest man ever chosen for the presidency of Harvard, but to Adams one of the best men ever chosen, irrespective of the fact that Locke had had to resign after only a few years in office, when his housemaid became pregnant. With his departure, in the words of one Harvard history, Locke was "promptly forgotten," but not by John Adams.

"Friendship," Adams had written to his classmate and cousin, Nathan Webb, "is one of the distinguishing glorys of man. . . . From this I expect to receive the chief happiness of my future life." When, a few years later, Webb became mortally ill, Adams was at his bedside keeping watch through several nights before his death.

His current friends—Sewall, Richard Cranch, Parson Anthony Wibird—were to be his friends to the last, despite drastic changes in circumstance, differing temperaments, eccentricities, or politics. When in time Adams became Richard Cranch's brother-in-law, he would sign his letters "as ever your faithful friend and affectionate brother, John Adams," meaning every word.

There was little he enjoyed more than an evening of spontaneous "chatter," of stories by candlelight in congenial surroundings, of political and philosophic discourse, "intimate, unreserved conversation," as he put it. And flirting, "gallanting," with the girls.

He was lively, pungent, and naturally amiable—so amiable, as Thomas Jefferson would later write, that it was impossible not to warm to him. He was so widely read, he could talk on almost any subject, sail off in almost any direction. What he knew he knew well.

Jonathan Sewall had already concluded that Adams was destined for greatness, telling him, only partly in jest, that "in future ages, when New England shall have risen to its intended grandeur, it shall be as carefully recorded among the registers of the literati that Adams flourished in the second century after the exode of its first settlers from Great Britain, as it is now that Cicero was born in the six-hundred-and-forty-seventh year after the building of Rome."

Yet Adams often felt ill at ease, hopelessly awkward. He sensed people were laughing at him, as sometimes they were, and this was especially hurtful. He had a way of shrugging his shoulders and distorting his face that must be corrected, he knew. He berated himself for being too shy. "I should look bold, speak with more spirit." In the presence of women—those he wished to impress above all—he was too susceptible to the least sign of approval. "Good treatment makes me think I am admired, beloved. . . . So I dismiss my guard and grow weak, silly, vain, conceited, ostentatious."

Determined to understand human nature, fascinated by nearly everyone he encountered, he devoted large portions of his diary to recording their stories, their views on life, how they stood, talked, their facial expressions, how their minds worked. In the way that his literary commonplace book served as a notebook on his reading, the diary became his notebook on people. "Let me search for the clue which led great Shakespeare into the labyrinth of human nature. Let me examine how men think."

He made close study of the attorneys he most admired, the Boston giants of the profession, searching for clues to their success. Jeremiah Gridley's "grandeur" emanated from his great learning, his "lordly" manner. The strength of James Otis was his fiery eloquence. "I find myself imitating Otis," wrote Adams.

His portraits of "original characters" in and about Braintree were extraordinary, detailed, full of life and color, and written obviously, like so much of the diary, out of the pure joy of writing. Possibly he knew what a gift he had as an observer of human nature. In another time, under different circumstances, he might have become a great novelist.

That so many disparate qualities could exist in one person was of never-ending fascination to him. He longed to understand this in others, as in himself. The good-natured, obliging landlady of a friend was also a "squaddy, masculine creature" with "a great staring, rolling eye," "a rare collection of disagreeable qualities." A tavern loafer of "low and ignoble countenance," one Zab Hayward of Braintree, who had no conception of conventional grace in dancing or anything else, was nonetheless regarded as the best dancer in town. Adams sat one night in a local tavern observing from the sidelines. "Every room . . . crowded with people," he recorded. "Negroes with a fiddle. Young fellows and girls dancing in the chamber as if they would kick the floor through." When at first Zab "gathered a circle around him . . . his behavior and speeches were softly silly, but as his blood grew warm by motion and liquor, he grew droll.

> He caught a girl and danced a jig with her, and then led her to one side of the ring and said, "Stand there, I call for you by and by." This was spoken comically enough, and raised a loud laugh. He caught another girl with light hair and a patch on her chin, and held her by the hand while he sung a song. . . . This tickled the girl's vanity, for the song which he applied to her described a very fine girl indeed.

Adams's new friend, Pastor Anthony Wibird, who had assumed the pulpit of Braintree's First Church during the time Adams was away at Worcester, also became the subject of some of his most vivid sketches.

Older than Adams by several years, Wibird was, as would be said in understatement, "somewhat eccentric," yet warmly esteemed. His pastorate would be the longest in the annals of the parish, lasting forty-five years, and the friendship between Adams and Wibird, equally enduring. Privately, Adams wrote of him with the delight of a naturalist taking notes on some rare and exotic specimen:

> P[arson] W[ibird] is crooked, his head bends forward. . . . His nose is a large Roman nose with a prodigious bunch protuberance upon the upper part of it. His mouth is large and irregular, his teeth black and foul and craggy. . . . His eyes are a little squinted, his visage is long and lank, his complexion wan, his cheeks are fallen, his chin is long, large, and lean. . . . When he prays at home, he raises one knee upon the chair, and throws one hand over the back of it. With the other he scratches his neck, pulls the hair of his wig. . . . When he walks, he heaves away, and swags one side, and steps almost twice as far with one foot as the other. . . . When he speaks, he cocks and rolls his eyes, shakes his head, and jerks his body about.

Wibird was "slovenly and lazy," yet—and here was the wonder—he had great "delicacy" of mind, judgment, and humor. He was superb in the pulpit. "He is a genius," Adams declared in summation.

Parson Wibird was one of the half dozen or so bachelors in Adams's social circle. The two closest friends were Jonathan Sewall, a bright, witty fellow Harvard man and struggling attorney from Middlesex County, and Richard Cranch, a good-natured, English-born clockmaker who knew French, loved poetry, and delighted in discussing theological questions with Adams. Bela Lincoln was a physician from nearby Hingham. Robert Treat Paine was another lawyer and Harvard graduate, whom Adams thought conceited but who, like Wibird and Sewall, had a quick wit, which for Adams was usually enough to justify nearly any failing.

The preferred gathering place was the large, bustling Josiah Quincy household at the center of town, where a great part of the appeal was the Quincy family. Colonel Quincy, as an officer in the militia and possibly the wealthiest man in Braintree, was its leading citizen, but also someone Adams greatly admired for his polish and eloquence. (Nothing so helped one gain command of the language, Quincy advised the young man, as the frequent reading and imitation of Swift and Pope.) In addition to the lawyer son Samuel, there were sons Edmund and Josiah, who was also a lawyer, as well as a daughter, Hannah, and a cousin, Esther, who, for Adams and his friends, were the prime attractions. Esther was "pert, sprightly, and gay." Hannah was all of that and an outrageous flirt besides.

While Jonathan Sewall fell almost immediately in love with Esther, whom he would eventually marry, Adams, Richard Cranch, and Bela Lincoln were all in eager pursuit of the high-spirited Hannah. Sensing he was the favorite, Adams was soon devoting every possible hour to her, and when not, dreaming of her. Nothing like this had happened to him before. His pleasure and distress were extreme, as he confided to his friend and rival Cranch:

> If I look upon a law book my eyes it is true are on the book, but imagination is at a tea table seeing that hair, those eyes, that shape, that familiar friendly look. . . . I go to bed and ruminate half the night, then fall asleep and dream the same enchanting scenes.

All this was transpiring when the amorous spirits of the whole group appear to have been at a pitch. Adams recorded how one evening several couples slipped off to a side room and "there laughed and screamed and kissed and hussled," and afterward emerged "glowing like furnaces."

After an evening stroll with Hannah through Braintree—through "Cupid's Grove"—Adams spent a long night and most of the next day with Parson Wibird, talking and reading aloud from Benjamin Franklin's *Reflections on Courtship and Marriage*.

"Let no trifling diversion or amusement or company decoy you from your books," he lectured himself in his diary, "i.e., let no girl, no gun, no cards, no flutes, no violins, no dress, no tobacco, no laziness decoy you from your books." Besides, he had moments of doubt when he thought Hannah less than sincere. "Her face and heart have no correspondence," he wrote.

Then came the spring night he would remember ever after. Alone with Hannah at the Quincy house, he was about to propose when cousin Esther and Jonathan Sewall suddenly burst into the room and the moment passed, never to be recovered. As it was, Bela Lincoln, the Hingham physician, increased his attentions and in a year he and Hannah Quincy would marry.

Seeing what a narrow escape he had had, Adams solemnly determined to rededicate himself. Only by a turn of fate had he been delivered from "dangerous shackles." "Let love and vanity be extinguished and the great passions of ambition, patriotism, break out and burn," he wrote.

Yet, when he met Abigail Smith for the first time later that same summer of 1759, he would not be greatly impressed, not when he compared her to Hannah. Abigail and her sisters Mary and Elizabeth were the daughters of Reverend William Smith of Weymouth, the small seaport town farther along the coast road. Adams's friend Cranch had lately begun calling on Mary, the oldest and prettiest of the three. On the evening he invited Adams to go along with him to meet Abigail, the middle sister, it was for Adams anything but love at first sight. In contrast to his loving, tender Hannah, these Smith sisters were, he wrote, neither "fond, nor frank, nor candid." Nor did Adams much like the father, who seemed a "crafty, designing man." Adams's first impressions were almost entirely bad and, as he would come to realize, quite mistaken.

THE HEAVIEST BLOW of his young life befell John Adams on May 25, 1761, when his father, Deacon John, died at age seventy, the victim of epidemic influenza that took a heavy toll in eastern Massachusetts and on older people especially. In Braintree, seventeen elderly men and women died. Adams's mother was also stricken, and though she survived—as she was to survive one epidemic after another down the years—she was too ill to leave her bed when her husband was buried.

On the back of the office copy of his father's will, Adams wrote in his own hand the only known obituary of Deacon John:

> The testator had a good education, though not at college, and was a
> very capable and useful man. In his early life he was an officer of the
> militia, afterwards a deacon of the church, and a selectman of the
> town; almost all the business of the town being managed by him in
> that department for twenty years together; a man of strict piety,

and great integrity; much esteemed and beloved wherever he was known, which was not far, his sphere of life being not extensive.

With his father gone, Adams experienced a "want of strength [and] courage" such as he had never known. Still, as expected of him, he stepped in as head of the family, and as time passed, those expressions of self-doubt, the fits of despair and self-consciousness that had so characterized the outpourings in his diary, grew fewer.

With his inheritance, he became a man of substantial property by the measure of Braintree. He received the house immediately beside that of his father's, as well as forty acres—ten of adjoining land, plus thirty of orchard, pasture, woodland, and swamp—and slightly less than a third of his father's personal estate, since alone of the three sons he had been provided a college education.

Adams was a freeholder now and his thoughts took a decided "turn to husbandry." He was soon absorbed in all manner of projects and improvements, working with several hired men—"the help," as New Englanders said—building stone walls, digging up stumps, carting manure, plowing with six yoke of oxen, planting corn and potatoes. He loved the farm as never before, even the swamp, "my swamp," as he wrote.

His love of the law, too, grew greater. He felt privileged, blessed in his profession, he told Jonathan Sewall:

Now to what higher object, to what greater character, can any mortal aspire than to be possessed of all this knowledge, well digested and ready at command, to assist the feeble and friendless, to discountenance the haughty and lawless, to procure redress to wrongs, the advancement of right, to assert and maintain liberty and virtue, to discourage and abolish tyranny and vice?

In the house that was now his own, in what had once been the kitchen, before a lean-to enlargement was added at back, he established his first proper law office. The room was bright and sunny and in winter warmed by what had been the old kitchen fireplace. In the corner nearest the road, he had an outside door cut so that clients might directly come and go.

His practice picked up. He was going to Boston now once or twice a week. Soon he was riding the circuit with the royal judges. "I grow more expert . . . I feel my own strength."

In November 1762 his friend Richard Cranch and Mary Smith were married, a high occasion for Adams that he hugely enjoyed, including the customary round of "matrimonial stories" shared among the men "to raise the spirits," one of which he happily included in his journal:

> The story of B. Bicknal's wife is a very clever one. She said, when she was married she was very anxious, she feared, she trembled, she could not go to bed. But she recollected she had put her hand to the plow and could not look back, so she mustered up her spirits, committed her soul to God and her body to B. Bicknal and into bed she leaped—and in the morning she was amazed, she could not think for her life what it was that had so scared her.

In the company of Richard Cranch, Adams had been seeing more and more of the Smith family, about whom he had had a change of heart. That his interest, at first informal, then ardent, was centered on Abigail was obvious to all. As an aspiring lawyer, he must not marry early, Jeremiah Gridley had warned. So it was not until October 25, 1764, after a courtship of nearly five years and just short of his twenty-ninth birthday, that John Adams's life changed as never before, when at the Weymouth parsonage, in a small service conducted by her father, he and Abigail Smith became husband and wife.

OF THE COURTSHIP Adams had said not a word in his diary. Indeed, for the entire year of 1764 there were no diary entries, a sure sign of how preoccupied he was.

At their first meeting, in the summer of 1759, Abigail had been a shy, frail fifteen-year-old. Often ill during childhood and still subject to recurring headaches and insomnia, she appeared more delicate and vulnerable than her sisters. By the time of her wedding, she was not quite twenty, little more than five feet tall, with dark brown hair, brown eyes, and a fine, pale complexion. For a rather stiff pastel portrait, one of a pair that she and John sat for in Salem a few years after their marriage, she posed with just a hint of a smile, three strands of pearls at the neck, her hair pulled back with a blue ribbon. But where the flat, oval face in her husband's portrait conveyed nothing of his bristling intelligence and appetite for life, in hers there was a strong, unmistakable look of good sense and character. He could have been almost any well-fed, untested young man with dark, arched brows and a grey wig, while she was distinctly attractive, readily identifiable, her intent dark eyes clearly focused on the world.

One wonders how a more gifted artist might have rendered Abigail. Long years afterward, Gilbert Stuart, while working on her portrait, would exclaim to a friend that he wished to God he could have painted Mrs. Adams when she was young; she would have made "a perfect Venus," to which her husband, on hearing the story, expressed emphatic agreement.

Year after year through the long courtship John trotted his horse up and over Penn's Hill by the coast road five miles to Weymouth at every chance and in all seasons. She was his Diana, after the Roman goddess of the moon. He was her Lysander, the Spartan hero. In the privacy of correspondence, he would address her as "Ever Dear Diana" or "Miss Adorable." She nearly always began her letters then, as later, "My Dearest Friend." She saw what latent abilities and strengths were in her ardent suitor and was deeply in love. Where others might see a stout, bluff little man, she saw a giant of great heart, and so it was ever to be.

Only once before their marriage, when the diary was still active, did Adams dare mention her in its pages, and then almost in code:

Di was a constant feast. Tender, feeling, sensible, friendly. A friend. Not an imprudent, not an indelicate, not a disagreeable word of action. Prudent, soft, sensible, obliging, active.

She, too, was an avid reader and attributed her "taste for letters" to Richard Cranch, who, she later wrote, "taught me to love the poets and put into my hands, Milton, Pope, and Thompson, and Shakespeare." She could quote poetry more readily than could John Adams, and over a lifetime would quote her favorites again and again in correspondence, often making small, inconsequential mistakes, an indication that rather than looking passages up, she was quoting from memory.

Intelligence and wit shined in her. She was consistently cheerful. She,

too, loved to talk quite as much as her suitor, and as time would tell, she
was no less strong-minded.

Considered too frail for school, she had been taught at home by her
mother and had access to the library of several hundred books accumulated by her father. A graduate of Harvard, the Reverend Smith was
adoring of all his children, who, in addition to the three daughters,
included one son, William. They must never speak unkindly of anyone,
Abigail remembered her father saying repeatedly. They must say only
"handsome things," and make topics rather than persons their subjects—sensible policy for a parson's family. But Abigail had views on
nearly everything and persons no less than topics. Nor was she ever to be
particularly hesitant about expressing what she thought.

Open in their affections for one another, she and John were also open
in their criticisms. "Candor is my characteristic," he told her, as though
she might not have noticed. He thought she could improve her singing
voice. He faulted her for her "parrot-toed" way of walking and for sitting
cross-legged. She told him he was too severe in his judgments of people
and that to others often appeared haughty. Besides, she chided him, "a
gentleman has no business to concern himself about the legs of a lady."

During the terrible smallpox epidemic of 1764, when Boston became
"one great hospital," he went to the city to be inoculated, an often har-
rowing, potentially fatal ordeal extending over many days. Though he
sailed through with little discomfort, she worried excessively and they
corresponded nearly every day, Adams reminding her to be sure to have
his letters "smoked," on the chance they carried contamination.

The rambling, old-fashioned parsonage at Weymouth and its furnishings were a step removed from the plain farmer's cottage of John's boyhood or the house Abigail would move to once they were married. Also,
two black slaves were part of the Smith household.

According to traditional family accounts, the match was strongly
opposed by Abigail's mother. She was a Quincy, the daughter of old John
Quincy, whose big hilltop homestead, known as Mount Wollaston, was a
Braintree landmark. Abigail, it was thought, would be marrying beneath
her. But the determination of both Abigail and John, in combination
with their obvious attraction to each other—like steel to a magnet, John
said—were more than enough to carry the day.

A month before the wedding, during a spell of several weeks when

they were unable to see one another because of illness, Adams wrote
to her:

> Oh, my dear girl, I thank heaven that another fortnight will
> restore you to me—after so long a separation. My soul and body
> have both been thrown into disorder by your absence, and a month
> or two more would make me the most insufferable cynic in the world.
> I see nothing but faults, follies, frailties and defects in anybody
> lately. People have lost all their good properties or I my justice or
> discernment.
>
> But you who have always softened and warmed my heart, shall
> restore my benevolence as well as my health and tranquility of mind.
> You shall polish and refine my sentiments of life and manners, ban-
> ish all the unsocial and ill natured particles in my composition, and
> form me to that happy temper that can reconcile a quick discern-
> ment with a perfect candor.
>
> Believe me, now and ever your faithful
>
> Lysander

HIS MARRIAGE to Abigail Smith was the most important decision of
John Adams's life, as would become apparent with time. She was in all
respects his equal and the part she was to play would be greater than he
could possibly have imagined, for all his love for her and what appreciation he already had of her beneficial, steadying influence.

Bride and groom moved to Braintree the evening of the wedding.
There was a servant to wait on them—the same Judah who had been the
cause of the family row years before—who was temporarily on loan from
John's mother. But as the days and weeks passed, Abigail did her own
cooking by the open hearth, and while John busied himself with his law
books and the farm, she spun and wove clothes for their everyday use.

Her more sheltered, bookish upbringing notwithstanding, she was to
prove every bit as hardworking as he and no less conscientious about
whatever she undertook. She was and would remain a thoroughgoing
New England woman who rose at five in the morning and was seldom
idle. She did everything that needed doing. All her life she would do her
own sewing, baking, feed her own ducks and chickens, churn her own

butter (both because that was what was expected, and because she knew her butter to be superior). And for all her reading, her remarkable knowledge of English poetry and literature, she was never to lose certain countrified Yankee patterns of speech, saying "Canady" for Canada, as an example, using "set" for sit, or the old New England "aya," for yes.

To John's great satisfaction, Abigail also got along splendidly with his very unbookish mother. For a year or more, until Susanna Adams was remarried to an older Braintree man named John Hall, she continued to live with her son Peter in the family homestead next door, and the two women grew extremely fond of one another. To Abigail her mother-in-law was a cheerful, open-minded person of "exemplary benevolence," dedicated heart and soul to the welfare of her family, which was more than her eldest son ever committed to paper, even if he concurred.

John and Abigail's own first child followed not quite nine months after their marriage, a baby girl, Abigail or "Nabby," who arrived July 14, 1765, and was, her mother recorded, "the dear image of her still dearer Papa."

A second baby, John Quincy, was born two years later, and again in mid-July, 1767, and Adams began worrying about college for Johnny, fine clothes for Nabby, dancing schools, "and all that." To Abigail, after nearly three years of marriage, her John was still "the tenderest of husbands," his affections "unabated."

For Adams, life had been made infinitely fuller. All the ties he felt to the old farm were stronger now with Abigail in partnership. She was the ballast he had wanted, the vital center of a new and better life. The time he spent away from home, riding the court circuit, apart from her and the "little ones," became increasingly difficult. "God preserve you and all our family," he would write.

But in 1765, the same year little Abigail was born and Adams found himself chosen surveyor of highways in Braintree, he was swept by events into sudden public prominence. His marriage and family life were barely under way when he began the rise to the fame he had so long desired. "I never shall shine 'til some animating occasion calls forth all my powers," he had written, and here now was the moment.

"I am . . . under all obligations of interest and ambition, as well as honor, gratitude and duty, to exert the utmost of abilities in this impor-

tant cause," he wrote, and with characteristic honesty he had not left
ambition out.

THE FIRST NEWS of the Stamp Act reached the American colonies during the last week of May 1765 and produced an immediate uproar, and in
Massachusetts especially. Starting in November, nearly everything written or printed on paper other than private correspondence and books—
all pamphlets, newspapers, advertisements, deeds, diplomas, bills,
bonds, all legal documents, ship's papers, even playing cards—were
required to carry revenue stamps, some costing as much as ten pounds.
The new law, the first British attempt to tax Americans directly, had
been passed by Parliament to help pay for the cost of the French and
Indian War and to meet the expense of maintaining a colonial military
force to prevent Indian wars. Everyone was affected. The *Boston Gazette*
reported Virginia in a state of "utmost consternation." In August,
Boston mobs, "like devils let loose," stoned the residence of Andrew
Oliver, secretary of the province, who had been appointed distributor of
the stamps, then attacked and destroyed the house of Lieutenant Governor Thomas Hutchinson, wrongly suspecting him of having sponsored
the detested tax.

Adams, who had earlier joined a new law club in Boston started by
Jeremiah Gridley, had, at Gridley's suggestion, been working on an essay
that would become *A Dissertation on the Canon and the Feudal Law*. It
was his first extended political work and one of the most salient of his life,
written at the age of thirty. Now, at the height of the furor, he arranged
for its publication as an unsigned, untitled essay in the *Gazette*. (It would
be published in England later, in a volume titled *The True Sentiments of
America*.) It was not a call to arms or mob action—with his countryman's
dislike of the Boston "rabble," Adams was repelled by such an "atrocious
violation of the peace." The Stamp Act was hardly mentioned. Rather, it
was a statement of his own fervent patriotism and the taproot conviction
that American freedoms were not ideals still to be obtained, but rights
long and firmly established by British law and by the courage and sacrifices of generations of Americans. Years later Adams would say the Revolution began in the minds of Americans long before any shots were fired
or blood shed.

"Be it remembered," he wrote in his *Dissertation*, "that liberty must at all hazards be supported. We have a right to it, derived from our Maker. But if we have not, our fathers have earned and bought it for us at the expense of their ease, their estates, their pleasure, and their blood.

> And liberty cannot be preserved without a general knowledge among the people who have a right from the frame of their nature to knowledge, as their great Creator who does nothing in vain, has given them understandings and a desire to know. But besides this they have a right, an indisputable, unalienable, indefeasible divine right to the most dreaded and envied kind of knowledge, I mean of the characters and conduct of their rulers.

He was calling on his readers for independence of thought, to use their own minds. It was the same theme he had struck in his diary at Worcester a decade before, in his turmoil over what to do with his life, writing, "The point is now determined, and I shall have the liberty to think for myself."

> Government is a plain, simple, intelligent thing, founded in nature and reason, quite comprehensible by common sense [the *Dissertation* continued]. . . . The true source of our suffering has been our timidity. We have been afraid to think. . . . Let us dare to read, think, speak, and write. . . . Let it be known that British liberties are not the grants of princes or parliaments . . . that many of our rights are inherent and essential, agreed on as maxims and established as pre-liminaries, even before Parliament existed. . . . Let us read and recollect and impress upon our souls the views and ends of our more immediate forefathers, in exchanging their native country for a dreary, inhospitable wilderness. . . . Recollect their amazing fortitude, their bitter sufferings—the hunger, the nakedness, the cold, which they patiently endured—the severe labors of clearing their grounds, building their houses, raising their provisions, amidst dangers from wild beasts and savage men, before they had time or money or materials for commerce. Recollect the civil and religious principles and hopes and expectations which constantly supported and carried them through all hardships with patience and resignation. Let us recollect it was liberty, the hope of liberty, for them-

selves and us and ours, which conquered all discouragements, dangers, and trials.

The essay began appearing in the *Gazette* on August 12, 1765, and it struck an immediate chord. "The author is a young man, not above 33 or 34, but of incomparable sense," wrote Boston's senior pastor, Charles Chauncey, to the learned Rhode Island clergyman and future president of Yale College, Ezra Stiles. "I esteem that piece one of the best that has been written. It has done honor to its author; and it is a pity but he should be known."

Soon afterward Adams drafted what became known as the Braintree Instructions—instructions from the freeholders of the town to their delegate to the General Court, the legislative body of Massachusetts—which, when printed in October in the *Gazette*, "rang" through the colony. "We have always understood it to be a grand and fundamental principle of the [English] constitution that no freeman should be subject to any tax to which he has not given his own consent." There must be "no taxation without representation"—a phrase that had been used in Ireland for more than a generation. And in rejecting the rule of the juryless Admiralty Court in enforcing this law, the instructions declared that there must be a trial by jury and an independent judiciary.

In amazingly little time the document was adopted by forty towns, something that had never happened before.

Now fully joined in Boston's political ferment, Adams was meeting with Gridley, James Otis, Samuel Adams, and others. Observing them closely, he concluded that it was his older, second cousin, Samuel Adams who had "the most thorough understanding of liberty." Samuel Adams was "zealous and keen in the cause," of "steadfast integrity," a "universal good character." The esteemed Otis, however, had begun to act strangely. He was "liable to great inequities of temper, sometimes in despondency, sometimes in rage," Adams recorded in dismay.

Otis, a protégé of Gridley, had been for Adams the shining example of the lawyer-scholar, learned yet powerful in argument. Now he became Adams's political hero, just as Thomas Hutchinson became Adams's chief villain. A lifetime later, Adams would vividly describe Otis as he had been in his surpassing moment, in the winter of 1761, in argument against writs of assistance, search warrants that permitted customs officers to enter and search any premises whenever they wished. Before the bench in the second-floor Council Chamber of the Province House in Boston, Otis had declared such writs—which were perfectly valid in English law and commonly issued in England—null and void because they violated the natural rights of Englishmen. Adams, who had been present as an observer only, would remember it as one of the inspiring moments of his life, a turning point for him as for history. The five judges, with Hutchinson at their head as chief justice, sat in comfort near blazing fireplaces, Adams recalled, "all in their new fresh robes of scarlet English cloth, in their broad hats, and immense judicial wigs." But Otis, in opposition, was a "flame" unto himself. "With the promptitude of classical illusions, a depth of research . . . and a torrent of impetuous eloquence, he hurried away all before him." By Adams's account, every one of the immense crowded audience went away, as he did, ready to take up arms against writs of assistance. "Then and there was the first scene of the first act of opposition to the arbitrary claims of Great Britain," Adams would claim. "Then and there the child independence was born."

But by 1765 it was the tragic decline of James Otis that gripped Adams. At meetings now, Otis talked on endlessly and to no point. No one could get a word in. "Otis is in confusion yet," Adams noted a year or so later. "He rambles and wanders like a ship without a helm." Adams began to doubt Otis's sanity, and as time passed, it became clear that Otis, his hero, was indeed going mad, a dreadful spectacle.

"The year 1765 has been the most remarkable year of my life," Adams wrote in his diary that December. "The enormous engine fabricated by the British Parliament for battering down all the rights and liberties of America, I mean the Stamp Act, has raised and spread through the whole continent a spirit that will be recorded to our honor, with all future generations."

"At home with my family. Thinking," reads the entry of a few nights later.

"At home. Thinking," he wrote Christmas Day.

WITH THE REPEAL of the Stamp Act by Parliament in the spring of 1766, and the easing of tensions that followed in the next two years, until the arrival of British troops at Boston, Adams put politics aside to concentrate on earning a living. He was thinking of politics not at all, he insisted.

He was back on the road, riding the circuit, the reach of his travels extending more than two hundred miles, from the island of Martha's Vineyard off Cape Cod, north to Maine, which was then part of the Massachusetts Bay Province, to as far west as Worcester. As recalled in the family years later, he was endowed for the profession of law with the natural gifts of "a clear and sonorous voice," a "ready elocution," stubbornness, but with the "counter-check" of self-control, and a strong moral sense. He handled every kind of case—land transfers, trespass, admiralty, marine insurance, murder, adultery, rape, bastardy, buggery, assault and battery, tarring and feathering. He defended, not always successfully, poor debtors, horse thieves, and smugglers. He saw every side of life, learned to see things as they were, and was considered, as Jonathan Sewall would write, as "honest [a] lawyer as ever broke bread."

In 1766, like his father before him, Adams was elected selectman in Braintree. But so active had his Boston practice become by 1768 that he moved the family to a rented house in the city, a decision he did not like, fearing the effect on their health. He established a Boston office and presently admitted two young men, Jonathan Austin and William Tudor, to read law with him, in return for fees of 10 pounds sterling. "What shall I do with two clerks at a time?" Adams speculated in his diary, adding that he would do all he could "for their education and advancement in the world," a pledge he was to keep faithfully. When Billy Tudor was admitted to the bar three years later, Adams took time to write to Tudor's wealthy father to praise the young man for his clear head and honest heart, but also to prod the father into giving his son some help getting started in his practice. Adams had seen too often the ill effect of fathers who ignored their sons when a little help could have made all the difference.

With the death of Jeremiah Gridley the year before and the mental collapse of James Otis, John Adams, still in his thirties, had become Boston's busiest attorney. He was "under full sail," prospering at last, and in the Adams tradition, he began buying more land, seldom more than five or ten acres of salt marsh or woodland at a time, but steadily, year after year. (Among his father's memorable observations was that he never knew a piece of land to run away or break.) Eventually, after his

brother Peter married and moved to his wife's house, John would purchase all of the old homestead, with its barn and fifty-three acres, which
included Fresh Brook, to Adams a prime asset. In one pasture, he reckoned, there were a thousand red cedars, which in twenty years, "if properly pruned," might be worth a shilling each. And with an appreciative
Yankee eye, he noted "a quantity of good stone in it, too."

He was becoming more substantial in other ways. "My good man is so
very fat that I am lean as a rail," Abigail bemoaned to her sister Mary.
He acquired more and more books, books being an acknowledged extravagance he could seldom curb. (With one London bookseller he had placed
a standing order for "every book and pamphlet, of reputation, upon the
subjects of law and government as soon as it comes out.") "I want to see
my wife and children every day," he would write while away on the court
circuit. "I want to see my grass and blossoms and corn. . . . But above all,
except the wife and children, I want to see my books."

In the privacy of his journal, he could also admit now, if obliquely, to
seeing himself as a figure of some larger importance. After noting in one
entry that his horse had overfed on grass and water, Adams speculated
wryly, "My biographer will scarcely introduce my little mare and her
adventures."

He could still search his soul over which path to follow. "To what
object are my views directed?" he asked. "Am I grasping at money, or
scheming for power?" Yes, he was amassing a library, but to what purpose? "Fame, fortune, power say some, are the ends intended by a
library. The service of God, country, clients, fellow men, say others.
Which of these lie nearest my heart?

> What plan of reading or reflection or business can be pursued by a
> man who is now at Pownalborough [Maine], then at Martha's Vine-
> yard, next at Boston, then at Taunton, presently at Barnstable,
> then at Concord, now at Salem, then at Cambridge, and afterward
> Worcester. Now at Sessions, then at Pleas, now in Admiralty, now at
> Superior Court, then in the gallery of the House. . . . Here and there
> and everywhere, a rambling, roving, vagrant, vagabond life.

Yet when Jonathan Sewall, who had become attorney general of the
province, called on Adams at the request of governor Francis Bernard to

offer him the office of advocate general in the Court of Admiralty, a plum for an ambitious lawyer, Adams had no difficulty saying no.

Politically he and Sewall were on opposing sides, Sewall having become an avowed Tory. Yet they tried to remain friends. "He always called me John and I him Jonathan," remembered Adams, "and I often said to him, I wish my name were David." Both understood that the office, lucrative in itself, was, in Adams's words, a "sure introduction to the most profitable business in the province." Sewall, with his large Brattle Street house in Cambridge, was himself an example of how high one could rise. Yet so open a door to prosperity, not to say the gratification to one's vanity, that a royal appointment might offer tempted Adams not at all.

With Boston full of red-coated British troops—sent in 1768 to keep order, as another round of taxes was imposed by Parliament, this time on paper, tea, paint, and glass—the atmosphere in the city turned incendiary. Incidents of violence broke out between townsmen and soldiers, the hated "Lobsterbacks."

The crisis came in March of 1770, a year already shadowed for John and Abigail by the loss of a child. A baby girl, Susanna, born since the move to Boston and named for John's mother, had died in February at a little more than a year old. Adams was so upset by the loss that he could not speak of it for years.

ON THE COLD MOONLIT EVENING of March 5, 1770, the streets of Boston were covered by nearly a foot of snow. On the icy, cobbled square where the Province House stood, a lone British sentry, posted in front of the nearby Custom House, was being taunted by a small band of men and boys. The time was shortly after nine. Somewhere a church bell began to toll, the alarm for fire, and almost at once crowds came pouring into the streets, many men, up from the waterfront, brandishing sticks and clubs. As a throng of several hundred converged at the Custom House, the lone guard was reinforced by eight British soldiers with loaded muskets and fixed bayonets, their captain with drawn sword. Shouting, cursing, the crowd pelted the despised redcoats with snowballs, chunks of ice, oyster shells, and stones. In the melee the soldiers suddenly opened fire, killing five men. Samuel Adams was quick to call

the killings a "bloody butchery" and to distribute a print published by
Paul Revere vividly portraying the scene as a slaughter of the innocent,
an image of British tyranny, the Boston Massacre, that would become
fixed in the public mind.

The following day thirty-four-year-old John Adams was asked to
defend the soldiers and their captain, when they came to trial. No one else
would take the case, he was informed. Hesitating no more than he had
over Jonathan Sewall's offer of royal appointment, Adams accepted, firm
in the belief, as he said, that no man in a free country should be denied the
right to counsel and a fair trial, and convinced, on principle, that the case
was of utmost importance. As a lawyer, his duty was clear. That he would
be hazarding his hard-earned reputation and, in his words, "incurring a
clamor and popular suspicions and prejudices" against him, was obvious,
and if some of what he later said on the subject would sound a little self-
righteous, he was also being entirely honest.

Only the year before, in 1769, Adams had defended four American
sailors charged with killing a British naval officer who had boarded their
ship with a press gang to grab them for the British navy. The sailors were
acquitted on grounds of acting in self-defense, but public opinion had
been vehement against the heinous practice of impressment. Adams
had been in step with the popular outrage, exactly as he was out of step
now. He worried for Abigail, who was pregnant again, and feared he was
risking his family's safety as well as his own, such was the state of emo-
tions in Boston. It was rumored he had been bribed to take the case. In
reality, a retainer of eighteen guineas was the only payment he would
receive.

Criticism of almost any kind was nearly always painful for Adams,
but public scorn was painful in the extreme.

"The only way to compose myself and collect my thoughts," he wrote
in his diary, "is to set down at my table, place my diary before me, and
take my pen into my hand. This apparatus takes off my attention from
other objects. Pen, ink, and paper and a sitting posture are great helps to
attention and thinking."

From a treatise by the eminent Italian penologist and opponent of
capital punishment Cesare, Marchese di Beccaria, he carefully copied the
following:

If, by supporting the rights of mankind, and of invincible truth, I shall contribute to save from the agonies of death one unfortunate victim of tyranny, or of ignorance, equally fatal, his blessings and years of transport will be sufficient consolation to me for the contempt of all mankind.

There were to be two conspicuously fair trials held in the new courthouse on Queen Street. The first was of the British captain, Thomas Preston, the opening of the trial being delayed until October when passions had cooled. The second was of the soldiers. In the first trial Adams was assisted by young Josiah Quincy, Jr., while the court-appointed lawyer trying the case was Josiah's brother, Samuel, assisted by Robert Treat Paine. Whether Captain Preston had given an order to fire, as was charged, could never be proven. Adams's argument for the defense, though unrecorded, was considered a virtuoso performance. Captain Preston was found not guilty.

Adams's closing for the second and longer trial, which was recorded, did not come until December 3, and lasted two days. The effect on the crowded courtroom was described as "electrical." "I am for the prisoners at bar," he began, then invoked the line from the Marchese di Beccaria. Close study of the facts had convinced Adams of the innocence of the soldiers. The tragedy was not brought on by the soldiers, but by the mob, and the mob, it must be understood, was the inevitable result of the flawed policy of quartering troops in a city on the pretext of keeping the peace:

We have entertained a great variety of phrases to avoid calling this sort of people a mob. Some call them shavers, some call them geniuses. The plain English is, gentlemen, [it was] most probably a motley rabble of saucy boys, Negroes and mulattoes, Irish teagues and outlandish jacktars. And why should we scruple to call such a people a mob, I can't conceive, unless the name is too respectable for them. The sun is not about to stand still or go out, nor the rivers to dry up because there was a mob in Boston on the 5th of March that attacked a party of soldiers. . . . Soldiers quartered in a populous town will always occasion two mobs where they prevent one. They are wretched conservators of the peace.

He described how the shrieking "rabble" pelted the soldiers with snowballs, oyster shells, sticks, "every species of rubbish," as a cry went up to "Kill them! Kill them!" One soldier had been knocked down with a club, then hit again as soon as he could rise. "Do you expect he should behave like a stoic philosopher, lost in apathy?" Adams asked. Self-defense was the primary canon of the law of nature. Better that many guilty persons escape unpunished than one innocent person should be punished. "The reason is, because it's of more importance to community, that innocence should be protected, than it is, that guilt should be punished."

"Facts are stubborn things," he told the jury, "and whatever may be our wishes, our inclinations, or the dictums of our passions, they cannot alter the state of facts and evidence."

The jury remained out two and a half hours. Of the eight soldiers, six were acquitted and two found guilty of manslaughter, for which they were branded on their thumbs.

There were angry reactions to the decision. Adams was taken to task in the *Gazette* and claimed later to have suffered the loss of more than half his practice. But there were no riots, and Samuel Adams appears never to have objected to the part he played. Possibly Samuel Adams had privately approved, even encouraged it behind the scenes, out of respect for John's fierce integrity, and on the theory that so staunch a show of fairness would be good politics.

As time would show, John Adams's part in the drama did increase his public standing, making him in the long run more respected than ever. Years later, reflecting from the perspective of old age, he himself would call it the most exhausting case he ever undertook, but conclude with pardonable pride that his part in the defense was "one of the most gallant, generous, manly and disinterested actions of my whole life, and one of the best pieces of service I ever rendered my country."

A SECOND SON, Charles, was born that summer of 1770, and for all the criticism to which he was being subjected, Adams was elected by the Boston Town Meeting as a representative to the Massachusetts legislature. It was his first real commitment to politics. Inevitably it would mean more time away from his practice, and still further reduction in income. When, the night of the meeting, he told Abigail of his apprehensions, she burst into tears, but then, as Adams would relate, said "she thought I had done as I ought, she was very willing to share in all that was to come."

But the complications and demands of both the law and politics became too much and Adams suffered what appears to have been a physical breakdown. "Especially the constant obligation to speak in public almost every day for many hours had exhausted my health, brought on pain in my breast and complaint in my lungs, which seriously threatened my life," he would later write. In the spring of 1771, he and the family moved back to Braintree, to "the air of my native spot, and the fine breezes from the sea," which "together with daily rides on horseback," gradually restored him.

Another child, Thomas Boylston, was born in September of 1772, and again Adams was off on the "vagabond life" of the circuit, carrying a copy of *Don Quixote* in his saddlebag and writing Abigail sometimes as many as three letters a day.

Business was good in Massachusetts in the calm of 1772 and Adams prospered once again. He appeared in more than two hundred Superior Court cases. Among his clients were many of the richest men in the colony, including John Hancock. At the conclusion of one morning in court, Adams was told people were calling him the finest speaker they had ever heard, "the equal to the greatest orator that ever spoke in Greece or Rome."

He could speak extemporaneously and, if need be, almost without limit. Once, to give a client time to retrieve a necessary record, Adams spoke for five hours, through which the court and jury sat with perfect patience. At the end he was roundly applauded because, as he related the story, he had spoken "in favor of justice."

At home, he filled pages of his journal with observations on government and freedom, "notes for an oration at Braintree," as he labeled them, though the oration appears never to have been delivered.

Government is nothing more than the combined force of society, or the united power of the multitude, for the peace, order, safety, good and happiness of the people. . . . There is no king or queen bee distinguished from all others, by size or figure or beauty and variety of colors, in the human hive. No man has yet produced any revelation from heaven in his favor, any divine communication to govern his fellow men. Nature throws us all into the world equal and alike. . . .

The preservation of liberty depends upon the intellectual and moral character of the people. As long as knowledge and virtue are diffused generally among the body of a nation, it is impossible they should be enslaved. . . .

Ambition is one of the more ungovernable passions of the human heart. The love of power is insatiable and uncontrollable. . . .

There is danger from all men. The only maxim of a free government ought to be to trust no man living with power to endanger the public liberty.

At the same time, he was vowing, at least in the privacy of his diary, to devote himself wholly to his private business and providing for his family. "Above all things I must avoid politics. . . ." But as tensions in the colony mounted, so did his pent-up rage and longing for action. On an evening with the Cranches, when a visiting Englishman began extolling the English sense of justice, Adams exploded, taking everyone by surprise, and Adams as much as any. "I cannot but reflect upon myself with the severity of these rash, inexperienced, boyish, raw and awkward expressions," he wrote afterward. "A man who has not better government of his tongue, no more command of his temper, is unfit for everything but children's play and the company of boys." There was no more justice in Britain than in hell, he had told the Englishman.

By the time of the destruction of the tea, what was later to become known as the Boston Tea Party in December 1773, he had again moved the family to Boston. His hatred of mob action notwithstanding, Adams was exuberant over the event. In less than six months, in May 1774, in reprisal, the British closed the port of Boston, the worst blow to the city in its history. "We live, my dear soul, in an age of trial," he told Abigail. Shut off from the sea, Boston was doomed. It must suffer martyrdom and expire in a noble cause. For himself, he saw "no prospect of any business in my way this whole summer. I don't receive a shilling a week."

Yet she must not assume he was "in the dumps." Quite the contrary: he felt better than he had in years.

In 1774, Adams was chosen by the legislature as one of five delegates to the First Continental Congress at Philadelphia, and with all Massachusetts on the verge of rebellion, he removed Abigail and the children again to Braintree, where they would remain.

In July he traveled to Maine, for what was to be his last turn on the circuit before leaving for Philadelphia. During a break from the court at Falmouth (later Portland), he and Jonathan Sewall, who was still attorney general, climbed a hill overlooking the blue sweep of Casco Bay, where they could talk privately.

Their friendship had cooled in recent years, as had been inevitable under the circumstances. In his diary Adams had grieved that his best friend in the world had become his implacable enemy. "God forgive him for the part he has acted," Adams had written, adding, "It is not impossible that he may make the same prayer for me." Now Sewall pleaded with Adams not to attend the Congress. The power of Great Britain was "irresistible" and would destroy all who stood in the way, Sewall warned.

As long as they lived, neither man would forget the moment. Adams told Sewall he knew Great Britain was "determined on her system," but "that very determination, determined me on mine." The die was cast, Adams said. "Swim or sink, live or die, survive or perish, [I am] with my country ... You may depend upon it."

Less than a year later, after the battle of Bunker Hill, Sewall would choose to "quit America." With his wife and family he sailed for London, never to return. "It is not despair which drives me away," he wrote before departure. "I have faith ... that rebellion will shrink back to its native hell, and that Great Britain will rise superior to all the gasconade of the little, wicked American politicians."

Not long afterward, in a series of letters to the *Boston Gazette* that he signed "Novangelus"—the New Englander—Adams argued that Americans had every right to determine their own destiny and charged the Foreign Ministry in London with corruption and venal intent. America,

Adams warned, could face subjugation of the kind inflicted on Ireland. Unless America took action, and at once, Adams wrote, they faced the prospect of living like the Irish on potatoes and water.

I I I

WITH JOSEPH BASS AT HIS SIDE, Adams crossed Long Bridge over the frozen Charles River and rode into Cambridge in the early afternoon of January 24, 1776, in time to dine with General Washington at the temporary quarters of Colonel Thomas Mifflin near Harvard Yard. Mifflin, a wealthy young Philadelphia merchant who served with Adams in the Continental Congress, had been one of the first to welcome Adams on his arrival in Philadelphia. As a "fighting Quaker," he had since become Washington's aide-de-camp.

Martha Washington was present with her husband, as were General Horatio Gates and his lady. When Martha Washington and Elizabeth Gates arrived in Cambridge by coach in December, it was remarked that they would surely be a welcome addition "in country where [fire] wood was scarce." Gates, a former British officer, was an affable, plain-faced man who, like Washington, had served during the French and Indian War on the disastrous Braddock expedition. As adjutant general he was Washington's right hand at Cambridge.

Washington and Adams were nearly the same age, Washington, at forty-three, being just three years older. Powerfully built, he stood nearly a head taller than Adams—six feet four in his boots, taller than almost anyone of the day—and loomed over his short, plump wife. The three officers, in their beautiful buff and blue uniforms, were all that Adams might imagine when picturing himself as a soldier.

Yet even they were upstaged by the main attractions of the gathering, a dozen or more sachems and warriors of the Caughnawaga Indians in full regalia who had been invited to dine, together with their wives and children. Adams had been fascinated by Indians since boyhood, when the aged leaders of the Punkapaug and Neponset tribes had called on his father. But he shared with Washington and Gates a dread fear of the British unleashing Indian war parties on the frontiers, as had the French twenty years before. Recalling what he had read and heard, Adams had earlier written to a friend, "The Indians are known to conduct their wars so entirely without faith and humanity that it would bring eternal infamy on the Ministry throughout all Europe if they should excite those savages to war. . . . To let loose these blood hounds to scalp men and to butcher women and children is horrid." Yet finding himself now unexpectedly in the actual presence of Indians was another matter, and he had a very different reaction.

The dinner, starting at two o'clock, was a diplomatic occasion. The Caughnawagas had come to offer their services to the Americans, and, gathered all about him, they presented a spectacle that Adams, to his surprise, hugely enjoyed. "It was a savage feast, carnivorous animals devouring their prey," he wrote in his diary. "Yet they were wondrous polite. The general introduced me to them as one of the Grand Council Fire at Philadelphia, upon which they made me many bows and cordial reception." To Abigail he reported himself decidedly pleased by the whole occasion.

What he could not risk telling her by letter was that the command at Cambridge had received the most heartening news, indeed the only good news, of the long, grim winter. An expedition led by young Henry Knox, a former Boston bookseller and colonel in Washington's army, had been sent to Lake Champlain to retrieve the artillery captured by Ethan Allen at Fort Ticonderoga and haul the great guns back over the snow-covered Berkshire Mountains all the way to Boston, a task many had thought impossible. Now the "noble train" was at Framingham, twenty miles to the west. It was a feat of almost unimaginable daring and difficulty and, ironically, only made possible by the severity of the winter, as the guns had been dragged over the snow on sleds.

Mounted and on their way again the next morning, with the temperature still in the twenties, Adams and Bass were joined by a newly elected Massachusetts delegate to Congress, young Elbridge Gerry. They rode out past the pickets and campfires of Cambridge and at Framingham stopped to see for themselves the guns from Ticonderoga, Adams making careful note of the inventory—58 cannon ranging in size from 3- and 4-pounders to one giant 24-pounder that weighed more than two tons. Clearly, with such artillery, Washington could change the whole picture at Boston.

The three riders pressed on through the grey and white landscape, making twenty to twenty-five miles a day. A "cold journey," Adams wrote. The weather was persistently wretched. There was more snow, wind, and freezing rain.

With dusk coming on by four in the afternoon and the bitter cold turning colder still, the glow and warmth of familiar wayside taverns was more welcome than ever. Under normal circumstances, Adams nearly always enjoyed such stops. He loved the food—wild goose on a spit, punch, wine, bread and cheese, apples—and a leisurely pipe afterward, while toasting himself by the fire. He picked up news, delighted in "scenes and characters," as he said, enough "for the amusement of Swift or even Shakespeare."

It was in such places that he had first sensed the rising tide of revolution. A year before the first meeting of Congress in 1774, riding the court circuit, he had stopped one winter night at a tavern at Shrewsbury, about forty miles from Boston, and as he would recall for Benjamin Rush years afterward, the scene left a vivid impression.

> ... as I was cold and wet I sat down at a good fire in the bar room to dry my great coat and saddlebags, till a fire could be made in my chamber. There presently came in, one after another half a dozen or half a score substantial yeomen of the neighborhood, who, sitting down to the fire after lighting their pipes, began a lively conversation upon politics. As I believed I was unknown to all of them, I sat in total silence to hear them. One said, "The people of Boston are distracted." Another answered, "No wonder the people of Boston are distracted; oppression will make wise men mad." A third said, "What would you say, if a fellow should come to your house and tell you he was come to take a list of your cattle that Parliament might tax you for them at so much a head? And how should you feel if he should go out and break open your barn, to take down your oxen, cows, horses and sheep?" "What would I say," replied the first, "I would knock him in the head." "Well," said a fourth, "if Parliament can take away Mr. Hancock's wharf and Mr. Row's wharf, they can take away your barn and my house." After much more reasoning in this style, a fifth who had as yet been silent, broke out, "Well it is high time for us to rebel. We must rebel sometime or other: and we had better rebel now than at any time to come: if we put it off for ten

or twenty years, and let them go on as they have begun, they will get a strong party among us, and plague us a great deal more than they can now. As yet they have but a small party on their side."

But now, at town after town, the atmosphere was edged with melancholy, the talk was of defeat at Quebec and the dire situation at Boston.

Snow lay deep most of the way. With drifts banked against buildings and stone walls, trees bare against the sky, the wind seldom still, no part of the journey was easy or uplifting to the spirits. Instead of welcoming committees and church bells, there was only the frozen road ahead.

The one bright note was young Gerry, who belonged to the so-called "codfish aristocracy" of Marblehead, his father having made a fortune shipping dried cod to Spain and the West Indies. Like Adams, indeed like every member of the Massachusetts delegation, Gerry was a Harvard graduate, a slight, birdlike man, age thirty-one, who spoke with a stammer and had an odd way of contorting his face, squinting and enlarging his eyes. But he was good company. Because of the family business, he had traveled extensively and was an ardent patriot. He and Adams talked all the way, making the journey, as Adams related to Abigail, considerably less tedious than it might have been. Their days together on the wintry road marked the start of what was to be a long, eventful friendship.

Like Adams, Gerry viewed mankind as capable of both great good and great evil. Importantly now, they were also of the same heart concerning what had to be done at Philadelphia.

Abigail had already said what John knew needed saying when, in November, a petition was circulated at home calling for reconciliation with Britain. "I could not join today in the petitions . . . for a reconciliation between our no longer parent state, by a tyrant state and these colonies," she wrote. Then, making a slight but definite dash mark with her pen before continuing, as if to signify her own break from the past, she said, "Let us separate, they are unworthy to be our brethren."

Passing through New York, Adams bought two copies of a small anonymous pamphlet, newly published under the title *Common Sense.* Keeping one, he sent the other on to her.

• • •

ADAMS AND HIS TWO COMPANIONS arrived at Philadelphia on Thursday, February 8, 1776, fifteen days after leaving Braintree.

His first letters from Abigail did not reach him until more than a month later and were filled with accounts of thrilling events. The American bombardment of Boston had begun March 2 and 3. "No sleep for me tonight," she wrote, as the house trembled about her. On March 5 she described a more thunderous barrage: "the rattling of the windows, the jar of the house and the continuous roar of the 24-pounders."

The night before, working at great speed, Washington's men had moved the guns from Ticonderoga to commanding positions on the high ground of the Dorchester Peninsula, south of Boston, looking over Boston Harbor and the British fleet. With hundreds of ox teams and more than a thousand American troops at work, breastworks had been set up and cannon hauled into place, all in a night and to the complete surprise of the British. Abigail was told that the British commander, on seeing what they had accomplished, remarked, "My God, these fellows have done more work in one night than I could make my army do in three months."

Days of fearful tension followed until Sunday, March 17, St. Patrick's Day, when she went again to the top of Penn's Hill to see a spectacle such as no one could ever have imagined—the British were abandoning Boston. General William Howe had struck an agreement with Washington. If allowed to depart in peace, the army would not leave Boston in flames.

The entire fleet, "the largest fleet ever seen in America," was lifting canvas in a fair breeze and turning to the open sea. "You may count upwards of one hundred and seventy-sail," she wrote. "They look like a forest."

The British had been outwitted, humiliated. The greatest military power on earth had been forced to retreat by an army of amateurs; it was a heady realization. As would be said by the Duke of Manchester before the House of Lords, "The fact remains, that the army which was sent to reduce the province of Massachusetts Bay has been driven from the capital, and the standard of the provincial army now waves in triumph over the walls of Boston."

With the departing fleet sailed a thousand Loyalists, many well known to John and Abigail Adams, including John's first mentor in the law, James Putnam of Worcester, and Samuel Quincy, brother of Hannah and Josiah, and Adams's opposing counsel in the Boston Massacre trials.

That such had come to pass, wrote Abigail, was surely the work of the Lord and "marvelous in our eyes."

CHAPTER TWO

TRUE BLUE

*We were about one third Tories, and [one] third
timid, and one third true blue.*

—John Adams

I

PHILADELPHIA, the provincial capital of Pennsylvania on the western
bank of the Delaware River, was a true eighteenth-century metropolis,
the largest, wealthiest city in British America, and the most beautiful.
Visitors wrote in praise of its "very exactly straight streets," its "many
fair houses and public edifices," and of the broad, tidal Delaware, alive in
every season but winter with a continuous traffic of ships great and small.

Though more than a hundred miles from the open sea, it was
America's busiest port, with wharves stretching nearly two miles along
the river. The topgallants of huge merchantmen loomed over busy Water
Street and Front Street. Cutters, shad boats, and two-masted shallops
tied up, moved in and out, in company with the great, flat-bottomed
Durham boats built to carry pig iron from the Durham Works upstream.
Shipbuilding was a thriving industry; seagoing trade, the city's lifeblood.
Ships outbound carried lumber and wheat, Pennsylvania's chief exports.
Inbound ships brought European trade goods and from the West Indies,
sugar, molasses, spices, and, increasingly now, European armaments and
supplies for war. With no means for producing arms or gunpowder, the
colonies were dependent on clandestine shipments from Europe by way
of the Caribbean, and particularly the tiny Dutch island of St. Eustatius.

One vessel reportedly docked at Philadelphia with 49,000 pounds of gunpowder.

Because of Pennsylvania's reputation for religious tolerance, and an abundance of good land available to the west, Philadelphia was the principal port of entry to America. The incoming tide of English, Welsh, Scotch-Irish, and Palatine Germans had been growing steadily. In numbers, if not in influence, Presbyterians and Baptists had long since surpassed the Quakers of the Quaker City.

Fifty years earlier, when young Benjamin Franklin arrived from Boston with a single "Dutch" (German) dollar in his pocket, Philadelphia had been a town of 10,000 people. By 1776 its population was approaching 30,000. Larger than New York, nearly twice the size of Boston, it was growing faster than either.

As conceived by its English Quaker founder, William Penn, in 1682, the plan of Philadelphia was a spacious grid, which to a man like John Adams, accustomed to the tangle of Boston's narrow streets, seemed a sensible arrangement. "I like it," Adams had declared in his journal at the time of the First Congress, when, newly arrived and filled with curiosity, he set off with his walking stick, resolved to learn his way about.

> Front Street is near the river, then 2nd Street, 3rd, 4th, 5th, 6th, 7th, 8th, 9th [he recorded]. The cross streets which intersect these are all equally wide, straight and parallel to each other, and are named for forest and fruit trees, Pear Street, Apple Street, Walnut Street, Chestnut Street, etc.

The main thoroughfare was High Street, commonly called Market Street, as it was the location of the immense public market. Most streets near the waterfront had brick footwalks and gutters and were lit at night by whale oil lamps, except when the moon was full. Many of the principal streets were lined with trees. "This is the most regular, neat, and convenient city I ever was in and has made the most rapid progress to its present greatness," declared an English visitor. But it was the public buildings and churches that made the greatest impression. The State House, where Congress met; and nearby Carpenters' Hall, which had been the setting for the First Congress; "noble" Christ Church, as

Adams called it, with its magnificent Palladian window and landmark spire; the new hospital; the new poorhouse; the new Walnut Street Prison, were all unusually handsome and substantial. Silas Deane of Connecticut thought the poorhouse, or "Bettering House," equal to anything of its kind anywhere. "All this is done by private donation and chiefly by the people called Quakers," he informed his wife. To another Connecticut delegate, Oliver Wolcott, the massive new jail more resembled a prince's palace than a house of confinement.

Public-spirited Philadelphians inspired by Benjamin Franklin had established the first volunteer fire company in the colonies, the first medical school, and a library. Franklin himself, Philadelphia's first citizen, was the most famous American alive—printer, publisher, philosopher, scientist, and, as inventor of the lightning rod, "the man who tamed the lightning." It was Franklin also who had led the way in establishing the American Philosophical Society, "for the promoting of useful knowledge," with the result that Philadelphia had become the recognized center of American thought and ideas. Other eminent members of the Philosophical Society included John Bartram, who west of town, on the banks of the Schuylkill River, had created the first botanical garden in America; Dr. Benjamin Rush, an enterprising young physician and champion of humanitarian reform; and David Rittenhouse, clockmaker, optician, instrument-maker and self-taught astronomer who, to study the transit of Venus in 1769, had erected an incongruous-looking observation platform that still stood on the grounds of the State House.

Topics of "consideration" at the Philosophical Society, as set forth in Franklin's initial proposal were, in the spirit of the age, all-embracing:

> all philosophical [scientific] experiments that let light into the nature of things, tend to increase the power of man over matter, and multiply the conveniences or pleasure of life . . . all new-discovered plants, herbs, trees, roots, and methods of propagating them. . . . New methods of curing or preventing diseases. . . . New mechanical inventions for saving labor. . . . All new arts, trades, manufacturers, etc. that may be proposed or thought of.

As it was, Philadelphia manufacturers and artisans produced more goods than in any city in America—boots, wigs, hardware, fancy carriages, Franklin stoves, mirror glass, and no end of bricks for a city where nearly everything was built of brick. Thomas Affleck produced furniture as fine as any made in the colonies, all in the fashionable style of the English cabinetmaker Chippendale. John Behrent on Third Street advertised what may have been the first piano made in America, "a just finished extraordinary instrument by the name of a pianoforte, made of mahogany, being of the nature of a harpsichord."

With twenty-three printing establishments and, by 1776, seven newspapers—more newspapers even than in London—Philadelphia was the publishing capital of the colonies. It was not only that Franklin's immensely popular *Poor Richard's Almanack* emanated from Philadelphia, but political pamphlets of such far-reaching influence as John Dickinson's *Letters from a Pennsylvania Farmer*, Thomas Jefferson's spirited *Summary View of the Rights of British America*, and now, *Common Sense*, which was selling faster than anything ever published in America.

Shops in nearly every street offered an array of goods and enticements such as most delegates to Congress could never find at home, everything from French brandy and Strasburg snuff to fancy chamber pots, artificial teeth, or ordinary pins of the kind John Adams purchased in "great heaps" to send home to Abigail. John Sparhawk, proprietor of the London Bookstore on Second Street, in addition to volumes on medicine and law, sold scientific instruments, swords, spurs, and backgammon tables.

There were as many as thirty bookshops and twice the number of taverns and coffeehouses, with names like Blue Anchor, Bunch of Grapes, Tun Tavern, Conestoga Wagon, Rising Sun, Half Moon, and each had its own clientele. The Free Masons convened at the staid old Indian King on Market Street. The London Coffee House, at the southwest corner of Front and Market, in the commercial center, was the favorite of the leading merchants and sea captains, indeed the place where much of the city's business was transacted, while the new, larger City Tavern on the west side of Second Street, between Walnut and Chestnut, had become the great gathering place for members of Congress. Adams, recording his first arrival in Philadelphia in August 1774, had written that "dirty, dusty, and fatigued as we were, we could not resist the importunity to go to the [City] Tavern," which, he decided, must be the most genteel place of its kind in all the colonies. It was there, at the City Tavern, a few days later, that Adams had first met George Washington.

Distilleries and breweries were thriving. Adams found the local beer so much to his liking that he temporarily abandoned his usual hard cider. "I drink no cider, but feast on Philadelphia beer," he acknowledged to Abigail.

To anyone unaccustomed to city life, the crowds and noise seemed overwhelming, and worst were market days, Wednesdays and Saturdays, when German-speaking country people came rolling into town in huge farm wagons loaded with produce, live chickens, pigs, and cattle. The "thundering of coaches, chariots, chaises, wagons, drays and the whole fraternity of noise almost continually assails our ears," complained a visiting physician. Delegate Stephen Hopkins from Rhode Island one day counted seventy farm wagons on Market Street.

Swarms of people moved up and down the sidewalks and spilled into the streets. At no point on the American continent could so many human beings be seen in such close proximity or in such variety. Sailors, tradesmen, mechanics in long leather aprons, journeymen printers, housepainters, sail-makers, indentured servants, black slave women, their heads wrapped in bright bandannas, free black stevedores and draymen, mixed together with Quaker merchants and the elegants of the city in their finery, everyone busy about something, and everyone, it seemed to visitors, unexpectedly friendly and polite.

Few delegates to Congress ever became accustomed to the bustle and noise; or to the suffocating heat of a Philadelphia summer; or to the clouds of mosquitoes and horseflies that with the onset of summer rose like a biblical scourge. Prices were high. Lodgings of even a modest sort were difficult to find. Conditions for the poor appeared little better than in other American cities. Misery, too, was on display. Delegates to Congress were frequently approached by beggars and, as in every city of the time, the scars and mutilations of disease and war were not uncommon among the passing crowds. Further, Philadelphia was notorious for its deadly epidemics of smallpox. During the most recent outbreak, in 1773, more than 300 people had died.

In his initial eagerness to see everything, Adams had made a tour of the new hospital. Led below ground to view the "lunaticks" locked in their cells, he saw to his horror that one was a former client from Massachusetts, a man he had once saved from being whipped for horse stealing. Afterward, upstairs, Adams walked between long rows of beds filled with the sick and lame, a scene of "human wretchedness" that tore at his heart. But if bothered by pigs loose in the streets, or the stench of rotting garbage and horse manure, he wrote nothing of it. Besides, like others, he found that to the west, toward the Schuylkill River, the city rapidly thinned out, beginning at about Sixth Street. By Eighth, beyond the hospital and the potter's burial ground, one was in open country. To a man who thought nothing of walking five to ten miles to "rouse the spirits," it was a welcome prospect. There were fields with wild strawberries in summer and scattered ponds, which in winter were filled with skaters, the most accomplished of whom, doffing their hats, performed something called the "Philadelphia Salute," a bow much like in a minuet.

One fair afternoon, as if to clear their heads, Adams and two or three others climbed the bell tower of Christ Church, up a series of dimly lit, narrow ladders, past the great bells in their yokes, to a point a hundred feet aboveground, where a trap door led to the open air of the arched lantern, above which rose the church spire. Steadying themselves on a slightly canted roof, they looked over the whole of the city, the long sweep of the river, and the farmland of New Jersey to the east. The breeze at that height was like nothing to be felt in the streets below.

With the rest of the Massachusetts delegation, Adams had moved into a lodging house kept by a Mrs. Sarah Yard on the east side of Second Street, across from City Tavern. A tally of his expenses shows charges for room and board of 30 shillings a week in Pennsylvania currency, not including firewood and candles, which were extra.

"My time is too totally filled from the moment I get out of bed until I return to it, [with] visits, ceremonies, company, business, newspapers, pamphlets, etc., etc., etc.," he had reported excitedly to Abigail.

On Sundays, the one day of respite from Congress, he was at church most of the day, attending services twice, even three times. With numerous denominations to choose from (everything except Congregational), he tried nearly all—the Anglican Christ Church, the meetinghouses of the Methodists, Baptists, Presbyterians, Quakers, the German Moravians—and passed judgment on them all, both their music and the comparative quality of their preaching. The Reverend Thomas Coombe of Christ Church was "sprightly" and distinct. "But I am not charmed," wrote Adams. "His style was indifferent." Indifference was a quality Adams found difficult to tolerate. The Methodist preacher was another matter. "He reaches the imagination and touches the passions very well."

One Sunday, "led by curiosity and good company," which included George Washington, Adams crossed a "Romish" threshold, to attend afternoon mass at St. Mary's Catholic Church on Fifth Street, an experience so singular that he reflected on it at length both in his journal and in a letter to Abigail. Everything about the service was the antithesis of a lifetime of Sabbaths at Braintree's plain First Church, where unfettered daylight through clear window glass allowed for no dark or shadowed corners, or suggestion of mystery. For the first time, Adams was confronted with so much that generations of his people had abhorred and rebelled against, and he found himself both distressed and strangely moved. The music, bells, candles, gold, and silver were "so calculated to take in mankind," that he wondered the Reformation had ever succeeded. He felt pity for "the poor wretches fingering their beads, chanting Latin, not a word of which they understood," he told Abigail.

> The dress of the priest was rich with lace—his pulpit was velvet and gold. The altar piece was very rich—little images and crucifixes about—wax candles lighted up. But how shall I describe the picture of our Savior in a frame of marble over the altar at full length upon the Cross, in the agonies, and the blood dropping and streaming from his wounds?

Yet Adams stayed through all of the long service. The music and chanting of the assembly continued through the afternoon, "most sweetly and exquisitely," and he quite approved of the priest's "good, short, moral essay" on the duty of parents to see to their children's temporal and spiritual interests. The whole experience, Adams concluded, was "awful and affecting"—the word "awful" then meaning full of awe, or "that which strikes with awe, or fills with reverence."

For one accustomed also to the plainest of domestic comforts and daily fare—and who loved to eat—the scale of Philadelphia hospitality in the opening weeks of the First Congress had been memorable. Not even in New York had he seen such display of private wealth, or dined and imbibed so grandly. At a great dinner for Congress in the banqueting hall at the State House, on September 16, 1774, a total of thirty-one toasts

had been raised before the affair ended. There were further elegant recep-
tions and dinners at the homes of the Mifflins, the Shippens, the Powels,
Cadwalladers, and Dickinsons, extended gatherings presided over and
attended by many of the most beautiful, fashionably dressed women of
Philadelphia.

"I shall be killed with kindness in this place," he told Abigail. "We go
to Congress at nine and there we stay, most earnestly engaged until three
in the afternoon, then we adjourn and go to dinner with some of the
nobles of Pennsylvania at four o'clock and feast on ten thousand delicacies, and sit drinking Madeira, claret and burgundy 'til six or seven."
Even plain Quakers, he reported, served ducks, hams, chickens, beef,
creams, and custards.

"A most sinful feast again," he recorded after another occasion, this in
the splendor of a great four-story mansion on Third Street, the home of
Mayor Samuel Powel, whose wealth and taste could be measured in
richly carved paneling, magnificent paintings, a tea service in solid silver
that would have fetched considerably more than the entire contents of
the Adams household at Braintree.

"Dined with Mr. [Benjamin] Chew, Chief Justice of the Province," he
began still another diary entry.

Turtle and every other thing. Flummery, jellies, sweet meats of
twenty sorts. Trifles, whipped syllabubs, floating islands . . . and
then a dessert of fruits, raisins, almonds, pears, peaches—wines most
excellent and admirable. I drank Madeira at a great rate and found
no inconvenience in it.

Within the walls of Congress, he was at first dazzled by the other delegates, who, he decided, comprised an assembly surpassing any in history.
Of the fifty-four in attendance, nearly half were lawyers and most had
received a college education. Several, like Washington, were known to be
men of great wealth, but others, like Roger Sherman of Connecticut, had
humbler origins. He had begun as a shoemaker.

As observant of people as ever, Adams recorded his impressions in
vivid, fragmentary notes of a kind kept by no other member of Congress.
Richard Henry Lee of Virginia was a "tall, spare . . . masterly man";
Roger Sherman spoke "often and long, but very heavily"; James Duane

of New York had a "sly, surveying eye," but appeared "very sensible." Joseph Galloway, a leading Philadelphia attorney and speaker of the Pennsylvania Assembly who would later resign from Congress and ultimately seek refuge with the British army, struck Adams at first meeting as having an air of "design and cunning."

John Dickinson, another prominent Philadelphian, was "a shadow . . . pale as ashes"; Adams doubted he would live a month. Caesar Rodney of Delaware was "the oddest looking man in the world . . . slender as a reed—pale—his face is not bigger than a large apple. Yet there is sense and fire, spirit, wit, and humor in his countenance."

Adams was amazed by the range and variety of talents. "The art and address of ambassadors from a dozen belligerent powers of Europe, nay, of a conclave of cardinals at the election of a Pope . . . would not exceed the specimens we have seen." Here were "fortunes, abilities, learning, eloquence, acuteness" equal to any. "Every question is discussed with moderation, and an acuteness and minuteness equal to that of Queen Elizabeth's privy council."

But after a month of such "acuteness and minuteness" over every issue at hand, irrespective of importance, Adams was "wearied to death." The business of Congress had become tedious beyond expression, he told Abigail.

> This assembly is like no other that ever existed. Every man in it is a great man—an orator, a critic, a statesman, and therefore every man upon every question must show his oratory, his criticism, and his political abilities.
>
> The consequence of this is that business is drawn and spun out to immeasurable length. I believe if it was moved and seconded that we should come to a resolution that three and two make five, we should be entertained with logic and rhetoric, law, history, politics, and mathematics concerning the subject for two whole days, and then we should pass the resolution unanimously in the affirmative.

Certain members began to irritate him. The perpetual round of feasting became only another burden of his "pilgrimage." Even Philadelphia lost its charm. For all its "wealth and regularity," Adams decided, Philadelphia was no Boston. Yet on departure from the First Congress in late October of 1774, after a stay of two months, he had written wistfully of the "happy, peaceful, the elegant, the hospitable, and polite city of Philadelphia," wondering if he would ever be back.

By the time he returned for the Second Continental Congress, in late spring 1775, a month after Lexington and Concord, Philadelphia had become the capital of a revolution. Troops were drilling; lavish entertaining was out of fashion. Congress was in the throes of creating an army, appointing a commander-in-chief, issuing the first Continental money. With several other delegates, Adams spent a day inspecting defenses on the Delaware.

"There are in this city three large regiments raised, formed, armed, trained, and uniformed under officers consisting of gentlemen of the very first fortune and best character in the place," Adams reported to Abigail's uncle, Isaac Smith, a prosperous Boston merchant whom Adams greatly admired. "All this started up since [the] 19th [of] April [since Lexington and Concord]. They cover the common every day of the week, Sundays not excepted."

The deliberations of Congress, meantime, had been moved from Carpenters' Hall to the larger, grander State House on the south side of Chestnut Street, between Fifth and Sixth Streets. Built some forty years before, it comprised a handsome main edifice, two stories tall with a bell tower and arcaded wings joining smaller "offices" at either end, all of it done in red brick. High on the exterior west wall of the main building, a large clock proclaimed the hour.

Congress convened in the Assembly Room on the first floor, to the left of the Chestnut Street entrance. An ample chamber, measuring forty by forty feet, it was notably devoid of decoration, "neat but not elegant," with whitewashed walls and flooded with daylight from high windows on both the north and south sides. On a low platform at the east end of the room stood a single, tall-backed chair for the president. There were two woodstoves and on the east wall, twin fireplaces, one on either side of the president's chair. Seats for the delegates, fifty or so Windsor chairs, were arranged in a semicircle facing the president's chair, these interspersed with work tables covered with green baize cloths and clustered according to region: New England on the left, middle colonies in the center, southern colonies on the right.

The Pennsylvania Assembly, having given up its space, had moved across the hall to the more elaborate Supreme Court Room, where the royal coat-of-arms hung. At the rear of the hall, a broad stairway led to the banqueting room that extended a hundred feet, the full length of the building.

Outside to the rear was the State House Yard, an open public green the size of a city block and enclosed the whole way around by a seven-foot brick wall. The Rittenhouse observation platform stood off to one side, and at the center of the far wall a huge single-arched wooden gate, twice the height of the wall, opened onto Walnut Street. In good weather, as a place for the delegates to stretch their legs and talk privately, the yard was ideal. Many days more business was transacted there than inside. And with the yard serving also now as a place to store cannon and barrels of gunpowder, the war was never far from consciousness.

All sessions of Congress were conducted in strictest secrecy behind closed doors because of the number of British agents in and about Philadelphia and the need to convey an impression of unity, that all members were perfectly agreed on the results of their deliberations. Consequently, like others, Adams could report comparatively little in his letters home, except that the hours were longer than ever, the issues of greater urgency, the strain worse on everybody.

His health suffered. His eyes bothered him to the point that he had difficulty reading. He wrote of the frustrations of "wasting, exhausting" debates. America was "a great, unwieldy body," he decided. "Its progress must be slow. It is like a large fleet sailing under convoy. The fleetest sailors must wait for the dullest and slowest."

Yet he would not give up or let down. "I will not despond."

A sweltering, fly-infested summer of 1775 was followed by an autumn of almost unceasing rains. Dysentery broke out in the military camps. Adams, though suffering from rheumatism and a violent cold, worked twelve to fourteen hours a day, in committee meetings from seven to ten in the morning, then to the full Congress till late afternoon, then back to committees from six to ten at night.

Politics were no less perplexing than ever. "Politics are a labyrinth without a clue," he wrote, but he had come to understand the makeup of Congress. He knew the delegates now as he had not before, and they had come to know him. That he was repeatedly chosen for the most important committees was a measure of his influence and of the respect others had for his integrity, his intellect, and exceptional capacity for hard work. He was the leading committeeman of the Massachusetts delegation, perhaps indeed of the whole Congress.

By October, at the time of Abigail's shattering ordeal with sickness and death at home, Adams was writing to say they must prepare themselves, "minds and hearts for every event, even the worst." Since his first involvement in the "Cause of America," he had known the crisis would never be settled peaceably and this, he told her in confidence, had been a source of much "disquietude."

> The thought that we might be driven to the sad necessity of breaking our connection with G[reat] B[ritain], exclusive of the carnage and destruction which it was easy to see must attend the separation, always gave me a great deal of grief.

II

POSSIBLY IT WAS HIS FIRST or second day back in Philadelphia, in early February 1776, after the long wintry journey from home, that Adams, in his room at Mrs. Yard's, drew up a list of what he was determined to see accomplished. Or as appears more likely, from its placement in his diary, the list had been composed earlier, somewhere en route. Undated, it included, "An alliance to be formed with France and Spain"; "Government to be assumed by every colony"; "Powder mills to be built in every colony and fresh efforts to make saltpetre [for the making of gunpowder]." And, on the second of the two small opposing pages in the diary, he wrote, a "Declaration of Independency."

Independence had been talked about privately and alluded to in correspondence, but rarely spoken of directly in public declamation, or in print. To Adams independence was the only guarantee of American liberty, and he was determined that the great step be taken. The only question was when to make the move. If a decision were forced on Congress too soon, the result could be disastrous; independence would be voted down. But every day that independence was put off would mean added

difficulties in the course of the larger struggle. Abigail, in one of her letters, aptly offered some favorite lines from Shakespeare:

> *There is a tide in the affairs of men,*
> *Which, taken at the flood, leads on to fortune;*
> *Omitted, all the voyage of their life*
> *Is bound in the shallows and in miseries . . .*
> *And we must take the current when it serves,*
> *Or lose our ventures.*

But just when to catch the tide was the question. By Adams's estimate, Congress was about equally divided three ways—those opposed to
independence who were Tories at heart if not openly, those too cautious
or timid to take a position one way or the other, and the "true blue," as he
said, who wanted to declare independence with all possible speed. So as
yet the voices for independence were decidedly in the minority. Indeed,
the delegates of six colonies—New York, New Jersey, Pennsylvania,
Delaware, Maryland, and South Carolina—were under specific instructions not to vote for independence.

The opposing argument hung on the lingering possibility of a last-
minute reconciliation with Britain. Were not the likes of Edmund Burke
speaking out in Parliament for American rights, it was said. Supposedly a
peace commission was on the way from London. To Adams such talk was
a phantom. "The Ministry," he wrote, "have caught the colonies as I
have often caught a horse, by holding an empty hat, as if it was full of
corn. . . ." But throughout the middle colonies, as in parts of the South,
great numbers of people had no wish to separate from the mother country. In Philadelphia such sentiment ran strong, and not just among the
city's numerous Tories. "The plot thickens. . . . Thinking people
uneasy," observed a local attorney. "The Congress in *equilibrio* on the
question of independence or no. . . . I love the cause of liberty, but cannot
heartily join in the presentation of measures totally foreign to the original
plan of resistance."

To many staunchly pacifist Quakers any step that led nearer to all-out
war was anathema. To them George III was "the best of kings," and they
spoke of those who called themselves patriots as "the violent people."

The mood of the city had become extremely contentious. "The malignant air of calumny has taken possession of almost all ranks and societies of people in this place," wrote Christopher Marshall, an apothecary and committed patriot (though a Quaker) who had become one of Adams's circle of Philadelphia friends.

> The rich, the poor, the high professor and the prophane, seem all to be infected with this grievous disorder, so that the love of our neighbor seems to be quite banished, the love of self and opinions so far prevails. . . . The [Tory] enemies of our present struggle . . . are grown even scurrilous to individuals, and treat all characters who differ from them with the most opprobrious language.

In Congress the strain was showing. From Virginia had come word that the royal governor, Lord Dunmore, having escaped to the safety of a British man-of-war, had called on all slaves to rebel, promising them their freedom if they joined the King's forces. On New Year's Day he had ordered the bombardment of Norfolk. Southern delegates were outraged. At the same time the bad news from Canada had had much the same effect witnessed by Adams in the wayside taverns en route from Massachusetts. "There is a deep anxiety, a kind of thoughtful melancholy," he reported to Abigail. Writing again, he stressed that the events of war were always uncertain. Then, paraphrasing a favorite line from the popular play *Cato* by Joseph Addison—a line that General Washington, too, would often call upon—Adams told her, "We cannot insure success, but we can deserve it."

With sickness widespread in Philadelphia there was much hacking and coughing in Congress and many a long, sallow look. When some of the delegates protested that smoke from the wood stoves in the chamber was the cause of such poor health, the stoves were removed. Other ailments struck. Thomas Lynch of South Carolina suffered a stroke from which he would not recover. Smallpox reappeared in the city, putting everyone further on edge. In March one of New England's most prominent delegates, Samuel Ward of Rhode Island, would die of the disease.

On February 27, word arrived that Parliament, in December, had prohibited all trade with the colonies and denounced as traitors all Americans who did not make an unconditional submission. The punishment for treason, as every member of Congress knew, was death by hanging.

A vast British armada was reported under way across the Atlantic and there were ominous rumors of the King hiring an army of German mercenaries. It was the New Englanders who held firm for independence, though two of the Massachusetts delegation, John Hancock and Robert Treat Paine, exhibited nothing like the zeal of either Samuel Adams or Elbridge Gerry. There were many, too, among the other delegations, who could be counted on, though unfortunately several of the most important were absent. Richard Henry Lee of Virginia would not appear at Philadelphia until the middle of March. Caesar Rodney of Delaware would be away until April. Thomas Jefferson of Virginia would not arrive for another three months, not until the middle of May. Meanwhile, time was wasting and a great deal needed doing.

Present nearly every day, notwithstanding his years and infirmities, was Benjamin Franklin, who, at age seventy, was popularly perceived to be the oldest, wisest head in the Congress, which he was, and the most influential, which he was not. Franklin wanted independence and considered Congress lamentably irresolute on the matter, as he told Adams. Franklin had no expectation of new terms from Britain and from long experience in London, as an agent for Pennsylvania, he knew the King and the Foreign Ministry as did no one else in Congress. But Franklin had no liking for floor debate. He was patient, imperturbable, and at times sound asleep in his chair. Never would he argue a point. Indeed, it was rare that he spoke at all or ventured an opinion except in private conversation, which to Adams, who was almost incapable of staying out of an argument, was extremely difficult to comprehend. "He has not assumed anything," Adams wrote in frustration, "nor affected to take the lead; but has seemed to choose that the Congress pursue their own sentiments, and adopt their own plans." That Franklin was quietly proposing to equip the Continental Army with bows and arrows must have left Adams still more puzzled.

For Adams any sustained equivalent of Franklin's benign calm would have been impossible. Knowing his hour had come and that he must rise to the occasion and play a leading part, he would play it with all that was in him.

Among the opposition there were only two whom he disliked, Benjamin Harrison and Edward Rutledge. Harrison, an outspoken Virginia planter, six feet four inches tall and immensely fat, was a fervent champion of American rights who liked to say he would have come to Philadelphia on foot had it been necessary. To Adams, nonetheless, he was a profane and impious fool. Rutledge, the youngest member, was dandified, twenty-six years old, and overflowing with self-confidence. At first, Adams judged him "smart" if not "deep," but the more Rutledge talked, the more he expressed disagreement with Adams, the more scathing Adams's assessment became, to the point where, in his diary, he appeared nearly to run out of words. "Young Ned Rutledge is a perfect Bob o' Lincoln, a swallow, a sparrow, a peacock, excessively vain, excessively weak, and excessively variable and unsteady—jejune, inane, and puerile."

Yet Adams remained pointedly courteous to both men, as to others of the anti-independence faction. Among the surprises of the unfolding drama, as tensions increased, was the extent to which the ardent, disputatious John Adams held himself in rein, proving when need be a model of civility and self-restraint, even of patience.

In later years Adams would recall the warning advice given the Massachusetts delegation the day of their arrival for the First Congress. Benjamin Rush, Thomas Mifflin, and two or three other Philadelphia patriots had ridden out to welcome the Massachusetts men, and at a tavern in the village of Frankford, in the seclusion of a private room, they told the New Englanders they were "suspected of having independence in view." They were perceived to be "too zealous" and must not presume to take the lead. Virginia, they were reminded, was the largest, richest, and most populous of the colonies, and the "very proud" Virginians felt they had the right to lead.

According to Adams, the advice made a deep impression, and among the consequences was the choice of George Washington to head the army. But Adams also wrote that he had "not in my nature prudence and caution enough" always to stand back. Years before, at age twenty, he had set down in his diary that men ought to "avow their opinions and defend them with boldness," and he was of the same mettle still.

THE BULWARK OF THE OPPOSITION, of the "cool faction," was the Pennsylvania delegation, and the greatly respected John Dickinson was its eloquent floor leader. Cautious, conservative by nature, Dickinson

was, as Adams had noted, a distinctive figure, tall and exceptionally slender, with almost no color in his face. Because of his *Letters from a Pennsylvania Farmer*, an early pamphlet on the evils of British policy, Dickinson
had become a hero. He was "the Farmer," his name spoken everywhere,
though he was hardly the plain man of the soil many imagined. Born to
wealth and raised on an estate in Delaware, he had trained in the law at
London and made his career in Philadelphia, where he had risen rapidly
to the top of his profession. Married to a Quaker heiress, he lived in grand
style, riding through the city in a magnificent coach-and-four attended
by liveried black slaves. His town house, catercornered to the State
House on Chestnut Street, was then undergoing extensive alterations
and thought to be too large and showy even by his wife, who preferred
their nearby country seat, Fairhill.

Dickinson had wished to make a good first impression on Adams, and
he succeeded. As a dinner guest at Fairhill during the First Congress,
Adams was charmed. Dickinson "has an excellent heart, and the cause of
his country lies near it," Adams had written. As for his initial concern
that the rigors of Congress might be too much for someone of such delicate appearance, Adams had learned better. Though afflicted with the
gout, Dickinson had since assumed command of a Philadelphia battalion
with the rank of colonel. He had become the politician-soldier of the sort
Adams so often imagined himself, yet it was with a determination no less
than Adams's own that Dickinson kept telling Congress that peaceful
methods for resolving the current crisis were still possible and greatly
preferable. He was not a Tory. He was not opposed to independence in
principle. Rather, he insisted, now was not the time for so dangerous and
irrevocable a decision.

Adams had come to believe that Dickinson's real struggle was with his
mother and his wife, both devout Quakers who bedeviled him with their
pacifist views. "If I had such a mother and such a wife," Adams would
reflect years later, recalling Dickinson's predicament, "I believe I should
have shot myself."

Outraged by Dickinson's insistence on petitions to the King as essential to restoring peace, even after Lexington, Concord, and Bunker Hill,
Adams had strongly denounced any such step. Like many other delegates, he had been infuriated by Congress's humble petition of July 8,
1775, the so-called Olive Branch Petition, that had been Dickinson's

major contribution. From the day he saw with his own eyes what the British had done at Lexington and Concord, Adams failed to understand how anyone could have any misconception or naïve hope about what to expect from the British. "Powder and artillery are the most efficacious, sure and infallible conciliatory measures we can adopt," Adams wrote privately.

In a speech on the floor of Congress, Dickinson warned the New England delegates that they would have "blood . . . on their heads" if they excluded the possibility of peace. Adams, springing to his feet, responded so vehemently that when he left the chamber Dickinson came rushing after, to confront him outside.

"What is the reason, Mr. Adams, that you New England men oppose our measures of reconciliation?" Dickinson angrily demanded, according to Adams's later account of the scene. "Look, ye! If you don't concur with us in our pacific system, I, and a number of us, will break off from you in New England and we will carry on the opposition by ourselves in our own way."

Though infuriated by Dickinson's "magisterial" tone, Adams replied calmly that there were many accommodations he would make in the cause of harmony and unanimity. He would not, however, be threatened.

Venting his "fire" in a private letter, Adams portrayed Dickinson as a "piddling genius" who lent a "silly cast" to deliberations. The letter was intercepted by British agents and widely published in Tory newspapers, with the result that Dickinson refused to speak when, one morning on their way to the State House, he and Adams passed "near enough to touch elbows," as Adams recorded that day.

> He passed without moving his hat or head or hand. I bowed and pulled off my hat. He passed haughtily by. . . . But I was determined to make my bow, that I might know his temper.
>
> We are not to be on speaking terms, nor bowing terms, for the time to come.

Others refused to speak to Adams, so great was the respect for Dickinson in Congress and in the city. A British spy in Philadelphia named Gilbert Barkley reported to his contact in London, "The Quakers and many others look on him [Adams], and others of his way of thinking, as the greatest enemies of this country." For weeks Adams was ostracized, "avoided like a man infected with leprosy," he would remember. He felt as he had after the Boston Massacre trials, "borne down" by the weight of unpopularity. Benjamin Rush would write sympathetically of Adams walking the streets of Philadelphia alone, "an object of nearly universal scorn and detestation."

Such was the support for Dickinson and the Olive Branch Petition that Adams and his colleagues were left no choice but to acquiesce. The petition was agreed to—only to be summarily dismissed by George III, who refused even to look at it and proclaimed the colonies in a state of rebellion.

Still, Dickinson and the anti-independents clung to the hope of a resolution to the crisis, insisting reconciliation was still possible, and so the wait for the peace commissioners had continued.

WHAT NEITHER JOHN DICKINSON nor John Adams nor anyone could have anticipated was the stunning effect of *Common Sense*. The little pamphlet had become a clarion call, rousing spirits within Congress and without as nothing else had. The first edition, attributed to an unnamed "Englishman" and published by Robert Bell in a print shop on Third Street, appeared January 9, 1776. By the time Adams had resumed his place in Congress a month later, *Common Sense* had gone into a third edition and was sweeping the colonies. In little time more than 100,000 copies were in circulation. "Who is the author of *Common Sense*?" asked a correspondent from South Carolina in the *Philadelphia Evening Post*. "He deserves a statue of gold."

Written to be understood by everyone, *Common Sense* attacked the very idea of hereditary monarchy as absurd and evil, and named the "royal brute" George III as the cause of every woe in America. It was a call to arms, an unabashed argument for war, and a call for American independence, something that had never been said so boldly before in print. "Why is it that we hesitate? . . . The sun never shined on a cause of greater worth . . . for God's sake, let us come to a final separation. . . . The birthday of a new world is at hand."

The British spy, Barkley, reported its publication as he did such other vital news items as the arrival of shipments of gunpowder from the West

Indies, or the sailing from Philadelphia of armed sloops and brigantines flying "what they call the American flag."

The anonymous author was revealed to be a down-at-the-heels English immigrant, Thomas Paine, who had landed at Philadelphia a year earlier with little more than a letter of introduction from Benjamin Franklin. Paine had been encouraged in his efforts by Benjamin Rush, who was himself the author of a pamphlet on the evils of slavery, and it was Rush who provided the title.

Friends in Massachusetts reported to Adams that because of *Common Sense* the clamor for a declaration of independence was never greater. "This is the time . . . we have never had such a favorable moment," wrote one. In a letter to Abigail, referring to the copy he had sent her, Adams said he expected *Common Sense* to become the "common faith," and on learning that in Boston, he, Adams, was presumed to be the author, he felt flattered. Writing to a former law clerk, he declared himself innocent, saying he could never have achieved a style of such "strength and brevity." But Adams was not without misgivings. The more he thought about it, the less he admired *Common Sense*. The writer, he told Abigail, "has a better hand at pulling down than building."

That Paine had attempted to prove the unlawfulness of monarchy with analogies from the Bible, declaring monarchy to be "one of the sins of the Jews," struck Adams as ridiculous. Paine had assured his readers that in a war with Britain, Americans, being such experienced seamen and willing soldiers and having such an abundance of war matériel at hand, would readily triumph. Adams had no illusions about the prospect of war with Britain. Almost alone among the members of Congress, he saw no quick victory, but a long, painful struggle. The war, he warned prophetically in a speech on February 22, could last ten years. What was more, as he confided to Abigail's uncle, Isaac Smith, he thought "this American contest will light up a general war" in Europe.

But it was Paine's "feeble" understanding of constitutional government, his outline of a unicameral legislature to be established once independence was achieved, that disturbed Adams most. In response, he began setting down his own thoughts on government, resolved, as he later wrote, "to do all in my power to counteract the effect" on the popular mind of so foolish a plan.

Meanwhile, for all the gloom and discord at the State House, Congress was making decisions. On February 26 there was enacted an embargo on exports to Britain. On March 2, Silas Deane was appointed a secret envoy to France to go "in the character of a merchant" to buy clothing and arms, and to appraise the "disposition" of France should the colonies declare independence. Oliver Wolcott, Deane's fellow delegate from Connecticut, sensed the approach of a moment that could "decide the fate of this country." Adams busily jotted notes:

> Is any assistance attainable from F[rance]? What connection may we safely form with her. 1st. No political connection. Submit to none of her authority. . . . 2nd. No military connection. Receive no troops from her. 3rd. Only a commercial connection.

In the hope that the Canadians could be persuaded to join the American cause as "the 14th colony," Congress organized a diplomatic expedition to Montreal with Benjamin Franklin at its head, and despite his age and poor health, Franklin departed on what was to be an exceedingly arduous and futile mission.

Adams joined in floor debate day after day, arguing a point, pleading, persuading, and nearly always with effect. No one spoke more often or with greater force. "Every important step was opposed, and carried by bare majorities, which obliged me to be almost constantly engaged in debate," he would recall.

> But I was not content with all that was done, and almost every day, I had something to say about advising the states to institute governments, to express my total despair of any good coming from the petition or of those things which were called conciliatory measures. I constantly insisted that all such measures, instead of having any tendency to produce a reconciliation, would only be considered as proofs of our timidity and want of confidence in the ground we stood on, and would only encourage our enemies to greater exertions against us.

Rarely did he prepare his remarks in advance other than in his mind, so that once on his feet he could speak from what he knew and what he strongly felt. He had tried writing his speeches but found it impossible. "I understand it not," he would tell Benjamin Rush. "I never could write declamations, orations, or popular addresses."

He had no liking for grand oratorical flourishes. "Affectation is as disagreeable in a letter as in conversation," he once told Abigail, in explanation of his views on "epistolary style," and the same principle applied to making a speech. The art of persuasion, he held, depended mainly on a marshaling of facts, clarity, conviction, and the ability to think on one's feet. True eloquence consisted of truth and "rapid reason." As a British spy was later to write astutely of Adams, he also had a particular gift for seeing "large subjects largely."

He would stand at his place, back straight, walking stick in hand, at times letting the stick slip between thumb and forefinger to make a quick tap on the floor, as if to punctuate a point. The "clear and sonorous" voice would fill the room. No one ever had trouble hearing what Adams had to say, nor was there ever the least ambiguity about what he meant. Nothing of what he or anyone said in the course of debate was officially recorded. But in later writings Adams recalled stressing certain points repeatedly:

> We shall be driven to the necessity of declaring ourselves independent and we ought now to be employed in preparing a plan for confederation of the colonies, [here might come the sharp tap of the stick] and treaties to be proposed to foreign power [tap] . . . together with a declaration of independence [tap]. . . .
>
> Foreign powers can not be expected to acknowledge us, till we have acknowledged ourselves and taken our station among them as a sovereign power [tap], an independent nation [tap].

On March 14, Congress voted to disarm all Tories. On March 23, in a momentous step, the delegates resolved to permit the outfitting of privateers, "armed vessels," to prey on "the enemies of the United Colonies," a move Adams roundly supported. In the advocacy of sea defenses he stood second to none. The previous fall he had urged the creation of an American fleet, which to some, like Samuel Chase of Maryland, had seemed "the maddest idea in the world." The fight began on the floor, and on October 13, to the extent of authorizing funds for two small swift-sailing ships, Congress founded a navy. By the end of the year Congress had directed that thirteen frigates be built. Adams was appointed to a naval committee that met in a rented room at Tun Tavern, and it was Adams who drafted the first set of rules and regulations for the new navy, a point of pride with him for as long as he lived.

Knowing nothing of armed ships, he made himself expert, and would call his work on the naval committee the pleasantest part of his labors, in part because it brought him in contact with one of the singular figures in Congress, Stephen Hopkins of Rhode Island, who was nearly as old as Franklin and always wore his broad-brimmed Quaker hat in the chamber. Adams found most Quakers to be "dull as beetles," but Hopkins was an exception. A lively, learned man, he had seen a great deal of life, suffered the loss of three sons at sea, and served in one public office or other continuously from the time he was twenty-five. The old gentleman loved to drink rum and expound on his favorite writers. The experience and judgment he brought to the business of Congress were of great use, as Adams wrote, but it was in after-hours that he "kept us alive."

> His custom was to drink nothing all day, nor 'til eight o'clock in the evening, and then his beverage was Jamaica spirits and water. . . . He read Greek, Roman, and British history, and was familiar with English poetry. . . . And the flow of his soul made his reading our own, and seemed to bring to recollection in all of us all we had ever read.

Hopkins never drank to excess, according to Adams, but all he drank was promptly "converted into wit, sense, knowledge, and good humor."

There was more to be done by sea and land than anyone knew, Adams kept saying. When on March 25 word arrived that the British had abandoned Boston, setting off jubilant celebration in Philadelphia, he lost no time in advocating the immediate fortification of Boston Harbor. "Fortify, fortify, and never let them in again," he urged a friend at home. On April 6, in another decisive step, Congress opened American ports to the trade of all nations except Britain.

Half measures would not answer, Adams knew. The tentative attitude of Dickinson and the "Quaker interests" was becoming more and more difficult to tolerate. Adams's sense of urgency grew greater by the day. "The middle way is no way at all," he wrote to General Horatio

Gates. "If we finally fail in this great and glorious contest, it will be by bewildering ourselves in groping for the middle way."

"This story of [peace] commissioners is as arrant an illusion as ever hatched in the brain of an enthusiast, a politician, or a maniac," he told Abigail in a letter in which he confided that he had been busy at something, "about ten sheets of paper with my own hand," that he would have to tell her about later.

Adams's *Thoughts on Government,* as it would be known, was first set forth in a letter to a fellow congressman, William Hooper, who, before returning home to help write a new constitution for North Carolina, had asked Adams for a "sketch" of his views. When another of the North Carolinians, John Penn, requested a copy, this, too, Adams provided, in addition to three more copies, all written out by hand, for Jonathan Sergeant of New Jersey and Virginians George Wythe and Richard Henry Lee, who with Adams's consent, had the letter published as a pamphlet by the Philadelphia printer John Dunlap.

For Adams the structure of government was a subject of passionate interest that raised fundamental questions about the realities of human nature, political power, and the good society. It was a concern that for years had propelled much of his reading and the exchange of ideas with those whose judgment he most respected, including Abigail, who had written to him the year before, "I am more and more convinced that man is a dangerous creature, and that power whether vested in many or few is ever grasping. . . .

> The great fish swallow up the small [she had continued] and he who is most strenuous for the rights of the people, when vested with power, is as eager after the prerogatives of government. You tell me of degrees of perfection to which human nature is capable of arriving, and I believe it, but at the same time lament that our admiration should arise from the scarcity of the instances.

Adams had accused Thomas Paine of being better at tearing down than building. In what he wrote in response, he was being the builder, as best he knew. To do this he had had "to borrow a little time from my sleep." He was exhausted, he acknowledged, but he seems also to have sensed the importance of what he had done.

"It has been the will of Heaven," the essay began, "that we should be thrown into existence at a period when the greatest philosophers and law-givers of antiquity would have wished to live. . . .

> a period when a coincidence of circumstances without example has afforded to thirteen colonies at once an opportunity of beginning government anew from the foundation and building as they choose. How few of the human race have ever had an opportunity of choosing a system of government for themselves and their children? How few have ever had anything more of choice in government than in climate?

He was looking beyond independence, beyond the outcome of the war, to what would be established once independence and victory were achieved. Much as he foresaw the hard truth about the war to be waged, Adams had the clearest idea of anyone in Congress of what independence would actually entail, the great difficulties and risks, no less than the opportunities. When arguing cases in court, he liked to draw on the fables of La Fontaine and to quote the line "in every thing one must consider the end."

The happiness of the people was the purpose of government, he wrote, and therefore that form of government was best which produced the greatest amount of happiness for the largest number. And since all "sober inquirers after truth" agreed that happiness derived from virtue, that form of government with virtue as its foundation was more likely than any other to promote the general happiness.

The greatest minds agreed, Adams continued, that all good government was republican, and the "true idea" of a republic was "an empire of laws and not of men," a phrase not original with Adams but that he had borrowed from the writings of the seventeenth-century philosopher James Harrington. A government with a single legislative body would never do. There should be a representative assembly, "an exact portrait in miniature of the people at large," but it must not have the whole legislative power, for the reason that like an individual with unchecked power, it could be subject to "fits of humor, transports of passion, partialities of prejudice." A single assembly could "grow avaricious . . . exempt itself from burdens . . . become ambitious and after some time vote itself perpetual." Balance would come from the creation of a second, smaller legislative body, a "distinct assembly" of perhaps twenty or thirty, chosen by the larger legislature. This "Council," as Adams called it, would be given "free and independent judgment upon all acts of legislation that it may be able to check and correct the errors of the others."

The executive, the governor, should, Adams thought, be chosen by the two houses of the legislature, and for not more than a year at a time. Executive power would include the veto and the appointment of all judges and justices, as well as militia officers, thus making the executive the commander-in-chief of the armed forces.

Essential to the stability of government and to an "able and impartial administration of justice," Adams stressed, was separation of judicial power from both the legislative and executive. There must be an independent judiciary. "Men of experience on the laws, of exemplary morals, invincible patience, unruffled calmness and indefatigable application" should be "subservient to none" and appointed for life.

Finally and emphatically, he urged the widest possible support for education. "Laws for the liberal education of youth, especially for the lower classes of people, are so extremely wise and useful that to a humane and generous mind, no expense for this purpose would be thought extravagant."

Little that Adams ever wrote had such effect as his *Thoughts on Government.* Yet he felt it was too rough, "crude" in execution. He regretted insufficient time to write "more correctly."

FROM ABIGAIL CAME LONG LETTERS filled with news from home—of family, of politics, of her day-to-day struggle to manage expenses, cope with shortages, and keep the farm going, a responsibility for which little in her background had prepared her. "Frugality, industry, and economy are the lessons of the day," she confided to a friend, "at least they must be so for me or my small boat will suffer shipwreck." To John she pleaded repeatedly for more news of his health and his outlook, and filled pages with her own feelings for all that was transpiring at Philadelphia.

She was particularly curious about the Virginians, wondering if, as slaveholders, they had the necessary commitment to the cause of freedom. "I have," she wrote, "sometimes been ready to think that the passion for liberty cannot be equally strong in the breasts of those who have been accustomed to deprive their fellow creature of theirs." What she felt about those in Massachusetts who owned slaves, including her own father, she did not say, but she need not have—John knew her mind on the subject. Writing to him during the First Congress, she had been unmistakably clear: "I wish most sincerely there was not a slave in the province. It always seemed a most iniquitous scheme to me—[to] fight ourselves for what we are daily robbing and plundering from those who have as good a right to freedom as we have."

It had been two weeks now since she had seen the British fleet sail out of Boston, and she viewed the approach of spring very differently than she had only a month before. Her world had been transformed. She was experiencing an uncommon *"gaiety de coeur,"* she wrote. "I think the sun shines brighter, the birds sing more melodiously." She longed to hear word of independence declared. Her spirit took flight at the thought:

> —and by the way in the new code of laws which I suppose it will be necessary for you to make, I desire you would remember the ladies, and be more favorable to them than your ancestors. Do not put such unlimited power into the hands of husbands.

Borrowing a line from a poem by Daniel Defoe that she knew he would recognize (for he had used it, too), she wrote, "Remember all men would be tyrants if they could.

> If particular care and attention is not paid to the ladies we are determined to foment a rebellion, and will not hold ourselves bound by any laws in which we have no voice or representation.
>
> That your sex are naturally tyrannical is a truth so thoroughly established as to admit of no dispute, but such of yours as wish to be happy willingly give up the harsh title of master for the more tender and endearing one of friend. Why then not put it out of the power of the vicious and the lawless to use us with cruelty and indignity with impunity. Men of sense in all ages abhor those customs which treat us only as vassals of your sex. Regard us then as being placed by providence under your protection and in imitation of the Supreme Being make use of that power only for our happiness.

She was not being entirely serious. In part, in her moment of spring-time *gaiety*, she was teasing him. But only in part.

Adams responded in a light spirit. "I cannot but laugh," he began.

We have been told that our struggle has loosened the bands of government everywhere; that children and apprentices were disobedient; that schools and colleges were grown turbulent; that Indians slighted their guardians and Negroes grew insolent to their masters. But your letter was the first intimation that another tribe more numerous and powerful than all the rest were grown discontented. This is rather too coarse a compliment but you are so saucy, I won't blot it out.

Depend on it, we know better than to repeal our masculine systems. Although they are in full force, you know they are little more than theory. We dare not exert our power in its full latitude. We are obliged to go fair and softly, and in practice you know we are the subjects. We have only the name of masters, and rather than give up this, which would completely subject us to the despotism of the petticoat, I hope General Washington and all our brave heroes would fight.

Others wrote from Massachusetts to question why it was taking so long to accomplish what everyone at home was demanding. "People can't account for the hesitancy they observe," said James Warren, while his wife, Mercy Otis Warren, who was a playwright and a woman Adams particularly admired, lectured him on the ideal republican government she foresaw for the future union of the colonies.

Replying to James Warren on April 16, Adams could hardly control his anger. "Have you seen the privateering resolves? Are not those independence enough for my beloved constituents? Have you seen the resolves opening our ports to all nations? Are these independence enough? What more would you have?"

But writing again to Warren, Adams tried to explain the concern and hesitation over independence. "All great changes are irksome to the human mind, especially those which are attended with great dangers and uncertain effects. No man living can foresee the consequences of such a measure."

The future was exceedingly dangerous, Adams felt certain. His mind was much on eventualities, given what he knew of human nature.

> We may please ourselves with the prospect of free and popular governments. But there is great danger that those governments will not make us happy. God grant they may. But I fear that in every assembly, members will obtain an influence by noise not sense. By meanness, not greatness. By ignorance, not learning. By contracted hearts, not large souls. . . .
>
> There is one thing, my dear sir, that must be attempted and most sacredly observed or we are all undone. There must be decency and respect, and veneration introduced for persons of authority of every rank, or we are undone. In a popular government, this is our only way.

To Mercy Warren, Adams counseled, "Patience! Patience! Patience!"

A week or so after denouncing the tyranny of men, Abigail wrote to say that in her loneliness and with so much riding on her shoulders, she scarcely knew which way to turn. "I miss my partner and find myself unequal to the cares which fall upon me. . . . I want to say many things I must omit. It is not fit to wake the soul by tender strokes of art, or to ruminate upon happiness we might enjoy, lest absences become intolerable."

She wished he would burn her letters, she said in postscript.

Sometimes he wrote to her from Congress itself. ("When a man is seated in the midst of forty people, some of whom are talking, and others whispering, it is not easy to think what is proper to write," he would tell her.) On April 18 she asked if he would be home in May or June, and to say she thought of him only "with the tenderest affection." He, on April 23, went on about his Philadelphia barber who more than anyone helped him maintain a sense of proportion. "He is a little dapper fellow . . . a tongue as fluent and voluble as you please, wit at will, and . . . never . . . at a loss for a story to tell . . . while he is shaving and combing me . . . he contributes more than I could have imagined to my comfort in this life."

But having received her letter, Adams became about as tender as he would allow on paper.

Is there no way for two friendly souls to converse together, although the bodies are 400 miles off. Yes, by letter. But I want a better communication. I want to hear you think, or to see your thoughts.

The conclusion of your letter makes my heart throb more than a cannonade would. You bid me burn your letters. But I must forget you first.

She followed at length, this time with thoughts on his concerns, writing that "a people may let a King fall, yet still remain a people, but if a King let his people slip from him, he is no longer a King. And as this is most certainly our case, why not proclaim to the world in decisive terms our own importance?"

"I think you shine as a stateswoman," he responded exuberantly, and in another letter wrote:

Your sentiments of the duties we owe to our country are such as become the best of women and the best of men. Among all the disappointments and perplexities which have fallen my share in life, nothing has contributed so much to support my mind as the choice blessing of a wife. . . .

I want to take a walk with you in the garden—to go over to the common, the plain, the meadow. I want to take Charles in one hand and Tom in the other, and walk with you, Nabby on your right hand and John on my left, to view the corn fields, the orchards . . .

Alas, poor imagination! How faintly and imperfectly do you supply the want of [the] original and reality!

SPRING HAD ARRIVED. Days of warm April rain and intermittent sunshine followed one after another. Trees were leafing out. In the enclosed backyards of the city, cherry blossoms burst into flower, followed by a profusion of lilacs in bloom.

Behind the closed doors of Congress the current of events seemed also to turn with the season as the delegates of three southern colonies, South Carolina, Georgia, and North Carolina, received instructions freeing them to vote for independence. Even among the opposition, there was growing agreement on the need for unanimity, "harmony," a healing of disputes. "It is a true saying of a wit," wrote Carter Braxton of Virginia, referring possibly to Benjamin Franklin, "we must hang together or separately."

Then, on the afternoon of Wednesday, May 8, Philadelphia heard the muffled but unmistakable thunder of cannon from thirty miles down the Delaware, as two heavily armed British ships, the frigate *Roebuck* and sloop-of-war *Liverpool*, tried to run the river defenses, a blockade of armed gondolas. The crash of cannon went on for two days before the ships turned back. No great damage was done, and to many it all seemed, as said in the *Pennsylvania Gazette*, "a most interesting spectacle." Thousands rushed by carriage and horseback to watch from the shoreline. But it had also been vivid proof that the war was no abstraction and could in fact come to Philadelphia in all its fury, a thought many had preferred not to face. The British fleet that evacuated Boston, it was now known, had sailed to Halifax, where presumably it was waiting for reinforcements before returning to attack New York.

By sundown May 9, the excitement down the river had ended. On the day after, Friday, May 10, came what many in Congress knew to be a critical juncture. Adams had decided the time was ripe to make his move.

With Richard Henry Lee, he put forth a resolution recommending that the individual colonies assume all powers of government—to secure "the happiness and safety of their constituents in particular, and America in general." Not only was it passed, but with surprising unanimity. It awaited only a preamble which, as drafted by Adams, was a still more radical statement. This brought on three days of fierce debate, during which Adams repeatedly took the floor, supported by Richard Henry Lee, while James Wilson of Pennsylvania argued in opposition. A decision that could clear the way to independence had at last arrived.

In contrast to the resolution, Adams's preamble put aside any possibility of reconciliation and all but declared the colonies immediately independent:

Whereas his Britannic Majesty, in conjunction with the lords and commons of Great Britain, has, by a late act of Parliament, excluded the inhabitants of these United Colonies from the protection of his crown; and whereas, no answer whatever to the humble petitions of the colonies for redress of grievances and reconciliation with Great Britain has been or is likely to be given; but the whole force of that kingdom, aided by foreign mercenaries, is to be exerted for the destruction of the good people of these colonies; and whereas it appears absolutely irreconcilable to reason and good conscience, for people of these colonies to take the oaths and affirmations necessary for the support of any government under the crown of Great Britain ... it is [therefore] necessary that the exercise of every kind of authority under the said crown should be totally suppressed, and all the powers of government exerted under the authority of the people of the colonies, for the preservation of internal peace, virtue, and good order, as well as the defense of their lives, liberties, and properties, against hostile invasions and cruel depredations of their enemies.

"Why all this haste?" James Duane demanded, according to notes that Adams kept. "Why all this driving?"

Samuel Adams, who rarely spoke in Congress, rose from his place. "I wonder the people have conducted so well as they have," he said.

James Wilson responded, "Before we are prepared to build a new house, why should we pull down the old one, and expose ourselves to all the inclemencies of the season?"

John Dickinson was absent, apparently indisposed, a victim of exhaustion.

What John Adams said was not recorded. But as the constant battler on the floor, with all that he had written, his work on committees, his relentless energy, industry, and unyielding determination, he had emerged a leader like no other, and when the breakthrough came at last on Wednesday, May 15, it was his victory more than anyone's in Congress.

The preamble was approved. When an exasperated James Duane told Adams it seemed "a machine for the fabrication of independence," Adams replied that he thought it "independence itself." He was elated. Congress, he wrote, had that day "passed the most important resolution that was ever taken in America."

Others agreed. Even "the *cool considerate men* think it amounts to a declaration of independence," wrote Caesar Rodney enthusiastically.

Most telling was the immediate effect in Pennsylvania, in Philadelphia itself, where popular opinion took a dramatic turn in support of independence.

At his lodgings two days later, Adams sat quietly writing to Abigail:

When I consider the great events which are passed, and those greater which are rapidly advancing, and that I may have been instrumental of touching some springs, and turning some wheels, which have had and will have such effects, I feel an awe upon my mind which is not easily described.

"I have reasons to believe," he added, "that no colony which shall assume a government under the people, will give it up."

III

THE DAYS HAD BECOME as warm as summer. "Fine sunshine," recorded Adams's Philadelphia friend Christopher Marshall one day after another. "Uncommonly hot . . . uncomfortable both to horse and man," registered Josiah Bartlett, who, returning to Congress from the cool of New Hampshire, was astonished to see fields of winter rye in New Jersey already full grown by the middle of May.

Thomas Jefferson, on reaching Philadelphia, decided, "as the excessive heats of the city are coming fast," to find lodgings "on the skirts of town where I may have the benefit of circulating air." He moved to spacious quarters in a new brick house at the southwest corner of Seventh and Market, in what was nearly open country. They were larger, more expensive accommodations than most delegates had—a suite of two rooms, bedroom and parlor on the second floor, with ample windows for "circulating air"—and unlike most delegates, he would reside alone, separate from the rest.

Jefferson had arrived on May 14 after a pleasant week's journey by horseback from the Piedmont of Virginia, accompanied by a single servant, a fourteen-year-old slave named Bob Hemings. Jefferson's road to Philadelphia, the reverse of Adams's, had been north by northeast, through the red-clay countryside of Virginia to Noland's Ferry on the

Potomac, then on into Maryland, winding past miles of prosperous-looking farms that became still more prosperous-looking as he crossed into Pennsylvania.

On resuming his seat in Congress, at the climax of debate over Adams's preamble, Jefferson had felt as nearly unsuited for the business at hand as for the stifling city climate. "I've been so long out of the political world that I am almost a new man in it," he wrote his college friend and confidant John Page. He worried about his ill wife at home. Given the choice, he would have preferred to be at Williamsburg, where a new Virginia constitution was being drafted. Of more immediate concern than the doings of Congress, it would appear from what he wrote Page, were some books, a two-volume French history of the Celts and a book on English gardens that he hoped Page would purchase for him from an estate sale.

At thirty-three Thomas Jefferson was the youngest of the Virginia delegates. He had not attended the First Congress, when Washington and Patrick Henry had been part of the delegation, and the Virginians with their liveried servants and splendid horses had ridden into the city like princelings. His role in the Second Congress had been on the whole modest. If he was conspicuous, it was mainly because of his height. At six feet two-and-a-half inches, he stood taller than all but a few and towered over someone like John Hancock, who at five feet four was perhaps the shortest man in the assembly. Standing beside John Adams, Jefferson looked like a lanky, freckled youth.

With eight years difference in their age, Adams was Jefferson's senior, both in years and political experience. The differences in physique, background, manner, and temperament could hardly have been more contrasting. Where Adams was stout, Jefferson was lean and long-limbed, almost bony. Where Adams stood foursquare to the world, shoulders back, Jefferson customarily stood with his arms folded tightly across his chest. When taking his seat, it was as if he folded into a chair, all knees and elbows and abnormally large hands and feet. Where Adams was nearly bald, Jefferson had a full head of thick coppery hair. His freckled face was lean like his body, the eyes hazel, the mouth a thin line, the chin sharp.

Jefferson was a superb horseman, beautiful to see. He sang, he played the violin. He was as accomplished in the classics as Adams, but also in mathematics, horticulture, architecture, and in his interest in and knowledge of science he far exceeded Adams. Jefferson dabbled in "improvements" in agriculture and mechanical devices. His was the more inventive mind. He adored designing and redesigning things of all kinds. Jefferson, who may never have actually put his own hand to a plow, as Adams had, would devise an improved plow based on mathematical principles, "a moldboard of least resistance," and find equal satisfaction in arriving at the perfect shape for a stone column or silver goblet.

Jefferson was devoted to the ideal of improving mankind but had comparatively little interest in people in particular. Adams was not inclined to believe mankind improvable, but was certain it was important that human nature be understood.

In contrast to Adams's need to fill pages of his diaries with his innermost thoughts and feelings, Jefferson kept neat account books. In an invariably precise hand, he recorded every purchase, every payment for meals, wines, books, violin strings, the least item of clothing. Unlike Adams, who, except for books, indulged himself in no expenditures beyond what were necessary, Jefferson was continually in and out of Philadelphia shops, buying whatever struck his fancy.

In the spirit of science, Jefferson maintained letter-perfect records of weights, measurements, and daily temperature readings. (Adams is not known even to have owned a thermometer.) "Nothing was too small for him to keep account of," one of his plantation overseers would remember of Jefferson. Yet he kept no personal diary, and for all the hours given to what he called "pen and ink work," Jefferson rarely ever revealed his inner feelings in what he wrote. He had nothing like Adams's fascination with human nature and, quite unlike Adams, little sense of humor. "He is a man of science," a close observer would later write of Jefferson. "But . . . he knows little of the nature of man—very little indeed."

It was Jefferson's graciousness that was so appealing. He was never blunt or assertive as Adams could be, but subtle, serene by all appearances, always polite, soft-spoken, and diplomatic, if somewhat remote. With Adams there was seldom a doubt about what he meant by what he said. With Jefferson there was nearly always a slight air of ambiguity. In private conversation Jefferson "sparkled." But in Congress, like Franklin, he scarcely said a word, and if he did, it was in a voice so weak as to be almost inaudible. Rarely would he object to a point or disagree with anyone to his face. "Never contradict anybody," he was advised by Franklin, whom he admired above all men, though it was advice he hardly needed. He "abhorred dispute," as he said, shrank from the contentiousness of politics, and instinctively avoided confrontation of any kind. It was as if he were trying to proceed through life as he had designed his moldboard plow to go through the red clay of Virginia, with the least resistance possible.

Years later, still puzzling over Jefferson's passivity at Philadelphia, Adams would claim that "during the whole time I sat with him in Congress, I never heard him utter three sentences together."

Jefferson himself would one day advise a grandson, "When I hear another express an opinion which is not mine, I say to myself, he has a right to his opinion, as I to mine.

> Why should I question it. His error does me no injury, and shall I become a Don Quixote, to bring all men by force of argument to one opinion? . . . Be a listener only, keep within yourself, and endeavor to establish with yourself the habit of silence, especially in politics.

Jefferson wished to avoid the rough and tumble of life whenever possible. John Adams's irrepressible desire was to seize hold of it, and at times his was to be the path of Don Quixote.

A departure from Jefferson's prevailing silence in Congress came late that summer when he stood in opposition to a proposal for a fast day, and in so doing appeared to cast aspersions on Christianity, to which Adams reacted sharply. Benjamin Rush reminded Adams of the incident in a letter written years later.

> You rose and defended the motion, and in reply to Mr. Jefferson's objections to Christianity you said you were sorry to hear such sentiments from a gentleman whom you so highly respected and with whom you agreed upon so many subjects, and that it was the only instance you had ever known of a man of sound sense and real genius that was an enemy to Christianity. You suspected, you told me, that

you had offended him, but that he soon convinced you to the contrary by crossing the room and taking a seat in the chair next to you.

In one regard only did Jefferson's behavior seem at odds with his usual placid way. If unwilling or unable to express anger, or passion, in his dealings with other men, he could be very different with his horse. As would be said within his own family, "The only impatience of temper he ever exhibited was with his horse, which he subdued to his will by a fearless application of the whip on the slightest manifestation of restiveness."

As the author of the *Summary View*, the young Virginian had, as Adams said, achieved "the reputation of a *masterly* pen," and however reticent in Congress, he proved "prompt, frank, explicit, and decisive upon committees and in conversation. . . ." That Jefferson, after attending the College of William and Mary, had read law at Williamsburg for five years with the eminent George Wythe, gave him still greater standing with Adams, who considered Wythe one of the ablest men in Congress. In his journal, Adams recorded a remark made by the New Yorker James Duane to the effect that Jefferson was "the greatest rubber off of dust" that Duane had ever met, and that he spoke French, Italian, and Spanish, and was working on German. The journal entry, dated October 25, 1775, was Adams's first recorded mention of Jefferson.

Sensitive to Adams's seniority and his importance in Congress—and possibly to Adams's vanity—Jefferson was consistently deferential to him. Clearly, too, for all their differences, they had much in common, not the least of which was their love of words, of books, and serious scholarship. They were as widely read, as learned as any two men in Congress. A list of the favorite authors of either could have served for the other. They had read the same law, distinguished themselves at an early age in the same profession, though Jefferson had never relished the practice of law as Adams had, nor felt the financial need to keep at it.

They were men who loved noble endeavor, who shared a disdain for indolence, and hated wasting time. Jefferson's devotion to home, to family, and his own native ground was quite as strong as Adams's. When Jefferson spoke of "my country," he usually meant Virginia, as Adams referred to Massachusetts as "my country." The one was as proudly a Virginian as the other a Yankee. The stamp of their origins was strong on both, and neither would have acknowledged any better place on earth than his "country," though neither, it is true, had yet seen much else. As Adams had never been farther south than Philadelphia, Jefferson had been no farther north than New York.

But in this, too, was the root of differences that ran deep and would prove long-lasting, for the reason that Massachusetts and Virginia were truly different countries. Indeed, it would be difficult for future generations to comprehend how much separated a man raised on a freeholder's farm in coastal New England from a son of Virginia such as Thomas Jefferson.

Jefferson had been born to respectable wealth achieved by his father, Peter Jefferson, a man of rugged vitality, tobacco planter and surveyor, and to an unassailable place in the Virginia aristocracy through his mother, Jane, who was a Randolph. His landholdings in Albemarle County, mostly inherited from his father, exceeded 5,000 acres. But where Adams, at his farm by Penn's Hill, lived very much like his father, and among the people of the town, Jefferson, very unlike his father or other Virginia planters, had removed to a mountaintop, removed from contact with everyday life, to create a palatial country seat of his own design in the manner of the sixteenth-century Italian architect Andrea Palladio.

It was a bold undertaking that spoke of unusually cultivated taste and high ambition, and was made possible by the added wealth that came with his marriage to Martha Wayles Skelton, a young widow.

He had started the project at the age of twenty-five, in 1768. Still only partly built, it had the high, columned porticoes of a classic Italian villa and carried a name, Monticello, meaning "little mountain" in old Italian. He had contracted for 100,000 bricks, ordered specially made window frames from London, and in Philadelphia purchased the unexpired servitude of an indentured servant, a stonecutter, to do the columns. It was a house and setting such as John Adams had never seen or could ever have imagined as his own, any more than he could have imagined the scale of Jefferson's domain. On his daily rounds by horseback, surveying his crops and fields, where as many as a hundred black slaves labored, Jefferson would commonly ride ten miles, as far as from Braintree to Boston, without ever leaving his own land. Further, he owned another 5,000-acre plantation to the southwest in Bedford County, an inheritance from his wife's father.

Jefferson had been raised and educated as the perfect landed gentleman of Virginia. He knew no other way. His earliest childhood memory was of being carried on a pillow by a slave and in countless ways he had been carried ever since by slaves, though they were never called that, but rather "servants" or "laborers." It was not just that slaves worked his fields; they cut his firewood, cooked and served his meals, washed and ironed his linen, brushed his suits, nursed his children, cleaned, scrubbed, polished, opened and closed doors for him, saddled his horse, turned down his bed, waited on him hand and foot from dawn to dusk.

By 1776, with the addition of the land inherited from his father-in-law, Jefferson reckoned himself a wealthy man and lived like one. With the inheritance also came substantial debts and still more slaves, but then in Virginia this was seen as a matter of course. The whole economy and way of life were built on slaves and debt, with tobacco planters in particular dependent on slave labor and money borrowed from English creditors against future crops. John Adams, by contrast, had neither debts nor slaves and all his life abhorred the idea of either.

In keeping with his background, Adams was less than dazzled by the Virginia grandees. In Virginia, he would say, "all geese are swans." Jefferson, for his part, knew little or nothing of New Englanders and counted none as friends. A man of cultivated, even fastidious tastes, Jefferson was later to tell his Virginia neighbor James Madison that he had observed in Adams a certain "want of taste," this apparently in reference to the fact that Adams was known on occasion to chew tobacco and take his rum more or less straight.

Jefferson had been slower, more cautious and ambivalent than Adams about resolving his views on independence. As recently as August 1775, less than a year past, Jefferson had written to a Tory kinsman, John Randolph, of "looking with fondness towards a reconciliation with Great Britain." He longed for the "return of the happy period when, consistently with duty, I may withdraw myself totally from the public stage, and pass the rest of my days in domestic ease and tranquillity, banishing every desire of afterwards even hearing what passes in the world." But in the same letter he declared that "rather than submit to the right of legislating for us assumed by the British parliament and which late experience has shown they will so cruelly exercise, [I] would lend my hand to sink the whole island in the ocean." His commitment now in the spring of 1776 was no less than Adams's own. And it was because of their common zeal for independence, their wholehearted, mutual devotion to the common cause of America, and the certainty that they were taking part in one of history's turning points, that the two were able to concentrate on the common purpose in a spirit of respect and cooperation, putting aside obvious differences, as well as others not so obvious and more serious than they could then have known.

Adams considered Jefferson his protégé at Philadelphia; Jefferson, impressed by Adams's clarity and vigor in argument, his "sound head," looked upon him as a mentor. They served on committees together, and as the pace quickened in the weeks after Jefferson's arrival, they were together much of the time. As would be said, each felt the value of the other in the common task.

IF THERE WAS "a tide in the affairs of men," as Abigail had reminded John, now was "the flood." "Every post and every day rolls in upon us independence like a torrent," he wrote on May 20.

Despite drenching rain, an open-air public meeting that day at the State House Yard drew a throng of thousands who listened as the May 15 resolve was read aloud, then voiced a demand vote for a new Pennsylvania constitution and a new legislature.

At week's end, on Friday, May 24, General Washington arrived for two days of meetings with Congress to report his heightened concern for the situation at New York, where a British attack was expected any time. The King, it was now known, had hired some 17,000 German troops to fight in America. At New York, Washington had at most 7,000 men fit for duty.

Three days later came word that on May 15, the Virginia convention at Williamsburg had resolved unanimously to instruct the Virginia delegation at Philadelphia "to declare the United Colonies free and independent states." An exultant John Adams wrote to Patrick Henry that the "natural course and order of things" was coming to pass at last. "The decree is gone forth, and it cannot be recalled, that a more equal liberty than had prevailed in other parts of the earth must be established in America."

On Friday, June 7, at the State House, Richard Henry Lee rose to speak. Sunshine streamed through the high windows. Lee, slim and elegant, was a spirited orator who was said to practice his gestures before a mirror. In a hunting accident years before, he had lost the fingers of his left hand, which he kept wrapped in a black handkerchief, and this, with his lithe figure and aquiline nose, gave him a decidedly theatrical presence. The importance of the moment was understood by everyone in the room.

> Resolved [Lee began]: . . . That these United Colonies are, and of a right ought to be, free and independent states, that they are absolved from all allegiance to the British Crown, and that all political connection between them and the state of Great Britain is, and ought to be, totally dissolved.

Adams immediately seconded the motion and the day following, Saturday, June 8, the debate began. Speaking in opposition, John Dickinson, James Wilson, Robert Livingston, and Edward Rutledge declared, according to notes kept by Jefferson, that while "friends of the measure," they opposed any declaration of independence until "the voice of the people" drove them to it. Further, should Congress proceed before hearing the "voice," then certain colonies "might secede from the union." It was the threat Dickinson in his anger had used earlier against Adams, but whether it was Dickinson speaking now, Jefferson did not record. Nor did he record what Adams, Lee, and George Wythe said, only that they declared public opinion to be ahead of Congress: that "the people wait for us to lead the way," that the European powers would neither trade nor treat with the colonies until they established independence, that "the present [military] campaign may be unsuccessful, and therefore we had better propose an alliance while our affairs wear a hopeful aspect." And that it was essential "to lose no time."

Intense debate continued past dark. Candles were brought in. "The sensible part of the house opposed the motion," wrote an irate Edward Rutledge. "No reason could be assigned for pressing into this measure, but the reason of every madman."

On Monday, June 10, after President John Hancock reconvened the assembly, Rutledge and the "cool party" succeeded in having the final vote delayed for twenty days, until July 1, to allow delegates from the middle colonies time to send for new instructions. Nonetheless, it was agreed that no time be lost in preparing a declaration of independence. A committee was appointed, the Committee of Five, as it became known, consisting of Jefferson, Adams, Roger Sherman, Robert Livingston, and Benjamin Franklin, who had by now returned from his expedition to Canada but was ill and exhausted and rarely seen.

On the floor above, meantime, in the Banqueting Hall of the State House, another revolution was transpiring as the Pennsylvania Assembly struggled over what instructions to give its delegation.

Adams, who had not written a word to Abigail in nearly two weeks, dashed off a letter saying, "Great things are on the tapis."

JEFFERSON WAS TO DRAFT the declaration. But how this was agreed to was never made altogether clear. He and Adams would have differing explanations, each writing long after the fact.

According to Adams, Jefferson proposed that he, Adams, do the writing, but that he declined, telling Jefferson he must do it.

"Why?" Jefferson asked, as Adams would recount.

"Reasons enough," Adams said.

"What can be your reasons?"

"Reason first: you are a Virginian and a Virginian ought to appear at the head of this business. Reason second: I am obnoxious, suspected and unpopular. You are very much otherwise. Reason third: You can write ten times better than I can."

Jefferson would recall no such exchange. As Jefferson remembered, the committee simply met and unanimously chose him to undertake the draft. "I consented: I drew it [up]."

Possibly neither of their memories served, and possibly both were correct. Jefferson may well have been the choice of the committee and out of deference or natural courtesy, he may well have offered Adams the honor. If there is anything that seems not in keeping, it is the tone of Adams's self-deprecation, which is more that of the old man he became than the Adams of 1776, who was anything but inadequate as a writer and who was by no means as unpopular as he later said. If he was thought "obnoxious," it would have been only by a few, and only he himself is known to have used the word. In all the surviving record of official and private papers pertaining to the Continental Congress, there is only one member or eyewitness to events in Philadelphia in 1776 who wrote disparagingly of John Adams, and that was Adams writing long years afterward. As critical as he could be in his assessment of others, the man he was inclined to criticize most severely was himself. In fact, the respect he commanded at Philadelphia that spring appears to have been second to none.

Unquestionably, Adams did value Jefferson's literary talents, but he knew also how much else he must attend to in the little time available, and the outcome of the "great question" was by no means certain. Already Adams was serving on twenty-three committees, and that same week was assigned to three more, including an all-important new Continental Board of War and Ordnance, of which he was to be the president.

That there would be political advantage in having the declaration written by a Virginian was clear, for the same reason there had been political advantage in having the Virginian Washington in command of the army. But be that as it may, Jefferson, with his "peculiar felicity of expression," as Adams said, was the best choice for the task, just as Washington had been the best choice to command the Continental Army, and again Adams had played a key part. Had his contribution as a member of Congress been only that of casting the two Virginians in their respective, fateful roles, his service to the American cause would have been very great.

ALONE IN HIS UPSTAIRS PARLOR at Seventh and Market, Jefferson went to work, seated in an unusual revolving Windsor chair and holding on his lap a portable writing box, a small folding desk of his own design which, like the chair, he had had specially made for him by a Philadelphia cabinetmaker. Traffic rattled by below the open windows. The June days and nights turned increasingly warm.

He worked rapidly and, to judge by surviving drafts, with a sure command of his material. He had none of his books with him, nor needed any, he later claimed. It was not his objective to be original, he would explain, only "to place before mankind the common sense of the subject."

Neither aiming at originality of principle or sentiment, nor yet
copied from any particular and previous writing, it was intended to
be an expression of the American mind, and to give to that expression the proper tone and spirit called for by the occasion.

He borrowed readily from his own previous writing, particularly from
a recent draft for a new Virginia constitution, but also from a declaration
of rights for Virginia, which appeared in the *Pennsylvania Evening Post*
on June 12. It had been drawn up by George Mason, who wrote that "all
men are born equally free and independent, and have certain inherent
natural rights . . . among which are the enjoyment of life and liberty."
And there was a pamphlet written by the Pennsylvania delegate James
Wilson, published in Philadelphia in 1774, that declared, "All men are,
by nature equal and free: no one has a right to any authority over another
without his consent: all lawful government is founded on the consent of
those who are subject to it."

But then Mason, Wilson, and John Adams, no less than Jefferson,
were, as they all appreciated, drawing on long familiarity with the semi-
nal works of the English and Scottish writers John Locke, David Hume,
Francis Hutcheson, and Henry St. John Bolingbroke, or such English
poets as Defoe ("When kings the sword of justice first lay down, / They
are no kings, though they possess the crown. / Titles are shadows,
crowns are empty things, / The good of subjects is the end of kings"). Or,
for that matter, Cicero. ("The people's good is the highest law.")

Adams, in his earlier notes for an oration at Braintree, had written,
"Nature throws us all into the world equal and alike. . . . The only maxim
of a free government ought to be to trust no man [kings included] to
endanger public liberty." The purpose of government, he had said in
his recent *Thoughts on Government*, was the "greatest quantity of human
happiness."

What made Jefferson's work surpassing was the grace and eloquence
of expression. Jefferson had done superbly and in minimum time.

I was delighted with its high tone and flights of oratory with which it
abounded [Adams would recall], especially that concerning Negro
slavery, which, though I knew his southern brethren would never
suffer to pass in Congress, I certainly would never oppose. There

were other expressions which I would not have inserted, if I had drawn it up, particularly that which called the King tyrant. . . . I thought the expression too passionate; and too much like scolding, for so grave and solemn a document; but as Franklin and Sherman were to inspect it afterwards, I thought it would not become me to strike it out. I consented to report it, and do not now remember that I made or suggested a single alteration.

A number of alterations were made, however, when Jefferson reviewed it with the committee, and several were by Adams. Possibly it was Franklin, or Jefferson himself, who made the small but inspired change in the second paragraph. Where, in the initial draft, certain "truths" were described as "sacred and undeniable," a simpler, stronger "self-evident" was substituted.

We hold these truths to be self-evident, that all men are created equal . . .

Adams had no doubt that there would be further changes called for and considerable debate over details and language once the declaration was submitted to Congress for approval. Still, he was confident enough about the draft that he laboriously transcribed the full text in his own hand, and later sent the copy to Abigail, who, understandably, thought he had written the Declaration.

THE PRESSURES OF RESPONSIBILITY grew greater for Adams almost by the hour. As head of the new Board of War, meeting every morning and evening, he was acutely aware of Washington's distress at New York. Dispatch riders from the general's headquarters brought repeated warnings that arms, lead, flints, medicines, and entrenching tools were all urgently needed. At Boston the troops were "almost mutinous in want of pay." In Canada, where the remnants of an American army were still holding out, the situation was gravely compounded by the ravages of smallpox.

On June 15, the provincial legislature of New Jersey had ordered the arrest of its royal governor, William Franklin, the estranged, illegitimate son of Benjamin Franklin, and authorized its delegates in Congress to vote for independence. To see that this was done, five new New Jersey delegates had been appointed.

In Maryland, delegate Samuel Chase, who had earlier gone to Canada with Benjamin Franklin, was rounding up support for independence, as perhaps no one else could have. A huge, red-faced young man of inexhaustible energy, Chase refused to accept the dictum that Maryland's delegates must vote down independence. "I have not been idle," he reported to Adams.

As he had for months now, Adams struggled to keep a balance with the need, on one hand, for all possible haste, and the need, on the other, to keep from pushing too fast, forcing events too soon. Some things, some people, must not be hurried. Time and timing were both of the essence, now more than ever. Reminders of time passing were everywhere about him: the great clock ticking away on the outside wall of the State House; bells at night striking the hour; the "clarions" of a hundred roosters calling across town as he began his day at first light.

"What in the name of *Common Sense* are you gentlemen of the Continental Congress about?" demanded a constituent writing from Massachusetts. "Is it dozing?"

"The only question is concerning the proper time for making a specific declaration in words," Adams replied.

> Some people must have time to look around them, before, behind, on the right hand, and on the left, and then to think, and after all this to resolve. Others see at one intuitive glance into the past and the future, and judge with precision at once. But remember you can't make thirteen clocks strike precisely alike at the same second.

No one in Congress had worked harder or done more to bring about a break with Britain. But it was the fact of independence more than the words on paper that concerned Adams, and especially for what it would do to unify the colonies and bring "spirit" to American military operations. Facts were "stubborn things," he had once argued in defense of the British soldiers after the Boston Massacre, and as stubborn as any of the large facts bearing heavily on his mind now was "the bloody conflict we are destined to endure."

On June 23 a conference of committees from every county in Pennsylvania declared that the delegates of Pennsylvania in Congress should vote for independence. "You see therefore," Adams wrote to Samuel Chase, "that there is such a universal expectation that the great question will be decided the first of July. . . . to postpone it again would hazard convulsions and dangerous conspiracies."

The birth of a new nation was at hand, perhaps truly, as Thomas Paine had written, a new world. "Solemn" was Adams's word for the atmosphere in Congress.

CHAPTER THREE

COLOSSUS OF INDEPENDENCE

[His] power of thought and expression . . . moved us
from our seats.

—Thomas Jefferson

I

Monday, July 1, 1776, began hot and steamy in Philadelphia, and before the morning was ended a full-scale summer storm would break. Adams, as usual, was out of bed before dawn. He dressed, wrote a long letter to a former delegate, Archibald Bulloch, who was the new president of Georgia, and following breakfast, walked to the State House, knowing what was in store. "This morning is assigned the greatest debate of all," he had said in the letter. "A declaration, that these colonies are free and independent states, has been reported by a committee some weeks ago for that purpose, and this day or tomorrow is to determine its fate. May heaven prosper the newborn republic."

He had wished Bulloch to know also that constant vigil was being kept for the arrival of the British at New York. "We are in daily expectation of an armament before New York, where, if it comes, the conflict may be bloody," he warned. Words in debate were one thing, the war quite another, but to Adams independence and the war were never disjunctive.

The object is great which we have in view, and we must expect a great expense of blood to obtain it. But we should always remember that a free constitution of civil government cannot be purchased at too dear a rate, as there is nothing on this side of Jerusalem of equal importance to mankind.

Presumably everything that could or need be said on the question of independence had been exhausted in Congress. Presumably, the question could be put and decided with little further ado. But it was not to be. John Dickinson had resolved to make one last appeal and Adams would be obliged to answer. They would rise to make their cases like the great lawyers they were, each summoning all his powers of reason and persuasion.

At ten o'clock, with the doors closed, John Hancock sounded the gavel. Richard Henry Lee's prior motion calling for independence was again read aloud; the Congress resolved itself into a committee of the whole and "resumed consideration." Immediately, Dickinson, gaunt and deathly pale, stood to be heard. With marked earnestness, he marshaled all past argument and reasoning against "premature" separation from Britain. "He had prepared himself apparently with great labor and ardent zeal," Adams would recall admiringly. "He conducted the debate not only with great ingenuity and eloquence, but with equal politeness and candor."

Though no one transcribed the speech, Dickinson's extensive notes would survive. He knew how unpopular he had become, Dickinson began. He knew that by standing firm, as a matter of principle, he was almost certainly ending his career. "My conduct this day, I expect, will give the finishing blow to my once great . . . and now too diminished popularity. . . . But thinking as I do on the subject of debate, silence would be guilt."

To proceed now with a declaration of independence, he said, would be "to brave the storm in a skiff made of paper."

When he sat down, all was silent except for the rain that had begun spattering against the windows. No one spoke, no one rose to answer him, until Adams at last "determined to speak."

He wished now as never in his life, Adams began, that he had the gifts of the ancient orators of Greece and Rome, for he was certain none of them ever had before him a question of greater importance. Outside, the wind picked up. The storm struck with thunder, lightning, and pelting rain. In his schoolmaster days at Worcester, Adams had recorded how such storms "unstrung" him. Now he spoke on steadily, making the case for independence as he had so often before. He was logical, positive, sensitive to the historic importance of the moment, and, looking into the future, saw a new nation, a new time, all much in the spirit of lines he had written in a recent letter to a friend.

Objects of the most stupendous magnitude, measures in which the lives and liberties of millions, born and unborn are most essentially interested, are now before us. We are in the very midst of revolution, the most complete, unexpected, and remarkable of any in the history of the world.

No transcription was made, no notes were kept. There would be only Adams's own recollections, plus those of several others who would remember more the force of Adams himself than any particular thing he said. That it was the most powerful and important speech heard in the Congress since it first convened, and the greatest speech of Adams's life, there is no question.

To Jefferson, Adams was "not graceful nor elegant, nor remarkably fluent," but spoke "with a power of thought and expression that moved us from our seats." Recalling the moment long afterward, Adams would say he had been carried out of himself, " 'carried out in spirit,' as enthusiastic preachers sometimes express themselves." To Richard Stockton, one of the new delegates from New Jersey, Adams was "the Atlas" of the hour, "the man to whom the country is most indebted for the great measure of independency. . . . He it was who sustained the debate, and by the force of his reasoning demonstrated not only the justice, but the expediency of the measure."

Stockton and two other new delegates from New Jersey, Francis Hopkinson and the Reverend John Witherspoon, famous Presbyterian preacher and president of the College of New Jersey at Princeton, had come into the chamber an hour or so after Adams had taken the floor and was nearly finished speaking. When they asked that Adams repeat what they had missed, he objected. He was not an actor there to entertain an audience, he said good-naturedly. But at the urging of Edward Rutledge, who told Adams that only he had the facts at his command, Adams relinquished and gave the speech a second time "in as concise a manner as I

could, 'til at length the New Jersey gentlemen said they were fully satisfied and ready for the question." By then he had been on his feet for two
hours.

Others spoke, including Witherspoon, the first clergyman to serve in
Congress, whose manner of speech made plain his Scottish origins. In all,
the debate lasted nine hours. At one point, according to Adams, Hewes of
North Carolina, who had long opposed separation from Britain, "started
suddenly upright, and lifting up both his hands to Heaven, as if he had
been in a trance, cried out, 'It is done! and I will abide by it.'"

But when later that evening a preliminary vote was taken, four
colonies unexpectedly held back, refusing to proclaim independence.
The all-important Pennsylvania delegation, despite popular opinion in
Pennsylvania, stood with John Dickinson and voted no. The New
York delegates abstained, saying they favored the motion but lacked
specific instructions. South Carolina, too, surprisingly, voted no, while
Delaware, with only two delegates present, was divided. The missing
Delaware delegate was Caesar Rodney, one of the most ardent of the
independence faction. Where he was or when he might reappear was
unclear, but a rider had been sent racing off to find him.

When Edward Rutledge rescued the moment by moving that a final
vote be postponed until the next day, implying that for the sake of unanimity South Carolina might change its mind, Adams and the others
immediately agreed. For while the nine colonies supporting independence made a clear majority, it was hardly the show of solidarity that
such a step ought to have.

The atmosphere that night at City Tavern and in the lodging houses
of the delegates was extremely tense. The crux of the matter was the
Pennsylvania delegation, for in the preliminary vote three of the seven
Pennsylvania delegates had gone against John Dickinson and declared in
the affirmative, and it was of utmost interest that one of the three, along
with Franklin and John Morton, was James Wilson, who, though a
friend and ally of Dickinson, had switched sides to vote for independence.
The question now was how many of the rest who were in league with
Dickinson would on the morrow continue, in Adams's words, to "vote
point blank against the known and declared sense of their constituents."

To compound the tension that night, word reached Philadelphia of the sighting off New York of a hundred British ships, the first arrivals of a fleet that would number over four hundred.

THOUGH THE RECORD of all that happened the following day, Tuesday, July 2, is regrettably sparse, it appears that just as the doors to Congress were about to be closed at the usual hour of nine o'clock, Caesar Rodney, mud-spattered, "booted and spurred," made his dramatic entrance. The tall, thin Rodney—the "oddest-looking man in the world," Adams once described him—had been made to appear stranger still, and more to be pitied, by a skin cancer on one side of his face that he kept hidden behind a scarf of green silk. But, as Adams had also recognized, Rodney was a man of spirit, of "fire." Almost unimaginably, he had ridden eighty miles through the night, changing horses several times, to be there in time to cast his vote.

Yet more important even than the arrival of Rodney were two empty chairs among the Pennsylvania delegation. Refusing to vote for independence but understanding the need for Congress to speak with one voice, John Dickinson and Robert Morris had voluntarily absented themselves from the proceedings, thus swinging Pennsylvania behind independence by a vote of three to two. What private agreements had been made the night before, if any, who or how many had come to the State House that morning knowing what was afoot, no one recorded.

Outside, more rain threatened, and at about ten came another cloudburst like the day before. New York continued to abstain, but South Carolina, as hinted by Edward Rutledge, joined the majority to make the decision unanimous in the sense that no colony stood opposed. The vote went rapidly.

So, it was done, the break was made, in words at least: on July 2, 1776, in Philadelphia, the American colonies declared independence. If not all thirteen clocks had struck as one, twelve had, and with the other silent, the effect was the same.

It was John Adams, more than anyone, who had made it happen. Further, he seems to have understood more clearly than any what a momentous day it was and in the privacy of two long letters to Abigail, he poured out his feelings as did no one else:

The second day of July 1776 will be the most memorable epocha in the history of America. I am apt to believe that it will be celebrated by succeeding generations as the great anniversary festival. It ought to be commemorated as the Day of Deliverance by solemn acts of devotion to God Almighty. It ought to be solemnized with pomp and parade, with shows, games, sports, guns, bells, bonfires, and illuminations from one end of this continent to the other from this time forward forever more.

Lest she judge him overly "transported," he said he was well aware of the "toil and blood and treasure that it will cost us to maintain this declaration." Still, the end was more than worth all the means. "You will see in a few days," he wrote in the second letter, "a Declaration setting forth the causes, which have impelled us to this mighty revolution, and the reasons that will justify it in the sight of God and man."

That the hand of God was involved in the birth of the new nation he had no doubt. "It is the will of heaven that the two countries should be sundered forever." If the people now were to have "unbounded power," and as the people were quite as capable of corruption as "the great," and thus high risks were involved, he would submit all his hopes and fears to an overruling providence, "in which unfashionable as the faith may be, I firmly believe."

THE "BAR OF SECRECY" notwithstanding, the news spread rapidly through the city. "This day the Continental Congress declared the United Colonies Free and Independent States," recorded a young artist newly established in Philadelphia, Charles Willson Peale, exuberant over the news. The facts, wrote Elbridge Gerry, were as well known in the taverns and coffeehouses of the city as in Congress itself.

But there could be no pause. There was too much still to be done. Congress had to review and approve the language of the drafted declaration before it could be made official. Deliberations of a different kind commenced at once, continuing through the next morning, July 3, when mercifully the temperature had dropped ten degrees, broken by the storm of the previous day.

For Thomas Jefferson it became a painful ordeal, as change after change was called for and approximately a quarter of what he had written was cut entirely. Seated beside Benjamin Franklin, the young Virginian looked on in silence. He is not known to have uttered a word in protest, or in defense of what he had written. Later he would describe the opposition to his draft as being like "the ceaseless action of gravity weighing upon us night and day." At one point Franklin leaned over to tell him a story that, as a printer and publisher over so many years, he must have offered before as comfort to a wounded author. He had once known a hatter who wished to have a sign made saying, JOHN THOMPSON, HATTER, MAKES AND SELLS HATS FOR READY MONEY, this to be accompanied by a picture of a hat. But the man had chosen first to ask the opinion of friends, with the result that one word after another was removed as superfluous or redundant, until at last the sign was reduced to Thompson's name and the picture of the hat.

Beyond its stirring preamble, most of the document before Congress was taken up with a list of grievances, specific charges against the King— *"He has plundered our seas, ravaged our coasts, burnt our towns. . . . He is at this time transporting large armies of foreign mercenaries to complete the works of death, desolation and tyranny. . . ."* And it was the King, *"the Christian King of Great Britain,"* Jefferson had emphasized, who was responsible for the horrors of the slave trade. As emphatic a passage as any, this on the slave trade was to have been the ringing climax of all the charges. Now it was removed in its entirety because, said Jefferson later, South Carolina and Georgia objected. Some northern delegates, too, were a "little tender" on the subject, "for though their people have very few slaves themselves yet they had been pretty considerable carriers. . . ."

In truth, black slavery had long since become an accepted part of life in all of the thirteen colonies. Of a total population in the colonies of nearly 2,500,000 people in 1776, approximately one in five were slaves, some 500,000 men, women, and children. In Virginia alone, which had the most slaves by far, they numbered more than 200,000. There was no member of the Virginia delegation who did not own slaves, and of all members of Congress at least a third owned or had owned slaves. The total of Thomas Jefferson's slaves in 1776, as near as can be determined from his personal records, was about 200, which was also the approximate number owned by George Washington.

John Dickinson, who owned eleven African men and women, was understood to be Philadelphia's second-largest slaveholder. Even Benjamin Franklin, who adamantly opposed slavery, had once owned two black house servants and had personally traded in slaves, buying and selling from his Market Street print shop. And though in recent years the Quakers of the city had been freeing more and more of their slaves, such notices as Franklin once published, offering "a likely wench about fifteen years old," were still to be seen in Philadelphia newspapers. One appearing that July in the *Pennsylvania Journal* read:

> TO BE SOLD: A large quantity of pine boards that are well seasoned. Likewise a Negro wench; she is to be disposed of for no fault, but only that she is present with child, she is about 20 years old . . . and is fit for either town or country business.

The president of Congress, John Hancock, had only in recent years freed the last of the slaves who were part of his lavish Boston household, and it was well known, as Jefferson said, that New Englanders had been "considerable carriers" in the lucrative slave trade. At one point, earlier in the century, approximately half the tonnage of New England shipping had been in transporting slaves, and the port of Boston prospered from the trade.

But it was also New Englanders who had assailed slavery in the most vehement terms. As early as 1700, before Jefferson or anyone in Congress was born, Judge Samuel Sewall of Boston, an eminent Puritan known for his role as a judge in the Salem witch trials, had declared in a tract called *The Selling of Joseph*, that "all men, as they are sons of Adam . . . have equal right unto liberty," and saw no justification, moral or economic, for making property of human beings. Slavery was evil. Of the slave trade, he wrote: "How horrible is the uncleanness, immorality, if not murder, that the ships are guilty of that bring crowds of these miserable men and women."

James Otis, in his famous speech on writs of assistance in 1761, had called for the immediate liberation of the slaves. "The colonists [of Massachusetts] are by the law of nature free born, as indeed all men are white and black. . . . Does it follow that it is the right to enslave a man because he is black?" When Samuel Adams and his wife were presented with a black slave girl as a gift in 1765, they had immediately set her free.

Of John Adams's circle in Philadelphia, the one to have taken the most assertive stand against slavery was the young physician Benjamin Rush, who from the time of the First Congress had been as close to all that went on as anyone not a delegate could have been and who, in another few weeks, would himself be elected to Congress, as one of the new Pennsylvania delegation. Rush—high-spirited, handsome, and all of thirty—had studied medicine in Edinburgh and in London, where he came to know Benjamin Franklin and once dined with Samuel Johnson and James Boswell. Overflowing with energy and goodwill, he was ardent for reform of all kinds: smallpox inoculation for the poor, humane care for the insane, reform of the penal code, but especially for the abolition of slavery. In 1773, Rush had published a pamphlet attacking slavery, and in 1774, the year the First Congress convened, he had helped organize the Pennsylvania Society for Promoting the Abolition of Slavery. He had appealed to the clergy to recognize slavery as a sin, and urged all legislators, "ye advocates for American liberty," to work for the liberty of blacks as well. The eyes of the world were watching, Rush charged. Yet he himself owned a slave.

On first meeting, Adams and Rush had misjudged each other. Adams thought Rush "a sprightly, pretty fellow," but "too much a talker to be a deep thinker," while Rush found Adams "cold and reserved." But they had quickly changed their minds, discovering much in common besides the love of talk. Like Adams, Rush was without affectation and unafraid to speak his mind, sometimes to the point of tactlessness. (Prudence, he was fond of saying, "is a *rascally* virtue.") Like Jefferson, the young physician seemed to take limitless interest in nearly everything under the sun.

Adams and Rush were of the same mind on slavery. Adams was utterly opposed to slavery and the slave trade and, like Rush, favored a gradual emancipation of all slaves. That it was, at the least, inconsistent for slave owners to be espousing freedom and equality was not lost on Adams, any more than on others on both sides of the Atlantic Ocean. In London, Samuel Johnson, who had no sympathy for the American cause, had asked, "How is it that we hear the loudest yelps for liberty from the drivers of Negroes?" Abigail, in her letters that spring, had questioned whether the passion for liberty could be "equally strong in the breasts of those who have been accustomed to deprive their fellow creatures of theirs," and had earlier pondered whether the agonies of pestilence and war could be God's punishment for the sin of slavery.

In time, Adams and Jefferson would each denounce slavery. Jefferson was to write of the degrading effects of the institution on both slave and master. Adams would call slavery a "foul contagion in the human character." In years past, as an attorney, Adams had appeared in several slave cases for the owner, never the slave, but he had no use for slavery. He never owned a slave as a matter of principle, nor hired the slaves of others to work on his farm, as was sometimes done in New England. He was to declare unequivocally in later years that "Negro slavery is an evil of colossal magnitude," and like Abigail, he felt this at the time.

But neither he nor any other delegate in Congress would have let the issue jeopardize a declaration of independence, however strong their feelings. If Adams was disappointed or downcast over the removal of Jefferson's indictment of the slave trade, he seems to have said nothing at the time. Nor is it possible to know the extent of Jefferson's disappointment, or if the opposition of South Carolina and Georgia was truly as decisive as he later claimed. Very possibly there were many delegates, from North and South, happy to see the passage omitted for the reason that it was so patently absurd to hold the King responsible for horrors that, everyone knew, Americans—and Christians no less than the King—had brought on themselves. Slavery and the slave trade were hardly the fault of George III, however ardently Jefferson wished to fix the blame on the distant monarch.

Of more than eighty changes made in Jefferson's draft during the time Congress deliberated, most were minor and served to improve it. The King's conduct was called one of "repeated" rather than "unremitting" injuries. The accusation that the King had "suffered the administration of justice totally to cease in some of these states" was edited to a simpler "He has obstructed the administration of justice."

But one final cut toward the conclusion was as substantial nearly as the excise of the passage on the slave trade, and it appears to have wounded Jefferson deeply.

To the long list of indictments against the King, he had added one assailing the English people, "our British brethren," as a further oppressor, for allowing their Parliament and their King "to send over not only soldiers of our common blood, but Scotch and foreign mercenaries to invade and destroy us." And therein, Jefferson charged, was the heart of the tragedy, the feeling of betrayal, the "common blood" cause of American outrage. "These facts have given the last stab to agonizing affection, and manly spirit bids us renounce forever these unfeeling brethren," he had written. "We must endeavor to forget our former love for them."

This most emotional passage of all was too much for many in Congress, and to it Jefferson had added a final poignant note: "We might have been a free and great people together." Nearly all of this was removed. There was to be no mention of a "last stab," or "love," or of the "free and great people" that might have been. Nor was there to be any mention of Scottish mercenaries, James Wilson and John Witherspoon both being Scots.

To no one's surprise, Adams did not sit silently by. He was present every hour, "fighting fearlessly for every word," as Jefferson would write.

No man better merited than Mr. John Adams to hold a most conspicuous place in the design. He was the pillar of its support on the floor of Congress, its ablest advocate and defender against the multifarious assaults encountered.

Finally, to Jefferson's concluding line was added the phrase "with a firm reliance on the protection of divine Providence," an addition that Adams assuredly welcomed. Thus it would read:

And for the support of this Declaration, with a firm reliance on the protection of divine Providence, we mutually pledge to each other our lives, our fortunes, and our sacred honor.

But it was to be the eloquent lines of the second paragraph of the Declaration that would stand down the years, affecting the human spirit as neither Jefferson nor anyone could have foreseen. And however much was owed to the writings of others, as Jefferson acknowledged, or to such editorial refinements as those contributed by Franklin or Adams, they were, when all was said and done, his lines. It was Jefferson who had written them for all time:

> We hold these truths to be self-evident, that all men are created equal, that they are endowed by their Creator with certain unalienable rights, that among these are life, liberty, and the pursuit of happiness. That to secure these rights, governments are instituted among men, deriving their just powers from the consent of the governed.

IN LATER YEARS the excessive summer heat of Philadelphia would frequently figure in accounts of Thursday, July 4, 1776. In fact, the day, like the one before, was pleasantly cool and comfortable. In Congress, discussion of the Declaration appears to have continued through the morning until about eleven o'clock, when debate was closed and the vote taken. Again, as on July 2, twelve colonies voted in the affirmative, while New York abstained. Again, John Dickinson was absent. It all went very smoothly.

Congress ordered that the document be authenticated and printed. But it would be another month before the engrossed copy was signed by the delegates. For now, only the President, John Hancock, and the Secretary of the Congress, Charles Thomson, fixed their signatures.

With passage of the Declaration of Independence thus completed, and having thereby renounced allegiance to the King and proclaimed the birth of a new United States of America, the Congress proceeded directly to other business. Indeed, to all appearances, nothing happened in Congress on July 4, 1776. Adams, who had responded with such depth of feeling to the events of July 2, recorded not a word of July 4. Of Jefferson's day, it is known only that he took time off to shop for ladies' gloves and a new thermometer that he purchased at John Sparhawk's London Bookshop for a handsome 3 pounds, 15 shillings.

But by the following morning, the fifth, printer John Dunlap had broadside editions available and the delegates were busy sending copies to friends. On July 6, the *Pennsylvania Evening Post* carried the full text on its first page.

The great day of celebration came Monday, July 8, at noon in the

State House Yard, when the Declaration was read aloud before an exuberant crowd. With drums pounding, five battalions paraded through the city and "on the common, gave us the *feu de joie* [thirteen cannon blasts], notwithstanding the scarcity of powder," as Adams recorded. Bells rang through the day and into the night. There were bonfires at street corners. Houses were illuminated with candles in their windows. In the Supreme Court Room at the State House, as planned, a half dozen Philadelphians chosen for the honor took the King's Arms down from the wall and carried it off to be thrown on top of a huge fire and consumed in an instant, the blaze lighting the scene for blocks around.

"Fine starlight, pleasant evening," recorded Adams's friend Christopher Marshall. "There were bonfires, ringing bells, with other great demonstrations of joy upon the unanimity and agreement of the Declaration." Another Philadelphia patriot, Charles Biddle, a wealthy merchant who had joined the crowd in the State House Yard to hear the Declaration read, recorded only that he had seen "very few respectable people present."

As mounted messengers carried the news beyond Philadelphia, celebrations broke out everywhere. In New York the next day, the Declaration was read aloud to Washington's assembled troops, and it was that night, at the foot of Broadway, that a roaring crowd pulled down the larger-than-life equestrian statue of George III. As in Philadelphia, drums rolled, bonfires burned, prayers were said, and toasts raised in town after town, North and South. When the news finally reached Savannah, Georgia, in August, it set off a day-long celebration during which the Declaration was read four times in four different public places and the largest crowd in the history of the province gathered for a mock burial of King George III. The feeling was that the air had been cleared at last. "The Declaration," said the Reverend Samuel Cooper of Boston, "must give new spring to all our affairs."

The actual signing of the document would not take place until Friday, August 2, after a fair copy had been elegantly engrossed on a single, giant sheet of parchment by Timothy Matlack, assistant to the secretary of Congress. Nothing was reported of the historic event. As with everything transacted within Congress, secrecy prevailed. To judge by what was in the newspapers and the correspondence of the delegates, the signing never took place.

In later years, Jefferson would entertain guests at Monticello with descriptions of black flies that so tormented the delegates, biting through their silk hose, that they had hurried the signing along as swiftly as possible. But at the time Jefferson wrote nothing of the occasion, nor did John Adams. In old age, trying to reconstruct events of that crowded summer, both men would stubbornly and incorrectly insist that the signing took place July 4.

Apparently there was no fuss or ceremony on August 2. The delegates simply came forward in turn and fixed their signatures. Also, a number of the most important figures in Congress were absent—Richard Henry Lee, George Wythe, Oliver Wolcott, Elbridge Gerry—and would sign later. A new representative from New Hampshire, Matthew Thornton, who had not been a member when the Declaration was passed, would add his name in November, and Thomas McKean of Delaware appears not to have signed until January 1777, which made him the last.

Like the others, Adams and Jefferson each signed with his own delegation, Adams on the right, in a clear and firm, plain hand, Jefferson at lower center with a signature more precise and elegant, but equally legible.

The fact that a signed document now existed, as well as the names of the signatories, was kept secret for the time being, as all were acutely aware that by taking up the pen and writing their names, they had committed treason, a point of considerably greater immediacy now, with the British army so near at hand.

Whether Benjamin Franklin quipped "We must all hang together, or most assuredly we shall hang separately" is impossible to know, just as there is no way to confirm the much-repeated story that the diminutive John Hancock wrote his name large so the King might read it without his spectacles. But the stories endured because they were in character, like the remark attributed to Stephen Hopkins of Rhode Island. Hopkins, who suffered from palsy, is said to have observed, on completing his spidery signature, "My hand trembles, but my heart does not."

The most encouraging result of the decision for independence was its almost immediate effect on "spirit," within Congress and among the people, but also among the rank-and-file militia. "The Declaration of Independence has produced a new era in this part of America," wrote Benjamin Rush, who had since taken his place in Congress in time to be a "signer." "The militia of Pennsylvania seem to be actuated with a spirit more than Roman. Near 2,000 citizens of Philadelphia have lately marched to New York." Such influence as the Declaration had had would have been "inconceivable" earlier. To Abigail, Adams wrote of the "gallant spirit prevailing in these middle colonies," and described the militia turning out in "great numbers and in high spirits." Samuel Adams, to whom the Declaration was "the decisive measure," wished only that it had come sooner.

Even those in Congress who had been so ardently opposed, now, by word or deed, committed themselves to the "Glorious Revolution." Robert Morris continued in his duties without pause, working as strenuously as anyone. "I think an individual that declines the service of his country because its councils are not comfortable to his ideas makes a bad subject," he wrote, still unable to see himself as other than a "subject." John Dickinson, though ill and exhausted from the strain of the past weeks, departed at the head of the first troops to march out of the city to join in the defense of New Jersey, a scene that made a deep impression on many, including John Adams. "Mr. Dickinson's alacrity and spirit," he told Abigail, "certainly becomes his character and sets a fine example."

II

THE SHIPS FLYING the Union Jack that arrived off New York at the end of June 1776—the fleet from Halifax that one eyewitness described as looking like "all London afloat"—had been only the start of an overwhelming show of British might come to settle the fate of the new United States of America.

By July 3, 9,000 troops led by General William Howe had landed on Staten Island, where hundreds of Tories were on hand to welcome them. Howe himself had gone ashore on July 2, the very day that Congress had voted for independence, and in the days following, up the Narrows between Staten Island and Long Island, came ever more British sails, including an armada of 130 warships and transports from England under command of the general's brother, Admiral Richard Lord Howe. By mid-August, 32,000 fully equipped, highly trained, thoroughly professional British and German (Hessian) soldiers—more than the entire population of Philadelphia—were ashore on Staten Island, supported by ten ships-of-the-line and twenty frigates, making in all the largest, most costly British overseas deployment ever until that time.

By contrast, the American army gathered in defense of New York, digging in on Manhattan and Long Island, was optimistically thought to number 20,000 troops, these nearly all poorly equipped amateurs led by Washington, who in his year as commander-in-chief had yet to fight a battle. From Long Island, one of Washington's ablest divisional commanders, Nathanael Greene, wrote to tell John Adams that in reality the American force might number 9,000; and as Adams knew, they had no naval support—not a single available warship or transport. When, on July 12, with the wind and tide in their favor, the British sent two men-of-war up the Hudson River to demonstrate who had control, there was nothing to stop them. As the huge ships passed upstream, American militia stood gawking onshore, which evoked an angry general order from Washington declaring such "unsoldierly conduct" could only give the enemy a low opinion of the American army.

From the flow of dispatches arriving at the War Office in Philadelphia, Adams was more aware of the situation than anyone in Congress and he was miserable, thinking about the consequences of a defeat at New York. He had not wanted the responsibility of heading the Board of War and felt "vastly unequal" to the multitude of problems and decisions to be grappled with. But it was also clear that they were all unequal to the task. No one in Congress was qualified. "We are all inexperienced in this business," he emphasized to Nathanael Greene.

The War Office consisted of rented space two blocks from the State House on Market Street. To a board of five members of Congress—Adams, Harrison, Rutledge, Sherman, and Wilson—fell the burden of virtually running the war. They were responsible for ordnance and fortifications, for appointing and promoting officers, for recruitment of enlisted men and raising rifle companies, for pay, provisions, and for somehow resolving the constant demand for flints, saltpeter and gunpowder, horses, wagons, tents, shoes, soap, and blankets. They dispatched ship carpenters where needed, appointed chaplains, and faced the incessant day-to-day frustrations of bickering, jealousies, and corruption. It was arduous, thankless work. He must be "very exactly and minutely acquainted with the state of every regiment," Adams was lectured by General Horatio Gates. And as all decisions required the approval of Congress, it was for the Board to prepare the reports on which to vote. It would be resolved that five tons of powder be sent to Williamsburg; or that British prisoners be moved from New Jersey to Pennsylvania; or that new positions of drum major and fife major be created; or that special commissioners be appointed to audit the accounts of the army of New York.

There were the ever-vexing complications of dealing in various colonial currencies of differing value, and the increasing worry over inflation and the fate of the new Continental money, the unbacked paper currency being produced in Philadelphia in steadily greater quantity. (One Nathan Sellers, a scrivener whose job it was to sign every bill by hand, recorded signing 4,800 bills in a single day that July.) "If that [the Continental currency] suffers in its credit, the Cause must suffer," Adams warned. "If that fails, the Cause must fail."

One of the committee assignments he shared with Jefferson was the Committee on Spies, charged with, among other things, drawing up a set of Articles of War—regulations and rules of discipline for the army. Knowing discipline to be a difficult and unpopular subject, Adams had recommended that they present a complete system at once and "let it meet its fate." And since, in his view, there was but one system of merit, that which had "carried two empires to the head of mankind," the Roman and the British (the second being drawn directly from the first), he recommended a straight-on borrowing of the British Articles of War, with only a few modifications. According to Adams, writing years later, "Jefferson in those days never failed to agree with me in everything of a political nature, and he very cordially concurred in this." But by midsummer the matter of the Articles of War had been passed over to the Board of War and had still to be considered by Congress.

Strongly opposed to the existing policy of short-term enlistments, Adams declared himself adamantly in favor of a regular army. But of his many worries the greatest was disease. Responding to the medical theories of young Dr. Rush, he pleaded for greater cleanliness among the troops. Smallpox worried him most of all. Smallpox was the "King of Terrors," the enemy to be feared more than any other. "Smallpox! Smallpox! What shall we do with it?" he asked Abigail. In a dispatch of July 11, Washington reported that an outbreak of smallpox in Boston had infected some of the troops and that every precaution was being taken to prevent the spread of infection to New York.

Adams's labors on the Board of War began usually at six in the morning and continued until nine, then resumed again in the evening. Between times, he was in the thick of debate in Congress over the Articles of Confederation. He knew it to be work of the greatest importance, but the strain was beginning to take a toll. He needed rest and for the first time hinted to Abigail the possibility of a "furlow."

Then, on July 16, came a letter from Abigail's uncle, Isaac Smith, reporting that Abigail, acting on her own, had decided that she and the children must be inoculated for smallpox. They had come to Boston to undergo the treatment, Smith himself having provided his large house on Court Street for their time of isolation.

Adams was beside himself. "Never—never in my life, had I so many cares upon my mind at once," he wrote to her. Under any other circumstances he would leave for Boston at once. As it was, he had no choice— he could only pray for their health. "I cannot leave this place, without more injury to the public now, than I ever could at any other time, being in the midst of scenes of business, which must not stop for anything."

Her letter of explanation, written July 13, did not reach Philadelphia for another week. Because of the outbreak of smallpox in Boston, thousands of people had come in from the surrounding countryside to be inoculated. It was there, in Boston, that smallpox inoculation had been introduced in America more than half a century earlier, and by a kinsman of Adams, Dr. Zabdiel Boylston, Adams's great uncle on his mother's side. The idea had come from a slave belonging to Cotton Mather, an African named Onesimus, who had said the practice was long established in Africa, where those with the courage to use it were made immune, and he had his own scar on his arm to show. The technique, the same as still practiced by Dr. Boylston, was to make a small incision, then with a quill scoop the "pus from the ripe pustules" of a smallpox patient into the open cut. A generally mild case of smallpox would result, yet the risk of death was relatively slight. The ordeal of the patient, however, could be considerable, as Adams knew from all he had seen at the time he was inoculated, and largely because of various purges that were thought essential to recovery.

"Such a spirit of inoculation" had never been known, Abigail reported. "The town and every house in it are as full as they can hold."

She and the children were part of a family contingent numbering seventeen that included the Cranches and their three children, Abigail's sister Elizabeth, a three-year-old daughter of brother William Smith, named Louisa, whom Abigail had taken under her wing, three servants, and two cousins—Cotton Tufts, Jr., and John Thaxter, Jr., a former law clerk of Adams's who had lately become the tutor for the Adams children.

We had our bedding, etc. to bring [Abigail wrote]. A cow we have driven down from B[raintree] and some hay I have had put into the stable, wood, etc., and we have really commenced housekeepers here. . . . Our little one [three-year-old Thomas] stood the operation manfully. . . . I wish it was so you could have been with us, but I submit.

"The little folks are very sick then and puke every morning, but after that they are comfortable," she continued. Now especially, he must keep writing to her. "Every expression of tenderness is a cordial to my heart. Unimportant as they are to the rest of the world, to me they are *everything*."

Though she herself was well enough to turn out on July 18 for Boston's celebration for the Declaration of Independence, the children's ordeal went on. The stay in her uncle's house would last nearly two months. "Nabby has enough of the smallpox for all the family beside," Abigail would report. "She is pretty well covered, not a spot of what is so sore that she can neither walk, sit, stand, or lay with any comfort." The pustules were the size of a large pea. Another time she would write of six-year-old Charles burning with fever and going into a delirium that lasted forty-eight hours.

In a letter to Isaac Smith, expressing his gratitude for all Smith was doing for his family, Adams said he would leave for Boston immediately if he could, but could not "in honor and duty to the public stir from this place. . . . We are in hourly expectation of some important event at New York." Writing to Abigail, he told her how proud he was of her for what she had done. He wished the whole populace could be inoculated. Yet he could not help being on "tenterhooks." It had taken ten days for her letter to reach him and heaven only knew what might have transpired in the interval.

It was the paradox of their lives that, as much as his public role kept them apart, he always needed to be with Abigail and she with him. They would never become accustomed to being separated. "I can do nothing without you," he was to tell her one way or another, time and again, and always from the heart. She would have him no other way than he was; she believed fervently in what he was doing, encouraged him in the role, and wished no other for him; she wanted him to be where he was doing his utmost for the country. And still she desperately wanted him with her. Each worried incessantly about the other's health and well-being, at times to the point of making themselves ill.

With sickness all about her now, Abigail sensed from John's letters that something was amiss with him. "Not one word respecting yourself," she wrote. "My anxiety for your welfare will never leave me but with my parting breath, 'tis of more importance to me than all this world contains besides."

Her suspicions were justified. By late July it had been six months since he and Joseph Bass had set off in the snow from Braintree, and the effect of the work, and unrelieved pressure, of too little sleep, no exercise, and increasing worries over her, had caught up with him. In fact, the whole Massachusetts delegation was in a bad way. Elbridge Gerry, sick and exhausted, had already departed for home. John Hancock was beset by gout. Robert Treat Paine, racked by a cough, seldom appeared in Congress. Samuel Adams was "completely worn out."

On July 25, having received no further news from Boston, Adams addressed a letter to the General Court of Massachusetts requesting a leave of absence, and to James Warren, who as Speaker of the General Court could help arrange such a leave, he declared, "My face is grown pale, my eyes weak and inflamed, my nerves tremulous, my mind as weak as water." He suffered "feverous heats by day and sweats by night," an infallible symptom, he was sure, of an approaching collapse. "I know better than anybody what my constitution will bear and what it will not," he told Warren, "and you may depend upon it, I have already tempted it beyond prudence and safety."

In 1760, twenty-two-year-old George III became King of Great Britain, Ireland, and the distant American provinces. He is shown in his coronation robes in a painting by Allan Ramsay.

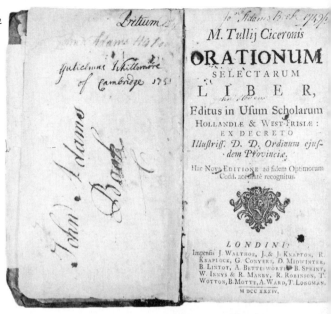

John Adams's well-worn schoolboy copy of Cicero, which he signed several times and dated 1750.

Harvard, America's first college, in an engraving by Paul Revere. To Adams, his years at Harvard were "total and complete happiness."

The Weymouth parson where Abigail Smith wa born and where she and John Adams were marr October 25, 1764.

British soldiers open fire on seemingly helpless citizens in a popular print by Paul Revere of the March 5, 1770, Boston Massacre. In one of the most courageous acts of his career, Adams agreed to defend the soldiers in court. Arguing that "facts are stubborn things," he won the case.

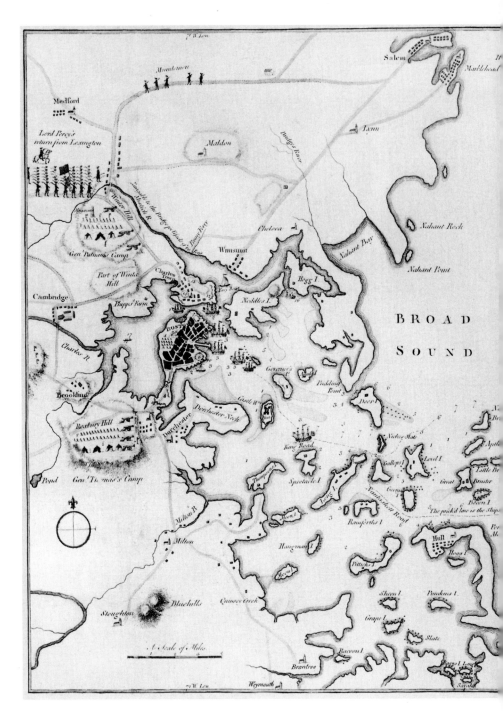

A 1775 map of Boston and vicinity shows troop placement
toward the end of the first year of the Revolution. Braintree
and Weymouth are at lower center.

Mem.

The Confederation to be taken up in Paragraphs.

An Alliance to be formed with France and Spain.

Embassadors to be sent to both Courts.

Government to be assumed in every Colony.

Coin and Currencies to be regulated.

Forces to be raised and maintained in Canada and New York. St. Lawrence and Hudsons Rivers to be secured.

Hemp to be encouraged and the Manufacture of Duck.

Powder Mills to be built in every Colony and fresh Efforts to make Salt Petre.

An Address to the Inhabitants of the Colonies.

The Bounties for Lead and Salt to be filled up, and Sulphur added to their Commission.

Money to be sent to the Pay master, to pay our Debts, and fullfill our Engagements. —

Taxes to be laid and levied, Funds established, New Notes to be given on Interest, for Bills borrowed. —

Treaties of Commerce with F. S. H. D. &c.

Declaration of Independency. Declaration of War with the Nation, Cruising on the british Trade, their East India Ships and Sugar ships.

prevent the Exportation of Silver and Gold.

John Adams was probably en route to the Continental Congress early in 1776 when he listed in a small notebook all that needed to be accomplished, including (at bottom) a "Declaration of Independency."

But the Day is past— The Second Day of July 1776, will be the most memorable Epocha, in the History of America.—

This unfinished engraving by Edward Savage of Congress voting independen
in 1776 is thought to be the most accurate rendering of the Assembly Room

dependence Hall. To John Adams (shown standing at center foreground), e "great day" was not July 4, but July 2, as he wrote at the time (above).

Young John Quincy Adams, who sailed twice for Europe with his father in the midst of war.

Drawings from John Quincy's journal. On the first voyage, at age ten, he learned the names of every sail.

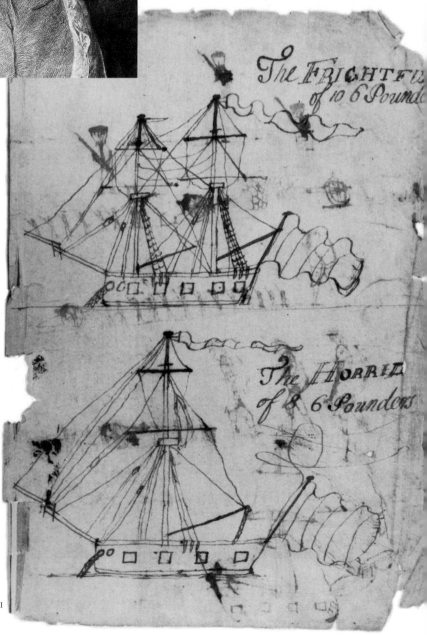

The FRIGHTF...
of 10 6 Pound...

The HORRID
of 8 6 Pounders

For the hon. John Adams Esq

1 Bushel Indian Meal
1 Cask Rum
1 Quere paper
2. Account Books
1/4. hundred Quills
30. Brown Sugar
1 Box Wafers
1 Bottle Ink
1 doz. pipes
2 lb Tobacco
2 Bottles Mustard
2 lb Tea
2. lb Chocolate. Theirs 14. one bo for Cabbin Stores
a Matrass & Bolster
a Leaden Case —

A list of personal supplies to be taken on the eventful voyage
of the 24-gun frigate *Boston* to France in the winter of 1778.

1

The adoration of Benjamin Franklin in Paris was of utmost value to the
American cause, as Adams recognized. But to his surprise, Adams found
Franklin to be lazy, neglectful of details, and not easy to work with.

The Comte de Vergennes, the powerful French Foreign Minister, who had little regard for John Adams and went out of his way to make life difficult for him.

Adams's French dictionary, one of the many books he purchased in Paris in a determined effort to learn French.

John Adams 1780
Paris. March 22.

LES

VERBES FRANÇOIS,

OU

NOUVELLE GRAMMAIRE,

EN FORME DE

DICTIONNAIRE.

CONTENANT,

La Conjugaison, tout au long, de tous les Verbes irréguliers de la Langue Françoise, avec les Décisions.

Autorisées & approuvées par l'Académie des *Inscriptions & Belles Lettres* pour leur Usage.

Cet ouvrage est rédigé d'une manière si aisée, que non seulement les commençants, mais encore ceux qui se piquent plus d'écrire cette Langue que la parler, pourront s'instruire & se perfectionner eux-mêmes sans recourir aux Maîtres.

Par M. DEMARVILLE.

SECONDE EDITION.

Revüe, corrigée, & augmentée par l'Auteur.

Quem penes arbitrium est, & jus, & norma loquendi.

A LONDRES:

15

16

Site of the Hôtel des Etats-Unis, America's first foreign legation, established by John Adams on the Fluewelen Burgwal, The Hague, in 1782.

The Treveszaal, or Truce Chamber, in the Binnenhof at The Hague, where Adams signed the Treaty of Commerce with the Dutch on October 8, 1782.

In an unfinished painting by Benjamin West, John Jay (standing left), Adams, Franklin, Henry Laurens, and William Temple Franklin, the secretary, gather for the signing of the Treaty of Paris that ended the Revolutionary War in 1783.

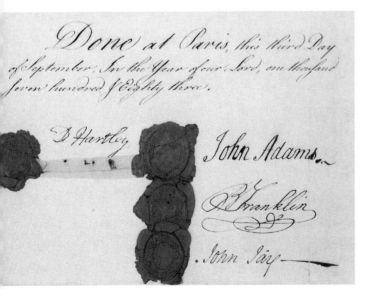

Adams signed first, in alphabetical order.

Home in France for the Adamses was a palatial house near Paris at Auteuil, which included five acres of garden and a staff of eight.

This Day 8 months I sailed for Europe since which many new and interesting scenes have presented themselves before me. I have seen many of the Beauties and some of the Deformities of this old World, I have been more than ever convinced that there is no Sumit of virtue, and no depth of vice which Humane Nature is not Capable of rising to on the one hand or sinking into on the other. I have felt the force of an observation which I have read, that "daily example is the most Suttle of poisons. I have found my taste reconciling itself to habits custom and fashions, which at first disgusted me.

In a letter to her sister Mary Cranch, February 20, 1785, Abigail Adams acknowledged that she had become reconciled to French habits, customs, and fashions that had at first "disgusted" her.

Most dazzling to Abigail was the Paris Opera, with its elegant crowds and dancers on stage, so thinly clad that at first she hardly dared look at them. "Their motions are as light as air and as quick as lightning . . . No description can equal the reality . . . I see them now with pleasure."

John Adams as diplomat,
by John Singleton Copley,
painted after the Revolution
at the artist's London
studio. (A study for the
portrait appears opposite
the title page.)

On June 1, 1785, Adams rode to
St. James's Palace to appear before
King George III as the first minister
of the new United States of America.
This is page one of the letter in
which Adams described the
historic encounter.

I went with his Lordship through the Levee Room
into the things Closet, the Door was Shut, & I was left with
his Majesty and the Secretary of State alone. I made my
three profound Bows, one at the Door, one about half
Way and a third before the Presence, according to the
established usage at this and all the Northern Courts of
Europe. I then addressed my self to his Majesty, in the follow
ing Words.

   Sir
     The United States of America have ap
pointed me, their Minister Plenipotentiary to your Majesty: and
have directed me, to deliver to your Majesty this Letter, which
contains the Evidence of it.

     It is, in Obedience to their Express Com
mands, that I have the Honour to assure your Majesty of their
unanimous Disposition and desire, to cultivate the most friendly
and liberal Intercourse between your Majestys Subjects and their
Citizens, and of their best Wishes for your Majestys Health and
Happiness, and for that of your Royal Family.

Philadelphia's customary steamy summer had returned in force. On a particularly sweltering Sunday, July 28, during which he appears never to have left his Market Street lodgings, Thomas Jefferson checked his thermometer no less than fourteen times, dutifully recording every reading, from a low of 76¾ at six-twenty in the morning to a high of 85 by midafternoon. At ten that night it was still 79¼.

Jefferson, too, was desperate to be gone. He was concerned about his wife and, like many in Congress, he continued to believe the war would be of short duration. The following day he wrote to Richard Henry Lee, who had been absent since mid-June, pleading for Lee to return and relieve him.

"For God's sake, for your country's sake, and for my sake, come," he implored. "I receive by every post such accounts of the state of Mrs. Jefferson's health that it will be impossible for me to disappoint her expectation of seeing me at the time promised."

Jefferson hoped to be home by mid-August, and had no intention of returning to Congress. The nature of his wife's ailment, however, was never explained. What expressions of worry or affection or frustration, what details of his own health he confided in the privacy of his letters to Martha Jefferson, or she to him, were not to be known, as he would one day, for reasons he never expressed, burn all their correspondence.

Earlier that spring in Virginia, Jefferson had himself suffered a severe breakdown following the sudden death of his mother. Excruciating headaches had kept him bedridden for weeks. Jefferson's feelings for his mother are difficult to gauge. He is not known to have ever expressed affection for her, and of her death he wrote all of one sentence, notable for its brevity and absence of the least sentiment. "My mother died at 8 o'clock this morning in the 57th year of her age," was all he chose to record. Possibly it was a deeply private love for his mother and the shock of her death coming so suddenly that explained his collapse. Or possibly it was worry over his wife's illness, or the stress of revolutionary politics. But there was no mistaking the intensity of his suffering. It had been necessary to delay his return to Congress for nearly six weeks.

Now, to his friend John Page, Jefferson wrote that it was only with "great pain" that he remained in Philadelphia.

. . .

WHILE THE BOARD OF WAR consumed much of Adams's time and energy, he was nonetheless in the thick of discussion and debate over the most pressing issue before Congress, the proposed "Articles of Confederation and Perpetual Union." With independence proclaimed, confederation—a working union of the colonies—had become the focus of "spirit" animating the delegates. Union was as essential as independence, nearly all contended—indeed, more important in the view of many—and the issues to be resolved were formidable.

Strict secrecy prevailed, much to Adams's disapproval. There was theory and there was practice in government, and Adams, the delegate who, as Rush said, could see "the whole subject at a glance," was determined that with theory now so eloquently proclaimed, practice be attended with equal diligence, and he wanted nothing about the deliberations to be concealed. In Massachusetts the idea of galleries for the public to watch the legislature was the custom. When Wilson of Pennsylvania, who agreed with him, moved that the doors be opened, galleries erected, or that Congress adjourn to some public building where the people might be accommodated, Adams enthusiastically seconded the motion, but to no avail.

As things were, Congress had no real legal authority. It could only pass resolutions, not laws. Having thus far dealt primarily with the "minutiae" of a plan for confederation, the delegates, by late July, had gotten down to the "great points of representation, boundaries, and taxation," in Jefferson's words; and as Josiah Bartlett wrote with New Hampshire understatement, "the sentiments of the members [were] very different on many of the articles." Nor was progress ever easy. "I find," wrote Rush, who had been in Congress all of a few weeks, "there is a great deal of difference between sporting a sentiment in a letter, or over a glass of wine upon politics, and discharging properly the duties of a senator."

To Adams, as he explained to Abigail, there were two especially knotty problems:

> If a confederation should take place, one great question is how shall we vote? Whether each colony shall count one? Or whether each shall have a weight in proportion to its numbers, or wealth, or exports or imports, or a compound ratio of all?
>
> Another is whether Congress shall have authority to limit the dimensions of each colony, to prevent those which claim, by charter,

or proclamation, or commission to the South Sea [the Pacific Ocean], from growing too great and powerful, so as to be dangerous to the rest.

More than that he felt he could not tell her, and for three days, July 30, 31, and August 1, Adams was engaged in passionate debate over the first of these problems.

As it stood, according to Article 17 of the proposed plan, each colony, irrespective of population or wealth, was to have one vote in deciding all questions concerning the confederation. Thirteen separate states would have thirteen equal votes, a concept Adams strongly opposed. He advocated voting in proportion to population, which was not surprising for someone from Massachusetts, one of the most populated and wealthy states. But he spoke more as an American than a New Englander. The individuality of the colonies was "a mere sound," he said, according to Jefferson's notes. "The confederacy is to make us one individual only; it is to form us, like separate parcels of metal, into one common mass. We shall no longer retain our separate individuality, but become a single individual as to all questions submitted to the confederacy."

Speaking for the small colonies, Hopkins of Rhode Island pointed out that the four largest would contain more than half the inhabitants of the confederacy and would thus govern the others as they pleased. But Benjamin Rush, in an eloquent first speech in Congress, declared, "The more a man aims at serving America the more he serves his colony." "We have been too free with the word independence. We are dependent on each other—not totally independent states. . . . When I entered that door, I considered myself a citizen of America."

With Franklin and Wilson, Rush moved that the vote be in proportion to numbers, insisting further that only freemen should be counted and that this would have the "excellent effect" of inducing the colonies to discourage slavery.

Jefferson was among those who remained silent, and the issue was not to be resolved then or for a long time to come. But on the second knotty problem, that concerning Virginia's claim that her boundaries extended to "the South Sea," which was debated August 2, the same day as the signing of the Declaration of Independence, Jefferson did speak up to say he protested the right of Congress to decide upon the right of Virginia.

· · ·

THE TENSION GREW EXTREME. John wrote to Abigail of being in constant "suspense, uncertainty, and anxiety" about the army at New York, and about "my best, dearest, worthiest, wisest friend in this world and all my children."

Even if he were granted a leave of absence, it would not come soon. Things being what they were, perhaps it would be better if she came to Philadelphia. If she were beside him, Adams wrote, he could stay on indefinitely, "proud and happy as a bridegroom." But thinking better of it, he decided she should inquire about horses to bring him home. "If Bass is in the land of the living, and is willing to take one more ride with his old friend, let him come."

Low in spirits, feeling misjudged and unappreciated by others in Congress, some of whom, he was sure, mistook his ardor for ambition, he succumbed to brooding and self-pity. Nobody understood him. "I have a very tender feeling heart," he wrote. "This country knows not, and never can know the torments I have endured for its sake." He would rather build stone walls upon Penn's Hill than hold the highest office in government, he told her, as though he believed every word.

His view of the prospects at New York grew steadily darker. "May Heaven grant us victory, if we deserve it," he prayed, "if not, patience, humility, and persistence under defeat."

But sensitive to Abigail's own anxiety and the long days of her confinement in Boston, he began writing at greater length and more frequently than he had, filling pages with his thoughts on a great variety of subjects, conscious that the mixture was often quite odd. Her pleasure in such letters was boundless. "I know not how you find the time amidst such a multitude of cares as surround you," she wrote. "I am really astonished at looking over the number [of letters] I have received during this month. . . . I hope 'tis your amusement and relaxation from care to be thus employed. It has been a feast to me."

A large wall map at the State House inspired a letter given over entirely to geography. (*The Map of the British Empire in America with the French and Spanish Settlements Adjacent Thereto*, by Henry Popple, measured nearly eight by eight feet, and was so detailed it even marked

Braintree, spelled "Bantry.") As a branch of knowledge, geography was "absolutely necessary to every person of public character," and to every child, Adams declared. "Really there ought not to be a state, a city, a promontory, a river, a harbor, an inlet or a mountain in all America, but what should be intimately known to every youth who has any pretensions to liberal education."

A sermon preached one Sunday by an unknown southern Baptist minister led to an extended essay on New England and southern preachers, the benefits of travel and education, Adams's own ambition to establish a Boston Philosophical Society, and concluded with a consideration of the shortcomings of his fellow New Englanders, in which he was also writing about himself.

> My countrymen want art and address. They want knowledge of the world. They want the exterior and superficial accomplishments of gentlemen upon which the world has foolishly set so high a value. In solid abilities and real virtues they vastly excel in general any people upon this continent. Our N[ew] England people are awkward and bashful; yet they are pert, ostentatious and vain, a mixture which excites ridicule and gives disgust. They have not the faculty of showing themselves to best advantage, nor the act of concealment of this faculty. An art and faculty which some people possess in the highest degree. Our deficiencies in these respects are owing wholly to the little intercourse we have had with strangers, and to our inexperience in the world. These imperfections must be remedied, for New England must produce the heroes, the statesmen, the philosophers, or America will be no great figure for some time.

He wrote of Benjamin Rush as the very model of a member of the American Philosophical Society, and described a rare moment away from the cares of Congress, a visit he had made to the studio of Charles Willson Peale on Arch Street, where he had had the pleasure of seeing portraits by Peale of Washington, Franklin, the young wife of Benjamin Rush, and various members of Peale's large family. Peale, a new star in the Philadelphia firmament, young, gifted, gregarious, was also a wholehearted patriot who only days earlier had signed on as a common soldier in a company of local militia. "He is ingenious," Adams wrote. "He has vanity, loves finery, wears a sword, gold lace, speaks French, is capable of friendship, and strong family attachments, and natural affections."

Adams was drawn particularly to a painting Peale had begun several years earlier following the death of a daughter who, like Adams's own Susanna, had died in infancy. "He showed me one moving picture. His wife, all bathed in tears, with a child about six months old, laid out upon her lap. This picture struck me prodigiously."

Encouraged by Adams's interest, Peale brought out books for him to see, showed him his sketches of Virginia plantation houses where he had stayed, including Washington's Mount Vernon. "He showed me several imitations of heads, which he had made in clay, as large as life, with his hands only. Among the rest, one of his own head and face, which was a very great likeness." Adams was delighted. How he wished he had the time and "tranquility of mind" for "these elegant and ingenious arts of painting, sculpture, statuary, architecture, and music."

But if Peale's portraits were all "very well done," he told Abigail, they were not so accomplished as those by John Singleton Copley, a view he knew would please her, since two particularly fine examples of Copley's work, companion portraits of Isaac Smith and his wife, Elizabeth, hung in the house where she was confined. "Copley," Adams assured her, "is the greatest master that ever was in America."

Writing of her days in the Smith house, Abigail told him she had discovered the joy of a room of her own. She had never coveted anything until now. It was a small room of her aunt's with a "pretty desk," bookshelves, and a window overlooking a garden. She wrote all her letters there, she explained, and kept his letters to her "unmolested" by anyone.

> Here, I say, I have amused myself in reading and thinking of my absent friend, sometimes with a mixture of pain, sometimes with pleasure, sometimes anticipating a joyful and happy meeting, whilst my heart would bound and palpitate with the pleasing idea, and with the purest affection I have held you to my bosom 'til my whole soul has dissolved in tenderness and my pen fallen from my hand.
>
> How often do I reflect with pleasure that I hold in possession a heart equally warm with my own, and fully as susceptible of the ten-

derest impressions, and who even now whilst he is reading here, feels all I describe.

"I must leave my pen to recover myself and write in another strain," she went on. "I wish for peace and tranquility. All my desires and all my ambition is to be esteemed and loved by my partner, to join with him in the education and instruction of our little ones, to set under our own vines in peace, liberty, and safety."

Then, almost as an afterthought, she said there was an odd report circulating in Braintree that he had been poisoned.

EARLY ON THURSDAY, August 22, an exceptionally clear, bright day in New York, the British commenced their invasion of Long Island. In wave after wave, first in small boats, then transports, 15,000 English, Scottish, and Hessian troops were rowed across the Narrows from Staten Island to land without opposition on the broad shoreline near Gravesend, eight miles to the rear of the American stronghold on Brooklyn Heights.

A violent storm the night before had cleared the air. The wind was out of the north. Everything sparkled in sunlight. An aide to Admiral Richard Lord Howe described the spectacle of a fleet "of above 300 ships and vessels with their sails open to dry, the sun shining clear upon them," of the green, wooded hills and meadows of Long Island, and the calm surface of the water as "one of the finest and most picturesque scenes that imagination can fancy"; and to this was added "the vast importance of the business and of the motions of the day."

Contrary to basic military doctrine, Washington had divided his forces between Manhattan and Long Island. Expecting a second, larger British landing on Manhattan, he remained there, while on Long Island his battalions braced themselves for the assault. But for days the British command under General William Howe made no move in force, not until August 27, when a furious battle was fought to the southwest of Brooklyn Heights. Washington was by then on the scene with reinforcements from Manhattan. Exhorting his men to conduct themselves like soldiers, he told them everything worth living for was at stake.

But the inexperienced Americans were outnumbered, outflanked, and overwhelmed in only a few hours. Most had never been in battle, and while many fought hard and courageously, many did not. Conceivably, as Adams speculated, had General Nathanael Greene remained one of their commanders, things would have gone differently. Ill of fever, Greene had been replaced by General John Sullivan, a former member of Congress from New Hampshire who knew nothing of the terrain and had little of Greene's ability. More than 1,000 Americans were captured, wounded, or killed, and among the prisoners were several generals, including Sullivan. British losses were perhaps 400.

Howe's forces had gone into action filled with contempt for the traitorous American rabble, and numbers of Americans were slaughtered after surrendering. One British officer happily reported, "The Hessians and our brave Highlanders gave no quarter; and it was a fine sight to see with what alacrity they dispatched the rebels with their bayonets after we had surrendered them so that they could not resist. . . . You know all stratagems are lawful in war, especially against such vile enemies to their King and country."

From a hill where with a telescope he watched a Maryland regiment fight its way back to the American lines against terrible odds, Washington was heard to say, "Good God! What brave fellows I must this day lose!"

When the remaining American army fell back to the defenses on Brooklyn Heights, General Howe, remembering the cost of his assault on Bunker Hill, chose not to press the attack, then or the following day.

Meantime, the wind held north, preventing any movement of British warships up the East River to cut off escape by the Americans, and on August 29 another storm blew in. A cold, drenching rain continued through the day and into the night. Before morning, a "peculiar providential" fog set in. When daylight came and the fog began to thin, the British discovered that the Americans had vanished.

Through the night, under the cover of darkness, rain, and fog, Washington's army had been ferried across the mile-wide East River, through powerful currents, in every conceivable kind of small boat, most of them manned by Massachusetts fishermen—some 9,000 to 10,000 troops with baggage and equipment, all moving with utmost silence.

The risks involved in so difficult a withdrawal had been extreme. Much had depended on those troops that remained behind, holding the lines until the last possible moment, an assignment given to two Pennsylvania battalions under Thomas Mifflin, who was by now a major general. "Our situation was very dangerous," an unnamed officer would write in the *Pennsylvania Evening Post*. "The retreat was conducted in the greatest secrecy, and by six o'clock in the morning we had everything embarked." But the hero was Washington. "There never was a man that behaved better upon the occasion than General Washington; he was on horseback the whole night, and never left the ferry stairs 'til he had seen the whole of his troops embarked."

NEWS OF WHAT HAPPENED did not reach Philadelphia until days later. It was only on August 27, the day of the battle of Long Island, that Congress even learned that the British had landed at Gravesend. The wait for further word seemed interminable and in such "strange uncertainty," John Adams sensed disaster. "Have we not put too much to the hazard in sending the greatest part of the army over to Long Island from whence there is no retreat?" he pondered.

It was not until August 31 that Congress learned of the battle and of Washington's withdrawal. And though the escape had been brilliantly executed and Washington was justly praised for saving his army, the defeat on the battlefield had been overwhelming, and the effect on Congress and on people everywhere as the news spread was devastating. "In general, our generals were outgeneralled," Adams would conclude.

Newspapers were filled with eyewitness accounts of the suffering and defeat. For days in Philadelphia the talk was of little else. Then, to compound the atmosphere of uncertainty, the captured General Sullivan appeared in the city. He had been paroled by the British to report to Congress that Admiral Lord Howe wished to confer privately about an accommodation.

Sullivan arrived on September 2, and it was on the following day, Tuesday, September 3, with the outlook as dark as it had ever been, that Jefferson decided to delay his departure no more. As it was, he had stayed three weeks longer than he had intended. Having settled his accounts, he mounted his horse, and with his young servant following behind, started for Virginia.

Adams, too, had reached a decision, as he explained to Abigail in a letter of September 4. Events having taken such a turn at Long Island, he would remain in Philadelphia. When Joseph Bass arrived the next day with the horses to take him home, it made no difference. "The panic may seize whom it will," Adams wrote, "it will not seize me."

WHEN JOHN SULLIVAN, a swarthy, arrogant man, appeared in Congress on September 3 to deliver Lord Howe's request for a conference, Adams was incensed. As Sullivan began his speech, Adams remarked under his breath to Benjamin Rush how much better it would have been had a musket ball at Long Island gone through Sullivan's head.

Taking the floor in protest, Adams called Sullivan a decoy duck sent to seduce Congress into renunciation of independence. But after four days of debate it was decided that a committee be sent to meet with Howe, a decision, said Caesar Rodney, made more to "satisfy some disturbed minds out of doors," than from any expectation of bringing about peace.

Adams remained adamantly opposed, convinced Howe was up to "Machiavellian maneuvers." But when unanimously chosen as one of a committee of three to go on the mission, he consented. "The staunch and intrepid, such as were enemies as much as myself to the measure, pushed for me, I suppose that as little evil might come of it, as possible," he wrote almost apologetically. The other two were Franklin and Edward Rutledge. Thus, New England, the middle states, and the South were to be represented, or, as also noted, it could be seen as a trio of the oldest, the youngest, and the most stouthearted of the members of Congress.

They were to meet His Lordship on Staten Island, and on the morning of September 9, in "fine sunshine," they set off, the whole city aware of what was happening. Franklin and Rutledge each rode in a high, two-wheeled chaise, accompanied by a servant. Adams went on horseback, accompanied by Joseph Bass. Congress, in the meanwhile, could only sit and wait, while in New York the admiral's brother, General Howe, temporarily suspended operations against the rebels.

Free of the city, out of doors and riding again, Adams felt a wave of relief from his cares and woes, even to the point of finding Edward Rutledge an acceptable companion. The road across New Jersey was filled with soldiers marching to join Washington, mostly Pennsylvania men in long brown coats. But for the "straggling and loitering" to be seen, it would have been an encouraging spectacle.

The journey consumed two days. With the road crowded, progress was slow and dusty. At New Brunswick the inn was so full, Adams and Franklin had to share the same bed in a tiny room with only one small window. Before turning in, when Adams moved to close the window against the night air, Franklin objected, declaring they would suffocate. Contrary to convention, Franklin believed in the benefits of fresh air at night and had published his theories on the question. "People often catch cold from one another when shut up together in small close rooms," he had written, stressing "it is the frowzy corrupt air from animal substances, and the perspired matter from our bodies, which, being long confined in beds not lately used, and clothes not lately worn . . . obtains that kind of putridity which infects us, and occasions the colds observed upon sleeping in, wearing, or turning over, such beds [and] clothes." He wished to have the window remain open, Franklin informed Adams.

"I answered that I was afraid of the evening air," Adams would write, recounting the memorable scene. "Dr. Franklin replied, 'The air within this chamber will soon be, and indeed is now worse than that without doors. Come, open the window and come to bed, and I will convince you. I believe you are not acquainted with my theory of colds.' " Adams assured Franklin he had read his theories; they did not match his own experience, Adams said, but he would be glad to hear them again.

So the two eminent bedfellows lay side-by-side in the dark, the window open, Franklin expounding, as Adams remembered, "upon air and cold and respiration and perspiration, with which I was so much amused that I soon fell asleep."

At Perth Amboy the morning of September 11, the three Americans were met by one of Lord Howe's officers who had crossed the narrow channel from Staten Island on the admiral's red-and-gilt barge and presented himself as a volunteer hostage. He would remain in Perth Amboy, he explained, as a guarantee that they would not be seized as prisoners. Adams told Franklin he thought the idea absurd. Franklin agreed and they insisted the officer go back with them on the barge.

Lord Howe was waiting as they came ashore at what was called Billopp's Point, at the southwestern tip of Staten Island. He was an impressive sight, spotless in the superbly tailored uniform of a Royal

Navy flag officer—knee-length navy blue coat of fine wool with white lapels, white cuffs, white lace below the cuffs, gleaming gold buttons and buttonholes edged with gold, gold-hilted dress sword at his side and on his head a magnificent black cocked hat with gold edging and a black silk cockade. To the rear stood a line of Hessian Guards with fixed bayonets—German fusiliers of the Lieb Regiment with striking uniforms of blue, yellow, and red—men chosen for their height and bravery, whose tall polished silver caps made them appear taller still.

Seeing his returned officer, Howe remarked, "Gentlemen, you make me a very high compliment, and you may depend upon it, I will consider it as the most sacred of things."

Franklin, who had known Howe in England, introduced Adams and Rutledge. There were the customary bows, after which they proceeded up a path to a large stone manor house, walking between the Hessian guards who looked, Adams remembered, "fierce as ten furies," as they presented arms, "making all the grimaces and gestures and motions of their muskets with bayonets fixed, which I suppose etiquette requires but which we neither understood nor regarded."

Considering the kind of military display the admiral might have provided—given the number of troops encamped still on Staten Island—or the impression he could have made had they met on board his flagship, this was an exceedingly modest show, suggesting both that the meeting was hastily arranged and that Howe, in the role of messenger of peace, felt any attempt at intimidation would be inappropriate.

The Billopp House belonged to a Tory, Christopher Billopp, and had been badly used by the Hessian Guard who were quartered there. Inside, it looked no better than a stable, except for the large parlor, where in a last-minute effort to decorate for the occasion—and dampen the smell—the floor had been spread with moss and green branches. A table was set and following a cold meal of "good claret," ham, and mutton, the admiral commenced the meeting.

A proud, stolid man with a prominent nose and large, sad eyes, Lord Richard Howe was fifty-five years old, older than Adams judged him. He had served in His Majesty's navy since the age of fourteen. He was considered an exceptionally able officer and, by reputation, had an exceptional gift for persuasion. Like his brother, the general, he was also known to be well disposed toward Americans. He was convinced, like most

Englishmen, that the great majority of Americans remained loyal to George III and that such men as the three seated before him at the table were an insignificant minority. It was with expressions of affection for America that he chose to open the discussion, stressing in particular his regard for Massachusetts.

Eighteen years earlier, during the French and Indian War, an older brother, Brigadier George Augustus, Viscount Howe, one of the outstanding British soldiers of the time, had been killed at Ticonderoga. The great William Pitt, then Britain's Secretary of State, had called him "a complete model of military virtue," and the Massachusetts Assembly had provided funds for a marble memorial in Westminster Abbey, an honor that Admiral Lord Howe said he esteemed "above all." He felt for America, said the admiral, as he did for a brother. "If America should fail, I should feel and lament it like the loss of a brother."

With a smile, Franklin replied, "My Lord, we will do our utmost endeavors to save your Lordship that mortification."

But the admiral did not smile. All would have been better, he observed, had he only arrived before the Declaration of Independence was signed. The Declaration had "changed the ground." Were it given up, however, he might possibly "effect the King's purposes . . . to restore peace and grant pardons," and thus such discussions as they were having could lead to a "re-union upon terms honorable and advantageous to the colonies as well as to Great Britain." Was there "no way of treading back this step of independency?"

It must be understood, he continued, that he could not confer with them as members of Congress—that he "could not acknowledge that body which was not acknowledged by the King, whose delegate he was," as his secretary recorded in the notes of the meeting—and that he therefore could only consider them "merely as gentlemen of great ability and influence," private persons and British subjects.

To this Adams immediately responded: "Your Lordship may consider me in what light you please," Adams said, "and indeed, I should be willing to consider myself, for a few moments, in any character which would be agreeable to your Lordship, except that of a British subject."

Further, as Howe's secretary, Henry Strachey, noted, Adams expressed "warmly" his determination "not to depart from the idea of independency." Turning to Franklin and Rutledge, Howe remarked gravely, "Mr. Adams is a decided character," the emphasis apparently on the word "decided."

Years afterward Adams would better understand the gloomy look on Howe's face, when he learned that before leaving London, Howe had been given a list of those American rebels who were to be granted pardons. John Adams was not on the list. He was to hang.

In the course of nearly three hours, Howe did most of the talking. But, as the committee would report to Congress, it had soon become obvious that Howe had no authority other than to grant pardons should America submit, which, as Franklin told him, meant he had nothing really to offer.

He was sorry that the gentlemen had had "the trouble of coming so far to so little purpose," Howe said at last. If the colonies could not give up "independency," negotiation was impossible.

"They met, they talked, they parted," wrote one of Howe's staff, "and now nothing remains but to fight it out against a set of the most determined hypocrites and demagogues, compiled of the refuse of the colonies, that ever were permitted by Providence to be the scourge of a country."

The Declaration of Independence had passed a first test. The war would go on.

THE BRITISH MOVED at once. On the morning of Sunday, September 15, with favorable winds and tide this time, five British warships sailed into the East River and commenced a thunderous, point-blank bombardment of American shore defenses on Manhattan. "So terrible and so incessant a roar of guns few even in the army and navy had ever heard before," wrote the admiral's secretary.

In a letter to Congress, Washington had earlier explained his intention of abandoning New York, and his larger conclusion that he and his army must avoid pitched battles with such a disciplined and numerous enemy, but rather fight a defensive war. But what happened when bargeloads of British and Hessian infantry began crossing from Long Island, coming through the smoke of the cannonade to land at Kips Bay, was no orderly evacuation of the kind Washington intended. Since the escape from

Brooklyn Heights, militia had been deserting in droves. Now those who remained abandoned their entrenchments and fled, never firing a shot. Entire units turned and ran. Galloping to the scene on horseback, Washington charged up and down among the fleeing men, trying to rally them to stand and fight. Outraged, Washington lost his celebrated self-control and began cursing and striking at officers with his riding crop.

Muskets, knapsacks, wagons, and cannon were left behind in the pell-mell rush to get away. Washington could only move with the troops, retreating rapidly northward, up the island of Manhattan to the rocky defenses of Harlem Heights.

For Washington and the American army it was a disastrous, shameful day, and when the news reached Philadelphia, the effect on Congress was decided. As Samuel Chase wrote, "Our affairs here wear a very unfavorable aspect."

His army was falling apart, Washington informed John Hancock in a bleak letter from Harlem Heights on September 25. For the moment, the British were again doing nothing, but unless "some speedy and effectual measures" were adopted by Congress, "our cause will be lost." The war, it was clear, was not to be "the work of a day." Short enlistments would no longer answer. There must be an army built on "a permanent footing," a standing army.

> To place any dependence upon militia is, assuredly, resting on a broken staff. Men just dragged from the tender scenes of domestic life, unaccustomed to the din of arms, totally unacquainted with every kind of military skill, which being followed by a want of confidence in themselves, when opposed to troops regularly trained, disciplined, and appointed, superior in knowledge, and superior in arms, makes them timid, and ready to fly from their own shadows.

Love of country and belief in the cause were noble sentiments, Washington continued, but even among the officers, those who acted "upon principles of disinterestedness" were "no more than a drop in the ocean." There must be good pay for officers. For the men, nothing would satisfy but a bounty and an offer of free land.

Stealing by his troops was rampant. If ever he was to bring discipline to bear, check this "lust for plunder," and stop wholesale desertions and widespread drunkenness, he must have new rules and regulations authorizing harsher punishments.

But Congress was ahead of him. It had already moved to make the changes Washington called for, and again it was Adams—Adams who had never thought it would be anything other than a long, difficult war—who had taken the lead, both as head of the Board of War and in floor debate.

On September 16, Congress adopted a new plan issued by the Board of War whereby every soldier who signed on for the duration was to be offered $20 and 100 acres of land. On September 20, a set of Articles of War—Adams's rendering of the British Articles of War—was agreed upon. The severity of punishments was increased, as Washington wished. Washington thought the maximum number of lashes allowed hitherto was hardly sufficient. For such crimes as drunkenness or sleeping on guard duty, Congress increased the punishment from thirty-nine to a hundred lashes, and increased as well the number of crimes for which the penalty was death. On October 1, Adams proposed the creation of a military academy. Although nothing would come of the motion until after the war, it was the first such proposal made.

Little that had happened through the summer had distressed Adams quite so much as the behavior of American troops, and especially reports that Massachusetts men had "behaved ill." "Unfaithfulness" was something he could not abide, and in his spells of gloom he pondered whether the fault was in the times.

> Unfaithfulness in public stations is deeply criminal [he wrote to Abigail]. But there is no encouragement to be faithful. Neither profit, nor honor, nor applause is acquired by faithfulness. . . . There is too much corruption, even in this infant age of our Republic. Virtue is not in fashion. Vice is not infamous.

One day, as he and Benjamin Rush sat together in Congress, Rush asked Adams in a whisper if he thought America would succeed in the struggle. "Yes," Adams replied, "if we fear God and repent our sins."

But the most direct and obvious response to the perilous state of Washington and his army, was the attention Congress turned to France.

Regrettable as it may have seemed to many, a large majority in Congress now saw that independence could not be won without something more than a people's army, or without help from the outside.

"We look only to heaven and France for succour," Rush wrote. At City Tavern and the London Coffee House toasts were now commonly raised to His Most Christian Majesty, young King Louis XVI of France, and to "a speedy alliance" between France and the United States.

Months before, in February, listing all that he was determined to see accomplished along with "independency," Adams had put an alliance with France at the head of the list. But in notes made in early March, at the time Silas Deane was appointed as a secret envoy, Adams had stressed that there must be no political or military connection with France, only a commercial connection. Later, in July, as head of the Committee of Treaties, he had written into the proposed Plan of Treaties an article that in quite blunt, undiplomatic language made clear his deep-seated distrust of France. Designed to safeguard the territorial integrity of the new United States, it stated that in case of any war "between the Most Christian King and the King of Great Britain, the Most Christian King shall never invade, nor under any pretense attempt to possess himself of" Canada, Florida, nor any city or town on the continent of North America, nor any island "lying near to the said continent."

By September, given the realities of the war, Adams had relinquished his earlier misgivings over a military connection with France, but when the Plan of Treaties was taken up in debate on the floor and motions were made to insert what he called "articles of entangling alliance," he fought them tooth and nail, and with success. As he wrote, the plan passed "without one particle" of such stipulations and, in fact, would remain the model for nearly all treaties of the United States for the next twenty-five years.

On September 26, Congress took the momentous step of appointing Benjamin Franklin and Thomas Jefferson as commissioners to the Court of France, to serve with Silas Deane.

In a letter to Jefferson, who had earlier requested just such an assignment, Richard Henry Lee stressed that it was the "great abilities and unshaken virtue" needed in carrying out such a mission that had directed Congress in its choice. In effect, Lee was telling Jefferson that Congress was counting on him and that there was no assignment more crucial to the fate of the country. "In my judgment, the most eminent services that the greatest of her sons can do America will not more essentially serve her and honor themselves than a successful negotiation with France."

When Jefferson wrote from Virginia to say that after days of deliberation he had decided he could not accept—because of "circumstances very peculiar in the situation of my family," which was understood to mean the health of his wife—Congress named, in his place, Arthur Lee, a brother of Richard Henry Lee, which was to prove an unfortunate choice.

AUTUMN BROUGHT CLEAR, cool days, with starlit nights cold enough for log fires at City Tavern, where Adams customarily dined. People were putting on flannels again. Wild geese were flying, their honking heard as they beat their way over the city in great V formations. Numbers of the staunchest members of Congress were departing for home, claiming the need for rest. Samuel Chase, Stephen Hopkins, and Joseph Hewes, like Thomas Jefferson, had left in September. In early October, Caesar Rodney and Roger Sherman took their leave. Franklin, who would sail for France on October 26, was already packing.

From Abigail came word that she and the children, having survived the long ordeal of inoculation in Boston, were at last home again in Braintree. Little Charles was still weak and having a "tedious time of it," but young Johnny, "Master John," as she now referred to him, had become her post rider, carrying the family mail to and from Boston.

"I have been here until I am stupefied," Adams told her in a gloomy letter of October 7. The suspense of what was to happen next in New York continued. Turning the situation over and over in his mind, Adams only grew more downcast.

But then four days later, as if a different man, he made his decision. "I suppose your Ladyship has been in the twitters for some time past, because you have not received a letter by every post as you used to," he wrote in high spirits. "But I'm coming home to make my apology in person." On Sunday, October 13, he and Bass saddled their horses and started for Braintree.

• • •

IT HAD BEEN a little more than eight months since Adams arrived in Philadelphia in February, and except for the few days taken up with the expedition to meet with Lord Howe, he had never strayed out of the city. True to his parting words to Jonathan Sewall on the hill above Casco Bay two summers before, he had shown unflinching devotion to the cause of his country, "swim or sink, live or die." He had never walked away from work that needed doing. He had never failed to speak his mind when it counted, to take a stand and fight for what he believed. Yet remarkably, he had never lost his temper or attacked anyone in a personal way, no matter the bitterness or inner fury to be found in some of his private writings.

For eight difficult, wearisome months, working under the greatest imaginable stress and with the full realization of all that was riding on what transpired in Congress, he had kept his head, kept driving toward the single surpassing objective of independence. The timing, the wording, the spirit of the Declaration, the plan of confederation, the approach to treaties, the winning of the war, were all, he saw, essential to achieving the large, overriding goal of an independent America. And beyond independence, as he consistently emphasized, was the ultimate need for a republican form of government built on a foundation of checks and balances.

Writing of Adams that September, Benjamin Rush told a friend, "This illustrious patriot has not his superior, scarcely his equal for abilities and virtue on the whole of the continent of America." Later, Rush would say of Adams, "Every member of Congress in 1776 acknowledged him to be the first man in the House." Jefferson was to remember Adams as "our colossus on the floor."

Few Americans ever achieved so much of such value and consequence to their country in so little time. Above all, with his sense of urgency and unrelenting drive, Adams made the Declaration of Independence happen when it did. Had it come later, the course of events could have gone very differently.

PART II

Distant Shores

*Fortune may have yet a better success in reserve for you,
and they who lose today may win tomorrow.*

—Cervantes

CHAPTER FOUR

APPOINTMENT TO FRANCE

I cannot but wish I were better qualified.

—John Adams

I

"WHEN DO YOU EXPECT to see Mr. Adams?" inquired Mercy Otis Warren in a hurried note from Plymouth.

Surely it must be a "great trial of patience and philosophy" to be so long separated from "the companion of your heart and from the father of your little flock," continued the older woman, whose tone in correspondence with Abigail Adams was customarily that of the wiser, slightly superior adviser.

Patience, fortitude, public spirit, magnanimity, and self-denial were called for, though she herself, wrote Mercy in candor, could not claim these "sublime" qualities. As Abigail knew, it had been only a short time past when Mercy urged her own husband to resign his commission as a general rather than serve outside New England, and James Warren had complied.

"But oh! the dread of losing all that this world can bestow by one costly sacrifice keeps my mind in continual alarms."

The note was dated October 15, 1776. By the time Abigail found a moment to reply, a new year had begun and John Adams had come and gone, riding away on still another winter day to still another session of Congress, heading for Baltimore accompanied by a new Massachusetts congressman, James Lovell.

"I had it in my heart to dissuade him from going and I know I could have prevailed," Abigail wrote to Mercy, "but our public affairs at the time wore so gloomy an aspect that I thought if ever his assistance was wanted, it must be at such a time. I therefore resigned myself to suffer some anxiety and many melancholy hours for this year to come."

Their separation was more grievous than any, for as she confided discreetly "circumstances" conspired. She was pregnant again. But she took heart, she said, from the late successes of General Washington, an affirming figure for a dark passage. "I am apt to think that our late misfortunes have called out the hidden excellencies of our commander-in-chief. 'Affliction is a good man's shining time,' " she wrote, quoting a favorite line from the English poet Edward Young.

In the aftermath of still further defeat in New York—at White Plains, and Fort Washington—the general had beat an inglorious retreat south through New Jersey to the Delaware, his army dwindling to less than 4,000 men, many of whom were without shoes and so thinly clad as to be unfit for service. With the onset of winter, the weather turned bitterly cold. "These are the times that try men's souls," wrote Thomas Paine, who was with the retreating army. "The summer soldier and the sunshine patriot will, in this crisis, shrink from the service of his country."

On December 7, Washington escaped to the Pennsylvania side of the Delaware, putting the river between his force and the enemy. Only days later, Congress evacuated Philadelphia and moved south to Baltimore, bag and baggage. The prospect for the American cause had never looked so bleak.

But when the British commander, General Howe, called a halt to the campaign on December 14, ordering his troops into winter quarters in New York and leaving New Jersey in the hands of small holding forces, Washington, to the astonishment of everyone, counterattacked. On Christmas night, in driving sleet and snow, he and his ragged army recrossed the Delaware and struck at Trenton the next morning, taking a drowsy Hessian guardpost completely by surprise. On January 2, he struck again, at Princeton, and again with stunning success. Measured by the numbers of troops involved, these were small engagements, but the effect on American spirits could hardly have been greater, and just when all seemed lost.

By mid-January 1777, Washington's army, too, was settled in winter quarters, miserably, at Morristown, New Jersey, while along the coast of Massachusetts, heavy snow fell in weather as severe as any in memory. In the wake of one February storm, howling winds piled drifts higher than a man's head. From her window beside the coast road, Abigail looked out at a world of white desolation, a small, slight figure, snow-bound with five children, including her niece, Louisa, and determined to be no summer soldier or sunshine patriot. She had never seen the road so obstructed, she informed John. For days not a soul passed her door.

"I want a bird of passage," she declared in early March, still having heard nothing from him. "Posterity who are to reap the blessings will scarcely be able to conceive the hardships and sufferings of their ancestors."

When a first letter from Baltimore arrived on March 9, filled with his distress over no word from her, she replied at once. Her health was as good as to be expected in her condition. Moreover, " 'Tis a constant remembrancer of an absent friend, and excites sensations of tenderness which are better felt than expressed."

By spring she had grown uncomfortably large and clumsy—young Johnny told her he never saw anyone grow so fat—but she was also uncommonly pale. She could never put the "cruel war" out of her mind. Her only brother, William Smith, had gone to sea, as a captain of marines on a privateer. Troops passed continually up and down the coast road— "not an hour in the day but what we see soldiers marching."

Adams, who by then had returned with the Congress to Philadelphia, wrote every week. He was homesick, weary with work. Attendance in Congress was down to a mere twenty. When Jefferson, claiming personal reasons, failed to return, Adams was especially disappointed. "We want your industry and abilities here extremely," he wrote to Jefferson. "Your country is not quite secure enough to excuse your retreat to the delights of domestic life." But Adams was not unsympathetic. "Yet for the soul of me, when I attend on my own feelings, I cannot blame you."

The Board of War was examining reports of atrocities committed by Hessian troops in New Jersey; Adams was sickened by what he heard. He was exasperated, too, by the constant squabbles of American officers. "They worry one another like mastiffs, scrambling for rank and pay like apes for nuts," he told Abigail.

I believe there is no one principle which predominates in human nature so much in every stage of life, from the cradle to the grave, in males and females, old and young, black and white, rich and poor, high and low, as this passion for superiority.

He wondered if he was sadly miscast in his public role. "I begin to suspect that I have not much grand in my composition. The pride and pomp of war, the continual sound of drums and fifes . . . have no charms for me." He would prefer the delights of a garden to dominion of a world. "I have nothing of Caesar's greatness in my soul. Power has not my wishes in her train."

He urged Abigail to keep up her cheer. Wondering what was in store for their children, he poured out heartfelt advice and admonitions to each of them.

You have discovered in your childhood a remarkable modesty, discretion, and reserve [he told Nabby]. You are now, I think, far advanced in your twelfth year—a time when the understanding opens, and the youth begin to look abroad into the world among whom they are to live. To be good, and to do good, is all we have to do.

"A taste for literature and a turn for business, united in the same person, never fails to make a great man," he counseled Johnny, while to Charles he expressed the hope that with the war over by and by he would have only to study "the arts of peace." To Thomas he offered the prospect of a career in medicine, warming so to the subject that he seemed to forget the boy was only five years old. "Would it not please you to study nature on all her wonderful operations, and to relieve your fellow creatures under the severest pains and distress to which human nature is liable?"

"I love to receive letters very much better than I love to write them," replied Johnny, who reported proudly that he was embarked on the third volume of Tobias Smollett's *History of England*.

History was the true source of "solid instruction," Adams wrote to the boy encouragingly. He must read Thucydides's history of the Peloponnesian War. There was no better preparation, whatever part he was called to play on "the stage of life." It was best read in the original Greek, of course, but he could find a reliable translation among his father's books. (Long afterward, writing of this time in his boyhood, John Quincy Adams would recall secreting himself in a closet to smoke tobacco and read Milton's *Paradise Lost*, trying without success to determine what "recondite charm" in them gave his father so much pleasure.)

RAMPANT INFLATION, shortages of nearly every necessity made the day-to-day struggle at home increasingly difficult. A dollar was not worth what a quarter had been, Abigail reported. "Our money will soon be as useless as blank paper." Bread, salt, sugar, meat and molasses, cotton and wool, had become dear beyond measure. Farm help, help of any sort, was impossible to find. Yet she managed—scrimped, saved, wove her own wool, made the family's clothes—determined not only to stay free of debt, but to make improvements. She would do her part in her way, as a patriotic duty but also because it was expected of her in his absence. "I believe nature has assigned each sex its particular duties and sphere of action," she would write, "and to act well your part, 'there all the honor lies.' "

"What will become of you, I know not," John wrote in anguish. "How you will be able to live is past my comprehension."

That spring James Warren reported to Adams that the farm never looked better and that Abigail was "like to outshine all farmers." But then Adams had never doubted that she could run things as well as he, or better.

She wanted him home by July in time for her delivery. Even the brutes of creation had the consoling company of their mates at such times, she reminded him. Beset by morbid premonitions, she imagined their separation as prelude to the "still more painful one" of his death, or her own. She longed for his soothing tenderness. "Is this weakness or is it not?"

His affection for her was of a kind that neither time nor place could abate, he insisted, knowing, as she did, that he could not abandon his duties.

On a night in early July, taken with a "shaking fit," she feared the life within was lost. Two weeks later, after an ordeal of several days, she wrote to tell him their baby, a daughter, had been stillborn. "It appeared to be a very fine babe, and as it never opened its eyes in this world, it looked as though they were only closed for sleep."

"The corn looks well, and [the] English grain promising," she bravely reported the week following. "We cannot be sufficiently thankful to a bountiful Providence that the horrors of famine are not added to those of war."

They had both wanted another child and hoped it would be another daughter. "The loss of this sweet little girl," wrote Adams after receiving her letter, "has most tenderly and sensibly affected me."

" 'Tis almost 14 years since we were united, but not more than half that time we had the happiness of living together," she wrote plaintively. "The unfeeling world may consider it in what light they please, I consider it a sacrifice to my country and one of my greatest misfortunes."

Remembering these years long afterward, Adams would tell Benjamin Rush they were "times that tried women's souls as well as men's."

THROUGH THE REST of the eventful summer of 1777, they exchanged news of the war. An immense enemy force under General John Burgoyne had started south from Canada, down the valley of Lake Champlain, in an audacious move to separate New England from the rest of the country. Fort Ticonderoga had fallen, abandoned by its American garrison, and enemy troops were pressing steadily on, hacking their way through the wilderness to reach the Hudson River. On July 22, Sir William Howe had sailed out of New York Harbor with a fleet of 267 ships carrying 18,000 soldiers, and vanished over the horizon, bound, it was thought, for Philadelphia. A week later the ships appeared in Delaware Bay, only to disappear again, which led to days of tension and speculation as to Howe's intentions. Adams interpreted such feints and maneuvers to mean the real objective was the Hudson, where Howe would join forces with Burgoyne, but then Adams decided an invasion of Philadelphia must be the plan after all. If Howe's army was at sea all this time, he speculated to Abigail, the men between decks must be suffering beyond expression.

Howe's fleet was sighted in Chesapeake Bay on August 21. Three days later, in a show of resolve, Washington paraded his troops through

Philadelphia, every man wearing a sprig of green as an emblem of hope. Adams felt a lift of heart at the sight. His hard work with the Board of War had had some effect. They looked well armed and tolerably well clothed, he thought, if a bit out of step.

Sixty miles below Philadelphia, the next day, August 25, Howe's army began coming ashore. On September 11, in a fierce, confused fight at Brandywine Creek, only twenty-five miles south of Philadelphia, Washington tried without success to check the advance of a superior enemy force. The battle, one of the largest of the war, raged until dark. The roar of cannon and of volleys of musketry could be heard plainly in Philadelphia. Washington lost more than 1,500 men killed, wounded, and taken prisoner. In no time the British were on the outskirts of the city, and before dawn on September 19, in response to urgent warning messages from a young officer on Washington's staff, Alexander Hamilton, Congress began departing with all possible speed—"chased like a covey of partridges," as Adams would say—to resettle in the little market town of York to the west. On September 26, Howe's columns marched in to occupy Philadelphia.

Privately, Adams questioned Washington's leadership. The Virginian had been "out-generaled" once again. "Oh, Heaven! grant us one great soul!" Adams wrote in his diary. "One leading mind would extricate the best cause from that ruin which seems to await it. . . . One active, masterly capacity would bring order out of this confusion and save this country."

But writing to Abigail, he showed no despair. The army had survived, the loss of Philadelphia did not matter, he assured her. She longed for "spirited exertions everywhere," for "some grand important actions to take place."

In October, as if in answer, came the stupendous news of the surrender of Burgoyne and his entire army at Saratoga to an American force commanded by Horatio Gates. In another few weeks, like most delegates to Congress, Adams was heading home.

Yet his stay this time was to be more abbreviated even than that of the year past, and Mercy Otis Warren would once more summon Abigail to noble sacrifice. "Great advantages are often attended with great inconveniences, and great minds called to severe trials," she wrote. "If your dearest friend had not abilities to render such important services to

his country, he would not be called. . . . I know your public spirit and fortitude to be such that you will throw no impediment in his way."

ADAMS REACHED MASSACHUSETTS by horseback in the last days of
November 1777 and for two weeks did little but relish the comforts of his
own fireside. He was home to stay, by preference and of necessity, he said.

> It was my intention to decline the next elections, and return to my
> practise at the bar. I had been four years in Congress, left my
> accounts in very loose condition. My debtors were failing, the paper
> money was depreciating. I was daily losing the fruits of seventeen
> years' industry. My family was living on my past acquisitions which
> were very moderate. . . . My children were growing up without my
> care in their education, and all my emoluments as a member of Con-
> gress for four years had not been sufficient to pay a laboring man on
> a farm.

But before leaving York, Adams had been told by Elbridge Gerry
that he was to be appointed a commissioner to France, in place of Silas
Deane, who was being recalled to answer charges of questionable conduct. According to Adams's later recollection, he said nothing to Gerry
about accepting the post, only that he felt unqualified. Gerry, too, would
describe Adams as "silent" on the matter, though Gerry would tell the
Congress that knowing Adams as he did, he was sure Adams would not
decline the duty. On November 27, Congress named Adams a commissioner to work with Franklin and Arthur Lee in negotiating a French
alliance.

A packet of letters and Adams's official commission to the Court of
France went off to Braintree by post rider. There was a formal letter of
notification from the new president of Congress, Henry Laurens of South
Carolina, and another from Richard Henry Lee and James Lovell on
behalf of the Committee for Foreign Affairs. ("We are by no means willing to indulge a thought of your declining this important service.") In a
separate letter, Lovell, the new Massachusetts representative, said that
all in Congress who understood the importance of the negotiations with
France were counting on Adams's acceptance, and that those sacrifices

Adams had already made of private happiness gave them confidence he would undertake "this new business." There was alarm over Franklin's age, Lovell said, adding, "We want one man of inflexible integrity on the embassy."

Lovell, the most active member of the Committee for Foreign Affairs and a dedicated patriot, was a shrewd, industrious man who loved intrigue and would make himself Congress's expert on cryptology. He and Adams had known each other for years, and Lovell professed only the warmest regard for Adams, as well as for Abigail. But Lovell was a practiced flatterer, sometimes to the point of impropriety. In a note to Abigail the summer before, accompanying some information on the war he thought she would want to see, Lovell had declared, "This knowledge is only part of the foundation of my affectionate esteem for you. Nor will I mention the whole." So an appeal to Adams's self-regard, by extolling his integrity to the point of implying that Franklin and Arthur Lee had none, was quite in the Lovell mode.

The official packet reached Braintree in mid-December, at about the time Washington's army was on the march west from Philadelphia to take up winter quarters at Valley Forge. Adams was away at Portsmouth, New Hampshire, representing a client in what was to be his last appearance ever in court as a private attorney. Thinking the packet must be urgent business, Abigail opened it and was stunned by what she read. Furious, she wrote straight away to Lovell, demanding to know how he could "contrive to rob me of all my happiness.

> And can I, sir, consent to be separated from him whom my heart esteems above all earthly things, and for an unlimited time? My life will be one continued scene of anxiety and apprehension, and must I cheerfully comply with the demand of my country?

The thought of John braving the North Atlantic in winter, and the very real possibility of his capture at sea, horrified her. No one put to sea from Boston in winter if it could possibly be avoided, even in peacetime.

News of the appointment had already reached Adams in New Hampshire. Thus, the day he dismounted from his horse at Braintree, December 22, he and Abigail knew they had reached one of the turning points of their lives. What was said between them, neither divulged. But the decision, difficult as it was, Adams made at once. There was no hesitation, no playing out the ordeal of deciding. If nothing else, he was decisive—they both were. Within twenty-four hours he had written his letter of acceptance to Henry Laurens. To James Lovell he wrote, "I should have wanted no motives or arguments to induce me to accept of this momentous trust, if I could be sure that the public would be benefited by it.

> But when I see my brothers at the bar here so easily making fortunes
> for themselves and their families . . . and when I see my own children
> growing up in something very like real want, because I have taken
> no care of them, it requires as much philosophy as I am master of, to
> determine to persevere in public life, and engage in a new scene for
> which I fear I am very ill qualified.

The question of whether Abigail should accompany him was discussed, and for a few days it appeared she might go, great as her fear was of crossing the water. It was the risk of capture by the enemy that weighed heaviest in the balance. But also the expense of living in Paris was bound to be more than they could afford, and clearly things at home would fall to ruin without her.

"My desire was, you know, to have run all hazards and accompanied him," Abigail would tell a friend, "but I could not prevail upon him to consent."

She would remain at home, but ten-year-old Johnny was to go with his father, as the boy ardently wished. It was the chance of a lifetime for him, an experience of inestimable value, Abigail recognized, her "thousand fears" notwithstanding. Assuredly he would encounter temptation, she wrote, but to exclude him from temptation would be to exclude him from the world in which he was to live. Later, in a long letter written after he had gone, she would assure him he was ever in her heart, but tell him also what was expected of him in his obligations to society, his country, and to his family:

> You are in possession of a natural good understanding and of spirits
> unbroken by adversity, and untamed with care. Improve your
> understanding for acquiring useful knowledge and virtue, such as
> will render you an ornament to society, an honor to your country,

and a blessing to your parents . . . and remember you are accountable to your Maker for all your words and actions.

He was to "attend" the advantages of such an experience and "attend
constantly and steadfastly to the precepts and instructions of your father
as you value the happiness of your mother and your own welfare."

THEY WERE TO SAIL on the new 24-gun frigate *Boston*, under the command of Captain Samuel Tucker of Marblehead. For weeks there was
much scurrying to get ready, much ado over packing and estimating the
food and supplies to be sent on board—for Adams, John Quincy, and a
Braintree man named Joseph Stephens, who would be going as Adams's
servant. The completed list included such immediate necessities for
Adams as ink, paper, account books, twenty-five quill pens, a dozen clay
pipes, tobacco, and a pocket-size pistol; but also two hogs, two "fat
sheep," six dozen chickens and five bushels of corn, fourteen dozen eggs, a
keg of rum, a barrel of madeira, four dozen bottles of port wine, tea,
chocolate, brown sugar, mustard, pepper, a box of wafers, a bag of Indian
meal, and a barrel of apples.

In view of the number of spies in and about Boston and the certainty
of British cruisers in New England waters, departure was to be managed
with all possible secrecy. Adams was not to go aboard at Boston. He
would be picked up near dark, at a rendezvous on the Braintree shore
known as Hough's Neck. As little as possible was to be said of the plan.
Adams would leave pressing legal matters unattended and without
explanation to his clients. Numbers of friends, even members of the family, never knew of his appointment to France until after he had gone.

One of the last letters he received before departure was from his
admiring friend Benjamin Rush, who in his usual flowing, assured hand
wrote that though he hated to see Adams go, he had every confidence
in him:

I am aware that your abilities and firmness are much wanted at the
Court of France, and after all that has been said of the advantages of
dressing, *powdering*, and *bowing* well as necessary accomplishments
for an ambassador, I maintain that knowledge and integrity with a

common share of prudence will outweigh them all. . . . I am willing to risk the safety of our country upon this single proposition, that you will effectually "baffle and deceive them all by being perfectly honest."

On a blustery morning in February, the *Boston* dropped anchor off Nantasket Roads. But with snow squalls and winds gathering to gale force, it was not until two days later that a barge was lowered.

Abigail did not go down to the shore to see her husband and son depart. The goodbyes were said at home.

THEY CROSSED THROUGH GREY TWILIGHT and blowing snow to a house by the shore, where sailors from the *Boston* were waiting out of the bitter wind. It was the home of a distant cousin whose wife, afflicted by "hysterical complaints," accosted Adams with a warning. He was embarking under bad signs. "The heavens frown, the clouds roll, the waves roar upon the beach," she declaimed. He was not enough of a Roman, Adams later said, to take this as an ill omen, but then neither was he a New Englander of the kind bred to the sea, for all that he loved its proximity and bracing air. He had never in his life sailed on a ship. His one venture had been by small boat in boyhood, and then only to go fishing at nearby Cohasset Rocks.

Now he was embarking on a 3,000-mile voyage on the North Atlantic in its most treacherous season, the risks far greater than he knew. The difference between what he understood of the perils to be faced and what the captain understood was hardly less than the difference between his understanding and that of his small son. A hardened seaman like Captain Tucker knew what the Atlantic could deliver up in February: the chances of being hit by a northeaster and driven onto the shoals of Cape Cod, graveyard of ships; the sheer terror of winter storms at sea when freezing spray aloft could turn to ice so heavy as to cause a ship to capsize. Navigation, never a simple matter, became difficult in the extreme from a violently pitching deck and with a horizon distorted by breaking seas, or, in the absence of sun and stars, quite impossible.

Adams was leaving his wife, children, friends, his home, his livelihood, everything he loved. He was risking his life and that of his small son, risking capture and who knew what horrors and indignities as a prisoner, all to begin "new business" for which he felt ill suited, knowing nothing of European politics or diplomacy and unable to speak French, the language of diplomacy. He had never in his life laid eyes on a King or Queen, or the Foreign Minister of a great power, never set foot in a city of more than 30,000 people. At age forty-two he was bound for an unimaginably distant world apart, with very little idea of what was in store and every cause to be extremely apprehensive.

But with his overriding sense of duty, his need to serve, his ambition, and as a patriot fiercely committed to the fight for independence, he could not have done otherwise. There was never really a doubt about his going.

If he was untrained and inexperienced in diplomacy, so was every American. If unable to speak French, he could learn. Fearsome as the winter seas might be, he was not lacking in courage, and besides, the voyage would provide opportunity to appraise the Continental Navy at first hand, a subject he believed of highest importance. And for all he may have strayed from the hidebound preachments of his forebears, Adams remained enough of a Puritan to believe anything worthy must carry a measure of pain.

"The wind was very high, and the sea very rough," he would record in his diary, "but by means of a quantity of hay in the bottom of the boat, and good watch coats with which we were covered, we arrived on board the *Boston* about five o'clock, tolerably warm and dry."

Continuing high winds and steep seas kept the ship at anchor in the roadstead another thirty-six hours. Then once under way, on a morning with the temperature at 14 degrees, the ship went only as far as Marblehead, where a sudden snowstorm blotted out all visibility, and nearly two days passed before Captain Tucker could put to sea. The weather was no warmer but fair at last, and the wind out of the northwest, exactly what was needed to clear Cape Cod on a broad reach.

The date was Tuesday, February 17, 1778, and, as Adams had no way of knowing, it marked the beginning of what would become a singular odyssey, in which he would journey farther in all, both by sea and land, than any other leader of the American cause.

"This morning weighed the last anchor and came under sail before breakfast," he recorded. "A fine wind and a pleasant sun, but sharp cold air. Thus I bid farewell to my native shore."

II

BY THOSE WHO KNEW, the *Boston* was judged a pretty ship. One of the smaller of the thirteen frigates commissioned by Congress, she had been built and launched at Newburyport in 1776. One hundred and fourteen feet on deck, and 514 tons, she had a theoretical complement of 200 men. As it was, there were 172 crowded on board, counting officers, crew, and 36 passengers, mostly French officers returning after service in the Continental Army. Of this French contingent, Adams took an immediate liking to an army surgeon named Nicholas Noel, who spoke English and thought well enough of John Quincy to begin schooling him in French.

As for Captain Tucker, Adams considered him able and attentive, though, to judge by the few books in his cabin, no doubt lacking in erudition. The son of a Marblehead sea captain, Tucker was thirty years old, a square, solid looking man with a booming voice who had been at sea since the age of eleven. But the *Boston* was a new command with a green crew, and the official instructions Tucker had received concerning his highly important passenger were unlike any in his experience. He had not only the responsibility of ensuring safe passage to France, but he was to consult with the Honorable John Adams on all important decisions.

> *You are to afford him on his passage every accommodation in your power, and to consult him on all occasions, with respect to your passage and general conduct, and the port you shall endeavor to get into, and on all occasions have great regard to the importance of his security and safe arrival.*

Adams showed an immediate interest in seeing everything about the ship and how it was run and, except for the tiny snug cabin that he and Johnny shared, little met his approval. Nor, characteristically, had he the least hesitation about letting Tucker know.

There was too much informality, too little discipline, and a "detestable" use of profanity that should never be tolerated. The men were insufficiently practiced in use of the guns; many hardly knew the ropes. Most disturbing was the same appalling indifference to sanitation that Adams knew from Dr. Rush to be the scourge of the Continental Army. Once walking through Potter's Field in Philadelphia the previous April, Adams had been overcome by the thought that more than 2,000 American soldiers had already been buried there, nearly all victims of smallpox and camp diseases. Dirty frying pans slayed more than swords, he had told Abigail. "Discipline, discipline is the great thing wanted." There could be no cleanliness without discipline, and death from disease among seamen was, he knew, exceedingly high. (For every sailor in the British navy killed in action or who died of wounds in the era of the American Revolution, seventeen died of disease.)

Meals on the *Boston* were wretched and served at the cook's pleasure. The reek of burning sea coal and the stench of stagnant water below-decks were dreadful, and contributed to everyone's misery when, after the first full day of "rolling and rocking" at sea, every passenger and half the crew became seasick.

Under ideal circumstances a crossing to France could be accomplished in about three weeks. As it was, the voyage would take six weeks and four days, excellent time, given that eight to ten weeks were the usual run in winter, and quite remarkable given all that happened.

In the first faint light of morning, the second day at sea, with wind and weather holding fair, from the masthead came a call of three ships bearing east on the northward horizon—three British frigates, as another hour would tell—that soon gave chase. After consultation with Adams, Captain Tucker determined to stand away from them. Two of the three ships eventually fell off, but one, the best sailor, kept in pursuit. "Sometimes we gained upon her, sometimes she upon us," Adams recorded. The chase went on all day and for two days following, when they crossed into the Gulf Stream.

> When night approached, the wind died away [Adams would write at the close of the third day], and we were left rolling and pitching in a calm, with our guns all out, our courses all drawn up, and every way

prepared for battle; the officers and men were in good spirits, and Captain Tucker said his orders were to carry me to France . . . he thought it his duty, therefore, to avoid fighting, especially with an unequal force, if he could, but if he could not avoid an engagement, he would give them something that should make them remember him.

In the night a sudden, violent storm struck with a blinding cannonade of thunder and lightning. The ship "shuddered . . . darted from side to side . . . all hands were called, and with much difficulty the guns were all got in and secured. It was with the utmost difficulty that my little son and I could hold ourselves in bed with both our hands, and bracing ourselves against the boards, planks, and timbers with our feet." There was a horrendous, terrifying crash as a bolt of lightning hit the main mast, very near the powder room. Twenty seamen were injured. One man, a hole burned in the top of his head, would die "raving mad."

The storm raged on. "The sea being very cross and high, forced me to scud before the wind under my foresail," recorded Captain Tucker. "Heavy gales and a dangerous sea running," he wrote the next day; "one thing and another continually giving way on board. . . . Pray God protect us."

Adams wanted to keep a running account of all that was happening but found it impossible. He was so drenched, everything was so soaking wet, that pen and paper were useless.

The ship was a wreck, its main mast split above and below the deck. No man could keep upon his legs, and nothing could be kept in its place [he later wrote]. The wind blowing against the current [of the Gulf Stream], not directly, but in various angles, produced a tumbling sea, vast mountains, sometimes dashing against each other . . . and not infrequently breaking on the ship, threatened to bury us all at once in the deep. The sails were all hauled down but a foresail . . . and we were left with bare poles entirely at the mercy of wind and water. The noises were such that we could not hear each other speak at any distance. The shrouds and every other rope in the ship exposed to the wind became a chord of very harsh music. Their vibrations produced a constant and a hideous howl.

In his diary later, Adams would confess to moments of severe regret that he had ever brought his son, but he wrote also of his extreme pride in the boy:

[His] behavior gave me a satisfaction that I cannot express. Fully sensible of our danger, he was constantly endeavoring to bear up under it with manly courage and patience, very attentive to me, and his thoughts always running in a serious strain. In this he was not singular. . . . I believe there was not a soul on board who was wholly thoughtless of a Divinity.

Appraising his own performance, Adams felt more than a little pleased, even some surprise, it would appear, that he had remained "perfectly calm."

The storm had driven the ship several hundred miles off course. But days of smooth sailing followed, and with the crew busy with repairs, Adams resumed lecturing the captain on order and improvements.

Tucker appears to have taken all that the insistent landsman had to say in remarkably good spirits and acted upon it as best he could, to Adams's considerable satisfaction. "I am constantly giving hints to the captain concerning order, economy and regularity," he wrote, "and he seems to be sensible of the necessity of them, and exerts himself to introduce them." As great a nuisance as Adams may have been, he got results; the ship took on a new look.

[Tucker] has cleared out between decks, ordered up the hammocks to be aired, and ordered up the sick, such as could bear it, upon deck for sweet air. This ship would have bred the plague or jail fever, if there had not been great exertions since the storm to wash, sweep, air and purify clothes, cots, cabins, hammocks and all other things, places, and persons.

Adams quite liked the salty, booming Tucker, and Tucker had come to appreciate Adams's company. Indeed, in remarks made later before the Navy Board, he would pay Adams as high a compliment as he knew. "I did not say much to him at first, but damn and bugger my eyes, I found him after a while as sociable as any Marblehead man."

On February 28, Adams could happily record in his diary that with smooth seas and a fine breeze the *Boston* had hardly any motion but forward. He was sleeping as soundly as in his bed at home.

The color of the ocean changed from blue to green as the Gulf Stream was left behind. "What is this Gulf Stream?" he pondered. "What is the course of it? From what point and to what point does it flow?" Flocks of gulls appeared astern, trailing the ship. "The wind is fresh, the ship sails at a great rate."

One fine day followed another. Life on board settled into a routine. With the captain's help, John Quincy had undertaken to learn the name of every sail and master the use of a mariner's compass. Father and son both worked on their French, Adams reading a bilingual edition of Molière's *Amphitryon*, one of several books he had brought from home.

He discussed medicine with the French surgeon Dr. Noel and encouraged the ship's first lieutenant, William Barron, to talk about his career and all that he had seen of the world. Barron, a Virginian, impressed Adams as exactly the kind of officer "much wanted in our infant navy."

One spectacular day, with all sails spread, the ship made an average of ten knots. Yet whatever the romance of the sea might be, it eluded

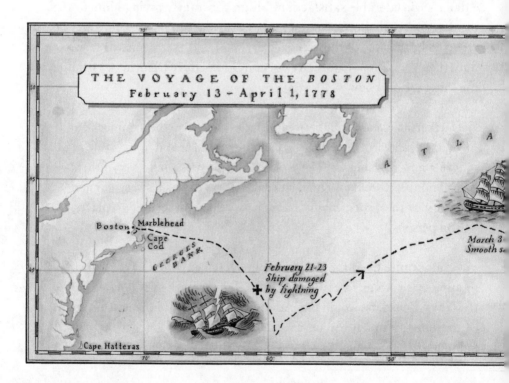

THE VOYAGE OF THE *BOSTON*
February 13 – April 1, 1778

Boston • Marblehead
Cape Cod
GEORGES BANK

February 21-23
Ship damaged
by lightning

Cape Hatteras

A T L A

March 3
Smooth s

Adams. "We see nothing but sky, clouds, and sea, and then seas, clouds, and sky."

"Oh that we might make [a] prize today of an English vessel lately from London with all the newspapers and magazines on board," he mused another morning.

"Nothing very remarkable this day," Captain Tucker wrote in his log. It had become a familiar entry. Once, after recording that the preceding twenty-four hours had both begun and ended with pleasant weather, he added, "Nothing more remarkable to my sorrow."

But suddenly life picked up again. "We spied a sail and gave her chase," a delighted Adams recorded. A ship hull-down on the southeastern horizon was thought to be a British cruiser. Tucker ordered the *Boston* cleared for action. Seeing Adams on the quarterdeck, he quickly explained the situation and, with Adams in agreement on a decision to attack, respectfully suggested that Adams go below, as "hot work" was to ensue.

The ship was a heavily armed merchantman flying the British flag, and in an hour or more they had all but closed on one another. The *Boston*, coming up bow-on, fired one shot, the merchantman fired three,

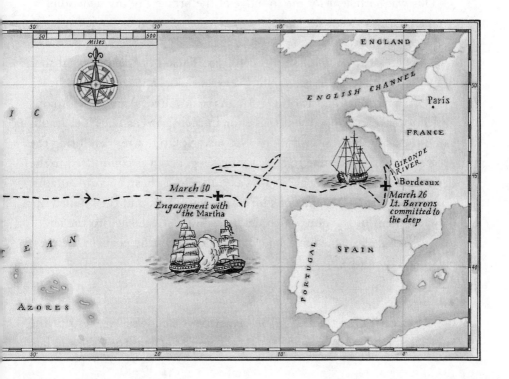

one ball splitting the *Boston*'s mizzen yard directly over the head of John Adams, who, as Tucker now saw, had taken a place in the heart of the action, musket in hand. When the *Boston* swung broadside, revealing for the first time her more formidable array of cannon, the British ship struck her colors.

It was a fine prize, the *Martha*, out of London and bound for British-held New York with a cargo valued at 70,000 pounds. The British captain and crew, prisoners now, were brought on board. Tucker assigned a picked crew to sail the prize to Boston, ordered a 7-gun salute, and proceeded on course. For Tucker especially, it was a moment of sweet triumph. The *Martha*, however, would soon be retaken by the British and delivered to Halifax.

Of the part Adams had played in the action, Tucker was to speak warmly, and later confirm how, at the height of the fray, he had discovered Adams "among my marines accoutered as one of them and in the act of defense.

> I then went unto him and said, "My dear sir, how came you here," and with a smile he replied, "I ought to do my share of the fighting." This was sufficient for me to judge of the bravery of my venerable and patriotic Adams.

Days later, approaching a French brig, Tucker ordered a signal shot fired. The gun blew to pieces, felling several sailors and shattering the leg of Lieutenant Barron, the officer Adams so admired. And it was Adams and Tucker who gripped young Barron in their arms as Dr. Noel amputated the limb. Barron died more than a week later, after "enduring the greatest pain," according to the captain's log, and was committed to the deep from the quarterdeck. "He was put into a chest," wrote Adams, "and ten or twelve pounds of shot put in with him, and then nailed up. The fragment of the gun which destroyed him was lashed to the chest, and the whole launched overboard through one of the ports in the presence of all the ship's crew."

ON MARCH 24, in the Bay of Biscay, Adams could see by telescope the snow-capped mountains of Spain. At the week's end, as the *Boston* at last entered the busy thoroughfare of Bordeaux, an Irish passenger from the *Martha* broke out a fiddle and played all afternoon as the sailors danced.

On Monday, March 30, with a French pilot aboard, the *Boston* moved up the Gironde, where the whole landscape struck Adams as extraordinarily beautiful. "Europe, thou great theater of arts, sciences, commerce, war, am I at last permitted to visit thy territories," he wrote that night in his diary, allowing that the sight of France at last gave him a kind of "pleasing melancholy."

When the *Boston* anchored at Bordeaux, he and Dr. Noel were invited to dine on a French warship lying close by. It was Adams's first exposure to French hospitality—in effect his first time in France—and he could not have been more pleased or impressed by the gentility of his hosts, the elegant cabin where the meal was served, the white stone plates, napkins, everything "as clean as in any gentleman's house," and food and wine, which, after the *Boston*, seemed heaven-sent.

His hosts spoke no English. But with the doctor serving as interpreter, Adams learned to his astonishment that as a consequence of the American triumph at Saratoga, France and the United States had already agreed to an alliance.

Thus, before he had even set foot on French soil, he found that the very purpose of his mission, to assist in negotiations for such an alliance, had been accomplished. The agreement, one of the most fateful in history, had been signed on February 6, 1778, or before Adams had even left home.

It was shortly after daybreak the next morning, April 1, All Fools' Day, when Adams, his son, and servant took leave of Captain Tucker and were rowed ashore. The relief felt by Tucker, his mission accomplished, may be imagined.

ADAMS WAS TO CROSS the Atlantic three more times, and John Quincy, too, in years to come would sail several times to and from Europe. But for neither was there ever to be an ocean voyage comparable to this, their first. Both would allude to it frequently—the novelty and high adventure, the savage storm, the battle at sea, the misery and terror and exhilaration of it all.

In a first letter from France to his "Hon[ore]d Mamma," the lines of his pen running up and down in waves, as though he were still on board ship, John Quincy would express what was felt deeply by both father and son: "I hope I shall never forget the goodness of God in preserving us through all the dangers we have been exposed to."

Years later, in a letter to Thomas Jefferson, Adams would describe the voyage on the *Boston* as symbolic of his whole life. The raging seas he had passed through, he seemed to be saying, were like the times they lived in, and he was at the mercy of the times no less than the seas. Possibly he saw, too, in the presence of John Quincy, how directly his determination to dare such seas affected his family and how much, with his devotion to the cause of America, he had put at risk beyond his own life. Besides, as he may also have seen, the voyage had demonstrated how better suited he was for action than for smooth sailing with little to do.

III

1778 April 4, Saturday
About ten o'clock we commenced our journey [by post chaise] to Paris and went about 50 miles.

April 5, Sunday
Proceeded on our journey, more than 100 miles.

April 6, Monday
Fields of grain, the vineyards, the castles, the cities, the gardens, everything is beautiful. Yet every place swarms with beggars.

April 8, Wednesday
Rode through Orleans and arrived in Paris about nine o'clock. For thirty miles from Paris or more the road was paved, and the scenes were extremely beautiful.

But for the beggars, France was nearly all beautiful in Adams's eyes, everything greatly to his liking. In Bordeaux he had been welcomed as a hero, cheered by crowds in the streets, embraced, escorted on a tour of the city, taken to his first opera ever, which he hugely enjoyed. With France and America now joined in common cause, he was no longer the envoy of a friendly nation but of an ally. "God save the Congress, Liberty, and Adams," an illuminated inscription proclaimed.

An American merchant in Bordeaux warned Adams of bad blood within the American commission at Paris, and some of the local citizenry had seemed disappointed to learn he was not Samuel Adams, *"le fameux Adams."* At a dinner in his honor a beautiful young woman seated beside him had opened the conversation with a question Adams found shocking. But though initially befuddled—"I believe at first I blushed"—he recovered and came off rather well, he thought.

"Mr. Adams," she had said, "by your name I conclude you are descended from the first man and woman, and probably in your family may be preserved the tradition which may resolve a difficulty which I could never explain. I never could understand how the first couple found out the art of lying together?"

Assisted by an interpreter, Adams replied that his family resembled the first couple both in name and in their frailties and that no doubt "instinct" was the answer to her question. "For there was a physical quality in us resembling the power of electricity or of the magnet, by which when a pair approached within striking distance they flew together . . . like two objects in an electrical experiment."

"Well," she retorted. "I know not how it was, but this I know, it is a very happy shock."

Rolling through the tollgates of Paris the night of April 8, crossing the Seine by the Pont Neuf, passing the Palace of the Louvre, Adams was astonished at the crowds, the numbers of carriages in the streets, the "glittering clatter" of Paris he had read of in books. Toward morning, awake in his hotel room on the Rue de Richelieu, he wondered at the stillness of so great a city—until first light when the clamor of bells and street cries and iron-rimmed carriage wheels on cobblestones was such as he had never heard.

The first call of the day was on Benjamin Franklin, and from that point on Adams was kept steadily on the move, with sights to see, social engagements, dinners, teas, the theater. There were important people he must meet, new faces, names to remember—endless, multitudinous French names—and in nearly every setting, awash in the rapid-fire conversation of what were, he was certain, the most polished people on earth, including a great number of exceedingly fashionable and opinionated women, he understood almost nothing.

It was Franklin who orchestrated the social rounds, insisting the first morning that they dine at the usual French hour of two o'clock with Jacques Turgot (Anne-Robert-Jacques Turgot, Baron de l'Aulne), the distinguished economist and, until recently, Minister of Finance. Adams had felt himself unsuitably "accoutered" to appear in such company, he told Franklin, but off they went.

Franklin lived in the gracious splendor of a garden pavilion, part of the magnificent Hôtel de Valentinois, a columned château on the heights of the village of Passy, overlooking the Seine, half an hour's ride from the city on the road to Versailles. It was the estate of a wealthy government contractor, former slave trader and generous friend of the American cause, Jacques Donatien Le Ray, the Comte de Chaumont, whose admiration for Franklin appeared boundless and who, with his stout figure and bald head, somewhat resembled him. As the guest of Chaumont, Franklin enjoyed the attention of nine liveried servants, a wine cellar of more than a thousand bottles, and virtually every comfort.

Receiving Adams with all customary cordiality, Franklin insisted that he move in with him to quarters previously occupied by Silas Deane. Arrangements were made for John Quincy to attend a nearby boarding school also attended by one of Franklin's grandsons, eight-year-old Benjamin Franklin Bache.

Franklin's friends, the "first people" of Paris as he spoke of them, must become Adams's friends, too, Franklin insisted. In addition to Chaumont and Turgot, there was the stately, white-haired Duchesse d'Enville (Marie-Louise-Elisabeth de La Rochefoucauld), one of the recognized "great ladies" of Paris, whom Adams liked at once, finding her observations, when translated, full of "bold, masculine and original sense." She was to be their hostess on several occasions. Her son, the Duc de La Rochefoucauld, grandson of the great French moralist of the previous century, François, Duc de La Rochefoucauld, was a scholar in his own right who, to Adams's relief, spoke perfect English. It was he who had done one of the earliest French translations of the Declaration of Independence.

Particularly appealing to the eye was Madame Brillon (Anne-Louise de Harancourt Brillon de Jouy), who was much spoiled by a wealthy, elderly husband and made an open show of her affection for Franklin, flirtatiously calling him "Cher Papa" while perched on his lap. Adams would later learn that another woman who appeared to be part of the Brillon family, a "very plain" person whom he presumed to be a companion of Madame Brillon, was in fact the mistress of Monsieur Brillon. "I was astonished that these people could live together in such apparent friendship and indeed without cutting each other's throats," Adams would write. "But I did not know the world."

There was also Franklin's particular friend and near neighbor at Passy, the flamboyant, once-beautiful Madame Helvétius, widow of the acclaimed philosophe Claude-Adrien Helvétius, who lived amid a menagerie of chickens, ducks, birds in aviaries, dogs, cats, and pet deer. There was the brilliant mathematician and political theorist Marie-Jean A. N. Caritat, Marquis de Condorcet, another of the philosophes of the French enlightenment, whose strange pallor Adams took to be the result of "hard study." And of supreme importance was the King's Foreign Minister, Charles Gravier, Comte de Vergennes, the most polished of all, a fleshy, majestic career diplomat who, during Adams's initial courtesy call at Versailles, expressed dismay that Adams understood nothing he said, but politely remarked that he hoped Adams would remain long enough in France to learn French perfectly.

Adams had never beheld such opulence—no American had—the exquisite dress, the diamonds on display, the bright rouge worn by the women, the time and money devoted to the elaborate coiffures of women and men alike. (Every morning in Paris some 7,000 barbers rushed through the streets to attend their customers.) Nor had he ever encountered such exquisite manners. Everyone was so exceedingly polite to everyone, and to foreigners most of all.

"The reception I have met in this kingdom has been as friendly, as polite, and as respectful as was possible," Adams assured Abigail in the first of his letters to reach her.

It is the universal opinion of the people here, of all ranks, that a friendship between France and America is in the interest of both countries and the late alliance, so happily formed, is universally popular; so much so that I have been told by persons of good judgment that the government here would have been under a sort of necessity of agreeing to it even if it have not been agreeable to themselves.

The delights of France are innumerable. The politeness, the elegance, the softness, the delicacy is extreme.

In short, stern and haughty republican that I am, I cannot help loving these people for their earnest desire and assiduity to please. ... The richness, the magnificence, and splendor is beyond all description.

But thinking perhaps he had strayed from his own true republican self a bit more than was seemly—and than Abigail would wish—he assured her that all such "bagatelles" meant nothing to him. "I cannot help suspecting that the more elegance, the less virtue in all times and countries."

In later years much would be written and said of John Adams's dislike of France, his puritanical disapproval of the French and their ways. But while, to be sure, there was much he disapproved of, and even disliked, much that he found shocking, such as the forwardness of the women, so also did most Americans of the day. Adams's objections stemmed not so much from a Puritan background—as often said—but from the ideal of republican virtue, the classic Roman stoic emphasis on simplicity and the view that decadence inevitably followed luxury, age-old themes replete in the writings of his favorite Romans. Like so many of his countrymen, then and later, Adams both loved and disapproved of France, depending in large degree on circumstances or his mood of the moment. What, in fact, was most interesting, as expressed repeatedly in his diary and private correspondence—and what seems to have struck him as most unexpected—was how very much about France he found appealing, how much he did truly love about the French and their approach to life. "If human nature could be made happy by anything that can please the eye, the ear, the taste or any other sense, or passion or fancy, this country would be the region for happiness," he wrote.

On an evening when the Comte de Chaumont took him in his carriage to a concert in the Royal Gardens of the Tuileries—the Concert Spirituel, which Adams was to attend many times—he was delighted to find that both men and women singers performed, and that the gardens were full of "company of both sexes walking," as he wrote in his diary. He did not, however, record the numbers of prostitutes that gathered regularly in the gardens, some standing on chairs to attract attention, even as decorous family parties strolled past.

He enjoyed particularly the company of women of fashion whose animated opinions were as much a part of every social occasion as those of the men. In such company no gentlemen would be tolerated in monopolizing a conversation. Adams thought women superior to men overall, as Abigail knew, and he was sure she would wish to know his views on the educated women of France.

> To tell you the truth, I admire the ladies here. Don't be jealous. They are handsome, and very well educated. Their accomplishments are exceedingly brilliant. And their knowledge of letters and arts, exceeds that of the English ladies, I believe.

His "venerable colleague" Franklin, he noted, had the enviable privilege, because of his advanced age, to embrace the ladies as much as he pleased and to be "perpetually" embraced by them in return. But then the adoration of Franklin to be found in all quarters was extraordinary, as Adams would later recount:

> His name was familiar to government and people, to kings, courtiers, nobility, clergy, and philosophers, as well as plebeians, to such a degree that there was scarcely a peasant or citizen, a *valet de chambre*, coachman or footman, a lady's chambermaid or a scullion in a kitchen, who was not familiar with it, and who did not consider him as a friend of humankind. When they spoke of him, they seemed to think he was to restore the golden age.

Crowds in the streets cheered the "good doctor." Fashionable women had taken to wearing a variation of his familiar bearskin hat. His likeness appeared everywhere—in prints, on medallions, on the lids of snuff boxes, making his face, as Franklin himself said, as well known as that of the man in the moon. Possibly the likeness of no one human face had been so widely reproduced in so many forms. Reputedly, the King himself, in a rare show of humor, arranged for it to be hand-painted on the bottom of a

Sèvres porcelain chamber pot, as a New Year's day surprise for one of Franklin's adoring ladies at Court.

Franklin was loved for his sober, homespun look—the fur hat, the uncurled, unpowdered hair, the spectacles on the end of his nose—and widely believed to be a Quaker, a misunderstanding he made no effort to correct. He was seen as the representative American, the rustic sage from the wilds of Pennsylvania (quite apart from the fact that he had lived sixteen years in London), and he agreeably played the part. Everything about him announced his "simplicity and innocence," observed an adoring French historian of the day.

But it was as a man of science that Franklin was most adored. It was the fame of his electrical experiments and overall inventiveness that made him one of the paragons of the age. Except for the aged Voltaire, who had only recently returned to Paris after years of exile and who had only a few months to live, there was in the eyes of the French no greater mortal.

It was that year, 1778, that Franklin sat for the celebrated sculptor Jean-Antoine Houdon, and that Franklin's host at the Hôtel de Valentinois, Le Ray de Chaumont, commissioned the painter Joseph-Siffred Duplessis, a favorite at the court, to do Franklin's portrait. For the Duplessis painting, which was to be a greater triumph at the Salon of 1779 than even Houdon's bust, Franklin wore his customary fur-collared russet coat and appeared perfectly at peace with himself and the world. Admirers saw strength of mind in the high, bald forehead, strength of character in the "robust" neck, unshakable serenity in the slight smile. But the lift of the brows lent a certain sardonic expression and the large, brown eyes looked sad and weary. No name was provided at the bottom of the elaborate frame, only a single-word inscription writ large in Latin, "VIR," meaning "man of character."

Whenever possible, Adams worked on his French, preferring the quiet of early morning, before Franklin was stirring. With lists of recommended books—French dictionaries, grammars, works of literature, histories of diplomacy—he went to one Paris bookseller after another until he had them all, and more. And as often as he could, he attended the theater, usually taking John Quincy with him. (For the boy it was the beginning of a lifelong love of the theater.) Adams would bring the text of the play in hand, so they could follow the lines as spoken. But as he would tell

Nabby in a letter, it was really the ladies "who are always to me the most pleasing ornaments of such spectacles."

At a performance of Voltaire's *Alzire*, at the Comédie Française, Voltaire himself was seated in a nearby box. Between acts, as the audience called his name, the eighty-three-year-old hero would rise and bow. "Although he was very advanced in age, had the paleness of death and deep lines and wrinkles in his face," Adams noted, there was "sparkling vitality" in his eyes. "They were still the poet's eyes with a fine frenzy rolling," Adams wrote, borrowing an expression from Shakespeare.

A few days later, Adams was present for what was felt to be one of the high moments in the Age of Enlightenment when, at the Academy of Sciences, Voltaire and Franklin, like two aged actors, as Adams described them, embraced each other in the French manner, "hugging one another in their arms, and kissing each other's cheeks."

ON FINE SPRING DAYS Adams could walk among the lilacs and *allées* of linden trees in the formal gardens of the Hôtel de Valentinois. The whole of France was one great garden, it seemed. "Nature and art have conspired to render everything here delightful," he wrote to Abigail. His health was good. He was extremely pleased with John Quincy's progress in French.

But he was also deeply troubled by the rancor within the American commission. Franklin had wasted no time confirming what Adams had heard at Bordeaux. It had been Adams's second day at Passy, during a moment of privacy, when Franklin spoke of the "coolness" between him and Arthur Lee, whom Franklin described as bad-tempered and extremely difficult to work with. Lee, said Franklin, was one of those "who went through life quarrelling with one person or another 'til they commonly ended in the loss of their reason." Lee was in league with another American, Ralph Izard, who, though appointed minister to the Grand Duchy of Tuscany, remained in Paris and only caused trouble. Franklin called Izard a man of violent passions and assured Adams that neither Lee nor Izard was liked by the French.

For their part, Lee and Izard were quick to assure Adams that Franklin was beneath contempt, expressing their views with a vehemence that astonished Adams as much as their choice of words.

Izard, a wealthy South Carolinian, was a devotee of the arts who with his wife had been living in Europe for several years. He was handsome, much infatuated with his own opinions, and an honest man, Adams believed.

Arthur Lee was known for his "mercurial temperament." As a commissioner to the court of France, Lee's importance, theoretically, was equal to that of Franklin and Adams. Also, with two brothers in Congress—Richard Henry and Francis Lightfoot Lee—he had more than a little political influence. Tall, erect, with a prominent Lee nose, he was as proud as any of his proud Virginia line, and spoke a passable French. He had trained in medicine at Edinburgh, where he was first in his class, then changed professions, taking up the law in London, where he became an agent for Massachusetts, first as an associate of Franklin, then succeeding him after Franklin's return to Philadelphia in 1775. It was in London that Lee had learned to dislike Franklin, and from the time he arrived in Paris, he had found it nearly unbearable to serve again in Franklin's shadow. Refusing to live with Franklin at Passy, Lee had arranged his own accommodations in the neighboring village of Chaillot.

Suspicious by nature, Lee had been the first to raise questions about Silas Deane's dealings as a commissioner. Lee was convinced that Deane, in buying supplies for the American army, had pocketed a fortune, and his letters to his brothers in Congress, charging Deane with corruption, had played a part in the decision of Congress to recall Deane. And, by the evidence, it appears that Deane had, indeed, let himself be bought. But Lee had suspected Franklin as well and was certain that Franklin was out to ruin him. (The thought that it might have been Jefferson, with his aversion to controversy, Jefferson who idolized Franklin, serving on the commission instead of Arthur Lee, was never lost on Franklin or Adams.) Indignant over Franklin's unwillingness to share confidences with him, Lee wrote an angry letter that Franklin left unanswered. "I am old, cannot have long to live, have much to do and no time for altercation," Franklin at last wrote to Lee in reply, but then never sent the letter. Writing to Samuel Adams, Lee described Franklin as "the most corrupt of all corrupt men."

John Adams had been predisposed to like Lee, largely out of admiration for Richard Henry Lee. But Adams was soon writing in his diary that Lee had confidence in no one. "He believes all men selfish, and no man honest or sincere." Still, Adams was never to doubt Lee's integrity or faithfulness to the American cause.

As for Franklin, Adams had come to France with few if any doubts or misgivings, fully expecting that he and Franklin could work as effectively together as at Philadelphia. That he greatly respected Franklin, there is no doubt. In private correspondence with James Warren, at the time of Franklin's arduous mission to Montreal in 1776, Adams had written:

> Franklin's character you know. His masterly acquaintance with the French language, his extensive correspondence in France, his great experience in life, his wisdom, his prudence, caution; his engaging addresses, united to his unshaken firmness in the present American system of politics and war, point him out as the fittest character for this momentous undertaking.

Their own expedition together to see Admiral Lord Howe at Staten Island had provided further opportunity for both men to know and appreciate one another. And though of different generations—and differing views on the effects of night air—they had in common, along with their Massachusetts origins, a lifelong love of the printed word, delight in amusing stories and turns of phrase. They were two staunch patriots who hated the British and shared the absolute conviction that for all the hazards and trials of the present, America was destined to be a "mighty empire."

From his student days at Harvard under John Winthrop, Adams had acquired an early admiration for Franklin as a man of science. Had Franklin done no more than devise the lightning rod, Adams liked to say, it would have been sufficient reason for the world to honor his name.

Franklin was a "great and good man," Adams had once assured Abigail in a letter from Philadelphia. Even in later years, when his opinion of Franklin had radically changed, Adams could still praise him for his genius and talents:

> He had wit at will. He had humor that, when he pleased, was delicate and delightful. He had a satire that was good-natured and caustic. Horace or Juvenal, Swift or Rabelais at his pleasure. He had talents

of irony, allegory, and fable that he could adapt with great skill to the promotion of moral and political truth.

But after several weeks at Passy, living together in close quarters, accompanying Franklin on his social rounds, observing the daily routine and how things were being run, Adams began to see another man than the idolized sage who, if not the villain portrayed by Lee and Izard, nonetheless gave Adams pause.

He found Franklin cordial but aloof, easygoing to the point of indolence, distressingly slipshod about details and about money. It was obvious time had taken its toll. Franklin was fat and stooped, his sloping girth larger than ever. Suffering terribly from the gout and from boils, he moved slowly and with difficulty, often with obvious pain. Some days he could barely get about.

The man who, as Poor Richard, had preached "Early to bed, early to rise," seldom rose before ten o'clock. (Adams found that by the time Franklin had finished breakfast he was able to receive only a few callers before it was time to depart for his midday dinner. Dinner over, Franklin often napped.) The man who had admonished generations of aspiring Americans to "Keep thy shop and thy shop will keep thee" seemed but vaguely interested in the day-to-day operations of the commission. "A little neglect may breed great mischief," Poor Richard had warned; Adams found more than a little neglect everywhere he turned. Public money was being spent, as Arthur Lee said, "without economy and without account." Adams would recall, "It was impossible for me to enter into any examination of what had passed before my arrival, because I could find no books, letters, or documents of any kind to inform or guide me."

"A thousand times I have desired that the public accounts might from time to time be made up, to which I have as constantly received evasive or affrontive answers," complained Arthur Lee. "So that now Mr. Adams and myself find that after the expenditure of more than five million livres, we are involved in confusion and debt."

Franklin acknowledged that frugality was a virtue he never acquired. As a wealthy man, he had no personal worries about money, and for all his supposed simplicity, he loved his pleasures and ease, as Adams noted. He rode in an elegant carriage, entertained handsomely. Adams worried about not only the cost but the appropriateness of such extravagance. He imagined the rent for their accommodations at the Hôtel de Valentinois to be exorbitant. When Franklin informed him that the Comte de Chaumont was charging nothing, that they were living there at no cost, Adams worried that that, too, was inappropriate, since, as everyone knew, Chaumont was one of the largest contractors furnishing supplies for the American army.

As time passed and his French improved, Adams further realized that Franklin spoke the language poorly and understood considerably less than he let on. Never verbose in social gatherings even in his own language, "the good doctor" sat in the salons of Paris, looking on benevolently, a glass of champagne in hand, rarely saying anything. When he did speak in French, he was, one official told Adams, almost impossible to understand. He refused to bother his head with French grammar, Franklin admitted to Adams, and to his French admirers this, with his odd pronunciation, were but another part of his charm, which only added to Adams's annoyance. Try as he might, Adams could never feel at ease in French society. Franklin, always at ease, never gave the appearance of trying at all.

From the time that news of the surrender at Saratoga first reached Paris, in December 1777, Franklin had found himself the center of attentions not just from the Court of His Most Christian Majesty Louis XVI, but from the British as well. Lord North, the Prime Minister, had delivered a conciliatory speech to Parliament; George III even recommended opening a channel of communication with "that insidious man" Franklin, with the result that a host of British agents began beating a path to Paris to ascertain what peace terms the Americans might consider.

Less than a mile from Passy, in the village of Auteuil, a cordial, well-to-do Scot named William Alexander established residence in order to be close to his dear old friend Dr. Franklin. Alexander was in and out of the Hôtel de Valentinois like one of the family, sometimes rousing Franklin from his bed before the usual hour to converse on the latest theory of latent heat or the increasing consumption of sugar in Britain. Alexander was outspoken in his contempt for British policy toward America. He thought the war an appalling blunder and favored unlimited independence for the United States.

Alexander, who was also a British spy, felt he could read Franklin's mind perfectly. However, the new resident commissioner at Passy, John Adams, required closer study, and in an effort to inform London, Alexander provided an especially perceptive appraisal:

John Adams is a man of the shortest of what is called middle size in England, strong and tight-made, rather inclining to fat, of a complexion that bespeaks a warmer climate than Massachusetts is supposed, a countenance which bespeaks rather reflection than imagination. His learning I suspect is pretty much confined to the classics and law. His knowledge of England and its constitution is [a] matter of real amazement to me. The most trite and common things as well as the more nice relative either to customs, manners, arts, policy, or constitution are equally known to him. He is an enthusiast, however, with regard to everything in this country [France] but the constitution and can conceive no country superior to it. I think he would be esteemed a bad politician in Europe in everything but discretion. He has, I believe, a keen temper which if he can command thoroughly, will be a great merit. His understanding lies, I think, rather in seeing large things largely than correctly. . . . In the conduct of affairs he may perhaps be able to take so comprehensive a view as to render invention and expedient unnecessary, but were they to become necessary, I think he would fail in these—and I am not clear as to the first, or whether much of his reputation may not arise from a very firm and decisive tone suited to the times, with a clear and perspicuous elocution.

Another frequent visitor, David Hartley, member of Parliament, old friend of Franklin's and an emissary from Lord North, struck Adams as a conceited dandy and almost certainly a spy. "I suppose as I did not flatter Mr. Hartley with professions of confidence which I did not feel," Adams would write, "and of so much admiration of his great genius and talents as he felt himself, he conceived a disgust at me." Hartley, as Adams himself would later relate, described Adams as "the most ungracious man" he ever met.

Warned repeatedly that he was surrounded by spies both French and British, the imperturbable Franklin declared he had no worry, since he had nothing to hide.

I have long observed one rule [he wrote to a friend] . . . to be concerned in no affairs that I should blush to have made in public, and
to do nothing but what spies may see. . . . If I was sure, therefore,
that my *valet de place* was a spy, as probably he is, I think I should
not discharge him for that, if in other respects I liked him.

Of the Americans around Franklin, the closest and most trusted was
Dr. Edward Bancroft, a New England physician in his mid-thirties and
another warm friend from Franklin's London years. Bancroft was
employed as secretary for the commission. An affable and unusually
accomplished man of many interests—writer, inventor, member of the
Royal Society, avid experimenter with inks and dyes—he was the ideal
companion for Franklin. He was consistently hardworking, fluent in
French, and had made himself all but indispensable to Franklin.

But what neither Franklin nor Adams was ever to know was that
Bancroft, too, was a British spy, his "emoluments" from the Crown
amounting to 500 pounds per year. Anything of importance that transpired within the American commission, or between Franklin and the
French Foreign Minister, all instructions received from Congress, any
confidences shared, were known by the British cabinet in London within
days. Bancroft's dispatches, written in invisible ink, were placed in a
sealed bottle that was deposited in a hole in a tree on the south terrace of
the Tuileries Gardens regularly every Tuesday evening after nine-thirty.
The system worked to perfection for several years.

Adams instinctively disliked Bancroft, thought him a gossip, found
his habitual mocking of Christianity offensive, thought him dishonest
and rightly suspected him of using inside information to profit on the
London stock market. Indeed, the mix of private and public business
beneath the roof of the Hôtel de Valentinois was considerable, with Bancroft, the Comte de Chaumont, and possibly even Franklin, all capitaliz-
ing on secret French support for the American war and a steady flow of
inside information. Bancroft's larger treachery, however, went unsus-
pected by Adams. Only Arthur Lee suspected that Bancroft was a spy,
but then Lee imagined spies everywhere.

Adams was concerned that Franklin, out of laziness, was leaving too
many decisions to Chaumont or Bancroft. But if Adams was disillu-
sioned by the Franklin he came to know at Passy, he also recognized that

Franklin had the confidence of Vergennes and the French Court as did no other American, and it was therefore the duty of all to treat him with respect. In all that he wrote in correspondence in his first nine months in France, Adams never criticized Franklin; and inclined as he may have been at times to side with Arthur Lee, he steadfastly refused to do so. Lee may have been justified in some of his anger at Franklin, Adams felt, but Lee was badly cast in his role, a dreadful aggravation to Franklin and also to the French, who not only disliked him but distrusted him, which was more serious.

As time passed, Adams's appreciation of the importance of France to America's future only increased. "The longer I live in Europe and the more I consider our affairs," he wrote, "the more important our alliance with France appears to me." Yet he felt he himself was in an impossible role. He saw the futility and unnecessary expense of having three commissioners, and after six weeks in Paris, as early as May 21, he was writing to Samuel Adams to say that one commissioner, Franklin, would be quite enough. As it was, he and Arthur Lee were superfluous.

ONE OF THE RARE OCCASIONS when the three American commissioners did anything together was the day of Adams's presentation to Louis XVI, on May 8, 1778. Accompanied by both Franklin and Lee, Adams arrived at Versailles in all-new French clothes, his wig dressed, and wearing a dress sword, as required at the palace.

They were received in the King's sumptuous, gilded bedchamber, as the King went through the elaborate morning ceremony of being dressed by officers of the state. In a brief, pleasant, inconsequential exchange, the Comte de Vergennes explained that the new American commissioner spoke no French, to which the young monarch responded, *"Pas un mot!"* ("Not a word!"), before passing into another room.

Adams detected "goodness and innocence" in the King's face. "He had the appearance of a strong constitution," Adams would write of the twenty-four-year-old Louis XVI, who was indeed kindhearted and robust, if painfully nearsighted and awkward, and who had it in his power to determine the fate of the United States of America.

In June at the public supper of the royal family, *le grand couvert*,

Adams was turned out again in attire "becoming the station I held, but not to be compared with the gold and diamonds and embroidery about me." Seated in close view, among ladies of "the first rank and fashion," he felt himself being gazed at in the way he and others had once gazed at the Indian chiefs who came to address Congress, except that he found it difficult to command such "power of the face" as the chiefs had.

The King, "the royal carver" at the table, "ate like a king and made a royal supper of solid beef and other things in proportion." But in the account Adams gave years afterward, it was the graceful Marie Antoinette, agleam in diamonds and finery, who remained most vivid in memory:

> She was an object too sublime and beautiful for my dull pen to describe. . . . Her dress was everything art and wealth could make it. One of the maids of honor told me she had diamonds upon her person to the value of eighteen million livres, and I always thought her majesty much beholden to her dress. . . . She had a fine complexion indicating her perfect health, and was a handsome woman in her face and figure. . . . The Queen took a large spoonful of soup and displayed her fine person and graceful manner, in alternately looking at the company in various parts of the hall and ordering several kinds of seasoning to be brought to her, by which she fitted her supper to her taste. When this was accomplished, her Majesty exhibited to the admiring spectators the magnificent spectacle of a great queen swallowing her royal supper in a single spoonful, all at once. This was all performed like perfect clockwork, not a feature of her face, nor a motion of any part of her person, especially her arm and her hand could be criticized as out of order.

THAT JUNE, 1778, Great Britain attacked French ships at sea. The war for American independence had set off a struggle for power in Europe. Britain and France were again at each other's throats. There was no declaration of war, nor would there be one. "Yet," Adams would rightly inform Samuel Adams, "there is in fact as complete a war as ever existed, and it will continue."

With little to do of a diplomatic nature, he took hold of administrative duties, striving to straighten out accounts and expedite correspondence, no less determined than he had been on board the *Boston* to see a badly run ship put in order. His long experience on the Board of War stood him in good stead. He drafted reports to Congress, sent off letters to various agents of Congress in France who had been drawing exorbitant bills on the commission, directing them to start providing regular account of their disbursements, and warning that they could be running up debts beyond available funds. He addressed the matter of prizes taken at sea by American privateers, and gave all possible attention to the vexing issue of what to do about American prisoners of war held by the British and those British prisoners taken on the high seas who were being held in France. The commissioners hoped for an exchange but were frustrated by British insistence that captive Americans were traitors and thus not conventional prisoners of war.

"I found that the business of our commission would never be done unless I did it," Adams wrote. "My two colleagues would agree on nothing ... and often when I had drawn the papers and had them fairly copied for signature, and Mr. Lee and I had signed them, I was frequently obliged to wait several days before I could procure the signature of Dr. Franklin on them."

If Franklin was slow to get under way in the morning, Arthur Lee found it impossible to arrive from Chaillot, only ten minutes away, earlier than eleven o'clock, by which time Adams, who rose at five, had been at his desk for hours.

Privately, he was distraught and painfully lonely. It had been more than three months since he left home and still there was no word from Abigail. He worried about her, longed for her, and in this felt still further removed from Lee, who had never married, and Franklin, whose wife was dead and who, when she was alive, had spent years apart from her with no apparent regret.

Franklin amused himself playing chess with his fashionable friends (including Madame Brillon while she bathed in her tub); Adams did not know chess. Franklin had his Masonic meetings; Adams was not a Mason. As at Philadelphia after his first weeks there, he began to tire of lavish hospitality, the "profusion of unmeaning wealth and magnificence." Such "incessant dinners and dissipations" were not the objects of his mission to France. "My countrymen were suffering in America and their affairs were in great confusion in Europe."

"Dined at home," became a frequent note in his diary. Through June there were few entries at all, so concerned had he become about "a house full of spies."

When a first letter from Abigail arrived on June 16, he wrote to her at once, but it would be midsummer before he heard from her again, and numerous letters that he wrote in the intervening time were either stolen, lost, or captured at sea—he would never know. Nor would it be known how many of her letters disappeared en route.

As once he had sent Abigail pins from Philadelphia, so now at her request he shipped off packages of European trade goods—handkerchiefs, ribbon, bolts of calico—which could "fetch hard money" at home and mean the difference to her financial survival. But, as with all correspondence, months must pass before he knew if any of the shipments were reaching her.

There was no news from Congress, no news of the war at home, which was as formidable a problem as any. Dispatches from Philadelphia that evaded capture at sea took at least six weeks to reach Paris under ideal sailing conditions. The great distance separating America from Europe, the inevitable long delay in any communication with Congress, or worse, the complete lack of communication for months at a stretch, would plague both Franklin and Adams their whole time in Europe, and put them at a decided disadvantage in dealing with European ministers, who maintained far closer, more efficient contact. Ships that were supposed to sail for America in a week or two, often lay in port for months, letters on board. By contrast, there was no European court to which an express could not be sent from Paris in ten or fifteen days, and an answer could be expected within approximately the same time. "There is, I imagine, no minister who would not think it safer to act by orders than from his own discretion," wrote Franklin in a letter explaining why he and the other Americans in Paris had to decide matters on their own most all of the time. To receive an answer from an inquiry to Philadelphia could take six months.

Relations between Franklin and Lee grew steadily more unpleasant, and Adams's role consequently became ever more frustrating, to the point where he felt he must unburden himself again to Samuel Adams, providing what was, in all, a very fair assessment:

> Between you and me, I have a difficult task [Adams wrote on August 7]. I am between two gentlemen of opposite tempers. The one may be too easy and good natured upon some occasions, the other too rigid and severe upon some occasions. The one may perhaps overlook an instance of roguery, from inadvertance and too much confidence. The other may mistake an instance of integrity for its opposite. . . . Yet both may be and I believe are honest men, and devoted friends to their country. But this is an ugly situation for me who does not abound in philosophy and who cannot and will not trim. The consequence of it may very probably be that I may have the entire confidence of neither. Yet I have hitherto lived in friendship with both.

With the passing of summer, Adams grew extremely disheartened. His one unfailing source of pleasure, "the joy of my heart," was John Quincy, who, he told Abigail proudly, was "esteemed" by all. A prominent figure in Franklin's circle, Marie Grand, wife of Ferdinand Grand, the French banker for American funds, was so impressed by the boy— indeed by both father and son—that she wrote Abigail to tell her so. In a conversation with Adams at a dinner, she recounted, he had remarked that in some cases it was the duty of a good citizen to sacrifice his all for the good of the country. She had found such a sentiment worthy of a Roman, yet rather hard to believe. Surely "nature," love of one's wife and children, would "operate more powerfully" than love of one's country. In reply, Adams said his wife felt as he did. And young John Quincy, too, Madame Grand told Abigail, "inherits the spirit of his father, and bids fair to be a Roman like him."

Adams had never had more to do in his life, he wrote, or so little to show for his efforts. Maintaining a position of impartiality between Franklin and Arthur Lee, playing mediator, had become a dreadful strain. In October, determined to improve the situation, Adams urged Lee to give up living at Chaillot and move in with them at the Hôtel de Valentinois.

"I am very sincere," he wrote. "There is room enough in this house to accommodate us all." He offered Lee his own quarters, saying he would move into the library.

> This arrangement will save a large sum of money to the public, and ... give us a thousand opportunities of conversing together, which now we have not.... It would remove the reproach we now lie under, of which I confess myself very much ashamed, of not being able to agree together.... I am, dear sir, with an earnest desire and a settled determination to cultivate a harmony, nay more a friendship with both my colleagues.

When Lee declined, strife within the commission grew worse. "The uncandor, the prejudices, the rage among several persons here, make me sick as death," Adams wrote in his diary. His two compatriots were men of honor and integrity, he still believed, but the one grew increasingly cunning and dissipated, the other sour, secretive, and no less cunning. "Virtue is not always amiable," Adams concluded.

Feeling his role was little better than that of a clerk, feeling forgotten by Congress, he labored on intensely, writing letters, struggling with accounts, trying to keep abreast of events through the London newspapers and magazines, where he now saw himself derided as pathetically out of place. "The English have got at me," he reported to Abigail. "They make fine work of me—fanatic, bigot, perfect cypher, not one word of the language, awkward figure, uncouth dress, no address, no character, cunning hardheaded attorney. But the falsest of it all is that I am disgusted with the Parisians." He hated playing second fiddle to Franklin, and by the year's end, to judge by a letter written to James Warren, Franklin's self-indulgent, self-serving ways had become nearly more than Adams could bear, for though he mentioned no name, it was obvious whom he meant.

> The longer I live and the more I see of public men, the more I wish to be a private one. Modesty is a virtue that can never thrive in public. Modest merit! Is there such a thing remaining in public life? It is now become a maxim with some, who are even men of merit, that the world esteems a man in proportion as he esteems himself.... I am

often astonished at the boldness with which persons make their pretensions. A man must be his own trumpeter—he must write or dic-
tate paragraphs of praise in the newspapers; he must dress, have a
retinue and equipage; he must ostentatiously publish to the world
his own writings with his name. . . . He must get his picture drawn,
his statue made, and must hire all the artists in his turn to set about
works to spread his name, make the mob stare and gape, and perpet-
uate his fame.

Yet the mood that poured from Adams's pen did not always match
the spirit with which he went about his daily business; and the gloom or
vitriol of one letter might be nowhere apparent in others written at the
same time, even the same day. He wrote little or nothing, for example, of
how he and Franklin worked together, yet live and work together they
did in close proximity for months on end while accomplishing much.

Once, several years earlier, in one of the many passages in his diary in
which he worked out his thoughts, Adams had written that concealment
of one's dislike for another was not a form of dishonesty or deception, but
an acceptable, even wise way of conducting the business of life.

There are persons whom in my heart I despise, others I abhor. Yet I
am not obliged to inform the one of my contempt, nor the other of
my detestation. This kind of dissimulation . . . is a necessary branch
of wisdom, and so far from being immoral . . . that it is a duty and a
virtue.

But this, he was quick to add, was a rule with definite limitations, "for
there are times when the cause of religion, of government, of liberty, the
interest of the present age of posterity, render it a necessary duty to make
known his sentiments and intentions boldly and publicly."

Whatever Franklin's failings and flaws, Adams never discounted the
value of his popularity and prestige. French esteem for the "good doctor"
remained of immense importance to the American cause, as Adams
knew. Arthur Lee, by contrast, was seldom anything but a handicap. His
dislike of the French was obvious. "His countenance is disgusting,"

Adams was to write. "His air is not pleasing . . . his temper is harsh, sour . . . his judgment of men and things is often wrong."

What most distressed Adams about Franklin was his approach with Vergennes. He "hates to offend and seldom gives any opinion 'til obliged," Adams noted. It was what had troubled Adams about Franklin in Congress. "Although he has as determined a soul as any man, yet it is his constant policy never to say yes or no decidedly but when he cannot avoid it." Franklin's concept of diplomacy was to ask for nothing that Vergennes would not give, be grateful for whatever help the French provided, and remain ever accommodating and patient. As Franklin's friend Condorcet would remark approvingly, Franklin as a diplomat "observed much and acted little."

Adams, no less than Franklin, felt the French alliance must be "cultivated with perfect faith and tenderness." But he was apprehensive of too much diffidence. He worried about the effect in the long run, as he explained to Roger Sherman in a letter he appears never to have sent. "There is [a] danger that the [American] people and their representatives [in Congress] may have too much timidity in their conduct towards this power, and that your ministers here may have too much diffidence of themselves and too much complaisance for the Court." Specifically, he warned of excessive attention to what the French thought, what France wanted, and "too much [French] influence in our deliberations."

In 1776, Adams had argued in Congress that any alliance with France must be commercial only. To James Warren, he had expressed his shame at the "whining" he heard that all was lost unless France stepped in. "Are we to be beholden to France for our liberties?" But now, with the end of the struggle no nearer in view, and with his newfound regard for the French, Adams saw things differently. France was "a rock upon which we may safely build," he told Warren. Like George Washington, Adams saw that sea power could decide the outcome of the war. Specifically he saw French naval support as the crucial necessity and felt duty-bound not just to voice his opinion to Vergennes, but to press for a greater commitment of French naval power, even at the risk of annoying the proud foreign minister.

Earlier in the summer, a French naval expedition under Admiral Charles-Henri Théodat d'Estaing, combined with an American land assault against the British at Newport, Rhode Island, had failed—news that didn't reach Paris until late in the year. Thus, to Adams, it was clear that more French ships were needed and no time was to be lost.

Franklin agreed, but counseled moderation. In December, Adams drafted a letter to Vergennes, which Franklin toned down. It was their most important undertaking together.

Signed by all three commissioners and submitted in the first week of January 1779, the letter stated that nothing would bring the war to a "speedy conclusion" more effectively than "sending a powerful fleet sufficient to secure naval superiority" in American waters. "Such a naval force, acting in concert with the armies of the United States, would in all probability take and destroy the whole British power in that part of the world."

Vergennes, however, chose to ignore the letter. His thoughts for the time being—and as probably the commissioners did not know—were taken up with the prospect of a French invasion of England.

On September 14, 1778, at Philadelphia, Congress named Benjamin Franklin minister plenipotentiary to the Court of Louis XVI. The three-man American commission was dispensed with. It was midwinter, however, before word reached Paris; the official dispatches did not arrive until February 12, 1779.

The new arrangement was exactly what Adams had recommended and the news was to leave him feeling more miserable than ever. He had been ill for the first time since coming to France, suffering from a violent cold and trying to cure himself in characteristic fashion by walking ten miles a day. Though he had clearly indicated that Franklin should be the one chosen, there had always been the possibility that Congress might pick him. Arthur Lee was dispatched to Madrid. But Congress had neglected to provide any instruction for what he, Adams, was to do, neither recalling him nor assigning him to a new post, which was both mystifying and insulting. Adams was not even mentioned in the communiqué.

Such being the case, he made the decision on his own, informing Vergennes that as he had been "restored to the character of a private citizen," he would depart. He submitted a request for passage on the next available ship bound for America, and to Congress addressed a long letter saying that since no notice appeared to have been taken of him, he could only assume that Congress "has no further service for me on this side of the water, and that all my duties are on the other."

"I shall therefore soon present before you your own good man. Happy—happy indeed—shall I be," he announced to Abigail, trying to see the bright side. To Richard Henry Lee, he claimed his new status as a private citizen "best becomes me, and is most agreeable to me." In truth, he was hurt and angry, and justifiably. He had been badly served by a Congress that told him nothing and showed no gratitude for all he had done. He felt himself strangely adrift, less able than ever in his life to sense what lay in store for him. In a letter to James Warren, he vowed never again to allow himself to be made the sport of wise men or fools.

His moods swung from high to low, then lower still with the arrival of a packet of letters from Abigail filled with abject loneliness and accusing him of neglecting her. "All things look gloomy and melancholy around me," she wrote. "You could not have suffered more upon your voyage than I have felt cut off from all communication with you." Adams claimed to have written nearly fifty letters to her between April and September, which was almost certainly an exaggeration, but whatever the number, she had received only two. "Let me entreat you to write me more letters at a time, surely you cannot want subjects." What he wrote, she said, was always too brief, cold, and impersonal. It was as if he had "changed hearts with some frozen Laplander."

Trying to respond as calmly as possible, Adams wrote and burned three letters in succession. One was too sad, the next too angry, a third too cheerful to reflect the truth, as he explained in a fourth and final version. Was it possible that "some infernal has whispered in your ear insinuations?" Had she forgotten the "unalterable tenderness of my heart?" he asked.

"For God's sake, never reproach me again with not writing or with writing scrips. Your wounds are too deep.

> You know not—you feel not—the dangers that surround me, nor those that may be brought upon our country.

Millions would not tempt me to write you as I used [to]. I have no
security that every letter I write will not be broken open and copied
and transmitted to Congress and the English newspapers. They
would find no treason or deceit in them, it is true, but they would find
weakness and indiscretion, which they would make as ill use of.

In another letter, written after receiving three from him, Abigail said
she had no doubt of his affection. "But my soul is wounded at a separation from you, and my fortitude is all dissolved in frailty and weakness."
She could not understand his reluctance to express his love. "The affection I feel for my friend is of the tenderest kind, matured by years, sanctified by choice and approved by Heaven. Angels can witness its purity,
what care I then for the ridicule of Britain should this testimony of it fall
into their hands?"

Adams enlisted support from John Quincy, who told his mother that
Papa could "write but very little because he had so many other things to
think of, but he can not let slip one opportunity without writing a few
lines and when you receive them you complain as bad or worse than if he
had not wrote at all and it really hurts him to receive such letters."

"If I were to tell you all the tenderness of my heart," Adams confided,
"I should do nothing but write to you. I beg you not to be uneasy."

As the time to leave drew nearer, he grew increasingly woeful. What
had he accomplished after all? Did anyone care?

"I am left kicking and sprawling in the mire. . . . It is hardly a state of
disgrace that I am in but rather of total neglect and contempt." What
was to become of him? He had never been in such a situation. "My present feelings are new to me."

Not since the most anguished diary entries of his youth had he
declared himself so overburdened with woe. "If ever I had any wit, it is all
evaporated. If ever I had any imagination, it is all quenched. . . . I believe
I am grown more austere, severe, rigid, and miserable than I ever was."

As ardently as he longed for home, he hated to leave Paris, hated to
leave France, and expected he would never return. "The climate is more
favorable to my constitution than ours," he acknowledged to Abigail.
He loved the food, the civility of everyday life. The French were "the
happiest people in the world . . . and have the best disposition to make
others so.

There is such a choice of elegant entertainments in the theatric way, of good company and excellent books that nothing would be wanting to me in this country but my family and peace to my country to make me one of the happiest of men.

The one tribute he received was a letter from Versailles, a letter Adams treasured. Vergennes, speaking for the King, offered praise for "the wise conduct that you have held to throughout the tenure of your commission," as well as "the zeal with which you have constantly furthered the cause of your nation, while strengthening the alliance that ties it to his Majesty."

What appears to have pleased Adams no less was the discovery during his parting call at Versailles that his French had so improved he could manage an extended conversation and speak as rapidly as he pleased.

THE TWO ADAMSES took their leave of Benjamin Franklin and others at Passy on March 8, 1779, and, with the servant Stephens, departed by post chaise for the coast of Brittany. At the bustling port of Nantes on the lower Loire, they settled into a hotel to wait for passage on the American frigate *Alliance*. Days passed, eventually weeks, during which father and son were together steadily. Biding their time, they walked about the town and along the river. Through long afternoons, Adams helped the boy in translating Cicero.

In late April, they moved on board the *Alliance*, only to learn later still, in a letter from Franklin, that orders had been changed and the ship was not to sail for America after all. However, a French frigate, *La Sensible*, was due to sail from Lorient, with a new French minister to the United States, Chevalier Anne-César de La Luzerne. Franklin gave instructions that the *Alliance* carry Adams to Lorient, but on arrival Adams found that Minister La Luzerne had been delayed. And so the wait went on, father and son remaining on board the *Alliance*.

In the days that followed, Adams spent considerable time with the daring young Scottish-American naval officer, John Paul Jones, who was fitting out an old French merchantman that he had renamed the *Bonhomme Richard*. They had met earlier at Passy, corresponded over naval matters, and Jones, quite unjustly, had decided that Adams, in his role as commissioner, was conspiring against him. Privately, Jones referred to Adams as a "wicked and conceited upstart," and expressed the wish that "Mr. Roundface" were at home minding his own business.

Having no part to play, no say in anything, no useful work, and no choice but to wait, was more nearly than Adams could bear. He began brooding. Imagining himself the victim of more than mere chance, he saw Jones and "the old conjurer" Franklin at the bottom of his troubles. He was being kept waiting, being humiliated, intentionally. "I may be mistaken in these conjectures, they may be injurious to J. and F., and therefore I shall not talk about them, but I am determined to put down my thoughts and see which turns out," Adams wrote in his diary.

> Do I see that these people despise me, or do I see that they dread me? Can I bear contempt—to know that I am despised? It is my duty to bear everything that I cannot help.

From time spent with Jones, Adams decided he was the most ambitious and intriguing officer in the American navy.

> Eccentricities and irregularities are to be expected from him. They are in his character, they are visible in his eyes. His voice is soft and small; his eye has keenness, and wildness and softness in it.

Adams never doubted that faces carried clues to character: the white-as-paper pallor of Condorcet bespoke dedication to hard study; the eyes of Voltaire with their "fine frenzy rolling" were the eyes of a poet; in the face of Louis XVI, Adams had seen "goodness and innocence" as clearly as he saw "keenness, and wildness and softness" in the eyes of young Jones.

But then studying his own face in the mirror, Adams did not like what he saw. There was nothing exceptional about him, he concluded, writing in his diary. "By my physical constitution, I am but an ordinary man. The times alone have destined me to fame." There was too much weakness and languor in his nature. "When I look in the glass, my eye, my forehead, my brow, my cheeks, my lips all betray this relaxation." Yet he could be roused, he knew. "Yet some great events, some cutting expressions, some mean scandals, hypocrisies, have at times thrown this assemblage of sloth, sleep, and littleness into a rage a little like a lion."

Most days, however, passed pleasantly enough. It was by his own choice that he dined often with Jones, spent hours in conversation with him and his officers, and as always, Adams was buoyed by talk. He and the surgeon of the *Bonhomme Richard*, an especially companionable man named Bourke, discussed everything from mathematics to rheumatism, Paris, London, the war at home, the war at sea, medicine at sea, the absence of profanity on French ships, and the nuances of the French language. At a dinner hosted by Jones at L'Épée Royale in town, the talk turned to the two ways most recommended for learning French, to take a mistress and to attend the Comédie-Française. When in good humor Dr. Bourke asked Adams which he preferred, Adams responded in like spirit, "Perhaps both would teach it soonest, to be sure sooner than either." But in his diary, he felt obliged to add, "The language is nowhere better spoken than at the Comédie."

"On board all day, reading *Don Quixote*," was the single entry for May 18.

It was June by the time the French minister, La Luzerne, arrived at Lorient. On June 17, Adams and John Quincy went aboard the *Sensible*, and that afternoon they were finally under way from France, Adams having no idea how very soon he would be returning.

I V

THERE WAS NO ADVANCE WORD of the arrival of the *Sensible*. The latest information Abigail had received, at the end of June in a letter written the first week of April, was that Adams was waiting to sail on the *Alliance*. But then in mid-July, Mercy Warren had passed along information received through James Lovell to the effect that Congress had in mind a new appointment for Adams, and that "Nobody seems to have an expectation of his return at present."

In the year and a half of her husband's absence, Abigail's distress had been worse than she had ever anticipated or, she was certain, than anyone could ever realize. "Known only to my own heart is the sacrifice I have made, and the conflict it has cost me," she had confided to her sister Elizabeth in the first weeks of his absence. "I wish a thousand times I had gone with him," she later told John Thaxter. For the first time in fourteen years of marriage she had had to face an entire winter on her own.

"How lonely are my days. How solitary are my nights," she had written to Adams in a letter that would not reach Passy until after he had departed.

Her sister Mary Cranch, of whom Abigail was extremely fond, continued to reside nearby in Braintree with her husband and family. But sister Elizabeth had married and moved away to Haverhill near the New Hampshire border. (Unimpressed by Elizabeth's choice in a husband, the young Reverend John Shaw, Abigail had tried to dissuade her, but without success. "Men are very scarce to be sure," Abigail had written by way of explanation to her own John.) And now Nabby, too, had gone off for an extended stay with the Warrens, leaving Abigail feeling more solitary than ever.

Earlier in the fall, when the French fleet put in at Boston, she had had her own encounter with French hospitality. A delegation of French officers, resplendent in royal blue and scarlet uniforms, had appeared in Braintree to pay their respects to the wife of the American commissioner. She was invited to dine on board one of their ships, which she did, twice, delighting in the perfect manners of the officers and the sense of being at the center of things. On another occasion, accompanied by Colonel Quincy, she dined with Admiral d'Estaing on board his magnificent flagship, *Languedoc*, possibly the finest warship in the world. "If I ever had any national prejudices [against the French] they are done away," she wrote, "and I am ashamed to own I was ever possessed of so narrow a spirit."

But in winter, surrounded by mountains of snow, secluded from all society, she could as well have been in Greenland, she said. In other times of separation, times of horrible duress with war at her doorstep and epidemic disease raging, she had somehow borne up, with so much to contend with, so little time to dwell on her own loneliness. "This is a painful situation," she wrote to James Lovell, "and my patience is nearly exhausted."

But there was a further, complicating element and that was Lovell himself. When Adams had wondered, from the tone of her letters, if some "infernal" might be whispering insinuations in her ear, he was not far from the truth.

In the first weeks after Adams's departure for France, Abigail had confided her state of mind to Lovell, who in response had written that her alarms and distress only afforded him "delight." More letters followed in which Lovell addressed her as Portia, presuming to use Adams's pet name for her, and inquiring whether he must limit himself to language devoid of sentiment. She replied saying, "I begin to look upon you as a very dangerous man . . . a most ingenious and agreeable flatterer." Yet she signed her letter "Portia."

Writing again, he appealed to her with a line from the Scottish poet Allan Ramsay, declaring if "ye were mine . . . how dearly I would love thee," and underscored the word love. When at the start of a new year she wrote to say Adams had been absent for a full eleven months, the reply from Lovell was closer to the raw double entendres of Laurence Sterne's *Tristram Shandy*, a book Abigail had never read: he expressed relief that her husband's "rigid patriotism" (again underscored) had not left her pregnant again.

Telling her not to imagine Adams doing anything in his private hours in Paris other than attending museums, Lovell, by insinuation, raised the question of what else Adams might be doing.

Lovell was a married man who, in five years in Congress, never once returned to Boston to see his wife and children. That he enjoyed the company of several women in Philadelphia was no secret there, but whether Abigail knew of this is not clear.

In Lovell's defense, it could be said that other men, too, would, as time went on, find Abigail Adams an irresistible correspondent—young John Thaxter, as an example, and most notably Thomas Jefferson. Her spirit and intelligence, her interest in their lives, her fund of opinions, seemed to elicit confidences such as they shared with few others, though none in the salacious manner of Lovell.

Abigail could have called a halt to the exchange with Lovell at any time, had she wished. But she did not. Clearly she enjoyed his flirtatious attention, but primarily she craved information—"intelligence"—and more than anyone in Congress, Lovell had shown himself willing and able to keep her supplied with news. He reported to her on the war, sent copies of the weekly *Journals of Congress*. As the most active member of the

Committee for Foreign Affairs, he was also in the best possible position to keep her posted on anything pertaining to her husband.

At no time was she indiscreet in what she wrote, and if he was, she refused to be intimidated. She needed him. That her affections rested entirely with her "dearest friend," and that she longed only for his return, she left no doubt. "I love everyone who manifests a regard or shows an attachment to my absent friend," she told Lovell, and however infrequently she heard from her absent friend, she kept writing to him at length with never a letup.

On August 2, 1779, a clear summer day with the blue waters of Boston sparkling in sunshine, the two Adamses and their servant were rowed from the *Sensible* to a point on the Braintree shore not far from where, under such different conditions, their adventures had begun. With no one expecting them, the shore was empty. Their arrival at home was a total surprise.

Try as he would through life, John Adams was never able to express adequately his attachment to home, his adoration of his wife and children. And the effect of his long absences since the onset of the war had only intensified these feelings. "I am, with an ardor that words have not power to express, yours," he had closed a letter to Abigail, and though her wish that he be less stringent in his expressions of affection was entirely understandable, there was never a question about the depth of his feelings or his devotion to her.

But at last there was no need for either to write anything. They were together again and their happiness—the happiness of the entire family— could not have been greater.

The farm would have been at its summer peak, and one may imagine John and Abigail walking their fields together, John glad for home ground beneath his feet again and delighting in the look of things under her management. There would be hard cider again, to start the day, fresh vegetables from the kitchen garden. There were relatives and old friends to see—his mother, the Cranches, Colonel Quincy, Parson Wibird. Neighbors stopped to bid him welcome. Together he and Abigail rode over Penn's Hill to visit with her father at the Weymouth parsonage. But mainly, it appears, Adams kept close to home, within familiar walls and the embrace of his family. The three children who had remained with their mother had all grown and changed. All had stories to tell him and hung on his own telling of his travels, the sights he had seen. The talk went on day and night, and doubtless John Quincy demonstrated his French to the amazement of all.

Time and again when away, Adams would profess preference for the simple domestic life by Penn's Hill above anything he knew; time and again, on reaching home, he would say that there and there only was everything he desired. It was a lifelong refrain, and his enjoyment now seemed to bear him out.

Sweet though it was, the interval was no time out of time. The war weighed too heavily on everyone's mind. The scarcities, inflation, taxes, and profiteering, the incessant worries and enmities of war, were all ever-present. Adams experienced firsthand the "amazing depreciation" of the currency, of prices so high as to be laughable under any other circumstances. Abigail and friends spoke bitterly of a selfish, avaricious spirit that had taken hold to a degree unthinkable earlier. A highly indignant James Warren told how "fellows who would have cleaned my shoes five years ago" had "amassed fortunes and are riding in chariots."

The news of the war was not encouraging. In the spring of 1778, Washington's army had emerged from the ordeal of winter at Valley Forge a stronger, more disciplined force. That June, when the British chose to evacuate Philadelphia and march back to New York, Washington had hit them at Monmouth, New Jersey, in a major battle which, though indecisive, had proven that his so-called "rabble" were well able to hold their own against the vaunted enemy. But then both armies were back where they had been before, with the British holding New York, the Americans outside keeping watch, and in the aftermath of the failed French and American effort at Newport that summer, the war appeared at a stalemate. Attention shifted to naval engagements between the French and British in the West Indies and to British forays into the South, where, in the spring of 1779, the Americans were defeated at Briar Creek, Georgia. There were British raids along the coast of Connecticut that summer, shortly before Adams returned, and apprehension along coastal Massachusetts that a major British strike there might be in the offing. But no one knew and nothing seemed to portend a resolution of the struggle.

• • •

ADAMS HAD BEEN HOME hardly a week when the town of Braintree chose him as a delegate to the state constitutional convention. Adams accepted and immediately began preparing himself.

There being as yet no national constitution, the form of government chosen by each of the states was a matter of utmost gravity. The constitution of an independent sovereign state had to stand on its own merits, not serve merely as a secondary component of a larger, overarching structure.

On September 1, Adams was off to Cambridge, to the First Church at the corner of Harvard Yard, where some 250 delegates gathered. In another few days he was chosen as one of a drafting committee of thirty who met in Boston on September 13 and in turn picked a subcommittee of three—Adams, Samuel Adams, and James Bowdoin, who was president of the convention—whereupon the other two picked Adams to draw up the state's constitution. He had become, as he later said, a sub-sub committee of one.

The work was to be his alone, and if ever he had a chance to rise to an occasion for which he was ideally suited, this was it. So many of his salient strengths—the acute legal mind, his command of the English language, his devotion to the ideals of the good society—so much that he knew of government, so much that he had read and written, could now be brought to bear on one noble task.

Nor could circumstances have been much more in his favor. He was rested, refreshed, inspired by the welcome home and by the honor his town and fellow delegates had bestowed on him. He could work at home in familiar surroundings, his books and papers about him, and with Abigail's steadying presence, which was always to his advantage. That his efforts were for his own Massachusetts was also of very great importance. After the frustrations and disappointments of France, such a chance to shine again must have seemed a godsend. Possibly, had there been no difficult time in France, no feelings of failure, his performance now would have been something less. In any event, the result was to be one of the most admirable, long-lasting achievements of John Adams's life.

To prepare, he had reviewed in detail those constitutions already framed by other states, and reread his own *Thoughts on Government*. He worked through the still-warm days of late September in his office just off the front hall. He worked at a plain, tall desk at which he wrote standing up or perched on a high stool, and he appears to have completed the draft sometime in early October. Printed copies, for the consideration of the convention, were ready at the end of the month, on or about October 30, 1779, his forty-fourth birthday.

It was titled "A Constitution or Form of Government for the Commonwealth of Massachusetts," Adams having chosen to use the word "commonwealth" rather than "state," as had Virginia, a decision he made on his own and that no one was to question. A tone of absolute clarity and elevated thought was established in the opening lines, in a Preamble, a new feature in constitutions, affirming the old ideal of the common good founded on a social compact:

> The end of the institution, maintenance, and administration of government is to secure the existence of the body politic; to protect it; and to furnish the individuals who compose it with the power of enjoying, in safety and tranquility, their natural rights and the blessings of life; and whenever these great objects are not obtained, the people have a right to alter the government, and to take measures necessary for their safety, happiness, and prosperity.
>
> The body-politic is formed by a voluntary association of individuals. It is a social compact, by which the whole people covenants with each citizen, and each citizen with the whole people, that all shall be governed by certain laws for the common good.

A Declaration of Rights, following the Preamble and preceding the Constitution itself, stated unequivocally that all men were "born equally free and independent"—words Adams had taken from the Virginia Declaration of Rights as written by George Mason—and that they had certain "natural, essential, and unalienable rights." It guaranteed free elections, and in one of a number of articles borrowed from the constitution of Pennsylvania, guaranteed "freedom of speaking" and "liberty of the press." It provided against unreasonable searches and seizures, and trial by jury. While it did not guarantee freedom of religion, it affirmed the "duty" of all people to worship "The Supreme Being, the great creator and preserver of the universe," and that no one was to be "hurt, molested, or restrained in his person, liberty, or estate for worshipping God in the manner most agreeable to the dictates of his own conscience," provided he did not disturb the public peace.

The people of Massachusetts were to have the sole and exclusive right of governing themselves, and in an article intended to prevent the formation of a hereditary monarchy, an expanded version of a similar article in the Virginia constitution, Adams wrote:

> No man, nor corporation or association of men have any other title to obtain advantages or particular and exclusive privileges distinct from those of the community, than what arises from the consideration of services rendered to the public . . . the idea of a man born a magistrate, lawgiver, or judge is absurd and unnatural.

In fundamental ways, the form of government was very like what Adams had proposed in his *Thoughts on Government*, and again, as in *Thoughts on Government*, he called for a "government of laws, and not of men." Founded on the principle of the separation and balance of powers, the Constitution declared in a single sentence that in the Commonwealth of Massachusetts "the legislative, executive and judicial power shall be placed in separate departments, to the end that it might be a government of laws, and not of men."

There would be two branches of the legislature, a Senate and a House of Representatives, an executive, the governor, who was to be elected at large annually and have veto power over the acts of the legislature. But it was the establishment of an independent judiciary, with judges of the Supreme Court appointed, not elected, and for life ("as long as they behave themselves well"), that Adams made one of his greatest contributions not only to Massachusetts but to the country, as time would tell.

In addition, notably, there was Section II of Chapter 6, a paragraph headed "The Encouragement of Literature, Etc.," which was like no other declaration to be found in any constitution ever written until then, or since. It was entirely Adams's creation, his original contribution to the constitution of Massachusetts, and he rightly took great pride in it.

Wisdom and knowledge, as well as virtue, diffused generally among the body of the people being necessary for the preservation of their rights and liberties; and as these depend on spreading the opportunities and advantages of education in various parts of the country, and among the different orders of the people, it shall be the duty of legislators and magistrates in all future periods of this commonwealth to cherish the interests of literature and the sciences, and all seminaries of them, especially the university at Cambridge, public schools, and grammar schools in the towns; to encourage private societies and public institutions, rewards and immunities, for the promotion of agriculture, arts, sciences, commerce, trades, manufactures, and a natural history of the country; to countenance and inculcate the principles of humanity and general benevolence, public and private charity, industry and frugality, honesty and punctuality in their dealings, sincerity, good humor, and all social affections, and generous sentiments among the people.

It was, in all, a declaration of Adams's faith in education as the bulwark of the good society, the old abiding faith of his Puritan forebears. The survival of the rights and liberties of the people depended on the spread of wisdom, knowledge, and virtue among all the people, the common people, of whom he, as a farmer's son, was one. "I must judge for myself, but how can I judge, how can any man judge, unless his mind has been opened and enlarged by reading," Adams had written in his diary at age twenty-five, while still living under his father's roof.

As had no constitution before, Adams was declaring it the "duty" of government not only to provide education but to "cherish" the interests of literature and science—indeed, the full range of the arts, commerce, trades, manufactures, and natural history.

In the last week of August, Adams had attended a dinner at Harvard in honor of the new French minister, the Chevalier de La Luzerne. The setting was the Philosophy Room of Harvard Hall, the old laboratory of Adams's favorite professor, Winthrop. There, among the "philosophical apparatus," Adams had offered to some of his dinner companions his dream of establishing a Society of Arts and Sciences at Boston, as a counterpart to the American Philosophical Society at Philadelphia. The idea was to be enthusiastically taken up; the American Academy of Arts and

Sciences would be founded in less than a year. But the dinner and the conversation were also an inspiration for what he wrote in the paragraph on education, and particularly the inclusion of natural history.

Because wisdom and education were not sufficient of themselves, he had added the further "duty" of government to "countenance and inculcate" the principles of humanity, charity, industry, frugality, honesty, sincerity—virtue, in sum. And amiability as well—"good humor," as he called it—counted for the common good, the Constitution of Massachusetts was to proclaim, suggesting that such delight in life as Adams had found in the amiable outlook of the French had had a decided influence.

He had written Section II of Chapter 6, in a burst of inspiration, the words "flowing" from his pen, but expected the convention to "show it no mercy," as he later said. "I was somewhat apprehensive that criticism and objections would be made to the section, and particularly that the 'natural history' and 'good humor' would be stricken out." To his surprise and delight, the whole of the paragraph passed intact, and, as he also noted, "unanimously without amendment!"

In the end, the convention approved nearly all of his draft, with only a few notable changes. Preferring what Jefferson had written in the Declaration of Independence, the convention revised the first article of the Declaration of Rights, that all men were "born equally free and independent," to read that all men were "born free and equal," a change Adams did not like and would like even less as time went on. He did not believe all men were created equal, except in the eyes of God, but that all men, for all their many obvious differences, were born to equal rights.

The reference to freedom of speech was removed, not to be reinstated until much later, and the worship of God was declared a right of all men, as well as a duty. The legislature was also given power to override the governor's veto, another change Adams regretted, as it was contrary to his belief in a strong, popularly elected executive.

None of the alterations, however, diminished his overall pride in what he and the convention had achieved, and the acclaim it brought. "I take vast satisfaction in the general approbation of the Massachusetts Constitution," he would tell a friend. "If the people are as wise and honest in the choice of their rulers, as they have been in framing a government, they will be happy, and I shall die content with the prospect for my children."

As time would prove, he had written one of the great, enduring documents of the American Revolution. The constitution of the Commonwealth of Massachusetts is the oldest functioning written constitution in the world.

ADAMS HAD PICKED UP on other business in the meantime, attending to some of his old law practice, and responding to those friends in Congress who wrote to welcome him home. Still wounded by the way Congress had treated him, he imagined that in the rancorous atmosphere of Philadelphia, with controversy swirling about the Deane affair and the hatred between Franklin and Arthur Lee, his own reputation was suffering. To his credit he had not rushed off to Philadelphia to see for himself, as someone less wise and less proud might have. If he had cause for complaint in such times of stress and uncertainty, so too, he knew, did others. "None of us have anything to boast of in these times, in respect to the happiness of life," he observed in one letter.

"We stand in greater need than ever of men of your principles," wrote his ever-devoted friend Benjamin Rush, who, like many, assumed that Adams would soon be reelected to Congress.

"Be assured you have not an enemy among us," declared James Lovell, who also made light of his prior "scrawls" to "lovely Portia." How much, if anything, Adams ever learned of Lovell's letters to Abigail is unknown.

Then, in October, out of the blue, came word from Philadelphia that Adams had been chosen by Congress to return to France as minister plenipotentiary to negotiate treaties of peace and commerce with Great Britain, a position he had neither solicited nor expected. The decision had been virtually unanimous. "Upon the whole I am of the opinion that in the esteem of Congress, your character is as high as any gentleman's in America," wrote Elbridge Gerry, knowing nothing would please Adams more.

Congress had voted him a salary of 2,500 pounds sterling. In addition, he was to have his own official secretary, Francis Dana, a Boston lawyer and member of Congress whom Adams knew and respected.

Henry Laurens, in a letter of congratulations, went out of his way to apologize for the fact that Adams had been so shabbily treated by Congress in his recent assignment, "dismissed without censure or applause," as Laurens said, but implored him, for the sake of the country, to accept the appointment.

From the Chevalier de La Luzerne came an offer of return passage on the *Sensible*, which was being refitted in Boston Harbor and soon to sail.

ADAMS DECIDED TO GO after even less discussion with Abigail than in 1777. That the same perils pertained went without saying.

Again Abigail was to remain behind, but this time nine-year-old Charles would also accompany his father, along with John Quincy. At first, John Quincy objected, saying he preferred to remain at home and prepare for Harvard, but his mother convinced him of the great opportunity inherent in such an experience.

In a heartfelt letter of farewell, she would liken the judicious traveler to a river that increases its volume the farther it flows from its source. "It will be expected of you, my son, that as you are favored with superior advantages under the instructive eye of a tender parent, that your improvements should bear some proportion to your advantages.

These are the times in which a genius would wish to live. It is not in the still calm of life, or the repose of a pacific station, that great characters are formed. The habits of a vigorous mind are formed in contending with difficulties. Great necessities call out great virtues. When a mind is raised, and animated by scenes that engage the heart, then those qualities which would otherwise lay dormant, wake into life and form the character of the hero and the statesman.

In addition to Francis Dana, John Thaxter would go as Adams's own private secretary and tutor for the boys. So including two servants, Stephens and another for Francis Dana, they made a company of seven.

There was no part he would rather play than that of peacemaker, Adams wrote to La Luzerne, but with a cautionary note: "Alas! When I reflect upon the importance, delicacy, intricacy and danger of the service, I feel a great deal of diffidence in myself."

Adams had no illusions of peace near at hand or of an easy path for himself. As he wrote forthrightly to Samuel Huntington, the new president of Congress, with so much at stake, his distress now was greater even than when he had last sailed for France.

Thus, a little more than three months after he had arrived home, Adams was again on his way across the ocean. The wind was favorable, he noted aboard the *Sensible*, November 15, under way past Cape Ann.

"My habitation, how disconsolate it looks!" Abigail wrote. "My table I sit down to it. But I cannot swallow my food. . . . My hopes and fears rise alternately. I cannot resign more than I do, unless life is called for."

CHAPTER FIVE

UNALTERABLY DETERMINED

[His] obstinacy. . . will cause him to foment a thou-
sand unfortunate incidents . . .

~The Comte de Vergennes

Thanks to God that he gave me stubbornness when I
know I am right.   ~John Adams

I

Two days out from Boston, in a stiff northeast wind, the *Sensible*, with 350 people on board, sprang a leak. A pump was put immediately in service, yet the leak grew worse day by day.

There was no sign of British cruisers, which to Adams were the worst of evils; but then the second week, off the Grand Banks, the wind began blowing from the northwest, the sea to run high. For one endless, miserable day, in howling winds, the old frigate labored under foresail only. A "very violent gale," recorded Adams, who, in order to write, had to get down on his cabin floor on hands and knees.

By the time the storm passed, the ship was leaking so badly that two pumps had to be manned day and night, unrelenting work in which all hands took part, passengers as well, including John Quincy. The situation was alarming. In the event of another storm or an encounter with the enemy, the captain explained, they would have no chance. The only choice was to make for the nearest friendly port, for Spain, "with all the sail the ship could prudently bear."

The *Sensible* labored slowly across the ocean, until finally, on the morning of December 8, 1779, running with the wind, she reached El Ferrol, on Spain's rocky northwestern tip. It had been a closer call than anyone liked to think. In less than an hour at anchor at El Ferrol, with the pumps stopped, there were seven feet of water in the hold.

"We have had an escape again," Adams began in a letter to Abigail from shore. "One more storm would very probably [have] carried us to the bottom of the sea," added John Quincy in his report to his mother.

Faced with the prospect of being marooned for weeks while repairs were made, Adams inquired about proceeding overland. The distance to Paris was 1,000 miles. The journey, east across Spain and over the Pyrenees to the French border, was one of extreme difficulty, he was warned, and never more so than in winter. But to sit still and wait again as he had in France, to let circumstance rule, or the whims or priorities of others, were not in his nature. He was determined to go, and talk of difficulties had little effect. Indeed, for a man so constituted as Adams, such talk could well have been the deciding factor. "The season, the roads, the accommodations for traveling are so unfavorable that it is not expected I can get to Paris in less than thirty days," he wrote in explanation to the president of Congress, Samuel Huntington. "But if I were to wait for the frigate, it would probably be much longer. I am determined, therefore, to make the best of way by land."

At first light, December 15, Adams, his sons, Francis Dana, John Thaxter, servants, Spanish guides and muleteers, and two additional Americans who had been aboard the *Sensible*, set off mounted on scrawny mules and looking, as John Thaxter noted, very like a scene from *Don Quixote*, and quixotic the whole undertaking turned out to be. Adams was exhausted before the journey began. In the week since landing he had hardly slept a night, so horrific was the torment of fleas and bedbugs, Spain's "enemies of all repose," as he said.

At the old city of La Coruña provisions were gathered. Three ancient calashes—clumsy, brightly painted two-wheeled carriages—were also added to the caravan, these remarkable for their cracked leather seats and broken harness patched together with rope and twine and pulled by mules with tiny, tinkling bells tied about their necks. As the calashes proved more uncomfortable than the mules, Adams, Dana, and Thaxter chose to go by mule most of the way.

We carried bread and cheese, meat, knives and forks, spoons, apples and nuts [Adams would write]. Indeed, we were obliged to carry . . . our own beds, blankets . . . everything that we wanted. . . . We got nothing at the taverns but fire, water . . . and sometimes the wine of the country.

From La Coruña, their route passed through Betanzos, once the capital of the kingdom of Galicia, then Lugo, Astorga, Burgos, and Bilbao. "There is the grandest profusion of wild irregular mountains I ever saw," Adams wrote. But the roads proved worse even than he had imagined, so rocky and treacherous it was necessary to go by foot a great part of the journey.

"We had nothing worth remarking today except we kept ascending," wrote John Quincy on December 31. Another day's journey was "almost perpendicular." With encouragement from his father, the boy had started a diary, the beginning of what was to be a lifelong enterprise lasting sixty-eight years.

To the Americans the wretchedness of the Spanish people, the squalor of the wayside taverns, were appalling. "Smoke filled every part of the kitchen, stable, and other part[s] of the house, as thick as possible so that it was . . . very difficult to see and breathe," Adams recorded at one tavern. "The mules, hogs, fowls and human inhabitants live . . . all together," he wrote of another overnight accommodation. Everywhere he saw poverty and misery, people in rags. "Nothing appeared rich but the churches, nobody fat but the clergy," he noted sadly.

There were days of rain, fog, and snow, mountains that went endlessly on and on, mountains like "a tumbling sea." The boys were sick with colds. Francis Dana became so ill there was a question whether he could continue. "We go along barking and sneezing and coughing as if we were fitter for a hospital than for travelers on the road," wrote Adams, whose own strength and spirits began to give out. He had never known a worse undertaking, he fumed in his diary. Given the choice of his first crossing on the *Boston*, or this, he would prefer the former with all its horrors. But only to Abigail, in a letter written at Bilbao, did he concede that he had made a mistake coming overland.

The one compensation of the journey was the warmth of the welcome they received along the route. Spain by now had entered the war, but as an ally of France only. John Jay of New York, the American minister to Spain, had been in Madrid for a year, and his mission had proven hopeless, as the Spanish Court had no interest in recognizing the independence of the United States. Still, no representative of any government would have been treated with more courtesy and friendship than were Adams and his party in town after town, as he was to report proudly.

At last in January, two weeks into the new year 1780, the travelers crossed the frontier at St.-Jean-de-Luz and by nightfall arrived at Bayonne. Leaving Spain, Adams regretted only that he had had no time for a detour to see the famous pilgrimage cathedral of Santiago de Compestela, and that he had to part with his mule, "as he was an excellent animal and had served me well."

Heading on by post chaise, he and his party were in Bordeaux in another few days, and despite fog and icy roads reached Paris on February 9, travel-worn but in "tolerable" health, nearly two months after departing from El Ferrol, three months after setting sail from Boston. A letter from Abigail filled with worry was waiting for him at the Hôtel de Valois on the Rue de Richelieu, which he planned to make his address this time.

LOSING NO TIME, Adams enrolled the boys the next morning in the boarding school at Passy, then called on Franklin. At Versailles the day after, accompanied by Franklin and Francis Dana, Adams "had the honor to wait on" the aged Prime Minister of France, Jean-Frédéric Phélypeaux de Maurepas, who was as old nearly as the century, older even than Franklin; as well as the Minister of Marine, Gabriel Sartine; and the all-important Foreign Minister, the Comte de Vergennes.

In Franklin's estimate, the "disposition" of the Court to the American cause was as favorable as it had ever been, and Adams came away from these initial discussions feeling even more sanguine. He had never heard the French Foreign Ministry "so frank, explicit, and decided," he stressed in a letter to Congress. Most encouraging was the talk of French naval support, and from all that he heard, he grew increasingly optimistic. The largest French fleet yet was preparing to sail. Four thousand troops under General Rochambeau were soon to depart.

"The French Court seemed to be now every day more and more convinced of the good policy, and indeed the necessity, of prosecuting the war with vigor in America," Adams informed James Warren. "They have been making great preparations accordingly, and are determined to maintain a clear superiority."

The one annoyance was Vergennes's apparent displeasure over Adams's mission. Adams offered a letter of explanation, saying he had been chosen by Congress as minister plenipotentiary to negotiate a peace with Great Britain, as well as a treaty of commerce. It was the wish of Congress, as a way to save time, that an authorized American envoy be present in Europe to treat with the ministers of the other powers the moment peace became possible. Further, it was the wish of Congress—as well as his own—to take no steps without consulting the ministers of his Most Christian Majesty.

Adams asked whether, "in the present circumstances of things," the British should be made aware of the purpose of his mission, and suggested that an official announcement be published such as had already appeared in the *Journals of Congress*.

His letter was written on February 12. In reply, February 15, Vergennes insisted that nothing be said of the matter until Conrad Gérard, the French minister to America who had been replaced by La Luzerne, arrived back in Paris, and explained Adams's instructions from Congress. In the meantime, Adams was told, "It is the part of prudence to conceal your eventual character [as peacemaker] and, above all, to take the necessary precautions that the object of your commission remain unknown to the Court of London."

Adams was astonished and deeply insulted. It was no affair of Gérard's to explain his instructions. It was also inconceivable that the British did not already know the nature of his business. The London papers had already carried news of his arrival in Europe and that he had come to "hear and receive any proposals of peace" from Great Britain. And as Vergennes was known to employ a veritable army of spies, he was hardly groping in the dark on such matters.

The proud, immensely shrewd French Foreign Minister had become one of the great figures of eighteenth-century Europe by dint of exceedingly hard work and by making himself a consummate man of the world. French support for the American war was his policy and he its champion from the start, despite the fearful drain it imposed on the treasury of

France. There was thus no one more deserving of American gratitude. But it was because of no abiding fervor for American liberty that he had persuaded his young king to come to America's aid. France was an absolute monarchy and Vergennes as stout a monarchist as could be found. His purpose, first, last, and always, was to weaken and humble Britain and, at the same time, expand French trade in America.

"Always keep in mind," Vergennes would tell the Minister of Finance, "that in separating the United States from Great Britain, it was above all their commerce we wanted."

Adams had no illusions about what determined the actions of nations. "It is interest alone which does it," he had once told Congress, "and it is interest alone which can be trusted." For Vergennes's American policy he had a vivid image: "He means . . . to keep his hand under our chin to prevent us from drowning, but not to lift our heads out of water."

As polite as Adams remained, Vergennes neither liked nor trusted him. He found Adams's manifest integrity unsettling; Adams's emphatic patriotism appealed not at all. The Foreign Minister was a man accustomed to deference, and exceedingly fond of having his way. Preferring to deal only with the ever obliging Franklin, he dreaded the prospect of Adams meddling in what he, Vergennes, regarded as his exclusive domain, the power politics of Europe. While all Paris might see Franklin as the authentic, homespun "natural" American, Vergennes knew better. It was precisely Franklin's subtlety, his worldliness, that made him invaluable as a diplomat. Adams, on the other hand, was truly a provincial. Worse, he was a novice; and there was no telling the damage such a man might do.

Vergennes's professed need to see the instructions Gérard was bringing was disingenuous, since Gérard had long since sent Vergennes a summary of Adams's instructions, in a dispatch from Philadelphia the very day they were adopted by Congress.

"The delicacies of the Comte de Vergennes about communicating my powers [to Britain] are not perfectly consonant to my manner of thinking," Adams wrote to Congress. Were he free to follow his own judgment, he would pursue a "bolder plan." But in the face of the Foreign Minister's directive there seemed little he could do. Franklin volunteered no support, nor did Adams ask for it.

At loose ends once again in Europe, and with no word from Congress,

Adams was nonetheless determined to make himself useful. If nothing else, he could write—Adams would *always* write. Another man might have relaxed and bided his time, just as another man might have waited at El Ferrol for his ship to be repaired, rather than striking out over the mountains of Spain.

Through that spring in Paris and on into summer, with able assistance from Francis Dana and John Thaxter, Adams produced letters by the score, reports, newspaper articles—a great outpouring of "intelligence" surpassing in quantity even his most ambitious literary efforts of other years. Determined to improve European understanding of the American cause, he became, with Vergennes's sanction, his own office of information and propaganda, supplying anonymous articles to the *Mercure de France*, a weekly journal edited by Edmé-Jacques Genêt of the Ministry of Foreign Affairs. "I can assure you of his [Vergennes's] pleasure in giving his approval to publish in the *Mercure* everything that shall come from such a good pen," wrote Genêt, who tried tactfully to convince Adams he would do better with his French readers if he were not quite so long-winded.

In addition, Adams turned out articles tailored for publication in the British press, these to be placed by an American in London named Edmund Jenings. Another American agent in London, Thomas Digges, was recruited to keep Adams supplied with items gleaned from the London papers. Jenings and Digges were somewhat shadowy figures who may have been double agents like Edward Bancroft, but Adams trusted both, relied heavily on them, and the system worked with great efficiency. Digges's reporting especially was fast and accurate. His dispatches, sent to C. F. Hoochera, a favorite bookseller of Adams's on the Pont Neuf, were addressed to Ferdinando Ramón San, a name Adams borrowed from one of the muleteers on the trek across Spain.

Adams and Dana got along well. In accepting the appointment as secretary, Dana had insisted that he be considered Adams's equal, a colleague, not an employee, and Adams, who had agreed, proved as good as his word. No less the New Englander than Adams, Dana was equally ill suited to trifling away his time. They were of like mind on most matters, including the underlying motives of the Comte de Vergennes.

Between times, on his own, Adams maintained correspondence with James Warren, James Lovell, Elbridge Gerry, Samuel Adams, and Benjamin Rush. And he wrote periodically to Vergennes, affirming his faith in the French-American alliance and passing along what little news from America came his way.

But much the greatest part of the outpouring was to Congress. From his rooms on the Rue de Richelieu, Adams issued almost daily correspondence, writing at times two and three letters a day, these addressed to President Samuel Huntington and filled with reports on British politics, British and French naval activities, or his own considered views on European affairs. In a letter dated April 18, he gave as clear-headed an appraisal as Congress was to receive from anyone in Europe.

> Although I am convinced by everything I see, and read and hear, that all the powers of Europe . . . rejoice in the American Revolution and consider the independence of America in their interest and happiness . . . yet I have many reasons to think that not one of them, not even Spain or France, wishes to see America rise very fast to power. We ought therefore to be cautious how we magnify our ideas and exaggerate our expressions of the generosity and magnanimity of any of these powers. Let us treat them with gratitude, but with dignity. Let us remember what is due to ourselves and our posterity as well as to them. Let us above all things avoid as much as possible entangling ourselves with their wars and politics . . . America has been the sport of European wars and politics long enough.

With still no response from Congress, after some forty-six letters, he kept steadily on. "I have written more to Congress since my arrival in Paris than they ever received from Europe put it all together since the revolution [began]," he told Elbridge Gerry without exaggeration. Franklin by contrast rarely wrote a word to Congress. By late July, Adams had produced no less than ninety-five letters—more than Congress wanted, he imagined—and never knowing whether anything had been received.

"I am so taken up with writing to Phil[adelphia] that I don't write to you as often as I wish," he told Abigail, to whom he had already written twenty times or more.

He saw his sons as often as he could and tried to keep watch on their progress at school. "Can't you keep a steadier hand?" he admonished John Quincy in response to a hurried scrawl from the boy listing his course of study. It was essential to learn to write well, Adams lectured. When another letter from John Quincy arrived, this beautifully executed on lightly penciled guide lines, Adams wrote at once to praise him and say how pleased he was. But unable to resist giving further advice, he told him to waste no time learning to do flourishes with his pen. "Ornaments of this kind, if not done with great skill, are worse than none," declared Adams in his notably plain hand.

Living at the center of Paris, he was able to see more of the city than ever before. The busy Rue de Richelieu was one of the most fashionable streets and the Hôtel de Valois, at 17 Rue de Richelieu, a premier residence. John Quincy would remember it as "magnificent." Close by were the gardens of the Palais Royal and the Tuileries, which, with their statuary, Adams thought beautiful beyond compare. On days when the boys could be with him, they walked the gardens and much of the city. He took them on his rounds of the bookshops on the Left Bank. They toured the Jardin du Roi, with its celebrated natural history displays. How long would it be, Adams wondered, before America had such collections.

"There is everything here that can inform understanding, or refine the taste, and indeed one would think that could purify the heart," he wrote of Paris to Abigail. Yet there were temptations. "Yet it must be remembered there is everything here, too, which can seduce, betray, deceive, corrupt and debauch," and in order to see to his duties, he must steel himself.

The conflict between the appeal of the arts and the sense that they were the product of a luxury-loving (and thus corrupt) foreign society played heavily on his mind. Delightful as it was to stroll the gardens of Paris, enticing as were science and the arts, he, John Adams, had work to do, a public trust to uphold. The science of government was his duty; the art of negotiation must take precedence.

Then, in a prophetic paragraph that would be quoted for generations within the Adams family and beyond, he wrote:

> I must study politics and war that my sons may have liberty to study mathematics and philosophy. My sons ought to study mathe-

matics and philosophy, geography, natural history, naval architecture, navigation, commerce, and agriculture in order to give their children a right to study paintings, poetry, music, architecture, statuary, tapestry, and porcelain.

How Americans deported themselves in Europe was a serious matter, Adams's convictions stemming more from patriotism than prudishness. So much more was at stake than one's own pleasure.

When a young New England merchant named Elkanah Watson, the son of a friend, wrote to inquire what sort of manners he should cultivate in anticipation of touring Europe, Adams's answer went far to explain his own conduct under the circumstances and the kind of guidance he was giving his sons.

You tell me, sir, you wish to cultivate your manners before you begin your travels . . . permit me to take the liberty of advising you to cultivate the manners of your own country, not those of Europe. I don't mean by this that you should put on a long face, never dance with the ladies, go to a play, or take a game of cards. But you may depend upon this, that the more decisively you adhere to a manly simplicity in your dress, equipage, and behavior, the more you devote yourself to business and study, and the less to dissipation and pleasure, the more you will recommend yourself to every man and woman in this country whose friendship or acquaintance is worth your having or wishing. There is an urbanity without ostentation or extravagance which will succeed everywhere and at all times. You will excuse this freedom, on account of my friendship for your father and consequently for you, and because I know that some young gentlemen have come to Europe with different sentiments and have consequently injured the character of their country as well as their own both here [and at home].

The boys were getting on splendidly, he assured their mother. Her "delicate" Charles was "hardy as flint," "speaks French like a hero." "He is a delightful little fellow. I love him too much."

Yet as before, Adams remained reluctant to profess his love for her, though it was from the heart that he wrote:

May Heaven permit you and me to enjoy the cool of the evening
of life in tranquility, undisturbed by the cares of politics and war—
and above all with the sweetest of all reflections that neither ambition, nor vanity, nor any base motive, or sordid passion through the
whole course of great and terrible events that have attended it, have
drawn us aside from the line of duty and the dictates of our con-
sciences. Let us have ambition enough to keep our simplicity, our
frugality, and our integrity, and transmit these virtues as the fairest
of inheritance to our children.

Peace was his dearest wish. But when ever would they see it? "The
events of politics are not less uncertain than those of war."

J OHN A DAMS WAS NOT UNSYMPATHETIC to the concerns of the
Comte de Vergennes and the Foreign Ministry. Nor was he ever so
obtuse about French sensibilities and the importance of maintaining
good relations with France as his detractors would later charge. "The
Court here have many differences to manage as well as we," he wrote
understandingly to Samuel Adams, "and it is a delicate thing to push
things in this country." While he believed candor essential in dealing
with the French, "harshness," he knew, was sure to ruin even the fairest
negotiations with them.

His great worry, as he reported to Congress, was that the French were
growing tired of the war. In fact, as Adams was unaware, Vergennes had
privately informed his king of a "need" for peace, while to a friend he
expressed but "feeble confidence" in the Americans. Further, Adams correctly suspected it was the French intention, once the war was ended, to
keep America poor and dependent—"Keep us weak. Make us feel our
obligations. Impress our minds with a sense of gratitude." He saw
acutely and painfully the dilemma of the French Alliance. Without
French help, the United States could not win the war, yet it was purely
for their own purposes that the French were involved.

Still, he felt no difficulty in dealing with Vergennes. Nor, interestingly, was he distressed with Franklin. In voluminous correspondence
with members of Congress and in his private writings, Adams had not a

complaining or disrespectful word to say about Franklin, nothing of the bitter disdain expressed in letters the year before.

But there now followed a chain of events that were to culminate in a serious rift with both Vergennes and Franklin. Probably it was inevitable.

On June 16, as had become routine, Adams sent Vergennes some latest items of news from America, these concerning the American currency. Three months before, on March 18, 1780, desperate to curb rampant inflation, Congress had resolved to devalue the dollar. It was a matter about which Vergennes already knew and, in passing along the information, Adams volunteered no opinion of Congress's policy. A few days later, however, Adams was summoned to Versailles for a discussion of the issue, during which he candidly voiced his approval of what Congress had done. Vergennes was as polite as always. "The conversation was long . . . very decent and civil on both sides," Adams would recall. But again Adams was telling the Foreign Minister what he already knew, since Adams had earlier expressed his views to Chaumont, who lost no time reporting the conversation to Vergennes.

Vergennes's situation was more complicated than Adams knew. There was dissension within the Foreign Ministry. The aged Prime Minister, Maurepas, was secretly making peace gestures to the British, and implying that the French might give way on support for American independence.

The easiest, most prudent step for Vergennes would have been to let the matter of the dollar cool for a while. Normally he would have taken it up with Franklin, the properly accredited minister to the Court, with whom he had never known the least discord. But it appears that he saw his chance. Having found no way to control Adams, he could now at last be rid of him.

In an official letter of June 21, Vergennes informed Adams that France opposed any revaluation of the American currency unless an exception were made for French merchants. He portrayed the measure as an act of bad faith on the part of America, implying it could have serious consequences to the alliance, and he called on Adams to request Congress to "retrace its steps and do justice to the subjects of the King."

If Vergennes was setting a trap—as it seems he was—Adams obliged by stepping into it, and perhaps knowingly. In a characteristically spirited, unambiguous letter, Adams made the case for revaluation and for no preferred treatment for French merchants, his purpose being to make clear his own views and those, he was sure, of Congress and the American people. "I thought it my indispensable duty to my country and to Congress, to France and the Count himself, to be explicit," he would say.

Revaluation was a necessity, he wrote. Congress had no other choice. And since most French merchants who dealt in armaments and military supplies had been paid in European currencies, they had little cause for complaint. Besides, their profits had been substantial. But the crux of the matter was that, in justice, no foreign merchant could possibly be granted better treatment than American merchants. It was that simple. "Foreigners, when they come to trade with a nation, make themselves temporary citizens, and tacitly consent to be bound by the same laws."

The letter was undoubtedly what Vergennes expected from Adams, and all that he needed—a written statement from Adams showing him to be in direct opposition to French policy and thus a threat to relations between France and America.

Adams, however, took this first real exchange of views with the aloof Foreign Minister as a long-awaited opportunity to broaden discussions on matters of more importance. The prospect of greater French military involvement in the war in America that had looked so promising earlier, appeared to have faded. While the army of Rochambeau had been sent to aid Washington, French warships had sailed not for the United States, as expected, but for the West Indies. Whatever the size of the armies of Washington and Rochambeau, Adams wrote emphatically, victory in America and an end to the war there would never come so long as the British were masters of the sea. The critical need was for a grand strategy whereby a French fleet would be deployed along the coast of the United States, to bottle up the British armies in the port cities where they were concentrated. Further, Adams argued, to keep a superior naval force on the coast of North America was "the best policy" for France, even were France to consider her own interests alone.

In another letter, raising again the naval question, Adams said he was "determined to omit no opportunity of communicating my sentiments to your excellency, upon everything that appears to me to be of importance to the common cause."

But Vergennes had had enough. On July 29, in a crushing reply, he ended any further communication with Adams. He would henceforth deal only with Franklin, he announced, and in a pointedly undiplomatic conclusion, informed Adams, *"Le Roi n'a pas eu besoin de vos sollicitations pour s'occuper des intérêts des États-Unis."* "The King did not stand in need of your solicitations to direct his attention to the interests of the United States."

A full set of Adams's letters were then delivered to Franklin, with an accompanying note from Vergennes saying, "The King expects that you will lay the whole before Congress." At the same time, a dispatch from the Foreign Minister went off to Philadelphia directing La Luzerne to see what could be done to have Adams recalled.

Franklin wrote a letter of his own to Congress, which he need not have. He could have merely forwarded the Adams letters as Vergennes requested and said little or nothing. But Franklin, too, it seemed had had enough of Adams. His letter was dated August 9, 1780, and while mild in tone and not entirely unfair in judgment, it was, as Franklin knew perfectly, a devastating indictment. Vergennes could not have wished for more, which may well have been Franklin's intent. "Mr. Adams has given extreme offense to the court here," it began.

> . . . having nothing else wherewith to employ himself, he seems to have endeavored to supply what he may suppose my negotiations defective in. He thinks, as he tells me himself, that America has been too free in expressions of gratitude to France; for that she is more obliged to us than we to her; and that we should show spirit in our applications. I apprehend that he mistakes his ground, and that this court is to be treated with decency and delicacy. The King, a young and virtuous prince, has, I am persuaded, a pleasure in reflecting on the generous benevolence of the action in assisting an oppressed people, and proposes it as a part of the glory of his reign. I think it right to increase this pleasure by our thankful acknowledgements, and that such an expression of gratitude is not only our duty, but our

interest. A different conduct seems to me what is not only improper and unbecoming, but what may be hurtful to us. Mr. Adams, on the other hand, who at the same time means our welfare and interest as much as I do or any man can do, seems to think a little apparent stoutness and greater air of independence and boldness in our demands will produce us more ample assistance. . . .

Mr. Vergennes, who appears much offended, told me yesterday that he would enter into no further discussions with Mr. Adams, nor answer any more of his letters. . . . It is my intention, while I stay here, to procure what advantages I can for our country by endeavoring to please this court.

Not for months was Adams to learn what Franklin had done. Nor was he to see Franklin or Vergennes again for an even longer time. For as Franklin also reported to Congress, Adams had by then departed Paris for Holland to see, as he told Franklin, "whether something might be done to render us less dependent on France."

II

IT WAS NOT HIS IDEA ALONE, or contrary to American intent. The prospect of securing financial help from the Dutch Republic had been talked about in Congress and at Paris for some time. The Dutch had been smuggling arms to America in quantity since before the French had become involved. More even than their French counterparts, Dutch merchants had grown rich in the trade, and so it seemed a reasonable prospect that Dutch money might also be available. Congress had considered sending a minister to Holland even before Adams left on his initial mission to France, and in his first months at Paris, he had reported that there was more friendship for America in Holland than generally understood. In advance of his second mission to Europe as peacemaker, Congress debated assigning Adams the additional task of negotiating a Dutch loan, but after concluding that a "distinct appointment" made better sense, named its former president, Henry Laurens of South Carolina, to seek a loan of $10 million. But Laurens was unable to depart for months to come, not until the summer of 1780.

Franklin, for his part, expressed strong disapproval of any such overt "suitoring" for alliances, preferring, as he said, that America, "a virgin state, should preserve the virgin character" and "wait with decent dignity for the applications of others." Apparently he saw no contradiction with his own "suitoring" at the Court of Versailles, or the irony that he, of all people, would preach the preservation of a "virgin character."

Adams, who had never lost interest in Holland, strongly disagreed, and from reports gathered since his return to Paris, he surmised that the chances for financial help from the Dutch were better than ever. He tried to convince Franklin and Vergennes of the need for a reconnaissance of the Low Countries, but without success. It was only when the strain of relations with Vergennes reached the breaking point that Vergennes acquiesced and provided Adams with the necessary passports, relieved to be rid of him.

With no support or consideration from either Vergennes or Franklin, Adams's position in Paris had become untenable. He longed for a change of scene. Above all, he longed to accomplish something, and was very quickly on his way to Amsterdam.

The venture was entirely of his own making. He went as a private citizen only, without authority, and, as it happened, wholly unaware that in June Congress had decided he should pursue exactly such a survey until Henry Laurens arrived. Optimism in Congress on the subject was as great as Adams's own.

For Adams, ever the independent man, it was a role of the kind he most loved—setting forth on his own against the odds in the service of the greatest of causes. For he genuinely believed the fate of the Revolution hung in the balance.

He removed his sons from the school at Passy and on July 27, accompanied by the servant Stephens, they were on their way north by coach, traveling fast over good roads to Compiègne and Valenciennes, through the finest farmland Adams had ever seen, at the height of one of the most abundant summers France had known. "The wheat, rye, barley, oats, peas, beans, and several other grains, the hemp, flax, grass, clover . . . the vines, the cattle, the sheep, in short everything upon this road is beautiful," observed the farmer from Braintree happily.

The boys, free from school and again in their father's company, felt a lift of spirits to match his own. "We passed by Mons, which is a city and a very pretty one," wrote thirteen-year-old John Quincy. "I never saw a more beautiful one in my life."

They rolled through Brussels and Antwerp. At Rotterdam, on a Sunday, attending services at an English church, they listened as the English preacher prayed that "a certain king" might have "health and long life and that his enemies might not prevail against him." Praying silently on his own, Adams asked that George III "be brought to consideration and repentance and to do justice to his enemies and to all the world."

From Rotterdam they continued by horse-drawn canal boat to Delft, then The Hague, the Dutch seat of government. On the approach to Amsterdam that evening the giant canvas sails of immense windmills turned ceaselessly on all sides, a spectacle such as they had never seen.

Holland was as far north as Adams had ever been in his travels and about as different from France as a place could be. Holland, the name commonly used for the Seven Provinces of the Netherlands (of which Holland was the richest and most populated province), had particular appeal to Americans. It was the tiny, indomitable republic which, in 1648, had formally won its independence from Spain, the mightiest empire of the time, after a war and truce that stretched over some eighty years. Like the United States, the Dutch Republic was born of war, and for more than a century had survived and prospered between two of the great, interminably warring powers of Europe, France and England. Adams would liken it to a frog hopping about between the legs of two battling bulls.

As America faced the challenge of a continental wilderness, Holland faced the North Sea. The extraordinary ingenuity and industry of the Dutch in wresting land from the sea were legendary. Still the actual spectacle of all that had been contrived and built, the innumerable canals, bridges, dams, dikes, sluices, and windmills needed to cope with water, to drain land, and hold back the sea—and that all had to be kept in working order so that life could go on—made first-time visitors stand back in awe, and New Englanders especially, knowing what they did of inhospitable climate and limited space. Francis Dana, when he arrived later, wrote of the Dutch living in a world made by hand. "The whole is an astonishing machinery, created, connected, constantly preserved by the labor, industry, and unremitting attention of its inhabitants at an expense beyond calculation."

Amsterdam alone had more than 500 bridges arching its web of canals. The pride of the city, its Town Hall, a massive structure of cut stone, stood, as almost every visitor was informed, on 13,659 wooden piles.

Predominantly Protestant, Holland was known for its tolerance, for allowing religious freedom to thousands of European Jews, French Huguenots, and other Christian sects. To New Englanders it was very nearly sacred ground, as the place where the English separatists known as the Pilgrims had found refuge in the seventeenth century, settling at Leyden for twelve years before embarking for Massachusetts.

The seventeenth century had been the Golden Age of the Dutch. In one of the most astonishing upsurges of commercial vitality in all history, they had become the greatest trading nation in the world, the leading shipbuilders and mapmakers. Amsterdam, the busiest port in Europe, became the richest city in the world, and with their vast wealth, the Dutch became Europe's money lenders.

In the arts and letters, it was the age of Rembrandt, Vermeer, Frans Hals, and van Ruysdael; of the poet Joost van den Vondel, of Grotius in theology and maritime law, Spinoza in philosophy. In the liberal atmosphere of seventeenth-century Holland, the French philosopher René Descartes found refuge and freedom to publish. John Locke, from whom Adams, Jefferson, and other American patriots drew inspiration, had published some of his earliest works while a political refugee in Amsterdam.

The Golden Age was long past by the time Adams arrived—Dutch maritime power and Dutch prestige were acknowledged to be "in decline"—yet business was thriving and visitors were struck by signs of Dutch prosperity on all sides. Amsterdam remained the commercial center of Europe. Its immense harbor thronged with shipping. "Wherever the eye ranges, masts and sails appear," wrote an English traveler. "Bells are sounding and vessels departing at all hours."

Beside the city's broad, tree-lined main canals, row upon row of elegant brick *grachtenhuizen* (canal houses) proclaimed the wealth of its merchant citizenry as did nothing else. Four and five stories tall, they were much alike in the Dutch manner, with stepped or bell-shaped gables and tall, sparkling windows of Dutch plate glass, which was considered something quite special. "The verdure of the trees reflecting strongly upon large windows which are kept bright and free of dust, add infinitely to their luster and magnificence," wrote a visiting American. The homes of the wealthiest families, the grandest houses of all, numbering in the hundreds along the Herengracht and the Keizersgracht (the Gentlemen's Canal and the Emperor's Canal), were as fine as any of the great city houses of Europe. And more even than the elegant façades, the interiors and furnishings of such houses—the marble floors, chinaware, leather-bound books, maps, and huge ebony-framed portraits of the merchants themselves or of their Golden Age patriarchs—bespoke generations of accumulated wealth and unrivaled position.

Commonly described as a kind of northern Venice, Amsterdam had none of the architectural grandeur of Venice and was subject to long, dank North Sea winters. Also, by late summer, the season when Adams arrived, many of the canals turned putrid-smelling, and "so laden with filth," an English woman wrote, "that on a hot day the feculence seems pestilential." Indeed, the Dutch climate was widely understood to be dangerous to the health. "Amsterdam fever" was a well-known and dreaded malady. Visitors who stayed too long could expect to be ill, it was said, though young James Boswell of London had written that one ought to experience no difficulty if one ate well, drank well, dressed properly, and took exercise. Of Amsterdam, however, Boswell had little to say beyond that it was a place where he could patronize brothels unobserved.

Adams found the city densely crowded and teeming with foreigners—French, English, and Americans, commercial agents, sea captains, journalists, tourists, and spies. In smoky cafés Dutch merchants and bankers drank coffee, pulled at clay pipes, and talked incessantly to all hours. The talk was open, spirited—an atmosphere made to order for Adams—and rife with high-blown speculation, most of which struck him as amusing, as he told Franklin in a friendly letter written soon after his arrival.

> One says America will give France the go by. Another that France and Spain will abandon America. A third that Spain will forsake France and America. A fourth that America has the interest of all Europe against her. A fifth that she will become the greatest manufacturing country and thus ruin Europe. A sixth that she will become a great and ambitious military and naval power, and consequently terrible to Europe.

Suspicious that there were too many Englishmen, and thus too many possible spies, in the hotel where he and the boys were staying, Adams found modest lodgings with an elderly widow, a "Madame La Veuve du Henry Schorn, of de Achterburgwal by de Hoogstrat," as he would give the new address.

To get his bearings he was out and about, walking the canals, studying the buildings, circumventing the entire city by foot, meeting people, glad to return to useful work. Through all his life Adams would be happiest when there was clear purpose to his days.

"Papa went out"; "Papa went out to dinner"; "Papa went out to take a walk," recorded John Quincy.

Adams knew no one, but from all that he saw and heard, and after meetings with a number of prominent Amsterdam bankers—Henrik Hooft, Jan de Neufville and son, Jacob and Nicholas van Staphorst—he grew highly optimistic. A "considerable" loan was entirely possible, he reported to Congress. Moreover, there was no better place in Europe in which to gather information or from which to circulate it.

In an exuberant letter to Abigail, he called Holland "the greatest curiosity in the world." He doubted there was any nation of Europe "more estimable than the Dutch, in proportion.

> Their industry and economy ought to be examples to the world. They have less ambition, I mean that of conquest and military glory, than their neighbors, but I don't perceive that they have more avarice. And they carry learning and the arts, I think, to a greater extent.

His only concerns were that the air was "not so salubrious" as that of France, and that the Dutch knew little at all about America, which he found astonishing.

When on September 16, Francis Dana turned up from Paris with the news that Congress had given Adams authority to work on securing a Dutch loan until Henry Laurens appeared, Adams notified John Thaxter to pack everything at the hotel in Paris and come at once. John Quincy and Charles were enrolled in Amsterdam's renowned Latin School, and Adams set to work. All his energy, zeal, stubborn determination, and his idealism, qualities that had seemed ill-suited at Versailles, were now to be brought to bear. In little time he cultivated an amazing range of friends among the press and in intellectual and financial circles, a number of whom were Jews who, Adams later said, were among the most liberal and accommodating of all.

He made a study of Dutch ways and temperament, read deeply in Dutch history, searching out ever more volumes in Amsterdam's numerous well-stocked bookshops. He struggled to learn the language, and in what seemed an equally daunting task, to fathom the complexities of the Dutch system of government.

Between times, he kept campaigning by mail for an American navy, his determination perhaps reinforced by a new appreciation of all that commerce at sea had meant to the Dutch. "If I could have my will, there should not be the least obstruction of navigation, commerce, or privateering," Adams wrote to Benjamin Rush, "because I firmly believe that *one* sailor will do us more good than *two* soldiers." To Congress he declared emphatically, *"A navy is our natural and only defense."*

In October, events took an unexpected turn, when word came from London that Henry Laurens, on his way to Amsterdam, had been captured at sea by a British man-of-war. Charged with high treason, Laurens was being held prisoner in the Tower of London, with "orders that no person whatever speaks to him," as Adams's London contact Thomas Digges reported. A sack containing Laurens's confidential papers had been thrown overboard from his ship too late and the British had hooked it from the sea. Among the papers was the draft of a proposed secret treaty between America and the Netherlands, a document of no real significance, but one the British were happy to use as a pretext for a show of angry indignation and threats of war, a possibility the Dutch dreaded as they did no other.

With the responsibility of securing a loan now squarely on his shoulders, and the likelihood of peace no nearer than before, Adams settled in for the long haul.

At home the war in the South was going badly. Charleston had fallen to the British. At Camden, South Carolina, General Horatio Gates had suffered a devastating defeat in a battle in which American soldiers had fled like sheep. Nearly 1,000 Americans had been killed and a thousand more captured. Gates had been a favorite general officer of the Congress and of Adams, and it had been one of the most disastrous defeats of the war.

But there must be no softening of resolve, Adams declared. "I think I see very clearly that America must grow up in war," he wrote to Congress. His own central task was to convince the Dutch that America would accept no outcome short of complete, irrevocable independence. Without that insurance, there would be no Dutch loan. Of this Adams was now absolutely certain.

> This country had been grossly deceived. It has little knowledge of the numbers, wealth, and resources of the United States, and less faith in their finally supporting independence, upon which alone a credit depends. They also have an opinion of the power of England vastly higher than the truth. Measures must be taken with great caution and delicacy to undeceive them.

With his phenomenal capacity for work—an attribute not lost on the industrious Dutch—he produced materials of every kind in an all-out effort to "undeceive" them, while at the same time providing Congress with some of the most astute political reporting of his diplomatic career. Help came from a number of his new Dutch friends, "people of the first character," as he said, who saw in the American struggle for independence hope for all humanity, and who, as Adams would long contend, never received the recognition they deserved.

Charles W. F. Dumas was a Dutch radical and friend of Franklin, a schoolmaster, linguist, and man of letters. Older than Adams by nearly fifteen years, he served faithfully as a translator and expert source of information.

John Luzac of Leyden, a lawyer, scholar, and editor, published in his *Gazette de Leyde* a steady variety of material supplied by Adams, including the first European translation of the new Massachusetts Constitution, which was to have an important effect in the Netherlands. In little time Luzac and Adams became the closest of friends.

Baron Joan Derk van der Capellen tot den Pol, a Dutch nobleman, had been the first and most prominent figure in the country to champion the American cause, and he greatly admired Adams's determination. Van der Capellen knew the majority of the Dutch sympathized with the

American Revolution, but astutely he advised Adams that only American success in the war would enlist Dutch credit, for all the expressions of good will and interest he would hear.

At The Hague, as Adams came to understand, there was little sympathy for the American cause, nor much hope for decisive action. The government of the country, maddeningly complicated to anyone unfamiliar with it, seemed devised intentionally to foster inertia. It was a republic, but with no real executive power, only a symbolic head of state, the hereditary Stadholder, William V, Prince of Orange, who was related to the British royal family and personally devoted to the status quo. As Adams explained to Congress, sovereignty resided in the national assembly, Their High Mightinesses, the States-General. Yet even they were but the deputies of the "regents" in the cities, a very select group of great influence. Thus, as Adams wrote, the true power lay in the cities and in Amsterdam in particular. "The burgomasters of Amsterdam . . . who are called the regency, are one integral branch of the sovereignty of the seven United Provinces, and the most material branch of all because the city of Amsterdam is one quarter of the whole Republic, at least in taxes."

Not until the government at The Hague took it upon itself to recognize the United States would anyone in the government be permitted to receive Adams officially. In actual practice nearly all would shun him. This being the case, it seemed only sensible to concentrate his efforts in Amsterdam, as both the money and the real political power were there.

But as Adams found, Dutch talk of financial support and an actual Dutch loan were decidedly different matters, his initial high expectations to the contrary. "No [banking] house that I have as yet thought it prudent to apply to dares to undertake the trust," he told Congress. The Netherlands had been too long allied with Britain, as a matter of commercial advantage. Dutch prosperity depended in large measure on British support for Dutch trade on the high seas. Dutch banks, moreover, held substantial loans to Britain. Hence, there was extreme reluctance to take any step, do anything rash, that might upset the British.

That November of 1780 the situation was further compounded by more dispiriting news from America. In September General Benedict Arnold had conspired to commit treason, to turn over the fortress at West Point to the British, and when found out, defected to the enemy. As Baron van der Capellen reported to Adams, Arnold's treachery, on top of the loss of Charleston and Gates's defeat at Camden, left Dutch confidence shattered. "Never has the credit of America stood so low," he told Adams, who advised Congress to "depend upon no money from hence."

All professions of Dutch friendship for America were but "little adulations to procure a share of our trade," and now even they had vanished like a vapor, as had his own prior exuberance and admiration for the Dutch.

A HARD NORTH SEA WINTER set in to match Adams's mood. Days were bitterly cold and raw, with darkness descending at four in the afternoon and the air of Amsterdam thick with chimney smoke. With the canals frozen, thousands of skaters took to the ice, a spectacle that provided what little cheer Adams found in life.

His health was suffering. He worried about his sons. At the Latin School, because he spoke no Dutch, John Quincy had been placed with elementary students. The boy grew restless and disheartened. The rector of the school thought him impertinent and merited a thrashing, as he informed his father. Adams's response was exactly what his own father's would have been. "Send the boys to me this evening," he answered. He had no wish to see his children subjected to such "littleness of soul," he explained to Abigail in a letter in which he gave vent not only to his indignation at the schoolmaster, but at what he had come to see as a decidedly unattractive side to the Dutch character that he had no desire to see rub off on his sons. "The masters are mean-spirited wretches, punching, kicking, and boxing the children upon every turn," he wrote.

No longer did he see the Dutch as "examples to the world," but perceived now, bitterly, "a general littleness arising from the incessant contemplation of stivers and doits [pennies and nickels], which pervades the whole people." Frugality and industry were virtues everywhere, but avarice and stinginess were not frugality.

> The Dutch say that without a habit of thinking of every doit before you spend it, no man can be a good merchant or conduct trade with success. This I believe is a just maxim in general. But I would never wish to see a son of mine govern himself by it. It is the sure and certain way for an industrious man to be rich. It is the only possible

way for a merchant to become the first merchant or the richest man in the place. But this is an object that I hope none of my children will ever aim at.

Through a young American named Benjamin Waterhouse, a student of medicine at the University of Leyden, Adams arranged for tutors for the two boys, and the opportunity for them to attend lectures at the university.

Such was the turmoil of Amsterdam that Adams now found it impossible even to arrange meetings. "Very few dare to see me," he reported. Searching desperately for a sign that all was not lost, the best he could come up with was the popularity of new songs full of patriotic resentment toward the English. A woman who sang one such song on an Amsterdam street corner sold six hundred copies in an hour, he informed Congress. But the hard truth was that after five months in the Dutch Republic, Adams had yet to meet a single government official of any importance.

In December, the veteran British ambassador to the Netherlands, Sir Joseph Yorke, began openly threatening the Dutch, setting off something very like panic. "War is to a Dutchman the greatest of evils," Adams wrote. "Yorke is so sensible of this that he keeps alive a continual fear of it." At year's end, "the high and mighty" Yorke abruptly departed and Britain commenced an undeclared war on Dutch shipping.

Convinced he must now gain recognition of American independence and arrange a Dutch-American alliance—and thus only, he had concluded, could he obtain a loan—Adams pressed Congress for greater authority. As winter progressed, his new commission arrived; Congress had designated him minister plenipotentiary to the Dutch Republic, which provided all the authority to be wished for.

Through February and March, despite the weather, Adams kept on the move, traveling back and forth between Amsterdam, Leyden, and The Hague, conferring with as many of his Dutch friends and contacts as possible. Again, as at Paris, the question was the timing of a formal announcement of his new powers.

Advised that his Amsterdam lodgings were too "obscure" for his new position, and that his effectiveness was being hurt by talk of this, Adams arranged for an American firm in Amsterdam to "hire" a suitable house—"the best house that is to be had at as cheap a rate as may be," he wrote—and to have it furnished "decent enough for any character in Europe to dine in with a republican citizen." In lengthy correspondence on the matter, he specified that the house be "large, roomy, and handsome, fit for the Hôtel des États-Unis d'Amérique." He would need two manservants and a "good cook" (whether male or female he did not care). A "genteel carriage" would be required, as well as a coachman, and Adams was particular that the livery be in the Paris mode: deep blue coat and breeches, scarlet cape and waistcoats. (He also wanted the clothes returned when the time came for the servants to leave.) This was "new work" for him, he added, having never set up housekeeping before.

At Versailles, meanwhile, the Comte de Vergennes was writing to his ambassador at Philadelphia to say that Adams, in his role in the Netherlands, had become an embarrassment, an observation that La Luzerne was expected to pass along to his numerous friends in Congress. Especially distressing to Vergennes was the thought of Adams ever having any say in a peace settlement. "[He] has a rigidity, an arrogance, and an obstinacy that will cause him to foment a thousand unfortunate incidents . . ."

BY ESTABLISHED DIPLOMATIC FORM, no emissary ever proclaimed his mission—his "public character"—until the government to which he was accredited was ready to receive him. To do otherwise was deemed not only appallingly bad form but altogether impractical.

By the time spring came, Adams had decided what he must do, no matter the diplomatic niceties. "America . . . has been too long silent in Europe," he wrote to Francis Dana. "Her cause is that of all nations and all men, and it needs nothing but to be explained to be approved."

Adams was by then at Leyden, settled temporarily with his sons, John Thaxter, and Benjamin Waterhouse, the medical student, in a house on a narrow street behind the Pieterskerk, the city's famous cathedral on the opposite side of the Rapenburg Canal from the university. It was the old quarter where the Pilgrims had lived during their years at Leyden, a connection deeply felt by Adams. A deacon at the cathedral would later relate, "Mr. Adams could not refrain from tears in contemplating this great structure."

On April 19, 1781, six years to the day from the battle of Lexington
and Concord, Adams completed and signed a sixteen-page memorial,
addressed to "Their High Mightinesses, the States-General of the United
Provinces of the Low Countries." A strong, even passionate appeal for
cooperation, it began by affirming that the American people were "unalterably determined" to maintain their independence and that if ever
there was a "natural alliance," it would be between the two republics of
the Netherlands and the United States. He recalled the years of asylum
that the Pilgrims had found among the Dutch. He recounted how New
York and New Jersey had been first settled by the Dutch, whose descendants and customs remained. Indeed, so close were the two republics in
history, religion, and government, Adams declared, "that every Dutchman instructed on the subject must pronounce the American revolution
just and necessary or pass a censure upon the greatest actions of his
immortal ancestors." And if such noble sentiments were not reason
enough for a Dutch-American bond, there was "the great and growing
interest of commerce," the "circumstance which perhaps in this age has
stronger influence than any other in the formation of friendships between
nations.

> It may not ... be amiss to hint that the central situation of this
> country, her extensive navigation, her possessions in the East and
> West Indies, the intelligence of her merchants, the number of her
> capitalists, and the riches of her funds, render a connection with her
> very desirable to America; and, on the other hand, the abundance
> and variety of the productions of America, the materials of manu-
> facturers, navigation, and commerce, the vast demand and con-
> sumption in America of the manufactures of Europe ... cannot
> admit of a doubt that a connection with the United States would be
> useful to this republic.

Adams was acutely aware of the magnitude of the step he was taking.
By breaking the rules of diplomatic convention—by embarking on his
own on what he called "militia diplomacy"—he was, he knew, risking
ridicule and enmity, and, in the event that things went sour, disgrace.
His entire mission was at stake, and who could say what the consequences would be at home if it were to fail. "But wise men know," he

would write, "that militia sometimes gain victories over regular troops, even by departing from the rules." It was the militia, after all, who had humiliated the British regulars at Lexington and Concord, on that earlier April 19.

For a man of such strong feelings and great inner tensions, these were days of extreme stress, during which he remained uncharacteristically silent, as Benjamin Waterhouse would recall in a telling description of Adams the morning he set off for The Hague, nine miles distant.

> I never shall forget the day and the circumstances of Mr. Adams's going from Leyden to The Hague with the memorial to their High Mightinesses, the States-General. . . . He came down into the front room where we were—his secretary, two sons, and myself—his coach and four at the door, and he, full-dressed, even to his sword, when with energetic countenance and protuberant eyes, and holding his memorial in his hand, said to us in a solemn tone, "Young men! Remember this day, for this day I go to The Hague to put seed in the ground that may produce good or evil—God knows which"—and putting the papers in his side pocket, he stepped into his coach and drove off alone, leaving us, his juniors, solemnized in thought and anxious, for he had hardly spoken to us for several days before—such was his inexpressible solitude.

At The Hague, Adams called first on the French ambassador, the young Duc de La Vauguyon, to inform him of his plan to present the memorial as soon as possible. La Vauguyon, a plump and personable young man whom Adams genuinely liked, spent the next several hours trying to dissuade him, urging that at the least he wait for an opinion from Vergennes. Adams refused. When, the following morning, La Vauguyon appeared at Adams's hotel to renew his plea, Adams again refused. He knew perfectly well that Vergennes would decide against him, Adams said, and there was no time to be lost.

> "What!" said the Duke [according to Adams's later rendition of the scene]. "Will you take responsibility of it upon yourself?" "Indeed, monsieur le Duc, I will; and I think I alone ought to be responsible, and that no other ambassador, minister, council, or court ought to be

answerable for anything concerning it. . . ." "Are you then determined?" "Determined, and unalterably determined, I am."

On Friday, May 4, 1781, at the Binnenhof, the Inner Courts, at The
Hague, Adams called on the Baron van Lynden van Hemmen, president
of the States-General for that week, and presented his memorial. And
with the energetic help of Dumas and Luzac, Adams had already
arranged for its publication in English, French, and Dutch, which was no
less important. Thousands of printed copies were made immediately
available. Newspapers were provided with the full text. In little time it
appeared throughout Europe.

That accomplished, Adams could do no more but wait for a reaction
from the Dutch government. They "will deliberate and deliberate and
deliberate," he wrote in despair, little imagining how right he was.

HE HAD BEEN AWAY from home now for more than a year, leaving Abigail to face two winters without him, the first of which had been the most
severe in forty years.

Her letters had never stopped, one season to another, though they
arrived sporadically and were nearly always five or six months out of
date. She wrote to him about the war and the severe weather. Sadly she
related the deaths of his brother Peter's wife, Mary, and of his mother's
husband, John Hall. His mother, she wrote, "desires her tenderest
regards to you, though she fears she shall not live to see your return."

Other letters were taken up with businesslike requests for trade goods,
as Adams was again supplying her with regular shipments. She ordered
silk gloves, ribbon, thread, fans, common calico, and handkerchiefs.
"Handkerchiefs will turn to good account for hard money," she reminded him. Only once did she request something for herself, a green
umbrella from Paris.

As she herself acknowledged, she found it impossible to write a short
letter, and to John Quincy and Charles came pages dispensing vigorous,
motherly exhortations. Strive to excel, she urged Charles. Anything
worth doing was worth doing well, she reminded them. Learning was not
attained by chance, but "must be sought for with ardor." She missed her
boys more than she could express, and worried more than ever once she

learned of the move to Holland, "a country so damp, abounding in stagnant water, the air of which is said to be very unfriendly to foreigners."

She tried to keep an even balance in her outlook, she told John. "I am not suddenly elated or depressed. I know America capable of anything she undertakes with spirit and vigor." No effort was too great for peace, no cost too dear, she wrote, and he must never doubt that his own part in serving that end meant everything to her.

> My whole soul is absorbed in the idea. The honor of my dearest friend, the welfare and happiness of this wide, extended country, ages yet unknown, depend for their happiness and security upon the able and skillful, the honest and upright discharge of the important trust committed to him. It would not become me to write the full flow of my heart upon this occasion.

Of the ordeal of separation, she said in closing, "I am *inured*, but not *hardened* to the painful portion. Shall I live to see it otherwise?"

Her letters were his great delight, he had assured her, so long as she did not complain, and she was determined to oblige. "I am wholly unconscious of giving you pain in this way since your late absence," she wrote as the second winter approached. "If I complained [before], it was from the ardor of affection which could not endure the least apprehension of neglect. . . . Sure I am that not a syllable of complaint has ever stained my paper in any letter I have ever written since you left me."

On Christmas Day, 1780, longing for him, she had written a letter he would not receive until nearly summer:

> My dearest friend,
>
> How much is comprised in that short sentence? How fondly can I call you mine, bound by every tie which consecrates the most inviolable friendship, yet separated by a cruel destiny, I feel the pangs of absence sometimes too sensibly for my own repose.
>
> There are times when the heart is peculiarly awake to tender impressions, when philosophy slumbers, or is over-powered by sentiments more conformable to nature. It is then that I feel myself alone in the wide world, without any one to tenderly care for me, or lend me an assisting hand through the difficulties that surround me. Yet

my cooler reason disapproves the ripening thought, and bids me bless the hand from which my comforts flow.

> *"Man active resolute and bold*
> *Is fashioned in a different mold."*

More independent by nature, he can scarcely realize all those ties which bind our sex to his. Is it not natural to suppose that as our dependence is greater, our attachment is stronger? I find in my own breast a sympathetic power always operating upon the near approach of letters from my dearest friend. I cannot determine the exact distance when this secret charm begins to operate. The time is sometimes longer, sometimes shorter. The busy sylphs are ever at my ear, no sooner does Morpheus close my eyes, than "my whole soul, unbounded flies to thee." Am I superstitious enough for a good Catholic?

A Mr. Ross [John Ross, a merchant from Nantes] arrived lately at Philadelphia and punctually delivered your letters. At the same time a vessel arrived from Holland and brought me yours from Amsterdam of the 25th of Sept[ember], which Mr. Lovell was kind enough to forward to me. I have written to you largely since Davis [Captain Edward Davis of the *Dolphin*] arrived here, though not in reply to the letters brought by him, for old Neptune alone had the handling of them. He was chased [by British cruisers] and foolishly threw over all his letters into the sea, to my no small mortification.

How many of Adams's letters had indeed been lost to Neptune, there was no reckoning. But for reasons unknown—and perhaps unknown even to him—Adams appears to have been writing to her hardly at all. In the first half of 1781, to judge by the letters she received, he wrote only once in the first three months and briefly, then briefly again in April, to say he had taken a house in Amsterdam beside the Keizersgracht. Another letter followed in May, another in June, which made four letters in six months and all mostly matter of fact, except that once he wrote, "Oh!Oh!Oh! that you were here."

He told her little of his work or about the boys—nothing, for example, of the fact that Charles had been severely ill at Leyden. It was as if all his concentration and energy were taken up by his dogged struggle. In the grip of constant uncertainty and stress—and having no successes to report—he preferred to keep silent. He was as preoccupied as he had ever been, and miserably unhappy; and in such a state of mind, as time would show, he was often disinclined to write to her. He abandoned his diary. Only to John Quincy, interestingly, did he pour forth in customary fashion, in letters filled with advice and affection.

IN THE TIME HE HAD SPENT with his eldest son since the voyage of the *Boston*, it had become clear to Adams that the boy was not only exceptionally bright, but capable of concentrated work to a degree well beyond his years, a judgment confirmed by Benjamin Waterhouse, who wrote of John Quincy bearing down on his lessons "with a constancy rarely seen at that age." (There was no longer a problem of language for the boy, since university lectures were conducted in Latin.)

"You are now at a university where many of the greatest men have received their education," Adams reminded him. He must attend all the lectures possible, in law, medicine, chemistry, and philosophy. He must make a study of all the departments and regulations of the celebrated university, "everything in it that may be initiated in the universities of your own country." Yet when John Quincy asked if he might buy ice skates that winter, Adams consented without hesitation, explaining that skating should be considered a fine art. "It is not simple velocity or agility that constitutes the perfection of it, but grace." Of riding, fencing, and dancing, he also approved, adding, "Everything in life should be done with reflection."

He sent a gift of several volumes of Pope, and a fine edition of a favorite Roman author, Terence, in both Latin and French. "Terence is remarkable, for good morals, good taste, and good Latin," Adams advised. "His language has simplicity and an elegance that make him proper to be accurately studied as a model." On hearing that John Quincy's course of studies did not include Cicero and Demosthenes, Adams could hardly contain his indignation. John Quincy must begin upon them at once, he declared, "I absolutely insist upon it." If forced to it, he would bring John Quincy back from Leyden and teach him himself.

Adams was writing about what he so dearly loved to the son he so dearly loved. That he was raising the boy to serve his country one day, there was never a question.

Latin and Greek were not all that mattered. John Quincy must neither forget nor fail to enjoy the great works of his own "mother tongue," and especially those of the poets. It was his happiness, too, that mattered.

> Read somewhat in the English poets every day. You will find them elegant, entertaining, and constructive companions through your whole life. In all the disquisitions you have heard concerning the happiness of life, has it ever been recommended to you to read poetry?
>
> . . . You will never be alone with a poet in your pocket. You will never have an idle hour.

"You will ever remember that all the end of study is to make you a good man and a useful citizen," Adams said at the close of a letter in May. "This will ever be the sum total of the advice of your affectionate father."

AT PARIS AND PHILADELPHIA all the while, movements were under way to dislodge John Adams as sole American peacemaker in Europe. Distressed by the mounting cost of the war, Vergennes was ready to see it concluded, and, if need be, to compromise with Britain on the question of American independence. Since he could not have the intractable Adams standing in the way, the French Foreign Minister sent specific instructions to La Luzerne to do whatever necessary to have Adams removed. La Luzerne, who had become a figure of conspicuous importance in Philadelphia, his influence with Congress as great as that of anyone, worked assiduously. With money to spend, he bribed at least one member of Congress, General John Sullivan, and possibly others besides.

Benjamin Franklin's letter of August 9, describing Vergennes's displeasure with Adams, had only recently arrived in Philadelphia and ignited sharp debate. On one side were those like Samuel Adams and James Lovell, who strongly supported John Adams's independent spirit and were unwilling that the United States give way always to the wishes of the French. On the other side stood those like John Witherspoon and young James Madison of Virginia, who trusted the French and believed French friendship and support of such critical importance that nothing should be allowed to put the alliance at risk, and who had little faith in John Adams's "stiffness and tenaciousness of temper," as Witherspoon said in his clipped Scottish way.

Appearing before a congressional committee considering the "conduct of Mr. Adams," La Luzerne stated the need for an American plenipotentiary who would "take no step without the approbation of his Majesty," and who, furthermore, would "receive his directions from the Comte de Vergennes."

On June 15, 1781, after hours of argument, Congress agreed to be governed by the dictates of the French Court. John Adams's powers as sole peacemaker with Britain were revoked. He was not to be recalled, as Vergennes wished and as La Luzerne had nearly succeeded in bringing about. Instead, he was to be one of five commissioners, each representing a major section of the country—Adams for New England, Franklin for Pennsylvania, John Jay for New York, Jefferson for Virginia, and Henry Laurens for the Deep South. But with Jay in Spain, Henry Laurens locked up in the Tower of London, Jefferson unlikely to leave Virginia, and Adams tied down with his assignment in Holland, there remained only Franklin to serve as the American negotiator at Paris, exactly as Vergennes desired.

Further, it was determined in a secret session of Congress that the commissioners were to do nothing in the negotiations for peace "without [the] knowledge and concurrence" of the ministers of their "generous ally, the King of France." Thus all decisions were subject to the approval of Foreign Minister Vergennes. In treating with the British, France was to have the final say, again exactly as Vergennes wished.

Congressman Thomas Rodney of Delaware, who had fought the measure, wrote that night to his older brother, Caesar. "I think it must convince even the French Court that we are reduced to a weak and abject state and that we have lost all that spirit and dignity which once appeared in the proceedings of Congress."

A few weeks later, and again in secret session, on a motion from James Madison, Adams's second prior commission, to negotiate a treaty of commerce with Britain, was also revoked.

At Braintree, Abigail had picked up word that Franklin was "blacking" the character of John Adams. "You will send me by first opportunity the whole of this dark process," she wrote straight away to James Lovell, and then let fly in a fury with her pen. Seldom in history has a wife so stoutly risen in defense of her "good man."

> Was the man [Adams] a gallant, I should think he had been monopolizing the women of the enchanter [Franklin]. Was he a modern courtier, I should think he had outwitted him in court intrigue. Was he a selfish, avaricious, designing, deceitful villain, I should think he had encroached upon the old gentleman's prerogatives.

"It needs great courage, sir, to engage in the cause of America," she added, fiercely proud of her "Mr. A."

> He is a good man. Would to heaven we had none but such in office. You know, my friend, that he is a man of principle, and that he will not violate the dictates of his conscience to ingratiate himself with a minister, or with your more respected body.
> Yet it wounds me, sir. When he is wounded, I bleed.

In early summer 1781, Francis Dana received notification from Congress that he was to proceed from Holland to St. Petersburg to seek recognition of the United States by the government of the Empress Catherine the Great of Russia. As Dana spoke little French and would need secretarial help, he asked Adams if John Quincy might accompany him. It would be an expedition of nearly 1,200 miles to a capital city few Americans had ever seen. But Adams thought highly of Dana, the boy excelled at French, and the experience, Adams felt, would stand him well for the future.

At the same time, Adams decided that young Charles, whose health remained uneven and who had become desperately homesick for his mother, should return to her in the care of Benjamin Waterhouse, who was on his way back to Boston.

"I consented [to the departure of both boys] . . . and thus deprived myself of the greatest pleasure I had in life," Adams later wrote. But before either departed, Adams himself was off to Paris, summoned by

Vergennes to take part in discussions of a possible mediation of the war by Russia and Austria. Nothing was more abhorrent to Adams than the prospect of a truce determined by France and other European powers and he headed south gravely worried.

John Quincy was gone on a "long journey with Mr. Dana . . . as an interpreter," was as much as he reported to Abigail in a letter from Paris dated July 11, John Quincy's fourteenth birthday. Charles was coming home, he also told her, but how or when he did not say, as probably he dared not for the boy's safety. "He is a delightful child, but has too exquisite sensibility for Europe." He himself was "distracted with more cares than ever," he wrote, "yet I grow fat. Anxiety is good for my health, I believe."

To Adams's immense relief, the discussions at Paris came to nothing, and by the month's end he was back in Holland in time to spend a few weeks with Charles. In mid-August, the eleven-year-old boy sailed on the *South Carolina*, which, after a troubled voyage, put in at La Coruña, Spain, where eventually he sailed on another American ship, *Cicero*, a privateer, and after more delays and adventures reached home at the end of January 1782, more than five months after leaving Amsterdam.

Adams was by then established in his commodious new residence in Amsterdam on the Keizersgracht. While not so grand as the houses along the Herengracht, the next canal nearer the center of the city, it was, as he had requested, perfectly "fit for the Hôtel des États-Unis d'Amérique"—a fine, red-brick canal house five stories tall, with a handsome front door at the top of a short flight of stone steps. There was a deep garden to the rear and the view from the large front windows included a pretty little arched bridge that crossed the Keizersgracht at the nearby corner, at Spiegelstraat, or Looking Glass Street. In the sunshine of summer, the trees bordering the canal cast lovely shadows on the water and on the façades of houses on the opposite side.

But to Adams, absorbed in his work, the outlook was bleak. Try as he could, the Dutch seemed to care only for their own commercial self-interests. He wondered if they were a people deficient in heart.

On August 24, with the arrival of a packet of letters from Congress sent on by Franklin from Paris, Adams learned that his commission as peacemaker had been revoked and a new commission established. He tried to maintain a good front. "Congress may have done very well to join

others in the commission for peace who have some faculties for it," he
wrote to Franklin. "My talent, if I have one, lies in making war."

Exhausted, his sons gone, Francis Dana gone, and with no reason to
think his mission to Holland anything but a failure, Adams fell ill. Nothing more was heard from him for six weeks.

THE ILLNESS, mild at first, grew steadily worse to the point that he lay
near death in the house by the canal. Several leading physicians came and
went. For several days he lost consciousness. Not until October was he
able to draft a letter, to say he had fallen victim to a "nervous fever," the
common, if imprecise, term used by the attending physicians. His fullest
description of what happened would be to Abigail, in a letter of October
9, when he was just barely able to hold a pen.

> Soon after my return from Paris, I was seized with a fever, of
> which, as the weather was and had long been uncommonly warm, I
> took little notice, but it increased very slowly and regularly, until it
> was found to be a nervous fever of a dangerous kind, bordering on
> putrid. It seized upon my head in such a manner that for five or six
> days I was lost, and so insensible to the operations of the physicians
> and surgeons as to have lost the memory of them. My friends were so
> good as to send me an excellent physician and surgeon whose skill
> and faithful attention, with the blessing of Heaven, saved my life.
> . . . I am, however, still weak, and whether I shall be able to recover
> my health among the pestilential vapors from these stagnant
> waters, I know not.

Writing a week later to the new president of Congress, Thomas
McKean, Adams added that the doctors had administered the "all powerful [Peruvian] bark"—quinine—and that this, too, had helped to save
him from a "nervous fever of a very malignant kind." To his Dutch colleague Charles Dumas, Adams wrote that "my feet had well nigh stum-
bled on dark mountains," and that he had recovered only through the
"wondrous virtue" of Peruvian bark.

In medical texts of the time, "nervous fever," or "slow nervous fever,"
was defined as an "insidious and dangerous" malady that began with list-

lessness, followed by chills, flushes of heat, "and a kind of weariness all over, like what is felt after a great fatigue.

> This is always attended with a sort of heaviness and dejection of spirit [wrote Dr. John Huxham, Fellow of the Royal College of Physicians at Edinburgh, in a treatise published in 1779] . . . the head grows more heavy, or giddy . . . the pulse quicker. . . .
>
> In this condition the patient often continues for five or six days. . . . About the seventh or eighth day the giddiness, pain, or heaviness of the head become much greater . . . and [this] frequently brings on delirium . . . Now nature sinks apace.

Most susceptible to the disease, it was thought, were those of "weak nerves," or who had experienced a "long dejection of spirits," or who had been "confined long in damp and foul air."

Quite possibly Adams had fallen victim to malaria, which in the heat of summer could be rampant in European seaports. Later, he would tell Abigail that the fever had "burnt up" half his memory and half his spirits. Like headache, fatigue, chills, and hot flashes, a subsequent depression or "melancholia" is also characteristic of the disease, which was thought then to emanate from stagnant water or foul air, "miasma," but, in fact, as would be learned a century later, is transmitted by mosquitoes.

But his "nervous fever" could also have been typhus, a disease characterized by high fever and delirium, and transmitted by lice.

That Adams's fatigue and "dejection of spirits" of that summer could have made him vulnerable to such a collapse is certainly possible. Notwithstanding his claim to Abigail to the contrary, anxiety was not at all good for his health. He himself would later say that excessive fatigue and anxiety concerning the state of his affairs in Holland, as well as the "unwholesome damps of the night," had brought him as "near to death as any man ever approached without being grasped in his arms."

More than a month would pass before Adams felt reasonably well again, and some symptoms of the fever would drag on, or recur long afterward, another characteristic of malaria. Six months later he would write of his "fever" and "feeble knees"; a year and a half later, he would tell Abigail the consequences of "Amsterdam fever" were still plaguing him.

In addition, others in the house—Thaxter, Stephens, and another of the servants—were stricken in the same way, which did little to improve the atmosphere. Adams would describe Stephens, a robust man who had never been ill, as "almost shaken to pieces" by fever, "reduced almost to a shadow." In all, it was as low a time as Adams ever knew.

His first letter to anyone, even before his letter to Abigail, was to Franklin on October 4, and in John Thaxter's hand. Only Adams's signature was his own. Having explained his long silence, he again stressed his acceptance of the new five-man peace commission, claiming he had actually been consoled by the change during the weeks when it appeared he might have nothing more ever to do with commissions of any sort. Particularly, he had been thinking about Jefferson and was eager to know if Franklin had any further word.

> Have you any information concerning Mr. Jefferson, whether he had accepted the trust? Whether he has embarked, or proposes to embark? I saw a paragraph in a Maryland paper which expressed apprehension that he was taken prisoner by a party of horse [cavalry] in Virginia?

In reply, Franklin expressed sincere concern for Adams's health, and said that while he had no further information on Jefferson, he very much doubted the truth of the story of his having been taken prisoner.

In mid-October, so low he could see no hope or purpose in anything, Adams wrote as downhearted a letter as any he ever sent to Congress. His efforts to raise money were "useless," his health wretched, his life in Europe so "gloomy and melancholy" and of such little use to the public "that I cannot but wish it may suit with the views of Congress to recall me." It was, as he doubtless knew, a request Congress would ignore.

Gradually his strength returned, his outlook improved. If nothing else, he could take his new reduced status as peace commissioner gallantly, put a good face on the matter, show no anger or disappointment, no animosity toward Congress or toward Franklin, and he urged Abigail to do the same. "Don't distress yourself... about any malicious attempts to injure me in the estimation of my countrymen. Let them take their course and go the length of their tether," he wrote. "The contemptible essays made by you-know-whom will only tend to their own confusion.... Say as little about it as I do."

He longed for his "dearest friend." "What a fine affair it would be if we could flit across the Atlantic as they say the angels do from planet to planet. I would dart to Penn's Hill and bring you over on my wings."

"Ah my dear John, where are you?" she was writing at home at almost the same time. "Two years, my dearest friend, have passed away since you left your native land." She was buying land in the new state of Vermont, she told him, a retreat in the woods where they could retire from the vexations and hazards of public life. In fact, she was well on the way to accumulating more than 1,000 acres in Vermont. "Do you not sometimes sigh for such a seclusion?" she asked.

There was talk of a future role for him in Massachusetts politics, but she had no such ambition. "I know the voice of fame to be a mere weathercock, unstable as water and fleeting as a shadow." Yet she did have pride, she conceded. "I know I have a large portion of it."

Her Vermont plans interested him not at all. "God willing I will not go to Vermont," he would write. "I must be within the scent of the sea."

AT THE END OF NOVEMBER came sensational news. On Friday, October 19, 1781, at Yorktown, Virginia, by Chesapeake Bay, the British General Cornwallis had surrendered his army to a combined American and French force under Washington and Rochambeau.

It was as decisive a defeat of the British as Saratoga and made possible by the arrival of Admiral de Grasse with the French West Indies fleet of twenty-eight ships of the line at exactly the right place at exactly the right time. The British had been trapped, just as Washington would have been on Long Island early in the war had the British fleet been able to close off the East River. More than 7,000 British troops had put down their arms, more even than at Saratoga.

To many on both sides of the Atlantic, it presaged a quick end to the war. In America, in the first flush of victory, Washington was hailed as "the deliverer" of his country; in London the British Prime Minister, Lord North, exclaimed, "Oh, God! It's all over."

Adams received "the glorious news" at Amsterdam the night of November 23. He was elated and took untold satisfaction from the knowledge that French sea power after all had proved decisive. It had been nearly three years since he told Vergennes that nothing would so guarantee a "speedy conclusion" to the war as a powerful French fleet in American waters, and now it had come to pass exactly as he had said.

Adams did not see Yorktown as the end of the struggle, however. The British still occupied major ports, including New York, and there would be no peace, he was sure, as long as a single company of British soldiers were at liberty anywhere in the United States. But if Yorktown did not mean an end to the war, it changed everything in Holland, as Adams saw at once. The chance to achieve his goal of Dutch recognition and financial support would never be better—Dutch merchants had no wish to be on the losing side.

Still "feebled" in health, he immediately met with the Duc de La Vauguyon and by mid-December could happily report to Congress that the French ambassador himself had said it was time Adams "demanded" an answer to his memorial of April, and do all in his power to secure a Dutch loan. "He thinks that I may now assume a higher tone, which the late *Cornwallization* will well warrant."

As the new year commenced, Adams was at The Hague audaciously demanding a "categorical answer." The president of the week, Bartholomeus van den Santheuvel, reported Adams's inquiry to Their High Mightinesses, the States-General, and so the question of American independence and Dutch-American relations became a matter of political debate throughout the country.

Adams then, in effect, took his case to the people of the Netherlands, calling for citizen petitions to the government for the recognition of the United States, and at the moment when popular sentiment against Britain was strongly on the rise. He went personally to the individual residences at The Hague for the delegations of eighteen cities in the province of Holland, each of which, as he explained to Congress, could be considered an independent republic. At every house, the reception was the same—approval, affection, esteem for the United States. Clearly, the campaign that he and his collaborators—Luzac, Dumas, van der Capellen—had launched to educate the Dutch people about the United States and its cause had not been in vain.

Nor did the collaborators cease to press for action. Van der Capellen in particular warned that alienating the Americans could damage trade with them and that it would be quite unwise to offend any further someone of such rectitude and importance as John Adams. "I know the unflinching character of Mr. Adams," he wrote. "I know that it has been a sore point, and I shudder for the consequences if we embitter a man of his influence, one of the principal founders of American freedom."

With the outlook brighter than it had ever been, Adams began receiving communications from Robert R. Livingston, who had been newly elected by Congress as the first Foreign Secretary—a choice the French ambassador, La Luzerne, boasted with some exaggeration to the Comte de Vergennes that he himself had arranged. Strongly allied with those in Congress who were well disposed toward the French, Livingston regarded Adams as imprudent and considered his April 19 memorial to the Dutch Court "a ridiculous display." In November he demanded that Adams explain his actions, and in a tone bound to infuriate Adams.

> We learned from Mr. Dumas that you have presented your credentials to the States-General. We are astonished that you have not written on so important a subject and developed the principles that induced you to declare your public character before the States were disposed to acknowledge it.

In a vigorous response, dated February 26, Adams recounted and explained his conduct in detail. The memorial had been exactly what the situation called for. The opposition of the Duc de La Vauguyon at the time had only confirmed the necessity of it. As for criticism of his own vanity or of his "militia diplomacy," he wrote: "The charge of vanity is the last resort of little wits and mercenary quacks, the vainest men alive, against me and measures that they can find no other objection to. . . . I have long since learned that a man may give offense and yet succeed."

It was a remarkable letter—lucid, knowledgeable, and candid, if flagrantly self-congratulatory. Warming to the subject of his memorial, he portrayed it as the great catalyst for turning the entire point of view of the Dutch and thus affecting all Europe. But then he recovered himself, and with appealing self-deprecation evoked a favorite image from Aesop: " 'What dust we raise,' said the fly upon the chariot wheel. It is impossible not to prove that this whole letter is not a similar delusion to that of the fly."

On February 26, 1782, the northern province of Friesland voted to instruct its delegates in the States-General to move formally to receive

John Adams as minister from the United States. "Friesland is said to be a sure index of national sense," Adams reported to Robert Livingston. "I am told that the Friesians never undertake anything but they carry it through."

Certain that full Dutch recognition was at hand, Adams and Charles Dumas purchased what they anticipated would be the American embassy at The Hague, a "large elegant" house on the Fluwelen Burgwal—Street of the Velvet Makers—beside one of the city's most beautiful canals.

"Your humble servant has lately grown much into fashion in this country," Adams reported to Abigail, having at last genuinely good news for her. "Some folks will think your husband a negotiator, but it is not to be, it is General Washington at Yorktown who did the substance of the work, the form only belongs to me."

ON MARCH 20 IN LONDON, in a dramatic appearance in the House of Commons, Lord North resigned, to be succeeded by Lord Rockingham, a friend of America whose earlier Ministry had repealed the Stamp Act. In a great shift of government, Charles James Fox, who was known to favor immediate recognition of American independence, became Foreign Secretary and to the post of Secretary of Colonial Affairs was named Lord William Shelburne, who, though he opposed American independence, sent a retired Scottish merchant named Richard Oswald to Paris to sound out Benjamin Franklin on the prospect of negotiations.

In the Netherlands the tide turned on March 28, when the Province of Holland recognized American independence. In rapid order the other provinces followed suit.

On Friday, April 19, a year to the day since Adams presented his memorial, the States-General resolved that "Mr. Adams shall be admitted and acknowledged in the quality of ambassador of the United States to Their High Mightinesses." When, the following day, Adams came to the assembly to present his letter of credence, it was as sweet a moment of triumph and vindication as he had ever known.

On Monday, April 22, at the Huis ten Bosch Palace at The Hague, Adams was received by His Most Serene Highness the Prince of Orange,

William V, and his wife Princess Wilhelmina in a ceremony of formal recognition. The day after, as Adams took particular pleasure in informing Robert Livingston, the French ambasador "made an entertainment for the *corps diplomatique* in honor of the United States, at which he introduced their minister to all the foreign ministers of this Court . . . and the Duc de La Vauguyon more than compensated for the stiffness of some of the others by paying more attention to the new brother than to the old fraternity."

All but speechless with pleasure, Adams heard the Spanish ambassador praise him for his determination and spirit, saying he had "struck the greatest blow that has been struck in the American cause, and the most decisive. It is you who have filled this nation with enthusiasm. It is you who have turned all on their heads." The tribute was one Adams would quote repeatedly in letters, and understandably, given his elation and the spirit of the moment.

The American minister became the toast of the Dutch Republic. Poems and songs were written in celebration of American independence; engraved portraits were published of the American heroes Washington and Adams. La Vauguyon, in a letter to Vergennes, reported that everywhere the recognition of America and the reception of Adams as envoy "arouses the liveliest transports of joy."

In May, Adams took up residence and put out a flag at the United States House, as he called it, the first American embassy anywhere in the world.

Yet for all this, his efforts to obtain Dutch financial help became no easier; and for all his own abundant self-satisfaction in the part he had played, he appreciated how much else had influenced the outcome. "The resolution which has taken place in this nation," he told Edmund Jenings, "is the result of a vast number and variety of events, comprising the great scheme of Providence. . . . When I recollect the circumstances, I am amazed, and feel that it is no work of mine."

AT LAST, on June 11, 1782, Adams negotiated with a syndicate of three Amsterdam banking houses—Willink, Van Staphorst, and De la Lande & Fynje—a loan of 5 million guilders, or $2 million at 5 percent interest.

It was not the $10 million Congress had expected Henry Laurens to secure, but it was an all-important beginning. It was money desperately needed at home and a foundation for American credit in Europe.

"If this had been the only action of my life, it would have been well spent," Adams wrote to Abigail, hoping she would "Pardon the vanity."

He was writing to her again and at length. He thought it unlikely that anyone would understand or appreciate the struggle and aggravation he had been through, the doubts, timidity, and hostilities he had had to contend with. "I have rendered a most important and essential service to my country here, which I verily believe no other man in the world would have done," he confided. "I don't mean by this that I have exerted any abilities here, or any action, that are not very common, but I don't believe that any other man in the world would have had the patience and perseverance to do and to suffer what was absolutely necessary."

Untrained in diplomacy and by temperament seemingly so unsuited for it, he had indeed succeeded brilliantly, as others and history would attest. He thought it no life for him—"I must be an independent man," he reminded her—and possibly he was as ready to give it up as he claimed. ("A child was never more weary of a whistle than I am of embassies.") But nothing he had done in the service of his country had given such satisfaction. No matter that the Dutch Republic was one of the "lesser theaters" of Europe, or that other events in which he had played a decisive part would rank higher in the balance. It had been his own path that he had taken, alone and in his own way. He had been ignored, ridiculed; he had very nearly died in the process. Yet he had persisted and succeeded.

Sometimes it was necessary to be "assuming," he observed in a letter to Edmund Jenings. Had he followed the advice and exhortations he was subjected to, and suspended operations to request instructions, he would have been forbidden to proceed as he had and most likely Holland would have signed a separate peace with England. "Thanks to God that he gave me stubbornness when I know I am right."

Ironically, a letter was en route that June from Robert Livingston demanding to know why in his reports to Congress Adams had included nothing about the dockyards and arsenals of Holland, or the ships preparing for sea, or anything about the leading members of the Dutch government. "You have not repeated your private conversations with them, from which infinitely more is to be collected than from all the pamphlets scattered about the streets," lectured Livingston, who had never set foot in Europe or served in a diplomatic role.

> If they avoid your company and conversation it is a more unfavorable symptom than any you have mentioned, and shows clearly that your public character should have been concealed 'til your address had paved the way for its being acknowledged. . . . None of your letters take the least notice of the French ambassador at The Hague. Is there no intercourse between you? If not, to what is it to be attributed?

The news that the Dutch Republic had recognized the United States did not reach Philadelphia until September, arriving by a Dutch ship named *Heer Adams*.

At noon, Tuesday, October 8, 1782, Adams arrived at the State House at The Hague to sign a treaty of commerce with the Dutch Republic. Deputies from the provinces of Holland and Zeeland stood waiting at the top of the stairs to escort him to the gilded Trèveszaal, or Truce Hall. With its elaborate frescoed ceiling and tall French doors overlooking a small lake and fountain, it could have been a chamber at Versailles, and as the ceremony proceeded ever so slowly, Adams had ample time to look about.

Finally, it was his turn, the treaty was signed and sealed, his work accomplished.

III

IN LATE SEPTEMBER, John Jay dispatched an urgent note to John Adams from Paris to report that the British emissary Richard Oswald had received a formal commission to treat with the United States on the matter of peace. Jay pressed Adams to come to Paris as soon as possible and cautioned that he "say nothing of this 'til you see me."

It was only with his treaty of commerce with the Dutch completed that Adams felt free to leave, but even then he seems to have been in no hurry to get to Paris. He hardly knew what to think about the prospect of making peace, he told Abigail. It could be "troublesome business," "another furnace of affliction," yet his spirits were high. "Yet I am very gay, more so than usual. I fear nothing. Why should I?"

The third week of October he started for Paris by carriage and six horses. With him were John Thaxter and an additional new secretary for the work at Paris, Charles Storer, a recent graduate of Harvard. Miserable weather slowed their progress. Unrelenting rain turned the road to a river of mud. The carriage broke down. But it was of Adams's own choice that he lingered over a private collection of Rubens altarpiece at Antwerp, and an altarpiece by Rubens that he thought "beautiful beyond description." Twenty-five miles north of Paris, he stopped again to tour the famous château at Chantilly, its stables and gardens, as though time were of no concern. It was a perfect autumn day that he would mark with a particularly lovely passage in his diary, revealing in a few lines the degree to which the hard-headed, intractable New Englander was, in the expression of the time, a man of "sensibility."

> While we were viewing the statue of Montmorency, Mademoiselle de Bourbon came out into the round house at the corner of the castle dressed in beautiful white, her hair uncombed, hanging and flowing about her shoulders, with a book in her hand, and leaned over the bar of iron, but soon perceiving that she had caught my eye and that I viewed her more attentively than she fancied, she rose up with that majesty and grace which persons of her birth affect if they are not taught, turned her hair off of both her shoulders with her hands in a manner that I could not comprehend, and decently stepped back into the chamber and was seen no more.

He reached Paris and the Hôtel de Valois that night. The following day, October 27, having bathed in a public bathhouse by the Seine and called for the services of a Parisian tailor and wigmaker, he was ready to take up his part in the negotiations.

Much had already transpired, as Adams learned from meetings with John Jay and a young American merchant named Matthew Ridley, whom Adams had met earlier in Holland and who, though he had no official role, seemed to know all that was going on.

Jay had arrived in Paris from Spain in June, and through most of the summer he and the British representative Richard Oswald had been in discussions centered on the recognition of American independence as a mandatory precursor to any talk of peace. Franklin had been absent from the talks, ill with the gout and bladder stones, and little progress was made. But in the last days of September, Oswald received word from London empowering him to treat with the ministers of the United States of America, not the American colonies, and at once the discussions took on a new air.

From their first meeting Jay and Adams found they were of like mind on most matters. "[Mr. Adams] is much pleased with Mr. Jay," Ridley wrote in his diary. "Mr. Adams is exceedingly pleased with Mr. Jay," Ridley added after several more meetings. Jay, in his diary, recorded only of Adams that he "spoke freely what he thought."

Jay was younger than Adams by ten years. Born to wealth and position in New York, tall, slim, and pale, he appeared somewhat haughty, carrying himself with a lift of the chin that made his hawk nose an even more pronounced feature. Like Adams, he had distinguished himself in the law and in Congress, where the two men had gotten along well enough, if frequently at cross purposes on issues. Jay, too, could be combative and stubborn, and as the descendant of French Huguenots, he had little liking for the Bourbon Court.

Jay refused to negotiate with the British until recognition of American independence was settled, and in so doing deliberately ignored the instructions of Congress to abide by the wishes of the French. Vergennes had wanted the discussions to proceed irrespective of the "point of independence." Let independence wait upon the treaty, he had told Franklin. In fact, Vergennes had sent a secret envoy to London to hint to Lord Shelburne that France did not support all the demands of the Americans.

Apparently it was not until he reached Paris, not until his initial meetings with Jay, that Adams learned for the first time of the commission's instructions from Congress to abide by the guidance of the French Foreign Ministry. Adams was outraged. America was not fighting a war for independence to be told what to do by the French. He wrote immediately to Robert Livingston to say he would rather resign than follow such instructions, and that he and Jay were "perfectly agreed" in their approach to the French.

I cannot express it better than in his own words: "to be honest and grateful to our allies, but to think for ourselves." I find a construction put upon one article in our instructions by some persons which, I confess, I never put upon it myself. It is represented by some as subjecting us to the French ministry, as taking away from us all right of judging for ourselves, and obliging us to agree to whatever the French ministers should advise us to do, and to do nothing without their consent. I never supposed this to be the intention of Congress. If I had, I never would have accepted the commission, and if I now thought it their intention, I could not continue in it. I cannot think it possible to be the design of Congress. If it is I hereby resign my place in the commission and request that another person may be immediately appointed in my stead.

Disappointed with the cramped accommodations available to him this time at the Hôtel de Valois, Adams changed lodgings, moving to the Hôtel du Roi on the Place du Carrousel, between the Palais Royal and the Quai du Louvre, which was to remain his headquarters.

Through most of the fall Paris had been shrouded with dark skies, cold rain and fog, and the same grim weather continued, adding nothing to anyone's spirits. For days Adams put off making contact with Franklin. After what Franklin had done to him, he told Matthew Ridley, he could hardly face the thought of going to Passy. When Ridley insisted he must, Adams agreed, but then, putting on his coat to leave, seemed to change his mind. It was only "with much persuasion [that] I got him at length to go," Ridley wrote.

It would be the first time Adams had seen Franklin since Franklin had written his devastating letter to Congress on August 9, 1780. Exactly when Adams found out about the letter, or read its content, are not clear, but once, and apparently only once, he unburdened his pent-up fury, in a letter written earlier that summer to Edmund Jenings. At the root of Franklin's behavior, Adams had convinced himself, was "base jealousy." The possibility that his own feelings toward Franklin could have the same root cause seems not to have entered his mind.

His base jealousy of me, and his sordid envy of my commission for making a treaty of commerce with Great Britain have stimulated him to attempt an assassination upon my character at Philadelphia, of which the world has not yet heard, and of which it cannot hear until the time shall come when many voluminous state papers may be laid before the public, which ought not to be until we are all dead.

Still, Adams was determined not to let personal ire stand in the way of his duty regarding the work at hand.

That I have no friendship for Franklin I avow. That I am incapable of having any with a man of his moral sentiments I avow. As far as fate shall compel me to sit with him in public affairs, I shall treat him with decency and perfect impartiality.

To Abigail he boasted that he and Jay had held the line on the point of independence, refusing to "speak or hear before we were put on an equal foot." Franklin, he told her, "as usual would have taken the advice of the C[omte] de V[ergennes] and treated without, but nobody would join him." But in this Adams was both overstating his own part and being blatantly unfair to Franklin, who had supported the recognition of American independence since the beginning, before Adams ever arrived on the scene.

Adams called on Franklin at Passy the same evening that Ridley talked him out the door. He stayed several hours and seized the opportunity to speak frankly of his opinion of the French Court, as well as to praise Jay for his "firmness." Franklin, wrote Adams afterward, "heard me patiently but said nothing."

However deep-seated his animosity toward Franklin, Adams did truly treat him with decency and managed to work effectively with him as he had in times past. Adams, Franklin, and Jay met and dined in Paris the next day and would repeatedly again in the weeks to come. As days passed, Adams found himself even admiring the "old conjurer."

The turning point came early, at one of the meetings prior to sitting down with the British negotiators, when Franklin, knowing the importance of a united front, told Jay and Adams, "I am of your opinion and will go on with these gentlemen in the business without consulting this [the French] Court."

It was a brave decision. In direct conflict with their instructions from

Congress, and at risk of alienating the French, they would ignore Vergennes. In his diary Adams described Franklin as "with us in entire harmony."

FORMAL SESSIONS WITH THE BRITISH NEGOTIATORS began the morning of October 30—Adams's forty-seventh birthday—and continued into the last week of November, as snow fell on the city day after day, only to melt as fog set in. Starting at eleven each morning, the meetings took place at Jay's lodgings at the Hôtel d'Orléans on the Rue des Petits-Augustins on the Left Bank; or at Adams's Hôtel du Roi; or the Hôtel de Valentinois at Passy, to spare Franklin the ride into Paris in such weather; or at Richard Oswald's quarters at the Grand Hôtel Muscovite, also on the Rue des Petits-Augustins.

Henry Laurens, who had been released from the Tower of London in exchange for General Cornwallis, was suffering poor health from his captivity and would not appear for the negotiations until the very end. As secretary for the American commissioners, Franklin had selected his grandson, William Temple Franklin, a decision that did not please Adams, who thought John Thaxter better qualified. (Temple Franklin was twenty-two, the illegitimate son of Franklin's illegitimate son, William, the former Tory governor of New Jersey who was living in London.) Also, among a half dozen other Americans who, like Matthew Ridley, were in and about the discussions, or dined with the negotiators as confidential matters were taken up, was Franklin's friend and associate, the spy Bancroft, as well as the young hero the Marquis de Lafayette, who was home from the war in America.

Richard Oswald continued as chief negotiator for the British. Oswald, a Scot, was a merchant who had made a fortune in government contracts and the slave trade. Elderly, blind in one eye, he was favorably inclined toward the American point of view, and agreeable to the point of being unsuited for politics. But he was joined now by Henry Strachey, the undersecretary of state, sent by Lord Shelburne to stiffen Oswald's resolve. Adams and Franklin had encountered Strachey once before, at Staten Island in 1776, at their meeting with Admiral Lord Howe, when Strachey, serving as Howe's secretary, had kept notes. Adams, who spelled the name "Stretchey," described him as an artful, insinuating man who "pushed and pressed every point," while a young British career diplomat, Alleyne Fitzherbert, who served as an assistant, struck Adams as refreshingly without airs.

In fact, the British envoys were not particularly impressive. In ability, experience, and resolve they were hardly a match for Adams, Franklin, and Jay, who, having started from scratch as diplomats, had come a long way in their time in Europe.

In his diary Adams compared the situation between Britain and America to that of an eagle and a cat. The eagle, soaring over a farmer's yard, swept and pounced on the cat, thinking it a rabbit. "In the air the cat seized her by the neck with her teeth and round her body with her fore and hind claws. The eagle finding herself scratched and pressed, bids the cat let go and fall down. 'No,' says the cat. 'I won't let go and fall. You shall stoop and set me down.' " The British, it appeared, were more ready to stoop and set America down than ever expected.

THE FUNDAMENTAL QUESTIONS to be dealt with, after acknowledgment of independence, were the boundaries of the United States, the right of navigation on the Mississippi River, debts, the interests of American Tories or Loyalists, and American fishing rights on the Grand Banks off Newfoundland, a main point with Adams.

The Americans insisted that Britain cede all territory between the Appalachian Mountains on the east and the Mississippi on the west, and to this the British agreed, thus at a stroke doubling the size of the new nation. The all-important right of the United States to navigation on the Mississippi was also settled.

On the question of private debts incurred by Americans to British merchants before the war, Franklin and Jay felt these had been counterbalanced by the American property confiscated or destroyed by the British army. But Adams strongly objected. Debts contracted in good faith should be paid, he insisted, and such a clause was included, though it would ultimately prove ineffective.

The British wanted compensation for the Loyalists. To Henry Strachey it was essential that such an article be included as proof to the thousands of American refugees that the British government, to which they had remained faithful, had not forgotten them. It was a point of view difficult for the Americans to accept, having, as they made clear, no sympathy for such people.

Strachey departed for London, taking the proposed articles for approval, and in the lull, Adams made his first visit to Versailles since his return to Paris. Vergennes, he had been informed by Lafayette, "took it amiss" that Adams had not been to see him.

Acutely sensitive to all that Vergennes had done to destroy his reputation with Congress, including enlisting Franklin to help make the case against him, Adams was no more eager to see Vergennes than he had been to see Franklin. He traveled the road to Versailles in a state of extreme apprehension, wondering, as he later wrote, whether he was to "hear an expostulation? a reproof? an admonition? or in plain vulgar English, a scolding? or was there any disposition to forget and forgive? and say all malice depart?"

What followed came as a total surprise. Invited to dine, Adams was made much of by both the Comte and Madame la Comtesse, who insisted he sit at her right hand and was "remarkably attentive" to him. Vergennes was overflowing with friendship. "The Comte, who sat opposite, was constantly calling out to me to know what I would eat and offer me *petits gateaux*, claret and Madeira, etc., etc.," Adams recorded. Never had he been treated with such respect at Versailles, and he was pleased beyond measure. "Good treatment makes me think I am admired, beloved. . . . So I dismiss my guard and grow weak, silly, vain," he had once written in his youth, in the throes of painful self-evaluation. Now he was in the full embrace of people who, as he said, made compliments a form of art. "French gentlemen. . . . said that I had shown in Holland that Americans understand negotiation as well as war. . . . Another said, *'Monsieur, vous êtes le Washington de la négociation.'* "

"It is impossible to exceed this," Adams continued in an effusive account in his diary that he was to regret having written. Somehow, perhaps by his own error, these pages from the diary, or "Peace Journal," as he called it, would be included with a report that went off to Philadelphia and were later read aloud in Congress to mock Adams for his abject vanity.

But what he wrote in the diary and how he responded to the moment were different matters. In the midst of such attentions, he kept his head. When Vergennes pressed for inside information on the course of the negotiations, Adams told him nothing. Nor did the pleasure he found in being so welcomed and fussed over by those who for so long had treated him with condescension or contempt, divert him even a little from the conviction that the way of the European powers and their leaders had never been and never would be to the benefit of the United States. When, another day, Richard Oswald charged Adams with being afraid of becoming the tool of the powers of Europe, Adams replied, "Indeed, I am."

"What powers?" says he. "All of them," says I. "It is obvious that all the powers of Europe will be continually maneuvering with us, to work us into their real or imaginary balances of power. . . . I think it ought to be our rule not to meddle, and that of all the powers of Europe not to desire us, or perhaps even to permit us, to interfere, if they can help it."

In the meantime, the Comte de Vergennes, through an emissary, had been letting the government in London know confidentially of his opposition to most of the American claims, and to his ambassador in Philadelphia he had written that France does not feel obliged to "sustain the pretentious ambitions" of the United States concerning either boundaries or fisheries.

ADAMS WAS AT HIS BEST in the final days of negotiations.

On November 25, Henry Strachey returned from London and the talks resumed at Oswald's lodgings at the Grand Hôtel Muscovite. Only two points remained to be settled: recompense for the Loyalists and American fishing rights on the Grand Banks off Newfoundland. Adams preferred that nothing be said of the Loyalists. Franklin was especially vehement in insisting that they receive no special treatment. In the end, after a "vast deal of conversation," the United States promised the Loyalists nothing. It was left that the individual states be requested to provide some form of compensation for property they had confiscated, a gesture that would prove largely meaningless.

Another day Henry Laurens appeared, like a stark reminder of the pain inflicted by a war that had still to end. To the lingering torments of his time in the Tower had been added the news that his son, Colonel John Laurens, had been killed in an unimportant action on a nameless battle-field in South Carolina almost a year after Yorktown. Laurens's one con-tribution to the proceedings was to provide a line to prevent the British army from "carrying away any Negroes or other property" when with-drawing from America. Oswald, who had done business with Laurens in former years, when they were both in the slave trade, readily agreed.

It was the argument over the fisheries that nearly brought negotia-tions to a halt when Adams, once again "unalterably determined," refused to accept any compromise that would impair New England's ancient stake in the sacred codfish. With the same vitality he had once brought to the courtrooms of Massachusetts and the floor of Congress, he championed the right of American fishermen, citing articles from treaties past and explaining in detail the migratory patterns of the cod, not to say the temperament of seafaring New Englanders. "How could we restrain our fishermen, the boldest men alive, from fishing in prohibited places?" he asked.

Then, just as agreement seemed near, Henry Strachey proposed to amend the line specifying the American "right" of fishing to read "lib-erty" of fishing, to which young Fitzherbert declared the word "right" to be "an obnoxious expression."

The moment was one made for Adams. Rising from his chair, smolder-ing with indignation, he addressed the British:

> Gentlemen, is there or can there be a clearer right? In former treaties, that of Utrecht and that of Paris, France and England have claimed the right and used the word. When God Almighty made the Banks of Newfoundland at 300 leagues distant from the people of America and at 600 leagues distance from those of France and En-gland, did he not give as food a right to the former as to the latter. If Heaven in the Creation have a right, it is ours at least as much as yours. If occupation, use, and possession have a right, we have it as clearly as you. If war and blood and treasure give a right, ours is as good as yours. We have been constantly fighting in Canada, Cape Breton, and Nova Scotia for the defense of the fishery, and have expanded beyond all proportion more than you. If then the right

cannot be denied, why then should it not be acknowledged? And put out of dispute?

It was settled—almost. Article III of the treaty would read, "It is agreed that the people of the United States shall continue to enjoy unmolested the right to take fish of every kind on the Grand Bank." However, on the matter of taking fish along the coast of Newfoundland and "all other of his Britannic Majesty's Dominions in America," the people of the United States were to have the "liberty," which, insisted the British negotiators, amounted to the same thing.

"We did not think it necessary to contend for a word," wrote a more mellow John Adams years afterward.

By the end of the day there was agreement on everything. Dining that evening at his hotel with Matthew Ridley, Adams was in high spirits. Asked if he would have fish, he laughed and declined, saying he had had "a pretty good meal of them" already that day.

Adams generously praised his fellow negotiators. Franklin, he told Ridley, had performed "nobly." But to Jay belonged the greatest credit, Adams said. Jay had played the leading part, Adams felt then and later, never failing to give Jay credit.

The following day, Saturday, November 30, 1782, all parties made their way through still another damp Paris snowfall, again to Oswald's quarters at the Grand Hôtel Muscovite for the signing of the preliminary treaty. Oswald was first to fix his name, followed by the four Americans in alphabetical order.

In effect, the Americans had signed a separate peace with the British. They had acted in direct violation of both the French-American alliance and their specific instructions from Congress to abide by the advice of the French foreign minister. To Adams there was no conflict in what they had done. The decision to break with the orders from Congress, and thus break faith with the French, had been clear-cut, the only honorable course. Congress had left them no choice. Congress had "prostituted" its own honor by surrendering its sovereignty to the French Foreign Minister. "It is glory to have broken such infamous orders," Adams wrote in his diary. "Infamous I say, for so they will be to all posterity."

To Franklin fell the unpleasant duty of breaking the news to Vergennes, and fortunately so, as in the parlance of diplomacy, it was a "delicate" moment.

As expected, Vergennes was extremely displeased, though "surprised" was the word he chose. "I am at a loss, sir, to explain your conduct, and that of your colleagues in this occasion," he wrote formally to Franklin. What had been signed, Franklin emphasized, were preliminary articles only. Nothing had been agreed to that ran contrary to French interests, and, of course, no peace could take place until the French and British concluded their talks and the definitive treaty was signed by all parties. Franklin apologized if he and his colleagues had been guilty of neglecting a point of *"bienséance"* (propriety), but this was from no want of respect for the King, "whom we all love and honor."

Then, with a cleverness of the kind he excelled in, Franklin included an afterthought. The English, he said, were now flattering themselves that they had divided the Americans from the French. So it were best that this "little misunderstanding" be forgotten and thereby prove the English mistaken.

Further, with amazing bravado, Franklin asked Vergennes for a loan of 6 million livres.

In truth, Vergennes thought well of the work done by the Americans at the negotiating table. He had no serious objections to the preliminary articles. Indeed, he thought Franklin, Jay, and Adams had obtained considerably more from the British than he had thought possible. "The English buy peace rather than make it," he remarked contemptuously to a French colleague. The "little misunderstanding" was "got over" in a matter of days and Vergennes agreed to the loan.

In a letter to Livingston that he never sent, Adams would later contend that Franklin would not have signed the treaty without the knowledge of Vergennes—that Vergennes, in fact, had been in on the whole thing. But Adams, exhausted in "strength and spirits," had by then succumbed to one of his spells of gloom during which he was incapable of seeing either Franklin or Vergennes in any but the darkest light.

It was not until late the following summer that the final, or definitive, Treaty of Paris was signed, and in the intervening time Adams fell once again into a black mood. Again, and with good cause, he felt Congress had forgotten him. He had received no expressions of gratitude or praise for what he had done, nor any sign of what, if anything, Congress had in mind for the future. To Abigail he described the "sharp fiery humors which break out in the back of my neck and other parts of me and plague me as much as the uncertainty in which I am in my own future destiny."

It was that summer, in a letter of July 22, 1783, to Robert Livingston, that Franklin described Adams in words that were never to be forgotten: "He means well for his country, is always an honest man, often a wise one, but sometimes and in some things, absolutely out of his senses."

In the first week of September the peacemakers convened to sign the definitive treaty. Henry Laurens was absent. Thus it was Adams, Franklin, and Jay who represented the United States at the ceremony at the Hôtel d'York on the Rue Jacob, and who signed their names in that order, along with a new representative of King George III, David Hartley.

In fixing his signature to the document, Adams, as he often did, put a little dash or period after his name, as if to say "John Adams, period."

The all-important first sentence of Article I declared, "His Britannic Majesty acknowledges the said United States . . . to be free, sovereign and independent states."

"Done at Paris," read the final line, "this third day of September, in the year of our Lord, one thousand seven hundred and eighty three."

The mighty Revolution had ended. The new nation was born.

IT HAD BEEN NINE YEARS since the First Continental Congress at Philadelphia, eight years since Lexington and Concord, seven since the Declaration of Independence, and more than three years since John Adams had last left home in the role of peacemaker.

To Thomas Jefferson, Adams would one day write, "My friend, you and I have lived in serious times." And of all the serious events of the exceedingly eventful eighteenth century, none compared to the arrival upon the world stage of the new, independent United States of America. Adams's part in Holland and at Paris had been profound. As time would tell, the treaty that he, Franklin, and Jay had made was as advantageous to their country as any in history. It would be said they had won the greatest victory in the annals of American diplomacy.

• • •

F OR HIS OWN PART, for the time being, Adams knew for certain only that he was exhausted and intended never again to be separated from Abigail for any extended period for as long as he lived. "You may depend upon a good domestic husband for the remainder of my life, if it is the will of Heaven that I should once more meet you," he wrote. And this, he told her, was a promise not lightly made. Whether he should come to her, or she to him, or how soon that could be, remained to be seen.

CHAPTER SIX

ABIGAIL IN PARIS

What a large volume of adventures may be grasped within this little span of life by him who interests his heart in everything.

—Laurence Sterne, *A Sentimental Journey*

I

As greatly as she wished it were not so, Abigail Adams was terrified of the sea. She who had held her ground against war, plague, and abject loneliness, who had faced one dread uncertainty after another through the worst of times, steadfastly, never flinching by all appearances, looked upon "hazarding" a voyage over the North Atlantic with nothing less than horror. The very thought, she told her husband, made a coward of her. It was not something she could change, he must understand, and as a measure of his love, he must come home to her with all possible speed. "I know not whether I shall believe myself how well you love me, unless I can prevail upon you to return."

Her mind was much on mortality. The same September of the Paris Peace Treaty, her adored father, the Reverend William Smith, had died in the Weymouth parsonage where she had been born and raised. The last of her "parental props" had fallen; one of the strongest of her ties to home was "dissolved." Her father had been among the reasons she had never felt free to leave for Europe. "I cannot consent to your going, child, whilst I live," he had told her. Still, though free now, she could not bring herself to go.

In the years when John served in Congress, Pennsylvania had seemed "that far country." Now her firstborn had seen Russia and returned to

Europe on his own by way of Finland, Sweden, Denmark, and Germany, as she knew from John's letters, though from the boy himself she had not had a line in two years. Her two youngest, Charles and Thomas, were away at Haverhill, boarding with her sister Elizabeth and the Reverend John Shaw, who was preparing them for college, Abigail having had a change of mind about John Shaw and his abilities. When she made the fifty-mile ride to Haverhill for a visit, it was the farthest from Braintree she had ever traveled.

Of her children, only Nabby remained at home, but at seventeen Nabby's life, too, was moving on. Fair-haired, pleasing in appearance, she was taller than her mother, more circumspect, less inclined to voice an opinion, a "fine majestic girl who has as much dignity as a princess," in Abigail's description, though she wondered if Nabby was too reserved, too prudent.

> She has stateliness in her manners which some misconstrue into pride and a haughtiness, but which rather results from too great reserve; she wants more affability, but she has prudence and discretion beyond her years. She is in her person tall, large, and majestic; Mamma's partiality allows her to be a good figure. Her sensibility is not yet which attracts whilst it is attracted. Her manners rather forbid all kinds of intimacy and awe whilst they command.

"Indeed, she is not like her Mamma," Abigail confided to John at last. "Had not her Mamma at her age too much sensibility to be *very prudent*."

A young lawyer named Royall Tyler had moved to town, boarding with the Cranches, and was showing interest in Nabby. Nor did he neglect to shower attention on Abigail, who thought highly of him. The son of a wealthy father, valedictorian of his class at Harvard, Tyler was handsome, witty, and well read. "If he is steady he will shine in his profession," she wrote. "His disposition appears extremely amiable." She seemed nearly as charmed by him as was Nabby.

But there was gossip of "dissipation" in the young man's past—that he had fathered an illegitimate child by a housemaid at Harvard and had, besides, squandered his inheritance. Abigail began having second thoughts, and wrote at length on the matter to her distant husband. A "growing attachment" between the two young people was plain to see. Tyler was spending more and more evenings by their fire, she reported. What should she do? "What ought I to say? I feel a powerful pleader within my own heart and well recollect the love I bore to the object of my early affections to forbid him to have hope." She wondered if perhaps a tender passion might be "just the thing for Nabby," to bring her out of herself.

Earlier, in a long, affectionate letter to his daughter, John had offered memorable advice on choosing a husband that, in sum, expressed what he valued most in a man and what he so struggled to be himself so much of his life:

> Daughter! Get you an honest man for a husband, and keep him honest. No matter whether he is rich, provided he be independent. Regard the honor and moral character of the man more than all other circumstances. Think of no other greatness but that of the soul, no other riches but those of the heart. An honest, sensible, humane man, above all the littleness of vanity and extravagances of imagination, laboring to do good rather than be rich, to be useful rather than make a show, living in modest simplicity clearly within his means and free from debts and obligations, is really the most respectable man in society, makes himself and all about him most happy.

On the matter of Royall Tyler he had shown little patience. "I don't like the subject at all," he told Abigail. The girl was too young for such thoughts. Nor did he like Tyler's method of "courting mothers." Abigail and Tyler both had "advanced too fast, and I should advise both to retreat.

> I don't like your word "dissipation" at all. I don't know what it means. . . . My child is a model, as you represent her and as I know her, and is not to be the prize, I hope, of any reformed rake. . . . In the name of all that is tender don't criticize your daughter for those qualities which are her greatest glory, her reserve and her prudence.

By the autumn of 1783, the romance had been suspended, though as Abigail reported, the young man's "attachment" had not lessened. As for Nabby, she would do nothing without her father's approval. It was another reason why John was needed at home, to appraise the situation for himself.

Abigail had a melancholy sense of life slipping away before she and John had had a chance to enjoy it. She had turned thirty-nine; the face in the mirror was a young woman no longer. And where, she asked in one especially plaintive letter, was that young "untitled" John Adams she had fallen in love with.

I recollect the untitled man to whom I gave my heart and in the agony of recollection, when time and distance present themselves together, wish he had never been any other. Who shall give me back my time? Who shall compensate to me those *years* I cannot recall? How dearly have I paid for a titled husband.

Hearing he might be appointed ambassador to the British Court, she begged him to refuse. She had no desire to live in England, no wish for the "parade and nonsense" of a public role. She was too inclined to wear her heart on her countenance, she reminded him. "I am sure I would make an awkward figure. And then it would mortify my pride if I should be thought to disgrace you." Her health was poor. She tired easily and suffered from headaches. "Neither of us appear built for duration," she wrote. "Would to heaven the few remaining days allotted to us might be enjoyed together."

His letters from Paris, written in September, pressed her to sail as soon as possible. Congress had appointed him to a new commission to negotiate a commercial treaty with Britain. She must come. She could sail for London, Amsterdam, or any port in France. The moment he heard of her arrival, he would fly to her—even by balloon if such travel were perfected in time, he added lightheartedly.

But it was only on hearing that he had suffered another serious illness that she changed her mind and resolved to go to him. Except for her marriage itself, it was the most important decision she had ever had to make.

A fever like that at Amsterdam had laid him low, she read in a letter written October 14, one of the last she was to receive before Boston's harbor was closed by winter ice. He was leaving for London for his health, and taking John Quincy with him. She must come soon. Concerning the courtship, the "family affair" on her mind, that could be managed quite well, Adams wrote. "The lady comes to Europe with you. If the parties preserve their regard until they meet again and continue to behave as they ought, they will still be young enough."

She began making plans, though not without dire apprehensions:

> You invite me to you. You call me to follow you. The most earnest wish of my soul is to be with you—but you can scarcely form an idea of the conflict in my mind. It appears to me such an enterprise, the ocean so formidable, the quitting of my habitation and my country, leaving my children, my friends, with the idea that perhaps I may never see them again, without my husband to console and comfort me under these apprehensions—indeed, my dear friend, there are hours when I feel unequal to the trial.

In January, after further consideration, John wrote again to say that if she thought it inadvisable to come to Europe, he would come to her. As for Nabby, he continued, "I can scarcely think it possible for me to disapprove of her final judgment formed with deliberation upon anything which so deeply concerns her whole happiness."

Then, having looked into the young man's background and reputation for himself, as much as that was possible at such a distance, Adams sent another letter, this to Tyler himself. "Sir, you and the young lady have my consent to arrange your plans according to your own judgment," Adams wrote, "and I pray God to bless and prosper you both whether together or asunder."

But neither letter would arrive in time.

SEEING TO THE NECESSARY ARRANGEMENTS kept Abigail occupied well into spring. As John had advised, she and Nabby were to be accompanied by two servants, Esther Field and John Briesler, both of Braintree. Uncle Isaac Smith, the Boston merchant, was to look into proper passage, while another uncle, Dr. Cotton Tufts of Weymouth, who had been advising Abigail on land investments, was to manage the family's financial affairs in her absence.

The farm was leased. But the house and all their possessions Abigail decided to leave in the care of a former slave of her father's named Phoebe, who had been freed by his will and was newly married to a free black man, William Abdee. "As there was no settled minister in Weymouth," Abigail told John, "I gave them the liberty of celebrating their nuptials here, which they did much to their satisfaction." That the couple would remain in her house in her absence, however long that might be, gave her particular peace of mind. "I have no doubt of their care and faithfulness, and prefer them to any other family."

In characteristic fashion she specified exactly how things were to be. "They are during the present year to have the use of the garden east of the house and that part of the great garden next to the road [and] all the fruit which grows in the garden," she instructed Cotton Tufts.

Phoebe is to be allowed a pint of milk a day. . . . I give her also a pig seven weeks old, 3 pounds [of] hog's lard, and what salt beef there is in the house. . . . The house and furniture are to be taken care of by opening and airing, rubbing, and cleaning it. . . . They are to be allowed use of the team in the fall to bring up a load of sea weed. . . . The library is to be under the care of Mr. Cranch. No books to be lent out unless to him and Mr. Tyler. . . . In November you will be so good as to give on my account the sum of 2 dollars to widow Abigail Field, 2 dollars to the widow Sarah Owen, who lives in the same house with her sister Field, 1 dollar to Mrs. Fuller and 1 dollar to the widow Mary Howard and 1 dollar to the wife of John Hayden, who is an aged woman and one of my pensioners—1 dollar to the widow Mary Green.

By the end of May, all was arranged. She had passage to England on the merchant ship *Active*, which was expected to sail within a few weeks. She had hoped to embark with friends. As it was, she knew none of the other passengers or the captain. She would not be sailing in winter, nor in the midst of war. Still, it was a venture that she had once thought nothing could ever tempt her to undertake. "But let no person say what they would or would not do, since we are not judges for ourselves until circumstances call us to act," she wrote to John on May 25, in her last letter before leaving.

Day by day, she had looked for some word from him, but there was none. "My thoughts are fixed, my latest wish depends on thee, guide, guardian, husband, lover, friend," she wrote, borrowing from one of her poets.

Abigail said her farewells in her front parlor on the morning of June 18, the house filled with neighbors, "not of unmeaning complimenters," she wrote, "but the honest yeomanry, their wives and daughters like a funeral procession, all come to wish me well and to pray for a speedy return." She had tried to prepare for the moment. "Knowing I had to act my little part alone, I had possessed myself with calmness, but this was too much for me." She and everyone around her were weeping as she shook hands one by one.

In Boston, at Isaac Smith's house the following day, Thomas Jefferson appeared out of the blue, to introduce himself and say that he, too, was soon to sail with his daughter, Martha, and a young mulatto slave, James Hemings. He had been appointed by Congress to join the commissioners, Franklin and Adams, in Paris. Thinking it important that he know more of the commercial interests of New England, he had been making a quick tour of Connecticut and Rhode Island, and had only just arrived in Boston. What Abigail's first impressions of Jefferson were during this encounter, or what he thought of her, neither recorded.

Jefferson intended to depart from New York in July and urged her to go with him. But her plans were made, her passage paid for. "I thanked him for his politeness," she reported to John, "but having taken my measures, I was determined to abide by them."

Like Abigail, Jefferson had never been to sea. As it turned out, he would sail from Boston after all, and only weeks later, crossing under sunny skies, the sea, as his daughter said, as calm as a river.

ABIGAIL SAILED on June 20, 1784. At age thirty-nine, having never been away from either her home or those of close relatives for more than a night or two in all her life, she, Nabby, their two servants, and a cow went on board the *Active* at Rowe's Wharf, and with a "fine wind" were quickly under way.

Among the few other passengers, as Abigail recorded, were a Colonel Norton from Martha's Vineyard, a Dr. Clark, a Mr. Foster, a Mr. Spear, a "haughty Scotchman" named Green, and one other woman whose name happened also to be Adams. No sooner had the ship passed the Boston lighthouse into rougher water than they were all horribly seasick. And so it was to be for days, everyone tossed about in cramped, "excessive disagreeable" quarters together.

"We crawled upon [the] deck whenever we were able, but it was so cold and damp that we could not remain long," Abigail wrote. The ship was filthy and carrying a cargo of whale oil and potash. With every roll of the waves the whale oil leaked, the potash "smoked and fermented," contributing further to the "flavor" below.

The staterooms for the women comprised two tiny, airless cabins opening onto the main cabin where meals were served and the men slept. Nabby and the other Mrs. Adams were in one cabin, while Abigail and Esther Field shared the other. At night, to keep from suffocating, they had to leave the doors open onto the main cabin. "We can only live with our door shut whilst we dress and undress," Abigail wrote in a journal she began for her sister Mary Cranch.

> Necessity has no law, but what should I have thought on shore to have layed myself down to sleep in common with a half dozen gentlemen. We have curtains it is true, and we only partly undress . . . but we have the satisfaction of falling in with a set of well behaved, decent gentlemen.

In a storm off the Grand Banks, with bottles and plates crashing to pieces all about them, the women had to be held fast in their chairs, "as some gentleman sat by us with his arm fastened in ours and his feet braced against a table or chair that was lashed down."

Afterward, the sailors assured her it had been only a breeze. Yet the hard rocking of the ship had so badly injured her cow that the animal had to be killed and cast overboard.

In the unrelieved dampness belowdecks Abigail suffered severely from rheumatism. The food was inedible. The cook she described as a "lazy, dirty Negro with no more knowledge of his business than a savage." But with a favorable turn in the weather, finding she could get about, her usual spirit returned, and very like John Adams on board the *Boston*, she proceeded to "make a bustle," in her expression. "And as I found I might reign mistress on board without any offense, I soon exerted my authority with scrapers, mops, brushes, infusions of vinegar, etc., and in a few hours you would have thought yourself in a different ship."

She "took up the direction of our cabin," as she wrote in another account for her sister Elizabeth, "taught the cook to dress his victuals, and have made several puddings with my own hands." When she mastered the names of all the masts and sails, the captain said he was sure she could take over at the helm as well.

Unlike John, she loved watching the sea. Wrapped in an old camblet cloak, she spent hours on deck, her soul filled with feelings of the sublime. After a night of brilliant phosphorescence in the water, a phenomenon she had longed to witness, she wrote in ecstasy of a "blazing ocean" as far as she could see. " 'Great and marvelous are Thy works, Lord God Almighty,' " she recorded reverently.

With Nabby she passed the time in the main cabin reading, writing, chatting, or playing cards with the other passengers, whose company she enjoyed. The doctor, John Clark, her favorite, was consistently cheerful, while Mr. Spear's "drollery" kept everyone in high spirits. From a book she was reading on medicine, she copied a passage about association with cheerful people being good for the health, and speculated whether her husband might not benefit from a little unbending of the mind.

There was only one of the group whom they would all have been happy to do without, the "haughty Scotchman," Mr. Green, who harped incessantly on the importance of rank and social position and who himself, Abigail concluded, had neither. He paid attention to her only because she was the wife of John Adams, she saw with distaste. "I know his politeness to me is not personally upon my own account, but because of my connection which gives me importance sufficient to entitle me to his notice.

He is always inquiring who was such [and such] a general? I have felt a disposition to quarrel with him several times, but have restrained myself, and only observed mildly that merit, not titles gave a man preeminence in our country, that I did not doubt it was a mortifying circumstance to the British nobility to find themselves so often conquered by mechanics and mere husbandmen—but that we esteemed it our glory to draw characters not only into the field, but into the senate, and believed no one would deny but what they had shone in both. All our passengers enjoyed this conversation.

One of the crew came to her with a story he felt he must tell her. He had been taken prisoner during the war and held in a jail in England. When he and several others escaped to Holland, the only help they were able to get was from John Adams, who gave them money from his own pocket.

What was ahead for her, she pondered in a diary she kept for herself only. Where would she be living? "No matter where," she wrote, "so that it only be in the arms of my dearest, best of friends. I hardly dare trust my imagination or anticipate the day. Cruel sleep how you have tormented me."

When, after a month at sea and the voyage nearly over, the ship lay becalmed, she found the wait intolerable. Motion, she decided, was the most desirable state. "Man was made for action. . . . I am quite out of conceit with calm."

Heading up the English Channel, the ship was caught in gale winds and for three days there was little sleep for anyone. At last, orders were given to drop anchor in the Downs, the roadstead of the Channel, within sight of the little town of Deal. The passengers were lowered over the side into an open pilot boat and in squally rain and the roar of heaving waves, with everyone soaked to the skin, they made for shore.

> We set off from the vessel now mounting upon the top of a wave as high as a steeple [Abigail would write], and then so low that the boat was not to be seen. I could keep myself up no other way than as one of the gentlemen stood braced up against the boat, fast hold of me and I with both arms around him. The other ladies were held in the same manner whilst every wave gave us a broadside.

Then with a sudden rush and a sound like thunder, an immense wave swept the boat broadside high up onto the beach. And thus it was, on

Tuesday, July 20, 1784, that Abigail and Nabby were "safely landed upon the British coast."

UNDER WAY BY POST CHAISE the next morning, they traveled hill and dale to Canterbury, then Chatham, then on to London, seventy-two miles all in a day. Beyond Chatham, they rolled with all possible speed to pass before dark the Black Heath, dreaded for its lurking highwaymen. Fear of the road, the threat of robbery or worse at the hands of highwaymen, was something foreign to Americans. At home it was not uncommon even for women to travel alone feeling perfectly safe. "Every place we passed, and every post chaise we met were crying out a robbery," Abigail later recounted. "The robber was pursued and taken in about two miles, and we saw the poor wretch, ghastly and horrible, brought along on foot." She judged him to be no more than twenty years old. Hearing that "the lad" was certain "to swing," she shuddered. "Though every robber may deserve death, yet to exult over the wretched is what *our* country is not accustomed to. Long may it be free of such villainies and long may it preserve a commiseration for the wretched."

Though a "monstrous great" city, London struck Abigail as more pleasant than ever she imagined. There was even sunshine, and the small, elegant Adelphi Hotel, on a narrow street just off the Strand, near the Thames, was "as quiet as at any place in Boston." That John and John Quincy had stayed there during their visit to London gave it further appeal.

She immediately dispatched a letter to John at The Hague reporting her arrival and her extreme desire to see him. "Heaven give us a happy meeting," she wrote.

Adams replied at once. Her letter had made him "the happiest man on earth," he said. "I am twenty years younger than I was yesterday." Because of the press of business, he was unable to "fly" to her just yet, but John Quincy was proceeding at once.

Hearing that John, while in London the previous fall, had had a full-length portrait done by Copley, and that the painting was on view at the artist's studio in Haymarket, she hurried off to see it. Adams, in court dress of brown velvet, stood holding a scroll in one hand—his memorial to the Dutch Republic, perhaps, or the Treaty of Paris—while with the other hand he pointed to a map of America spread on a table. Beside the table, a globe figured prominently. He was the picture of a statesman— firm of stance, his expression one of grave resolve. He wore lace at his sleeve and a gold-handled sword. If he looked a little older and stouter than when Abigail had last seen him, she thought it "a very good likeness . . . a most beautiful picture." She was delighted.

A steady stream of visitors left her little time to herself. They came every day, Americans in London who wished to pay their respects, including a number of Loyalists. She was told how young she looked, offered assistance, invited to tea. When not receiving visitors, she and Nabby went sightseeing (to Westminster Abbey, the British Museum) or shopping for new clothes, but astounded by the prices, they bought little. She was surprised at how familiar the faces of the English looked, so like Americans, that it was as if she had seen them before. "The London ladies," she also noted, "walk a vast deal and very fast."

On Friday, July 30, a servant came "puffing" up the stairs at the hotel to announce, "Young Mr. Adams." When John Quincy entered, Abigail hardly knew him. As tall as his father, he looked older than seventeen—a man nearly. The resemblance to his father was striking. Seeing him with Nabby made her feel very much the matron, she confided to her sister Mary, but "were I not their mother, I would say a likelier pair you will seldom see in a summer's day."

Nabby judged her brother a "sober lad," but one she was sure she would like once they were reacquainted. To a cousin at home John Quincy wrote, quite properly, "You can imagine what an addition has been made to my happiness by the arrival of a kind and tender mother, and a sister who fulfills my most sanguine expectations."

From The Hague, John Adams promised to be with them in a matter of days, but warned that there could be no lingering in London. He must join his colleagues in Paris.

ON THE MORNING OF SATURDAY, August 7, Nabby had been out for a walk. When she returned, she noticed a man's hat on the table with two books in it.

Everything around appeared altered, without my knowing in what particular [she wrote that night in her diary]. I went into my room, the things were moved; I looked around. . . . "Why are these things moved?"—All [this] in a breath to Esther. . . .

"Why is all this appearance of strangeness? Whose hat is that in the other room?" . . . " 'Tis my father's!" I said, "Where is he?"

"In the room above."

Up I flew, and to his chamber, where he was lying down, and received me with all the tenderness of an affectionate parent after so long an absence. Sure I am, I never felt more agitation of spirits in my life; it will not do to describe.

Abigail's only reference to the reunion with John was in passing in a letter to Mary Cranch: "You know my dear sister that poets and painters wisely draw a veil over those scenes which surpass the pen of one or the pencil of the other; we were indeed a very happy family once more met together after a separation of four years."

Early the following day they were all off for Paris.

II

THE JOURNEY WAS MADE in record time. They went by fast coach from London to the Channel, and by boat to Calais, landing on the shores of France at dawn the next morning, then sped on by coach-and-six. If Abigail felt still, as on shipboard, that motion was the preferred state, she must have been ecstatic.

The whole route from Calais to Paris, she and Nabby felt they were riding through scenes from a favorite novel, Laurence Sterne's *A Sentimental Journey*. There were all kinds of travelers, Sterne had written—inquisitive travelers, idle travelers, vain travelers—but the true value of travel was not in strenuous sight-seeing. It was in opening one's heart to feeling.

Adams had been away from Paris for nearly a year. In an effort to regain his strength after the illness that struck him down in the late summer of 1783, he had moved to a large house with a garden on the outskirts of the city, just beyond Passy in the still-rural village of Auteuil.

Long a believer in the therapeutic benefits of fresh air and exercise, he had become still more adamant on the subject during his years in Europe. If the dank atmosphere of Amsterdam had been the cause of his first terrible collapse, so the noisome air of Paris had laid him low the second time.

Like Passy, Auteuil was set on an airy hill above the Seine, and adjoined the beautiful Bois de Boulogne, where he could take his daily walks or ride horseback. But when his American doctor, James Jay, the brother of John Jay, had suggested a sojourn in England, he had gone off to London with John Quincy and later to Bath, to take the waters, an experience Adams had found little to his liking and that was cut short by a summons to return to Holland to secure still another desperately needed loan.

Adams again succeeded with the Dutch bankers, but only after one of the most horrendous episodes in all his earthly pilgrimage. Crossing a wintry North Sea, he and John Quincy had been caught in a storm. Landing on a desolate Dutch island, they had had to press on the rest of the way by foot and iceboat. "The weather was cold, we were all frequently wet," he wrote. "I was chilled to the heart, and looked I suppose, as I felt, like a withered old worn out carcass. Our polite skipper frequently eyed me and said he pitied the old man." Adams, by then forty-eight, felt that during the ordeal he had left one stage of life and entered another.

The four Adamses and their two American servants reached Paris on August 13, stopping at the Hôtel d'York on the Left Bank, where the Peace Treaty had been signed. Jefferson and his daughter had already arrived in the city the week before.

While Adams conferred with Jefferson and Franklin, Abigail and Nabby toured the city, John Quincy serving as their guide and interpreter. Then, after several days, the family moved to the rented house at Auteuil, where they were to remain for no one knew how long.

In Paris there had been talk of Jefferson succeeding Franklin as minister to France, a prospect that Adams rejoiced in. Whether Adams would be appointed to the British Court, as was also expected, remained unresolved, and though it was a position he longed for, as a capstone to his diplomatic service, he could not say so outright, and imagined quite correctly that there was stiff opposition in Congress.

Yet Adams was pleased beyond measure. "The house, the garden, the situation near the Bois de Boulogne, elevated above the river Seine and the low grounds, and distant from the putrid streets of Paris, is the best I could wish for," he recorded the day they moved in. It had been a long time since he had felt so well disposed. "I make a little America of my own family," he wrote to Arthur Lee. "I feel more at home than I have ever done in Europe," he told Cotton Tufts. He thought himself better off even than Franklin; besides, his rent was lower.

The house was enormous, three stories of trimmed limestone, and plainly in need of attention. It had once been the country villa of two extravagant, scandalous sisters, the Demoiselles Verrières—Marie and Claudine-Geneviève de Verrières. Depending on how one counted, there were forty or fifty rooms, including a small theater "gone to decay." Abigail, accustomed to a cottage of seven rooms, was nonplussed. Weeks later she would still be finding rooms she had not seen.

Reception salon, dining room, and kitchen were on the first floor, as well as quarters for the servants. The family "apartments" were above, where every room had French doors looking over the garden. The mirrors alone were said to have cost 30,000 livres. One octagonal room on the second floor was paneled entirely with mirrors.

"Why, my dear," wrote Abigail to her niece, Betsy Cranch, "you cannot turn yourself in it without being multiplied twenty times . . . [and] that I do not like, for being rather clumsy, and by no means an elegant figure, I hate to have it so repeated to me."

The furnishings were sparse; there were no carpets. The whole place could do with a good scrubbing, she saw, and wondered how cold it might be in winter.

The garden, however, was "delightful," very romantic in its neglect, and it was the garden she would come to love most. There were fully five acres with rows of orange trees, stone walks overhung with grapevines, circles and octagons of flowers in bloom, pots of flowers, a Chinese fence, a fish pond, a fountain that no longer worked, and a little summerhouse, "beautiful in ruins."

The weather, like the garden, enchanted her. The days and nights of late summer were ideal, "beautiful, soft, serene." And as time passed, her affection for the place grew appreciably. She would rent furniture, purchase new table linen, china, and glassware, hire servants, acquire a songbird in a cage, and see the garden fountain restored to running order. She felt "so happy" at Auteuil, "so pleasingly situated."

THE FRENCH AND THEIR WAYS were another matter, however. The shock experienced by John Adams on his first arrival in France was tepid compared to that of his wife.

From the morning of their landing at Calais, Abigail had been convinced that every coachman, porter, and servant was somehow trying to cheat her, an anxiety not helped by the fact that she understood nothing they said. Now the number of servants she was expected to employ and the division of labor insisted upon by them left her bewildered and exasperated. "One [servant] will not touch what belongs to the business of the other, though he or she has time enough to perform the whole," she wrote, in an effort to explain the system to her sister Mary. The coachman would do nothing but attend the carriage and horses. The cook would only cook, never wash a dish. Then there was the maître d'hôtel whose "business is to purchase articles into the family and oversee that nobody cheats but himself." Counting Esther Field and John Briesler, she eventually had eight in service, but that, she was told, was hardly what was expected.

She and John both worried about running into debt, given his salary from Congress of $9,000. While such a sum might be a great deal in Braintree, John wrote to Cotton Tufts, at Court it was but "a sprat in a whale's belly."

"We spend no evenings abroad, make no suppers . . . avoid every expense that is not held indispensable," Abigail reported to Mary.

The shock was not so much the exorbitant expense of public life in Europe, but that extravagance was taken as the measure of one's importance. "The inquiry is not whether a person is qualified for his office," she wrote to Uncle Isaac Smith, "but how many domestics and horses does he keep." The British ambassador had fifty servants, the Spanish ambassador, seventy-five.

Fashion ruled and fashion decreed that she and Nabby have their own hairdresser in residence, a young woman named Pauline, who, as a matter of pride, refused to dust or sweep. Both the sweeping and waxing of floors was reserved for a manservant called the *frotteur* who went tearing about from room to room with brushes strapped to his feet, "dancing here and there like a merry Andrew," and to whom was also assigned the unenviable task of emptying the chamber pots. Why, with so much land available, there was no proper privy, Abigail could not understand.

Even her two servants from home, Esther and John, felt obliged to have their hair dressed, such was the ridicule they were subjected to by the other servants. "To be out of fashion is more criminal than to be seen in a state of nature, to which the Parisians are not averse."

She thought Paris far from appealing, for all the splendor of its public buildings. And if she had not seen all of it, she had "smelt it." Given its state of sanitation, the stench was more than she could bear. With new construction under way everywhere, the narrow streets were cluttered with piles of lumber and stone, great mounds of rubble. Everything looked filthy to her. Even the handsomest buildings were black with soot. The people themselves were the "dirtiest creatures" she had ever laid eyes on, and the number of prostitutes was appalling. That any nation would condone, let alone license, such traffic, she found vile, just as she found abhorrent the French practice of arranged marriages among the rich and titled of society.

"What idea, my dear madame, can you form of the manners of a nation, one city of which furnishes (blush oh, my sex, when I name it) 52,000 unmarried females so lost to a sense of honor and shame as publicly to enroll their names in a notary office for the most abandoned purposes and to commit iniquity with impunity," she wrote in outrage to Mercy Warren. "Thousands of these miserable wretches perish annually with disease and poverty, whilst the most sacred of institutions is prostituted to unite titles and estates."

On a visit later to a Paris orphanage run by Catholic Sisters of Charity, she was shown a large room with a hundred cribs and perhaps as many infants. It was a sight both pleasing and painful—pleasing because all was so admirably clean, and the nuns especially attentive and kind, but painful because of the numbers of abandoned babies, "numbers in the arms, great numbers asleep . . . several crying." In an average year 6,000 children were delivered to the orphanage, she was told by the head nun. Even as they talked, one was brought in that appeared to be three months old. In various parts of the city, it was explained, there were designated places with small boxes in which a baby could be "deposited." In winter one child in three died of exposure.

> Can we draw a veil over the guilty cause [Abigail wrote], or refrain from comparing a country grown old in debauchery and lewdness with the wise laws and institutions of one wherein marriage is considered as holy and honorable, wherein industry and sobriety enable parents to rear numerous offspring, and where the laws provide resource for illegitimacy by obliging the parents to maintenance, and if not to be obtained there, they become the charge of the town or parish where they are born?

The whole French way of life seemed devoted to little else but appearances and frivolity, everybody bent on a good time, going to the theater, to concerts, public shows and spectacles. She wondered when anyone ever did any work. In London she had seen streets swarming with people, but there they appeared to have business in mind. Here pleasure alone seemed to be the business of life and no one ever to tire of it. Not even on the Sabbath was there pause. Sundays were more like election days at home, as all of Paris "poured forth" into the Bois de Boulogne, where the woods resounded with "music and dancing, jollity and mirth of every kind."

The few resident Americans she met, like the famously beautiful Anne Bingham of Philadelphia and the naval hero John Paul Jones, did not greatly impress her. Young Anne Bingham, who was married to the immensely wealthy William Bingham, was, Abigail agreed, "very handsome," but "rather too much given to the foibles" of France. "Less money and more years may make her wiser," Abigail wrote. And John Paul Jones was a decided disappointment. She had pictured him a "rough, stout, war-like Roman." Instead, he was tiny, soft-spoken, and a favorite with the French ladies, whom he flattered excessively. "I should sooner think of wrapping him up in cotton wool and putting him into my pocket, than sending him to contend with cannon ball."

But most memorable was her first encounter with a "great lady" of France. The occasion was a dinner given by Franklin at his house in Passy, shortly after the Adams family arrived. In recent years Franklin had become increasingly attached to the "sweet society" of the celebrated Madame Helvétius, whose own small estate was close by in Auteuil. Franklin had even proposed marriage to Madame Helvétius, who declined, saying they were past the age for romance. Yet she remained prominent in his life and always the center of attention at his social gatherings. Franklin told Abigail she was to meet one of the best women in the world, and Abigail, curious to see what so charmed "the good Doctor," rode to Passy full of anticipation, only to be appalled by the woman from the moment she appeared.

She entered the room with a careless, jaunty air [Abigail began in a vivid sketch, in a letter to her niece, Lucy Cranch]. Upon seeing ladies who were strangers to her, she bawled out, "Ah, mon Dieu! where is Franklin? Why did you not tell me there were ladies here?" You must suppose her speaking all this in French. "How do I look?" said she, taking hold of a dressing chemise made of tiffany which she had on over a blue lutestring, and which looked as much upon the decay as her beauty, for she was once a handsome woman.

Her hair was fangled [done in the latest style]; over it she had a small straw hat, with a dirty half gauze handkerchief round it, and a bit of dirtier gauze than ever my maids wore was sewed on behind. She had a black gauze scarf thrown over her shoulders.

She ran out of the room. When she returned, the Doctor entered at one door, she at the other, upon which she ran forward to him, caught him by the hand, "Hélas, Franklin!" then gave him a double kiss, one upon each cheek, and another upon his forehead. When we went into the room to dine, she was placed between the Doctor and Mr. Adams. She carried on the chief conversation at dinner, frequently locking her hands in the Doctor's, and sometimes spreading her arms upon the backs of both gentlemen's chairs, then throwing her arm carelessly upon the Doctor's neck.

I should have been greatly astonished at this conduct, if the good Doctor had not told me that in this lady I should see a genuine

Frenchwoman, wholly free of affectation or stiffness of behavior, and one of the best women in the world. For this I must take the Doctor's word, but I should have set her down for a very bad one, although 60 years of age and a widow. I own I was highly disgusted, and never wish for an acquaintance with any ladies of this cast.

After dinner she threw herself upon a settee, where she showed more than her feet. She had a little lap-dog who was, next to the Doctor, her favorite. This she kissed, and when he wet the floor, she wiped it up with her chemise.

To the Yankee matron from Braintree, the sloppy, ill-mannered, egotistical old woman seemed the very personification of the decadence and decay inherent in European society. Abigail hoped there might be other French ladies whose manners were more consistent with her own ideas of decency; otherwise she would wind up a recluse in France.

YET THESE WERE only early impressions, she conceded. "I have been here so little while that it would be improper for me to pass sentence, or form judgments of people," she told Mercy Warren, implying that with time she might come to see things differently. And change—or at least soften—she did, and especially as she discovered the pleasures and glamour of the Paris theater.

Abigail had always loved to read plays, but with no theaters in Boston, she had never actually seen one performed on stage until arriving in London. Now she could go as often as she wished and in the French manner, with or without the company of her husband. She quickly became a devotee of both the new Comédie-Française and the Opéra. As little as she understood the language, she loved the actors who were "beyond the reach of my pen." The performances were far superior to what she had seen in London, the crowds considerably more polite. If only the cleanliness of the British could be joined with the civility of the French, she told Mercy, it would be a "most agreeable assemblage."

For her sister, Elizabeth, Abigail described in loving detail the Comédie-Française, with its great Doric columns, its magnificent chandeliers, one of which, in the sky-blue theater itself, had two hundred candles ablaze.

Fancy, my dear Betsy, this house filled with 2,000 well dressed gentlemen and ladies!... Suppose some tragedy represented which requires the grandest scenery, and the most superb habits of kings and queens, the parts well performed, and the passions all excited, until you imagine yourself living at the very period.

One evening the four Adamses went by carriage to the Comédie-Française to see *The Marriage of Figaro*, then a sensation in Paris. The work of the dashing Beaumarchais—who had been an early supporter of the American Revolution and thickly in league with Silas Deane, shipping supplies to America—the play was a satire about the triumph of virtuous servants over their aristocratic employers. In the fifth act came the famous denunciation of his master by the valet, Figaro, that invariably brought an outburst of approval from the audience.

Because you are a great noble, you think you are a great genius! Nobility, a fortune, a rank, appointments to office: all this makes a man so proud! What did you do to earn all this? You took the trouble to get born—nothing more.

Some weeks later, when her own servants, Esther and Pauline, came home from a performance thrilled by what they had seen, Abigail was delighted.

The opera was more enthralling still, the dancing such as she had never imagined, "the highest degree of perfection." At first, she was shocked, but not for long. As she wrote to sister Mary, "I have found my taste reconciling itself to habits, customs and fashions which at first disgusted me.

The dresses and beauty of the performers were enchanting, but no sooner did the dance commence that I felt my delicacy wounded, and I was shamed to be seen looking at them. Girls clothed in the thinnest silk and gauze, with their petticoats short, springing two feet from the floor, poising themselves in the air, with their feet flying, and as perfectly showing their garters and drawers, as though no petticoats had been worn, was a sight altogether new to me. Their motions are as light as air and as quick as lightning.

While the opera house was not as impressive a building as the French theater, it was more lavishly decorated, and the costumes on stage more extravagant. "And oh! the music, vocal and instrumental, it has a soft persuasive power and a dying, dying sound."

She was changing in outlook, she knew. The more she saw of Paris and French society, the more entranced she was with the "performance" of French life, and especially the women of fashion, most of whom, she was relieved to find, were nothing like Madame Helvétius. It was as if the whole of society were a stage. Life itself was a theatrical production and Frenchwomen, raised on theater, had achieved as perfect a command of the art as anyone actually on stage. Abigail could hardly take her eyes off them, studying their every expression and gesture, charmed by the sound of their voices and by their intelligence.

They are easy in their deportment, eloquent in their speech, their voices soft and musical, and their attitude pleasing. Habituated to frequent theaters from their earliest age, they became perfect mistresses of the art of insinuation and the powers of persuasion. Intelligence is communicated to every feature of the face, and to every limb of the body; so that it may be in truth said, every man of this nation is an actor, and every woman an actress.

However greatly she deplored the dictates of fashion, on principle, she was utterly fascinated by the dress of the French ladies, which she described as being like their manners, "light, airy, and genteel." She had made clothes for herself and her family for years, and little about the design and exquisite workmanship of what passed before her now escaped her eye. The fashionable shape for women was that of the wasp, "very small at the bottom of the waist and very large round the shoulders," she reported to a cousin at home, adding ruefully, "You and I, madam, must despair of being in the mode."

With her limited French and limited means, she found her social circle inevitably limited as well. But of the Frenchwomen she came to know, by far the most engaging, and the one whose company she greatly preferred, was the "sprightly" young wife of the Marquis de Lafayette—Adrienne Françoise de Noailles—whose family, the Noailles, was among the wealthiest, most distinguished of France. In years past, after dining at their Paris mansion, Adams had written at length of all he had seen, the gardens, walks, pictures, and furniture, "all in the highest style of magnificence," and family portraits "ancient and numerous." Adrienne was one of five daughters of Jean de Noailles, Duc d'Ayen, and Henriette d'Arguesseau, and to Adams they constituted the most "exemplary" family he had met since arriving in Paris. Adrienne, who was still in her twenties when she and Abigail met, had been married to Lafayette in 1774 when she was fourteen and he sixteen. In contrast to most French-women, and very like Abigail, she remained openly devoted to her husband and children. Importantly, she spoke English and despite her wealth and position dressed simply and disliked pretentious display quite as much as did Abigail. Lafayette, a hero in Paris no less than in America, and himself one of the richest men in France, had recently acquired a palatial house on the Rue de Bourbon, which he made a center of hospitality for Americans in Paris.

"You would have supposed I had been some long absent friend who she dearly loved," Abigail wrote to Mary Cranch of the greeting she had received the day of her first call on Madame Lafayette, and for the rest of her stay she would never fail to enjoy the young woman's company. "She is a good and amiable lady, exceedingly fond of her children . . . passionately attached to her husband!!! A French lady and fond of her husband!!!" How aware Abigail may have been of the husband's frequent infidelities is not known.

Nabby, who felt she, too, had found a compatible soul in Madame Lafayette, began to see sides to French life that her own country might take lessons from. "I have often complained of a stiffness and reserve in our circles in America that was disagreeable," wrote the daughter whose mother worried that she was too stiff and reserved. "A little French ease adopted would be an improvement."

HOW WERE HER TWO "dear lads" at home, Abigail asked in a letter to Elizabeth Shaw. "I have got their profiles [silhouettes] stuck up which I look at every morning with pleasure and sometimes speak to as I pass, telling Charles to hold up his head."

But in time came letters from sisters Elizabeth and Mary both, assuring her that all was well at home, the boys well behaved and enjoying perfect health. Braintree had become a dull place without her, wrote Mary, who faithfully reported all that Abigail would wish to know about her house, farm, the doings of the town—who had been married, who had been born in her absence, who had taken ill, and who had died—and the health of John's mother, who at seventy-five still walked to meeting each Sunday. Her house, Abigail was told, was just as she would wish. "Phoebe keeps it in perfect order. It is swept and everything that wants it, rubbed once a week." Her every letter was treasured and read aloud to the delight of all. When Mary called on John's mother, to say she had come to read Abigail's letters to her, the old lady replied, "Aya, I had rather hear that she is coming home."

Abigail was to have no worries over her boys, wrote Elizabeth. "I shall always take unspeakable pleasure in serving them." The Reverend John Shaw reported the progress being made under his tutelage and offered a benediction for John Adams: "May Heaven reward him for the sacrifices he has made, and for the extensive good he has done to his country."

It still took two to three months for letters to cross the ocean, sometimes longer, but the three sisters kept up their correspondence without cease. In her letters to Mary Cranch, Abigail was more inclined to share the details of her life and her innermost feelings, while with sister Elizabeth—and perhaps because the Reverend Shaw, too, would be reading what she wrote—she was often moved to evoke the creed they had been raised on in the Weymouth parsonage. "I am rejoiced to find my sons have been blessed with so large a share of health since my absence," she told Elizabeth.

> If they are wise they will improve . . . the bloom of their health in acquiring such a fund of learning and knowledge as may render them useful to themselves, and beneficial to society, the great purpose for which they were sent into the world. . . . To be good, and do good, is the whole duty of man comprised in a few words.

"I wish I could give you some idea of the French ladies," Nabby wrote to Elizabeth another time. "But it is impossible to do it by letter, I should absolutely be ashamed to write what I must if I tell you truths. There is not a subject in nature that they will not talk upon. . . . I sometimes think myself fortunate in not understanding the language."

III

FOR ABIGAIL AND JOHN it was the long-dreamed-of chance to enjoy life together again, as husband and wife in a world at peace, and removed from the contentiousness and stress of politics at home, that made the time in France an interlude such as they had never known. No more wars and no more separations became their common creed. With Nabby and John full-grown and the best of companions, they could all four come and go together, do so much that had never been possible before, delighting in each other's company, indeed preferring it.

To compound the pleasure and stimulation of the new life, there was the bonus of Jefferson and the flourishing of a friendship that under normal circumstances at home would most likely never have happened. The vast differences between Jefferson and Adams, in nature and outlook, were as great as ever; and much had happened in Jefferson's life since 1776 to change him. But brought together as they were in Paris, in just these years between one revolution and another, none of them knowing what was over the horizon for France or their own country, or for any of them individually, the bonds that grew were exceptional. None of them would think of Paris ever again without thoughts of the other.

In addition to the time he spent working with Adams, Jefferson dined at Auteuil repeatedly, almost from the day the family moved in, and they in turn with him in Paris, once he was settled in a rented house in what was called the Cul-de-Sac Taitbout, near the Opéra. John Quincy, with Jefferson's encouragement, came to regard Jefferson's quarters as his own private refuge when in the city, and struck up friendships with Jefferson's two young aides, Colonel David Humphreys and William Short. The interest Jefferson showed in John Quincy pleased the young man exceedingly and was not lost on his parents. "He appeared to me as much your boy as mine," Adams would remind Jefferson fondly in later years.

"Dined at Mr. Jefferson's" became a familiar entry in John Quincy's diary. "In afternoon, went . . . to Paris, Mr. Jefferson's." "Spent evening with Mr. Jefferson, whom I love to be with."

One afternoon in September the Adams family, Jefferson, and "eight or ten thousand" others attended one of the celebrated Paris spectacles of the time, a balloon ascension from the Tuileries Gardens. "Came home and found Mr. Jefferson again," Nabby would record another day. "He is an agreeable man."

When Arthur Lee wrote to tell John Adams that Jefferson's supposed genius was in fact mediocre, his affectation great, his vanity greater, and warned Adams to judge carefully how much he confided in Jefferson, Adams would have none of it, replying, "My new partner is an old friend . . . whose character I studied nine or ten years ago, and which I do not perceive to be altered. . . . I am very happy with him."

For Adams so much had changed about the atmosphere in which he lived and worked that it was as if Paris had become an entirely different place, and he, a different man. There were none of the intense pressures and uncertainties of his previous years in Europe. With his family about him, with John Quincy serving as his secretary, he was perfectly at ease, never lonely. "If you and your daughter were with me," he had once written to Abigail from Paris, "I could keep up my spirits." And he was as good as his word: his pleasure in her company was palpable to all. "He professes himself so much happier having his family with him, that I feel amply gratified in having ventured across the ocean," Abigail wrote to her sister Elizabeth. Nothing, it seems, upset him. Not even Franklin bothered him anymore. The old man had become too afflicted with age and the agonies of his ailments, "too much an object of compassion, to be one of resentment," Adams noted. And the pleasure of working with Jefferson stood in such vivid contrast to the ill will and dark suspicions Adams had had to contend with when dealing with Arthur Lee. As Abigail would confide to Jefferson, there had seldom been anyone in her husband's life with whom he could associate with such "perfect freedom and unreserve," and this meant the world to her. Jefferson, she wrote, was "one of the choice ones of the earth."

She was charmed by his perfect manners, his manifold interests and breadth of reading, and, though she did not say it in so many words, by the attention he paid to her. Knowledge of the repeated tragedies that had befallen him also strongly affected her, as others. That Jefferson had vowed, as he told his family, to "keep what I feel to myself," only made him a more interesting and sympathetic figure, and particularly to those, like Abigail and John, who had known heartbreak themselves.

IN THE YEARS SINCE JEFFERSON and John Adams had last seen one another in Philadelphia, Jefferson had suffered the loss of two children— an unnamed infant son who died two weeks after his birth, and a baby girl, Lucy Elizabeth, who died in 1781, at age four-and-a-half months. Then, on September 6, 1782, at Monticello, the worst day of Jefferson's life, his wife Martha had died at age thirty-three, apparently from complications following the birth in the previous spring of still another child, a second Lucy Elizabeth.

As the story was related to the Adamses, Jefferson had been led from his wife's deathbed all but insensible with grief and for weeks kept to his room, pacing back and forth, seeing no one but his daughter Patsy. He "confined himself from the world," Nabby wrote in her journal, and then for weeks afterward, as Patsy herself would relate, he "rode out . . . incessantly on horseback, rambling about the mountains," she still his constant companion and "solitary witness to many a violent burst of grief."

At thirty-nine, Jefferson had been left a widower with three young children, his political career over, he thought, his political ambitions dissolved.

In the years immediately after his return from Philadelphia, his influence and accomplishments as a member of the Virginia General Assembly had been second to none. He had labored steadily, revising laws, writing legislation to eliminate injustices and set the foundation for a "well-ordered" republican government. And to a degree he had succeeded, although one of his proudest achievements, a bill for the establishment of religious freedom, a subject of extreme controversy, was not passed by the legislature until several years hence, after he departed for France.

Jefferson was infrequently at Williamsburg, however. His principal work, the revising and writing of laws, was carried on at Monticello, where he remained more or less in isolation, absorbed in his "darling pleasures," as his friend John Page said—with continuing work on his house, gardens, and orchards, his scholarly pursuits, management of the plantation, and the interests of his family. In February 1778, when Adams and John Quincy were bound for France aboard the *Boston*, Jefferson was placing orders for another 90,000 bricks, and overseeing the first planting of peas for the year and several varieties of fruit trees.

He had seen nothing of the war. Its principal adverse effects on his way of life were spiraling inflation, and the loss of twenty-two of his slaves who ran off in the hope of joining the British side and gaining their freedom. Any connection he had with the larger struggle was through correspondence. His only contact with the enemy was with prisoners. When 4,000 British and Hessian troops who had surrendered at Saratoga were marched to Charlottesville to be quartered outside of the town, Jefferson arranged for proper housing for the officers on neighboring plantations and saw no reason not to offer his friendship and hospitality. Indeed, he took delight in having such welcome additions to his social circle. One Hessian officer would write warmly that while all Virginians were apparently fond of music, Jefferson and his wife were particularly so. "You will find in his house an elegant harpsichord, pianoforte, and some violins. The latter he performs well upon himself...." Possibly, John and Abigail Adams learned of this while in Paris. In any event, for them to have entertained the enemy under their own roof while war raged would have been unthinkable.

But the detachment Jefferson enjoyed from the war had ended abruptly in the spring of 1779 when the Virginia Assembly chose him to succeed Patrick Henry as the wartime governor, a role he disliked and that was to prove the low point of his public career, as probably he foresaw. Only weeks later he was writing that the day of his retirement could not come soon enough. He had no background or interest in military matters. Furthermore, the real political power was not in the office of the governor, but in the Assembly, as Jefferson himself, distrusting executive authority, had helped to establish. After the rarefied life at Monticello, the everyday confusion, endless paperwork and frustrations of administering a state at war—trying to cope with inflation, taxes, allocations of money and supplies—was torturous and only grew worse.

In the first of two one-year terms, he and his family lived as had his colonial counterparts in the Governor's Palace at Williamsburg, a stone's throw from the home of George Wythe, where Jefferson had once boarded and read law. In the second term, when the capital was moved further inland to the struggling hamlet of Richmond, he, Martha, and the children occupied a rented house there and again lived in style. But it was his bad luck to be governor in one of the darkest times of the war, as the British shifted their campaign South. Word that Charleston had fallen reached him only days after his reelection. During that summer of 1780 came the humiliating rout at Camden. Virginia troops performed badly, but the defeat meant also the loss of precious cannon, wagons, tents, and muskets. Called on for reinforcements, Virginia could only send unarmed men. Enlistments were down, the state treasury empty.

Jefferson did what he could, and, by his own assessment, was ineffectual. By September he found his duties "so excessive," his execution of them "so imperfect," he would have retired but for the urging of friends. Then early in 1781 the British invaded Virginia. The traitor Benedict Arnold led a sudden, daring raid on Richmond, and with the advance of spring, the British under Cornwallis swept through the state almost at will, scattering the legislature to the hills and very nearly capturing the governor.

The Assembly had withdrawn to Charlottesville, theoretically safe from Cornwallis. Jefferson was at Monticello once more, his long-desired retirement scheduled to begin in a few days, as he informed George Washington in a letter of May 28. His term as governor expired on Saturday, June 2.

At sunrise, Monday, June 4, a lone horseman came pounding up the mountain to warn Jefferson that British cavalry were on the way to capture him and the legislature. Captain Jack Jouett of the Virginia militia had made a wild, forty-mile ride through the night. His face was cut and streaked with blood, where it had been lashed by low-hanging branches. Had it not been for a nearly full moon, he might not have arrived in time.

Reportedly, a calm, cheerfully hospitable Jefferson insisted that Jouett have a glass of his best Madeira before continuing on to Charlottesville. "I ordered a carriage to be readied to carry off my family," Jefferson would write in his account of the morning. Remaining behind, he spent another several hours gathering up papers and making sure the silver and china were hidden away. It was only when he saw by telescope that the streets of Charlottesville in the valley below were filled with British soldiers that he at last mounted his horse and took off through the woods, narrowly escaping the detachment of cavalry that arrived on the mountaintop only minutes later.

The British left Monticello untouched, but at another of Jefferson's farms, known as Elk Hill, where Cornwallis made his headquarters, they burned barns, crops, and fences, slaughtered sheep and hogs, carried off horses, cut the throats of horses too young for service, and took away with them some thirty slaves.

To have fled as he did had been Jefferson's only realistic recourse, but it had cost him in reputation. He was accused by political enemies of having taken flight in panic, of abandoning his duties in the face of the British—as if by allowing himself to be captured, he would have somehow better served his country.

The Assembly had also fled west over the Blue Ridge to Staunton in the Shenandoah Valley, but when the House of Delegates reconvened in Staunton on June 12, a young member named George Nicholas called for an inquiry into the conduct of Thomas Jefferson. No specific charge was made, and by the year's end, after Jefferson appeared before the House to defend his actions, he was officially cleared of any blame.

For someone of his extreme sensitivity, it was a painful ordeal. As he told his friend James Monroe, he had suffered "a wound in my spirit which will only be cured by the all-healing grave."

Word that Jefferson had been taken captive by the British spread rapidly and as far as Europe, where it had so distressed John Adams. In fact, Jefferson and his family had headed south to the seclusion of Poplar Forest, his other, more remote plantation in Bedford County. There they remained for six weeks, during which Jefferson, in a fall from his horse, shattered his left wrist. To occupy himself, through what had become as low a time as he had known, he began making notes in answer to a series of questions sent by a French aristocrat, the Barté-Martois, on the state of Virginia, notes that would one day be published as a book, Jefferson's first and only book.

When at summer's end he was asked to become one of the peace commissioners in Europe, he declined, telling friend and kinsman Edmund Randolph in a letter from Monticello, "[I] have retired to my farm, my family and books from which I think nothing will ever more separate me." A month later, Cornwallis surrendered at Yorktown to the combined American and French forces under Washington and Rochambeau.

Approaching Monticello by horseback afterward, an officer from Rochambeau's army, the Marquis de Chastellux, saw the great house "shining alone" on its summit, and described how, arriving on top, he found the "Sage" of Monticello wholly "retired from the world and public business."

Several days in Jefferson's company disappeared like minutes, Chastellux later wrote. They talked of art, literature, and natural history, as work on the house continued about them. The clutter and racket of construction were hardly the tranquil setting one would imagine for a sage, but Chastellux thought the house admirably unlike anything he had seen in his American travels. Of Martha Jefferson, then in the ninth month of pregnancy, he wrote only that she was "mild and amiable," which, regrettably, was no more than conventional compliments for the woman about whom so very little was ever recorded.

With the death of Martha less than five months later, everything changed. In a letter to Chastellux, Jefferson described himself as emerging from a "stupor of mind which had rendered me as dead to the world as she. . . ." He had lost all interest in Monticello, believing he could never be happy there again. But before the year was out, Congress again called for him to go to France—an idea set in motion by his close political ally, James Madison—and this time Jefferson accepted at once. When the assignment was postponed and the Virginia General Assembly (again at Madison's request) chose him as a delegate to Congress, he readily accepted that, too, and served six months, though always with an eye on France and what was happening there.

Madison, who had never met John Adams, reported to Jefferson that Adams's letters to Congress from France revealed nothing so much as his vanity, his prejudice against the French Court, and "venom" against Franklin. When Jefferson learned that Adams was again to collaborate with Franklin at Paris, he was incredulous and in a coded letter to Madison offered a private view of Adams that was anything but an unqualified endorsement. He was at a loss even to imagine how Adams might behave in any negotiation, Jefferson wrote, and likened Adams to a poisonous weed.

He hates Franklin, he hates Jay, he hates the French, he hates the English. To whom will he adhere? His vanity is a lineament in his character which had entirely escaped me. His want of taste I had observed. Notwithstanding all this he has a sound head on substantial points, and I think he has integrity. I am glad therefore that he is of the commission and expect he will be useful in it. His dislike of all parties, and all men, by balancing his prejudices, may give the same fair play to his reason as would a general benevolence of temper. At any rate honesty may be expected even from poisonous weeds.

No sooner was Jefferson named by Congress, in May 1784, to replace John Jay at Paris, than he was ready to go. Talk of retirement to Monticello was heard no more. He had not time even to return to Virginia to say goodbye to his two small children, six-year-old Polly and Lucy Elizabeth, now two, who had been left in the care of his wife's sister, Elizabeth Eppes. He gathered up Patsy, who had been living and studying in Philadelphia and, with the young servant James Hemings, was on his way to Boston and ultimately to Paris.

To John Adams, Jefferson's presence in Paris was a godsend. The Virginian seemed entirely his old self, in ability and in his devotion to their common tasks as commissioners. "Jefferson is an excellent hand. You could not have sent a better," Adams wrote in December to Elbridge Gerry, the spirit of his observations markedly different from what Jefferson had written privately of him.

He appears to me to be infected with no party passions or national prejudices, or any partialities, but for his own country. . . . Since our meeting upon our new commissions, our affairs have gone on with utmost harmony and nothing has happened to disturb our peace. I wish this calm will continue and believe it will.

In a letter to Henry Knox, Adams wrote proudly, "You can scarcely have heard a character[ization] too high of my friend and colleague, Mr. Jefferson, either in point of power or virtues. . . . I only fear that his unquenchable thirst for knowledge may injure his health."

• • •

THAT JEFFERSON WAS OFTEN ILL during their time with him in France was of great concern to the Adamses, though Jefferson himself gamely dismissed it as no more than the "seasoning" required of all newly arrived strangers to the country. But privately, Jefferson, now forty-one, told Abigail he did not expect to live more than a dozen years longer.

When feeling fit, which was much of the time, he was out and about, and as before in Philadelphia, proved an irrepressible shopper. At first chance he bought a new dress sword, silver forks and spoons, candlesticks, wine, violin strings, the model of a hydraulic engine, every purchase recorded in his tidy accounts. He bought new French clothes for himself—French lace cuffs, French shirts and lace ruffles, French gloves—new clothes for Patsy, new clothes for James Hemings, whom he put on regular wages.

The young man had been Jefferson's personal servant from the time Jefferson was governor of Virginia. He was nineteen years old, the son of a slave named Betty Hemings, who had belonged previously to Jefferson's late father-in-law, John Wayles, who reportedly was James's father—which, if true, meant that James was Jefferson's own half-brother-in-law. Since slavery was forbidden in France, James was to be quietly considered a free man for the time being. He would be apprenticed to one of the finest chefs in Paris, that he might one day bring the haute cuisine of France home to Monticello.

Jefferson was still in arrears—the income from his operations at Monticello and his other farms failed to cover his debts—and, like the Adamses, he fretted that his salary was insufficient for the manner in which he was expected to live, and to which, unlike the Adamses, he was long accustomed.

In matters of economy, as in other aspects of his life, Jefferson did not practice what he preached. He would insist to his daughter Patsy that she keep to the rule of "never buying anything which you have not the money in your pocket to pay for," and warned that "pain to the mind" of debt was greater by far than having to do without "any article whatever which we may seem to want." Yet this was hardly how he lived. A chronic acquirer, Jefferson is not known to have ever denied himself anything he wished in the way of material possessions or comforts. Once settled in Paris, he never held back, spending for example, more than 200 francs for an initial stock of fifty-nine bottles of Bordeaux—200 francs being the equivalent of three months' wages for the average French worker.

The rented house on the Cul-de-Sac Taitbout was smaller than he liked and would not long satisfy, as he already foresaw; all the same, he proceeded to remodel two rooms and spent half his salary buying more and finer furniture than needed. He rented a pianoforte, hired six additional servants. A chariot he fancied wound up costing 15,000 francs by the time repairs were made and it had been fitted out as he wished with green morocco leather.

With the United States behind on payments on its loans, Jefferson found Paris bankers reluctant to advance him sufficient sums to cover his expenses. In distress, he turned to Adams, who arranged a loan with banks in Amsterdam, as Adams had on occasion for his own expenses. Later, unable to repay the advance, Jefferson would turn to private creditors and go still deeper in debt.

Like Adams, Jefferson wrote repeatedly to friends at home and in Congress, urging that the commissioners' salaries be raised to a realistic level. That the Adamses were able to make ends meet as they did, Jefferson attributed to what he regarded as an extremely "plain" style of life, and even more to Abigail's management of expenses. As Jefferson would explain in a letter to George Washington, John Adams had the advantage of being "under the direction of *Mrs. Adams*, one of the most estimable characters on earth, and the most attentive and honorable economists."

Yet at no point did Jefferson's financial plight slow his spendthrift ways. Faithfully, almost obsessively, he kept recording every purchase and expenditure, but it was as if somehow he could never bring himself to add up the columns. At home, in his voluminous farm records, he never in his life added up the profit and loss for any year, and perhaps for the reason that there was almost never any profit.

On principle, Jefferson abhorred cities and their teeming throngs, quite as much as he abhorred debt. The mobs of great cities were like cancerous sores, he had written in his book on Virginia, a state entirely without cities. Nonetheless, he showed no interest now to live as Franklin and Adams did in semirural retreat outside Paris, where the panoramic views over the Seine were more like what he was accustomed to at home, and where the rent was appreciably less. He would reside by choice in the heart of the city his entire time in France, openly delighting in so much that was not to be found in Virginia. He relished all that Paris offered in the way of luxurious shopping, architecture, painting, music, theater, the finest food, the best wine, and the most cultivated society in his experience—never mind what he may have written about cities or the expenses he incurred.

Paris booksellers soon found they had an American patron like no other. In the bookshops and stalls along the Seine were volumes in numbers and variety such as Jefferson had never seen, and his pleasure was boundless. To Madison he would describe the surpassing pleasure of "examining all the principal bookstores, turning over every book with my own hand and putting by everything related to America, and indeed whatever was rare and valuable to every science." There were weeks when he was buying books every day. In his first month in Paris, he could not buy them fast enough, and ran up bills totaling nearly 800 francs. Nor was the book-buying spree to end. The grand total of books he acquired in France was about 2,000, but he also bought books by the boxful for Washington, Franklin, and James Madison.

With the purchase of works of art, he was tentative at first, buying only two "small laughing busts," as he recorded, then a plaster statue of Hercules and two portraits that he itemized only as "heads." Then, in a spasm of bidding at an estate auction, he bought five mostly religious paintings, including a large *Herodias Bearing the Head of Saint John*, which, like some of the others, was a copy, in this case of a popular work by Guido Reni. Before he was finished, Jefferson would buy sixty-three paintings in France as well as seven terra-cotta busts for 1,100 livres by the greatest sculptor of the day, Jean-Antoine Houdon, whom, at the request of the Virginia legislature, Jefferson also commissioned to do a life-size statue of George Washington.

Devoted to chess, eager to try his skill with some of the expert players of Paris, Jefferson found his way to a chess club, but was so decisively beaten in several games that he never went back.

Though he could read French well enough, Jefferson was never to speak the language with the fluency Adams attained. Further, he was considerably more disapproving of the outspokenness and apparent promiscuity of French women than ever Adams had been. While Adams, on first arriving in Paris, had reported to Abigail how much he admired the Frenchwomen he met—for their accomplishments, education, their views on serious matters—Jefferson felt that the decadent state of government in France was owing in good part to the influence of such women.

He had at once placed twelve-year-old Patsy in the most fashionable and most expensive convent school in Paris, the Abbaye Royale de Panthemont on the Left Bank, where to Protestant students, he was assured, no word was ever spoken of religion, but where presumably she would be safe from social influences he thought wholly unsuitable for her.

She wore a crimson uniform and was soon speaking French better than her father, who visited her frequently, enjoying the walk over the Seine by the Pont Neuf. One morning in October, Jefferson, Adams, Abigail, John Quincy, and Nabby went together to the convent to see two young nuns take the veil in a ceremony that Nabby would describe in her diary as an "affecting sight" for all. "I could not refrain from tears; everyone seemed affected."

Jefferson's devotion to his daughter, his obvious pleasure in her company and her equally obvious devotion to him, were to the Adamses greatly to his credit. "She is a sweet girl, delicacy and sensibility are read in every feature," Nabby wrote of Patsy, "and her manners are in unison with all that is amiable and lovely; she is very young." Tall for her age and freckled, she was commonly said to resemble her father.

With the onset of winter, Jefferson took ill again. He was confined to the house for six weeks. Sunshine was his great physician, he liked to say, and there was too little of it in Paris.

Then, in the last week of January, came crushing news from Virginia. His two-year-old daughter, Lucy, had died of whooping cough. Of six children, now only two remained alive. The shadow of his unspeakable sorrow fell on everyone around him. The whole Adams household was in mourning. Jefferson, as so often in his life, retreated into silence and went on with his work.

I V

To the diplomatic tasks at hand, Franklin, Adams, and Jefferson, the old Revolutionary trio, gave due attention, working steadily and in easy accord. "We proceed with wonderful harmony, in good humor, and unanimity," acknowledged Adams, whose sole complaint was a gnawing feeling of "inutility." The issues before them were commercial treaties with the nations of Europe, but it was extremely slow, unexciting work and with no notable progress. The new independent United States faced commercial barriers everywhere, while desperately in need of markets for American surpluses. The American position was free trade, but very little interest was shown.

With Franklin confined to his quarters at Passy, most of the commissioners' working sessions were held there. They carried on correspondence, drew up reports, and, as obliged, appeared each Tuesday at the King's levee at Versailles, where afterward they dined with the Comte de Vergennes and the rest of the diplomatic corps. "It is curious to see forty or fifty ambassadors, ministers or other strangers of the first fashion from all the nations of Europe, assembling in the most amicable manner and conversing in the same language," wrote Jefferson's aide, Colonel Humphreys. "What heightens the pleasure is their being universally men of unaffected manners and good dispositions."

The three American commissioners tried not to get discouraged. But as Jefferson observed, "There is a want of confidence in us." Ultimately, for all their efforts, only one commercial treaty would be negotiated, that with Prussia.

Writing to a correspondent at home, Adams said philosophically, "Public life is like a long journey, in which we have immense tracks of waste countries to pass through for a very few grand and beautiful prospects. At present, I scarcely see a possibility of doing anything for the public worth the expense of maintaining me in Europe."

An equitable trade agreement with Britain was much the most important and pressing objective. But British-American relations had been strained since the Paris Peace Treaty, and the British remained maddeningly obdurate until that winter, when the commissioners were informed that His Majesty's government would welcome an American minister to "reside constantly" at the Court of St. James's. It seemed a hopeful shift in tide, but as such a matter could be decided only by Congress, the inevitable wait began.

In letters to Congress stressing the need for an envoy to Britain, Adams neither offered recommendations nor said anything of his own

feelings, as ardently as he wanted the assignment. To Abigail there was
no question that he would be chosen—it was his "destiny," she told
Mary Cranch—and she was equally unambiguous about Jefferson's fit-
ness for his role in France. Jefferson, she assured Cotton Tufts, was "an
excellent man . . . and will do honor to his country."

In marked contrast to both Franklin and Jefferson, Adams remained
the picture of health. He had rarely ever looked or felt better. And indeed,
life for the Adams family had settled into a routine which, if unspectacular, seemed to agree with all of them. Together almost constantly, they
enjoyed a contentment such as they had seldom known.

Their days began early. With breakfast finished, weather permitting,
John and John Quincy customarily set off for a five- or six-mile walk in
the Bois de Boulogne before getting down to work. At two in the afternoon the family gathered for dinner. Most afternoons Adams was at
Passy with Franklin and Jefferson. Tea was usually at five, by which
time it was dark. In the evenings the family convened in the second-floor
sitting room, to read or play cards, except for John Quincy, who was at
his studies again, it having been agreed that he would return home soon
to enter Harvard. Many nights Adams worked with him, happily playing the schoolmaster again and with his star pupil.

At seventeen the boy was extraordinarily accomplished. In his seven
years away from home and from conventional schooling, he had benefited immeasurably from his father's interest and encouragement. His
travels, his reading, the time spent in the company of men like Francis
Dana and Thomas Jefferson had given him a maturity, made him conversant on a breadth of subjects that people found astonishing. He had
already seen more of Europe and Russia than any American of his generation. His French was virtually perfect. He was broadly read in English
and Roman history. "If you were to examine him in English and French
poetry, I know not where you would find anybody his superior," wrote
Adams proudly to the boy's former tutor and guardian at Leyden, Dr.
Benjamin Waterhouse.

He has translated Virgil's *Aeneid* . . . the whole of Sallust and Taci-
tus' *Agricola* . . . a great part of Horace, some of Ovid, and some of
Caesar's *Commentaries* . . . besides Tully's [Cicero's] *Orations*. . . .
In Greek his progress has not been equal; yet he has studied

morsels of Aristotle's *Politics*, in Plutarch's *Lives*, and Lucian's *Dialogues*, *The Choice of Hercules* in Xenophon, and lately he has gone through several books in Homer's *Iliad*.

In mathematics I hope he will pass muster. In the course of the last year . . . I have spent my evenings with him. We went with some accuracy through the geometry in the *Preceptor*, the eight books of Simpson's *Euclid* in Latin. . . . We went through plane geometry . . . algebra, and the decimal fractions, arithmetical and geometrical proportions. . . . I then attempted a sublime flight and endeavored to give him some idea of the differential method of calculations . . . [and] Sir Isaac Newton; but alas, it is thirty years since I thought of mathematics.

The picture of father and son, heads together at a table, absorbed in their work, brought Abigail satisfaction of a kind she had been long denied. "The table is covered with mathematical instruments and books, and you hear nothing 'til nine o'clock but of theorem and problems bisecting and dissecting tangents and se[quents]," she recorded one evening at Auteuil, "after which we are often called upon to relieve their brains by a game of whist."

By Nabby's account, "Pappa's hour" for bed was ten o'clock, after which she and John Quincy would have "a little conversation among themselves." "We see but little company, and visit much less," wrote Nabby, who found Auteuil less sociable than she desired. Still in a quandary over Royall Tyler, she had had almost no word from him, and while John Quincy's plans seemed neatly resolved, hers were not.

No one liked the thought of John Quincy leaving. "I feel very loath to part with my son and shall miss him more than I can express," Abigail wrote to her sister Mary. But "Master John" was now also "a man in most respects, all I may say but age," and it was his wish to go home.

She herself felt waves of extreme homesickness. A heavy snow falling over Paris filled her with emotion because it "looked so American." "What a sad misfortune it is to have the body in one place and the soul in another," she told Mary. The time in France had made her love her own country more than ever. And from the little experience she had had making the adjustment to foreign ways, and foreign speech, from what she knew now that she had not before of the intricacies and difficulties of diplomacy, she wondered how in the world "Mr. Adams" had ever "lived through the perplexing scenes he has had to encounter." Her regard for her country and for her husband had never been greater.

But of all that Abigail wrote of life *en famille* in the house at Auteuil, perhaps the most memorable vignette was in a letter to her niece Lucy Cranch, dated January 5, 1785. Describing a festive scene at the dinner table, she managed to capture much that was essential about each of them, including herself, but of her Mr. Adams in particular.

You must know that the religion of this country requires [an] abundance of feasting and fasting, and each person has his particular saint, as well as each calling and occupation. Tomorrow is to be celebrated *le jour des rois*. The day before this feast it is customary to make a large paste pie, into which one bean is put. Each person cuts his slice, and the one who is so lucky as to obtain the bean is dubbed king or queen. Accordingly, today, when I went in to dinner, I found one upon our table.

Your cousin Nabby began by taking the first slice; but alas! poor girl, no bean and no queen. In the next place, your cousin John seconded her by taking a larger cut, and as cautious as cousin T__ when he inspects merchandise, bisected his paste with mathematical circumspection; but to him it pertained not. By this time I was ready for my part; but first I declared that I had no cravings for royalty. I accordingly separated my piece with much firmness, nowise disappointed that it fell not to me.

Your uncle, who was all this time picking his chicken bone, saw us divert ourselves without saying anything. But presently he seized the remaining half, and to crumbs went the poor paste, cut here and slash there; when behold, the bean! "And thus," said he, "are kingdoms obtained!" But the servant who stood by and saw the havoc, declared solemnly that he could not retain the title, as the laws decreed it to chance, and not to force.

WHEN DURING THAT SPRING of 1785 Queen Marie Antoinette gave birth to a son, the Duke of Normandy, a Te Deum was sung in thanks at

Notre Dame, with the King himself taking part. As intended, it was one of the grandest occasions of the reign of Louis XVI and his Queen, and the four Adamses and Thomas Jefferson, along with everyone of fashion in Paris, were in attendance. Of the spectacles the Americans beheld in Paris, this was surpassing and would be recalled for years afterward, when such memories of France had become part of a vanished world.

The crowds en route to the cathedral were greater than any they had ever seen in their lives. Jefferson speculated to Nabby that there were as many people in the streets as in all of Massachusetts.

"There was but just space sufficient for the carriages to pass along," wrote John Quincy, "and had there not been guards placed on both sides at a distance not greater than ten yards from one another, there would have been no passage at all for the coaches. For as it was, the troops had the utmost difficulty to restrain the mob."

Thanks to Madame Lafayette, they were seated in a gallery overlooking the choir, "as good a place as any in the church," thought John Quincy, who in a long description of the spectacle in his diary demonstrated that besides being precociously erudite, he had learned, as his father urged, to observe the world around him and was well started on becoming an accomplished writer. He described the Parliament lined up to the right side of the choir, robed in scarlet and black, the Chambre des Comptes on the left, in robes of black and white; the bishops arriving two by two, "a purple kind of mantle over their shoulders," the Archbishop of Paris, "a mitre upon his head," and finally the arrival of the King.

> . . . and as soon as his Majesty had got to his place and fallen upon his knees, they began to sing the Te Deum, which lasted half an hour, and in which we heard some exceeding fine music.
> . . . What a charming sight: an absolute king of one of the most powerful empires on earth, and perhaps a thousand of the first personages of that empire, adoring the divinity who created them, and acknowledging that He can in a moment reduce them to the dust from which they spring.

Another day he wrote of the show of fashion and wealth at Longchamps in the Bois de Boulogne during the week before Easter.

There are perhaps each of these days a thousand carriages that come out of Paris to go round and round one of the roads in the wood one after another. There are two rows of carriages, one goes up and the other down so that the people in every carriage can see all the others. Everybody that has got a splendid carriage, a fine set of horses, or an elegant mistress, send them out on these days to make a show at Longchamps.

After so many years of living and traveling in Europe, the prospect of returning to "the pale of college" was more than a little discouraging to the boy. But like his father, he was "determined that as long as I shall be able to get my own living in an honorable manner, I will depend on no one.

My father has been so much taken up all his lifetime with the interests of the public that his own fortune has suffered by it. So that his children will have to provide for themselves, which I will never be able to do if I loiter away my precious time in Europe.

With the return of fair weather in April, life picked up. Jefferson, his health recovered, became notably sociable and by choice spent part of nearly every day with some or all of the Adamses. For all that would be said later of Jefferson's love of the French and regard for the philosophes, he clearly preferred to be with the Adamses whenever possible. His pleasure in Abigail's company was overflowing and delighted her, while Franklin, as she wrote, was "vastly social and civil." She loved the feeling of being included at the center of things, in much the way she had felt while dining on board the French warships in Boston Harbor.

ON THE EVENING OF APRIL 26, Jefferson rode out from Paris to deliver a letter that had just arrived from Elbridge Gerry informing Adams that he had been named minister to the Court of St. James's. It was requested that he be in London no later than the King's birthday on June 4.

Within days Jefferson learned that he was indeed to replace Franklin as minister to France, and it was with considerable sadness that Jefferson and the Adamses realized the end was at hand to a time like none other they had known. Nobody said goodbye to Paris without some sadness, Abigail was told. Gone from her writing were accounts of the dirt and dissipations of the French. Instead, she regretted leaving for the harsher climate of London, regretted leaving her garden, regretted especially the loss of Jefferson's society.

John Adams, too, for all his ambition to serve in London, seemed anything but eager to leave the setting of such sustained contentment. "I shall find nowhere so fine a little hill, so pleasant a garden, so noble a forest and such pure air and tranquil walks, as at Auteuil," he wrote to Richard Cranch. "I shall part with Mr. Jefferson with great regret."

Adams took his new assignment with utmost seriousness, rightly confident that he had given as much thought to British-American relations, and issues of war and peace, as had any American. What "friendly and decent terms" could be achieved in the next few years would be crucial for both nations.

Concerned about protocol in London, worried how he might be received, dreading the thought of people staring at him, he turned for advice to the British ambassador to France, the Duke of Dorset, whom he liked and trusted. In his diary afterward Adams recorded the essence of the conversation:

> He said that Lord Carmarthen was their Minister of Foreign Affairs, that I must first wait on him, and he would introduce me to his Majesty.... I asked Lord Carmarthen's age. He said 33. He said I should be stared at a great deal. I told him I trembled at the thought of going there. I was afraid they would gaze with evil eyes.

When another diplomat, assuming that Adams welcomed the change in assignment, remarked that no doubt Adams had a number of relatives in England, Adams took offense. No, he declared, he had no relatives there. "I have not one drop of blood in my veins but what is American." Writing to Mercy Warren earlier, Adams had said emphatically that he was no John Bull, he was John Yankee, "and such shall I live and die."

At Versailles, in parting conversation with the Comte de Vergennes,

Adams listened as Vergennes grandly told him that it was, of course, a step down to go from the Court of France to any other court, even if a "great thing to be the first ambassador from your country to the country you sprang from!"

When Jefferson called on the aging Foreign Minister, he demonstrated perfectly why he would be so welcome at the French Court.

"You replace Mr. Franklin, I hear," said Vergennes.

"I *succeed*," said Jefferson. "No one can replace him."

What passed between Adams and Franklin at their final parting was not recorded. Doubtless both were perfectly cordial. There would be further work to transact between them, further correspondence to maintain. But it was the last time they were ever to see one another.

At the house at Auteuil, everyone began packing. In the second week of May, John Quincy set off for Lorient, on the first leg of the long journey home to America. He would sail on a French packet and, as part of his passage, was to look after a gift from Lafayette to George Washington of seven hunting dogs.

THE FINAL DEPARTURE OF JOHN, Abigail, and Nabby from the house at Auteuil, the afternoon of May 20, 1785, was wrenching for everyone present. The servants whom Abigail had once found such a trial clustered about the carriage in tears. When she requested that her songbird be put inside the carriage with her, it fluttered so frantically in its cage that she had to give it up to her chambermaid, and it was on that melancholy note the family departed for Calais.

"We journeyed slowly and sometimes silently," Abigail wrote to Jefferson. John passed the time en route to the Channel reading the book Jefferson had presented as a parting gift, his own *Notes on the State of Virginia*, one of two hundred copies he had had privately printed in Paris. The book, Adams would write to Jefferson, was "our meditation all the day long," implying that he had been reading it aloud to Abigail and Nabby as they rolled toward Calais. The passages on slavery, said Adams, were "worth diamonds."

Alone at his desk at Poplar Forest, where more than a hundred slaves labored in the fields beyond his window, Jefferson had written one of the most impassioned denunciations of his life, decrying slavery as an extreme depravity:

> The whole commerce between master and slave is a perpetual exercise of the most boisterous passions [Jefferson had written], the most unremitting despotism on the one part, and degrading submissions on the other. Our children see this, and learn to imitate it.... The parent storms, the child looks on, catches the lineaments of wrath, puts on the same airs in the circle of smaller slaves, gives a loose to his worst passions, and thus nursed, educated, and daily exercised in tyranny, cannot but be stamped by it with odious peculiarities. The man must be a prodigy who can retain his manners and morals undepraved by such circumstances.... if a slave can have a country in this world, it must be any other in preference to that in which he is to be born to live and labor for another ... or entail his own miserable condition on the endless generations proceeding from him.... Indeed, I tremble for my country when I reflect that God is just: that his justice cannot sleep forever.

Continuing, Jefferson offered as "a suspicion only" that blacks were inferior to whites in both mind and body. "Their inferiority," he wrote, "is not the effect merely of their condition of life.... It is not their condition ... but nature, which has produced the distinction." Besides their differences in color and hair, he noted, black people secreted less by the kidneys and more by the glands of the skin, "which gives them a very strong and disagreeable odor." They were "more tolerant of heat, and less so of cold, than whites.... more ardent after their female," but love seemed with them "to be more an eager desire, than a tender delicate mixture of sentiment and sensation. Their griefs are transient ... their existence appears to participate more of sensation than reflection."

What John and Abigail Adams may have thought of this from the man who had professed to believe that all men are created equal is not known.

"The departure of your family has left me in the dumps," Jefferson wrote to Adams from Paris. "My afternoons hang heavily on me."

Crossing the Channel on board the Dover packet days later, Abigail offered to share the family's cabin with a desperately seasick young man who, in gratitude for her kindness, gave her two songbirds of his own. "As they were quite accustomed to traveling, I brought them here in safety, for which they happily repay me by their melodious notes," she would write to Jefferson in her first letter from London, knowing his love of music.

CHAPTER SEVEN

LONDON

An ambassador from America! Good heavens what
a sound!
                                    —London Public Advertiser

---

I

HIS MAJESTY THE KING of England and the new American minister to the Court of St. James's were not without common interests and notable similarities. Like John Adams, King George III was devoted to farming. Seldom was His Majesty happier than when inspecting his farms, or talking crops and Merino sheep with his farm workers at Windsor. Like Adams, the King had a passion for books. The difference, as with the farming, was mainly a matter of scale. His private library was one of the treasures of Britain. During Adams's earlier stay in London, the American painter Benjamin West had arranged a tour of the royal quarters at Buckingham House, and for Adams the high point had been seeing the King's library. He wished he could stay a week, Adams had said.

George III was to turn forty-seven on June 4, which made him two years younger than Adams, and though taller, he had a comparable "inclination to corpulence." Like Adams, he was an early riser, often out of bed before five. He, too, kept to a rigorous schedule and was an exuberant talker. Adams would later say George III was the greatest talker he had ever known. He was obstinate, affectionate, devoted to his wife and children, who numbered fifteen—again it was a matter of scale. He was deeply religious and, like Adams, sincerely patriotic.

Yet for all they had in common, the principal difference between the two was vast and paramount. One was the King of England, the other a Yankee farmer's son—John Yankee—who spoke now for an upstart nation the survival of which was anything but assured. Indeed, in England as in Europe it was generally thought that the experiment in democracy across the water had little chance of success.

With his appointment to the Court, Adams felt he had attained the pinnacle of his career, and, with the retirement of Franklin, he was now America's most experienced diplomat. But from Elbridge Gerry he had learned that the appointment had come only after rancorous dispute in Congress, and that the central issue, as Gerry reported with blunt candor, was Adams's vanity, his "weak passion."

Gerry's letter had arrived in the last days at Auteuil. Deeply hurt, Adams had written an extraordinary reply, a dissertation on the subject of vanity set forth in his clearest, plainest hand, as if intended for posterity as much as for Gerry. There were all kinds of vanity, Adams wrote—of material possessions, of physical appearance, of ribbons and titles—but there was also that which came from years spent in the service of other men, without attention to oneself, in the face of exhausting toil and at risk of life. This latter kind was a vanity, a pride, he knew. He had experienced that "joy," and for him to deny it or try to conceal it would be rank hypocrisy:

> If at times I have betrayed in word or writing such a sentiment, I have only to say in excuse for it that I am not a hypocrite, nor a cunning man, nor at all times wise, and that although I may be more cautious for the future, I will never be so merely to obtain the reputation of a cunning politician, a character I neither admire nor esteem.

Apologizing for the length of the letter, Adams added finally in a small hand at the bottom of the page, "When a man is hurt he loves to talk of his wounds." But after further thought—and possibly on the advice of Abigail—he put the letter aside. It was never sent.

The old charge of vanity, the character flaw that Adams so often chastised himself for, had been made again, and on the floor of Congress, just as he was to assume his most important role. So now more than ever he felt bound to do all in his power to serve honorably, succumbing neither to vanity nor political craftiness.

On arrival in London, he went promptly as instructed to confer with young Lord Carmarthen. Informed that his private audience with the King was arranged for June 1, he began preparing himself for what he knew would be an occasion of historic importance for his country and one of the great events of his life. Told that he must deliver a brief speech before the King, and that it be as complimentary as possible, he worked and reworked what he would say until he knew it by heart.

OF THE TIMES when Adams felt himself uncomfortably alone at center stage, there were few to compare to the afternoon in London, when at the end of a short ride through the rain with Lord Carmarthen in his carriage, they approached the arched gatehouse at St. James's Palace. Doors opened for them, Adams was led up a flight of stairs and down a hall to a room crowded with ministers of state, lords, bishops, and courtiers, all eyes on him as he and Carmarthen stood waiting outside the King's bedchamber, which was not where the King slept, but a formal reception room.

When the door opened, they proceeded, Adams, as instructed, making three bows, or "reverences," one on entering, another halfway, a third before "the presence."

"The United States of America have appointed me their minister plenipotentiary to Your Majesty," Adams began, nearly overcome by emotion.

"I felt more than I did or could express," he later wrote. Before him, in the flesh, was the "tyrant" who, in the language of the Declaration of Independence, had plundered American seas and burned American towns, the monarch "unfit to be the ruler of a free people," while to the King, he himself, Adams knew, could only be a despised traitor fit for the hangman's noose.

"The appointment of a minister from the United States to Your Majesty's Court will form an epoch in the history of England and of America," he continued.

I think myself more fortunate than all my fellow-citizens, in having the distinguished honor to be the first to stand in your Majesty's royal presence in a diplomatic character; and I shall esteem my self the happiest of men if I can be instrumental in recommending my country more and more to your Majesty's royal benevolence, and of restoring an entire esteem, confidence, and affection, or, in better words, the old good nature and the old good humor between people who, though separated by an ocean and under different governments, have the same language, a similar religion, and kindred blood.

I beg your Majesty's permission to add that although I have some time before been intrusted by my country, it was never in my whole life in a manner so agreeable to myself.

Brief as it was, he got through the speech only with difficulty, his voice at times quaking, and the King, too, was greatly moved. "The King listened to every word I said, with dignity but with apparent emotion," Adams would report to Foreign Secretary John Jay. "Whether it was in the nature of the interview, or whether it was my visible agitation, for I felt more than I did or could express, that touched him, I cannot say. But he was much affected, and answered me with more tremor than I had spoken with.

The circumstances of this audience are so extraordinary, the language you have now held is so extremely proper, and the feelings you have discovered so justly adapted to the occasion, that I must say that I not only receive with pleasure the assurance of the friendly dispositions of the United States, but that I am very glad that the choice has fallen upon you to be their minister. I wish you, sir, to believe, and that it be understood in America, that I have done nothing in the late contest but what I thought myself indispensably bound to do by the duty which I owed to my people. I will be very frank with you, I was the last to consent to separation; but the separation having been made, and having become inevitable, I have always said, as I say now, that I would be the first to meet the friendship of the United States as an independent power.

25

John Adams was born in 1735 in the Braintree farmhouse on the right. He and Abigail made their first home in the nearly identical house on the left. Both houses still stand.

27

Two pastels done by Benjamin Blythe at Salem, in 1766, are the earliest known portraits of Abigail and John Adams. Her decided nature is clearly evident, while he might be almost any untested, well-fed young man of the time.

In London, at the height of their friendship, John Adams and Thomas Jefferson each sat for the young American painter Mather Brown. The Adams portrait was done in 1785, that of Jefferson the year after.

This of Jefferson, however, is a copy by Brown of the original, which later disappeared. It is the first known portrait of Jefferson and, unlike all others, shows him looking very like a European dandy.

John Quincy Adams at age twenty-nine, in a portrait by John Singleton Copley.

30

31

Charles Adams, the seco[nd] son and "the most a gent[le] man," at twenty-seven[.] Artist unknown.

32

Thomas Boylston Adams, the third son, who had "a spice of fun in his composition," at twenty-three.

Nabby Adams at nineteen by Mather Brown. To her father the portrait caught both her "drollery and modesty."

John Trumbull painted the Vice President of the United States
in 1793, when John Adams was fifty-seven. To Adams there was
"no penance like having one's picture done."

Painted over several years, Gilbert Stuart's portrait of Abigail
Adams was begun in 1800, while she still presided over the President's
House in Philadelphia. Stuart remarked to a friend that as a young
woman she must have been a "perfect Venus."

This portrait by Gilbert Stuart is thought to have been painted in Philadelphia in 1798 but may have been done later. It is considered the finest of several Stuart portraits of John Adams as President of the United States.

John Adams was nearly eighty-nine when, at the request of
John Quincy, he posed one last time for Gilbert Stuart. "He lets
me do as I please," Adams said of the artist, "and keeps me
constantly amused with conversation."

He could not vouch that these were the exact words, Adams cautioned in his letter to Jay, for the King's manner of speaking had been so odd and strained. (It was Adams's first encounter with the famous stutter of George III.) "He hesitated some time between his periods, and between the members of the same period. He was indeed much affected."

Smiling, the King changed the subject. "There is an opinion among some people that you are not the most attached of all your countrymen to the manners of France," he said.

Adams, embarrassed, replied, "I must avow to your Majesty, I have no attachment but to my own country."

"An honest man will never have any other," the King said approvingly, and with a bow signaled that the interview was ended.

> I retreated [Adams wrote], stepping backwards, as is the etiquette, and, making my last reverence at the door of the chamber, I went my way. The Master of Ceremonies joined me . . . and accompanied me through the apartments down to my carriage, several stages of servants, gentlemen-porters, and under-porters roaring out like thunder as I went along, "Mr. Adams' servants, Mr. Adams' carriage."

It had all gone superbly. Adams's remarks had been graceful, dignified, appropriate, and, with the possible exception of his reference to "kindred blood," altogether sincere. He had proven a diplomat of first rank, almost in spite of himself.

The King, too, had been the essence of courtesy and poise, as Adams later acknowledged. But any thought that the interview presaged an overall cordial welcome for the new minister was dashed soon enough by the London press, which dismissed the meeting as nothing more than a curious anecdote for future historians. "An ambassador from America! Good heavens what a sound!" scoffed the *Public Advertiser*. The *London Gazette* expressed rank indignation at the very appointment of such a "character" as Adams to the Court. To the *Daily Universal Register* it had been a notably cool reception, while the *Morning and Daily Advertiser* described Adams as so pitifully embarrassed as to be tongue-tied.

Beneath the polite English surface lay burning animosity, surmised Abigail, who, like John, felt she was taking part in an elaborate stage play.

UNTIL A SUITABLE HOUSE could be found, the three Adamses were residing in the Bath Hotel in Piccadilly, where, after the quiet of Auteuil, the noise of the streets seemed horrendous. Abigail hated the thought of having to hire servants again and making the necessary domestic arrangements on her own. "I cannot bear to trouble Mr. Adams with anything of a domestic kind, who from morning until evening has sufficient to occupy all his time," she wrote to her sister Mary. Still, she delighted in being once more where her own language was spoken. A performance of Handel's *Messiah* at Westminster Abbey was "sublime beyond description," she wrote to Jefferson. "I most sincerely wished for your presence, as your favorite passion would have received the highest gratification. I should have sometimes fancied myself amongst the higher order of beings."

Three weeks after Adams's private audience with the King came the Queen's circle, or "drawing room." This time all three of the family were to attend, as well as Colonel William Stephens Smith of New York, who had been appointed by Congress as secretary of the American legation and was also newly arrived in London. Smith had served with distinction in the Continental Army. At the battle of Long Island he had made the night withdrawal across the East River and later served on Washington's staff. He was a graduate of the college at Princeton and, with his soldierly carriage and dark good looks, made a handsome addition to the group.

Days were consumed in preparation. She must look "elegant but plain as I could possibly appear with decency," Abigail instructed her dressmaker. The dress she wore was of white silk trimmed with white crepe and lilac ribbon, over an enormous hoop. "A very dress cap with long lace lappets, two white plumes and a blonde lace handkerchief; this is my rigging," she informed Mary in high spirits. "I should have mentioned two pearl pins in my hair, earrings and necklace of the same kind." Nabby's attire, too, was in white, only with a petticoat, "the most showy part," and included a cap with three immense feathers.

Mother and daughter had seldom if ever looked so glorious. "Thus equipped we go in our own carriage," wrote Abigail. "But I must quit my pen to put myself in order for the ceremony which begins at two o'clock."

"Congratulate me, my dear sister, it is over," she commenced the next installment, settling in to describe in detail and with wry humor all that had transpired, and leaving little doubt as to what she thought of such business overall, or whether she was capable of meeting the test, even if it meant four hours on her feet.

Of the English novelists, Abigail was especially fond of Samuel Richardson, whose popular works, *Pamela* and *Clarissa*, were tales told through the device of extended letters. Richardson, "master of the human heart," had "done more towards embellishing the present age, and teaching them the talent of letter-writing, than any other modern I can name." That her own outpouring of letters was influenced by Richardson, Abigail would have readily agreed. In Richardson's hands events unfolded in letters written "to the moment," as things happened. "My letters to you," she would tell Mary, "are first thoughts, without correction."

At the palace the Adamses were escorted to a large drawing room, where two hundred selected guests, including foreign diplomats and their wives, were arranged in a large circle. "The King enters the room and goes round to the right, the Queen and princesses to the left," Abigail began her account for Mary.

Only think of the task the royal family have, to go round to every person and find small talk enough to speak to all of them. Though they very prudently speak in a whisper, so that only the person who stands next can hear what is said. . . . The Lord in Waiting presents you to the King and the Lady in Waiting does the same to Her Majesty. The King is a personable man, but my dear sister, he has a certain countenance which you and I have often remarked, a red face and white eyebrows. . . . When he came to me, Lord Onslow [Arthur Onslow, lord of the royal bedchamber] said, "Mrs. Adams," upon which I drew off my right glove and His Majesty saluted my left cheek, then asked me if I had taken a walk today. I could have told His Majesty that I had been all morning preparing to wait upon him, but I replied, "No, Sire." "Why don't you love walking?" says he. I answered that I was rather indolent in that respect. He then bowed and passed on. It was more than two hours after this before it came my turn to be presented to the Queen. The circle was so large that the company were four hours standing. The Queen was evidently embarrassed when I was presented to her. I had disagreeable feelings, too. She, however, said, "Mrs. Adams, have you got your house? Pray how do you like the situation of it?" Whilst the Princess Royal [Charlotte Augusta Matilda, the oldest daughter of George III and Queen Charlotte] looked compassionate, and asked me if I was much fatigued, and observed that it was a very full drawing room. Her sister who came next, Princess Augusta, after having asked your niece if she was ever in England before, and her answering, "Yes," inquired me how long ago, and supposed it was when she was very young. And all this is said with much affability and ease and freedom of old acquaintance.

The two princesses were quite pretty, "well shaped," "heads full of diamonds." Queen Charlotte, however, was neither pretty nor well shaped, and on the whole, Abigail told Mary, the ladies of the Court were "very plain, ill-shaped, and ugly, but don't tell anybody that I say so."

All things considered, the royal family was surprisingly affable, but certainly the life they led was not to be envied. Nor should anyone imagine that Abigail remained anything other than herself: "I could not help reflecting with myself during the ceremony, what a fool I do look like to be thus accoutered and stand for four hours together, only to be spoken to by 'royalty.' "

THE SUITABLE HOUSE was found and, their furniture having arrived from France, the family moved to the quiet of Grosvenor Square in the West End. The tree-shaded square with its neat gravel walks covered five acres—exactly the size of the garden at Auteuil—and was framed by elegant town houses belonging to a number of London's most eminent citizens, including Lord Carmarthen.

The house the Adamses rented—what became the first American

legation in London—was No. 8, at the northeast corner. The front entrance opened onto a large hall. There was a dining room spacious enough for entertaining on the first floor and another ample room that Adams made his office for public business. Drawing room and library were on the floor above, bedrooms on the third floor. The kitchen was in the English basement, and a stable was to the rear. Once the servants were hired and in place "below stairs," the staff consisted of Esther Field, now elevated to lady's maid, a butler, a housemaid, a cook, a kitchen maid, two footmen (one of whom was John Briesler), and a coachman. This made a total of eight, as at Auteuil, and again Abigail would have preferred fewer who worked harder. Adams, after several weeks in residence, allowed that after so long in France he was "not so pleased" with English cookery.

But these were quibbles. The house suited perfectly. For Adams the location was ideal. Abigail had a small room of her own with a view of the square, a place to write and be alone with her thoughts, and to Nabby, it was all a decided improvement over Auteuil. "We shall live more as if we were part of the world," she wrote to John Quincy.

That "world"—London of the 1780s—was a city grown all out of proportion, with nearly a million souls. Though a city still of "smoke and damp," in Adams's words, it was an appreciably cleaner, healthier, less violent place than it had been earlier in the century. It was both the political capital of Britain and the center of manufacturing, finance, and trade. The Thames, its foul, mud-colored main artery and portal to the world, carried more traffic than any river in Europe. One had only to stand on any London bridge, said a guidebook, to see fleets of ships "carrying away the manufactures of Britain and bringing back the produce of the whole earth," a spectacle illustrating Adams's chief concern as ambassador, since none was American.

The great dome of St. Paul's Cathedral rose high above what seemed a forest of towers, turrets, and church spires, very unlike the skyline of Paris. A thousand hackneys plied the streets, and innumerable sedan chairs, each propelled by four strong men, usually Irish, who could shout and muscle their way through traffic faster than the hackneys. All was "tumult and hurry," just as portrayed in English novels. Bond Street shops were thought superior to those of Paris. London coffeehouses, taverns, theaters, and concert halls surpassed anything of the kind elsewhere in the British empire, and for the young and aspiring, London remained the great magnet. Exhilaration of the kind voiced by young James Boswell of Edinburgh upon seeing the city for the first time in 1762 was felt still by thousands who kept coming from the hinterlands. In London was to be found the full tide of human existence, Boswell's hero, Samuel Johnson, had said, declaring famously, "When a man is tired of London, he is tired of life."

The extravagance of the ruling class was notorious. At such exclusive clubs as Brooks or Boodles on St. James's Street, fortunes were reputedly gambled away at the turn of a card, and, nightly, young men drank themselves into a stupor. This was not quite true, but the stories would never die, and the clothes, carriages, the sheer weight of gold braid on the livery of servants, left little doubt as to how vast was the wealth of the wealthiest. Yet, as the Adamses found, one could hardly go anywhere without encountering such spectacles of poverty and misery as to tear at the heart—people in tatters, hunger and suffering in their faces, as Abigail wrote. And who was to answer for the wretched victims "who are weekly sacrificed upon the gallows in numbers sufficient to astonish a civilized people?" Compounding her sorrow was the realization that every night and in all weather abandoned children by the hundreds slept beneath the bushes and trees of nearby Hyde Park.

The English historian and novelist Tobias Smollett had written of the inevitable distrust felt by every visitor to London, the underlying fear of being taken. For his part, Adams was determined to be neither stingy nor a fool. Approached by the representative of a group known as His Majesty's Royal Bell Ringers, who asked that he share some of his "honorable bounty" and said two guineas were customary, Adams gave the man one guinea and said he would look into what was customary.

James Boswell could still be seen on occasion holding forth at the Globe Tavern on Fleet Street; the novelist Fanny Burney was soon to become a lady in waiting to Queen Charlotte; Richard Brinsley Sheridan was still part owner and manager of the famous Drury Lane Theater. But the giants of London's literary world, authors to whom the Adamses were devoted—Richardson, Sterne, Smollett, Samuel Johnson—were all dead and gone. And so, too, was Hogarth. The reigning artists were the rivals Thomas Gainsborough and Joshua Reynolds and the American Benjamin West, who did elegant portraits and historical scenes, rather than graphic renditions of the dark side of London life.

As much as anything, it was a city of entertainments, and this to Abigail was its saving grace. She joked about seeing a "learned pig, dancing dogs, and a little hare that beats a drum," amusements fit for children; but she openly enjoyed them and with Nabby went more than once to Sadler's Wells music hall, to delight in the "wonderful feats" of a troupe of tumblers.

The three Adamses went often to the theater, and to Ranelagh Gardens in Chelsea, where, in company with fashionable London society, they strolled garden paths, sipped imperial tea, listened to music, or gazed at paintings within an immense gilded rotunda. Smollett had described Ranelagh as looking like "the enchanted palace of a genie . . . crowded with the great, the rich, the gay, the happy and the fair." To Abigail, the "fair" on display were more stunning by far than any to be seen at Court.

Pleased to be in a Protestant country once more, the family attended church regularly, riding to the village of Hackney to hear the celebrated liberal preacher and champion of America, Richard Price, who was to become a valued friend. Once, for no reason other than intellectual curiosity, Adams rode to Windsor to call on the famous English astronomer Sir William Herschel, whose crowning achievement had been the discovery of the planet Uranus. Greeting Adams affably, Herschel was delighted to talk of his work, and Adams returned to Grosvenor Square elated. Nabby recorded that she had never known her father so gratified by a visit of any kind.

But neither the Reverend Price's friendship nor William Herschel's reception was representative. With the exception of tradesmen and a few officials of the government, the British overall were decidedly cool toward the new American minister and his family—perfunctory, but no more. And they did stare as Adams had worried they would, and not in a friendly way. "The English may call the French starers," wrote Nabby to John Quincy, "but I never saw so little civility and politeness in a stare in France as I have here." To Jefferson, with whom she had commenced regular correspondence, Abigail described the atmosphere as "not the pleasantest in the world." In truth, the American minister and his family were being pointedly ignored.

Their "society" was confined almost entirely to other Americans living in London, or to such openly avowed friends of America as Richard Price. A few of the Americans were acquaintances from Boston, like the aspiring young architect Charles Bulfinch. Jefferson's aide, William Short, came on errands from Paris, and the duplicitous Dr. Edward Bancroft showed up, affable as always. Whether Bancroft was serving still as a spy for the British government is not known, though in all likelihood he was.

Friendliest and most helpful were the American painters Benjamin West and John Singleton Copley, who introduced the family to their protégés, young Mather Brown of Boston and John Trumbull of Connecticut, a veteran of the Revolution. A rage for painters and painting had seized the household, Nabby reported excitedly to John Quincy, after Mather Brown set up his easel at Grosvenor Square to do portraits of all three of the Adamses. Her delight was extreme. (The young man was so striking-looking as to be commonly spoken of as "handsome young Brown," as though that were his name.) Brown's portrait of her was quite "tasty," she thought. Wearing a wide-brimmed hat with ribbons and feather, she sat with her hands in her lap, looking directly ahead, a lovely, poised, somewhat wistful young woman at the threshold of adulthood. Her father was charmed, it was "her exactly," he said.

For his own portrait Adams posed at his writing desk, with quill and paper in hand, and Jefferson's *Notes on the State of Virginia* prominently displayed to one side. Adams believed his strongest attributes were, as he said, "candor, probity, and decision," but these he failed to find in the face that looked back from the finished canvas, and he expressed disappointment. In Brown's portrait, he appeared composed, leaner than Copley had portrayed him, and reflective. It was a fine study of an eighteenth-century gentleman of consequence, but nothing about the pose or the expression gave any suggestion of his characteristic alertness and vitality, or sense of humor—let alone "candor, probity, and decision."

Brown's rendering of Abigail was thought "a good likeness," but the painting would ultimately disappear.

Meantime, West and Copley in particular opened doors for Adams in London as did no one else. "I did not ask favors or receive anything but cold formalities from ministers of state or ambassadors," he would explain. "I found that our American painters had more influence at Court to produce all the favors I wanted."

"Economies" remained a constant concern. The cost of living in London was higher even than in Paris, and to make matters worse, Congress had cut Adams's salary by a fifth, from 2,500 to 2,000 pounds. A dinner guest from Scotland would describe a meal with the Adamses as "good" but "plain," while Jefferson, visiting later, would be astonished by how "very plain" they lived. Writing to Mercy Warren after the first year in London, Adams would confide, "I am driven to my wits' end for means."

Lavish entertainment of the kind expected of an ambassador to the Court was out of the question. But then neither did the Adamses have any great desire for London society. She was too old-fashioned, Abigail said, for keeping company with "midnight gamblers and titled gamesters," whose way of life she had seen something of and may have enjoyed more than she was willing to admit. At a party given by the Swedish ambassador, pressed to fill an empty place at one of the card tables, she won four games straight.

Worst of all was being patronized by the British. One of the few British women to call on Abigail since the move to Grosvenor Square, the wife of a member of Parliament remarked, in an effort to make conversation, "But surely you prefer this country to America?" British prejudice toward the French struck Abigail as ludicrous, now that she had lived in France, and made her realize how greatly she disliked prejudice in any form. But then unexpectedly, she was brought up short to find it in herself.

Having read and loved the plays of Shakespeare since childhood, she was thrilled by the chance to see an actual stage production. The great English tragedienne Sarah Siddons, who had come out of retirement the year before, appeared in *Macbeth* for the first time and was acclaimed a triumph. That Mrs. Siddons then appeared in *Othello*, making the transition from Lady Macbeth to Desdemona, was declared the mark of genius, and the Adamses were among the glittering audiences that filled the Drury Lane for both productions. To Abigail, Mrs. Siddons was brilliant but miscast as Lady Macbeth. It was in *Othello*, as Desdemona, that she was "interesting beyond any actress I had ever seen."

Yet to read of Desdemona in the arms of a black man was, Abigail found, not the same as seeing it before her eyes. "Othello [played by John Kemble] was represented blacker than any African," she wrote. Whether it was from "the prejudices of education" or from a "natural antipathy," she knew not, "but my whole soul shuddered whenever I saw the sooty heretic Moor touch the fair Desdemona." Othello was "manly, generous, noble" in character, so much that was admirable. Still she could not separate the color from the man. Filled with self-reproach, she affirmed that there was "something estimable" in everyone, "and the liberal mind regards not what nation or climate it springs up in, nor what *color* or *complexion* the man is of."

Attacks on Adams in the press continued. He was called a nobody, ridiculed for having insufficient means to conduct himself in proper fashion. The *Public Advertiser* reminded its readers that all so-called American patriots were cowards, murderers, and traitors, and described Adams as looking "pretty fat and flourishing" considering "the low estate he is reduced to." In letters to the editor he was decried as a "pharisee of liberty," an "imposter." Every hireling scribbler was set to vilify them, wrote Abigail, who in her time in London acquired a dislike of the press that would last a lifetime.

From Paris, where he was well supplied with London papers, Jefferson expressed astonishment at such slanders, as well as admiration for Adams's fortitude. "Indeed a man must be of rock who can stand all this," he wrote to Abigail. "To Mr. Adams it will be but one victory the more." Then, in a rare revelation of inner feeling, a confession of weakness such as he seldom made to anyone, Jefferson told her:

> It would have ill suited me. I do not love difficulties. I am fond of quiet, willing to do my duty, but [made] irritable by slander and apt to be forced by it to abandon my post. These are weaknesses from which reason and your counsels will preserve Mr. Adams.

Possibly, he postulated, it was "the quantity of animal food eaten by the English which renders their character unsusceptible of civilization."

He had been taken up by the Paris "literati," he reported happily, and acquired a larger, more expensive house for himself. Located at the corner of the Champs-Élysées and the Rue de Berri, the newly built Hôtel de Langeac had twenty-four rooms, an indoor toilet, and a "clever garden."

Not satisfied with it as it was, Jefferson proceeded to redesign and reconstruct much of the house to suit his fancy, thus adding further to the expense and despite grave concern over his own private finances.

To his brother-in-law, Francis Eppes, who was managing his affairs at home, Jefferson wrote, "The torment of mind I endure till the moment shall arrive when I shall owe not a shilling on earth is such really as to render life of little value." But what could he do? He could not sell any more of his land, he wrote: he had sold too much as it was, and land was his only provision for his children. "Nor," he added, "would I willingly sell the slaves as long as there remains any prospect of paying my debts with their labors."

Had Jefferson been as forthcoming with Adams as with his brother-in-law, Adams, the farmer's son, would have had no argument with Jefferson's faith in land as the only true wealth. But that Jefferson could so matter-of-factly consider selling off his slaves—not freeing them—and so readily transfer the burdens of his own extravagances to the backs of those he held in bondage, would have struck Adams as unconscionable, and would no doubt have been a serious test of his respect, if not affection, for the man. But such matters as these Jefferson never mentioned or discussed with Adams.

Meanwhile, he and Abigail exchanged shopping requests. Jefferson purchased French shoes and lace for her, and hunted down French dessert platters of a kind she had her heart set on for her dining table. For her part, Abigail was to pick out a dozen English shirts for him, a tablecloth and napkins sufficient for a seating of twenty. "But when writing to you," he declared at the close of one letter, "I fancy myself at Auteuil and chatter on till the last page of my paper awakes me from my reverie."

OCCASIONS AT COURT grew increasingly tedious and strained for Adams and his family. "Do you go out much for a walk," the King kept inquiring of Abigail and Nabby at each and every reception, though the King, they thought, at least dissembled better than the Queen, whose countenance, said Nabby, was "as hard and unfeeling as if carved out of an oak knot."

Particularly grating to Adams was the oft-spoken assumption among many of the British that sooner or later America would "of course" return to the British fold.

> There is a strong propensity in this people [he wrote to Richard Henry Lee] to believe that America is weary of her independence; that she wishes to come back; that the states are in confusion; Congress has lost its authority; the governments of the states have no influence; no laws, no order, poverty, distress, ruin, and wretchedness; that no navigation acts we can make will be obeyed; no duties we lay on can be collected . . . that smuggling will defeat all our prohibitions, imposts and revenues. . . . This they love to believe.

There was indeed "a new order of things arisen in the world," Adams emphasized to another correspondent at home, but British statesmen refused to comprehend this. Overall, the attitude toward America, he had come to realize, was hardly less hostile than it had been during the war. "They hate us," he wrote to a friend. One Englishman had declared in his presence, "I had rather America had been annihilated, than that she should have carried her point."

Much of this he and Abigail attributed to "venom" spread by American Loyalists in London. One vehement figure, Harrison Gray, once the treasurer of Massachusetts, said in a letter to the press that if it were left to him, he would have John Adams hanged.

Adams remained remarkably calm, nonetheless, conducting himself with model composure, and refusing to have any contact with Loyalists, with one exception. Taking the initiative, he hunted up his old friend Jonathan Sewall, whom he had not seen since the day they bid farewell at Casco Bay in what seemed a lifetime before. Adams rode to Sewall's London lodgings, and as Sewall wrote afterward, it was a memorable reunion. "When Mr. Adams came in, he took my hand in both his, and with a hearty squeeze, accosted me in these words, *'How do you do, my dear old friend!'* Our conversation was just such as might be expected at the meeting of two old sincere friends after a long separation."

They talked for two hours. Neither had changed his views on the Revolution, nor his enmity for the side the other had chosen, though apparently nothing of this was said. Through the years of the war Sewall had taken heart from every American defeat, every report of dissension in the American army, and from the news of Benedict Arnold's return to his proper allegiances. Like many Loyalists living in exile in England, Sewall had had a difficult time getting by. Exiled from their homeland, unappreciated in their adopted country, most Loyalists had a hard life.

Sewall had grown bitter and resentful. His hatred of New England patriots was worse than ever: "those sanctified hypocrites," he called them, those "rebellious, ungenerous, ungrateful sons of bitches." Suffering bouts of melancholia, he had largely withdrawn from life, seldom leaving his rooms. Noticeably aged, he lived only for his two sons, he confessed to Adams, and for their sakes planned to remove to Canada.

Adams urged Sewall and his wife, Esther Quincy, to come and take a family dinner at Grosvenor Square, and "in a way so friendly and hearty," wrote Sewall, that he almost complied, but could not, would not.

"Adams has a heart formed for friendship, and susceptible to its finest feelings," Sewall continued in his account of the reunion. "He is humane, generous and open, warm in his friendly attachments, though perhaps rather implacable to those he thinks his enemies." Clearly, Adams did not regard Sewall as his enemy.

Each felt he knew the other as well as he knew any man, and privately Adams thought Sewall, in 1774, had tragically sacrificed principle for position, while Sewall, as he wrote, thought Adams's own "unbounded ambition" was at fault; this and "an enthusiastic zeal for the imagined or real glory and welfare of his country" had overcome Adams's better self, "his every good and virtuous social and friendly principle." With some understandable resentment perhaps, Sewall concluded that Adams had gone as far as his ambition would take him, and further that he was ill suited for his present role.

> He is not qualified by nature or education to shine in courts. His abilities are undoubtedly equal to the mechanical parts of his business as ambassador; but this is not enough. He cannot dance, drink, game, flatter, promise, dress, swear with the gentlemen, and small talk and flirt with the ladies; in short, he has none of the essential arts or ornaments which constitute a courtier. There are thousands who, with a tenth of his understanding and without a spark of his honesty, would distance him infinitely in any court in Europe.

For all the warmth of the reunion, the expressions of brotherhood, the two hours were difficult. Adams came away deeply saddened. He would forever think of Sewall as one of the casualties of the war. According to Adams, when Sewall died in New Brunswick a number of years later, it was of a broken heart.

I I

OF THE MULTIPLE ISSUES in contention between Britain and the new United States of America, and that John Adams had to address as minister, nearly all were holdovers from the Treaty of Paris, agreements made but not resolved, concerning debts, the treatment of Loyalists, compensation for slaves and property confiscated by the British, and the continued presence of British troops in America. All seemed insoluble. With its paper money nearly worthless, its economy in shambles, the United States was desperate for trade, yet without the power or prestige to make demands, or even, it seemed, to qualify for respect. British complacency was massive. The British saw no cause for haste in fulfilling any of the agreements with their poor, weak, former adversary. Nor were they the least inclined to lessen or jeopardize in any way their primacy at sea. British reluctance to be accommodating was quite as great as the American need for equitable resolutions. The British continued to exclude American vessels from both Canada and the West Indies, as well as from Britain. Further, no American products could be shipped anywhere within the British Empire except in British vessels.

To Adams the first priority must be to open British ports to American ships. But his efforts came to nothing, while at home, under the Articles of Confederation enacted in 1781, Congress was without power to regulate commerce. It was thus a sad and humiliating situation.

Adams went repeatedly to Whitehall to meet with Lord Carmarthen. He called at 10 Downing Street for an exchange with the Prime Minister, William Pitt, the younger, who was all of twenty-four years old, who never stopped talking and impressed Adams not at all. Whatever Adams proposed, whatever inquiries he made to the Ministry, he received no answers. Long days and nights were spent reporting to Foreign Secretary Jay and composing memorials to Carmarthen. One particularly important memorial, calling for the withdrawal of British garrisons from the Northwest, as agreed in the Treaty of Paris, went unanswered for three months. When at last Carmarthen replied, it was to say only that this violation of the treaty was no different from the failure of Americans to pay the debts due British creditors.

Adams was hardly surprised. From his first meeting with Pitt, he had been convinced that Britain would never willingly give up the forts, any more than they would open the way to American trade with the West Indies.

When Adams talked of "commercial reciprocity," the British thought him naïve. Like Jefferson, Adams believed in free trade in theory, but faced with British intransigence, he began losing hope of ever attaining such an agreement and cautioned Jefferson, "We must not, my friend, be the bubbles of our own liberal sentiments." Presently, the picture no brighter, he told Jefferson that if the British Court refused to act a reasonable and equitable part, the United States should enter into "still closer and stronger connections with France."

Commercial relations with France, however, were no more promising than with Britain. Jefferson, who was as dedicated to close ties with the French as ever Franklin had been, had thus far succeeded in attaining a single agreement, one whereby American whale oil would be admitted to French markets, and this for a limited time only. Since the end of the war, the French, for their part, had attained nothing like the flourishing American trade that Vergennes had imagined. The demand for French goods in America was low and not likely to improve. When in a meeting with Lord Carmarthen, Adams summoned all his old intensity to warn that the attitude of the British, if continued, would inevitably strengthen commercial ties between the United States and France, it had no effect whatever. He saw no hope, Adams reported to Jefferson.

Correspondence between Grosvenor Square and Paris remained steady and candid. In eight months' time, from late May 1785, when Adams first assumed his post in London, until February 1786, he wrote twenty-eight letters to Jefferson, and Jefferson wrote a nearly equal number in return. Entirely trusting of one another, the two ministers exchanged news, opinions on issues, speculations on potential markets for American tobacco in Europe. One long letter from Adams was devoted to Portugal's need for American timber, tar, turpentine, and salt fish, as well as the corresponding future market in America for Portuguese wine and olive oil. When Jefferson asked Adams to inquire about insuring the life of the sculptor Houdon, who was sailing for America to do the statue of Washington, discussion of the matter went back and forth in several letters before Adams had things arranged.

A small but noteworthy difference in the letters was that Jefferson regularly signed himself in conventional fashion, "Your obedient and humble servant," or "Your friend and servant," while Adams wrote, "Yours most affectionately," or "With great and sincere esteem," or "My dear friend adieu."

Increasingly their time and correspondence was taken up by concerns over American shipping in the Mediterranean and demands for tribute made by the Barbary States of North Africa—Algiers, Tripoli, Tunis, and Morocco. To insure their Mediterranean trade against attacks by the "Barbary pirates," the nations of Europe customarily made huge cash payments. It was extortion and an accepted part of the cost of commerce in that part of the world. France paid $200,000 a year to Algiers alone; Britain paid even more, as much as $280,000 annually. In past years, before the war, when American trade in the Mediterranean flourished, American ships had come under the protection paid for by the British. But after 1776, such protection no longer pertained. Nor would France now foot the cost of guaranteeing respect for the American flag off the shores of North Africa. Tribute (bribes) would have to be paid and it would cost the United States dearly, Vergennes had advised Adams earlier; otherwise, there would be no peace with the Barbary States.

Just weeks after Adams arrived in London, in July 1785, two American ships were seized by Algerian pirates. Twenty-one American sailors were taken captive and forced into slave labor. News spread that Benjamin Franklin, en route from France to Philadelphia, had been captured by Barbary pirates, and though untrue, the story caused a sensation.

From Philadelphia, John Jay sent instructions to negotiate with the Barbary States. Funds were made available by Congress up to $80,000. But Adams and Jefferson had no money at hand. When Jefferson inquired whether Adams might borrow again from the Dutch, and reported that French officers in Paris were angry over not having been paid what they were due for services in the Revolution, Adams was helpless to do anything. It was not at all certain, he answered, that there would be funds sufficient even to cover "your subsistence and mine."

On a chill evening in February came what Adams took to be an opening. At the end of a round of ambassadorial "visits," he stopped to pay his respects to a new member of the diplomatic corps in London, His Excellency Abdrahaman, envoy of the Sultan of Tripoli. It was apparently a spur-of-the-moment decision on Adams's part and resulted in an amazing, smoke-filled exchange that Adams, delighted by the humor of the scene, happily recounted for Jefferson.

Adams and his host settled into two large chairs before a great fire, while a pair of factotums stood by at attention. As His Excellency Abdrahaman spoke no English, they got by on scraps of Italian and French. His Excellency wished to know about American tobacco. That grown in Tripoli was far too strong, the American much better, he said, as two immensely long pipes were brought in, ceremoniously filled, and lighted.

> It is long since I took a pipe, but [Adams wrote]... with great complacency, [I] placed the bowl upon the carpet... and smoked in awful pomp, reciprocating whiff for whiff... until coffee was brought in. His Excellency took a cup, after I had taken one, and alternately sipped at his coffee and whiffed at his tobacco... and I followed the example with such exactness and solemnity that [one of] the two secretaries... cried out in ecstasy, "Monsieur, vous êtes un Turk!"

The conversation turned to business. America was a great nation, declared His Excellency, but unfortunately a state of war existed between America and Tripoli. Adams questioned how that could be, given there had been no injury, insult, or provocation on either side. The Barbary States were the sovereigns of the Mediterranean all the same, he was told, and without a treaty of peace there could be no peace between Tripoli and America. His Excellency was prepared to arrange such a treaty.

Two days later, at the stroke of noon, His Excellency appeared at Grosvenor Square, flanked by servants in orange robes and turbans. Time was critical, Adams was informed. The sooner peace was made between America and the Barbary States the better. Were a treaty delayed, it would be more difficult to make. A war between Christian and Christian was mild, prisoners were treated with humanity; but, warned His Excellency, a war between Muslim and Christian could be horrible.

The man was either a consummate politician or truly benevolent and wise—Adams could not tell which—and though apprehensive that the sums demanded would be exorbitant, he felt there was no time to lose. He dispatched Colonel Smith to Paris with a letter urging Jefferson to come as quickly as possible. His visit, Adams suggested, could be attributed to his desire to see England and pay his respects at Court.

JEFFERSON ARRIVED on March 11, 1786, to find London brightened by a light dusting of snow. He settled into rooms on Golden Square for a stay, as it turned out, of nearly two months, during which the ties of friendship with John and Abigail became stronger than ever.

Since they had last seen him, Jefferson had become noticeably more elegant in attire. He had taken to powdering his hair and acquired a French *valet de chambre*, Adrien Petit, who had earlier worked for the Adamses. He looked every inch the polished courtier and, with his height and slim good looks, drew attention everywhere they went.

At a meeting with Ambassador Abdrahaman, Adams and Jefferson were told that peace with Tripoli would cost 30,000 guineas for his employers, as His Excellency put it, plus 3,000 pounds sterling for himself. Payments were to be in cash on delivery of the treaty signed by his sovereign. The two Americans protested that the figure was too high. His Excellency assured them it was his lowest price and allowed that peace with all Barbary states might cost from 200,000 to 300,000 guineas. They could only refer the matter to Congress, Adams and Jefferson replied, and the meeting ended.

Compared to such demands, the sum Congress had authorized them to spend was, as they reported to John Jay, "but a drop in the bucket."

Several meetings with Lord Carmarthen were no more encouraging with Jefferson present than they had been for Adams for months past. Jefferson felt insulted by Carmarthen's seeming "aversion to have anything to do with us."

When Adams presented Jefferson at the King's levee at St. James's on March 15, George III could not have been "more ungracious" in his "notice of Mr. Adams and myself," according to an account later provided by Jefferson. Later still a grandson of Adams's would take this to mean the King had turned his back on them, and the story would become rooted in history. But almost certainly no such incident occurred. Jefferson said nothing to the effect at the time. Nor did any of the numerous ministers, courtiers, members of Parliament, and other diplomats present who were ever watchful for the slightest sign of royal disapproval or anything the least out of the ordinary. Nothing untoward was reported or hinted at in the newspapers, and importantly, nothing was ever said or written by John Adams, who, of all men, would have been enraged by any disrespect shown a minister of the United States being presented under his sponsorship.

Whatever the truth of the situation, Jefferson's sensitivity to British hauteur was real, his dislike of the British sufficient to last a lifetime. "They require to be kicked into common good manners," he told Colonel Smith. The fact that his debts were largely to English creditors may well have had something to do with such feelings.

Of London, he thought only the shops worthy of attention, and devoted ample time to them, spending lavishly on shoes, boots, a flintlock rifle, a reading lamp, plated harness and stirrups, and a set of chessmen. His major, most costly purchases were British-made scientific instruments, which, he conceded, were the finest available. Possibly at the urging of Abigail, he also paid a shilling to see the "learned pig."

As at Auteuil, Jefferson was a frequent presence at the house on Grosvenor Square, delighting all with his sparkling conversation and fund of information. Abigail gave several dinners in his honor. John arranged a tour of the King's library. There were repeated evenings at the theater—Jefferson would see three performances by Mrs. Siddons in three different roles—and a late night at the French ambassador's ball, in the splendorous Hôtel de France on Hyde Park, an occasion marked by the presence of many "very brilliant ladies of the first distinction," as Abigail noted.

Appraising the figure she herself cut in such gatherings, Abigail was good-naturedly realistic. She had grown as large as her two sisters combined, she claimed to Mary Cranch, and John was keeping pace with her. Pity the poor horse that would ever have to carry both of them, she wrote.

Recording in his diary the names of the few specimens of the British aristocracy who "ventured" conversation with him at the French ambassador's ball, Adams noted, "This people cannot look me in the face: there is a conscious guilt and shame in their countenances when they look at me. They feel they have behaved ill, and that I am sensible of it."

When, after weeks of waiting, there was still no more word from Lord Carmarthen, and the ambassador from Portugal, the one European minister to have shown any interest in opening trade negotiations, was reported too ill to see them, Adams and Jefferson decided to take a break from London and go off on a tour of English gardens, what Abigail called "their little journey into the country."

She and John had not been apart since they were reunited in London the summer of 1784, not for a year and eight months, which, she noted, was the longest time they had had together since they were married. Time away in Jefferson's company would, she was sure, do John great good.

THEY SET OFF on April 4, traveling by hired coach, sharing expenses, and accompanied by their two servants, John Briesler and Adrien Petit. They moved rapidly and covered a great deal of ground in just six days, relying on Jefferson's copy of *Observations on Modern Gardening* by Thomas Whately as their guide, the last word on English gardens.

Their direction was west along the Thames where the English countryside was in its April glory. Mornings were often cool, but with hazy sunshine breaking through by midday. Willow trees were in leaf. There were cherry blossoms and an abundance of daffodils in bloom, and the more miles that passed, the more the landscape opened up, with broad green hillsides covered with sheep and scampering newborn lambs by the hundreds.

In the long, eventful lives of Adams and Jefferson, it was an excursion of no importance to history. But it was the one and only time they ever spent off on their own together, free of work and responsibility, and at heart both were countrymen, farmers, with an avid interest in soils, tillage, climate, and "improvements." "There is not a sprig of grass that grows uninteresting to me," Jefferson was fond of saying, and Adams, in the spirit of eighteenth-century hyperbole, might well have agreed. Each kept occasional notes on the journey, and while Jefferson showed more interest in "practical things," where Adams was inclined to remark on the historical or literary associations of the places they saw, this does not necessarily preclude a comparable interest in most everything encountered. Adams was quite as interested in proper land management as Jefferson; Jefferson possibly cared as much for Shakespeare as did Adams.

The first stops were two that Jefferson had already made a few days earlier on his own, but was happy to repeat. Both—Alexander Pope's garden beside the Thames at Twickenham and Woburn Farm—were prime examples of the "modern," or "new-style" English landscape gardening that was so radically different from the highly symmetrical gardens made fashionable by the French, and particularly by the work of André LaNôtre at Versailles in the time of Louis XIV. In the new style, there was no "regularity." Instead, a seemingly natural arrangement of open grasslands, winding paths, clumps and groves of trees, in combination with an abundant presence of water in the form of serpentine lakes, streams, and artificial cataracts, was intended to evoke the look of an idealized English landscape. It was all to appear to be the work of the hand of God, but was in fact the doing of the "master-hand" of the landscape gardener or architect. Everything was chosen for effect. The "disposition" of trees was of particular importance, and among the trees and lakes were nearly always arranged a variety of classic temples or pavilions, a faux ruin or grotto, all very romantic in spirit, their size and number depending on the wealth or fancy of the client.

Such gardens could extend over hundreds of acres. They were not flower gardens, but private parks. Architects, gardeners, and clients thought of themselves as working like landscape painters, only on a vast scale and with scores of laborers at their bidding. Whole valleys were carved out, hilltops removed, streams rerouted, thousands of trees planted to achieve the desired look. The colossal expense seemed of no concern.

"Gardening, in the perfection to which it has been lately brought in England, is entitled to a place of considerable rank among the liberal arts," declared the ultimate authority, Thomas Whately. While Adams noted Woburn's beauty, Jefferson concentrated on the distribution of labor. "Four people to the farm, four to the pleasure garden, four to the kitchen garden," he recorded.

Another day, April 6, they toured the ultimate expression of the new style. Stowe, a true eighteenth-century marvel, was the largest, grandest, most famous landscape garden in England. It had been praised in poetry by Pope, acclaimed by Rousseau, and was the work, in part, of the most famous English landscape gardener of the day, Lancelot Brown, "Capability" Brown, as he was known, for his habit of extolling to clients the "capabilities" of their property. But it was also the design of architect William Kent and of its late owner and guiding spirit, Richard Grenville-Temple, Lord Cobham.

Set in a rolling sweep of land that lent a feeling of even grander scale, the estate comprised approximately 400 acres and was approached through a tremendous Corinthian arch. In addition to a columned manor house commanding one ridge, there were all the requisite lakes and waterfalls, bridges and architectural niceties—a Temple of Victory, Temple of Venus, Temple of Bacchus, a faux Gothic temple—everything romantic in spirit. For a panoramic view, said to take in five counties, Adams climbed a circular stairway to the top of a 115-foot observation tower built in His Lordship's memory. "I mounted . . . with pleasure," Adams wrote, "as Lord Cobham's name was familiar to me from Pope's works."

Whether Jefferson made the climb is not clear, as he recorded nothing of it, but then neither did he say a word in his notes about a beautiful bridge done in the manner of his adored Palladio, or the Temple of Victory, the honey-colored showpiece of the garden, which was very like the Maison Carrée, the Roman temple at Nîmes, which Jefferson was later to see on his travels in southern France and take as the model for his design for the capitol of Virginia. What he did record was that thirty-three men and boys were required to tend the grounds, and that he considered the huge Corinthian arch useless, inasmuch as it had "no pretension to direction."

Adams found the total effect greatly to his liking, but thought temples to Venus and Bacchus unnecessary, as mankind had "no need of artificial incitements to such amusements."

If Stowe was the ultimate in fashionable private splendor, the Shakespeare house in Stratford-on-Avon, the next stop, was as humble as could be imagined. Told that an old wooden chair in a corner by the chimney was where the bard himself had sat, the two American tourists cut off souvenir chips, this "according to the custom," as Adams was quick to note. But he was distressed by how little evidence remained of Shakespeare, either of the man or the miracle of his mind. "There is nothing preserved of this great genius . . . which might inform us what education, what company, what accident turned his mind to letters and drama," Adams lamented. Jefferson noted only that he paid a shilling to see the house and Shakespeare's grave. But years afterward Adams would claim that Jefferson, on arriving at Stratford-on-Avon, had actually gotten down on his knees and kissed the ground.

At Edgehill, scene of the first great battle of the English civil war, and later at Worcester, the setting of Cromwell's final victory over Charles II in the year 1651, it was Adams's turn to be deeply moved. This was history he knew in detail. Here were "scenes where freemen had fought for their rights," he wrote in his diary. Finding some of the local residents sadly ignorant of the subject, he gave them an impromptu lecture.

"And do Englishmen so soon forget the ground where liberty was fought for?" he asked. "Tell your neighbors and your children that this is holy ground, . . . All England should come in pilgrimage to this hill once a year."

To Adams it appeared his exhortation had "animated" and "pleased" his audience. What the expression may have been on Jefferson's face, there is no telling. Nor regrettably did either man write of what passed between them along the way—what they talked about mile after mile in their rocking coach, or in the evenings as they dined together, what questions were asked, what observations made on life, politics, the law, the books they loved, their families, the future of their country. It was the closest time they ever spent in each other's company and neither recorded a word about the other. But then neither wrote very much about anything, as if they had both declared a holiday from "pen work," in Jefferson's expression.

Birmingham, where they stopped at the Swann Inn, was the most distant point of the excursion, and the famous nearby farm known as Leasowes, once the home of the poet William Shenstone, was for Jefferson the most anticipated stop of the entire journey. Jefferson had long admired Shenstone's pastoral verse, but of greater importance had been the influence of Shenstone's own highly romantic description of Leasowes on Jefferson's plans for Monticello.

Leasowes, one of the earliest of all the new-style gardens, was considerably smaller than the others, set in gentle farmland, with a view of low hills to the south and west. But Leasowes had fallen into neglect since the poet's death, and Jefferson was greatly saddened and disappointed. It was nothing like what he had imagined. "This is not even an ornamental farm," he wrote. "It is only a grazing farm with a path around it, here and there a seat of a board, rarely anything better. Architecture has contributed nothing." Let Leasowes be an object lesson, he concluded. Shenstone had ruined himself financially with all he had spent on the farm, and so "died of the heartaches which debt occasioned him." It was a lesson that Jefferson, alas, would not heed.

To Adams, on the other hand, Leasowes was preferable to anything they had seen. The small scale of the place was more to a New Englander's liking. It was "the simplest and plainest," the "most rural of all," and thus particularly appealing, Adams thought. "I saw no spot so small that exhibited such a variety of beauties."

From Leasowes the travelers turned and headed south again, in the direction of London, stopping in the course of the next few days at Hagley Hall, a Palladian great house on a hill with a sweeping view somewhat like that of Monticello, Blenheim Palace at Woodstock, and then nearby Oxford, where they visited the university's botanical garden beside the river Cherwell. By nightfall, April 9, they were back in London.

According to Adams's count, they had toured twenty country places in all and he thought them high entertainment. Later, after a visit with Abigail to Pains Hill on the outskirts of London, at Surrey, where an immense ornamental park with lakes, grottoes, hermit's hut, even a facsimile tent of an Arab prince, had been created from a "heap of sand," Adams declared it "the most striking piece of art" of any. Yet he hoped it would be a long time before such gardens ever became the fashion at home, where nature had done greater things on a nobler scale. How anyone could improve on Penn's Hill, Adams could not imagine.

· · ·

In London, Jefferson resumed his shopping spree, buying, among other things, another microscope and a pair of satin "Florentine" breeches. With the three Adamses and Colonel Smith, he toured the British Museum and, at Adams's urging, sat for Mather Brown.

Commissioned by Adams, it was Jefferson's first portrait and quite unlike anything done of him thereafter. A bust by Houdon, for example, sculpted in Paris a few years later, would be Jefferson in the heroic mode, chin lifted, eyes on a distant horizon—Jefferson as frontiersman. In this by Brown he might have been the perfect European dandy, magnificent in ruffled shirt, hair dressed and powdered. He had a wistful, almost mournful expression and there were dark circles under his eyes. It was Jefferson as courtier and romantic, and while some who saw it thought it a poor likeness, the Adamses appear to have been quite pleased.

As requested, Brown would do a copy of the Jefferson portrait for them, as well as a copy of the Adams portrait for Jefferson. The original painting of Jefferson would ultimately disappear. The copy, which was hung prominently in the house on Grosvenor Square, would remain a proud possession in the Adams family for generations.

On April 26, he and Adams having accomplished nothing in the way of diplomatic progress, and with no reason to expect a change in their prospects, Jefferson said his goodbyes and departed for Paris. Officially his mission had been "fruitless." But of Adams, Jefferson had more to say, writing from Paris to his friend Madison as he had before on the subject. The difference this time was that Jefferson seemed to go out of his way, almost apologetically, to explain how Adams, with all his faults, had won his heart.

You know the opinion I *formerly* entertained of *my friend Mr. Adams*. Yourself and the governor were the first who *shook* that opinion. I afterwards saw proofs which *convicted* him of a degree of *vanity* and of *blindness* to it, of which no germ *had appeared* in Congress. A *7-months'* intimacy with him *here* and as many *weeks* in *London* have given me opportunities of studying him closely. *He is vain, irritable and a bad calculator* of the force and probable effect of the motives which govern men. This is *all* the *ill* which can be *said of him*. He is as disinterested as the Being which made him: he is profound in his views, and accurate in his judgment *except where knowl-edge of the world* is necessary to form a judgment. He is so amiable that I pronounce you will love him if ever you become acquainted with him.

III

FROM THE TIME of his arrival in their lives the previous year, Colonel William Smith had impressed John and Abigail as entirely deserving of his reputation as an admirable young man of great promise. "He possesses a high sense of honor and as independent a spirit as any man I ever knew, and . . . we have every reason to believe that his character will bear the strictest scrutiny," Abigail had written earlier to Cotton Tufts. "His character is not only fair and unblemished," she informed John Quincy, "[but] at age 21 he commanded a regiment, and through the whole war conducted with prudence and bravery and intrepidity, when armed against the foe." She wished John Quincy to know this, because Colonel Smith was "like to become your brother."

William Smith's interest in Nabby, and hers in him, had been apparent for months, but only after Nabby had formally broken her engagement to Royall Tyler would Abigail permit any mention of the new "connection."

The contrast between the character of Smith and Tyler was clear enough, she stressed to John Quincy, in an effort to explain his sister's decision. Besides, had not Shakespeare observed that "a heart agitated with the remains of a former passion is most susceptible to a new one"?

Having concluded from day-to-day observation that his young secretary possessed all the qualifications necessary to make a "faithful and agreeable" companion for Nabby, John Adams left it to her to determine her own future. But Abigail spent hours with Nabby in close conversation. "I begged her to satisfy herself that she had no prepossession left in her mind and heart, and she answered me she never could be more determined!"

Abigail, however, as she confided to her sister Mary, had begun to find life increasingly empty and pointless. Her health was uneven; she was bothered by recurring rheumatism and severe headaches. She was tired of London and longed for home. When Mary apologized for filling her letters with too many Braintree "particulars," Abigail replied, "Everything however trivial on that side of water interests me. Nothing here." "Can there be any pleasure in mixing company where you care for no one and nobody cares for you?"

She dwelled increasingly on the fate of their brother, William, whose drinking and errant ways had been a secret worry for years and who by now, after abandoning his wife and children, had more or less disappeared. In correspondence among themselves the three sisters never referred to William by name, only as "this unhappy connection," the "poor man," or "our dearest relative."

Who was looking after him, Abigail wondered. What had been different about his childhood in the Weymouth parsonage? What might be in store for her own children?

"I cannot, however, upon a retrospect of his education, refrain from thinking that some very capital mistakes were very indesignedly made," she would tell Mary. "I say this to you who will not consider it as any reflection upon the memory of our dear parents, but only as a proof how much of the best and worthiest may err, and as some mitigation for the conduct of our deceased relatives."

IN THE FINAL DAYS of May 1786, John Adams was called on to hurry to Amsterdam once again, to secure still another desperately needed Dutch loan for the United States.

On June 12, Adams having returned, Nabby and Colonel William Smith were married in the house on Grosvenor Square, in a small ceremony with only a few friends present—the Copleys, among others. In another few weeks bride and groom moved to a new address on Wimpole Street.

"The young couple appear to be very happy," was all that Adams had to say, in a letter to James Warren, while to Mary Cranch, Abigail described the ceremony as too solemn and important an event for her not to have experienced "an agitation" equal to what she had felt at her own wedding. The night before the wedding, she further confided, she had dreamed of Royall Tyler, and strangely found herself feeling sorry for him.

Abigail and Nabby had been faithful companions for years, through all of John's endless absences. They had been virtually inseparable and the change now was difficult for Abigail. She had made the young couple promise to dine at Grosvenor Square every day; still, she was as "lonesome" as she had ever been. To boost her spirits she imagined a marriage between John Quincy and Patsy Jefferson, and to Jefferson playfully proposed the idea. While it was true, she wrote, that in losing her daughter she had gained a son, she already had three sons. What she needed was another daughter. "Suppose you give me Miss Jefferson and in some [fu]ture day take a son in lieu of her. I am for strengthening [the] federal union."

At home in Massachusetts, meantime, John Quincy had been denied admission to Harvard until he completed several months of tutoring in Greek with the Reverend Shaw at Haverhill. But then in March 1786, John Quincy, too, had become a "son of Harvard."

He must not study too hard, Adams cautioned kindly. "The smell of the midnight lamp is very unwholesome. Never defraud yourself of sleep, nor your walk. You need not now be in a hurry." What was essential, Adams advised, was an inquisitive mind. John Quincy must get to know the most exceptional scholars and question them closely. "Ask them about their tutors; manner of teaching. Observe what books lie on their tables. . . . Ask them about the late war . . . or fall into questions of literature, science, or what you will."

The more Adams thought about the future of his country, the more convinced he became that it rested on education. Before any great things are accomplished, he wrote to a correspondent,

> a memorable change must be made in the system of education and knowledge must become so general as to raise the lower ranks of society nearer to the higher. The education of a nation instead of being confined to a few schools and universities for the instruction of the few, must become the national care and expense for the formation of the many.

That his own exceptional, eldest son, with the advantages he had, could one day play a part in bringing about such a "memorable change," he had every confidence.

When Elizabeth Shaw wrote that as agreeable as John Quincy might be in company, he could be in private conversation "a little too decisive and tenacious" in his opinions, Abigail responded with a strong letter of motherly advice to the young man. "Watchfulness over yourself" was called for, lest his knowledge make him arrogant.

> If you are conscious to yourself that you possess more knowledge upon some subjects than others of your standing, reflect that you have had greater opportunities of seeing the world, and obtaining a knowledge of mankind than any of your contemporaries. That you have never wanted a book but it has been supplied to you, that your whole time has been spent in the company of men of literature and science. How unpardonable would it have been in you to have been a blockhead.

By now Charles, too, had entered Harvard, at age fifteen. More outgoing than his older brother, Charles was thought to be too easily distracted from his studies. Where John Quincy required a warning against the perils of the midnight lamp, Charles needed reminding that such a lamp existed.

Remembering so much that went on in his own days at Harvard other than classwork and studies, Adams wrote affectionately to his second son, "You have in your nature a sociability, Charles, which is amiable, but may mislead you. A scholar is always made alone. Studies can only be pursued to good purpose by yourself. Don't let your companions then, nor your amusements, take up too much of your time."

ADAMS WAS HIMSELF spending increasing amounts of time alone, working intently and seldom to good purpose, he felt. The impasse over the withdrawal of British troops from the American Northwest and the payment of American debts to British creditors continued. Lord Carmarthen readily agreed that by the Paris Treaty His Majesty's armed forces were to depart from the United States "with all convenient speed," but, as he liked also to point out, the same treaty stipulated that creditors on either side "shall meet with no lawful impediment to the recovery of the full value in sterling of all *bona fide* debts." "I flatter myself, however, sir," Carmarthen told Adams, "that whenever America shall manifest a real determination to fulfill her part of the treaty, Great Britain will not hesitate to prove her sincerity."

For Adams, who had argued emphatically at Paris for full repayment of American debt and had never deviated from that view, American reluctance, or inability, to make good on its obligations was a disgrace and politically a great mistake. When word reached London that some states, including Massachusetts, had passed laws against compliance with the treaty, Adams was appalled. Any such suspension of British debts, however colored or disguised, was a direct breach of the treaty, he wrote in a fury to Cotton Tufts, who had become a member of the Massachusetts Senate. "Our countrymen have too long trifled with public and private credit." He would make good on all outstanding debt to British creditors, and if the British posts in America were not then immediately evacuated, he would declare war.

But he had written this when "wroth and fretted." War was the last thing he wanted. Any war now would be calamitous for the United States and must be avoided at almost any cost, he wrote another day.

What was implicit in all "oratorical utterance" from Whitehall, Adams knew, was that to the British there was as yet no proper American government and so it would be pointless to undertake serious transactions until such existed. To Adams it was particularly offensive that the British thus far had not thought it necessary even to appoint an ambassador to the United States.

In an exchange of letters between London and Paris, meantime, he and Jefferson considered the question of whether to pay tribute to the Barbary pirates or wage war with them. Jefferson recommended war as more honorable and proposed that an American fleet be built. Adams agreed in principle and promised, "I will go all lengths with you in promoting a navy." Like Jefferson, he detested the prospect of paying bribes. But given that there was no American navy at present and that it would be years most likely before Congress voted such a resolution, Adams thought it sensible to pay the money. "We ought not fight them at all, unless we determine to fight them forever," he told Jefferson, who willingly deferred to Adams's judgment. Later in January 1787, they would sign a pact with Morocco, whereby the United States, like France and Britain, agreed to pay for protection.

. . .

EAGER FOR A BREAK from the doldrums of summer in London, with Parliament in recess and "everyone fled from the city," the Adamses decided to see some of the English countryside. With Nabby and Colonel Smith, they set off for a weeklong excursion to Essex. Adams had expressed interest in visiting the village of Braintree, expecting they might find some connection with their own Braintree, but poking about in the village graveyard, he found no familiar names and the village itself was sadly disappointing, poor and "miserable." Still, the trip was a welcome departure—and for Abigail especially—and even more welcome was the wholly unexpected journey that followed immediately afterward.

Adams was needed at The Hague to exchange ratification of the treaty with Prussia, the one European trade agreement that he and Jefferson, for all their efforts, had succeeded in accomplishing. The treaty, signed in July 1785, had been ratified only that May of 1786, so late that unless it were signed within a matter of weeks, it would expire. Since Prussia had no minister in London or Paris, but only at The Hague, Adams was needed there without delay or the treaty would come to nothing. Jefferson excused himself from attending, saying it was on too short notice.

"As this presents a good opportunity for seeing the country [Holland]," Abigail wrote happily, "I shall accompany him." In fact, they were both extremely pleased to be going. Little could have delighted Adams more than the chance to show her the country that meant so much to him, where success had been his, where, as they both appreciated, he had helped change the course of history, and where he was still the accredited American minister, Congress having never bothered to replace him.

They were gone five weeks, stopping first at The Hague for the signing ceremony on August 8, then moving on at a pace sufficient to see just about everything—Rotterdam, Delft, Leyden, Haarlem, Amsterdam, Utrecht—with Abigail supplying colorful comment in her letters. "Not a hill to be seen," she wrote, incredulous. The people were "well-fed, well-clothed, contented," the women notable for their beautiful complexions. ("Rouge is confined to the stage here," she reported approvingly to

Nabby.) She saw no poverty such as in Paris and London. The cities were amazingly clean and orderly. "It is very unusual to see a single square of glass broken, or a brick out of place." Leyden was the cleanest city she had ever seen in her life; and if Braintree in Essex had failed to evoke feelings of ancestral ties, the church of the Pilgrims at Leyden more than made up for it. In its stillness, she felt the same wave of emotion that had moved Adams to tears on his first visit. At the Amsterdam Stock Exchange, by contrast, the "buzz" of business being transacted reminded her of nothing so much as "the swarming of bees."

The reception they were given by the Dutch was warm and heartening, "striking proof, not only of their personal esteem," Abigail wrote, "but of the ideas they entertain with respect to the Revolution which gave birth to their connection with us. . . . The spirit of liberty appears to be all alive with them."

At Utrecht they witnessed the swearing in of new magistrates of the city, as a result of major constitutional reforms enacted by the Patriot party. It was a ceremony conducted, as Adams wrote, "in the presence of the whole city," and it moved him profoundly. To John Jay he would claim it to be the first bearing of fruit of the American Revolution in Europe.

THE AUTUMN OF 1786 produced no improvement in relations with the British, whose icy civility Adams found all the more galling after the respect and affection he had been shown in Holland. Yet his spirits were high, his health excellent. Besides, he and Abigail knew by then that they were to become grandparents. Nabby was pregnant, her baby expected in April. Not even the news from home of an uprising of aggrieved farmers in western Massachusetts seemed to distress Adams.

Shays's Rebellion, as it would come to be known, after one of its leaders, Daniel Shays, a former captain in the Continental Army, was in protest of rising taxes and court action against indebted farmers who, in many cases, were losing their land in the midst of hard times. The insurgents had prevented the sitting of the state supreme court at Springfield. But thus far there had been no violence.

"Don't be alarmed at the late turbulence in New England," Adams counseled Jefferson. "The Massachusetts Assembly had, in its zeal to get the better of their debt, laid on a tax rather heavier than the people could bear." He was confident all would be well and concluded prophetically, "This commotion will terminate in additional strength to the government."

Inexplicably, correspondence from Jefferson had dwindled to a standstill. On returning from Holland, Abigail had found but one letter waiting, this only to say he did not understand her proposed trade of her son for his daughter, and to relate again his delight in the French. ("They have as much happiness in one year as an Englishman in ten.") After that there had been no further word. A letter to Adams concerning whale oil, sent in late September, was written and signed for Jefferson by his aide, William Short. Then at the end of October came a brief note to Adams, awkwardly written by Jefferson with his left hand.

"An unfortunate dislocation of my right wrist has for three months deprived me of the honor of writing to you," he at last explained to Abigail before Christmas. But his reason for writing was to tell her that his eight-year-old daughter Polly was on her way to London by ship from Virginia, in the care of a nurse, and that he had taken the liberty to tell those who arranged the voyage "that you will be so good as to take her under your wing till I can have notice to send for her."

What Jefferson said nothing of was that he had been spending as much time as possible through August and September with a beautiful young woman named Maria Cosway. Born of English parents but raised in Italy, she was the wife of a wealthy, dandified English artist, Richard Cosway, and was herself an artist. She was fluent in several languages, musical, slim and delicate, with sparkling blue eyes and a mountain of fashionably dressed blond hair that made her several inches taller than her tiny, almost dwarf-like husband. The Cosways were a bright fixture in London society, and Abigail and Nabby are known to have met her on at least one social occasion.

Maria was twenty-six years old, Jefferson forty-three, and the attraction of each to the other was instantaneous. If not in love, Jefferson was wholly infatuated. Wishing only to be with her, he canceled every social engagement he could. As he would tell her, "Lying messengers were dispatched into every corner of the city with apologies." He bought tickets to the theater, the opera; they rode through Paris in Jefferson's carriage behind a pair of fine new horses, and strolled the gardens at Marley, near

Versailles. Sometimes, Richard Cosway was with them, more often they were alone.

Whether it was on a walk in the Cours-la-Reine, as commonly said later, that Jefferson dislocated his wrist, attempting to impress her by vaulting a fence, is not certain. But the accident put an end to their outings, and the pain of the injury was excruciating. For a month Jefferson was virtually confined to his house, and by early October the Cosways had returned to London.

Struggling to write with his left hand, he labored over a carefully composed letter to her in which he described a debate between "Head" and "Heart," a conventional literary device of the day, and by the end of twelve pages it appeared "Head" was the winner. In any case, when Maria Cosway returned to Paris the next summer, Jefferson showed noticeably less interest in her.

To his friends the Adamses, he said nothing of any of this and possibly they never knew. But then, as the news of Shays's Rebellion grew more alarming, an exchange of views on the subject set Abigail and Jefferson sharply in opposition for the first time.

To many on both sides of the Atlantic, it seemed from reports of the "tumults" in Massachusetts that the new nation was already breaking apart. To the British, accounts in the newspapers only confirmed what they had been predicting all along, while to many Americans who little understood the suffering of the Massachusetts farmers, and this included Abigail, the situation was an outrage, intolerable. "For what have we been contending against the tyranny of Britain," she asked, writing to Mary Cranch, "to become the sacrifice of a lawless banditti? . . . Will my countrymen justify the maxim of tyrants, that mankind is not made for freedom?"

With the arrival of the new year, and still more sensational reports of mob violence in Massachusetts, she let Jefferson know her opinion in no uncertain terms. "Ignorant, restless desperadoes, without conscience or principles, have led a deluded multitude to follow their standard under pretense of grievances which have no existence but in their imaginations." She had no patience with mobs crying out for paper money or the equal distribution of wealth. She saw only the need for "the wisest and most vigorous measures to quell and suppress" the revolt.

It was almost as an afterthought that she told him she would be pleased to look after his daughter as requested.

When Jefferson wrote to say he hoped the captured rebels would be pardoned, Abigail was appalled. "The spirit of resistance to government is so valuable on certain occasions, that I wish it to be always kept alive," he lectured. "I like a little rebellion now and then. It is like a storm in the atmosphere."

How sincerely Jefferson meant what he had written, how much was hyperbole among friends, is difficult to gauge. He had a fondness for the imagery of storms. To Maria Cosway he had described how "sublime" it was high on his mountaintop at Monticello "to look down into the workhouse of nature, to see her clouds, hail, snow, rain, thunder, all fabricated at our feet!" Moreover, in the same letter to Abigail, he offered the thought that the only hope for change among the ever lighthearted French was not rebellion but to pray for good kings.

Abigail took his wish for "a little rebellion now and then" quite to heart and was not pleased. When Jefferson left Paris at the end of February for a long, leisurely tour of southern France and Italy, ostensibly to see if the mineral springs at Aix-en-Provence might help his still-painful wrist, John Adams kept on writing to him. But Abigail did not. It was the end of June before she could bring herself to write again, and then only to tell Jefferson his daughter had safely arrived.

Interestingly, only months afterward, Jefferson would write a letter to her new son-in-law, Colonel Smith, to say he hated the thought of America not having a rebellion such as had occurred in Massachusetts, every twenty years or so. What were a few lives lost? Jefferson asked. "The tree of liberty must be refreshed from time to time with the blood of patriots and tyrants. It is a natural manure." But of this letter, Abigail apparently knew nothing.

ON APRIL 2, 1787, Nabby gave birth to "a fine boy," William Steuben Smith, who was declared to have "the brow of his grandpapa." "I feel already as fond of him as if he was my own son, nay, I can hardly persuade myself that he is not," Abigail wrote to Lucy Cranch.

On June 26, life picked up still more with the arrival of little Polly Jefferson. She was escorted by the captain of the ship she had sailed on, Andrew Ramsay, to whom she had become so attached that his parting was extremely upsetting for her.

"I show her your picture [the Mather Brown portrait]," Abigail wrote to Jefferson. "She says she cannot know it, how should she when she should not know you."

The one surprise, she informed Jefferson, was the nurse who had accompanied the child. "The old nurse who you expected to have attended her was sick and unable to come. Instead she has a girl about 15 or 16 with her, the sister of the servant you have with you," she said, tactfully avoiding the word slave.

For Abigail and John Adams it was their one encounter with Sally Hemings, who was actually fourteen, younger even than Abigail supposed, and who was to figure years afterward in a sensational scandal surrounding Jefferson's private life. She was also the only slave known ever to have lived under the Adamses' roof.

To Abigail, Sally seemed nearly as much a child as Polly. In the opinion of Captain Ramsay, as Abigail also related, she would be of "so little service" that he recommended taking her back to Virginia. Abigail told Jefferson he would have to be the judge. "She seems fond of the child and appears good natured." On further acquaintance, however, Abigail concluded that the nurse might need more care than the child and that without supervision would be incapable of her responsibilities.

At first, Polly seemed a handful for anyone. Her weeks on board ship had made her "as rough as a little sailor." Abigail warmed to her at once. She took her shopping for new clothes and books, kept her at her side as if she were her own. She was a "lovely child," the favorite of everyone in the household, Abigail wrote. Adams, as he himself said, was entirely won over.

From Polly they learned her pitiful story. Having no memory of her mother, she had been living with an aunt, Jefferson's sister Elizabeth Eppes, whom she adored and had refused to leave when Jefferson sent for her. Deceived into believing that a visit with her cousins on board Captain Ramsay's ship in a Virginia harbor was only for a day or two, she had awakened to find her cousins gone, the ship under way. The deception had made her angry and suspicious, as was still readily evident.

Jefferson was at last heard from. Rather than come himself to fetch the child, he was sending his valet, Petit. Having only just returned to Paris from his travels in the South, Jefferson explained, he had "the arrearages of three or four months all crowded on me at once." To the Adamses it must have seemed a lame excuse, knowing as they did how little there could be of a truly pressing nature to keep Jefferson in Paris and how competent William Short was to handle what business there was for a week or so, just as he had been doing for months.

Abigail was crestfallen. She and the child had both been expecting Jefferson to appear any day. She was distraught, too, at the prospect of sending Polly off with someone who spoke no English. "I am really loath to part with her," she wrote to Jefferson on July 6, "and she, last evening upon Petit's arrival, was thrown into all her former distresses, and bursting into tears told me it would be as hard to leave me as it was her Aunt Eppes."

The day of her departure, Polly clung to Abigail's neck weeping, "almost in a frenzy." Abigail, too, was crying. To no one, she said, had she ever become so attached in so few days as this little girl, and as time would show, the love she felt for the child was to be her one enduring tie to Jefferson.

IV

"POPULARITY WAS NEVER my mistress, nor was I ever, or shall I ever be a popular man," Adams had written to James Warren at the start of the year, 1787, to say he had just completed a book that was almost certain to make him unpopular. "But one thing I know, a man must be sensible of the errors of the people, and upon his guard against them, and must run the risk of their displeasure sometimes, or he will never do them any good in the long run."

It was, as Warren doubtless appreciated, about as concise a synopsis of Adams's course through public life as could be found.

Once, in 1776, writing to Abigail about Thomas Paine's *Common Sense*, Adams had said of Paine that he was "a better hand at pulling down than building." Now again he observed to Warren, "It is much easier to pull down a government, in such a conjuncture of affairs as we have seen, than to build up at such season as present." It was Adams's intention to turn to building again.

For months after the journey to Holland he had remained in "a state of philosophic solitude," at work in his library on a consideration of comparative government based on "reading and reason." When, the week of Christmas, Abigail went off with the Smiths for a sojourn at Bath, Adams kept steadily at his labors. "Don't be solicitous of me. I shall do very well," he wrote to her Christmas Day. If cold in the night, he would take a "Virgin" to bed—that, he explained, being the English term for a hot water bottle.

He felt an urgency like that of 1776. Great events were taking place at home. Support for a stronger central government was gaining ground— and largely in reaction to Shays's Rebellion, as Adams had foreseen. A constitutional convention was in the offing, and as he had been impelled in 1776 to write his *Thoughts on Government*, so Adams plunged ahead now, books piled about him, his pen scratching away until all hours. "He is so much swallowed up in the pursuit of his subject that you must not wonder if you do not receive a line from him," Abigail explained to John Quincy. But having read what he was writing, she worried. "I tell him they will think in America that he is setting up a king."

By early January, 1787, Adams had rushed the first installment of his effort to a London printer. Titled *A Defence of the Constitutions of Government of the United States of America*, it was, in finished production, more a pamphlet than a book, in octavo form, and included on the title page a line from Pope: "All nature's difference keeps all nature's peace." Copies were sent off at once to the United States and to Jefferson in Paris.

Adams conceded that the writing suffered from too great haste. He called it a "strange book," which in many ways it was, much of it a hodge-podge overloaded with historical references and extended borrowings from other writers and usually without benefit of quotation marks. Yet in all he had achieved something quite out of the ordinary, thoughtful, high-minded, and timely. To a considerable extent the book was an expanded, more erudite rendition of the case for checks and balances in government that he had championed in his *Thoughts on Government*, and later put into operation in his draft of the Massachusetts constitution.

The people of America now had "the best opportunity and the greatest trust in their hands" that Providence ever ordained to so small a number since Adam and Eve. There must be three parts to government—executive, legislative, and judicial—and to achieve balance it was essential that it be a strong executive, a bicameral legislature, and an independent judiciary. On the role of the executive Adams was emphatic:

> If there is one central truth to be collected from the history of all ages, it is this: that the people's rights and liberties, and the democratical mixture in a constitution, can never be preserved without a strong executive, or, in other words, without separating the executive from the legislative power. If the executive power, or any considerable part of it, is left in the hands of an aristocratical or democratical assembly, it will corrupt the legislature as necessarily as rust corrupts iron, or as arsenic poisons the human body; and when the legislature is corrupted, the people are undone.

Nonetheless, the legislative power was "naturally and necessarily sovereign and supreme" over the executive.

In all history, he declared, there was no greater statesman and philosopher than Cicero, whose authority should ever carry great weight, and Cicero's decided opinion in favor of the three branches of government was founded on a reason that was timeless, unchangeable. Were Cicero to return to earth, he would see that the English nation had brought "the great idea" nearly to perfection. The English constitution, Adams declared—and knowing he would be taken to task for it—was the ideal. Indeed, "both for the adjustment of the balance and the prevention of its vibrations," it was "the most stupendous fabric of human invention" in all history. Americans should be applauded for imitating it as far as had been done, but also, he stressed, for making certain improvements in the original, especially in rejecting all hereditary positions.

A hereditary monarchy could be a republic, Adams held, as England demonstrated, and hereditary aristocracies could be usefully employed in balanced governments, as in the House of Lords. But Adams adamantly opposed hereditary monarchy and hereditary aristocracy in America, as well as all hereditary titles, honors, or distinctions of any kind—it was why he, like Jefferson and Franklin, strongly opposed the Society of the Cincinnati, the association restricted to Continental Army officers, which had a hereditary clause in its rules whereby membership was passed on to eldest sons.

As he explained to Jefferson, much of what he wrote was in response to the dangers of radical French thought. Specifically he had written in defence (hence the title) against the theories of the philosophe Turgot, who espoused perfect democracy and a single legislature, or as he wrote, "collecting all authority into one center, that of the nation." To Adams this was patent nonsense. A simple, perfect democracy had never yet existed. The whole people were incapable of deciding much of anything, even on the small scale of a village. He had had enough experience with town meetings at home to know that in order for anything to be done certain powers and responsibilities had to be delegated to a moderator, a town clerk, a constable, and, at times, to special committees.

Reliance on a single legislature was a certain road to disaster, for the same reason reliance on a single executive—king, potentate, president—was bound to bring ruin and despotism. As the planets were held in their orbits by centripetal and centrifugal forces, "instead of rushing to the sun or flying off in tangents" among the stars, there must, in a just and enduring government, be a balance of forces. Balance, counterpoise, and equilibrium were ideals that he turned to repeatedly. If all power were to be vested in a single legislature, "What was there to restrain it from making tyrannical laws, in order to execute them in a tyrannical manner?"

At home every state but Pennsylvania and Georgia had a bicameral legislature, and because of the obvious shortcomings of the one-house Congress under the Articles of Confederation, agreement on the need for a bicameral Congress was widespread. So to a considerable degree Adams was preaching what had become accepted doctrine at home.

Drawing on history and literature, some fifty books altogether, he examined what he called the modern democratic republics (the little Italian commonwealth of San Marino, Biscay in the Basque region of Spain, the Swiss cantons), modern aristocratic republics (Venice, the Netherlands), and the modern monarchical and regal republics (England, Poland); as well as the ancient democratic, aristocratic, and monarchical republics including Carthage, Athens, Sparta, and Rome. There were frequent citations in Latin, Greek, and French, extended use of Swift, Franklin, Dr. Price, Machiavelli, Guicciardini's *Historia d'Italia*, Montesquieu, Plato, Milton, and Hume, in addition to scattered mentions of Aristotle, Thucydides, Hobbes, La Rochefoucauld, and Rousseau, as well as Joseph Priestley, whom Adams had lately come to know in London.

But for all this it remained at heart a lawyer's brief for what he had said in his *Thoughts on Government*, and what he had helped establish in practice in the Massachusetts constitution. Where it departed most notably from what he had written before was in its pronouncements on human nature.

To Adams nothing had changed about human nature since the time of the ancients. Inequities within society were inevitable, no matter the political order. Human beings were capable of great good, but also great evil. Thus it had always been and thus it would ever be. He quoted Rousseau's description of "that hideous sight, the human heart," and recounted that even Dr. Priestley had said that such were the weaknesses and folly of men, "their love of domination, selfishness, and depravity," that none could be elevated above others without risk of danger.

How he wished it were not so, Adams wrote. Thucydides had said the source of all evils was "a thirst of power, from rapacious and ambitious passions," and Adams agreed. "Religion, superstition, oaths, education, laws, all give way before passions, interest, and power."

As to the ideal of a nation of equals, such was impossible. "Was there, or will there ever be a nation whose individuals were all equal, in natural and acquired qualities, in virtues, talents, and riches? The answer in all mankind must be in the negative."

Even in America where there was "a moral and political equality of rights and duties," there were nonetheless inequalities of wealth, education, family position, and such differences were true of all people in all times. There was inevitably a "natural aristocracy among mankind," those people of virtue and ability who were "the brightest ornaments and the glory" of a nation, "and may always be made the greatest blessing of society, if it be judiciously managed in the constitution." These were the people who had the capacity to acquire great wealth and make use of political power, and for all they contributed to society, they could thus become the most dangerous element in society, unless they and their interests were consigned to one branch of the legislature, the Senate, and given no executive power. Above all, the executive magistrate must have sufficient power to defend himself, and thus the people, from all the "enterprises" of the natural aristocracy.

Adams believed in a "government of laws not of men," as he had written in his *Thoughts on Government* and in the Massachusetts constitution but, as he stressed now in conclusion, "The executive power is properly the government; the laws are a dead letter until an administration begins to carry them into execution."

Through the months of work on the *Defence*, Adams knew it was time to wind things up in London. He had achieved nothing in his diplomatic role and could expect no improvement in his prospects. Within weeks after the first copies of his *Defence* were ready at the printer, he had written to John Jay to ask that he be recalled. So while noble in intent, the *Defence* may also have been partly intended as a way of reintroducing himself to his countrymen and influencing the debate on the Constitution. And however apprehensive he may have been over what the reaction might be, he moved ahead without pause, working on two more installments.

In February came warm praise from Paris. "I have read your book with infinite satisfaction and improvement," wrote Jefferson. It would do "great good," he predicted. "Its learning and its good sense will I hope make it an institute for our politicians, old as well as young."

Such approbation was "vast consolation," Adams responded, conceding that it had been a "hazardous" and "hasty" enterprise, and that he was pursuing it further. There were just two aspects of life in Europe that he regretted leaving. One was access to books, the other was "intimate correspondence with you, which is one of the most agreeable events in my life."

In time came more praise and approval. From Philadelphia, where the Constitutional Convention had assembled, Benjamin Rush, a member of the Convention, wrote that the *Defence* had "diffused such excellent principles among us, that there is little doubt of our adopting a vigorous and compound federal legislature." James Madison, who had taken the lead in drafting the so-called Virginia Plan, providing for three equal branches in the new government, and who had seldom ever had anything complimentary to say about Adams, declared in a letter to Jefferson that while men of learning would find nothing new in the book, it was certain to be "a powerful engine in forming public opinion," and, in fact, had "merit."

But as both John and Abigail had anticipated, there were others who perceived dark intent in what he had written. Cotton Tufts warned that there were people sowing discord, claiming Adams was all for monarchy and planned to put an English prince on a throne in America. In Virginia, the president of the College of William and Mary, a cousin of Madison's, the Reverend James Madison, saw a "secret design" in the book—that Adams, under the influence of a foreign Court, was "plotting" to overturn the American government.

LATE THAT SUMMER of 1787, in Philadelphia, the Constitutional Convention was nearing the completion of its efforts. In Paris parading mobs and incidents of public disrespect for the royal family had caught many by surprise, including the American ambassador. Suddenly all tongues had been let loose in Paris, Jefferson reported excitedly to Adams. There were placards all over the city, and though the mobs had ceased, the Queen had received a "general hiss" while attending the theater. "The King, long in the habit of drowning his cares in wine, plunges deeper and deeper; the Queen cries out, but sins on."

WHEN COPIES of the new Constitution of the United States, signed at Philadelphia on September 17, reached London that autumn, Adams read it "with great satisfaction." He would have preferred more power in the presidency than provided—particularly the authority to make presidential appointments without Senate approval. But of greater concern was the absence of a bill of rights, in the spirit of what he had written for the constitution of Massachusetts.

"What think you of a Declaration of Rights? Should not such a thing have preceded the model?" Adams wrote straight off to Jefferson.

Writing from Paris a few days later, before receiving Adams's letter, Jefferson said nothing about a bill of rights, only that there were "things" in the Constitution that "stagger all my dispositions to subscribe" to it.

His great concern was the office of the President, which, as conceived, struck him as "a bad edition of a Polish king.

> He may be reelected from four years to four years for life. . . . Once in office, and possessing the military force of the union, without either the aid or check of a council, he would not be easily dethroned, even if the people could be induced to withdraw their votes from him. I wish that at the end of the four years, they made him ever ineligible a second time.

Here was the difference between them, Adams replied prophetically. "You are afraid of the one, I, the few. We agree perfectly that the many should have full, fair, and perfect representation [in the House]. You are apprehensive of monarchy; I, of aristocracy. I would therefore have given more power to the President and less to the Senate."

He was not so concerned about a President staying long in office, Adams said, as he was about too frequent elections, which often brought out the worst in people and increased the chances of foreign influence.

While Jefferson would have much to say about the Constitution and the need for a bill of rights in subsequent private correspondence with Madison, he made no public statement for the time being, whereas Adams sent off a strong endorsement to John Jay that was to be widely quoted at home. As once he had seen the Declaration of Independence uniting the different and often disputatious states in common cause, Adams now saw the Constitution as the best means possible "to cement all America in affection and interest as one great nation." Indeed, if there was a consistent theme in all that Adams wrote and strived for, it was the need for a binding American union.

> The public mind cannot be occupied about a nobler object than the proposed plan of government. It appears to be admirably calcu- lated to cement all America in affection and interest as one great nation. A result of accommodation and compromise cannot be sup- posed perfectly to coincide with any one's ideas of perfection. But as all the great principles necessary to order, liberty, and safety are respected in it, and provision is made for corrections and amend-

ments as they may be found necessary, I confess I hope to hear of its adoption by all the states.

On December 6, writing to Jefferson, Adams reported that at last his recall had been approved by Congress, "and how we say at sea, 'Huzza for the new world and farewell to the old one.'"

For the second and, she hoped, the last time in her life, Abigail was making arrangements to cross the North Atlantic, and with hardly less apprehension than the time before.

There was a great accumulation of clothes, books, china, and furniture to pack, a York rosebush she was determined to take. The furniture included pieces purchased originally for the houses at Amsterdam and The Hague. There was a four-post Dutch bed, a great Dutch chest with heavy brass pulls and claw feet, tables of different sizes, a set of six cushioned Louis XV chairs and a settee, these with delicate floral carvings. Adams's desk, a beautiful French escritoire of veneered satinwood and ebony, which he had bought in Paris after the war, was his particular pride and joy.

All were considerably finer, more elegant pieces than the Adamses had ever owned in years past and would have looked quite out of place in the farmhouse at Braintree. But, as they now knew, they were not to reside in the old homestead. Through Cotton Tufts, Adams had arranged the purchase of what was known as "the Vassall-Borland place," which Adams had had his eye on for years and which, in memory, seemed quite grand. Built more than fifty years before, about 1731, as the summer villa of a wealthy sugar planter from the West Indies, Leonard Vassall, the house had stood empty through much of the war, after Vassall's daughter, the widow Borland, a Loyalist, fled to England. When Adams heard the place was available, he made his decision. Located on the coast road, on the north side of town, the property included house, farm buildings, and some eighty acres at a purchase price of 600 pounds. Adams envisioned it as the ideal setting for his retirement.

There were friends in London for Abigail to say goodbye to, last letters to get off to her sisters, and to John Quincy, who, having finished Har-

vard, was now studying law and not very pleased about it. When Mary
Cranch wrote to report that their brother William had died, Abigail was
devastated.

Reflection on such bad news was too painful for her, she wrote in reply.
Nor was there time for reflection. Her maid, Esther Field, had discovered
with an astonishment equal nearly to Abigail's own, that she was pregnant with the child of the ever-faithful footman, John Briesler, and both
wished to be married before sailing for home.

The first week in February, Adams paid a final call at Whitehall. On
February 20, he had his "audience of leave" with George III, who in
parting said, "Mr. Adams, you may with great truth, assure the United
States that whenever they shall fulfill the treaty on their part, I, on my
part, will fulfill it in all its particulars." More than this, however, Adams
was to remember the King's graciousness toward him.

Then, out of the blue and to his utter dismay, Adams was called on to
make one last emergency trip to Holland, and in the worst possible season
to cross the North Sea. It was essential that he take formal leave of his
ambassadorial post there, he was informed, and to secure yet another
loan, this to enable the United States to make its payments on earlier
loans from the Dutch.

To Adams the journey was punishment for sins unknown. The single
consolation was that Jefferson was to meet him at Amsterdam. Together
they succeeded with the Dutch bankers and in high spirits agreed that
when the time came that Adams was at last on his way to heaven, he
would surely have first to negotiate another Dutch loan. It was the last
time they ever collaborated in a public matter.

To Abigail, Jefferson had written, "I have considered you while in
London as my neighbor, and look forward to the moment of your departure from thence as to an epoch of much regret and concern to me. . . .
My daughters join me in affectionate adieus. Polly does not cease to
speak of you with warmth and gratitude. Heaven send you, Madam, a
pleasant and safe passage."

It was a charming letter of the kind at which Jefferson excelled and
that by now he was writing to a number of women within his Paris circle
who, in addition to Maria Cosway, included Anne Bingham and another
equally striking American, Angelica Church, as well as several Frenchwomen of note, all of whom, interestingly, were married.

Writing to Jefferson "in the midst of the bustle and fatigue of packing," Abigail said simply and sincerely that she could not leave without sending "a few lines to my much esteemed friend, to thank him for all his kindness and friendship towards myself and family."

THE AMERICAN MINISTER, his wife, and two American servants departed London for the last time on Sunday, March 30, 1788, by coach for Portsmouth, where they were to sail on the American ship *Lucretia*, bound for Boston. The Smiths, with their infant son, were to sail on another ship for New York, the temporary federal capital, where Colonel Smith planned to pursue his career.

"Mr. Adams, the late envoy from the American states, set off for Portsmouth on Sunday last, to embark for his return," read a small item in the *Whitehall Evening Post*. "That gentleman settled all his concerns with great honor; and whatever his political tenets may have been, he was much respected and esteemed in this country."

Because of bad weather, it was another three weeks before the Adamses were truly under way.

As Abigail fervently wished, she and John were never to see England or Europe again. Henceforth, she wrote on board in her diary, she would be quite content to learn what more there was to know of the world from the pages of books.

Adams is not known to have recorded any of his thoughts during the voyage home, but earlier he had said his great desire was "to lay fast of the town of Braintree and embrace it with both arms and all my might. There live, there to die, there to lay my bones, and there to plant one of my sons in the profession of law and the practices of agriculture, like his father."

Only Nabby, it seems, strongly objected. Their father had still more to do for his country, she had written to John Quincy.

By his opinions, advice, and recommendations, he has, I believe, in his power to do as much, perhaps the most, towards establishing her character as a respectable nation of any man in America—and shall he retire from the world and bury himself amongst his books, and live only for himself? No—I wish it not.... The Americans in

Europe say he will be elected Vice President. Besides, my brother, independent of other considerations, he would not, I am well convinced, be happy in private life.

John Adams was fifty-two. Except for the few months he had spent in Massachusetts in 1778, he had been away for ten years. In that time he had traveled thousands of miles in France, Spain, the Netherlands, and England; he had repeatedly crossed the English Channel and the North Sea; and his voyage home now marked his fourth crossing of the Atlantic. Altogether by land and sea he journeyed more than 29,000 miles, farther than any leading American of his time in the service of his country, never once refusing to go because of difficulties or unseasonable conditions, or something else that he would have preferred to do.

He had first sailed for Europe in the midst of war. He was returning now after more than five years of peace. For him personally, the homeward passage marked as clear an end to one chapter of his life, and the beginning of another, as had his initial voyage out. The intervening years in Europe had been as memorable and important, he felt, as any in his life.

Through the first years in France, for all his troubles with Franklin, he had worked steadily with the old patriot and often with telling effect. That he had pressed doggedly for a greater part in the war by the French navy would stand as one of his own proudest efforts, and with reason, given what happened at Yorktown.

With his success obtaining Dutch loans at the critical hour of the Revolution, he felt, as did others, that he had truly saved his country. That he had embarked on such an unprecedented mission on his own initiative, that he had undertaken his own one-man diplomatic campaign knowing nothing initially of the country, its language, and with no prior contacts or friendships to call upon, and yet carried through to his goal, were simply extraordinary and a measure of his almost superhuman devotion to the American cause.

His part in the Paris Peace Treaty would stand the test of time, Adams believed, as much as anything he had ever done. If the years and effort at London had come to naught, he at least knew he had given devoted service, conducting himself with consistent aplomb and dedication. No one could fault him for a false step. Nor could it be imagined that another of his countrymen in the same role could have done better.

Of the overwhelming convulsion soon to come in France, of the violent end in the offing for the whole European world Adams had come to know, he appears to have had few if any premonitions, no more than anyone else.

What changes had taken place at home in his absence he could only imagine, but clearly, with the advent of the new Constitution, a new epoch had opened in the history of his country.

For her part, Abigail speculated privately that any further role in politics might be "a little like getting out of the frying pan and into the fire."

Part III

Independence Forever

Our obligations to our country never cease but with our lives.

~John Adams

CHAPTER EIGHT

HEIR APPARENT

Gentlemen, I feel a great difficulty how to act. I am
Vice President. In this I am nothing, but I may be
everything.

—John Adams

I

On the crystal-clear morning of Tuesday, June 17, 1788, the keeper of the Boston lighthouse, Thomas Knox, sighted the *Lucretia* making good speed on the northeast horizon, and by prearranged plan he set in motion a welcome home such as John Adams had never imagined.

The landmark lighthouse, the first built in America, stood ten miles out from Boston on a tiny rock island at the head of the harbor. For more than half a century, since before Adams was born, it had taken the brunt of the open Atlantic, only to be blown up by the British in 1776. Rebuilt since the war, it stood again as before, and for those on board the inbound ship, after a rough crossing of fifty-eight days, its granite tower gleaming in the sunshine of a perfect morning was a thrilling sight.

At the signal from lightkeeper Knox, cannon boomed at the fort on Castle Island, to alert the town. Losing no time, Knox then set sail by pilot boat to meet the *Lucretia* and deliver an official welcome to Minister Adams and his lady from Governor John Hancock.

"My coach will be at the end of Long Wharf," Hancock had written. The Adamses were to proceed to a reception in their honor at his Beacon Hill home, where he hoped they would "tarry till you have fixed upon your place of abode."

As the ship cleared the lighthouse and swept into the harbor, the green hills of Braintree stood forth on the port side, while ahead rose Boston's multiple church steeples. Again cannon thundered from Castle Island, in official salute, and in little time the ship was tying up at dockside, where a crowd of several thousand was gathered.

People were cheering, church bells ringing, as the Adamses came ashore. Along the route to Beacon Hill, more throngs lined the streets. "The bells in the several churches rang during the remainder of the day— every countenance wore the expressions of joy," reported the *Massachusetts Centinel*.

For John and Abigail, who in their long absence had often felt unappreciated or forgotten, such an outpouring was inexpressibly gratifying, but also difficult to take in. Hancock, who adored ceremony and show, was so delighted by the excitement, he insisted the next day that he escort them to Braintree in his coach, and that they go accompanied by cavalry. But the Adamses had had enough fanfare and departed Boston on their own. At Braintree they moved in quietly with the Cranches until their furniture could be delivered from the ship.

THE FIRST DAYS at Braintree were a continuing round of emotional reunions—with the Cranches, sons Charles and Thomas, and John's astonishingly spry mother, now seventy-nine; John's brother Peter, Cotton Tufts, and Parson Wibird; plus a score of Quincys, Basses, and other old friends and neighbors. John Quincy arrived by horseback from Newburyport, where he was reading law.

Adams rejoiced in the sight of his sons. Charles, eighteen, and Thomas, fifteen, both Harvard scholars now and inches taller than their mother, had been small boys when he last saw them. John Quincy, soon to turn twenty-one, was clearly a grown man, and his father's pride and joy were no less than ever.

> The oldest has given decided proofs of great talents, and there is not a youth his age whose reputation is higher for abilities, or whose character is fairer in point of morals of conduct [he wrote to Nabby]. The youngest is as fine a youth as either of the three, if a spice of fun in his composition should not lead him astray. Charles wins the heart, as usual, and is the most a gentleman of them all.

"Busy unpacking during the whole day," recorded John Quincy, once the furniture and belongings arrived and the move to the new house began. Another day was devoted to unpacking his father's books, "yet [we] did not get half enough."

The Shaws arrived from Haverhill. There were teas and dinners at the Cranches. At church on Sunday the combined family filled several pews. "Parson Wibird preached in his usual dull, unanimated strain," fumed John Quincy, who had never understood his father's admiration for the eccentric preacher.

To Abigail's great disappointment, the new house, the "old Vassall-Borland place," once thought an elegant country seat, was found to be in poor repair and distressingly small and cramped after what she had known in Europe. Her sense of scale had changed more than she knew. The white clapboard house was handsome enough and stood by itself, uncrowded by the side of a main road, with farmland stretching before and behind. But there were just six rooms and ceilings were low. "In height and breadth, it feels like a wren's house," she wrote.

For days house and grounds were overrun with carpenters, masons, and farmhands. Some of her furniture had been badly damaged at sea. "But you know there is no saying nay," she added gamely.

Adams could not have been more pleased with his new "estate," as he wrote to an English friend. "It is not large, in the first place. It is but the farm of a patriot."

Spirits high, he plunged into the farmer's life, tramping his fields and pastures, inspecting walls, appraising livestock, hiring help, discussing weather and crops, and delegating projects. A French writer, J. P. Brissot de Warville, stopping at Braintree on a tour of America "to examine the effects of liberty upon men, society, and government," described farmer Adams as "like one of the generals and ambassadors of the golden ages of Rome and Greece . . . forgetful of his books and royal courts." (After a visit to Mount Vernon, Brissot would write much the same of George Washington.)

But another French traveler would be astonished to find a man of such consequence as Adams living in a house so small that, as he wrote, "no Paris lawyer of the lowest rank would choose [it] for a country seat."

Speculation on Adams's political future was rampant. He was talked of as governor, senator, Vice President, everything but President.

According to the *Centinel*, it was already certain he would become Vice President, and if not that, Chief Justice of the Supreme Court. "And who can object to Mr. Adams?" asked the paper which, after enumerating his many abilities and attainments, observed that he happened also to be "providentially" unemployed.

Henry Knox and Benjamin Lincoln, two stalwarts of 1776 and now of formidable political importance, came to talk. Benjamin Rush wrote from Philadelphia, warmly endorsing the prospect of his old friend as Vice President. Ezra Stiles, president of Yale, in a letter informing Adams that he had received an honorary degree from Yale, said he rejoiced at the thought of Adams for Vice President.

In keeping with the unwritten rule of the time that any display of ambition would be unseemly, Adams kept silent. But, in fact, he had decided from the time he arrived home that he would accept the vice presidency, and that role only, any other being "beneath him," as Abigail put it confidentially in a letter to Nabby.

The makeup of political leadership in the country had greatly changed in Adams's absence. Many with whom he had served in the Continental Congress had passed from the scene—some, like Benjamin Rush, were retired from public life; others deceased. Fourteen of those who had signed the Declaration of Independence were dead, including Stephen Hopkins and Caesar Rodney, and much about politics was now in the hands of "new men," "smart young men," known to Adams only by reputation. Madison of Virginia was still in his thirties. Hamilton of New York and Fisher Ames of Massachusetts were younger still.

Because Washington, a Virginian, was certain to become President, it was widely agreed that the vice presidency should go to a northerner, and Adams was the leading choice. That Adams could be blunt, stubborn, opinionated, vain, and given to jealousy was understood. Further, some of the "new men," notably Hamilton and Madison, questioned how willingly and loyally Adams might serve in second place to Washington, in view of the difficulties he was said to have had with Franklin in Paris.

The one visitor known to have recorded a firsthand impression of Adams that fall of 1788 found him quite at peace with life and surprisingly approachable. Judith Sargent Murray, a young woman from Gloucester traveling with her husband on their honeymoon, stopped at

Braintree in October and saw in "the countenance of Mr. Adams" a "most pleasing benevolence" she had not anticipated, as well as the marks of "deep thinking" customarily associated with "the sage, the philosopher," and "unbending integrity." Here was a man who had "stood before kings upon an equal level," she wrote. "I expected to be inspired with a painful awe, but strange to tell, every idea of distance was immediately banished." Of Abigail she observed: "It is evident the domestic as well as the more brilliant virtues are all her own. We were soon grouped in familiar chat. It was with [difficulty] I remembered they were not friends of ancient date."

Winter approached, and still Adams remained silent on politics. Abigail left for New York to be with Nabby for the arrival of another baby, a second son, John Adams Smith, leaving Adams alone with his ruminations. "I think of my poor dear and pity him," Abigail wrote from New York to Mary Cranch. But Adams wanted no one to feel sorry for him. Whatever the outcome—whether he was denied the vice presidency or whether the honor was to be his—he would be the winner either way, he insisted. "If they mortify my vanity, they give me comfort. They cannot deprive me of comfort without gratifying my vanity."

To Jefferson in Paris he wrote, "The new government has my best wishes and most fervent prayers for its success and prosperity; but whether I shall have anything more to do with it, besides praying for it, depends on the future suffrage of freemen."

BY PROCEDURE established in the new Constitution, the President was to be chosen by "electors" named by the state legislatures. Each elector was to cast one ballot with the names of two choices for President. The person with the most votes in the final tally was to become President, the runner-up, Vice President. In the event of a tie, the decision would go to the House of Representatives, a prospect so disturbing to Alexander Hamilton that he "deemed [it] an essential point of caution" to see that John Adams did not wind up with such a strong showing in the electoral count as to embarrass Washington. He was not against Adams, Hamilton explained privately. "Mr. A, to a sound understanding, has always appeared to me to add an ardent love for the public good." But Hamilton was taking no chances. Working quietly through the winter, he did what he could to convince leading politicians in several states to withhold votes from Adams.

The scheme succeeded. When the electors met in February 1789, Washington was chosen President unanimously with 69 votes, while Adams, though well ahead of ten others, had 34 votes, or less than half. Adams was humiliated by the news, his pride deeply hurt, but of Hamilton's part, he knew nothing.

Yet the fact remained that at age fifty-three, he, John Adams, the farmer's son from Braintree, had been chosen to serve as the first Vice President of the United States, the second-highest office in the land.

Abigail was to remain at home until he found a suitable place for them to live in New York. And thus the morning of his departure there was much that was reminiscent of other days as he bid goodbye, heading off again with a single servant, John Briesler. The difference this time was that Adams went accompanied by cavalry, a sight such as had never been seen in Braintree. It was April 13, 1789, one of the signal days of Adams's life and also, as it happened, Thomas Jefferson's forty-sixth birthday.

Boston provided a hero's send-off, with cannon salutes and exuberant crowds. The grand cavalcade that escorted Adams out of the city included more than forty carriages.

> Merit must be conspicuously great when it can thus call forth the voluntary honors of a free and enlightened people [wrote the *Massachusetts Centinel*]. But the attentions shown on this occasion were not merely honorary—they were the tribute of gratitude due to a man who after retirement from trials and services which were of 18 years unremitted continuance, hath again stepped forth to endeavor to establish and perpetuate that independence . . . and which his exertions have so greatly contributed to produce.

All through Massachusetts and Connecticut people lined the road to cheer Adams as one of their own, a New England man. At Hartford he was presented a bolt of locally manufactured brown broadcloth considered worthy for an inaugural suit. New Haven gave him the "Freedom of the City." That ideal weather accompanied the procession day after day was taken as auspicious.

At four o'clock the afternoon of April 20, after a week on the road, Adams arrived at the bridge at Spuyten Duyvil Creek, at the northern tip of Manhattan Island. A troop of New York cavalry and a "numerous concourse of citizens" led by John Jay and several members of Congress were waiting to escort him south to the city and Jay's palatial home on Broadway.

ONCE, IN THE MIDST of negotiations for the Paris Peace Treaty, John Adams had predicted that thirteen United States would one day "form the greatest empire in the world." It was a faith he had first expressed at age nineteen, when a fledgling schoolmaster at Worcester, writing to his kinsman Nathan Webb; and it remained a faith no less in 1789, for all the skepticism and derision he had heard expressed abroad, and despite the many obstacles confronting the new nation.

Much about the state of things, much that Adams had seen or heard since his return, was heartening. On a visit to Harvard, he had crossed a magnificent new bridge over the Charles River, said to be the finest bridge in America. New England shipping and ocean trade were reviving after a slump that followed the war. A Salem vessel, *Grand Turk*, had been to China and back and was the talk of Massachusetts.

There was a rise in demand for American farm products. In Virginia, work had started on canals for both the James and Potomac Rivers. At Philadelphia an inventor named John Fitch had demonstrated a steamboat on the Delaware River. But as striking as any sign of the country's burgeoning energy and productivity was the "Grand Federal Procession" held in Philadelphia that July 4 of 1788, in which many hundreds of tradesmen marched, grouped by guilds: shipbuilders, rope-makers, instrument-makers, blacksmiths, tin-plate workers, cabinetmakers, printers, bookbinders, coppersmiths, gunsmiths, saddlers, and stonecutters, some fifty different groups carrying banners and the tools of their trade.

As a result of the Paris Peace Treaty, the size of the nation was double what it had been, greater in area than the British Isles, France, Germany, Spain, and Italy combined, and if the American population was small by the standards of Europe, it was expanding rapidly, which to Adams was the most promising sign of all. From 2 million or so in 1776, the population had grown to nearly 4 million by 1789, and this despite seven years of

violent war, the departure of perhaps 100,000 Loyalists, and comparatively little immigration during the war years. Philadelphia, still the
largest city, had increased to a population of 40,000. New York counted
18,000 and, like Philadelphia, surged with growth. Of the thirteen states,
Virginia remained the richest and most populous, and thereby maintained the greatest political influence.

But wages were still low everywhere, and money was scarce. There was
no standard American coinage or currency. British, Spanish, French, and
German coins were all still in use, along with the coins of the different
states, their value varying appreciably from one state to another. In New
England, for example, six shillings made a dollar, while in New York eight
shillings made a dollar. In the entire country there were only three banks.

Travel was slow and arduous everywhere, the roads appallingly bad
and worst in the South. Largely because of bad roads, the new Congress,
scheduled to convene in New York on the first Wednesday in March
1789, would not have a sufficient number present to make a quorum in
either house until weeks afterward.

The nation had no army to speak of—about 700 officers and men. The
Continental Navy had disappeared. The sea power that Adams had
envisioned and worked so hard to attain was nonexistent.

The great majority of Americans lived and worked on farms, and fully
two-thirds of the population was concentrated in a narrow band along
the eastern seaboard from Maine to Spanish Florida. Nearly everything
else was wilderness. The whole country, concluded one visitor, was "a
vast wood." In Massachusetts it was thought that less than a third of the
land had been cleared, and it was the same in New York and Pennsylvania. Pittsburgh, at the end of the rough-hewn wagon road over the
Allegheny Mountains, was the westernmost town of any consequence in
the country and had fewer than 500 souls.

Approximately half the territory of the United States in 1789 was still
occupied by American Indians, most of whom lived west of the Appala-
chians, and though no one knew how many there were, they probably
numbered 100,000.

That a new America was steadily taking form beyond the Appala-
chians was one of the clearest signs of the times. Down the same road
Adams traveled that spring to New York came small caravans from
Massachusetts, New Hampshire, and Connecticut—families with chil-

dren and household belongings piled onto heavy wagons, bound for Ohio, a journey of more than 700 miles. At the same time, settlers from Virginia and the Carolinas were crossing into Kentucky and Tennessee. George Washington himself, known to have great confidence in the future of the West, had landholdings in the Ohio River country of more than 20,000 acres.

But to many the immense size of the country and the shift of population westward were serious concerns. With people spread so far and communication so slow and unreliable, what was to hold the nation together? Such republics of the past as Adams had written about in his *Defence of the Constitutions* were small in scale—so what hope was there for one so inconceivably large? "What would Aristotle and Plato have said, if anyone had talked to them, of a federative republic of thirteen states, inhabiting a country of five hundred leagues in extent?" Adams pondered.

Besides, the country had no tradition of union. Indeed, Americans were long accustomed to putting the interests of region or state ahead of those of the nation, except during war, and not always then. Following the Revolution, General Nathanael Greene had written to Washington from South Carolina that "many people secretly wish that every state be completely independent and that as soon as our public debts are liquidated that Congress should be no more."

North and South, the new Constitution had been vehemently opposed as a threat to the rights of the states and thus to individual liberty. Two sides had formed, the Federalists, who wanted a strong federal government, and the Anti-Federalists, who held to the sentiment of Thomas Paine, "That government is best which governs least." And the outcome had been anything but certain. Not until June 1788, the week the Adamses were unpacking at Braintree, had the Constitution been finally secured, when New Hampshire became the ninth state to ratify.

"The only way to keep us from setting up for ourselves is to disunite us," young schoolmaster Adams had written in his percipient letter to Nathan Webb, and to Adams now, as to others, dissolution remained the greatest single threat to the American experiment. "The fate of this government," he would write from New York to his former law clerk, William Tudor, "depends absolutely upon raising it above the state goverments." The first line of the Constitution made the point, "We the people, in order to form a more perfect union."

Of the potentially divisive threats to "the more perfect union," none surpassed slavery. The slave population, too, had burgeoned to nearly 700,000 men, women, and children who had no freedom whatever. There were slaves still in every state but one—only Massachusetts had eliminated slavery thus far—but with the overwhelming majority of slaves, fully 500,000 or more, centered in Maryland, Virginia, and the Carolinas, the difference between North and South was if anything greater than ever.

For Adams, who had seen far more of Europe than of his own country, the different Americas of the West and the South could only be imagined. But more disturbing to him than almost anything was the view heard in many circles that the old ideal of devotion to the public good had been supplanted by rampant avarice; the love of country, by a love of luxury. Mercy Warren had written to the Adamses while they were still in London that the current "avidity for pleasure" in America was certain to lead to trouble. Money, wrote James Warren bitterly, was all that mattered anymore. "Patriotism is ridiculed," he had warned Adams. "Integrity and ability are of little consequence."

The Warrens were among those who had adamantly opposed the Constitution, convinced it would only encourage speculation and vice. Certain that America was going the way of imperial Rome, James Warren had turned tiresomely sour and querulous. And though saddened by the change in his friend, Adams sensed he was right, that a moral shift had taken place. Nabby, appraising the politicians she encountered in New York, including Governor George Clinton, surmised there were few for whom personal aggrandizement was not the guiding motivation. She felt herself "in a land of strangers." It was a feeling not unknown to her father.

"I find men and manners, principles and opinions, much altered in this country since I left it," he confided to her. But this only made his dedication to union all the stronger.

II

AT THE START of every new venture of importance in his life, John Adams was invariably assailed by grave doubts. It was a life pattern as distinct as any. The boy of fifteen, riding away from home to be examined for admission to Harvard, suffered a foreboding as bleak as the rain clouds overhead. The delegate to the first Continental Congress, preparing to depart for Philadelphia, felt "unalterable anxiety"; the envoy sailing for France wrote of "great diffidence in myself." That he always succeeded in conquering these doubts did not seem to matter. In advance of each large, new challenge, the painful waves rolled in upon him once again.

Part of this was stage fright, part the consequence of an honest reckoning of his own inadequacies. Mainly it was the burden of an inordinate ability to perceive things as they were: he was apprehensive because he saw clearly how much there was to be apprehensive about. And so it was as he approached the untried office of Vice President.

With issues of such immense national consequence to be addressed, policies to be considered and resolved, precedents to establish, laws to enact, an entire new structure for the governance of the nation to be brought into being, could he, given his nature, do justice to the essentially passive, ceremonial role he had been chosen to fill? Action had been his metier, advocacy his strength, and the vice presidency offered opportunity for neither. "The Vice President of the United States," stipulated Article I, Section 3, of the Constitution, "shall be President of the Senate, but shall have no vote, unless they be equally divided." So could he with his passion, his fund of opinion, his love of debate, possibly keep from speaking his mind? "I am but an ordinary man," he had once written. "The times alone have destined me to fame." But had "the times" now cast him in a role for which he was wholly unsuited?

Such worries weighed heavily through the journey to New York, for all the "parade and show" in his honor, and in advance of his first appearance in the Senate, he prepared a brief speech in which, with marked understatement and honesty, he identified the problem: "Not wholly without experience in public assemblies, I have been more accustomed to take a share in their debates than to preside in their deliberations." Some months later, after one of the most unfortunate passages in a long public life, he would acknowledge succinctly to John Quincy that, in truth, the office he held was "not quite adapted to my character," that it was too inactive, too "mechanical," and that mistakenly he was inclined to think he must "throw a little light on the subject" when need be.

He had left home not knowing where he and Abigail might live, not knowing what salary Congress would provide, and worries over money troubled him exceedingly. Adams had strong views on the matter of recompense for officeholders. He was adamantly opposed to the notion espoused by some that in the ideal republican government public officials should serve without pay—an idea that had been supported by both Franklin and Washington, two of the wealthiest men in the nation. Were a law to be made "that no man should hold an office who had not a private income sufficient for the subsistence and prospects of himself and family," Adams had written earlier while in London, then the consequence would be that "all offices would be monopolized by the rich; the poor and the middling ranks would be excluded and an aristocratic despotism would immediately follow." He thought public officials should not only be paid, but that their salaries should be commensurate with their responsibilities and necessary expenses. And as one of the "middling ranks" himself, he viewed with great concern the expenses of living in New York.

Having had no word from Washington, he knew nothing of what might be on the General's mind, and one wonders how much worse he might have felt had he known. "May Heaven assist me," Washington had written privately, "for at present I see nothing but clouds and darkness before me." If Adams was concerned about making ends meet, Washington had had to arrange a loan to cover personal debts and the expense of moving to New York. Greatest was his worry that the country would expect too much of him.

FEDERAL HALL, where Congress met, was a handsomely proportioned stone building at the junction of Broad and Wall Streets distinguished by its glassy cupola and colonnaded front balcony. Formerly City Hall, it had been transformed according to designs by Major Pierre Charles L'Enfant, a young French engineer and architect who had served as a volunteer in the Revolution. Local citizens had provided the funds in the hope that an edifice worthy of the new republic would inspire Congress to make New York the permanent capital. When costs ran to twice the initial estimates, few complained, so appealing were the results.

It was the first building in America designed to exalt the national spirit, in what would come to be known as the Federal style. Emblazoned in the pediment of the front portico was an immense American eagle. Stars and laurel wreaths were a decorative motif inside and out, and all greatly admired. The meeting room of the House of Representatives, on the ground floor, had "spacious galleries open to all," so that visitors could observe the proceedings. The Senate Chamber, on the floor above, was a handsome room with high windows, fireplaces of fine American marble, and a ceiling patterned with thirteen stars and suns. Like the building, the Senate Chamber was neither overly grand nor imposing, but stately and filled with light. But there were no galleries for visitors, as the Senate was to meet behind closed doors.

Senator Oliver Ellsworth of Connecticut, on first seeing the building, said it surpassed any in the country. "I wish the business expected to be transacted in it may be as well done and as universally admired as the house is."

Adams was formally received at the door of Federal Hall and escorted upstairs to the Senate on the morning of Tuesday, April 21, two days before George Washington arrived in New York, crossing the harbor in a velvet-lined barge and landing to a stupendous ovation. There was no swearing-in ceremony for Adams—the wording of an oath for the Senate was among the host of matters still to be resolved. He was simply greeted by the president pro tempore of the Senate, John Langdon of New Hampshire, and conducted to his chair at the head of the chamber.

Unfolding two sheets of paper, Adams proceeded with his prepared remarks, "cheerfully and readily" accepting the duties of Vice President. Before him, seated in a semicircle, were most of the newly elected members of the Senate, a number of whom he knew from times past, including Langdon, Ellsworth, Richard Henry Lee, Ralph Izard of South Carolina, Robert Morris of Pennsylvania, and Tristram Dalton of Massachusetts, who had been a classmate at Harvard.

Adams said how moved he was to be once again among old friends, so many "defenders of the liberties" of the country. He offered congratulations to the American people on the formation of the Constitution and spoke warmly of the "commanding talents and virtues" of Washington. The part played by the hand of God in the choice of such a man to head the nation, said Adams, was so clear as to be apparent to all.

Having acknowledged the concern he felt over his ability to sit silently by during the debate and preside only, he said it would be his "constant endeavor" to behave toward all members with the consideration and decorum befitting their station and character.

> But if from inexperience or inadvertency, anything should ever escape me inconsistent with propriety, I must entreat you, by putting it to its true cause and not to any want of respect, to pardon and excuse me.

"A trust of the greatest magnitude is committed to this legislature," he said in conclusion, "and the eyes of the world are upon you."

Questions of ceremony and etiquette, such matters as how properly to address the President, required prompt attention, and to Adams these were no small concerns. If it was largely a ceremonial role he was to play, then best to get it right, he felt, and starting with his own place in the scheme of things, should the President choose to address the Senate. "Gentlemen, I feel a great difficulty how to act," he said. "I am Vice President. In this I am nothing, but I may be everything. But I am President also of the Senate. When the President comes into the Senate, what shall I be?"

There was silence from the floor, until Oliver Ellsworth, considered an authority on the Constitution, rose to his feet. "I find, sir," he said, "it is evident and clear, sir, that whenever the Senate are to be there, sir, you must be at the head of them. But further, sir, I shall not pretend to say."

Later, when Adams raised the question of whether the Senate should be seated or standing when the President addressed them, Richard Henry Lee offered that in England when the King spoke before a combined session of Parliament, members of the House of Lords sat and those of the House of Commons stood. Lee was followed by Ralph Izard, who said he could attest from personal observation of such occasions at Parliament that members of the House of Commons stood because in the House of Lords there were no seats for them.

On the day of his inauguration, Thursday, April 30, Washington rode to Federal Hall in a canary-yellow carriage pulled by six white horses and followed by a long column of New York militia in full dress. The air was sharp, the sun shone brightly, and with all work stopped in the city, the crowds along his route were the largest ever seen. It was as if all New York had turned out and more besides. "Many persons in the crowd," reported the *Gazette of the United States*, "were heard to say they should now die contented—nothing being wanted to complete their happiness ... but the sight of the savior of his country."

In the Senate Chamber were gathered the members of both houses of Congress, the Vice President, and sundry officials and diplomatic agents, all of whom rose when Washington made his entrance, looking solemn and stately. His hair powdered, he wore a dress sword, white silk stockings, shoes with silver buckles, and a suit of the same brown Hartford broadcloth that Adams, too, was wearing for the occasion. They might have been dressed as twins, except that Washington's metal buttons had eagles on them.

It was Adams who formally welcomed the General and escorted him to the dais. For an awkward moment Adams appeared to be in some difficulty, as though he had forgotten what he was supposed to say. Then, addressing Washington, he declared that the Senate and House of Representatives were ready to attend him for the oath of office as required by the Constitution. Washington said he was ready. Adams bowed and led the way to the outer balcony, in full view of the throng in the streets. People were cheering and waving from below, and from windows and rooftops as far as the eye could see. Washington bowed once, then a second time.

Fourteen years earlier, it had been Adams who called on the Continental Congress to make the tall Virginian commander-in-chief of the army. Now he stood at Washington's side as Washington, his right hand on the Bible, repeated the oath of office as read by Chancellor Robert R. Livingston of New York, who had also been a member of the Continental Congress.

In a low voice Washington solemnly swore to execute the office of President of the United States and, to the best of his ability, to "preserve, protect, and defend the Constitution of the United States." Then, as not specified in the Constitution, he added, "So help me God," and kissed the Bible, thereby establishing his own first presidential tradition.

"It is done," Livingston said, and turning to the crowd, cried out, "Long live George Washington, President of the United States."

With the crowd in raptures, cannon pounding, church bells clanging, Washington bowed still again and then, Adams at his side, moved back to deliver his inaugural address to a seated Congress.

If the Vice President had seemed hesitant or nervous performing his small part earlier, the President was no better. Washington's hands trembled holding his speech, which he read in a voice so low that many in the room had difficulty hearing what he said. No part of the address was particularly distinguished or memorable and the delivery was monotonous throughout. Several times his voice quavered. Yet none of this seemed to matter. He was Washington and many in the room had tears in their eyes. Representative Fisher Ames of Massachusetts later wrote of sitting "entranced," as though he were witnessing "an allegory on which virtue was personified." A French diplomat, Louis-Guillaume Otto, wrote with amazement at the effect Washington had. Never had "a citizen of a free country enjoyed among his compatriots a confidence as pure and as universal . . . a real merit and a faithful virtue must be the basis of it."

Adams provided no comment on the day's events. Writing to Abigail late the following day, he reported only that at a reception at the President's house, Washington had greeted him "with great cordiality . . . affection, and confidence," and that all had gone "very agreeably."

Days later, in Paris, where he had only just learned of Adams's election, Jefferson wrote warmly, "No man on earth pays more cordial homage to your worth or wishes more fervently your happiness." Having requested temporary leave from his duties in France to settle private affairs at home, Jefferson hoped to reach Virginia by late summer.

But little at all went agreeably for Adams in the weeks to follow. In the Senate, the issue of titles, and particularly the question of how the President was to be addressed, superceded all other business. In the House a move to consider titles met with quick defeat. The House voted that the chief executive should be addressed simply as "George Washington, President of the United States." But in the Senate the discussions became heated, with Adams taking part more than the members deemed appropriate.

According to some accounts it was the Virginian, Richard Henry Lee, who raised the issue, saying that titles were in use everywhere in the world, that there was something in the human makeup that responded to them, and that they were perfectly appropriate. Senator Izard, expressing agreement, moved that "Excellency" be the President's title. When Senator Ellsworth observed how very ordinary the mere appellation of President sounded, Adams immediately concurred from the Chair. There were presidents of fire companies and cricket clubs, Adams observed.

A committee appointed to consider the issue reported back with the suggested title "His Highness the President of the United States of America and Protector of the Rights of the Same." But it was Adams who took the lead in advocating titles, voicing his views in direct opposition to a strong-willed senator from Pennsylvania, William Maclay. Indeed, had it not been for Adams and Maclay the issue might have come to little more than it did in the House. Instead, it occupied the Senate for nearly a month.

Only Maclay was keeping a private journal of what transpired, and being the only account, it would be quoted repeatedly by latter-day historians. Maclay's rendition of Adams was devastating. Adams's version of what happened, written a few years later, would be quite different. According to Adams, his supposed passion for titles amounted merely to a reasonable request for advice from the Senate on how to address Washington:

> Whether I should say, "Mr. Washington," "Mr. President," "Sir," "may it please your Excellency," or what else? I observed that it had been common while he commanded the army to call him "His Excellency," but I was free to own it would appear to me better to give him no title but "Sir" or "Mr. President," than to put him on a level with a governor of Bermuda.

Adams believed everything possible should be done to bring dignity and respect to the central government and thus strengthen the union. If the central government was to have greater authority and importance than the state governments, then the titles of federal office ought to reflect that. It was thus essential to adorn the office of the President, the highest office, with commensurate "dignity and splendor." Titles were symbols, just as impressive buildings were symbols, except that titles, unlike buildings, cost nothing.

Like Richard Henry Lee, Adams believed the need for "distinctions" ran deep in human nature and that to deny this was unrealistic. The love of titles was like the love of parades and pageantry. The title did not make the man, of course, but it enhanced the standing of the man in the eyes of others. Rank and distinction were essential to any social organization, be it a family, a parish, or a ship, Adams would say. He cared intensely about the future of the republic and, as he had tried to explain in his *Defence of the Constitutions*, he saw men of education, ability, and wealth as "the natural aristocracy," the great strength and blessing of society, but potentially also a great threat to liberty, if their power and energies were misdirected. These were not hereditary titles he was proposing, but titles conferred by society for merit and that went only with positions of high federal responsibility. He was convinced that the modest compensation and heavy burdens of public service—the disruption of family life, the criticism and insults one was subjected to—must be compensated for, if ever people of ability were to take part. He believed that honorable titles of a kind not to be acquired in any other line of work could make a difference. To him personally, he insisted, they mattered not at all. It was his thought that Washington should be called "His Majesty the President," or something of the sort.

But there was no popular support for grand titles. Adams was woefully out of step with the country. Had he been in New York two years earlier, almost certainly he would have seen a play called *The Contrast*, if for no other reason than it was written by Nabby's former suitor, Royall Tyler. The first American play to be produced on stage, it opened with the lines:

> *Exult each patriot heart! This night is shown*
> *A piece which we may fairly call our own:*
> *Where the proud titles of "My Lord!" "Your Grace!"*
> *To humble "Mr." and plain "Sir" give place.*

One wonders, too, what effect Abigail might have had on her husband had she been with him during his first weeks as Vice President. It was not titles that gave men preeminence in America, she had lectured the "haughty Scotchman" on her voyage to England and to the solid approval of her shipmates.

James Madison, in an address to the House, had expressed the conviction of most Americans when he said, "The more simple, the more republican we are in our manners, the more national dignity we shall acquire."

But Adams would not be stilled. It was almost as if he had to go against the current, lest anyone doubt his independence. He repeatedly intruded on the Senate's time to voice his views, even lecturing the Senate, as if back at his schoolmaster's desk. "For forty minutes he harangued us from the chair," wrote Senator Maclay of one such disquisition.

Maclay, the most radical and outspoken Anti-Federalist in the Senate, was a rough-hewn lawyer from Harrisburg, Pennsylvania who stood six feet three and believed he was serving among a "set of vipers." Caustic, opinionated, he disliked just about everyone. In the privacy of his journal he called Alexander Hamilton "a damnable villain"; Robert Morris, "the greatest blackguard"; and referred to James Madison as "His Littleness." For Adams he felt only contempt. Earlier Benjamin Rush had encouraged Maclay to support Adams for Vice President and to be friendly to him after Adams took office, with a view to the help Adams might provide in making Philadelphia the capital. "We knew his vanity," Maclay wrote, "and hoped by laying hold of it to render him useful among the New England men in our scheme of bringing Congress to Pennsylvania." Accordingly, Maclay treated Adams with feigned deference, hating every moment of it, as he wrote in his journal. He thought Adams "silly," said he had "the face of folly." Whenever he looked at the Vice President presiding in his chair, wrote Maclay, "I cannot help thinking of a monkey just put into breeches."

It was the spirit of the Constitution that most Americans wanted, Maclay insisted, rising repeatedly to address the Senate. "Let us read the Constitution," he declared. *"No title of nobility shall be granted by the United States."* Any such attributes were "contraband language" in America.

To judge by what Maclay recorded, Adams made a fool of himself every time he opened his mouth, while he, Maclay, remained the voice of reason and the people's will. Possibly, Adams was as ludicrous as Maclay portrayed him. But given Maclay's contempt for Adams—a contempt so blatant that some in the Senate urged him to exercise some self-restraint—it is hard to imagine that what he wrote was not highly colored by bias.

Persisting in his futile effort, Adams made himself a mockery, even among some who were on his side. When Ralph Izard suggested that Adams himself be bestowed with a title, "His Rotundity," the joke rapidly spread. In the House, Representatives John Page of Virginia, Jefferson's lifelong friend, and Thomas Tucker of South Carolina relieved the tedium of extended debates by penning and exchanging doggerel at the Vice President's expense. "In gravity clad, He has nought in his head, But visions of Nobels and Kings," wrote Tucker, as a poetic query, to which Page responded:

> *I'll tell in a trice—*
> *'Tis old Daddy Vice*
> *Who carries of pride an ass-load;*
> *Who turns up his nose,*
> *Wherever he goes,*
> *With vanity swelled like a toad.*

On May 14, exactly as the House had done, the Senate voted that Washington's title be simply and only "The President of the United States."

Clearly the issue had been blown out of proportion. As even Madison admitted on the floor of the House, it was not a question of vital importance. Nor had Adams proven himself a monarchist, as some like Maclay kept insisting. Privately, Adams knew what a bad start he had made, and to be the butt of jokes, after all he had been through, was hurtful. But as any adverse or critical comment on Washington, any ridicule at all, would have been considered unacceptable at this stage, Adams served as a convenient target for mockery and humor, and would again, just as he would be subject to the easiest, most damaging of smear words: monarchist. He was the first, but by no means the last, Vice President to take abuse in the President's place, though much of it, to be sure, he brought on himself.

Most serious perhaps was the damage he had done to his standing with Washington, who was privately advised that the fuss over titles had made Adams not just unpopular in Virginia but "odious." Washington was thereafter to maintain an appreciable distance from Adams, thus diminishing still more the importance of the vice presidency and Adams's part in the scheme of things.

Yet through it all, true to his promise, Adams had shown no anger or acted discourteously to anyone. At one point he also conceded from the chair that perhaps he had been out of the country too long and failed to know the temper of the people.

To compound his troubles, word had been passed to him for the first time explaining the "dark and dirty intrigue" used to deny him votes for Vice President, and it sickened him. "Is not my election to this office in the scurvy manner in which it was done a curse rather than a blessing?" he asked Benjamin Rush in a letter charged with disgust. He had not yet learned who was behind the scheme, only that it had originated in New York, and the more he observed of life in New York, the more disconsolate he grew. To William Tudor, he railed against the "corruption of ambition," the "ungovernable rage" for money and luxury he saw on all sides. Later, Adams would attribute such "scrawls" to "gloomy times and desperate circumstances." He felt miserably alone. His accommodations with John Jay were the finest possible, and occasional Sundays with Nabby and her family helped greatly. But his need for Abigail, his ballast, was acute.

By mid-May he had located a house and posted an urgent plea for her to come at once. From her letters he knew the trouble she was having finding someone to lease the farm, and that she was short of funds. He told her to borrow whatever she needed, or sell off some of the livestock, "anything at any rate" rather than delay a day longer. If no one would take the place, she should "leave it to the birds of the air and the beasts of the field," he told her. In the meantime, he was desperate for books to be sent—Hume, Johnson, Priestley, Livy, Tacitus, Cicero, "and a Plutarch in French or English."

As to the nature of his "difficulties," he gave no explanation. Of all that had been going on in the Senate and his part in it, he said only that he had survived largely through prayer.

"My sincere thanks to Mr. Wibird for his remembrance of me in his prayers," he told Abigail. "It is to me a most affecting thing to hear myself prayed for, in particular as I do every day in the week, and disposes me to bear with more composure, some disagreeable circumstances that attend my situation."

The suspicion that Adams was a monarchist at heart grew stronger, and understandably, as in his *Defence of the Constitutions of Government* he did seem to lean in that direction. Distraught over what he had heard, Benjamin Rush wrote to caution his "dear friend" to think again and remember all he had espoused at the start of the Revolution.

In fact, Adams had done serious damage to his reputation and among others besides Rush whose opinions he most valued. It appeared that the man who put such stress on balance in government was himself a little unbalanced. Writing Madison from Paris, Jefferson dismissed the Senate's proposed title for Washington as "the most superlatively ridiculous thing" he had ever heard of, and called Adams's part in such business "proof" that Franklin's characterization of Adams as "sometimes absolutely mad" was the right one.

As so often before when feeling battered and unappreciated, Adams poured out his fury and frustration on paper. To Rush he insisted he was as much a republican as ever. Still, he did not see hereditary monarchy and aristocracy as necessarily contrary to human nature. Nor was it beyond reason to imagine that the time could come when America, of necessity, might have to resort to something of the kind—as "an asylum against discord, seditions, and civil war"—in order to preserve the laws and liberties of the people. He did not expect to see anything like this happen in his lifetime. He was only saying it was conceivable.

"I am a mortal and irreconcilable enemy to monarchy," he would later tell Rush, after Rush expressed worry that Adams had abandoned the ideals of 1776. "I am no friend to *hereditary limited* monarchy in America," Adams wrote explicitly. "Do not, therefore, my friend, misunderstand me and misrepresent me to posterity.

> I deny an "attachment to monarchy," and I deny that I have "changed my principles since 1776." . . . The continent is a kind of whispering gallery and acts and speeches are reverberated around from New York in all directions. The report is very loud at a distance when the whisper is very gentle in the center.

But this was written later, when the new government, as well as Adams's own role in it, had become more stable. In the meanwhile, even Rush conceded that he was equally distraught over the moral temper of the times and the long-range prospects for America. "A hundred years hence, absolute monarchy will probably be rendered necessary in our country by the corruption of our people," wrote the usually optimistic physician. He asked only that the republican ideal be given a fair chance, which Adams was not only willing, but determined, to do.

Many years afterward, reflecting on his friend Adams and the charge that he had been corrupted by his years in Europe, Rush wrote that, in fact, there had been no change at all. Adams was as "familiar and unaffected" as ever, "strictly upright," and "a real American in principle and conduct."

As distressing as almost anything for Adams was the flood of requests for his help in securing government jobs. His response was to refuse them all on the grounds that only the President had the power to make appointments. He himself, he insisted, had no say on patronage. Even appeals from deserving friends were denied. When Mercy Warren asked him to arrange a suitable position for her husband James, Adams replied huffily that he had no such influence and that even if he did he could not possibly allow the authority entrusted to him to become "subservient to my private views, or those of my family or friends."

Adams detested the idea of friends trying to use him, but he could readily have done something for the Warrens, and with perfect propriety.

One further aggravation were the reports from home about young Charles, who had gotten into a scrape at Harvard. Abigail wrote of suffering "anxious hours" over what she had heard, though given the company Charles had been keeping, she was not surprised. She thought the boy belonged with his father. To Cotton Tufts, who apparently supplied more details on the matter, Adams wrote helplessly, "What shall I do with that tender-hearted fool?"

The exact nature of Charles's difficulties was never defined in the correspondence, but from fragmentary Harvard records it appears that one student was expelled, others reprimanded, when the one, or all, ran naked through Harvard Yard, and the implications are that there had been drinking involved. In any event, Charles was with Abigail when she arrived by packet boat in New York at the start of summer, and life for the Vice President took a decided turn for the better.

ALL THE FRUSTRATIONS and feelings of stagnation that went with the vice presidency, all that so many others who followed in the office were to bemoan down the years, were felt intensely by the first Vice President. Yet for Adams it was by no means a time of unrelieved misery. Indeed, in their private lives, it was as happy a stretch of years as he and Abigail knew, beginning from the day of her arrival, June 24, 1789. "We are all very happy," wrote Adams to Cotton Tufts. And so they were.

He had rented a proper country seat, Richmond Hill, a mile north of town on a high promontory beside the Hudson, with sweeping views and nearly always a breeze. Adams loved the location and that the rent was considerably less than for a comparable house in town. His salary as Vice President, a subject of much debate in Congress, would be set at $5,000, a figure lower than previously understood, and whether he could thus afford to live in a style befitting the office remained a worry.

"We are delightfully situated," Abigail reported to Mary Cranch. "The prospect all around is beautiful to the highest degree." Sailing ships of every kind were constantly in view, passing up and down the wide tidal river.

> On one side we see a view of the city and of Long Island. The river [is] in front, [New] Jersey and the adjacent country on the other side. You turn a little from the road and enter a gate. A winding road with trees in clumps leads to the house, and all around the house it looks wild and rural as uncultivated nature. . . . You enter under a piazza into a hall and turning to the right hand ascend a staircase which lands you in another [hall] of equal dimensions of which I make a drawing room. It has a glass door which opens into a gallery the whole front of the house which is exceeding pleasant. . . . There is upon the back of the house a garden of much greater extent than our Braintree garden, but it is wholly for a walk and flowers. It has hawthorne hedge and rows of trees with a broad gravel walk.

She had her usual complaints—repairs were needed, good servants impossible to find, the local prices outrageous—but the longer she stayed at Richmond Hill, the more attached she became, and Adams concurred. "Never," he wrote, "did I live in so delightful a spot."

They were both happy to be near Nabby and the grandchildren, and Abigail unhesitatingly assumed her social obligations as the wife of the Vice President, making and receiving calls. "At Richmond Hill it is expected that I am at home both to gentlemen and ladies whenever they come out, which is almost every day . . . besides it is a sweet morning ride." After she and Nabby paid a first call on Mrs. Washington, Abigail expressed complete approval. "She is plain in dress, but that plainness is the best of every article. . . . Her hair is white, her teeth beautiful." Having attended several of the President's levees, Abigail could attest that the "court" of the Washingtons was as crowded, the company as brilliantly dressed as at St. James's, with the difference that here she thoroughly enjoyed herself. Her "station" at levees, she explained to Mary, was to the right of Mrs. Washington—though this Mary must keep to herself, "as *all distinction* you know is unpopular." If someone mistakenly stood in her place, the President never failed to see the situation corrected without anyone being offended. He "has so happy a faculty of appearing to accommodate and yet carrying his point that if he was not really one of the best intentioned men in the world, he might be a very dangerous one.

> He is polite with dignity, affable without formality, distant without haughtiness, grave without austerity, modest, wise, and good. These are traits in his character which peculiarly fit him for the exalted station he holds, and God grant that he may hold it with the same applause and universal satisfaction for many, many years, as it is my firm opinion that no other man could rule over this great people and consolidate them into one mighty empire but he who is set over us.

After Paris and London, however, she found New York extremely dull. There was but one theater and the local preachers were unbearably ponderous. Still being at the center of politics more than made up for it. "I am fearful of touching upon political subjects," she wrote. "Yet perhaps there is no person who feels more interested in them."

Through the sweltering summer, Adams never missed a day in the Senate, rolling in each morning from Richmond Hill in a one-horse chaise, not the fine carriage portrayed in hostile newspaper accounts. A Judiciary Act was deliberated and passed, establishing a federal court system, and set the size of the Supreme Court. Then a proposal that the Senate have a say in the removal of cabinet officers—a proposal put forth by Senator Maclay—set off fierce debate. To the Federalists, the bill was a flagrant attempt to diminish the power of the President to the benefit of the Senate, and they adamantly objected, arguing that the removal of ranking officials in the executive branch must be at the sole discretion of the President. Adams met with several senators—he was "busy indeed, running to everyone," according to Maclay's journal. Most important, he convinced Tristram Dalton of Massachusetts to withdraw his support for Maclay's bill. Then, when the vote proved a tie, Adams performed his only legislative function and cast his vote against the measure.

Afterward, James Lovell wrote from Massachusetts to tell Adams people were saying he had cast his vote with the President only because he "looked up to that goal." Of course he looked up to it, Adams answered. How could it be otherwise? "I am forced to look up to it, and bound by duty to do so, because there is only one breath of one mortal between me and it."

Another confidant, the Connecticut jurist John Trumbull, who had once clerked in Adams's law office, told Adams the southern aristocrats naturally held him in contempt and remained his enemies because he was a New Englander without "advantages from pride and family." They "suppose themselves born to greatness and cannot bear to be eclipsed by merit only."

"You talk of my enemies, but I assure you I have none," Adams said in spirited reply. That he was a New Englander, there was no denying. As for having no pride of family, there was little he was more proud of.

> My father was an honest man, a lover of his country, and an independent spirit and the example of that father inspired me with the greatest pride of my life. . . . My father, grandfather, great grandfather, and great, great grandfather were all inhabitants of Braintree and all independent country gentlemen. I mean officers in the militia and deacons in the church. . . . The line I have just described makes about 160 years in which no bankruptcy was ever committed, no widow or orphan was ever defrauded, no redemptor intervened and no debt was contracted with England.

The old, stubborn independence of his forebears kept playing on his thoughts. It had been the bedrock of their integrity, and he was resolved to see it sustained. When his son Thomas wrote, expressing an interest in public life, Adams felt he was answering for generations of their line:

> Public business, my son, must always be done by somebody. It will be done by somebody or other. If wise men decline it, others will not; if honest men refuse it, others will not. A young man should weigh well his plans. Integrity should be preserved in all events, as essential to his happiness, through every stage of his existence. His first maxim then should be to place his honor out of reach of all men. In order to do this he must make it a rule never to become dependent on public employments for subsistence. Let him have a trade, a profession, a farm, a shop, something where he can honestly live, and then he may engage in public affairs, if invited, upon independent principles. My advice to my children is to maintain an independent character.

OTHER THAN A FEW stiff social occasions, Adams had little contact with the President and no influence, but as yet it seemed no one had any influence with Washington. "He seeks information from all quarters and judges more independently than any man I ever saw," Adams wrote approvingly. In the choice of the cabinet, Adams is not known to have been asked an opinion, or to have offered any.

It was to be a geographically balanced cabinet, with New England, the Middle States, and the South represented, and all four positions were promptly confirmed by the Senate: Hamilton of New York as Secretary of the Treasury; Jefferson, Secretary of State; Edmund Randolph of Virginia, Attorney General; and Henry Knox of Massachusetts as Secretary of War. (If not the most intellectually outstanding of the four, Knox was certainly the most physically noticeable, having acquired over the years an immense girth, to the point of weighing nearly three hundred pounds.) For Chief Justice of the Supreme Court, Washington chose John Jay.

It was thus to be a government led by revolutionaries, all men who had taken part in the Revolution. Washington, by common agreement, was the greatest man in the world, and in Adams, Hamilton, Jefferson, Madison, and Jay, the American people could fairly claim to have the best minds in the country. And however striking their differences in temperament or political philosophy, they were, without exception, men dedicated primarily to seeing the American experiment succeed.

Adams approved of all the choices for the cabinet. Such was his regard for Hamilton at this point, he arranged for young Charles to clerk in Hamilton's Wall Street law office until Hamilton commenced his duties as Secretary of the Treasury, when Charles moved on to another firm. So through late summer father and son could be seen riding off to work together each morning in the one-horse chaise.

III

IN SEPTEMBER, as Congress took up the question of where to locate the permanent capital, and the President prepared for a tour of New England, news came of revolution in France. It was a bolt out of the blue, catching everyone by surprise, and the event that was to make the already difficult business of founding the new American government still more complicated and contentious. In the life of John Adams the old issue of America's relations with France was to bear heavily and fatefully yet again.

On July 14 an enraged mob had stormed and captured the Bastille, the ancient Paris prison that had come to symbolize an intolerable regime. All its prisoners, numbering just seven and none of them political, had been set free. Its commander had been beaten to death and decapitated, his dripping head then carried through the streets on a pike. In the days that followed, as rampaging mobs took over the city, one elderly Paris official was hanged from a lamppost, another cut to pieces, his heart torn from his body and brandished from a window of the Hôtel de Ville.

The headline of the *New York Daily Gazette*, September 19, 1789, announced, A COMPLETE REVOLUTION IN FRANCE. The National Assembly was proceeding to form a new constitution. France, friend and ally in America's struggle for freedom, was now herself taking up the cause, and nearly everywhere in America the news was greeted with enthusiasm.

France seems travailing in the birth of freedom [wrote William Maclay]. Her throes and pangs of labor are violent. God give her a happy delivery! Royalty, nobility, and vile pageantry, by which a few of the human race lord it over and tread on the necks of their fellow mortals, seem like to be demolished with their kindred Bastille, which is said to be laid in ashes. Ye gods, with what indignation do I review the late attempt of some creatures among us to revive the vile machinery. Oh Adams, Adams what a wretch thou art!

For Adams the news from France had the effect of an alarm bell. Heedless of the troubles he had already brought on himself with his *Defence of the Constitutions*, he took up his pen and launched into a series of newspaper essays, determined to show again the evil effects of unbalanced governments. He consulted no one, asked for no advice or opinion from others. Working under intense, self-imposed pressure, he wrote straight out, on and on, never pausing to rewrite or edit himself, which would have helped and for which he later apologized.

He labored at these essays for months, during which Congress adjourned and he returned to Massachusetts to join Washington for part of his visit there, proudly escorting the President on a tour of Harvard. But even before the first of the essays appeared, he let it be known that while he understood the reasons for the revolution in France—the oppressive abuses of the government, the overbearing and costly "armies of monks, soldiers, and courtiers"—and though he strongly supported the ideals espoused by French patriots, he viewed the situation with dire misgivings. "The French Revolution," he wrote to a Dutch friend, Francis van der Kemp, "will, I hope, produce effects in favor of liberty, equity, and humanity as extensive as this whole globe and as lasting as all time." Yet, he could not help foresee a tragic outcome, in that a single legislative assembly, as chosen by the French, could only mean "great and lasting calamities."

To the Reverend Richard Price in London, who had preached a widely publicized sermon in support of what was happening in France, Adams acknowledged feeling a sense of satisfaction and triumph in the revolution. Nor did he doubt its immense historic importance: "It appears to me that most of the events in the annals of the world are but childish tales compared to it," Adams declared. Later, having read Price's sermon, he said such principles and sentiments as Price expressed had been "from the year 1760 to this hour, the whole scope of my life."

But he had "learned by awful experience to rejoice with trembling." He could not accept the idea of enshrining reason as a religion, as desired by the philosophes. "I know not what to make of a republic of thirty million atheists."

From experience he knew the kinds of men such upheavals could give rise to, Adams told another correspondent. In revolutions, he warned, "the most fiery spirits and flighty geniuses frequently obtained more influence than men of sense and judgment; and the weakest man may carry foolish measures in opposition to wise ones proposed by the ablest." France was "in great danger." Ahead of anyone in the government, and more clearly than any, Adams foresaw the French Revolution leading to chaos, horror, and ultimate tyranny.

In London, meanwhile, the fiery Irish-born statesman Edmund Burke, who had once been the American Revolution's strongest friend in Parliament, declared in a speech that the French were proving themselves the ablest architects of ruin who ever existed. "In one summer they have done their business . . . they have completely pulled down to the ground their monarchy, their church, their nobility, their law, their revenue, their army, their navy, their commerce, their arts, and their manufacturers." The French, said Burke, sounding very like Adams, had "destroyed all balances and counterpoises which serve to fix a state and give it steady direction, and then they melted down the whole into one incongruous mass of mob and democracy."

Burke adamantly opposed such English enthusiasm for the revolution in France as espoused by Richard Price, which he thought woefully irresponsible, and the speech, which was published in full in New York in the *Gazette of the United States,* was but a prelude to what would be Burke's most famous book, *Reflections on the French Revolution,* published late in 1790.

Adams, too, took up the architectural theme, in a letter to his old fellow revolutionary Samuel Adams. "Everything will be pulled down. So much seems certain," he wrote. "But what will be built up? Are there any principles of political architecture? . . . Will the struggle in Europe be anything other than a change in impostors?"

. . .

THAT SEPTEMBER, Jefferson with his daughters Patsy and Polly, and slaves James and Sally Hemings, landed at Norfolk, Virginia, where he learned for the first time that he had been named Secretary of State.

He had left Paris well after the fall of the Bastille, and though he had witnessed none of the bloodshed of the summer, he had known what was happening and approved, convinced the violence would soon end and that for France, a glorious new day had dawned.

When Jefferson arrived at Monticello, according to traditional family accounts, his slaves were so overjoyed to see him they unhitched his horses and pulled his carriage up the last ridge of the mountain, then carried "Master" in their arms into his house. "It seemed impossible to satisfy their anxiety to touch and kiss the very earth which bore him," Patsy Jefferson would write.

Jefferson remained at Monticello through the winter, for nearly three months, during which Patsy, at seventeen, was married to a cousin, Thomas Randolph, Jr., after little or no courtship. As a wedding present, Jefferson gave the young couple 1,000 acres and twelve families of slaves, and helped in the eventual purchase of a nearby plantation for them called Edgehill—all of which necessitated an additional loan of several thousand dollars, this time from bankers in Amsterdam.

In early March, Jefferson started for New York, stopping briefly at Philadelphia to pay a last visit to Benjamin Franklin, who was mortally ill. Calling on Benjamin Rush shortly afterward, Jefferson assured his old friend he was as faithful a republican as ever and "deplored" the change in John Adams. He regarded Adams "with respect and affection as a great and upright man," Jefferson said, but "the greatest man in the world," he had lately concluded, was Madison.

At New York, Jefferson took a lease on a house on Maiden Lane, and immediately—inevitably—ordered that extensive alterations be made inside and out, despite the fact that New York was not expected to remain the capital much longer. James Hemings, now accomplished in the art of French cookery, was installed in the kitchen, and a letter went off to Paris telling Adrien Petit to come as soon as possible.

With the death of Franklin on April 17, Philadelphia staged the greatest public homage that had ever been given a deceased American. In New York, the House of Representatives voted to put on mourning, but the

Senate declined. When Jefferson proposed to Washington that the executive department follow the example of the House, Washington, too, declined, saying he would not know where to draw the line if he once began such a ceremony.

Adams's only known response to the news of Franklin's demise was in a letter to Rush in which he lamented the lies history would tell of "our revolution." "The essence of the whole will be *that Dr. Franklin's electrical rod smote the earth and out sprung General Washington. That Franklin electrified him with his rod and thenceforward these two conducted all the policy, negotiation, legislation, and war.*"

The reunion of the Adamses and Jefferson in New York was appropriately amicable. They saw each other socially at dinners and presidential levees, and on more than one occasion, Jefferson rode out to Richmond Hill. "Jefferson is here and adds much to the social circle," Abigail noted, but that was all. Jefferson in his letters home to Patsy (whom he addressed as Martha, now that she was a married woman) made no mention of the Adamses.

The *Gazette of the United States* had by now carried the text of a formal reply by Jefferson to the welcome he had received from his Virginia neighbors. It was a declaration of his faith in reason and democracy that he had taken great pains over.

> It rests now with ourselves to enjoy in peace and concord the blessings of self-government so long denied to mankind: to show by example the sufficiency of human reason for the care of human affairs and that the will of the majority, the natural law of every society, is the only sure guardian of the rights of man. Perhaps even this may sometimes err, but its errors are honest, solitary and short-lived. Let us then, my dear friends, forever bow down to the general reason of society.

But to Adams the "sufficiency" of reason alone for the care of human affairs was by no means clear, and it was exactly the will of the majority, particularly as being exercised in France, that so gravely concerned him. He was certain France had "severe trials" to endure, as he wrote to a friend. The will of the majority, if out of hand, could lead to "horrible ravages," he was sure. "My fundamental maxim of government is never to trust the lamb to the wolf," and in France, he feared, the wolf was now the majority.

Adams's series of articles also commenced in the *Gazette of the United States* that spring of 1790, on April 27, and would continue for a year, endlessly, it seemed to many. Though they were unsigned, the identity of the author was common knowledge. Titled "Discourses on Davila," and ultimately published as a book, they were largely a translation of a history of the French civil wars of the sixteenth century, a once-popular work, *Historia delle guerre civili di Francia*, by the Italian Enrico Caterino Davila, published first in 1630. More than he had in his *Defence of the Constitutions*, Adams stressed the perils of unbridled, unbalanced democracy, and in what he called "useful reflections" he dealt with human nature, drawing heavily on the works of Adam Smith, Samuel Johnson, Shakespeare, and Voltaire, and on Pope's *Essay on Man*.

In the initial installments, he wrote again, as he had as far back as his teaching days at Worcester, of the natural *"passion for distinction"* in all men and women—"whether they be old or young, rich or poor, high or low, wise or foolish, ignorant or learned, every individual is seen to be strongly actuated by a desire to be seen, heard, talked of, approved and respected."

"To be wholly overlooked, and to know it, are intolerable," wrote the man who, as Vice President, felt himself so consistently overlooked.

He ruminated on avarice, poverty, fame, and honor. No one, he wrote, better understood the human heart than the Romans, who "considered that as reason is the guide of life, the senses, the imagination and affections are the springs of activity." Unlike Jefferson, Adams was not only fascinated by "the passions," but certain they ruled more often than others were willing to concede. "Reason holds the helm, but passions are the gales."

The world was growing more enlightened, Adams conceded. "Knowledge is more diffused. . . . Man, as man, becomes an object of respect." But, he insisted, there was "great reason to pause and preserve our sobriety.

Amidst all their exultations, Americans and Frenchmen should remember that the perfectibility of man is only human and terrestrial perfectibility. Cold will still freeze, and fire will never cease to burn; disease and vice will continue to disorder, and death to terrify mankind.

Between Jefferson and Adams there was no discussion of their diverging views. To Jefferson, Adams had become an embarrassment, and while always pleasant in social encounters, Jefferson had as little as possible to do with him. On matters of foreign relations, where Adams's judgment could have been of value, Jefferson would never seek his counsel or include him in deliberations. Washington seldom asked Adams for views, but Jefferson, who in Europe had deferred repeatedly to Adams, asked for them not at all.

Like Washington and many others, Adams had become increasingly distraught over the rise of political divisiveness, the forming of parties or factions. That political parties were an evil that could bring the ruination of republican government was doctrine he, with others, had long accepted and espoused. "There is nothing I dread so much as a division of the Republic into two great parties, each arranged under its leader and converting measures in opposition to each other," Adams had observed to a correspondent while at Amsterdam, before the Revolution ended. Yet this was exactly what had happened. The "turbulent maneuvers" of factions, he now wrote privately, could "tie the hands and destroy the influence" of every honest man with a desire to serve the public good. There was "division of sentiments over everything," he told his son-in-law William Smith. "How few aim at the good of the whole, without aiming too much at the prosperity of parts!"

Then, in May, with the weather unseasonably wet and cold and influenza rampant in the city, Washington was suddenly taken so ill it appeared the one unifying force respected by all was in mortal jeopardy.

In the first six months of his presidency, Washington had lived in a comparatively modest house on Cherry Street, but had since moved to grander quarters, a mansion on Broadway, where now the street was cordoned off to give him some quiet. One doctor after another came and went at the front door. For several days, until the fever broke, it appeared the President was dying. Senator Maclay, on a call at the house, found "every eye full of tears." When the President's presiding physician allowed that death was all but certain, alarm swept through the city. Calamity faced the country.

For the Adamses, they were days of extreme anxiety. When the crisis passed, Abigail tried to convey to Mary Cranch the degree to which the union and permanency of the government depended on Washington's life. "At this early day when neither our finances are arranged, nor our government sufficiently cemented to promise duration, his death would, I fear, have had most disastrous consequences." The prospect of anyone succeeding to Washington's place was unthinkable, but the realization that there was indeed "only one breath," as John had put it, between him and the presidency, and that it would be he who would have to face the "disastrous consequences," had struck her full force as it had not before. "I feared a thousand things which I pray I never may be called to experience," she continued. "Most assuredly I do not wish for the highest spot. I never before realized what I might be called to do, and the apprehension of it only for a few days greatly distressed me."

Meantime, the entire household at Richmond Hill was stricken with influenza, with the exception of the Vice President. James Madison had been laid up. One congressman died. Jefferson was out of circulation for a month, confined to his house in the grip of excruciating headaches.

That one had to keep "a good heart," come what may, was Abigail's lifelong creed. "A merry heart doeth good like a medicine," she loved to say, quoting *Proverbs*. "I hate to complain," she now wrote. "No one is without difficulties, whether in high or low life, and every person knows best where their own shoe pinches."

That June of 1790, with the President recovered, the French diplomat, Louis-Guillaume Otto, summing up the situation in New York for his government, reported that the influence and importance of the Vice President were "nil." If Washington had an heir apparent, by all rights it was Jefferson.

> It appears certain at present that he [Adams] will never be President and that he will have a very formidable competitor in Mr. Jefferson, who, with more talents and knowledge than he, has infinitely more the principles and manners of a republican.

THAT SUMMER Congress worked itself to a fever pitch over two issues certain to be of long-lasting consequence. The question of where to locate the national capital had been a topic of rancorous discussion since the summer before, and was again at the forefront, along with a proposal for the federal government to assume some $25 million in debts incurred by the states during the Revolution. The "assumption" plan was the work of the youthful Hamilton, who, since his appointment, had swiftly made the Treasury the most creative department in the government, and was commonly recognized as having extraordinary ability.

An immigrant of illegitimate birth, Hamilton had arrived in New York from the West Indies at age fifteen. In less than ten years he had distinguished himself as a scholar at King's (later Columbia) College, served as Washington's aide in the war, led an assault at Yorktown, and married into the wealthy, influential Schuyler family of New York, which did him no harm when, after the war, he turned his energies to the law and politics. Brilliant to the point of genius, he exuded vitality and could turn on great charm when needed. His capacity for hard work was almost superhuman. Though somewhat shorter than Adams—about five feet seven—he was attractively slender, handsome, with clear blue eyes and sandy red hair, and dressed so as never to be lost in a crowd, in perfectly tailored coats, waistcoats, and breeches in a rainbow of colors. Even his ambition seemed to become him—Adams wrote of Hamilton's "high-minded ambition"—and his incurable love of intrigue had thus far alienated no one.

As one of the principal authors, along with Madison, of the *Federalist Papers*, Hamilton ranked as a leading proponent of a strong central government, and his name was commonly linked with that of Madison, with whom he remained on friendly terms. Further, both were highly esteemed by the President, which was of considerable importance.

Madison, a tiny, sickly-looking man who weighed little more than a hundred pounds and dressed always in black, had emerged as the most formidable figure in the House, largely on the strength of a penetrating intelligence and a shrewd political sense. Adams thought him overrated, but in time Adams would change his mind.

Hamilton's assumption plan had first been laid before Congress the previous January, 1790, as part of a large report in which he argued that a sound public credit was essential to economic growth and national unity. He had called for the central government to pay off all federal debt and to assume the debt of the states as well, on the grounds that they had been incurred in the common cause of independence. Boldly, Hamilton argued that such an increase in the national debt would be a blessing, for the greater the responsibility of the central government, the greater its authority.

He was vehemently opposed, however, by those who saw it as an over-reaching and very unrepublican move to concentrate power in the central government to the detriment of the states. To southerners in the Congress the scheme would not only reduce the importance of the states, but would lead to a dangerous, ultimately corrupting concentration of wealth and power in the North. And it was Madison now, breaking with Hamilton, who led the opposition in the House, where assumption was put to the vote on April 12 and narrowly defeated.

Still, the battle continued, and at the same time that the location of the capital—the "residence" issue—had become a subject of equal rancor. New Yorkers, eager to keep the capital where it was, had begun building an executive mansion for Washington by the Battery, with a grand panorama of the harbor. New Englanders also favored New York, it being much the easiest location for them to reach, though Philadelphia, adamantly espoused by the Pennsylvanians, was considered an acceptable alternative.

The Virginians wanted no part of either of the northern cities and were strongly committed to bringing the capital south to a site on the Potomac River not far from Washington's home at Mount Vernon. Those "most adjacent to the seat of legislation will always possess advantages over others," said Madison, who feared that the South and its agrarian way of life would suffer were the capital to remain in the North.

In the Senate, charges and countercharges were voiced with increasing vehemence. Adams struggled to keep order and apparently with little effect. "John Adams has neither judgment, firmness of mind, nor respectability of deportment to fill the chair of such an assembly," scoffed the ever-splenetic William Maclay.

Then, on a morning in June, the historic "compromise of 1790" began to take form, when Hamilton and Jefferson met outside the President's house and Hamilton, taking Jefferson by the arm, walked him up and down for half an hour, urging him, for the sake of the union, to join in "common cause" and resolve acceptance of the assumption bill. Professing that reasonable men ought to be able to reach a compromise, Jefferson invited Hamilton and Madison to dine at his house the next day. And there, over a bottle of Jefferson's best wine, the bargain was struck. In return for southern support for the assumption bill, Hamilton agreed to do all he could to persuade the Pennsylvanians to vote for a permanent capital by the Potomac, if it were agreed to move the capital temporarily to Philadelphia. Madison said he would not vote for assumption, but then neither would he be "strenuous" in opposition.

Whether, in fact, the outcome was resolved in this fashion is not altogether clear, but certainly Jefferson believed the bargain had been settled, for on July 1 he wrote William Short in Paris to have his furniture and paintings shipped to Philadelphia.

The crucial vote on residence, however, was made not in the House but in the Senate, where apparently an agreement had already been reached between the Pennsylvanians and the Virginians. When a last-minute motion to keep the capital in New York for two more years resulted in a thirteen-to-thirteen tie, Adams cast a nay vote.

By July 12 both houses of Congress had voted to relocate the capital in Philadelphia for ten years—until the turn of the century—after which it would move to a permanent site on the Potomac. The Pennsylvanians went along with the agreement, convinced that once the capital was located in Philadelphia it would never move. Adams was inclined to agree. A capital, he said, ought to be in a great city, an idea no Virginian would ever have entertained.

With the passage of the assumption bill at the end of the month came cries of "intrigues, cabals, and combinations." New Yorkers were outraged. Senator Maclay speculated that, if the truth were known, Washington was behind the whole arrangement, which indeed he was, and in the first public criticism of the President, the *New York Advertiser* charged him with gross ingratitude to the city of New York.

As soon as Congress adjourned on August 12, the government began packing for the move. The President and Mrs. Washington departed for Mount Vernon, while the Vice President set off for Philadelphia to find a house, leaving Abigail in despair over the thought of leaving Richmond Hill, and particularly as Nabby gave birth to a third child that summer, another boy, named Thomas.

By late fall the Adamses were resettled in a substantial brick house two miles west of Philadelphia overlooking the Schuylkill. Called Bush Hill, it was another setting of idyllic charm, except that the British army, during the occupation, had left hardly a tree or bush standing.

Washington arrived and moved into the Robert Morris house on Market Street, considered the grandest residence in Philadelphia. (General Sir William Howe had made it his headquarters during the occupation.) Jefferson, too, took a house on Market, just blocks away, where his additions this time included a library, stable, and garden house. He had furniture sent on from Monticello and eventually his treasures from France arrived in no less than eighty packing cases, a quantity of purchases such as no one American had ever brought back from Europe.

On Monday, December 6, Congress reconvened in Congress Hall, formerly the Philadelphia County Courthouse, a two-story red-brick building erected since the war on the west side of the State House. As at Federal Hall in New York, the House of Representatives met on the first floor, the Senate on the floor above. The Supreme Court would sit in what had been City Hall, a corresponding brick building on the east side of the State House.

For all that Philadelphia had grown and changed, it was familiar territory for Adams, filled with memories. He was happy to be back, and once she had overcome another spell of poor health, Abigail was writing of her delight in seeing "the dazzling Mrs. Bingham again," and of Mrs. Washington's Friday evenings, where "fine ladies show themselves, and as candlelight is a great improver of beauty, they appear to great advantage." The President was as fond of theater as were the Adamses, and invited them to accompany him and Mrs. Washington to performances at the Southwark Theater. They dined several times at the presidential mansion, and the President and his lady, in a rare exception to his rule of accepting no invitations, came to dine at Bush Hill.

So bone-chilling was the cold of that winter, every fireplace at Bush Hill had to be kept blazing and Abigail's principal problem with new servants this time was that they were so frequently drunk. But her house was full of life, as she wrote. Son Thomas, having finished at Harvard, came to live with his mother and father. Charles rode down from New York for periodic visits, bringing his customary good cheer. When John Quincy traveled from Boston for a stay in February, Abigail was able to report to sister Mary that for the first time in years she had all three sons together under her roof.

Like her husband, Abigail had the highest hopes for their eldest son. The time would come, she said, when "this young man will be sought as a jewel of great price." But John Quincy did not look well and seemed to have lost "much of his sprightliness and vivacity." The year before, while still at Newburyport, he had fallen in love with a fifteen-year-old girl, Mary Frazier, and was strongly advised by his parents that both he and the girl were too young for a serious "attachment." By autumn the romance was broken off. Now, Abigail reported to Mary Cranch, the young man fretted that his Boston law practice was so slow taking hold. "We all preach patience to him."

But her greater worry was Nabby, whose husband, with a growing family and no profession, had suddenly gone off to England on some kind of speculative venture.

Happily, America was prospering, commerce and agriculture both flourishing, and there was increasing confidence everywhere. Secretary Hamilton's proposed national bank, the centerpiece of his plan and now before Congress, had the support of nearly everyone, Abigail reported to Cotton Tufts. There was not a doubt that the bill would pass and by a considerable majority, she assured the trusted family adviser.

As she predicted, the bill for the Bank of the United States passed by a sizable majority, despite opposition from Madison and Jefferson, who urged the President to exercise a veto on constitutional grounds. But Hamilton's views carried greater weight with Washington, who signed the bill on February 25.

Better versed on financial matters than her husband, Abigail wanted to invest immediately in government securities, but as she told Cotton Tufts, "Mr. Adams held to his faith in land as true wealth."

Indeed, Adams not only put his trust in land as the safest of investments, but agreed in theory with Jefferson and Madison that an agricultural society was inherently more stable than any other—not to say more virtuous. Like most farmers, he had strong misgivings about banks, and candidly admitted his ignorance of "coin and commerce." Yet he was as pleased by the rise of enterprise and prosperity as anyone, and in moments of discouragement over public life, even contemplated going into the China trade! As strong as his attachment to life lived close to the land may have been, Adams liked what he saw happening. "Never since I was born was America so happy as at this time."

Had the Adamses invested in government securities as Abigail wished, they would, almost certainly, have wound up quite wealthy.

NOWHERE IN THE DOZENS of personal letters they had written in more than a year had either John or Abigail made mention of Jefferson. To judge by their correspondence he might still have been in France. It was not that they never saw him. Rather, it seems that if they had nothing good to say, they said nothing. But then that spring of 1791, Adams and Jefferson were caught up in a public controversy that neither anticipated or wanted and that put the first severe strain on their already cooling friendship. The effect on national politics would be profound, and as was perhaps inevitable, the root cause was the revolution in France.

In furious response to Edmund Burke's book *Reflections on the Revolution in France*, Thomas Paine, who was then in England, had produced a pamphlet, *The Rights of Man*, that attacked Burke and set forth an impassioned defense of human rights, liberties, and equality. Jefferson, on receiving an early copy, promptly passed it on to a Philadelphia printer with a note warmly endorsing it as the answer to "the political heresies that have sprung up among us." When the printer published a first American edition, Jefferson's endorsement appeared prominently on the title page and was attributed to the Secretary of State.

The endorsement caused a sensation. Jefferson claimed to be astonished but privately confirmed that by "political heresies" he meant the writings of John Adams. In a letter of explanation to Washington, he said he was "mortified" to be "thus brought forward on the public stage . . . against my love of silence and quiet, and my abhorrence of dispute." He greatly regretted that "the indiscretion of a printer" had doubtless offended his "friend Mr. Adams, for whom, as one of the most honest and disinterested men alive, I have cordial esteem," despite "his apostasy to hereditary monarchy." But to Adams, Jefferson said nothing. Weeks passed, during which Adams, deeply offended, kept silent, then returned to Braintree for a brief visit.

Presently, when a series of spirited letters signed "Publicola" began appearing in Boston's *Columbian Centinel*, attacking *The Rights of Man* and its sponsor, Jefferson, like many readers, assumed "Publicola" was Adams. In fact, it was John Quincy, who, rising to the defense of his father, took Jefferson to task for claiming that a difference in political opinion might be declared "heresy," and those who differed in view from the Secretary of State were therefore heretics.

> I am somewhat at a loss to determine [he wrote] what this very respectable gentleman means by political heresies. Does he consider this pamphlet of Mr. Paine's as a canonical book of political scripture? As containing the true doctrine of popular infallibility, from which it would be heretical to depart in one single point? . . . I have always understood, sir, that the citizens of these States were possessed of a full and entire freedom of opinion upon all subjects civil as well as religious; they have not yet established any infallible criterion of *orthodoxy*, either in church or state . . . and the only political tenet which they could stigmatize with the name of heresy would be that which should attempt to impose an opinion upon their understandings, upon the single principle of authority.

Jefferson let three months pass before sending Adams a rather stiff letter of apology and explanation, which, though well intentioned, hardly sufficed. Written at Philadelphia, the letter was dated July 17, 1791. He had taken up his pen a dozen times and as often put it down, "suspended between opposing considerations," Jefferson began. "I determine, however, to write from a conviction that truth between candid minds can never do harm." He had written what he had about "heresies," he said, only "to take off a little of the dryness of the note." He had been "thunderstruck" by the printer's use of the note. He had hoped it would attract no attention and implied it might not have but for the fuss over the "Publicola" series. It was because of "Publicola" that "our names [were] thrown on the public stage as public antagonists.

> That you and I differ in our idea of the best form of government is well known to us both, but we have differed as friends should do, respecting the purity of each other's motives, and confiding our differences of opinion to private conversation. And I can declare with truth in the presence of the Almighty that nothing was further from

my intention or expectation than to have either my own or your name brought before the public on this occasion. The friendship and confidence which has so long existed between us required this explanation from me, and I know you too well to fear any misconstruction of the motives of it.

Never in his life, Jefferson added, had he written anything for newspapers anonymously or under a pseudonym, and he never intended to.

He did not tell Adams, as he had Washington, that he had Adams specifically in mind as the perpetrator of "heresies." Nor did he say that he knew by then that "Publicola" was John Quincy. Jefferson's source was Madison, who had also observed that the young man's style was notably less clumsy than that of the father.

Adams answered Jefferson at once and with obvious feeling. He accepted Jefferson's account of what had happened, but allowed that the printer had "sown the seeds of more evils" than he could ever atone for. He, Adams, had been held up to ridicule in one newspaper after another for his meanness (the *New Haven Gazette* had called him an "unprincipled libeler"), his love of monarchy, his antipathy to freedom. Adams vehemently denied that he favored monarchy. "If you suppose that I have or ever had a design or desire of attempting to introduce a government of Kings, Lords, and Commons, or in other words a hereditary executive, or a hereditary senate, either into the government of the United States or that of any individual state in this country, you are wholly mistaken. . . . If you have ever put such a construction on anything of mine, I beg you would mention it to me, and I will undertake to convince you that it has no such meaning."

The problem was that so many who criticized his writings had never bothered to read them, Adams said. Some misunderstood them, others willfully misrepresented them. Either way, he had been made the victim of "tempestuous abuse." That Jefferson himself had once praised his *Defence of the Constitutions*, apparently finding no heresies therein, Adams, to his credit, made no mention.

He took issue only with Jefferson's claim that their differences on the best form of government were well known to both of them. This was simply not so, Adams wrote. "You and I have never had a serious conversation together that I can recollect concerning the nature of government."

He was not "Publicola," and he had had no hand in writing the essays, Adams assured Jefferson, but refrained from identifying the author. What troubled him most, he said, was the mounting enmity between public men. "I must own to you that the daring traits of ambition and intrigue, and those unbridled rivalries which have already appeared, are the most melancholy and alarming systems that I have ever seen in this country." If this was what politics came to, then the sooner he was out of it, the happier he would be.

At the last, Adams left no doubt of how much Jefferson and his friendship meant to him.

> I thank you, sir, very seriously for writing to me. It is high time that you and I should come to an explanation with each other. The friendship that has subsisted for fifteen years between us without the smallest interruption, and until this occasion without the slightest suspicion, ever has been and still is very dear to my heart. There is no office which I would not resign, rather than give a just occasion to one friend to foresake me. Your motives for writing to me, I have not a doubt, were the most pure and the most friendly; and I have no suspicion that you will not receive this explanation from me in the same candid light.

Jefferson would have been better off had he let the matter drop. Instead, he wrote again, speciously insisting that blame for the controversy rested with "Publicola." Then, in what must have been an effort to spare Adams's feelings, he went further. In direct contradiction to what he told Washington, Jefferson denied to Adams that he ever had him in mind when he wrote to the printer: "Indeed, it was impossible that my note should occasion your name to be brought into question; for as far from naming you, I had not even in view any writing which I might suppose to be yours. . . . Thus I hope, my dear sir, that you will see me to have been innocent *in effect* as I was in intention."

In sum, Jefferson refused to take any responsibility for what had happened. To Washington he cited the "indiscretion of a printer"; to Adams he said John Quincy was the cause of the trouble, and that he himself was innocent of ever even thinking of Adams in the first place.

But it was not Jefferson who had suffered abuse and ridicule in the press. It was Adams, and the damage done was extreme, given the overwhelming popularity of both Thomas Paine and the French Revolution.

From this point on, Adams and Jefferson were seldom to be perceived as anything other than archrivals. The public stage that Jefferson said he wished to avoid, the growing enmity between public men that Adams abhorred, had made them in the public mind symbols of the emerging divisions in national politics. Further, in what he had written to Madison, and in what he had said in his note to the printer, Jefferson had tagged Adams with being both mentally unsound and a monarchist, the two charges most commonly and unjustly made against him for the rest of his life.

Adams let the matter drop. He made no reply to Jefferson's last letter, and there would be no further correspondence between them for several years. The "explanation with each other" that Adams hoped for would have to wait for more than two decades.

IN THE AUTUMN of 1791, alarmed to find they were living beyond their means, Abigail and John moved from Bush Hill to a modest dwelling in town at Fourth and Arch Streets. Servants were let go, except for Briesler and a cook, "a clever, sober, honest," free black woman, as Abigail reported to Mary Cranch. "We live sociably and friendly together," she wrote, and in many ways felt they were all better off living in town.

But with winter came the inevitable siege of illnesses, and for Abigail, beset mainly by rheumatism "attended with a violent fever," it was as miserable a time as she had known. Her eyes became so inflamed she could not bear any light in her room, "not even the fire to blaze." After six weeks in bed she was still too feeble to go downstairs without being carried. "I have scarcely any flesh left in comparison to what I was." Dr. Rush came several times to draw blood, and, in the mistaken belief that the human body contained more blood than it actually does, it was his practice to bleed patients far more than customary. At times he was known to remove as much as eighty ounces, which could well explain Abigail's feeble state.

The news that Colonel Smith, newly returned from London, was to sail again on the next packet, and would be taking Nabby and the children with him, left her feeling still more dreadful. The "everlasting fever" hung on, she wrote weeks later, confiding also that the "critical period" of midlife compounded her troubles. She brooded over the brevity of life. "How soon may our fairest prospects be leveled with the dust and show us that man in his best estate is but vanity and dust?" she wrote on March 21, 1792, after a particularly bad night of "nerves." It was already another election year, the end of the President's and the Vice President's terms of office. Who knew what was to come? Southern members of the House seemed determined not just to oppose the Secretary of the Treasury but to destroy him, while much of the press joined in the assault. Not even the President escaped their venom any longer. Oddly it was only the Vice President now who was allowed to "sleep in peace," though this hardly compensated for Abigail's worry for the country.

"I firmly believe," she darkly forecast to Mary, "if I live ten years longer, I shall see a division of the Southern and Northern states, unless more candor and less intrigue, of which I have no hopes, should prevail."

Adams was more sanguine. If frequently exhausted by his labors and distressed over her ailments, he appears to have come to terms with his marginal role in the order of things. It had been a painful process, but he had at last learned the part he was supposed to play and to a large degree accepted its limitations. Rarely did he speak in the Senate anymore. Rarely if ever did he intrude on Senate business. If the role of Vice President made him a political cipher—as it would anyone—he could at least serve faithfully.

He was in the chair every day, all day, without fail, which was a point of pride with him, but also of some worry, since he knew such sedentary confinement to be good neither for the body nor the spirit of "a man habituated for a long course of years to long voyages and immense journeys."

Though loyal to Washington and the administration, Adams was but nominally a Federalist, refusing steadfastly to be, or to be perceived as, a party man. That he had allowed "no party virulence or personal reflections" to escape him was also a matter of pride and consolation. If called upon to maintain order in the Senate now, he apparently had only to tap gently with his silver pencil case on the small mahogany table before him.

In mid-April, her health sufficiently restored for her to travel, Abigail returned to Massachusetts. Adams followed in May, once Congress adjourned, and the long summer at home, far removed from the hornets' nest of election-year politics at the capital, did much to restore them both.

The one big change at home was that their part of town, the old, first-settled North Precinct, had been broken off from the rest of Braintree and renamed Quincy. Otherwise, town life and days on the farm went on refreshingly the same as always.

AMONG CLOSE ASSOCIATES the President had been expressing a strong desire to return to private life. He was weary of the demands of office, weary and disheartened, Washington said, by party rancor and a severely partisan press that had taken to calling him the American Caesar.

Many of the harshest attacks on Hamilton's economic policies—and some of the more biting comments on Washington himself—came from the *National Gazette*, a newspaper newly established in Philadelphia as an antidote to the partisan Federalist views of the *Gazette of the United States*, to which Alexander Hamilton was a regular contributor of essays and money. But when it became known that the editor of the new *National Gazette*, Philip Freneau, had been encouraged to establish the paper by Madison and Jefferson, and that he was also employed by Jefferson as a translator in the Department of State, it appeared Jefferson himself had a hand in the attacks on the President and the administration. The most vicious assaults, however, were aimed at Hamilton, whom Freneau delighted in vilifying, and to add to the insults, such diatribes were nearly always accompanied by lavish praise for Jefferson.

Washington claimed to disregard newspaper abuse but privately asked Jefferson to intercede with Freneau and remove him from the State Department. Jefferson insisted that Freneau and his paper were saving the country from monarchy and persuaded Washington that it would be a grave misstep to impede on freedom of the press.

Even more aggravating for the President was the unrelenting feud between Jefferson and Hamilton, the two highest officers in his cabinet, and the most gifted. Animosity between them had reached the point where they could hardly bear to be in the same room. Each was certain the other was a dangerous man intent on dominating the government; and each privately complained of the other to the President.

The one, Hamilton, disliked and distrusted the French, while, for the good of the American economy, strongly favoring better relations with Britain. The other, Jefferson, disliked and distrusted the British, while seeing in France and the French Revolution the embodiment of the highest ideals of the American Revolution. To Jefferson, Hamilton was "not only a monarchist, but for a monarchy bottomed on corruption." To Hamilton, Jefferson belonged among those "pretenders to profound knowledge" who were "ignorant of the most useful of all sciences—the science of human nature." The day would come, Hamilton warned, when Jefferson would be revealed as a voluptuary and an "intriguing incendiary."

Washington urged "mutual forebearances, and temporizing yieldings on all sides." To Hamilton, he expressed a deep melancholy that "a fabric so goodly, erected under so many providential circumstances," should be "wracked by controversy and brought to the edge of collapse."

On one issue only were Hamilton and Jefferson in agreement—that for the sake of the country, Washington must serve a second term, as he alone could hold the union together. "North and South will hang together if they have you to hang on," Jefferson told Washington. There were very few such uniquely eminent individuals upon whom society had peculiar claims, Jefferson insisted. Among that indispensable few, however, Jefferson did not count himself. His own intention was to retire.

In the *National Gazette*, Freneau warned that "plain American republicans" stood to "be overwhelmed by those monarchical writers on Davila, etc.," who were spreading "their poisoned doctrines throughout this blessed continent." To commemorate July 4, the paper declared, "Another revolution must and will be brought about in favor of the people."

Seeing themselves as representing the true spirit of republican ideals, Jefferson, Madison, Freneau, and others allied with them had begun calling themselves Republicans, thus implying that the Federalists were not, but rather monarchists, or monocrats, as Jefferson preferred to say. And while there was as yet some question whether it was Jefferson or Madison who led the Republicans, there was no doubt about who led the Federalists. It was Hamilton, who was more than a match for anyone.

Hamilton, for his part, had no intention of diverting votes from Adams this time around. Aaron Burr, a New York Republican and Hamilton's nemesis, was in the running for Vice President and so Hamilton was happy now to laud Adams as "a real friend to genuine liberty, order and stable government."

Early in September, Hamilton sent an urgent letter to Quincy telling Adams he must return to Philadelphia with all possible speed. Adams's absence from the scene, Hamilton warned, was benefiting the candidacy of yet another, more serious rival for the vice presidency, the popular governor of New York, George Clinton, a long-time Anti-Federalist now in the Republican camp. "I am persuaded you are very indifferent personally to the event of a certain election, yet I hope you are not so as to the cause of good government," Hamilton wrote.

But with Congress not due to reconvene for another two months and the President still declining to say whether he would serve again, Adams saw no need for hurry and remained where he was. What annoyed him exceedingly, he confided to Abigail, was the idea that George Clinton could ever be regarded as a serious rival, given the immense difference in their sacrifices for the country, differences in experience and knowledge. To Adams this was not a question of vanity but of plain fact.

THE NEWSPAPERS, meanwhile, were filled with increasingly lurid news from Paris. With the whole country beset by chaos and violence, France by now was also at war with much of Europe. The King was being held a virtual prisoner in the Palace of the Tuileries, while the extreme radicals of the revolution, the Jacobins—Marat, Danton, Robespierre—were riding high.

The *Massachusetts Centinel* carried a report from London dated August 14, describing how, on August 10, a riotous mob of thousands had marched on the Tuileries to proclaim the King a traitor and call for his head. The paper reported that 130 of the King's Swiss guards were cut down, countless others murdered, and "numerous heads, stuck on poles, were carried about the streets." Actually more than 500 Swiss guards had been slaughtered, and at least 400 of the besiegers.

An October edition of the Boston paper carried a report of massacres in September in which 6,000 to 7,000 people had been slain, which was an exaggeration. Yet the truth of the September Massacres was hardly less appalling. Some 1,400 political prisoners—including more than 200 priests—were butchered in the name of the revolution. "Let the blood of traitors flow. That is the only way to save the country," cried Marat, who had once been a physician pledged to save lives.

From London, Nabby wrote to her mother of reports from Paris "too dreadful to relate." "Ship loads of poor, distressed, penniless priests and others are daily landing upon this island." The Marquis de Lafayette had fled France and was being "kept a close prisoner by the Austrians." Madame de Lafayette had escaped to Holland. That the French King and Queen would soon "fall sacrifice to the fury of the *mobites*," Nabby had no doubt. "I wonder what Mr. Jefferson says to all these things?"

As it happened, William Short was writing to Jefferson from The Hague at the same time, and his descriptions of events greatly distressed Jefferson. In a stinging confidential reply of January 1793, Jefferson called them "blasphemies." "The tone of your letters had for some time given me pain," he informed Short, "on account of the extreme warmth with which they censured the proceedings of the Jacobins of France." Jefferson would hear no more of it. "I consider that sect as the same with the Republican patriots (of America). . . ." He deplored the loss of life, Jefferson said, but only as he would deplore the loss of life in battle. Then Jefferson, whose personal philosophy was to get through life with the least pain possible, who shunned even verbal conflict, made as extreme a claim as any of the time.

> The liberty of the whole earth was depending on the issue of the con-
> test . . . rather than it should have failed, I would have seen half the
> earth desolated. Were there but an Adam and an Eve left in every
> continent, and left free, it would be better than it now is.

He warned Short to take care in the future how he reported events in France. "You have been wounded by the sufferings of your friends, and have by this circumstance been hurried into a temper of mind which would be extremely disrelished if known to your countrymen."

. . .

NOT UNTIL NOVEMBER did Washington announce that he would accept a second term, and only then did Adams conclude it was time to return to Philadelphia, setting off by public coach in heavy winter weather. Her health again a concern, Abigail remained at home, a temporary measure as they both supposed.

Snowbound in a tavern at Hartford, Adams fell into conversation with another traveler who happened not to recognize him. Knowing how greatly it would amuse Abigail, he described how the man had launched into a harangue on the state of national politics, declaring that the trouble with John Adams was that "he had been long in Europe and got tainted."

> I told him that it was hard if a man could not go to Europe without being tainted, that if Mr. Adams had been sent to Europe upon their business by the people, and had done it, and in doing it had necessarily got tainted, I thought the people ought to pay him for the damage the taint had done him.

Though the electoral vote would not be known until February, it was clear by Christmas that Washington was again the unanimous choice for President, and that Adams, for all that had been said against him, had won a clear second place, far ahead of George Clinton. In the final count Adams received 77 votes; Clinton, 50; Jefferson, 4; Aaron Burr, 1.

IV

"MONDAY AFTERNOON and all Tuesday it rained, then cleared up, very cold and blustering," Abigail began a Sunday evening letter to her "Dearest Friend."

> On Friday came a snow storm, wind very violent, at North East. It continued so through Friday night and Saturday, even until Sunday morning, when the snow was over the tops of the stone wall and so

banked that no wheel[ed] carriage can stir. We had not any meeting today, and some person[s] had their sheep to dig out from under the snow banks.

Separation had become a burden they must bear once again, and again an extended correspondence resumed, after a hiatus of nearly nine years, one letter following another, back and forth between Quincy and Philadelphia, week upon week. Abigail's intention to remain at home only temporarily proved wishful thinking. Traveling had become too difficult for her. Since Congress was only in session approximately six months of the year, and John could be at home the rest of the time, she chose to stay in Quincy through the whole of his second term as Vice President.

The state of her health was a prime consideration, but so also was economic necessity, as she would confide to Nabby. "A powerful motive for me to remain here during the absence of your father is the necessity there is that such care and attention should be paid to our affairs at home as will enable us to live in a humble state of independence whenever your father quits public life, which he daily becomes more and more anxious to do." "He has ever sustained the character of the independent freeman of America," she added modestly, neglecting to mention the part she had played in making that possible.

For both Abigail and John the stress of separation now was no less severe than in times past, for all the changes in their station in life.

My days of anxiety have indeed been many and painful in years past, when I had many terrors that encompassed me around [Abigail wrote on January 7, 1793, after John had been gone little more than a month]. I have happily surmounted them, but I do not find that I am less solicitous to hear constantly from you than in times of more danger. . . . Years subdue the ardor of passion but in lieu thereof friendship and affection deep-rooted subsists which defies the ravages of time, and whilst the vital flame exists.

For his part, Adams assured her, "I am with all the ardor of youth, yours." "To a heart that loves praise so well, and received so little of it," he told her another day, "your letter is like laudanum," which someone had told him was "the Divinity itself."

"I want to sit down and converse with you, every evening," she would write. "I sit here alone and brood over possibilities and conjectures."

"You apologize for the length of your letters," he told her in a long letter of his own. "[They] give me more entertainment than all the speeches I hear. There are more good thoughts, fine strokes, and mother wit in them than I hear in the whole week."

To further reduce expenses, Adams had given up the small house in Philadelphia and taken a room with the secretary of the Senate, Samuel Otis, and his wife, who did not normally accommodate boarders but felt the Vice President of the United States should have something better than the usual lodging house. Never again would he spend money he did not have just to keep up appearances, Adams vowed. "I am so well satisfied with my present simplicity that I am determined never to depart from it." He had a sunny room with a southern exposure and a fireplace that he kept going most of the time. "I am warm enough at night, but cannot sleep since I left you."

They exchanged views on politics, events in France, family finances, reported on the weather and the doings of their scattered family. They wrote on everything from the price of clover seed to the meetings of the American Philosophical Society, where Adams had been asked to be a member. Reflecting on the outcome of the election, Abigail saw it as proof not only of the wisdom of the people, but their faith in the administration. The "newspaper warfare" had only strengthened support for the government, she felt certain.

"There must be, however," Adams responded, "more employment for the press in favor of the government than there has been, or the sour, angry, peevish, fretful, lying paragraphs which assail it on every side will make an impression on many weak and ignorant people."

Almost from the moment the election was decided—and the Republican campaign to unseat Adams had failed—the Republican press shifted its attacks almost entirely to the President, striking the sharpest blows Washington had yet known. Now it was he who had the deplorable inclination to monarchy. The "hell hounds" were in full cry, wrote Adams, who wondered how well Washington might bear up under the abuse. "His skin is thinner than mine."

For himself it appeared he had been granted temporary immunity. He was even warmly received on his return to the Senate, where, for the moment, a mood of "tranquility" had settled. He felt, Adams wrote, as though he were receding slowly into the background, yet professed to mind not at all.

The Secretary of the Treasury and the Secretary of State, meanwhile, were under constant fire from one side or the other. Jefferson was busy behind the scenes in a campaign to drive Hamilton from office. If unwilling to attack Hamilton directly himself, or to write under an assumed name, he was not above urging others to do so. "For God's sake, my dear sir," Jefferson would admonish Madison, "take up your pen, select the most striking heresies, and cut him to pieces in the face of the public."

Jefferson's certainty that monarchists were poised to destroy the republic had become an obsession. Yet with Adams he remained on speaking terms—in part because he knew Adams to be too independent ever to be in league with Hamilton, and because he sincerely wished for no further rupture in their friendship. When Adams attended his first meeting of the Philosophical Society, Jefferson was "polite enough to accompany me," as Adams reported to Abigail.

It was Adams's impression that Jefferson was pulling back from his habitual extravagances. To cut costs, the Secretary of State had sold a horse and some of his furniture. Jefferson's debt to his British creditors was a colossal 7,000 pounds, Adams had learned, which led him to ponder whether this might account for Jefferson's antipathy to the central government. If only someone could pay off Jefferson's debt, indeed pay off the personal debt of all Virginians, Adams speculated, then perhaps Jefferson's reason might return, "and the whole man and his whole state would become good friends of the Union."

What vexed Adams most was Jefferson's "blind spirit of party." In theory, Jefferson deplored parties or faction no less than did Adams or anyone. In practice, however, he was proving remarkably adept at party politics. As always, he avoided open dispute, debate, controversy, or any kind of confrontation, but behind the scenes he was unrelenting and extremely effective. To Jefferson it was a matter of necessity, given his hatred of Hamilton and all that was riding on what he called the "beautiful" revolution in France. To Adams, Jefferson had become a fanatic. There was not a Jacobin in France more devoted to faction, he told Abigail.

Continuing accounts of the chaos and bloodshed in France left both Adamses filled with pity and contempt. The French government was by now fully in the grip of the extreme radicals, and Adams shuddered at the thought. "Danton, Robespierre, Marat, and co[mpany] are furies," he wrote. "Dragon's teeth have been sown in France and come up monsters."

It was known that the Duc de La Rochefoucauld, philosopher and lover of liberty, one of the first in France to translate the Declaration of Independence, and one of the first, with his mother, to befriend Adams in Paris, had been stoned to death by a mob before his mother's eyes. Louis XVI, stripped of all power, was to go on trial for treason. But Adams was incapable of exulting as others were over the plight of the French monarch. He had no heart for "king-killing," Adams said. Indeed, he was tired of reading all newspapers, he told Abigail on the eve of Washington's second inauguration. "The whole drama of the world is such tragedy that I am weary of the spectacle."

On Monday, March 4, 1793, in an inaugural ceremony of record brevity, Adams looked on respectfully as Washington took the oath of office. The event, held in the Senate, was simple and dignified. Washington's address, all of two paragraphs, lasted but minutes, and Adams, like others present, was soon on his way home, Congress having adjourned until December.

The prospect of months on his farm doing as he pleased gave Adams a lift of heart as little else could have. But the tragic drama that he had grown so weary of only worsened. No sooner was he home than the news arrived that on January 21, Louis XVI had been beheaded. The papers described the King's last ride, the scaffold where "his head was severed from his body in one stroke" by the guillotine, the cries of *"Vive la Nation!"* from the crowds, then hats thrown in the air.

Like Washington, Adams could not bring himself to say anything publicly. But to a correspondent in England, he warned, "Mankind will in time discover that unbridled majorities are as tyrannical and cruel as unlimited despots," and he lamented that so much more blood would have to flow before the lesson was learned.

Jefferson, who had once called Louis XVI "a good man," "an honest man," observed privately that monarchs were "amenable to punishment like other criminals." It was the view expressed in a letter in the *New York Journal* signed "A Republican":

> Mankind is now enlightened. They can discover that kings are like other men, especially with respect to the commission of crimes and an inordinate thirst for power. Reason and liberty are overspreading the world, nor will progress be impeded until the towering crown shall fall, and the spectre of royalty be broken in pieces, in every part of the globe. Monarchy and aristocracy must be annihilated, and the rights of the people firmly established.

Great Britain and Spain, too, had by now declared war on France. Britain's declaration came on February 1, 1793, and as no one could then have foreseen, Britain and France would be at war for another twenty-two years, well into the next century.

In early April, "Citizen" Genêt landed at Charleston, South Carolina, causing a sensation. Edmund Charles Genêt, the audacious new envoy from Jacobin France, was the son of Edmé Genêt, the French foreign office translator, with whom Adams had once worked in Paris, turning out propaganda for the American Revolution. Young Genêt had been dispatched to America with instructions to rouse American support for France, spread the principles of the French Revolution, and encourage privateering against British shipping by American seamen. From the welcome he received at Charleston and along his whole four-week journey north to Philadelphia, he concluded all Americans were in sympathy with the French radicals and would, in keeping with the French-American alliance of 1778, gladly join France again in common cause. Jacobin clubs—pro-French democratic societies—sprung up along his route, and Genêt liberally dispensed money to outfit American privateers.

But on April 22 in Philadelphia, before Genêt arrived, Washington issued a Proclamation of Neutrality, a decision Adams had no part in but affirmed what he had long said about keeping free from the affairs of

Europe. "Let us above all things avoid as much as possible entangling ourselves with their ways and politics," he had written from France fourteen years earlier.

The welcome for Genêt at Philadelphia was rapturous. Jefferson estimated that the crowd the night of Genêt's arrival, May 16, numbered 1,000. Genêt said 6,000, and gloried in the "perpetual fetes" that followed in the next several weeks. To the thrill of hundreds of dinner guests Genêt sang the "Marseillaise" and rendered rousing new lines to a tune from a French operetta:

> Liberty! Liberty, be thy name adored forever,
> Tyrants beware! Your tott'ring thrones must fall;
> Our int'rest links the free together,
> And Freedom's sons are Frenchmen all.

"All the old spirit of 1776 is rekindling," exuded Jefferson, who saw in Genêt's popularity eloquent testimony by the people against "the cold caution" of their own government.

Washington decided to receive the young emissary, and in a manner which, if not cold, was strictly formal. American neutrality remained firm, which led Genêt, who knew nothing of American politics, to conclude he must rally the American people against the President. Only later would he admit his mistake, and blame Jefferson and the Republicans for deceiving him for their own purposes.

Many years afterward Adams would wildly exaggerate the tumult caused by Genêt, claiming that 10,000 people had roamed the streets threatening "to drag Washington out of his house" and compel the government to declare war on Britain. Adams's alarm at the time was extreme, but he was by no means alone in wondering if a revolution were hatching. The flourishing pro-French democratic societies were secret political clubs verging on vigilante groups and seemed truly bent on gaining French control over American politics.

Then, with summer, came the two calamities for which the year 1793 would be forever remembered. In France the Reign of Terror commenced, a siege of vicious retribution that would send nearly 3,000 men and women to the guillotine in Paris alone, while in the provinces the slaughter was even more savage. At Lyon, where the guillotine was thought too slow a means of dispensing with antirevolutionaries, hundreds were mown down by cannon fire. At Nantes, 2,000 people were herded onto barges, tied together, taken to the middle of the Loire and drowned.

In Philadelphia, beginning in August, yellow fever raged in the worst epidemic ever to strike an American city. Reports of what was happening in Paris would not reach America for months, but accounts of the "pestilence" in Philadelphia filled the newspapers soon enough. At Quincy the Adamses were in anguish over the welfare of young Thomas, from whom there was no word.

By the last weeks of August people were dying in Philadelphia at a rate of more than twenty a day. In September, as the death toll rose rapidly, Benjamin Rush and other physicians, helpless to stop the plague, advised all who could leave the city to do so without delay. The federal government and most businesses shut down. Bush Hill, where the Adamses had lived, was converted to an emergency hospital. To avoid contamination people stopped shaking hands and walked in the middle of the streets.

According to common understanding, the cause of yellow fever was the foul, steaming air of late summer in cities like Philadelphia—"a putrid state of air occasioned by a collection of filth, heat, and moisture," as Abigail explained to her sister Elizabeth—and the "proof" was that the disease always vanished with the return of cold weather. That yellow fever, like malaria, is transmitted by mosquitoes (which also vanish with cold weather) would not be understood for another hundred years.

Hamilton and his wife became dangerously ill but would recover. Jefferson, who had earlier given up living in town and moved to a house beside the Schuylkill, wrote of the crowds fleeing to the countryside, and allowed that he, too, would leave except that he did not wish to give the appearance of panic. When the President and Mrs. Washington departed for Mount Vernon, Jefferson was soon on his way to Monticello.

By October the death rate reached more than a hundred a day. People were dying faster than they could be buried. Numbers of physicians and ordinary citizens performed heroically, doing all they could for the stricken, and no one more so than Rush, though whether his ministrations—his insistence on "mercurial purges" and "heroic bloodletting"—

did more good than harm became a subject of fierce controversy. Eventually Rush, too, fell ill, but survived.

At Quincy worry over Thomas did not end until mid-October, when the young man wrote to say he had fled to New Jersey and, though perfectly well, was "pretty short of *cash*."

The epidemic ended with the first hard frost in November. In all, more than 5,000 had perished and Philadelphia would be a long time recovering from the fearful loss.

In France, however, there was no cease to the slaughter. That October, Marie Antoinette went to the guillotine, as did Brissot de Warville, who had visited the Adamses in Quincy. "Would to Heaven that the destroying angel would put up his sword," wrote Abigail, who seems to have felt the horror of what was happening more even than her husband.

But the Terror only accelerated, eventually consuming those who set it in motion. Marat was murdered; Danton and Robespierre went to the guillotine. The final toll would eventually reach 14,000 lives. Among those executed in the last few days of the Terror, as Abigail would later learn, to her horror, were the grandmother, mother, and sister of her friend Madame Adrienne Lafayette.

ARRIVING AT PHILADELPHIA in late November, Adams was pleased to find the President reinstated and most of Congress back to business. Moving in with the Otises again, Adams resumed his thoroughly unspectacular, rather solitary routine: "I go to the Senate every day, read the newspapers before I go and the public papers afterward, see a few friends once a week, go to church on Sundays; write now and then a line to you and Nabby, and oftener to Charles than to his brothers to see if I can fix his attention and excite some ambition."

Adams harbored no illusions about his importance, any more than during his first term. "My country in its wisdom contrived for me the most insignificant office that ever the invention of man contrived or his imagination conceived," he told Abigail. The measure of his insignificance was that all parties could afford to treat him with some respect. "They all know that I can do them neither much good nor much harm."

It was not just that the vice presidency offered so little chance to say or do anything of consequence, but that at a time when party politics were becoming increasingly potent and pervasive, he would not, could not, be a party man. And so, for both reasons, he was becoming more and more a man apart.

Genêt was still stirring up trouble, but then, to Adams, Genêt was a fool whose head had been turned by too much popular attention, and there was far more harmony over the issue of neutrality than Adams had expected. Even Jefferson, who had so warmly welcomed Genêt at first, now professed strong agreement with the President's stand.

Jefferson's conflict with Hamilton, however, had become intolerable. As Jefferson wrote to his daughter Martha, he was "under such agitation of mind" as he had never known. On December 31, 1793, Jefferson resigned as Secretary of State, news that led Adams to write at length on the subject of his friend, saying things in several family letters he had not said before and that he wished to remain confidential. He had admired Jefferson's abilities and disposition for so long, Adams told Abigail, that he could not help feel some regret at his leaving. "But his want of candor, his obstinate prejudices of both aversion and attachment, his real partiality in spite of all his pretensions, his low notions about many things, have so utterly reconciled me to [his departure] . . . that I will not weep." On January 6, he reported, "Jefferson went off yesterday, and a good riddance of bad ware."

What might be in store for Jefferson in Virginia politics, Adams had no way of knowing, but of this he was certain: if Jefferson were to retire to his "rural amusements and philosophical meditations" at Monticello, he would soon wither away. For instead of being "the ardent pursuer of science" that some imagined, Jefferson was the captive of ambition, and ambition, Adams told John Quincy, was "the subtlest beast of the intellectual and moral field . . . [and] wonderfully adroit in concealing itself from its owner.

> Jefferson thinks he shall by this step get a reputation of a humble modest, meek man, wholly without ambition or vanity. He may even have deceived himself into this belief. But if the prospect opens, the world will see . . . he is as ambitious as Oliver Cromwell. . . . Though his desertion may be a loss to us of some talent, I am not sorry for it on the whole, because his soul is poisoned with ambition.

Ambition was something he knew about, Adams acknowledged, for he himself had been struggling for thirty years to conquer "the foul fiend."

Jefferson had once described Adams as a poor judge of human nature—"a bad *calculator* of the force and probably the effect of the motives which govern men," Jefferson had said in a letter to Madison. But with the exception of Madison, Adams understood Jefferson as well as anyone did, or perhaps ever could. And as exasperated as Adams was with him, as critical as he sounded, he refused to let the friendship slip away.

In April he sent Jefferson the gift of a book, with a note of congratulations on the arrival of spring at Monticello, far from the "din of politics and the rumors of war." It was the first letter Adams had written to Jefferson in more than two years. Jefferson replied at once, saying he had returned to farming "with an ardor which I scarcely knew in my youth," and in answer Adams said he knew the very same ardor every summer on his own farm.

Rural life was a topic on which they could readily agree, just as they could on the increasing threat of war. The British had begun stopping American ships and taking off sailors, claiming they were British citizens. In the West Indies they captured American trading vessels. War fever swept the country. When a bill that would have suspended all trade with Britain resulted in a tie vote in the Senate, the Vice President "determined the question in the negative."

He had had enough of one war to wish ever to see another, Jefferson wrote, and to this Adams concurred wholeheartedly. The President, he reported to Jefferson, was sending Chief Justice John Jay as a special envoy to London to "find a way to reconcile our honor with peace." He had "no great faith in any very brilliant success," Adams said, "but [I] hope he may keep us out of war."

A modest correspondence would continue for two years. At the end of another long stretch at Quincy, Adams would write of a summer spent "so deliciously in farming that I return to the old story of politics with great reluctance," and Jefferson would profess that "tranquility becomes daily more and more the object of my life, and of this I certainly find more in my present pursuits than those of any other part of my life." Jefferson portrayed himself as living plainly, "farmerlike," as though he had little more on his mind than crops and weather. "We have had a hard winter and backward spring," he would report to Adams from his mountaintop the following May.

> This has injured our wheat so much that it cannot be made a good crop by all the showers of heaven which are now falling down on us exactly as we want them. Our first cutting of clover is not yet begun. Strawberries not ripe till within this fortnight, and everything backward in proportion. . . . I am trying potatoes on a large scale, as a substitute for Indian corn for feeding the animals.

Once, briefly, a difference in philosophy was touched upon, when Jefferson observed that the "paper transactions" of one generation should "scarcely be considered by succeeding generations," a principle he had earlier stated to Madison as "self-evident," that " *'the earth belongs in usufruct to the living':* that the dead have neither the power or rights over it." Adams, however, refused to accept the idea that each new generation could simply put aside the past, sweep clean the slate, to suit its own desires. Life was not like that, and if Jefferson thought so, it represented a fundamental difference in outlook.

"The rights of one generation of men must depend, in some degree, on the paper transactions of another," Adams wrote. "The social compact and the laws must be reduced to writing. Obedience to them becomes a national habit and they cannot be changed by revolutions that are costly things. Men will be too economical of their blood and property to have recourse to them very frequently." Jefferson's wish for "a little rebellion now and then to clear the atmosphere," as he had once put it to Abigail, did not stand to reason, Adams was telling him. Nor did reason have any bearing on what was happening in France, Adams insisted in another letter:

> Reasoning has been all lost. Passion, prejudice, interest, necessity have governed and will govern; and a century must roll away before any permanent and quiet system will be established. . . . You and I must look down from the battlements of Heaven if we ever have the pleasure of seeing it.

Politics, Jefferson answered, was "a subject I never loved, and now hate."

Nowhere in his correspondence with Adams did Jefferson suggest he was suffering anything like what Adams had predicted retirement to Monticello would do to him. Only to Madison did he reveal in a letter of April 1795, "My health is entirely broken down within the last eight months." And only years later, in a letter to his daughter Polly, warning her against a life of seclusion, would Jefferson acknowledge that in fact he had suffered a breakdown very like what Adams had foreseen.

> I am convinced our own happiness requires that we should continue to mix with the world, and to keep pace with it. . . . I can speak from experience on the subject. From 1793 to 1797, I remained closely at home, saw none but those who came there, and at length became very sensible of the ill effect it had upon my own mind, and of its direct and irresistible tendency to render me unfit for society, and uneasy when necessarily engaged in it. I felt enough of the effect of withdrawing from the world then to see that it led to an anti-social and misanthropic state of mind, which severely punishes him who gives in to it; and it will be a lesson I never shall forget as to myself.

Adams's supposition that Jefferson was cutting back on his extravagant ways was, however, mistaken. To the contrary, the Virginian had resolved to live in grander style than ever, and plunged into the largest, most costly project of his life. He had decided to transform Monticello—to tear off the entire second floor and more than double the size of the house—along the lines of an elegant new residence he had seen in Paris, a palatial house with a dome called the Hôtel de Salm, on the Left Bank of the Seine. All the building and remodeling he had done thus far—the renovation of rented houses in Paris, New York, and Philadelphia, even the initial construction of Monticello itself—had been but prelude to what was now under way.

It was as if he were helpless to do otherwise. He must draw up plans, design and redesign everything down to the smallest detail, build, rebuild, take apart, take down, and put up again, no matter the cost or impracticality of it all.

The existing eight-room Palladian country house was to become a great domed villa with twenty-one rooms. It was designed to accommodate lavish hospitality and to answer all his own private needs and comforts. His mind brimmed with French ideas and niceties. There were to be beds in alcoves as in France, elongated windows and French doors, a magnificent parquet floor replicated from one he had seen in the country estate of a French friend, as well as ample space to display the paintings and busts, the gilded pier mirrors, clocks, and furniture he had shipped home from France.

He had already begun ordering window sash from Philadelphia, and set his slaves to quarrying limestone and making bricks. To Adams he mentioned his new "nail manufactory" and the time devoted to counting and measuring nails, but of the larger project he said nothing, knowing what the frugal New Englander would think of it.

FOR RELIEF from the tedium of his "insignificant" labors, Adams took long walks through Philadelphia as he often had in years past, his pace only somewhat slower. Exercise was indispensable, he explained to Charles, who had complained of feeling lethargic. "Move or die is the language of our Maker in the constitution of our bodies." One must rouse oneself from lethargy. "When you cannot walk abroad, walk in your room. . . . Rise up and then open your windows and walk about your room a few times, then sit down again to your books or your pen."

To many in Congress, Adams was an old man, an assessment he thought perfectly valid. His teeth tormented him—it had been necessary to have several pulled—and he worried over a tremble in his hands. In keeping with the changes of fashion, he had given up wearing a wig and was by now quite grey and bald. He was overweight; his eyes were often red and watery from too much reading.

It was "painful to the vanity of an old man to acknowledge the decays of nature," he wrote. So weak were his eyes, such was the trembling of his hand, he told John Quincy, that "a pen is as terrible to me as a sword to a coward." He wondered how much longer he could continue in public life. Yet he devoted hours each day to writing letters, and often at great length. On his walks he generally covered three to five miles, thinking little of it. Nor does there appear to have been any appreciable slowing down on the quantity of books he read.

He had much to be grateful for—"good parents, an excellent wife, and promising children, tolerable health on the whole and competent fortune," as he told Abigail. With Thomas recently admitted to the Philadelphia bar, he could now claim three lawyer sons. Increasingly his thoughts turned to their careers and their future, more than to his own.

"Much more depends on little things than is commonly imagined," he cautioned John Quincy. "An erect figure, a steady countenance, a neat dress, a genteel air, an oratorical period, a resolute, determined spirit, often do more than deep erudition or indefatigable application."

With Charles he shared his private views on the current clamor over the subject of equality. "How the present age can boast of this principle as a discovery, as new light and modern knowledge, I know not." The root of equality, Adams said, was the Golden Rule—"Love your neighbor as yourself." Equality was at the heart of Christianity. When he had written in the Massachusetts Declaration of Rights that "all men are by nature free and equal," he meant "not a physical but a moral equality."

> Common sense was sufficient to determine that it could not mean that all men were equal in fact, but in right, not all equally tall, strong, wise, handsome, active, but equally men . . . the work of the same Artist, children in the same cases entitled to the same justice.

Nabby and her family had returned from England, where William Smith's financial ventures appeared to have brought them a measure of welcome prosperity. Adams was pleased for Nabby, but worried over what his son-in-law would ultimately make of himself. "I know not what he is in pursuit of," he told Abigail.

John Quincy had lately distinguished himself with a series of newspaper essays denouncing Citizen Genêt and seemed well launched as an attorney in Boston, if still unresolved about aspiring to a public career. When Washington requested of France that Genêt be recalled, Adams, with a father's pride, was certain that John Quincy's essays had played a decisive part. Yet he could not help feeling sympathy for Genêt, his old friend's son. Ordered home to Paris, to face charges of misconduct, which meant almost certain death by guillotine, Genêt chose to stay on in New York, where eventually he married the daughter of George Clinton and settled down to the life of a country gentleman on the Hudson.

From the tone of the letters that arrived week after week from Philadelphia, Abigail sensed a change in her husband. There seemed to be little or none of the old anger, but far more acceptance of life. "I am happy to learn," she wrote, "that the only fault in your political character, and one which has always given me uneasiness, is wearing away. I mean a certain irritability which has sometimes thrown you off your guard."

When reports reached him that his mother was gravely ill, Adams, assuming the worst, was saddened almost beyond words. "My aged and venerable mother is drawing near the close of a virtuous and industrious life," he wrote to Nabby. "May her example be ever present with me! May I be able to fulfill the duties of life as well as she has done." But the old lady's resilience was astounding. She revived, to his great relief, and his thoughts returned to his children.

To Abigail, late in the spring of 1794, he wrote of John Quincy's rising reputation, implying he knew more than he was saying. "I have often thought he has more prudence at 27 than his father at 58." "All my hopes are in him," he said in another letter, "both for my family and my country."

At last, on May 26, Adams sent off a confidential letter to John Quincy with the biggest news he had been able to report in years. He had been informed that day that the President would nominate John Quincy to be minister to the Netherlands. If Adams had played a part in the decision, as possibly he could have, he never said so. To his mind there was not a shadow of doubt that John Quincy was the ideal choice, as he told him. Annoyed that he had not been consulted on the appointment, John Quincy replied, "I rather wish it had not been made at all." But as an Adams, he had little choice, and so began another long career in public service. His father was presiding as usual the day the Senate confirmed the appointment.

Slightly taller than his father, John Quincy had become notably handsome, his youthful face lean and finely chiseled. In a magnificent portrait by Copley done in London a year later, he might be the beau ideal of the time. He was also more widely traveled and more conversant with French and Dutch than any American diplomat yet dispatched across the Atlantic. He sailed from Boston that September of 1794, taking his brother Thomas along with him to serve as his private secretary.

THE ATTENTION OF THE COUNTRY, meanwhile, had shifted to western Pennsylvania where an insurrection had broken out over a federal excise tax on distilleries, the only internal tax thus far imposed by the federal government. At home at Quincy through the summer, Adams had kept abreast of the crisis in the newspapers. An army of fully 12,000 volunteers marched over the Alleghenies in an unprecedented show of force, Washington himself riding at the head part of the way, with Hamilton second in command. By the time Adams returned to Philadelphia in December and established himself in different lodgings, at the Francis Hotel, the so-called Whiskey Rebellion had ended. It was a victory the Federalists were happy to drink to, but the Republicans soon had their own cause to celebrate, when Alexander Hamilton announced he would retire. Convinced he had accomplished all he could, the brilliant, headstrong Secretary of the Treasury returned to his lucrative New York law practice. No one, however, expected him to abandon politics.

With the retirement also of Secretary of War Henry Knox in December, the sense of an administration in ebb was strongly felt. Only Edmund Randolph, now Secretary of State, remained of Washington's original cabinet.

The threat of embroilment in the European war continued, America at the "precipice," as Adams said, and still there was no word from John Jay in London. Adams's days went on much as before, the greater part of his time given to his duties in the Senate. At the Francis Hotel he occupied a small but comfortable room looking onto Franklin Court, and at meals he appears to have enjoyed the company of the other guests, most of whom were members of Congress. A young English visitor staying at the hotel, Thomas Twining, was delighted to find the Vice President "superior to all sense of superiority" and in appearance more like "an English country gentleman who had seen little of the world, than a statesman who had seen so much of public life."

I was always glad [he wrote years later] when I saw Mr. Adams enter
the room and take his place at our table. Indeed, to behold this distinguished man . . . occupying the chair of the Senate in the morning, and afterwards walking home through the streets and taking his
seat among his fellow citizens as their equal, conversing amicably
with men over whom he had just presided . . . was a singular spectacle, and a striking exemplification of the state of society in America
at this period.

By the time the Jay Treaty at last reached the President in the spring
of 1795, Philadelphia was in a frenzy of speculation over what it might
contain. On June 8, the day Washington called a special session of the
Senate to consider the treaty, he invited Adams to dine alone with him.
The meeting was confidential, and Adams said nothing about it, except
to caution Abigail that "mum-mum-mum" was the word.

That the terms of Jay's treaty would ignite a storm of protest was
plain at once. Jay had given up virtually every point to the British, in
return for very little. Conspicuously absent was any guaranteed protection of American seamen from British seizure. Further, the British had
refused to open their ports to American trade, except in the West Indies,
but there only to ships of less than seventy tons. The one important
British concession was to remove the last of their troops from forts in the
northwest by the end of the year.

But Jay had gained peace with Britain—"To do more was impossible," he told the President—and Washington, though disappointed, concluded it was enough. The treaty, with his prestige behind it, went to the
Senate for approval. Through thirteen days of furious debate behind
closed doors, Adams could only watch and listen. What felt like a tropical
heat wave descended on the city, making the cooped-up chamber all but
unbearable. Finally, on June 24, by exactly the required two-thirds margin, the Senate consented to ratification.

Senators were enjoined to disclose nothing until the treaty was signed
by the President. But in a matter of days the full text was published by
the *Philadelphia Aurora*, which had replaced Freneau's *National Gazette*
as the leading Republican newspaper. It was the first scoop in American
newspaper history and a "battle royal" commenced at once. Mobs in the

streets declared Jay a traitor and burned him in effigy. There were riots in New York and Boston. The President was assailed in print as never before, and nowhere more than in the *Aurora*, which was edited by young Benjamin Franklin Bache, the grandson of Franklin who had once been John Quincy's schoolmate in France.

From the distance of Monticello, Jefferson saw what Jay had wrought as a "monument of venality" and sent a letter to the new French ambassador at Philadelphia to assure him of his own continuing enthusiasm for France.

Adams, who knew from experience—knew better than anyone—what Jay had been up against in dealing with the British, never doubted that a flawed treaty was far preferable to war with Britain. He stood by the President, unwavering in his support.

The common accusations notwithstanding, Adams was no Anglophile. As greatly as he admired the British constitution and the British structure of government, he considered the British as insolent as ever, and the unfortunate "mad" George III (by now the victim of porphyria), a hopeless blunderer. The day might come when America would have to "beat down" the "insolence of John Bull," Adams told Abigail, but he prayed it would not be soon.

The furor over the treaty would continue until the House took up the necessary appropriations the following year. But that summer Washington's troubles grew still worse, when Edmund Randolph resigned as Secretary of State after being accused of taking money from France to influence the administration against Britain—a charge never proven.

With the departure of Randolph the brilliant cabinet that Washington had started with was entirely gone, replaced by men who were by and large mediocrities. Whether, in view of the charges and the abuse he was subjected to, Washington would agree to stand for election again, no one could say, but in his usual fashion, he would keep his thoughts to himself for as long as possible.

For the Adamses the summer at Quincy passed uneventfully. Their one private worry was over Charles, who, just as his law career was getting under way, had fallen in love with Sally Smith, the pretty younger sister of Nabby's husband. Abigail and John both objected to the romance, and with the same line of reasoning they had used earlier with

John Quincy. Charles agreed to a moratorium, but after several months candidly told his father, "Were I to declare that I did not entertain the same opinion of Sally Smith that I ever did, I should declare a falsehood."

When the news reached Quincy early that fall that Charles and Sally had been married in New York, his parents were devastated. But Charles assured them he was never happier, and Nabby affirmed it to have been the best possible step for him. "After all the hairbreadth scrapes and imminent dangers he has run, he is at last safe landed," she reported.

Stopping at New York en route to Philadelphia in December, Adams was delighted to find Charles well established in a "commodious" home and office on Front Street, and pleased, too, with Sally, who "behaved prettily in her new sphere." "My love to Daughter Adams, the first I have had since your sister changed her name," he later wrote affectionately to Charles.

V

"I AM HEIR APPARENT, you know," Adams reminded Abigail after arriving in Philadelphia for the opening of the Fourth Congress.

The prospect of Adams succeeding Washington had been ever-present for seven years, but now, separated again by hundreds of miles, they addressed themselves to the growing likelihood of his actually becoming President, exchanged thoughts and feelings on the challenge in a way that apparently they never had before, and that perhaps they would have found impossible except at a distance. As Abigail had said herself in a letter years before, "My pen is always freer than my tongue." Were it for her alone to decide, were personal considerations all that mattered, she wrote, she would unhesitatingly tell him to retire. But with a decision of "such momentous concern," she dared not try to influence him. "I can say only that circumstances must govern you . . . [and] pray that you have superior direction." If, however, he entertained any thought of continuing as Vice President under someone other than Washington, he must forget it. "I will be second under no man but Washington," she declared.

Adams expressed concern over the toll the presidency could take on his health. He felt perfectly strong, he assured her, but twice mentioned the tremble in his hands, and remarked that he could see the President rapidly aging before his eyes.

Early in February 1796, on the same day Benjamin Franklin Bache declared in the *Aurora* that "good patriot" Jefferson was the inevitable and ideal choice to replace Washington, Adams professed to be tired of politics. "I am weary of the game," he told Abigail, then added with characteristic honesty what she had long understood, "Yet I don't know how I would live out of it."

No successor to Washington could expect such support as Washington had, she warned. "You know what is before you—the whips, the scorpions, the thorns without roses, the dangers, anxieties, the weight of empire." Still, the presidency would be a "glorious reward" for all his service to the country, should Providence allot him the task.

"I have looked into myself," he wrote in another letter, "and see no dishonesty there. I see weakness enough. But no timidity. I have no concern on your account but for your health."

> I hate speeches [he continued], messages, addresses, proclamations and such affected, constrained things. I hate levees and drawing rooms. I hate to speak to 1,000 people to whom I have nothing to say. Yet all this I can do.

When she reminded him that he was sixty years old, he replied, "If I were near I would soon convince you that I am not above forty."

In MARCH, when the House of Representatives took up the Jay Treaty, it appeared a constitutional crisis was in the offing. The Republicans had pounced on the treaty with all their "teeth and . . . nails," as Adams reported. "The business of the country . . . stands still . . . all is absorbed by the debates. . . . Many persons are very anxious and forebode a majority unfavorable, and the most pernicious and destructive results." It was hard to imagine the Republicans being that "desperate and unreasonable," but should they be, he told Abigail, "this Constitution cannot stand. . . . I see nothing but a dissolution of government and immediate war."

He was again invited to dine alone with the President, who in the course of the evening mentioned three times that he would likely retire. "He detained me there 'til nine o'clock," Adams wrote, "and was never more frank and open about politics. I find his opinions and sentiments are more like mine than I ever knew before, respecting England and France and our American parties."

To Adams, time was moving all too fast. ("Long! Nothing is long! The time will soon be gone and we shall be surprised to know what has become of it.") Then, the first week in May, he could happily send Abigail word that the Jay Treaty bills had passed both Houses, "and good humor seems to be returning." The constitutional crisis had passed, the threat of war was greatly diminished.

Requesting a leave of absence, he was on his way home by May 6. His time as Vice President was virtually over. He had served longer than in any other post in his career, and in all he had served extremely well— dutifully as president of the Senate and with unfailing loyalty to Washington. He had cast tie-breaking votes in the Senate of historic importance—in protecting the President's sole authority over the removal of appointees, for example, and in the several stages leading to the location of the national capital. In all, Adams cast thirty-one deciding votes, always in support of the administration and more than by any vice president in history.

AT QUINCY he threw himself into his other life as farmer Adams with greater zest than ever, as though determined to make the most of what might be his last extended stay for a long while.

It had been a particularly fine spring along the coast of Massachusetts, with warm days and ample rain. The farm "shines very bright," he wrote. For the first time in years he revived his diary, keeping note of all daily activity and progress. He decided to build a substantial new barn, the first such project he had ever undertaken. "This day my new barn was raised near the spot where . . . my father . . . raised his new barn in 1737," he recorded on July 13. He thought it looked "very stately and strong."

He kept three to ten men at work through the summer, including John Briesler, another of the numerous Bass family, Seth Bass, and a hard-drinking neighbor named Billings, who was an especially hard worker.

After the sedentary life of the Senate, Adams relished the days out of doors. He loved the work, the tangible results, the feeling that he had not only returned home, but returned, if only for a while, to the ways of his father and generations of Adamses.

July 15, Friday
... Went with three hands ... [to] cut between 40 and 50 red cedars, and with a team of five cattle brought home 22 of them at a load. We have opened the prospect so that the meadows and western mountain may be distinctly seen. ...

July 16
... We got in two loads of English hay. ...

July 20
... Walked in the afternoon over the hills and across the fields and meadows, up to the old plain. The corn is as good there as any I've seen. ...

August 2
... finished the great wall on Penn's Hill.

August 5
... Sullivan and Mr. Sam Hayward threshing—Billings and Bass carting earth and seaweed and liming the compost.

He was up each morning with the birds, drank his usual gill of hard cider, and with Abigail passed quiet evenings reading, writing letters, or keeping up with his diary, where along with the chronicle of daily enterprises, he wrote of clear summer skies and described a morning shower as "a soft, fine rain in a clock calm ... falling as sweetly as I ever saw in April ...." Ever the realist, he wrote, too, of rattlesnakes and corn worms, Hessian flies and "mosquitoes numerous."

Though Abigail's health remained a worry, she apparently felt well enough to entertain Parson Wibird at dinner and to ride to Weymouth to dine with Cotton Tufts, whose salted beef, shell beans, and whortleberry pudding Adams proclaimed "luxurious."

"Of all the summers of my life," he recorded, "this has been the freest from care, anxiety, and vexation to me. The sickness of Mrs. A. excepted."

"Billings and Prince laying wall," he wrote September 8. "Briesler and James picking apples and making cider. Stetson widening the brook.

> I think to christen my place Peacefield, in commemoration of the peace which I assisted in making in 1783, of the thirteen years peace and neutrality which I have contributed to preserve, and of the constant peace and tranquility which I have enjoyed in this residence.

THOUGH POLITICS through the summer of 1796 had been in "a perfect calm," as Abigail noted, neither she nor John had any illusions about what was to come. Mischief was surely brewing in "the Jacobin caldron," she wrote, as "venomous as Macbeth's hell broth." When the Boston papers carried news of Washington's retirement and the text of his "Farewell Address" of September 17, it was, as said, as if a hat had been dropped to start the race.

Adams and Jefferson were the leading candidates in what was the first presidential election with two parties in opposition, an entirely new experience for the country. Jefferson remained at Monticello, Adams at Peacefield, neither taking any part in what quickly became a vicious, all-out battle.

Adams was pilloried in the Republican press as a gross and shameless monarchist—"His Rotundity," whose majestic appearance was so much "sesquipedality of belly," as said Bache's *Aurora*. Adams, declared the widely read paper, was unfit to lead the country, and beneath a headline declaring AN ALARM, Bache warned that unless by their votes the people were to call forth Thomas Jefferson, "the friend of the people," Adams, the "champion of kings, ranks, and titles," would be their President. Were Adams to be elected, warned the *Boston Chronicle*, the principle of hereditary succession would be imposed on America, to make way for John Quincy. With Jefferson, said the paper, no one need worry since Jefferson had only daughters.

To add further fuel to the fire, Thomas Paine, in a fury over the Jay Treaty, unleashed an unprecedented attack on George Washington in the pages of the *Aurora*. Writing from Paris, Paine called Washington a creature of "grossest adulation," a man incapable of friendship, "a hypocrite in public life," apostate and impostor.

For their part, the Federalists were hardly less abusive. Jefferson was decried as a Jacobin, an atheist, and charged with cowardice for having fled Monticello from the British cavalry in 1781. "Poor Jefferson is tortured as much as your better acquaintance," Adams wrote to John Quincy.

The candidates for Vice President were Aaron Burr of New York for the Republicans, and for the Federalists, Thomas Pinckney of South Carolina, thus providing regional balance on both sides. Adams was expected to carry New England, Jefferson, the South, while the Middle States could go either way.

To add to Adams's troubles, Alexander Hamilton was up to his old tricks behind the scenes, urging the strongest possible support for Thomas Pinckney, ostensibly as a way to keep Jefferson from becoming Vice President, but also, it was suspected, to defeat Adams as well and make Pinckney president—Pinckney being someone Hamilton could more readily control.

The rumors of this that reached Adams at Quincy would be confirmed before the year was out by his old friend Elbridge Gerry, who was a presidential elector for Massachusetts and, like Adams, an ardent antiparty man. For both John and Abigail, Gerry's report marked the end of whatever remaining trust or respect they had for Hamilton. Abigail henceforth referred to him privately as Cassius. John called him "as great a hypocrite as any in the U.S. His intrigues in the election I despise."

For all the clamor over politics, the country was still at peace and more prosperous than ever. If there was a prevailing sentiment overall concerning national politics, it was one of regret, even sadness, that Washington would soon be stepping down. Abigail expressed what most Americans felt when, quoting Shakespeare, she wrote of Washington, "Take his character all together, and we shall not look upon his like again."

On November 23, Adams bid her goodbye and started for Philadelphia, and again by public conveyance, John Briesler his sole companion. "Fear takes no hold of me," he assured Abigail, as if to boost both their spirits. He reached Philadelphia on December 4, and the night of December 7, struggling with the prospect of defeat, he wrote again:

> I laugh at myself twenty times a day, for my feelings, and [the] meditations and speculations in which I find myself engaged: Vanity suffers. Cold feelings of unpopularity. Humble reflections. Mortifications. Humiliation. Plans of future life. Economy. Retrenching expenses. Farming. Returning to the bar, drawing writs, arguing causes, taking clerks.
>
> I can pronounce Thomas Jefferson to be chosen P[resident] of [the] U[nited] S[tates] with firmness and a good grace that I don't fear. But here alone abed, by my fireside, nobody to speak to, pouring upon my disgrace and future prospects—this is ugly.

But in a week or so, in an entirely different mood, he was writing to tell her it appeared he would be elected President. Though the final count would not be known until February, when the electors met, it was being said openly in and out of Congress that he had won, and that Jefferson was to be Vice President.

Overnight, Adams was being treated as though suddenly he had become a different man, and this he found most remarkable. Even Bache's *Aurora* seemed to experience a miraculous change of heart. John Adams, the paper now declared, was clearly preferable to Washington.

> There can be no doubt that Adams would not be a *puppet*—that having an opinion and judgment of his own, he would act from his own impulses rather than the impulses of others—that possessing great integrity he would not sacrifice his country's interests at the shrine of party. . . . In addition . . . it is well known that Adams is an aristocrat only in *theory*, but that Washington is one in *practice*— that Adams has the simplicity of a republican but that Washington has the ostentation of an eastern bashaw—that Adams holds none of his fellow men in slavery, but Washington does. . . . The difference is immense.

To Adams's particular delight, one of the most partisan of all the young Republicans, Representative William Branch Giles of Virginia, had been heard to say of him, "The old man will make a good President, too."

At Monticello, Jefferson received word from Madison that he should be prepared for the likelihood of finishing second, and that for the good of the country and the "valuable effect" of his influence on Adams, he must accept the vice presidency. In reply, Jefferson expressed no reluctance to serve under Adams, since "he had always been my senior, from the commencement of my public life." Then, three days after Christmas, Jefferson took up his pen to write an extraordinary letter to Adams.

From his latest information, Jefferson said, it appeared Adams's election to the "first magistracy" was an established fact. But to Jefferson this had never been in doubt. "I have never one single moment expected a different issue." And though he knew he would not be believed, it was true nonetheless that he never wished it otherwise. He warned that Hamilton had been up to some of his usual schemes, but doubted it would change the outcome.

I leave to others the sublime delights of riding in the storm, better pleased with sound sleep and a warm berth below, with the society of neighbors, friends and fellow laborers of the earth, than of spies and sycophants. No one then will congratulate you with purer disinterestedness than myself. . . . I have no ambition to govern men. It is a painful and thankless office. . . . I devoutly wish you may be able to shun for us this war by which our agriculture, commerce, and credit will be destroyed. If you are, the glory will be all your own; and that your administration may be filled with glory and happiness to yourself and advantage to us is the sincere wish of one who though, in the course of our voyage through life, various little incidents have happened or been contrived to separate us, retains still for you the solid esteem of the moments when we were working for our independence, and sentiments of respect and affectionate attachment.

It was a fine show of magnanimity in defeat, as well as one of the warmest expressions of friendship Jefferson ever wrote or that anyone had ever addressed to Adams. But after finishing the letter, Jefferson had second thoughts and sent it on to Madison in Philadelphia—"open for your perusal"—so that if anything he had written "should render the delivery of it ineligible in your opinion, you may return it to me."

Madison was appalled. He saw the letter as a dreadful mistake, and decided it must go no further. As he explained delicately to Jefferson, friendship was one thing, politics another. Adams already knew of his friendship, Madison advised, and were Adams to prove a failure as President, such compliments and confidence in him as Jefferson had put in writing could prove politically embarrassing.

The letter was never sent. It remained in Madison's possession, in a file only a few blocks from where Adams resided.

For Adams it could have been one of the most important letters he ever received. Jefferson's praise, his implicit confidence in him, his rededication to their old friendship would have meant the world to Adams, and never more than now, affecting his entire outlook and possibly with consequent effect on the course of events to follow.

Not long after, however, Adams did receive a letter from Abigail, written at Quincy on January 15, 1797:

> The cold has been more severe than I can ever before recollect. It has frozen the ink in my pen, and chilled the blood in my veins, but not the warmth of my affection for him for whom my heart beats with unabated ardor through all the changes and vicissitudes of life, in the still calm of Peacefield, and the turbulent scenes in which he is about to engage.

CHAPTER NINE

OLD OAK

The task of the President is very arduous, very
perplexing, and very hazardous. I do not wonder
Washington wished to retire from it, or rejoiced in
seeing an old oak in his place.

—Abigail Adams

I

THE INAUGURATION of the second President of the United States commenced in the first-floor House Chamber of Congress Hall in Philadelphia just before noon, Saturday, March 4, 1797.

The room was filled to overflowing, every seat taken by members of the House and Senate, justices of the Supreme Court, heads of departments, the diplomatic corps, and many ladies said to have added a welcome note of "brilliancy" to the otherwise solemn occasion.

There was a burst of applause when George Washington entered and walked to the dais. More applause followed on the appearance of Thomas Jefferson, who had been inaugurated Vice President upstairs in the Senate earlier that morning, and "like marks of approbation" greeted John Adams, who on his entrance in the wake of the two tall Virginians seemed shorter and more bulky even than usual.

It was a scene few who were present would ever forget. Here were the three who, more than any others, had made the Revolution, and as many in the audience supposed, it was to be the last time they would ever appear on the same platform. Adams felt as he had when he first appeared before George III—as if he were on stage playing a part. It was, he later told Abigail, "the most affecting and overpowering scene I ever acted in."

Jefferson's height was accentuated by a long blue frock coat. Washington was in a dress suit of black velvet. Adams, the plainest of the three, wore a suit of grey broadcloth intentionally devoid of fancy buttons and knee buckles.

Resolved to keep things as understated as possible, he had ridden to Congress Hall from his lodgings at the Francis Hotel in a "simple but elegant enough" carriage drawn by just two horses. The grand carriage and six white horses of Washington's first inauguration had been dispensed with. Nor would Adams allow an official retinue to march in procession with him. As he confided to Abigail, he wanted few if any of the "court" trappings of his predecessor. On learning that she had had the Quincy coat-of-arms painted on her carriage at home, he told her to have it painted out. "They shall have a republican President in earnest," he wrote.

Overcast skies had cleared by noon. The day turned bright and cloudless. But for Adams there was little cheer. With none of his family present, he felt miserably alone. He had been unable to sleep the night before, sick with worry that he might not make it through the ceremony without fainting. But he succeeded with flying colors, delivering an address that left little doubt as to where he stood on the Constitution, partisan politics, domestic concerns, France, and the pressing issue of peace or war.

Though in print the speech would seem a bit stilted, it was delivered with great force and effect. Stirred by emotion, and in a strong voice, Adams recalled the old ardor of the American Revolution and spoke of the "present happy Constitution" as the creation of "good heads prompted by good hearts." In answer to concerns about his political creed, he expressed total attachment to and veneration for the present system of a free republican government. "What other form of government, indeed, can so well deserve our esteem and love?" He spoke of his respect for the rights of all states, and of his belief in expanded education for all the people, both to enlarge the happiness of life and as essential to the preservation of freedom. The great threats to the nation, Adams warned, were sophistry, the spirit of party, and "the pestilence of foreign influence."

He paid gracious tribute to Washington's leadership. He lauded American agriculture and manufacturing, pledged himself to a spirit of "equity and humanity" toward the American Indian, "to meliorate their condition by inclining them to be more friendly to us, and our citizens to be more friendly to them."

To Abigail he would later write, "I have been so strangely used in this country, so belied and so undefended that I was determined to say some things as an appeal to posterity." But the strongest lines, those underscoring his determination to maintain American neutrality, were delivered directly for the benefit of Congress and the foreign diplomats present, not to say the opposition press. It was his "inflexible determination" to maintain peace with all nations, Adams declared, then expressed a personal esteem for France, stemming from a residence of nearly seven years there. Finally he affirmed an "unshaken confidence" in the spirit of the American people, "on which I have often hazarded my all."

Then, having issued a solemn invocation of the Supreme Being, he stepped down from the platform to a table at the front of the chamber, where Chief Justice Oliver Ellsworth administered the oath of office, Adams energetically repeating the words.

And so Adams became President of the nation that now—with the additions of Vermont, Kentucky, and Tennessee—numbered sixteen states. Having never in his public life held an administrative position, having never played any but a marginal role in the previous administration, having never served in the military, or campaigned for a single vote, or claimed anything like a political bent, he was now chief executive and commander-in-chief.

Many in the chamber were weeping, moved by his words, but still more, it seems, by the prospect of Washington's exit from the national stage. "A solemn scene it was indeed," Adams wrote, noting that Washington's face remained as serene and unclouded as the day. "Me thought I heard him think, 'Ay! I am fairly out and you are fairly in! See which of us will be the happiest!' "

Approval came from all sides. Federalist Senator Theodore Sedgwick of Massachusetts called it "the most august and sublime" occasion he ever attended. Praise in the Federalist press, too, was not so much for Adams as for the occasion—"Thus ended a scene the parallel of which was never before witnessed in any country." But Republicans openly extolled what the new President had said. In the pages of the *Aurora*, Benjamin Franklin Bache proclaimed John Adams a hero in a way incon-

ceivable before, lauding the "Republican plainness" of Adams's appearance, his "true dignity," his "incorruptible integrity." In all, it was one of
the handsomest tributes ever paid to Adams.

> It is universally admitted that Mr. Adams is a man of incorruptible
> integrity, and that the resources of his own mind are equal to the
> duties of his station; we may flatter ourselves that his measures will
> be taken with prudence, that he will not become the head of a party,
> and that he will not be the tool of any man or set of men. His speech
> on the inauguration augers well to our country. . . . He declares him-
> self the friend of France and of peace, the admirer of republicanism,
> the enemy of party, and he vows his determination to let no political
> creed interfere in his appointments. How honorable are these senti-
> ments; how characteristic of a patriot!

It was praise Adams took with a large grain of salt, suspecting Bache
of wanting only to create a "coolness between me and Mr. Washington."
More to his liking was an item in a Baltimore paper describing him as "an
old fielder," which as he explained to Abigail, "is a tough, hardy, labori-
ous little horse that works very hard and lives upon very little, very useful to his master at small expense."

BOTH BEFORE AND AFTER his inauguration dozens of old friends,
including some like Benjamin Rush who had supported Jefferson in the
election, made a point of expressing confidence in Adams. Elbridge Gerry
likened him to a ship ballasted with iron, capable of riding out any storm.
Cotton Tufts, in a letter lamenting the "vexation" Adams was bound to
encounter, wrote, "I will not, however, admit this to be of weight sufficient to deter or prevent a great and good man." A letter from Samuel
Adams, then in his seventy-fifth year, may have meant the most of all. "I
congratulate you as the first citizen of the United States—I may add the
world. I am, my dear sir, notwithstanding I have been otherwise represented in party papers, your old and unvaried friend."
    Except for his siege of anxiety the night before the inauguration,
Adams's state of mind had remained quite steady. He had never felt
"easier," he assured Abigail, and a diary entry of the wife of the British

ambassador seems to bear him out. At a dinner given by Washington in mid-January, Henrietta Liston found herself seated between the President and the Vice President—"between the rising and setting suns"— and though she found Washington as noble as expected, Adams proved surprisingly entertaining. "There is a good deal of amusement in the conversation of Adams, a considerable degree of wit and humor," she recorded happily.

While he knew much patience would be called for in time to come, Adams reminded Abigail that he had had a "good education" in patience in his years in public life, and could "look at a storm with some composure." Constituted as he was, he may even have welcomed a storm. When in the predawn hours of January 27, a terrible fire ripped through the home and shop of the Philadelphia printer and publisher of the *Federal Gazette*, Andrew Brown, taking the lives of his wife and children, Adams was conspicuous among the men handing up buckets to fight the blaze. Brown, as all knew, had for some time been excoriating the Vice President at every chance.

In February, when the outcome of the election became official, it had been Adams's role, as president of the Senate, to open and read the final votes in the electoral college. He had won by only a narrow margin, with 71 votes to Jefferson's 68. (Pinckney had 59, Burr, 30, Samuel Adams, 11.) As Adams himself observed, he was President by three votes. Yet he appears to have taken it in stride. "I am not alarmed," he told Nabby, who had written to express her concern. "If the way to do good to my country were to render myself popular, I could easily do it. But extravagant popularity is not the road to public advantage." To Abigail he wrote simply, "The die is cast."

With the inauguration still to come, he had taken one of the most fateful steps of his presidency. Rather than choosing a new cabinet of his own, Adams asked Washington's four department heads to stay on, convinced this was the surest way to preserve Federalist harmony. "Washington had appointed them and I knew it would turn the world upside down if I removed any one of them," he later wrote. "I had then no particular objection to any of them." Also, there was no tradition of cabinet members resigning their positions at the end of a President's term. Washington himself had encouraged them to remain; nor did any express a wish to leave.

They were Secretary of State Timothy Pickering of Salem, Massachusetts; Secretary of the Treasury Oliver Wolcott, Jr., of Connecticut; Secretary of War James McHenry of Maryland; and Charles Lee of Virginia, the Attorney General. All were younger men than Adams. Wolcott, the youngest at thirty-seven, was the son of the Oliver Wolcott with whom Adams had served in the Continental Congress. A plump, rather pleasant-looking lawyer who had been educated at Yale, he was thought trustworthy and affable. McHenry, an even friendlier and more likable man, had been born and raised in County Antrim, Ireland, and spoke with a trace of an Irish accent. Charles Lee, like Wolcott, was still in his thirties, a graduate of the College of New Jersey at Princeton and, while perfectly competent, was distinguished primarily for being a Lee of Virginia.

None were of oustanding ability, but all were Federalists, and Wolcott and McHenry, like Secretary of State Pickering, were extreme Federalists, or High Federalists. They belonged to the ardently anti-French, pro-British wing of the party who considered Alexander Hamilton their leader, and because of this, and the fact that they had served in the Washington cabinet, they were inclined to look down on John Adams.

But of the four it was Timothy Pickering who held the strongest views and, as Secretary of State, was the most important, given the precarious nature of a world at war, as well as his own obdurate personality. Pickering was not an easy man to like or get along with even under normal circumstances, as Adams knew. In many ways Pickering might have served as the model New Englander for those who disliked the type. Tall, lean, and severe-looking, with a lantern jaw and hard blue eyes, he was Salem-born-and-bred, a Harvard graduate, proud, opinionated, self-righteous, and utterly humorless. After brief service on Washington's staff during the war, he had been promoted to adjutant general. Later he became the first Postmaster General, and from there moved over to replace Henry Knox as Secretary of War. When Secretary of State Edmund Randolph was forced to resign under a cloud of suspicion—a cloud largely of Pickering's making—Pickering was named to succeed him, but only after Washington had been turned down by five others to whom he offered the position.

To his credit, Pickering was energetic and conscientious. He was fond of music and enjoyed a happy marriage that had produced ten children. Adams, who had known him for years, though not well, was willing to give him—indeed all of his cabinet—the benefit of the doubt. "Pickering and all his colleagues are as much attached to me as I desire," he told Elbridge Gerry.

To many the great question was the part Jefferson might play concerning relations with France—the Republicans hoping it would be considerable, the Federalists determined he should have no say whatever. Privately, Adams was ambivalent on the subject. While he had forgiven Jefferson most of his past trespasses, he had by no means forgotten them. "I may say to you that his patronage of Paine and Freneau and his entanglements with characters and politics which have been pernicious are and have been a source of inquietude and anxiety to me," Adams confided to Tristram Dalton. "He will have too many French about him to flatter him, but I hope we can keep him steady."

To Elbridge Gerry, however, Adams expressed greater confidence. In view of Jefferson's good sense and long friendship, Adams thought he could expect from his Vice President support of the kind he himself had given Washington, "which is and shall be the pride and boast of my life." Benjamin Rush, meantime, had written to Jefferson to say what a lift it gave him to hear Adams "speak with pleasure of the prospect of administering the government in a connection with you. He does justice to you upon all occasions . . ."

Arriving in Philadelphia just days before the inauguration, Jefferson had called on Adams at the Francis Hotel, where Jefferson, too, was to stay. They had not seen one another for three years, and apparently the reunion went well. As a matter of courtesy, one such visit between the President and Vice President would have sufficed, but the fact that Adams promptly returned the call the next morning was taken as a clear signal that Adams meant truly to pursue a policy above party divisions.

According to Jefferson's account of the meeting, written years later, Adams "entered immediately" into discussion of the crisis at hand and his wish for Jefferson to play a lead part in resolving it. Faced with the prospect of war with France, Adams was determined to make a fresh effort at negotiations in Paris, to bring about a reconciliation, which he believed possible and desirable. "Great is the guilt of an unnecessary war," he had written to Abigail.

The government of France, led since 1795 by a five-headed executive commission known as the Directory, had chosen to interpret the Jay Treaty as an Anglo-American alliance. In an effort to improve relations with France, Washington had recalled the American minister, James Monroe, and sent in his place a staunch Federalist, General Charles Cotesworth Pinckney of South Carolina. But as yet there was no word from Pinckney.

It was the "first wish of his heart," Adams told Jefferson, to send him to Paris, though he supposed this would be out of the question. "It did not seem justifiable for him to send away the person destined to take his place in case of an accident to himself," Jefferson would recall; "nor decent to remove from consideration one who was a rival for public favor."

Jefferson agreed with Adams's reasoning. Irrespective of whether the Constitution would allow it, he was sick of residing in Europe, Jefferson said, and hoped never to cross the Atlantic again as long as he lived.

That being so, Adams continued, it was his plan to send two emissaries to join Pinckney, making it a bipartisan three-man commission, which by its "dignity" ought to satisfy France, and by its geographical and political balance satisfy both parties and all parts of the country. He had in mind Elbridge Gerry and James Madison, who had recently retired from Congress. Jefferson said he was certain Madison would not accept, but at Adams's request agreed to inquire.

This was on March 3, the day before the inauguration. The next morning, in his own brief inaugural remarks before the Senate, Jefferson made a point of commending Adams as that "eminent character," and spoke of their "uninterrupted friendship." For a fleeting interlude the prospect of truly nonpartisan cooperation between them appeared attainable. "I am much pleased," one Supreme Court justice wrote, "that Mr. Adams and Mr. Jefferson lodge together. The thing looks well; it carries conciliation and healing with it, and may have a happy effect on parties."

The day following the inauguration, however, when President Adams asked others, including Washington, for their opinion on sending Madison to Paris, he heard only stiff objections. To such High Federalists as Timothy Pickering and Secretary of the Treasury Wolcott, Madison was as unacceptable as Jefferson would have been. Wolcott told the President that sending Madison would "make dire work among the passions of our parties in Congress." When Adams said he refused to be intimidated by party passions, Wolcott threatened to resign.

As Jefferson would recall, it was that evening while walking down Market Street with Adams, after a farewell dinner given by Washington, that he informed Adams of Madison's refusal to go to France. Adams indicated that in any event the issue was now academic. There had been a change of mind due to objections raised. To Jefferson it was clear that Adams, who imagined he might "steer impartially between the parties," had been brought abruptly back into the Federalist fold. But it was also clear to Adams that neither Jefferson nor Madison had the least desire to work with the administration, and thus he could expect no help from any of the Republicans.

It was there on Market Street, according to Jefferson, that he and Adams reached the breaking point. Adams never again mentioned a word to him on the subject of France, "or ever consulted me as to any measures of the government."

Whether the parting was quite so clear-cut as Jefferson remembered is uncertain. But as Adams, too, later acknowledged, they "consulted very little together afterward." Adams was to call on his Vice President for advice no more than Washington had called on him. The great difference, however, was that Jefferson was of the opposing party, with differing objectives and principles, and Adams consequently could never count on such loyalty from Jefferson as he had given Washington. Adams never knew when Jefferson might be working secretly to undercut or thwart him, for Jefferson's abiding flaw, Adams had concluded, was "want of sincerity."

In his Farewell Address, Washington had warned against "the baneful effects of the spirit of party." Particularly in governments of "popular form," he had said, "it is seen in its greatest rankness and is truly their worst enemy." Yet party spirit and animosities were as alive as ever, as Adams had been shown in the bluntest of terms in little more than twenty-four hours since taking office.

On March 8, Washington called at the Francis Hotel to say goodbye to

Adams and wish him well. They were parting on good terms. For all his long coolness toward Adams, Washington before leaving office had written an unsolicited letter expressing the *"strong hope"* that as President, Adams would not withhold "merited promotion" from John Quincy. "I give it as my *decided opinion,"* Washington wrote, "that Mr. [John Quincy] Adams is the most valuable public character we have abroad, and there remains no doubt in my mind that he will prove himself to be the ablest of all our diplomatic corps if he is now to be brought into that line, or into any other public work." Little that Washington might have said or done could have meant more to Adams.

"The President is fortunate to get off just as the bubble is bursting, leaving others to hold the bag," Jefferson wrote to Madison. "Yet, as his departure will mark the moment when the difficulties begin to work, you will see, that they will be ascribed to the new administration."

Jefferson, too, would depart shortly, after a quick farewell to Adams. "He is as he was," Adams noted cryptically.

So MUCH HAD HAPPENED in John Adams's life—he had done so much, taken such risks, given so much of himself heart and soul in the cause of his country—that he seems not to have viewed the presidency as an ultimate career objective or crowning life achievement. He was not one given to seeing life as a climb to the top of a ladder or mountain, but more as a journey or adventure, even a "kind of romance, which a little embellished with fiction or exaggeration or only poetical ornament, would equal anything in the days of chivalry or knight errantry," as once he confided to Abigail. If anything, he was inclined to look back upon the long struggle for independence as the proud defining chapter.

In this sense the presidency was but another episode in the long journey, and, as fate would have it, he was left little time to dwell overly on anything but the rush of events and the increasingly dangerous road ahead.

"My entrance into office is marked by a misunderstanding with France, which I shall endeavor to reconcile," he wrote to John Quincy, "provided that no violation of faith, no stain upon honor is exacted. . . . America is not *scared.*"

On the evening of March 13, or possibly the next morning, Adams was hit with stunning news. The French Directory had refused to receive General Pinckney. Forced to leave Paris as though he were an undesirable alien, Pinckney had withdrawn to Amsterdam and was awaiting instructions.

To make matters worse, Adams learned of further French seizures of American ships in the Caribbean and that by decrees issued in Paris, the Directory had, in effect, launched an undeclared war on American shipping everywhere. The crisis had come to a head. Adams faced the threat of all-out war.

Days were consumed by tedious meetings. The weather was miserable, he reported to Abigail. "I have a great cold. The news is not pleasant." Such confidence in his cabinet as he had expressed to Elbridge Gerry was badly shaken. From what he wrote privately to Abigail, it appears he already sensed what trouble was in store from that quarter. "From the situation where I now am, I see a scene of ambition beyond all my former suspicions or imagination. . . . Jealousies and rivalries . . . never stared me in the face in such horrid forms as in the present."

On March 21 he moved into the President's House vacated by Washington, but what should rightfully have been a fulfilling moment proved only more demoralizing.

> The furniture belonging to the public is in the most deplorable condition [he reported to Abigail]. There is not a chair to sit in. The beds and bedding are in a woeful pickle. This house has been a scene of the most scandalous drinking and disorder among the servants that I ever heard of. I would not have one of them for any consideration. There is not a carpet nor a curtain, nor a glass [mirror], nor linen, nor china, nor anything.

Rent for the house was an exorbitant $2,700 a year, plus another $2,500 for carriages and horses. Though Congress would allot $14,000 to purchase furniture, Adams worried that on his salary of $25,000, it would be impossible to make ends meet. They would be more "pinched" than ever in their lives, he warned Abigail. "All the glasses, ornaments, kitchen furniture . . . all to purchase. All the china . . . glass and crockery.

... All the linen besides. . . . Secretaries, servants, wood, charities . . . the
million dittoes." Yet not a word could they say. "We must stand our
ground as long as we can." To no one but her could he ever complain.

The work was more taxing than he had been prepared for, "very dry,
dull," "perplexing," and "incessant." But again nothing could be
said. "Don't expose this croaking and groaning. . . . I should lose all
my character [reputation] for firmness. . . . Indeed, I sometimes suspect
that I deserve a character of peevishness and fretfulness, rather than
firmness."

But more was happening than he let on. On Saturday, March 25, he
called for Congress to reconvene in special session on May 15, "to consult
and determine on such measures as their wisdom shall be deemed meet
for the safety and welfare of the United States." War clouds gathered
over the capital—to the angry indignation of the Republicans. The Federalist press declared the United States had been grievously insulted by
France; the Republican press affirmed American friendship with the
French and, while expressing the hope that the President would remain
true to his inaugural pledge to seek peace, reported that a "certain
ex-Secretary" (Hamilton) was secretly preaching war to further his political ambitions.

A lively new newspaper had begun publication in Philadelphia, in
answer to Bache's *Aurora*. *Porcupine's Gazette* was the work of an English
printer and bookseller, William Cobbett, who wrote under the pen name
"Peter Porcupine" and immediately demonstrated that he could be as
biased, sarcastic, and full of invective as Bache, and attract no less attention. Headlines in *Porcupine's Gazette* announced that war with France
was all but certain:

MR. PINCKNEY, THE AMERICAN MINISTER AT PARIS, HAVING RECEIVED
ORDERS TO QUIT THE TERRITORIES OF THE FRENCH REPUBLIC, HAS
ACTUALLY TAKEN HIS DEPARTURE ACCORDINGLY. WAR BETWEEN
THESE TWO POWERS MAY THEREFORE BE CONSIDERED INEVITABLE.

Cobbett not only expected and wanted war with France, but favored the
alliance with Britain that was bound to result—an increasingly popular
view in many quarters.

It is manifestly the design of the French party to lull the people into a fatal security, to deaden their national energy and to defeat in this way those measures of defense which would secure to us our independence. With this view they will fabricate reports of accommodation with France—for this end they are constantly preaching up the improbability of a war with that nation, and some of the base traitors have even declared that in the event of war they will join France.

Adams remained silent, but in letters to Henry Knox and John Quincy said he would do everything possible to settle all disputes with France. To Abigail he confessed to being totally exhausted and begged her to come to his rescue. The more at odds he felt with his cabinet, the less he trusted their judgment, the greater his need for her insight and common sense, her presence in his life. His pleas for her to come grew more urgent even than those he had sent during his difficult debut as Vice President.

"I must go to you or you must come to me. I cannot live without you," he wrote. And again: "I must entreat you to lose not a moment's time in preparing to come on, that you may take off from me every care of life but that of my public duty, assist me with your councils, and console me with your conversation."

"The times are critical and dangerous, and I must have you here to assist me," he told her. "I must now repeat this with zeal and earnestness. I can do nothing without you."

ABIGAIL HAD BEEN corresponding faithfully the whole time, offering advice, opinions on people, often saying more than she knew she should as the wife of a president. "My pen runs riot," she allowed. "I forget that it must grow cautious and prudent." She had encouraged his confidence in Jefferson. Like others, she had thought the odd circumstance of having a President and Vice President of "differing sentiments" could prove a blessing were both to "aim at the same end, the good of their country." Conceivably the combination of two well-meaning men could serve to continue the Union as Washington had managed all alone.

When Adams confided that he hoped to keep Hamilton at a safe distance, she provided a withering farsighted assessment. "Beware that spare Cassius has always occurred to me when I have seen that cock sparrow," she wrote. "Oh, I have read his heart in his wicked eyes. The very devil is in them. They are lasciviousness itself."

She prayed that " 'things which made for peace may not be hid from your eyes.' " Her feelings were not those of pride or ostentation, but "solemnized" by the knowledge of the obligations and duties he had assumed. "That you may be enabled to discharge them with honor to yourself, with justice and impartiality to your country, and with the satisfaction to this great people, shall be the daily prayer of your A.A."

Her own days were taken up with all that would have preoccupied him had he been home, and more. She kept house, ran the farm, settled issues among the hired men, managed the family finances, and tried not to complain about her health or loneliness.

In a particularly memorable letter, she recounted a crisis that arose when the youngest of her hired hands, James Prince, a free black boy she had taken under her wing in Philadelphia, came to ask if he might attend evening classes in town at a new school for apprentices. Abigail, who had taught him herself to read and write, warmly approved, but was soon asked by a neighbor to withdraw James. If she did not, she was told, the other boys would refuse to attend and the school would close. Had James misbehaved, Abigail asked. No, she was informed, it was because he was black. Did these other boys object when he attended church? No, they did not.

"The boy is a freeman as much as any of the young men, and merely because his face is black is he to be denied instruction?" she asked. "How is he to be qualified to procure a livelihood? Is this the Christian principle of doing unto others as we would have others to do to us?"

She requested that the boys be sent to her. "Tell them . . . that I hope we shall all go to Heaven together." And this, she was pleased to report to Adams, ended the crisis. She heard no more on the subject; James continued in the school.

As ever, a very considerable part of her time was devoted to correspondence with the rest of the family, about whom she reported to John, seldom withholding her own opinions.

John Quincy was in love again, this time with Louisa Catherine Johnson, the daughter of the American consul in London whom the Adamses knew. Though John Quincy assured his mother that his "matrimonial prospects" were still uncertain, she could not help worrying, as she told him, whether the young woman was right for him, whether she might be too young, too accustomed to the splendors and attractions of Europe—meaning her expensive tastes might be more than he could afford.

"All your observations on the subject are received by me with gratitude, as I knew them to proceed from serious concern and purest parental affection," answered the young diplomat. The lady in question had "goodness of heart and gentleness of disposition, as well as spirit and discretion," and would "prove such a daughter as you would wish for your son."

"My fear arose from the youth and inexperience of the lady," Abigail wrote in reply, and asked John Quincy to please tell Louisa that "I consider her already my daughter."

Her greater concern was still over Nabby, whose husband, Colonel Smith, Abigail had sadly concluded, was "a man wholly devoid of judgment." He had deceived himself with his visionary schemes and "led his family into a state of living which I fear his means will not bear him out."

In April, as Abigail was preparing to leave for Philadelphia, the weather turned unseasonably hot. Then as suddenly the temperature plunged and John's aged mother went into a sharp decline. "The good old lady is sure she shall die now [that] her physician and nurse are about to leave her, but she judges with me that all ought to be forsaken for the husband," Abigail informed John.

Refusing to leave, she was with his mother until the end came on April 21, and it was she who made arrangements for the funeral in her front parlor.

"I prepare to set out on the morrow," she wrote to John on April 26. "Our aged parent has gone to rest. . . . She fell asleep, and is happy. . . . I am ready and willing to follow my husband wherever he chooses."

The obituary that appeared in the Boston papers, noted that Susanna Boylston Adams Hall, mother of the President of the United States, who died in the eighty-ninth year of her life, had "afforded the present generation a living example of that simplicity of manners and godly sincerity for which the venerable settlers of this country were so justly esteemed."

From Philadelphia, Adams wrote to Abigail to express his grief and the wish that he had been at Quincy to give her help and comfort.

> Our ancestors are now all gone, and we are to follow them very soon to a country where there will be no war or rumor of war, no envy, no jealousy, rivalry or party.
>
> You and I are entering on a new scene, which will be the most difficult and least agreeable of any in our lives. I hope the burden will be lighter to both of us when we come together.

Her journey south was extremely difficult, because of heavy rains and washed-out roads. She felt like Noah's dove, Abigail wrote, her thoughts always returning to the ark she had left. The part she must play now, as wife of the President, though "enviable no doubt in the eyes of some," was one she had never envied or wanted. "That I may discharge my part with honor and give satisfaction is my most earnest wish."

Stopping to see Nabby at East Chester, she was stunned to find that Colonel Smith was off again on another of his uncertain ventures, and Nabby too upset even to talk about it, except to say she had no idea where he was. "My reflections upon prospects there took from me all appetite for food," Abigail confided to her sister Mary, "and depressed my spirits, before too low."

Expecting her to arrive at Philadelphia on May 10, Adams set off that morning by carriage and met her about twenty-five miles outside the city.

> I quitted my own carriage, and took my seat by his side [she wrote]. We rode on to Bristol, where I had previously engaged a dinner, and there upon the banks of the Delaware, we spent the day, getting into the city at sunset.

It took several days for her to recover from the trip. But in little time she, too, was caught up in the tumult of events.

ONE DAY LATER, on May 11, Thomas Jefferson arrived in Philadelphia from Monticello to find the city astir over a private letter he had written more than a year before that had just appeared in print in the *New York*

Minerva, a strongly Federalist paper, edited by Noah Webster. Writing to an Italian friend, Philip Mazzei, during the debate over the Jay Treaty, Jefferson had described America as a country taken over by "timid men who prefer the calm of despotism to the boisterous sea of liberty," and by leaders who were assimilating "the rotten as well as the sound parts of the British model." Then, in the line that caused the stir, Jefferson wrote:

> It would give you a fever were I to name to you the apostates who have gone over to those heresies, men who were Samsons in the field and Solomons in the council, but who have had their heads shorn by the harlot England.

Successive translations of the letter from English to Italian to French, then back to English again had changed and intensified some of the wording by the time it appeared in the *Minerva*—"harlot" had become "whore," for example—but the meaning was essentially unchanged and the letter was taken by many as an unconscionable attack on Washington.

Jefferson said nothing in his defense, and Washington, too, remained silent. But great damage had been done to Jefferson by the "Mazzei Letter," notwithstanding the many prominent Republicans who claimed he had only been telling the unvarnished truth.

II

THE PRESIDENT entered Congress Hall at midday, May 16, 1797, absolutely clear in his mind about his intentions and walked to the dais knowing he had the support of his cabinet in what he was about to say. Indeed, some of the language in the speech he carried was their own, arrived at after he had asked for their answers to a list of specific questions, a technique employed by his predecessor. Long a man of decided temperament, Adams was as determined as he had ever been to maintain the policy of neutrality established by Washington, while refusing to submit to any indignities or to sacrifice American honor—he was determined, in essence, to fulfill his own inaugural promises.

But as an old realist, and one who had read more of history and experienced more of it than any of those in his audience, he also knew how extremely difficult, if not impossible, neutrality would be to achieve and maintain in a world at war. He knew how much could happen in France or Britain or on the high seas, or within his own country, over which he had no control. Regional and party differences had made a tinderbox of American politics. It was not only that Republicans were divided from Federalists, but Federalists were sharply at odds with themselves, and the roll of the strident, often vicious press was changing the whole political atmosphere.

Nor was Adams like George Washington immensely popular, elected unanimously, and all but impervious to criticism. He had no loyal following as Washington had, no coterie of friends in Congress. Further, there was the looming reality that America at the moment had no military strength on land or sea. With authorization from the Republic of France, French privateers continued to prey on the American merchant fleet at will and there was no way to stop them.

In a calm, steady voice, Adams said the French had "inflicted a wound in the American breast," but that it was his sincere desire to see it healed, and to preserve peace and friendship with all nations. He was therefore calling for both "a fresh attempt" at negotiation with France, and a buildup of American military strength.

> While we are endeavoring to adjust all our differences with France by amicable negotiation, with the progress of the war in Europe, the depredations on our commerce, the personal injuries to our citizens, and the general complexion of our affairs, render it my duty to recommend your consideration of effectual measures of defense.

This was not an act of belligerence, but a measure to give added weight and respect to the mission he planned to send to Paris.

As was remarked at the time, the speech bore a strong resemblance to the American eagle, an olive branch in one talon, and in the other the "emblems of defense." Federalist papers hailed Adams's patriotic fire. He had "shone forth" as in times of old, exciting "the liveliest approbation of all real Americans."

It may be justly called a *true American speech* [said the *Gazette of the United States*]. It breathes in every line true American patriotism. It came from the heart of a tried patriot, and was addressed to the hearts of patriots alone. There was nothing wavering in it; no little trick to catch a transitory approbation from the discontented, or to soothe the fractious. It was the explicit language of the first magistrate of the nation, disclosing to his fellow citizens the honest sentiments of his heart, expressing with proper feeling and sensibility the wrongs done to his injured country, and his determination to attempt to obtain redress; while at the same time it manifested humane anxiety to avert the calamities of war by temperance and negotiations.

Federalist approval was emphatic and widespread. From Mount Vernon, Washington wrote that the President had "placed matters upon their true ground."

Republicans were enraged. Adams had not only failed to express sufficient sympathy for the French but had sounded a "war-whoop." How, if he wanted to avoid war, could he press Congress to build up the navy?

Benjamin Bache turned with a fury on the President he had so recently lauded as a prudent, high-minded man of integrity. In almost daily attacks in the *Aurora*, Adams was belittled as "The President by Three Votes," mocked again as "His Rotundity," excoriated as a base hypocrite, a tool of the British, "a man divested of his senses." He was charged again and again as a creature of Hamilton and the Federalist war hawks.

In fact, most Federalists at this point, including Hamilton, recognized the need for a renewed effort to treat with France, and as Adams did not know, it was largely because of Hamilton's influence that the cabinet had given their full support to the peace mission.

Within days Adams appointed two special envoys who, with General Pinckney, would comprise a new commission to proceed to Paris. He chose John Marshall of Virginia, whom he did not know, and his own former aide in Paris, Francis Dana. But when Dana declined because of poor health, Adams named Elbridge Gerry.

Marshall, a forty-two-year-old lawyer, was an ardent champion of

George Washington under whom he had served gallantly in the war. A cousin of Jefferson's, but not an admirer of the Vice President, he was known to be able, skilled in the law, and, as mattered greatly, he was one of Virginia's few Federalists. Secretary of State Pickering and others in the cabinet strongly approved the choice.

Elbridge Gerry, however, was unacceptable to Pickering and the cabinet, who thought him too independent and unreliable. "It is ten to one against his agreeing with his colleagues," Secretary of War McHenry warned the President. Even Abigail questioned the choice. But Adams insisted. He needed someone on the commission whose friendship and loyalty were beyond doubt. He knew Gerry—"I knew Gerry infinitely better than any of them," he later said. The old bond of 1776 was still a tie that held Adams to Rush and even to Jefferson, for all the strains of politics. From the time of their ride to Philadelphia by horseback in the crisis winter of 1776, Adams had felt Gerry was someone to count on, and he was prepared to do just that in the present crisis. With the exception of his own son, John Quincy, there was perhaps no man in whom Adams placed more trust. Also, importantly, of the three envoys Gerry was the most sympathetic to France and, with his open admiration of Jefferson, came the closest to making it a bipartisan commission.

Later, when Marshall arrived in Philadelphia, Adams felt still better about the makeup of the commission. He and Marshall liked each other at once, even used virtually the same words to describe one another. Marshall judged Adams a "sensible, plain, candid, good tempered man," while Adams wrote of Marshall, "he is a plain man, very sensible, cautious, and learned in the law of nations."

In Paris the three American envoys would be dealing with the extremely wily and charming new French Foreign Minister, Charles-Maurice de Talleyrand-Périgord. A former bishop in the Catholic Church, Talleyrand had only recently returned to France after more than two years in exile in Philadelphia, where he had been well treated. Adams had known him but only slightly, not enough to have a sense of what to expect.

THE UNDECLARED WAR at sea continued. That spring Adams was informed that already the French had taken more than 300 trading vessels. American seamen had been wounded. In March the French captors of a ship out of Baltimore, the *Cincinnatus,* had tortured the American captain with thumbscrews in an unsuccessful attempt to make him say he was carrying British cargo.

"The task of the President is very arduous, very perplexing, and very hazardous. I do not wonder Washington wished to retire from it, or rejoiced in seeing an old oak in his place," observed Abigail, who in her letters to her sister Mary was to provide an inside look at the Adams presidency like no other, much as she had in portraying their life in France and London years before, writing always to the moment and with untrammeled candor.

Adams was in his office in the President's House most of every day and from "such close application" looked exhausted. She took charge of the large house, supervised the staff, and sent off orders to Mary for shipments of the President's favorite New England cheese, bacon, white potatoes, and cider. In keeping with "old habit," she told Mary, their day began at five in the morning. Breakfast was at eight, and they saw each other again at dinner, customarily served at three. "I begin to feel a little more at home, and less anxiety about the ceremonious part of my duty," Abigail allowed. "I am obliged every day to devote two hours for the purpose of seeing company."

> The day is past, and a fatiguing one it has been [she closed another letter at eight o'clock in the evening]. The ladies of Foreign Ministers and the Ministers, with our own secretaries and ladies have visited me today, and add to them, the whole levee today of Senate and House. Strangers, etc. making near one hundred asked permission to visit me, so that from past 12 till near 4:00, I was rising up and sitting down.

She was both involved and vitally interested in her husband's world. She read all the newspapers, and in time came to know the names and faces of everyone in Congress, their background and political views. Little transpired in the capital that she did not know about. Yet her interest in matters at home never flagged. She kept contact with nieces and nephews, inquired regularly about the welfare of her pensioners: Parson Wibird, who had grown old and infirm, and her aged former servant

Phoebe, to whom she sent money and made sure she had sufficient firewood and whatever other necessities were wanting.

The President's worries and burdens were never out of mind. "Mrs.
Tufts once styled my situation 'splendid misery,'" Abigail reminded
Mary. Interestingly, it was a phrase Vice President Jefferson also used to
describe the presidency.

When Adams named John Quincy to be minister to Prussia, more
Republican protest erupted. Washington had never appointed relatives
to office, it was said, not even distant relatives. The President must
resign, charged the *Aurora*, "before it is too late to retrieve our deranged
affairs." When Congress chose to leave some matters to the "discretion"
of the President, the *Aurora* attacked Adams for his excessive vanity.

"We may truly say we know not what a day will bring forth," Abigail
observed in her running account. "From every side we are in danger. We
are in perils by land, and we are in perils by sea, and in perils by false
brethren." Whom she meant by false brethren, she did not say. But the
Vice President all the while did nothing whatever to help his former
friend the President. Further, he made no secret of his belief that Adams
was leading the nation straight to war.

After years of seclusion at Monticello, Jefferson had, with amazing
agility, stepped back into the kind of party politics he professed to abhor,
and in no time emerged as leader of the opposition. With Madison in
retirement, and the vice presidency providing ample free time, Jefferson
kept extremely busy as a "closet politician," in one man's expression,
writing letters and lending support—ideas, information, and money—to
the Republican press, including such "gladiators of the quill" as a dis-
solute Scottish pamphleteer and scandalmonger named James T. Callender, who wrote for the *Aurora* and specialized in attacks on John Adams.

The Francis Hotel, where Jefferson continued to lodge, became headquarters for the Republican inner circle. Any pretense of harmony
between the President and Vice President was dispensed with. Like other
Republicans, Jefferson failed to understand how Adams could reconcile
negotiation for peace with measures of defense, and in private correspondence accused Adams of willfully endangering the peace. When some
of this got back to Adams, he angrily declared it bespoke a mind "eaten
to a honeycomb with ambition, yet weak, confused, uninformed, and
ignorant."

Yet given all that Jefferson was doing, and the combustible atmosphere of the moment, Adams's rancorous comments were remarkably few and mild. Many in the Federalist party suspected Jefferson of outright treachery against his own country.

Convinced that the best hope for the world was the defeat of Britain by France, and that such an outcome was imminent, Jefferson privately advised the French chargé d'affaires in Philadelphia, Philippe-Henry-Joseph de Letombe, that the Directory should show the three American envoys all proper courtesy but "then drag out the negotiations at length."

Letombe wrote of the meeting with "the wise Jefferson," in a report to his Foreign Minister, dated June 7, 1797. America, Jefferson had impressed upon Letombe, was "penetrated with gratitude to France" and would "never forget that it owes its liberation to France." The new President of the United States was another matter, however. Jefferson was unsparing: "Mr. Adams is vain, irritable, stubborn, endowed with excessive self-love, and still suffering pique at the preference accorded Franklin over him in Paris." But Adams's term of office was only four years, Jefferson reminded Letombe. Besides, Adams did not have popular support. "He only became President by three votes, and the system of the United States will change along with him."

Possibly these were not Jefferson's exact words; possibly his assessment of Adams was not as harsh and patently disloyal as Letombe's account would make it appear. But if what Letombe recorded was all that Jefferson had to say for Adams, this would seem to have proved the end of a long friendship. And whatever Jefferson's exact words may have been, clearly the chargé d'affaires was led to conclude that the difficulties of the moment were not a question of American regard for France, but of the difficult, unpopular, aberrant old man who temporarily held office as President.

The truth, it happens, was that Adams and Jefferson both wanted peace with France and each was working to attain that objective, though in their decidedly different ways.

SUMMER MARKED the departure of the envoys, Gerry sailing from Boston, Marshall from Philadelphia, where Congress sweltered and fumed trying to wind up business, before "the sick season" came on.

She could not wait to start for home, Abigail wrote. She longed for a sea breeze and her rose bush. "The President really suffers for want of a journey, or rather for want of some relaxation," she told Mary Cranch.

Today will be the fifth great dinner I have had, about 36 gentlemen today, as many more next week, and I shall have to get through the whole of Congress, with their appendages. Then comes the 4th of July, which is a still more tedious day, as we must then have not only all Congress, but all the gentlemen of the city, the Governor and officers and companies. . . . I hope the day will not be hot.

The Fourth turned out to be a "fine, cool day," and her reception a great success.

. . . my fatigue arose chiefly from being dressed at an early hour, and receiving the very numerous sets of company who were so polite as to pay their compliments to me in succession in my drawing room after visiting the President below, and partaking of cake, wine, and punch with him. To my company were added the ladies of foreign ministers and Home Secretaries with a few others. The parade lasted from 12 until four o'clock.

To at least one of those present, she and the President seemed the picture of calm good cheer. Henrietta Liston, the British ambassador's wife, described Adams as "steady and resolute," while "Mrs. Adams . . . has spirit enough to laugh at Bache's abuse of her husband, which poor Mrs. Washington could not do."

In days the city had become a bake house again, as Abigail wrote. "The hot weather of July has weakened us all. Complaints of the bowels are very frequent and troublesome." Strangely, cats were dying all over the city. The streets were filled with dead cats. No one had an explanation, and no one in Congress wished to delay departure an hour longer than necessary.

On July 10, exhausted, irritable members of both houses started for home convinced the special session had only aggravated party divisions.

Adams had hoped it would help unite the country, and in this plainly he had failed.

There was some consolation, however. After a good deal of fuss and bickering, Congress had at last approved an Act Providing a Naval Armament. It was hardly what Adams had called for, but it was a start, providing funds to equip and man three frigates, the *Constitution*, the *United States*, and the *Constellation*, which had been built during the Washington administration but remained unequipped for service.

With a cooling rain falling, the Adamses started for home on July 19. Why, asked the *Aurora*, had the President of the United States "absconded" from the seat of government at a time when the public mind was "exceedingly agitated"?

III

It was a summer without incident. There was no news from France, no worsening or lessening of the crisis. For Adams the pleasures of August and September at Peacefield had all the desired effect. By the time they were heading back to Philadelphia, he and Abigail were both rested and revived. Abigail wrote of feeling better than she had in years.

Also, one news item appears to have added considerably to their outlook. John Quincy and Louisa Catherine Johnson had been married, as the Adamses learned just before leaving home. The small announcement in a Boston paper, like the first word from John Quincy himself, appeared two months after the fact. The young couple were married on July 26 in the ancient Anglican church known as All Hallows Barking by the Tower of London.

"I have now the happiness of presenting to you another daughter," read John Quincy's letter to his "Dear and Honored Parents," each of whom responded with an appropriately warm letter of congratulations. "And may the blessing of God Almighty be bestowed on this marriage and all its connections and effects," wrote Adams in benediction.

The departure from Quincy took place in the first week of October, but the Adamses were not to reach the capital for more than a month. Yellow fever again raged in Philadelphia, as they learned en route, and so it was necessary to stop and wait at East Chester with Nabby. Adams was kept apprised by daily reports. Two-thirds of the population of Philadelphia had fled the city. The government had scattered to various outlying towns. He imagined members of Congress stranded along the way all up and down the country, all waiting as he was, "in a very disagreeable, awkward, and uncertain situation." Told there had been an attempt to break into the President's House and asked if a guard should be posted, Adams said no, lest a sentinel at the door lead people to think the situation worse than they knew.

The wait at East Chester was not easy, as much as he and Abigail adored Nabby and the four grandchildren. The house was small, and the continued absence of Colonel Smith cast a shadow. Abigail found East Chester itself unbearably dull. She worried about Nabby living there, and urged her to come with the children to Philadelphia. "I cannot leave her here this winter with not a single creature within 20 miles of her to speak a word to, or shorten the long solitary winter evening," she told Mary. But Nabby refused. "I cannot say as much as is in my mind," wrote Abigail, "the subject being a very delicate one."

Adams went to New York for a dinner in his honor. Otherwise, to fill the time there was little but the newspapers and talk of a sensational scandal involving Alexander Hamilton. Possibly for Abigail, who claimed to have seen "the very devil" in Hamilton's eyes, the story came as no surprise.

The "Reynolds Affair" was a complicated tangle of financial dealings, adultery, blackmail, and alleged corruption in the Department of the Treasury, all dating back five years. In 1792, while his wife and children were away, Hamilton had become involved in an "improper connection" with a young woman named Maria Reynolds. Her husband, James Reynolds, a speculator with an unsavory reputation, commenced to blackmail Hamilton, until the point when he, Reynolds, went to prison for an earlier swindle. It was then, while in prison, that Reynolds, in an effort to ease his case, got word to three Republican members of Congress, including Senator James Monroe, that Hamilton was not only an adulterer, but, as Secretary of the Treasury, secretly profiteering with government funds. When the three confronted Hamilton with the charges, he denied any corrupt act as a public official, but acknowledged the affair with Mrs. Reynolds and the blackmail plot, with the understanding that they, as gentlemen, would keep silent, which they did to a degree. A few more were let in on the secret, including the Republican clerk of the House, John Beckley, and Thomas Jefferson.

But it was not until that summer of 1797 that the story broke in a series of unsigned pamphlets produced by James Callender, the unscrupulous writer for the *Aurora*, whose source apparently was Beckley.

Callender dismissed the adulterous affair as a cover story and accused Hamilton of being a partner with Reynolds in corrupt financial dealings. In response, Hamilton published his own pamphlet, *Observations on Certain Documents . . . in which . . . the Charge of Speculation against Alexander Hamilton . . . is Fully Refuted*. He denied any improper speculation with James Reynolds, but confessed to the adulterous affair. "My real crime," Hamilton wrote, "is an amorous connection with his wife."

Hamilton's disgrace was a windfall for the Republicans and all who had long thought him corrupt. Presumably the scandal would put a finish to his public career.

Jefferson appears to have made no comment on the Reynolds Affair. Nor did Adams, though it is certain he and Abigail heard plenty, such was the mood in Philadelphia when in November they arrived back at the President's House, after an absence of fully four months. "Alas, alas, how weak is human nature," wrote Abigail to her son Thomas.

There was still no report from the three envoys to France. Speaking before Congress on November 23, Adams could acknowledge only that the "unpleasant state of things" continued. The wait would go on, and the lack of information, plus the suspicion that some people knew more than they were saying, only put nerves further on edge.

Feelings ran deep, dividing the parties, dividing old friends. "Men who have been intimate all their lives," wrote Jefferson, "cross the streets to avoid meeting and turn their heads another way, lest they should be obliged to touch their hats."

IN EUROPE, French armies had been sweeping across Italy and Austria, in a campaign of French aggrandizement led by young General Napoleon Bonaparte, who appeared invincible. Now, with the start of a new year, 1798, Bonaparte had been given command of all forces on land and sea to carry the war across the Channel to Britain, and as John Quincy reported to his father, the expedition was "in great forwardness." Bonaparte shortly was to change his mind and lead his forces to Egypt instead, as John Quincy would also report. The French had become formidable as never before.

January 1798 in Congress Hall in Philadelphia, by contrast, was marked by a battle royal on the floor of the House. Vicious animosity of a kind previously confined to newspaper attacks broke out in the first physical assault to occur in Congress. In the midst of debate, when Federalist Roger Griswold of Connecticut insulted Republican Matthew Lyon of Vermont, Lyon crossed the chamber and spat in Griswold's face. Soon after, Griswold retaliated with a cane. Lyon grabbed fire tongs from the fireplace, and the two went at each other until, kicking and rolling on the floor, they were pulled apart.

To some the scene provided comic relief. To others it was sad testimony to how very far the republican ideal had descended. It was also apt prelude to much that would follow.

Step by step, events were moving toward the precipice, as Adams said. The first hint of trouble with the mission to France had been in a letter to Adams from General Pinckney in November, but it was a hint only, nothing to go on. In January, again in a private letter, came word from John Marshall by way of The Hague warning that the mission might not be received by the French Directory. In February, to make the tension still worse, Adams had to inform Congress that a French privateer had actually attacked a British merchant ship inside Charleston Harbor.

"We are yet all in the dark respecting our envoys," Abigail wrote on February 16; and again in another week: "Our envoys have been near six months in Paris but to this hour not a line has been received."

In the meanwhile, as the President was unaware, his cabinet—Wolcott and McHenry in particular—were receiving continued advice and directions from Alexander Hamilton, who had supposedly retired from public life.

Hamilton was still opposed to war with France. "It is an undoubted fact that there is a very general and strong aversion to war in the minds of the people of the country," he wrote to McHenry. "It is an undoubted fact that there is a very general indisposition toward the war in the minds of the people of the United States," McHenry dutifully advised the President four days later. But should the present attempt to negotiate fail, then the President must address the Congress in a style "cautious, solemn, grave, and void of asperity," declared McHenry—Hamilton also having told him this was what he was to say.

At last, late the evening of March 4, a year to the day since Adams became President, official dispatches arrived in Philadelphia and were delivered immediately to Timothy Pickering's desk at the Department of State at Fifth and Chestnut Streets. Four of the dispatches were in cipher and it would be several days before they were decoded. But the message of the fifth dispatch was clear. Seething with indignation, Pickering pulled on a coat and hurried three blocks to the President's House.

What Adams read was extremely unsettling. The government of France had refused to see the envoys. The mission had failed. Furthermore, the Directory had decreed all French ports closed to neutral shipping and declared that any ship carrying anything produced in England was subject to French capture.

Promptly the next morning, Monday, March 5, Adams sent the uncoded dispatch to Congress. But there was more to the story, as he soon learned with the decoding of the other dispatches.

After arriving in Paris in the first week of October, the three American envoys were kept waiting for several days and then were granted a meeting with Foreign Minister Talleyrand for all of fifteen minutes. More days of silence followed. Then began a series of visits from three secret agents representing Talleyrand—Jean Conrad Hottinguer, Pierre Bellamy, and Lucien Hauteval—who were referred to by the Americans in their dispatches as X, Y, and Z. The Foreign Minister was favorably disposed toward the United States, the American envoys were informed, but in order for negotiations to proceed, a *douceur* (a sweetener) would be necessary, a bribe of some $250,000 for Talleyrand personally. In addition, a loan of $10,000,000 for the Republic of France was required as compensation for President Adams's "insults" in his speech before Congress the previous May.

Pinckney, Marshall, and Gerry refused to negotiate on such terms. M. Hottinguer, the X of X, Y, and Z, reminded them of the "power and violence of France," as Marshall recorded, but the Americans held their ground. "Gentlemen," said Hottinguer, "you do not speak to the point.

It is money. It is expected that you will offer the money. . . . What is your answer?" to which General Pinckney emphatically replied, "No! No! Not a sixpence."

The last of the dispatches was not entirely decoded until March 12, and for several days Adams struggled over what to do, listening to advice and scribbling his thoughts on paper as his mood swung one way then another. He wrote of the "continued violences" of the French at sea, of their "unexampled arrogance" in refusing to receive the envoys, and declared such "injury, outrage, and insult" more than a self-respecting nation should ever have to submit to. But he also noted that peace might still be attainable, and, in fact, peace with honor was still his determined objective.

Wild rumors swept the city. It was said France had already declared war on the United States, that the French were moving to take possession of Florida and Louisiana.

Adams's message to Congress on March 19 revealed only that the diplomatic mission had failed, and thus he must call again for the measures necessary to defend the nation in the event of attack. It was as mild a statement as he could have made under the circumstances. There was not a word about war, nor anything said of the contents of the dispatches, except that they had been examined and "maturely considered."

The Republicans immediately decried the message as a declaration of war. In a letter to Madison, Jefferson called it "insane" and commenced lobbying for ways to delay action and allow time for Bonaparte to invade Britain. Jefferson proposed that members of Congress adjourn at once and go home to consult their constituents on the great crisis. "The present period . . . of two or three weeks," he told Madison in a burst of hyperbole, "is the most eventful ever known since that of 1775, and will decide whether the principles established by that contest are to prevail, or give way to those they subverted."

Convinced that Adams was deliberately withholding information favorable to the French, Republicans in and out of Congress began insisting that the documents be made available at once. Any delay would be a sign of further duplicity. The *Aurora* taunted Adams for being "afraid to tell."

"Beds of roses have never been his destiny," Abigail wrote of her husband. Whether he would reveal more of the dispatches was something only he could determine, she told Mary; but "clamor who will," great care must be taken that nothing endanger the lives of the envoys who were still in Paris. The Republicans, French agents, and the "lying wretch" Bache intended to abuse and misrepresent the President until they forced him to resign, "and then they will reign triumphant, *headed by the man of the people,*" Jefferson.

The respect she had expressed for Jefferson the year before had vanished. How different was the President's situation from that of Washington, whose Vice President had "never combined with a party against him . . . never intrigued with foreign ministers or foreign courts against his own government . . . never made Bache his companion and counsellor." John Adams was no warmonger. In self-defense the country might become involved in a war, and for that the country should be prepared, which was the President's intent. Of what possible benefit could a war be to him? she asked. "He has no ambition for military glory. He cannot add by war to his peace, comfort, or happiness. It must accumulate upon him an additional load of care, toil, trouble, malice, hatred, and I dare say, revenge."

On Monday, April 2, on the floor of the House, Representative Albert Gallatin of Pennsylvania, who had replaced Madison in the leadership of the Republicans, stood to propose that the President be requested to turn over the text of the dispatches. Republicans who had been clamoring for disclosure were now joined by a number of High Federalists who had gotten wind of the damaging content of the dispatches and were happy to help the Republicans step into a trap of their own making. By a vote of 65 to 27 the House demanded that the full text be delivered at once.

Adams, who had apparently concluded that the envoys were by now safely out of France, released the documents the next day, and with the galleries cleared of visitors and the doors secured, the House went into executive session.

The revelation that the crisis was not less than the administration implied, but far worse, hit the Republicans like a hammer. They were "struck dumb, and opened not their mouths," wrote Abigail. Many representatives privately voiced outrage over the effrontery of Talleyrand and his agents. Some offered lame new arguments. It was said that the whole XYZ story was a contrivance of the Federalist warmongers, that the breakdown of negotiations was the fault of the American envoys. Jefferson, while refusing to comment publicly, privately blamed Adams for past insults to the French, and insisted that Talleyrand and his agents were not, after all, the French government, which was "above suspicion."

Once the Senate voted to have copies of the documents printed for use within Congress only, it was only a matter of days before they were public knowledge.

In the House, Gallatin had urged that the dispatches not be published, certain that they would dash any surviving hope of a settlement with France—which, it appears, was exactly the fear that troubled the President. And, indeed, High Federalists were claiming it was too late for preaching peace any longer. The Federalist press protested the "damnable outrages" of the French, and a wave of patriotic anti-French anger swept the city and the country with unexpected passion. As Abigail reported to Mary Cranch and John Quincy, public opinion in the capital changed overnight. The tricolor cockade of France that Republicans had been wearing in their hats all but disappeared from sight. No one was heard singing French patriotic songs in public as before, or espousing the cause of France.

The *Aurora*, in turn, lashed out at the President as a man "unhinged" by the "delirium of vanity." Had Adams refrained from insulting the French, had he chosen more suitable envoys, the country would never have been brought to such a pass. But in a matter of days subscriptions and advertising fell off so drastically that it appeared the paper might fail. Anger at Bache and Callender was as intense nearly as at the French. John Fenno, editor of the rival *Gazette of the United States*, asked, "In the name of justice and honor, how long are we to tolerate this scum of party filth and beggerly corruption . . . to go thus with impunity?" In the heat of the moment, it was a question many were asking, including the wife of the President. Bache and his kind had the "malice and falsehood of Satan," wrote Abigail, whose dislike of the press, dating from the attacks on Adams by London newspapers a decade before, had nearly reached the breaking point.

For the first time, she began to fear for her husband. "Such lies and falsehoods were continually circulated," she wrote to Mary, "and base and incendiary letters sent to the house addressed to him, that I really have been alarmed for his personal safety. . . . With this temper in a city like this, materials for a mob might be brought together in ten minutes."

THE COUNTRY BEGAN to prepare for war. On April 8, 1798, Representative Samuel Sewall, a Federalist from Marblehead, Massachusetts, called on Congress to give the President all he had asked for and slowly, somewhat reluctantly, Congress swung into action. Measures were passed for arming merchant ships. Substantial funds—nearly $1 million—were voted for harbor fortifications and cannon foundries. In May a bill passed empowering United States warships to capture any French privateer or cruiser found in American waters.

"The merchant vessels along the wharf in this city begin to wear a warlike appearance," reported *Porcupine's Gazette*. "I dare say the French spies have been writing many, many a melancholy letter on the subject to their partisans who are laying off the coast."

Led by Gallatin, the Republicans mounted vigorous resistance, and nothing passed by large majorities. The "Executive Party," Gallatin argued, was creating the crisis only to "increase their power and to bind us by the treble chain of fiscal, legal and military despotism."

A bill for a "provisional army" was passed, but not before it was cut from 25,000 men to 10,000, which was still more than Adams had asked for or wanted. For though he was the greatest advocate of the navy of any American statesman of his generation, Adams deplored the idea of a standing army.

The rebirth of the navy—the "wooden walls" he wanted above all for defense of the country—and a new Department of the Navy, separate from the War Department, were his pride and joy. Little that he achieved as President would give him greater satisfaction, and with his choice of the first Secretary of the Navy, the able, energetic Benjamin Stoddert of Maryland, he brought into his administration the one truly loyal ally he had close at hand.

From every part of the country came hundreds of patriotic "addresses" to the President—expressions of loyalty and "readiness" from state legislatures, merchant groups, fraternal orders, college students, small towns and cities. Suddenly, Adams was awash in a great upswelling of patriotism. His popularity soared. Never had he known such attention and acclaim, which some thought surpassed even what Washington had known while in office.

Abigail, making her social calls about the city, found people stopping on the street to bow to her or lift their hats, something she had not experienced before. "People begin to see who have been their firm unshaken friends, steady to their interests and defenders of their rights and liberties," she wrote. "In short, we are now wonderfully popular except with Bache & Co., who in his paper calls the President, old, querulous, bald, blind, crippled, toothless Adams."

At the New Theater on Chestnut Street a young performer named Gilbert Fox was stopping the show each night singing "Hail Columbia," which was "The President's March" with new lyrics composed by Joseph Hopkinson of Philadelphia, son of a signer of the Declaration of Independence, Francis Hopkinson. Abigail was part of the full house the night of its premiere, April 25, when Fox was called back to sing it three more times and cheers from the audience, according to Abigail, might have been heard a mile away. "The theater, you know," she reminded Thomas, "has been called the pulse of the people."

A few nights later, with the President in the audience as Fox sang "Hail Columbia," the response was still more stupendous. The song was called for "over and over." The audience joined in the singing, danced in the aisles.

> Firm, united let us be. Rallying 'round our liberty.
> As a band of brothers joined,
> Peace and safety we shall find.

When a lone man tried to sing "Ciera," the marching song of the French Revolution, there were shouts to throw him out.

Even the High Federalists heartily approved of John Adams as they never had. The President, it was said, had awakened the nation from its "fatal stupor."

Adams himself, exhilarated by such unprecedented popularity, appeared to be as caught up in the spirit of the moment as anyone. Deeply touched by the patriotic addresses that kept pouring in, he spent hours laboring to answer them, as if obliged to respond to each and every one, and in some of what he wrote, he appeared ready to declare war anytime. "To arms then, my young friends," he said in reply to the youth of Boston, "to arms, especially by sea."

One May afternoon crowds lined Market Street as a thousand young men of Philadelphia marched two-by-two to the President's House, wearing in their hats, as a sign of their support, black cockades like those worn by Washington's troops in the Revolution, Adams received a delegation of them in the Levee Room wearing a dress uniform and sword.

Yet here and there in his replies to the patriotic addresses were to be found clear signs that peace, not war, remained his objective. "I should be happy in the friendship of France upon honorable conditions, under any government she may choose to assume," he said in a letter to the citizens of Hartford, Connecticut.

When he called for a day of fasting and prayer, he was roundly mocked in the Republican press, but on the day itself the churches were filled. To Vice President Jefferson, it was as though an evil spell had been cast over the capital. He called it a "reign of witches," and saw no difference between Adams and the "war party." The new navy, in Jefferson's view, was a colossal waste of money.

When a fight broke out between two street gangs wearing the black and tricolor cockades, the cavalry was called in. It had become dangerous to set foot outside the door at night, Jefferson wrote. "Politics and party hatreds destroy the happiness of every being here," he told his daughter Martha. "They seem, like salamanders, to consider fire as their element." One French emigré would remember people acting as though a French army might land at any moment. "Everybody was suspicious of everybody else; everywhere one saw murderous glances."

Benjamin Bache's house was assaulted, his windows smashed. It was rumored that French agents were plotting to burn the city. At the presidential mansion, Adams finally consented to have a sentry posted at the door.

What Adams's thoughts were through all this he did not record. His personal correspondence had dried up. He wrote almost no letters at all of the kind in which he customarily unburdened himself—in large part because Abigail was with him, but also because he had almost no time to himself.

By all signs, however, he was still of two minds in addressing the crisis. In the image of the American eagle, he still clutched both olive branch and arrows, even if, on occasion in his public poses, his head, unlike the eagle's, was turned to the arrows.

In his physical appearance, Adams was noticeably changed. He was uncharacteristically pale and had lost weight—"he falls away," Abigail noted. If not exactly toothless, as Bache said, he had suffered the loss of several more teeth, about which he was quite self-conscious. Abigail worried that he was smoking too many cigars and working to the point of collapse.

> Some afternoons he is called from his room twenty times in the course of it, to different persons, besides the hours devoted to the ministers of the different departments, the investigation necessary to be made of those persons who apply for offices or are recommended, the weighing the merits, and pretentions of different candidates for the same office, etc., etc., etc.

"I dare not say how really unwell he looks," she told Cotton Tufts. To Mary Cranch she confided, "I think sometimes that if the [Congress] does not rise and give the President respite, they will have Jefferson sooner than they wish."

Yet his spirits were fine, his resolve unwavering in the face of Talleyrand and the Directory. "Poor wretches," she wrote, "I suppose they want him to cringe, but he is made of oak instead of willow. He may be torn up by the roots, or break, but he will never bend."

ON JUNE 12, Adams received news that rocked him more than he dared show. A letter arrived from William Vans Murray, who had replaced John Quincy as minister at The Hague. Dated April 12, two months past, it revealed that while envoys Pinckney and Marshall had left Paris, Elbridge Gerry had remained behind. It seemed France wished to treat with Gerry alone.

For Adams, who had banked so much on Gerry against the advice of nearly everyone, it was a painful, infuriating turn of events, as once again Abigail reported to Mary.

Can it be possible, can it be believed that Talleyrand has thus declared and fascinated Mr. Gerry, that he should dare to take upon him such a responsibility? I cannot credit it, yet I know the sin which most easily besets him is obstinacy, and a mistaken policy. You may easily suppose how distressed the President is at this conduct, and the more so because he thought Gerry would certainly not go wrong, and he *acted* [on] his own judgment, against his counsellors, "who have been truer prophets than they wish themselves." Gerry means the good of his country, he means the peace of it, but he should consider it must not be purchased by national disgrace and dishonor. If he stays behind he is a ruined man in the estimation of his countrymen. This is all between ourselves.

How could Gerry possibly stay "among the wolves?" Mary would ask in response. She felt great distress for the President, she said, but then "he ought not have infallibility demanded of him."

On June 17, John Marshall arrived by ship in New York, and in another two days received a hero's welcome in Philadelphia. Marshall said nothing about going to war with France, however. Indeed, for all he had been through, Marshall was confident, he told Adams, that the French did not want a war with the United States.

Marshall was an impressive man, tall, solidly handsome, unmistakably intelligent, and without airs. Further, unlike all the others advising Adams, he had met with the French and strongly advocated caution and moderation. In effect, Marshall told Adams that there need not be a war, which had been Adams's instinctive sense all along. Marshall also informed him that Elbridge Gerry had remained behind in Paris because he had been told by Talleyrand that if he left, war would follow. Gerry had made his decision for the good of the country, aware of the scorn he would be subjected to at home.

If Adams had had any thought of asking for a declaration of war before Congress adjourned, he changed his mind. Instead, he sent a message of all of four sentences, the fourth and most important of which was: "I will never send another minister to France without assurances that he will be received, respected, and honored as the representative of a great, free, powerful, and independent nation."

But with the war clamor at a pitch, all talk of an alternative solution was limited to private discussion. More common was the opinion that a formal declaration of war could not come too soon, a view most strongly held by those nearest Adams, including his wife. In a letter to John Quincy, Abigail described how the town of Newburyport had taken upon itself to build a 20-gun warship to loan to the government, and that all down the coast other cities were following the example. A few weeks later she would write to him again of further progress with the "subscription" ships, her enthusiasm for the burgeoning navy clearly as great as that of her husband. Philadelphia had raised $80,000 to build a 36-gun frigate. New York had subscribed a nearly equal sum for a comparable ship. Baltimore had done the same. "Boston outstrips them all," she wrote.

Just months earlier Abigail had questioned the very idea of war. Now, one senses, had she been called upon to serve, she would have signed up and marched off without hesitation. "This city, which was formally torpid with indolence and fettered with Quakerism," she reported proudly, "has become *one* military school, and every morning the sound of the drum and fife lead forth, 'A Band of Brothers Joined.' " Writing to Mary Cranch, Abigail berated Congress for being so slow to vote a declaration of war. "Why, when we have the thing, should we boggle at the name?"

CONTRARY TO THE expectations of nearly everyone, Adams did not ask for a declaration of war against France. Had he done so, the Congress would assuredly have obliged. Instead, they turned their attention to the enemies at home.

Another Philadelphia summer had arrived. The temperature in the last week of June was in the 90s, "the weather so hot and close, the flies so tormenting," Abigail wrote, she hardly had energy to move. "Not a leaf stirs till nine or ten o'clock . . . It grows sickly, the city noisome." In two sweltering weeks, their popularity and confidence never higher, the Federalist majority in Congress passed into law extreme measures that Adams had not asked for or encouraged. But then neither did he oppose them, and their passage and his signature on them were to be rightly judged by history as the most reprehensible acts of his presidency. Still, the infamous Alien and Sedition Acts of 1798 must be seen in the context of the time, and the context was tumult and fear.

Adams later spoke of the Alien and Sedition Acts as war measures. It was how he saw them then, and how he chose to remember them. "I knew there was need enough of both, and therefore I consented to them," he would write in explanation long afterward, and at the time, the majority of Congress and most of the country were in agreement.

There was rampant fear of the enemy within. French emigrés in America, according to the French consul in Philadelphia, by now numbered 25,000 or more. Many were aristocrats who had fled the Terror; but the majority were refugees from the slave uprisings on the Caribbean island of San Domingo. In Philadelphia a number of French newspapers had been established. There were French booksellers, French schools, French boardinghouses, and French restaurants. The French, it seemed, were everywhere, and who was to measure the threat they posed in the event of war with France?

In addition to the French there were the "wild Irish," refugees from the Irish Rebellion of 1798 who were thought to include dangerous radicals and in any case, because of their anti-British sentiment, gladly joined ranks with the Republicans. James Callender was sometimes cited as a prime example of this type, apart from the fact that Callender was a Scot.

Beyond that, the United States was at war—declared or not—and there were in fact numbers of enemy agents operating in the country.

The Alien Acts included a Naturalization Act, which increased the required period of residence to qualify for citizenship from five to fourteen years, and the Alien Act, which granted the President the legal right to expel any foreigner he considered "dangerous." In the view of the Vice President, the Alien Act was something worthy of the ninth century. Jefferson and others imagined a tempestuous John Adams expelling foreigners by the shipload. As it was, they need not have worried. Adams never invoked the law and this despite the urging of Secretary of State Pickering, who did indeed favor massive deportations.

Of greater consequence was the Sedition Act, which made any "False, scandalous, and malicious" writing against the government, Congress, or the President, or any attempt "to excite against them . . . the hatred of the good people of the United States, or to stir up sedition," crimes punishable by fine and imprisonment. Though it was clearly a violation of the First Amendment to the Constitution guaranteeing freedom of speech, its Federalist proponents in Congress insisted, like Adams, that it was a war measure, and an improvement on the existing common law in that proof of the truth of the libel could be used as a legitimate defense. Still, the real and obvious intent was to stifle the Republican press, and of those arrested and convicted under the law, nearly all were Republican editors.

Such stalwart, respected Federalists as Senators Theodore Sedgwick of Massachusetts and James Lloyd of Maryland were strongly in support of the Sedition Act. Noah Webster, editor, author, lexicographer, and staunch Federalist, declared it time to stop newspaper editors from libeling those with whom they disagreed, and to his friend Timothy Pickering wrote to urge that the new law be strictly enforced.

Even George Washington privately expressed the view that some publications were long overdue punishment for their lies and unprovoked attacks on the leaders of the union.

Vice President Jefferson, having no wish to be present for the inevitable passage of the Sedition Act, or anything more that might take place in such an atmosphere, quietly packed and went home to Monti-cello.

There were some Federalists who had mixed feelings about the Sedition Act, and John Marshall was openly opposed. Were he in Congress, Marshall said, he would have voted against it.

Though Adams appears to have said nothing on the subject at the time, it is hard to imagine him not taking a measure of satisfaction from the prospect of the tables turned on those who had tormented him for so long. And if Adams was reluctant to express his views, Abigail was not. Bache and his kind would inevitably provoke measures to silence them, she had predicted to Mary Cranch. They were "so criminal" that they ought to be brought to court. "Yet daringly do the vile incendiaries keep up in Bache's paper the most wicked and base, violent and culminating abuse," she wrote another day, sure that "nothing will have effect until Congress passes a Sedition Bill."

It was not uncommon in Philadelphia—or in Massachusetts—to hear talk of the unrivaled influence Abigail Adams had on her husband and of her political sense overall. Fisher Ames once observed that she was "as complete a politician as any lady in the old French Court." That Adams valued and trusted her judgment ahead of that of any of his department heads there is no question, and she could well have been decisive in persuading Adams to support the Sedition Act. "Bearing neither malice or ill will towards anyone, not even the most deluded . . . I wish the laws of our country were competent to punish the stirrer up of sedition, the writer and printer of base and unfounded calumny," she wrote, and the key word to her was "unfounded." She wanted proven lies to be judged unacceptable. This, she was sure, would "contribute as much to the peace and harmony of our country as any measure, and in times like the present, a more careful and attentive watch ought to be kept over foreigners."

But it was also possible that Adams needed no persuading, and that in what she wrote to Mary Cranch, Abigail was speaking for both of them. Nor, importantly, was her influence always decisive, as shown by his choice of Elbridge Gerry as an envoy to France and, most importantly, his continued reluctance to declare war.

ON JULY 2, to meet the cost of the military buildup, the House voted a first direct tax on the people, a tax on land. Also, on July 2, to the surprise of many, Adams nominated George Washington as commander-in-chief of the new provisional army. "It was one of those strokes which the prospect and exigency of the times required," wrote Abigail, "and which the President determined upon without consultation." In addition, Adams submitted a list of proposed general officers that included Alexander Hamilton, but also several Republicans, most notably Aaron Burr, as well as his own son-in-law, Colonel Smith.

In a matter of days, Congress abrogated the French-American treaties of 1778, created a permanent Marine Corps, passed the Sedition Act, and approved the nomination of Washington as supreme commander. War fever was at a pitch.

On July 9, Secretary McHenry left for Mount Vernon by the express mail stage carrying Washington's commission and a letter from Adams saying that were it in his power to appoint Washington President, he would gladly do so.

On July 16, Congress adjourned and departed the city with a rush. By July 25, when the Adamses set off, people were already dying in what would become the worst yellow fever epidemic since 1793.

I V

THE YEAR 1798, the most difficult and consequential year of John Adams's presidency, was to provide him no respite. His stay at Quincy would be longer even than the year before, but the stress of the unde-clared war—the Quasi-War, as it came to be known, or Half-War, as he called it—combined with the threatening ambitions of Alexander Hamil-ton and growing dissension within Adams's own cabinet, filled his days with frustration and worry. There was precious little peace to be found at Peacefield in the summer of 1798, and especially as Abigail fell so ill that she very nearly died.

The first days at home were supposed to have been an even greater delight than usual, for unbeknown to Adams, a huge improvement to the house had taken place in their absence. An entire wing with a spacious parlor and a library above, had been added to the east end, and the whole house "new painted" inside and out. Abigail had secretly arranged it all that spring through Cotton Tufts, as a surprise for Adams. It was a "wren's house" no more. She had doubled its size, much as Jefferson had done at Monticello, except on a considerably smaller scale and with the difference that she did it entirely to her own wishes, paying for it out of money she saved from household expenses at Philadelphia, and never asking for Adams's permission or opinion. "I meant to have it all done snug ... before I come," she had told Mary Cranch in April. "I know the President will be glad when it is done, but he can never bear to trouble himself about anything of the kind, and he has not the taste for it."

The parlor was for Abigail, the second-floor library, or "Book room," for Adams, and like the parlor, it was to have a handsome fireplace and windows on three sides. It must accommodate all his books "in regular order and be a pleasant room for the President to do business in," Abigail had directed.

But in late June, just as the project was nearly finished, a Quincy neighbor on his way through Philadelphia stopped to pay his respects and revealed the whole secret to Adams, who, Abigail was happy to report, responded with a hearty laugh.

Whatever pleasure they might have found in their expanded quarters was foreclosed before they ever reached home. Abigail was taken ill on the journey and confined to her bed from the day they arrived, August 8.

She was "very weak," Adams wrote to Oliver Wolcott. Some days later he reported to Timothy Pickering, "Mrs. Adams is extremely low and in great danger." In fact, she was as sick as she had ever been and it was with difficulty that Adams was able to concentrate on anything else.

Nabby, who with her daughter Caroline had come for an extended visit, hoping to be of help, wrote to John Quincy that it had become a different house. "The illness of our dear mother has cast a gloom over the face of everything here, and it scarce seems like home without her enlivening cheerfulness."

To Secretary of War McHenry, Adams would describe it as "the most gloomy summer" he had known, but he could as easily have called it one of the most gloomy passages of his life, second only to his own siege of illness and despair in Amsterdam. Writing to George Washington later, after two months at home, Adams would say that Abigail's fate was still very precarious "and mine in consequence of it."

Yet to judge from the volume of correspondence, the number and variety of issues he dealt with, he worked no less diligently than usual, spending long hours at his desk in the new library across the hall from Abigail's sickroom. Official reports from Philadelphia, dispatches from department heads, documents requiring his signature, requests for pardons, applications for jobs, reports of all kinds, arrived in assorted bundles, daily by post rider. Decisions were called for on matters large and small. Benjamin Rush asked that his brother be considered for the Supreme Court. There was a request for the President's approval to build a lighthouse at Cape Hatteras, a request from Secretary Wolcott for authority to borrow up to $5,000,000 on behalf of the United States, reports from Wolcott on the yellow fever epidemic. Secretary McHenry sent an extended review, numbing in detail, of expenditures required for the Department of War. (*"I have supposed that the items in the table of the Quarter Master's supplies and contingent expenses for the eight additional companies and privates to the old establishment and for the six additional companies of dragoons may be covered by the appropriations for the original army and that the 600 thousand dollars stated by the Quarter Master's Department for the 12 regiments will procure all the camp equipage not provided for by the table."*) Nor was there any letup in the stream of patriotic addresses.

Adams struggled to read it all and respond. "Wooden walls have been

my favorite system of warfare and defense for three and twenty years,"
he wrote in reply to an address from the Boston Marine Society. "Americans in general, cultivators as well as merchants and marines, begin to
look to that source of security and protection." After reading Wolcott's
report on the ravages of yellow fever at the capital, Adams sent an anonymous contribution of $500.

Most pressing was an unfortunate dispute that developed between
Adams and Washington. At the heart of the issue was whether Alexander
Hamilton should be made the second-highest-ranking officer in the new
army, as Washington preferred and as Hamilton desperately desired.

When McHenry had gone off by express stage to Mount Vernon in
early July, he had carried, in addition to Washington's commission from
the President, a letter from Hamilton about which Adams was told nothing. "The arrangement of the army may demand your particular attention," Hamilton wrote, referring to Washington's choice of a general
staff. In this regard Washington was advised that the judgment of the
President ought not to be a consideration. "The President," Hamilton
wrote, "has no relative ideas, and his prepossessions on military subjects
in reference to such a point are of the wrong sort," meaning, presumably,
that Adams cared more for the navy than the army.

The view that Adams was unsuited to prepare the nation for war and
that Hamilton, by contrast, was the ideal choice for second-in-command
was shared by McHenry and Secretary Pickering alike. Indeed, Pickering had already said as much in a letter to Washington.

Thus, both the Secretary of War and the Secretary of State were
secretly campaigning for Hamilton, supplying him with inside information, and undermining the intentions of their President, whom they saw
riding for a fall. Sending Hamilton copies of secret government documents that summer, McHenry attached a note saying, "Do not, I pray
you, in writing or otherwise betray the confidence which has induced me
to deal thus with you or make extracts or copies. . . . Return the papers
immediately."

Washington had accepted his commission in an entirely cordial letter
to Adams, but with the understanding that as head of the new army he
could choose his own principal officers. Then he made known his intention to name Hamilton as second-in-command, with the rank of major
general. Since no one expected Washington to take the field at his age, or

to command except in name, the proposed arrangement meant, in effect, that Hamilton was to be in command—it was to be Hamilton's army.

In a letter that went off from Quincy to McHenry on August 29, Adams wrote that Washington had conducted himself with "perfect honor and consistency." But the "power and authority are in the President," Adams reminded his Secretary of War. "There has been too much intrigue in this business," he added, suggesting he knew more, or suspected more, than he appeared to. In a letter to Oliver Wolcott that he most likely never sent, Adams said angrily that were he to consent to the appointment of Hamilton to second rank under Washington, he would consider it the most reprehensible action of his life. "His talents I respect. His character—I leave . . ."

But Washington had left Adams no way out. To raise the new army Washington's prestige was essential, as Hamilton, McHenry, Pickering, and Wolcott all understood. On September 30, Adams relinquished the final say to Washington.

September 30 was a Sunday, which makes it unlikely that the letter went off until the following day, October 1, the same day Elbridge Gerry arrived home from France, bringing news that gave a very different cast to the whole picture. Gerry's ship appeared off Boston that morning. Losing no time, he dispatched a letter to Adams before the ship docked. But whether Gerry's letter reached Adams before Adams's letter went off to McHenry with the morning post is not known.

The French wanted peace, Gerry reported.

Three days later, on Thursday, October 4, Gerry presented himself at Quincy, and he and Adams settled in for a long private talk.

In his few days ashore Gerry had been thoroughly ostracized in Boston. "Not a hat was moved" as he walked up State Street, according to one account from the time. Angry crowds shouted insults outside his Cambridge home. But the welcome from Adams was warm, and the more Gerry talked, the more Adams must have realized that the current had turned his way at last. Talleyrand, Gerry assured him, was ready to treat seriously with the United States.

It was a critical moment in Adams's presidency. Among other things, Gerry had more than justified Adams's confidence in him. What he was telling Adams, to be sure, was what Adams desperately wanted to hear. The last thing in the world Adams wished to do was to lead the country into a needless war. But more to the point, he judged quite correctly that Gerry was telling the truth.

John Marshall had said much the same thing, and so had John Quincy in some of his correspondence with his father, but as Adams was to write, the assurances of Gerry—"my own ambassador"—were "more positive, more explicit, and decisive."

Gerry's letter of October 1, Adams later said, "confirmed these [earlier] assurances beyond all doubt in my mind, and his conversations with me at my own house in Quincy, if anything further had been wanting, would have corroborated the whole."

It was the week after Gerry's return when a letter arrived from Washington. Written on September 25, it did not reach Adams until October 8. Were he to be denied the deciding voice in the selection of his general staff, Washington informed the President, he would resign his commission.

Adams sent off an immediate reply, agreeing to Washington's wishes. As he had accepted Washington's cabinet in the interest of unanimity, so he now accepted Washington's choice of Hamilton. But he also had reason to believe now that Hamilton and the army might not be needed at all.

As a matter of form, he reminded Washington a bit lamely that by the Constitution it was the President who had the authority to determine the rank of officers. Washington promoted Hamilton to be inspector general.

In the contest of who was in charge, Adams, it seemed, had been put in his place, outflanked not so much by Washington as by his own cabinet, and ultimately Hamilton, which left Adams feeling bruised and resentful. But at the same time, it gave Hamilton, and those in Adams's cabinet whose first loyalty was to Hamilton, an inflated sense of their own importance and authority.

From continued discussion with Gerry at Quincy and from new dispatches from William Vans Murray at The Hague, Adams became convinced that Gerry's conduct in Paris had not only been proper, but courageous. On October 20, writing to Pickering to ask for suggestions on the content of his forthcoming message to Congress, Adams made it plain that he was thinking of sending a new minister to France "who may be ready to embark . . . as soon as . . . the President shall receive from the Directory satisfactory assurance that he shall be received and entitled to all the prerogatives and privileges of the general laws of nations." Further, he offered a list of those he had in mind for the assignment that included Patrick Henry and William Vans Murray.

Then, in a letter to his Secretary of War expressing his full support for Washington's judgment, Adams added two pointed observations. Maintaining armies was costly business and could become quite unpopular in the absence of an enemy to fight, he reminded McHenry. Of what possible use could a large army be, Adams was saying, if a French invasion never took place? In closing, he observed, "At present there is no more prospect of seeing a French army here than there is in heaven."

ABIGAIL'S ILLNESS dragged on. She never left her sickbed, her "dying bed," as she said. Talk of sickness and death—of insomnia, melancholy, her persistent, baffling fevers—dominated the domestic scene, just as sickness and death filled the newspapers, week after week, as yellow fever spread in Boston, New York, Baltimore, and worst of all in Philadelphia.

By September nearly 40,000 people had evacuated Philadelphia. Yet the newspapers continued to report more than a hundred new cases a day. "The best skill of our physicians . . . have proved unequal to the contest of this devouring poison," reported the *Aurora*. By the time the plague ran its course in Philadelphia, more than 3,000 lost their lives, including, as the Adamses were stunned to read, the mayor of the city and both Bache of the *Aurora*, who had died on September 10 at age twenty-nine, and his arch nemesis, Fenno of the *Gazette of the United States*, who died just days before. The list of victims also included four of the servants at the President's House, as Abigail was duly informed.

The melancholy that beset her was unrelenting, suggesting the fever she suffered may have been malaria, but she was also distressed over further troubles within the family.

Before leaving on his diplomatic assignment abroad, John Quincy had left his savings, some $2,000, in the trust of his brother Charles. In the time since, however, Charles had managed to lose nearly all of it through bad investments, and then kept silent about what had happened, refusing to answer John Quincy's queries, in the hope that, with a little more time, he might somehow recover at least part of the money. Only that summer had the truth become known within the family, and it was devastating to both parents, but especially to Abigail, who had so long and so diligently managed the family affairs.

"I have not enjoyed one moment's comfort for upwards of two years on this account," Charles wrote to his mother in midsummer. "My sleep has been disturbed, and my waking hours embittered."

"He is not at peace with himself," she would write later to John Quincy, during her convalescence, "and his conduct does not meet my wishes.

> He has an amiable wife . . . two lovely children. I hope my letters will in time have their effect. I have discharged my duty I hope faith-fully, but my dying bed was embittered . . . with distress for the only child whose conduct ever gave me pain.

Abigail was bedridden at Quincy altogether for eleven weeks. It was early November before she was well enough to come downstairs, and it was early November before Philadelphia was declared once more free of yellow fever.

On November 12, leaving Abigail behind, Adams headed off in the presidential coach behind two spirited horses and accompanied by his young nephew William Shaw—Billy Shaw, as he was known—a recent graduate of Harvard who had been lame since birth and had lately become the President's secretary.

"I strive to divert the melancholy thoughts of our separation, and pray you do the same," Adams wrote to Abigail at the end of his first day on the road.

CHAPTER TEN

STATESMAN

Great is the guilt of an unnecessary war.

~John Adams

I

ADAMS WAS ON THE MOVE AGAIN, gobbling up the miles. The weather was clear and cool, the road dry. "Our horses go like birds," he wrote. Some days they made thirty miles. "We glided along unforeseen, unexpected, and have avoided all noise, show, pomp, and parade," he reported to Abigail from Connecticut.

He wrote nearly a letter a day. His teeth and gums ached; one side of his face was badly swollen. Yet, he assured her, he was neither "fretful nor peevish." Indeed, the speed at which he moved, his joy in horses that could fly like birds, suggest he was heading for the capital knowing there was a way out of the impasse he had faced since taking office—that out of the gloomiest of times at home had come a first real sense that he might succeed after all in his main objective.

A recurring rumor did much for his spirits. It was said a British fleet under Admiral Horatio Nelson had overwhelmed the French off the coast of Egypt. "Nelson's victory is mightily believed along the road," Adams wrote. If true, the chance of a French invasion of America had all but vanished.

There was snow in New York and the horses required a day's rest. Adams stopped to see his son Charles, but of this he wrote nothing.

Crossing New Jersey, the horses flying again, they made forty-five miles in a day, to arrive on November 24 in Philadelphia, where it was known for certain that Nelson had destroyed the French fleet at the battle of the Nile, four months earlier on August 1.

The city was in a bustle. Throngs of people were returning to resume daily life, opening boarded-up shops, airing out houses, scrubbing everything with a will, now that the epidemic had passed. The weather was brisk. Congress was back, and to the delight of the city, George Washington had returned and could be seen coming and going from temporary headquarters at a boarding house on Eighth Street.

The general had entered Philadelphia on November 10 with full military flare, on horseback and in uniform, and accompanied by cavalry. "Almost the whole of the military corps were drawn up on the commons to receive him," reported the *Aurora*, which had suspended publication following the death of Benjamin Bache, but was back in business under Bache's wife, Margaret. "This morning arrived in town the Chief who unites all hearts," exclaimed another paper, the *American Daily Advertiser*.

While the war fever of summer had by no means vanished like the yellow fever, the spirit of opinion heard in the shops and taverns, and within the councils of government, was noticeably more moderate, and in large part because of the British victory at the Nile. Albert Gallatin wrote to his wife that he felt an honorable accommodation with France was now within the power of the administration, perhaps even "certain."

Soon after his arrival, Adams met with a Philadelphia physician named George Logan, who had recently returned from France. As a Quaker and ardent Republican, Logan was not the sort of man Adams was known to favor. To Federalist war hawks he was contemptible, since he had presumed to conduct his own peace mission to France. Roundly castigated as a dangerous, possibly disloyal meddler, Logan found it impossible to get a fair hearing within the administration. When he called on the Secretary of State, to say he had been told by high officials in the French government that France was ready to make peace, Pickering gave him short shrift and showed him to the door. To see George Washington, Logan had accompanied a Philadelphia clergyman when he called at the house on Eighth Street. But Washington had refused to speak to Logan, directing what few comments he had to the clergyman only.

Adams, however, received Logan courteously, and tea was served. He had conversed directly with Talleyrand and a principal member of the Directory, Logan said, and they had expressed the wish to settle all disputes with America.

Adams showed displeasure only once, when Logan insisted that the Directory was ready to receive a new American minister. According to Logan, Adams leaped from his chair, saying that only if a Republican were sent would the French receive him. "But I'll do no such thing," Adams said. "I'll send whom I please."

"And whomever you do please to send will be received," Logan assured him.

Whether he knew it at the time, Logan had made a strong impression. "I had no reason to believe him a corrupt character, or deficient in memory or veracity," Adams later wrote.

Secretaries Pickering and McHenry remained certain that war was inevitable. Nonetheless, they joined the consensus among the President's advisers that, given the mood of the country and the Congress, a declaration of war at this point would be "inexpedient." But it was also the unanimous conclusion of the cabinet that another mission to France would be an act of humiliation and was therefore unacceptable. If there were to be peace overtures, they must come from France. Let a French mission cross the ocean this time.

On December 7, 1798, Adams walked to Congress Hall, and in the presence of Generals Washington and Hamilton, Secretary of State Pickering, and both houses of Congress, he affirmed again America's need for defensive strength and America's desire for peace. The speech had been written by Pickering and Wolcott, and except for the addition of one phrase, Adams had made few changes. It must, he said, be "left with France . . . to take the requisite step" of assuring that any American mission sent to Paris would be properly received. So while preparation for war would continue, Adams had signaled that the door to peace remained ajar. It was only a question of French intent and sincerity.

The speech infuriated the Republicans and the Vice President, and no less was the anger of the High Federalists in Congress, who had expected a declaration of war. If Adams lacked the fortitude to take the step, then Congress would, they declared. But their efforts failed. Congress was not inclined to declare war.

The martial ambitions of the inspector general were undampened, however. With his new command, Hamilton dreamed now of grand conquest with himself riding at the head of a new American army.

The idea was to "liberate" Spanish Florida and Louisiana, possibly all of Spanish America, in a bold campaign combining a British fleet and American troops. First proposed by an impassioned apostle of Spanish-American freedom, Francesco de Miranda of Venezuela, the scheme had been around for years. Adams had learned of it and dismissed it out of hand. "We are friends with Spain," he had told Pickering. But the British had shown interest, and in secret Hamilton had lately become involved, seeing possibilities for national empire and personal glory beyond the vision of lesser men. In a letter to one of his generals in Georgia, Hamilton stressed the need for a buildup of military supplies. "This you perceive, looks to offensive operations," he wrote. "If we are to engage in war, our game will be to attack where we can. France is not to be considered as separate from her ally [Spain]. Tempting objects will be within our grasp."

Adams knew in general, if not in detail, what Hamilton, Pickering, and others were up to and would later speak of it as a colossal absurdity. "The man is stark mad or I am," he would remember thinking of Hamilton. But at the time, he kept his own counsel, waiting to make his move. He wanted all "to be still and calm," and told his department heads no more than they needed to know. For he understood now that their first loyalty was not to him.

For someone supposedly suspicious by nature, Adams had been inordinately slow to suspect the worst of his closest advisers, and to face the obvious truth that keeping Washington's cabinet had been a mistake. Still, somehow, he must avoid a war and keep Hamilton from gaining the upper hand with his "mad" schemes. As Abigail had warned the summer before, "That man would . . . become a second Bonaparte."

AT THE NAVY DEPARTMENT and the President's House that December, with a foot of snow in the streets outside and sleigh bells sounding, Adams, Gerry, McHenry, Secretary of the Navy Stoddert, and others gathered about large maps of the West Indies. Four squadrons, twenty-one ships in total, virtually the whole of the American naval force, were now assigned to the Caribbean. The largest squadron, which included the heavy frigates *United States* and *Constitution*, was under Commodore John Barry, who was admonished in his orders that "a spirit of enterprise and adventure cannot be too much encouraged in the officers under your command. . . . We have nothing to dread but unactivity."

The fleet was to cruise the Lesser Antilles, from St. Christopher (St. Kitts) to Tobago. San Domingo (Haiti) was to have increasing importance. Toussaint L'Ouverture, leader of the slave rebellion on San Domingo, had written to Adams to suggest they become allies. Desperate for food for his starving troops, Toussaint wanted the American embargo lifted from the former French colony. In effect, he wanted recognition of the black republic, and Adams was interested. Thus, in December, a representative from Toussaint, Joseph Bunel, dined with Adams, marking the first time a man of African descent was the dinner guest of an American President.

American ships would be welcome and protected in all San Domingo ports, Adams was told. John Quincy had earlier written his father to say he hoped something could be done for Toussaint, that he wished to see San Domingo "free and independent." And with Secretary Pickering strongly of the same mind, Adams responded promptly. Commodore Barry was instructed to show himself "with the greatest part of the fleet at Cape François, to Genl. Toussaint, who has a great desire to see some ships of war belonging to America." And the issue of de facto recognition, "Toussaint's clause," would go before Congress.

General Washington was rarely seen. He was working seven days a week with Hamilton drawing up plans for the army, reviewing applications, and choosing qualified officers for twelve new regiments that were all still largely on paper. Satisfied with what had been accomplished, Washington departed the city for the last time on December 14.

MUCH HAD BEEN SAID of Washington's cheerful demeanor. Even the *Aurora* commented on his "good health and spirits," while Adams, by contrast, looked drawn and weary and was seldom cheerful. The old streak of irritability, his single flaw, according to Abigail, had been made worse by the presidency, as he himself acknowledged. He was weary from work, "weary of conjectures," as he said. "If you come on, you must expect to find me cross," he had written to her in fair warning. It was not just that the work was unending, but that it was so tiresome. "A peck of troubles in a large bundle of papers often in a handwriting almost illegible comes every day . . . thousands of sea letters . . . commissions and patents to sign. No company. No society. Idle, unmeaning ceremony."

Adams's earlier proposal of Colonel Smith for the general staff had been turned down by the Senate (as had his proposed commission for Aaron Burr). Smith was unacceptable, Adams was told, because he was a bankrupt. This Adams had not denied, but praised his son-in-law as a brave and able soldier who had more than proven himself in the Revolution. Against his better judgment, Adams agreed to try again, this time nominating Smith for a colonel's commission, which in spite of "warm opposition," the Senate approved.

In a letter to Smith, telling him the news, Adams made clear what an embarrassment the whole business had been for him, and warned Smith bluntly that, if unchecked, his pride and extravagances would bring ruin.

His own children would be his undoing, Adams complained to Abigail. "My daughter and son [Charles] bring down my gray hairs with sorrow to the grave, if I don't arouse my philosophy. The daughter, too, without a fault. Unfortunate daughter! Unhappy child!"

Snow fell again for several days. Christmas morning dawned clear and bright, and Adams succeeded in rousing his philosophy to a considerable degree. There was no mistaking his age or the burdens of the presidency, he wrote to Abigail. "I am old, old, very old and never shall be very well—certainly while in this office, for the drudgery of it is too much for my years and strength." But he took joy in the day. "It is Christmas and a fine day," he wrote. He had a cold, but was over it now. "I sleep well, appetite is good, work hard, conscience is neat and easy. Content to live and willing to die. . . . Hoping to do a little good."

THE VICE PRESIDENT, having departed Monticello on December 18 and traveled "dreadful" winter roads north by public coach, arrived at Philadelphia that same Christmas morning in time for breakfast at the Francis Hotel. Jefferson had been absent for six months, during which he had raised no voice as head of the Republican party, but had kept extremely busy, writing letters and secretly drafting a set of resolutions to be introduced in the legislature of Kentucky. Written in response to the Alien and Sedition Acts, Jefferson's Kentucky Resolutions declared that each state had a "natural right" to nullify federal actions it deemed unconstitutional. The states were thus to be the arbiters of federal authority. At the same time, James Madison undertook a version of his own resolutions for Virginia.

The Kentucky Resolutions, which had passed in November, were an open challenge to the authority of the central government and a measure both of Jefferson's revulsion over the Alien and Sedition Acts and the seriousness with which he regarded states' rights. Possibly he failed to see the dire threat to the union embodied in what he had written, but a letter he wrote to Madison strongly suggests otherwise. He was confident, Jefferson said, that the American people with their "good sense" would "rally with us round the true principles of the federal compact," but, he wrote in chilling conclusion, he was "determined, were we to be disappointed in this, to sever ourselves from the union we so much value, rather than give up the rights of self-government."

Tormented by the thought of his old enemy Hamilton riding high as inspector general and federal power in the grip of a "military enclave," Jefferson saw the country on the verge of civil war. He feared a federal army under Hamilton might march on the South at any time. His advice to Madison and other close associates was to stay calm and quiet. "Firmness on our part, but passive firmness, is the true course," Jefferson cautioned after returning to Philadelphia.

He was distressed also about the bill before Congress to lift the embargo on San Domingo and commence trade with the "rebellious Negroes under Toussaint." When "Toussaint's clause" was passed, Jefferson noted bleakly, "We may expect therefore black crews and . . . missionaries" pouring "into the Southern states. . . . If this combustion can be introduced among us under any veil whatever, we have to fear it."

It had been more than a year since the President and Vice President had spoken to each other. Except for passing pleasantries at a few ceremonial occasions, conversation and correspondence between them had ceased. Had they been able to compare notes, they would have discovered how much more they shared in common than met the eye or than either had any idea.

Both complained privately of poor health. They were each extremely lonely and longed for home. Much of what Jefferson wrote to his daughters from Philadelphia in the opening weeks of the New Year, 1799, might have been taken from Adams's letters to Abigail. Jefferson battled a head cold and suffered from inflammation of the eyes. "The circle of our nearest connections is the only one in which a faithful and lasting affection can be found," he wrote to Polly. And in a letter to Martha he could hardly have sounded more like Adams in his own days as Vice President: "Environed here in scenes of constant torment, malice, and obliquy, worn down in a station where no effort to render service can avail anything, I feel not that existence is a blessing, but when something recalls my mind to my family or farm."

Had Jefferson known Adams's mind at this juncture, he would have been quite surprised. Most striking was their common dislike and fear of Hamilton. The worries Jefferson had about Hamilton's threat to the nation were more than matched by Adams's, as Adams revealed in private conversation with Elbridge Gerry at the President's House. "[Adams] thought Hamilton and a party were endeavoring to get an army on foot to give Hamilton the command of it, and thus to proclaim a regal government and place Hamilton as the head of it, and prepare the way for a province of Great Britain," wrote Gerry. Plainly, Adams feared a military coup by the second "Bonaparte," which goes far to explain what was soon to take place.

Closing his Christmas letter to Abigail, Adams said, "I write to you nothing about public affairs because it would be useless to copy the newspapers which you read. And I can say nothing more."

How much was implied by this, she could only try to imagine.

Three weeks later, in mid-January, to Adams's utmost joy, his son Thomas, now twenty-seven, arrived in Philadelphia after four years abroad. "Thomas is my delight," he wrote. It was also of no small consequence that Thomas carried word from John Quincy assuring his father that the French were ready to negotiate.

II

ON MONDAY, February 18, 1799, Adams made his move. Having consulted no one, and without advice from Abigail, he took the most decisive action of his presidency. Indeed, of all the brave acts of his career—his defense of the British soldiers in the Boston Massacre trials, the signing of the Declaration of Independence, his crossing the Atlantic on the *Boston* in the winter of 1778, the high risks of his mission to Holland—one brief message sent to the United States Senate was perhaps the bravest.

It was carried by a courier to the second-floor Senate Chamber, where an astonished Vice President interrupted the business on the floor to read it aloud:

> Always disposed and ready to embrace every plausible appearance of probability of preserving or restoring tranquility, I nominate William Vans Murray, our minister resident at The Hague, to be minister plenipotentiary of the United States to the French Republic.
>
> If the Senate shall advise and consent to his appointment, effectual care shall be taken in his instructions that he shall not go to France without direct and unequivocal assurances from the French government, signified by their Minister of Foreign Relations, that he shall be received in character, shall enjoy the privileges attached to his character by the law of nations, and that a minister of equal rank, title, and powers shall be appointed to treat with him, to discuss and conclude all controversies between the two Republics by a new treaty.

The "war-monger" who the summer before had refused to declare war had declared, if not peace, then, at least, that the door to peace was now wide open.

Republicans were astounded. Federalists were momentarily speechless, then filled with "surprise, indignation, grief, and disgust." Particularly galling to them was the fact that it was Jefferson who read the message.

The Secretary of State was enraged. The "*honor* of the country is prostrated in the dust—God grant that its safety may not be in jeopardy," Timothy Pickering wrote to George Washington. In a letter to William Vans Murray, Pickering would declare "every real patriot . . . was thunderstruck." Adams, he said, was "suffering the torments of the damned." "I beg you to be assured that it is *wholly his own act*," Pickering reported to Hamilton.

Senator Theodore Sedgwick of Massachusetts, who had greatly admired Adams, worked for his election, and thought he had thus far played "a noble part" as President, felt personally betrayed. Barely able to contain his fury, he wrote of the "vain, jealous, and half frantic mind" of John Adams, a man ruled "by caprice alone." "Had the foulest heart and the basest head in the world been permitted to select the most embarrassing and ruinous measure, perhaps it would have been precisely the one which has been adopted."

Another riled Federalist, Robert G. Harper of South Carolina, Hamilton's chief spokesman in the House, privately expressed the hope that on Adams's way home to Quincy, his horses might run away with him and break his neck.

Hamilton himself allowed that if anything coming from John Adams could astonish, certainly this had.

To Thomas Jefferson it was the "event of events," but strangely—regrettably—he was unable to accept what Adams had done at face value, or to give him any credit. Rather, Jefferson took pleasure in the "mortification" of the Federalists, which proved, he said, that war was always their intent. To Madison he wrote that Adams had only made the nomination "hoping that his friends in the Senate would take on their own shoulders the odium of rejecting it."

In the *Aurora*, Margaret Bache and her new editor, William Duane, would concede only that Adams deserved "fair applause" for prudence.

But for all the indignant fuming of the High Federalists, no motions were made in the Senate for a resolution opposing a new mission to France. When a Senate committee led by Sedgwick came to see Adams a few days later, it was to object only to the choice of Murray, who was thought too young, not "strong enough," for an assignment of such importance. They wished to have the nomination retracted, which Adams refused to do. Murray was a man of experience and ability through whom communications with Talleyrand were already established, Adams answered. Further, Murray had the advantage of being on the scene.

Accounts differ whether the meeting was amicable or acrimonious, but a compromise resulted in any event. Instead of Murray alone serving as minister plenipotentiary, Adams nominated Patrick Henry and Chief Justice Oliver Ellsworth to join Murray as envoys to France, making a commission of three. The Senate immediately confirmed the appointments and a day later, March 4, Congress adjourned. Afterward, when Patrick Henry declined for reasons of health, Adams chose another southerner, the Federalist governor of North Carolina, William Davie.

In Massachusetts, infuriated Federalists were saying that had the President's "old woman" been with him in Philadelphia none of this would have happened—she being the more stouthearted of the two. "This was pretty saucy," Abigail wrote to John of the gossip, "but the old woman can tell them they are mistaken." She considered his decision a "master stroke."

By the second week of March, as Adams was preparing to leave for Quincy, word reached Philadelphia that the American frigate *Constellation*, under Captain Thomas Truxtun, had captured the French frigate *L'Insurgent*, after a battle near the island of Nevis in the Leewards, the first major engagement of the undeclared war at sea. Where would it all end, people were asking in Philadelphia. But Adams was anything but alarmed or displeased. Of Captain Truxtun he wrote, "I wish all other officers had as much zeal."

While his entire political standing, his reputation as President, were riding on his willingness to make peace, Adams was no less ardent for defense. In fact, he was convinced that peace was attainable only as a consequence of America's growing naval strength. To Secretary Stoddert he even proposed that some of the fast new ships might be used to cruise the coast of France.

Nor do I think we ought to wait a moment to know whether the French mean to give us any proofs of their desire to conciliate with us. I am for pursuing all the measure of defense which the laws authorize us to adopt, especially at sea.

. . .

CONVINCED he could run the government as well from Quincy as at Philadelphia, Adams stretched his stay at home from late March to September, fully seven months. From the views expressed by his vociferous critics, it was hard to say which annoyed them more, his presence at the capital or his absence. At worst, his absence seemed an arrogant abdication of responsibility. At best, it seemed a kind of eccentric scholarly detachment.

Some moderate Federalists and old friends warned Adams he could be doing himself and the country great harm by remaining too long in seclusion. "The public sentiment is very much against your being so much away from the seat of government. They did not elect your officers, nor do they . . . think them equal to govern without your presence and control," wrote a correspondent who feared a plot against Adams could be hatching in his absence. "I speak the truth when I say that your real friends wish you to be with your officers, because the public impression is that the government will be better conducted."

There had been criticism of his long absence the year before, irrespective of Abigail's illness, but the criticism now was greater, and with reason. Adams's presence at the center of things was what the country rightfully expected, and could indeed have made a difference.

But stay he did at Peacefield, and to his mind with more than sufficient justification. Washington, too, had spent long sessions at Mount Vernon (though never for seven months), and with Philadelphia hit by yellow fever every summer and fall, the government barely functioned there for several months. He could accomplish his work quite as readily at home as at the capital, so long as Congress was not in session. Were he ever unable to appear when Congress was sitting, Adams said, he would resign.

He worked dutifully. He read everything that was sent to him, read several newspapers assiduously, wrote some seventy letters to his department heads during the time he was absent, twenty-eight of which were to his Secretary of State. If there were delays in the system, they were nearly always at Philadelphia, not at his end.

Beyond all that, Adams recognized there was only so much he could do, that he could effect the roll of events only to a point. Writing to Washington earlier, he had expressed much of his philosophy as President in two sentences: "My administration will not certainly be easy to myself.

It will be happy, however, if it is honorable. The prosperity of it to the country will depend upon Heaven, and very little on anything in my power."

Frequently he would interject a similar refrain in thoughtful letters to his department heads when passing down decisions or judgments on matters of government business. For Adams the ultimate command rested always beyond the reach of mortal men, just as the very natures and actions of men themselves were often determined by their Maker. In an official letter to Secretary of the Navy Stoddert written the summer of 1799, Adams began, "It always gives me pain when I find myself obliged to differ in opinion from any of the heads of departments; but, as our understandings are not always in our own power, every man must judge for himself." When Secretary of War McHenry stressed the importance to the nation of a substantial army and of "genius in the command of it," Adams responded that "Genius in a general is oftener an instrument of divine vengeance than a guardian angel."

In health and outlook he always benefited from time on his farm, and Abigail's health, too, was soon greatly improved. Given his nature and so much that burdened his mind, he undoubtedly had moments of despair and anger. Once when General Knox and Adams's old friend from the years in Holland, Dr. Benjamin Waterhouse, came to call, Adams sat the whole time reading a newspaper. Still, he attended the Harvard commencement, a Fourth of July celebration in Boston, and the launching of the frigate *Boston*.

On July 23, Adams watched from an upstairs window as the *Constitution* headed out to sea from Boston under full sail. "After a detention of nine days by contrary winds," he wrote, "the *Constitution* took advantage of a brisk breeze, and went out of the harbor and out of sight this afternoon, making a beautiful and noble figure."

According to Abigail, in a midsummer report to John Quincy, the President was in "very good humor."

LATE IN THE DAY, August 5, Adams received a dispatch from Pickering containing a letter from Talleyrand dated May 12, assuring that the American envoys would be received with all appropriate respect.

It was the word Adams had been waiting for. At his desk at Peacefield the next morning, he wrote a letter to Pickering leaving no doubt of his intentions, his sense of urgency, or who was the senior diplomat between them, *and* that he expected immediate action taken. It was in all a strong summary of what had been his policy from the start. It also included a flash of Adams's temper—in what he said in response to Pickering's umbrage over the impatience Talleyrand had expressed about the time the Americans were taking to get things moving.

"It is far below the dignity of the President of the United States to take any notice of Talleyrand's impertinent regrets, and insinuations of superfluities," Adams lectured. "You or Mr. Murray may answer them as you please."

That said, Adams got to the essential point, lest Pickering have any misconceptions:

> I will say to you, however, that I consider this letter as the most authentic intelligence yet received in America of the successes of the coalition. That the design is insidious and hostile at heart, I will not say. Time will tell the truth. Meantime, I dread no longer their diplomatic skill. I have seen it, and felt it, and been the victim of it these twenty-one years. But the charm is dissolved. Their magic is at an end in America. Still, they shall find, as long as I am in office, candor, integrity, and, as far as there can be any confidence and safety, a pacific and friendly disposition. If the spirit of exterminating vengeance ever arises, it shall be conjured up by them, not me. In this spirit I shall pursue the negotiation, and I expect the cooperation of the heads of departments.

American defenses by sea and land were not to be relaxed. As to the mission, he wished "to delay nothing."

> My opinions and determinations in these subjects are so well made up, at least to my satisfaction, that not many hours will be necessary for me to give you my ultimate sentiments concerning the matter or form of the instructions to be given to the envoys.

But just as it seemed Adams had set his course, news came from Paris of a breakup of the Directory—"chaos," according to reports. To his cabinet it brought a surge of hope that peace could be postponed, a view strongly reinforced by Inspector General Hamilton.

Secretary of the Navy Stoddert, Adams's consistently loyal supporter, urged him to come at once to Trenton, New Jersey, where the government had set up emergency quarters until the yellow fever epidemic passed in Philadelphia. Although not inclined to go just yet, Adams told Stoddert that should "considerable difference" arise between the heads of departments, he would come at all events.

On September 13, Stoddert wrote again, filled with apprehension "that artful designing men might make such use of your absence" as to disrupt the peace initiative and "make your next election less honorable than it would otherwise be." This and a letter from Pickering proposing suspension of the peace mission were all Adams needed to hear. Abigail would follow once she had things in order at home.

He would be in Trenton by October 15 at the latest, Adams wrote Stoddert. "I have only one favor to beg, and that is that a certain election may be wholly laid out of this question and all others."

Adams left Peacefield on the last day of September, ready for what he had to face. But stopping at East Chester to see Nabby, he was struck a blow for which he was wholly unprepared. While the details are sparse, it could only have been one of the most dreadful moments of his life. To make matters worse, he had begun to feel ill en route and so arrived at East Chester already in a low state.

From his distraught daughter-in-law, Charles's wife, Sally, who with her two small daughters was staying with Nabby, Adams learned for the first time that Charles, who had disappeared, was bankrupt, faithless, and an alcoholic.

"I pitied her, I grieved, I mourned," Adams wrote to Abigail in anguish, "but could do no more." David's son Absalom at least had enterprise, he said. "Mine is a mere rake, buck, blood, and beast." If he felt pity for Charles, he did not express it.

"I love him too much," Adams had once written of his small second son when they were in Paris. "Charles wins the heart as usual, and is the most gentleman of them all," he had said upon seeing him again, after the return from England. Now Charles had become "a madman possessed of the devil." And, declared Adams, "I renounce him."

As time passed, the Adamses would say comparatively little about

Charles. It was as though the downfall of Abigail's brother William were repeating itself, and the family returned to the old ways of keeping "calamity" private. Only now and then would Abigail make mention of it, usually in letters to Mary Cranch, and almost never referring to Charles by name. "Any calamity inflicted by the hand of Providence, it would become me in silence to submit to," she wrote some weeks later, "but when I behold misery and distress, disgrace and poverty brought upon a family by intemperance, my heart bleeds at every pore." A "graceless child," he was, but she did not renounce him.

To push on to Trenton, "loaded with sorrow," was almost more than Adams was up to. He felt wretchedly ill with a cold so severe that he thought he might have yellow fever, which he did not.

Trenton, a village no larger than Quincy under normal conditions, was overflowing with refugees from Philadelphia, in addition to several hundred government officials and military officers. The best that could be arranged for the President were a small bedroom and sitting room in a boardinghouse kept by two maiden sisters named Barnes, one of whom provided the ailing Adams with a down comforter, while the other dosed him with a purgative of rhubarb and calomel.

Adams arrived expecting to meet directly with his cabinet to straighten out the impasse on the mission to France, and as miserable as he felt, he was ready to summon them without delay. What he had not expected was the presence in Trenton of General Hamilton, who had come to make a personal appeal to Adams to suspend the mission.

Hamilton had ridden over from Newark, where his troops were encamped and where by protocol he ought to have remained until called for, should the President wish to see him. That he had chosen to come to Trenton uninvited was taken by some as the kind of bold move Hamilton was known and admired for, but it also strongly suggested an element of desperation.

Hamilton called on Adams at the Barnes boardinghouse, where presumably they drew up chairs in Adams's tiny sitting room—two proud, pertinacious men who by now hated each other, one ambitious for war, the other peace, and each determined to have his way.

According to Adams, who provided several accounts of the confrontation, then and later, he received the general with appropriate civility, saying nothing of politics. But at first chance Hamilton commenced to "remonstrate" against the mission to France. "His eloquence and vehemence wrought the little man up to a degree of heat and effervescence. . . . He repeated over and over again . . . [his] unbounded confidence in the British empire . . . with such agitation and violent action that I really pitied him, instead of being displeased." The British had the upper hand in the war, Hamilton insisted, and would soon help restore the Bourbons to power in France. America must join with the British and have no dealings whatever with the present French government.

Adams was astonished by Hamilton's "total ignorance" of the situation in Europe. He would as soon expect the sun, moon, and stars to fall from their orbits as to see the Bourbons restored, he told Hamilton. But even were that to happen, what injury could it mean for the United States to have envoys there?

The meeting lasted several hours, through which, by his account, Adams sat patiently listening as Hamilton with his famous powers of persuasion talked steadily on. "I heard him with perfect good humor, though never in my life did I hear a man talk more like a fool."

On October 15, Adams summoned the cabinet to a session that lasted until eleven o'clock that night. Pickering, Wolcott, and McHenry, like Hamilton, adamantly opposed the mission. Secretary of the Navy Stoddert supported it, as did Attorney General Lee, the only member of the cabinet not present at Trenton, but who had expressed his views in a letter.

Adams's decision was given the next morning, Wednesday, October 16, 1799. "The President has resolved to send the commissioners to France," wrote a thoroughly dispirited Hamilton to George Washington. "All my calculations lead me to regret the measure." The commission sailed for France on November 15.

If Hamilton and his admirers in the cabinet had outmaneuvered Adams in the contest over command of the army, Adams had now cut the ground out from under Hamilton. Whatever dreams Hamilton entertained of military glory and empire, America was to have no need of either a standing army or a Bonaparte, which, it is fair to say, was as clear an objective in Adams's mind as was peace with France.

III

"I ENCLOSE THE SPEECH," Abigail wrote to Mary Cranch. "It has been received here with more applause and approbation than any speech which the President has ever delivered."

She was reinstated in the President's House and in the President's life, resuming her role where she had left off, despite all she had been through, and all, Mary knew, she suffered because of Charles. There would be grumbling over the speech, Abigail wrote. There would always be grumbling, she had come to understand.

Addressing a joint session of the new Congress, at the usual noon hour, December 3, 1799, Adams had delivered the most moderate, peaceable speech since his inaugural message, stressing a "pacific and humane" American stance before the world. Gone were calls for a new navy or a new army. Though the "measures adopted to secure our country against foreign attacks," must not be renounced, the national defense must be "commensurate with our resources and the situation of our country." War drums were out of season. Adams evoked instead "prospects of abundance," "the return of health, industry, and trade, to those cities which have lately been afflicted with disease."

Let the grumblers wake up to the "brightest, best and most peaceful days they now see," declared Abigail. Her old delight in being at the center of things had returned in full flower. In unseasonably mild weather, she was out and about taking walks, making calls, receiving visitors, and enjoying the current spectacle of Philadelphia society. For in its last winter as the nation's capital, the city "intended to shine." "I have heard of 'Once a man and twice a child' and the ladies' caps are an exact copy of baby's caps," Abigail began her report to Mary on "gay attire," showing no less delight in details—sleeves, buttons, petticoats, hairstyles—than once she had when writing from Paris.

Then, in an instant, the entire mood of the city changed. On December 14, 1799, as if to give period to the passing of the century and the Federal era, George Washington died at Mount Vernon. The cause of death was a heavy cold—a streptococcus infection. He had been sixty-seven, and until a few days before, in good health. The news reached Philadelphia the night of the seventeenth. In the morning the muffled bells of Christ Church commenced to toll and Congress adjourned.

The Adamses were stunned. The nation, said the President in a formal message to the Senate, had lost "her most esteemed, beloved, and admired citizen. . . . I feel myself alone, bereaved of my last brother." No man was more deservedly beloved and respected, wrote Abigail. A "universal melancholy has pervaded all classes of people."

The door of the presidential mansion, Congress Hall, Washington's pew at Christ Church, were draped in black. In Boston Harbor every ship displayed "the melancholy signal of mortality." "Our pulpit is hung with black," Mary Cranch reported from Quincy.

The day after Christmas, the official day of mourning in the capital, troops of light infantry and cavalry passed through the city to the slow military beat of muffled drums, in a grand solemn procession that began at Congress Hall and included a host of federal and state leaders, city magistrates, Masons, and a riderless white horse with reversed boots in the stirrups. Washington had been interred in the family vault at Mount Vernon, but this was the nation's funeral for its first President and greatest hero. The line of march was south on Fifth Street, east on Walnut, then north on Fourth, crossing Chestnut, Market, and Arch Streets to the German Lutheran Church at Fourth and Cherry, which had the largest seating capacity of any church in the city.

"The President of the United States and his Lady . . . and a vast concourse of other citizens," were present for services led by Bishop William White of Christ Church, with an oration by Representative Henry Lee of Virginia—General "Light-Horse Harry" Lee—who extolled Washington as "first in war, first in peace, first in the hearts of his countrymen."

When the service ended after four and a half hours, several hundred people crowded into the President's House. "The gentlemen all in black," Abigail noted, while the ladies had not let their grief "deprive them in their taste for ornamenting." They wore black military sashes, "epaulets of black silk . . . black plumes . . . black gloves and fans."

But as the encomiums to Washington continued, in speeches, sermons, and editorials—tributes that seemed often as contrived for show as the black plumes and fans—Abigail grew extremely impatient. When a minister at Newburyport, in a rapturous eulogy spoke of Washington as the "savior" of the country, she turned indignant. At no time, she wrote, had the fate of the country rested on the breath of one man, not even

Washington. "Wise and judicious observations about his character are those only which will outlive the badges of mourning," she told Mary. "Simple truth is his best, his greatest eulogy."

For the time being, the President said no more than he already had. But the Vice President was not known to have said anything about Washington. In some quarters it was being observed that because of his shame over the "Mazzei Letter," Jefferson had deliberately delayed his departure from Monticello to avoid the ceremonies in Washington's memory. Jefferson, who could have been in Philadelphia in time, did not arrive until two days later, on December 28, after an absence of ten months.

"I CONGRATULATE YOU on the New Year and the New Century," Adams wrote to his old friend Cotton Tufts on January 1, 1800, adding a line from Virgil, "*Aspice venturo laetentur ut omnia!* [Look how they are full of joy at the age to come!]."

If Adams had any thoughts or feelings about the passing of the epochal eighteenth century—any observations on the Age of Enlightenment, the century of Johnson, Voltaire, the Declaration of Independence, the American Revolution, the French Revolution, the age of Pitt and Washington, the advent of the United States of America—or if he had any premonitions or words to the wise about the future of his country or of humankind, he committed none to paper. His thoughts, to judge by what he said to Cotton Tufts, were on home and some marshland he wished to buy, overpriced though it might be.

Across the water, events had moved on dramatically. In February came the news from France of a coup on November 9—18 Brumaire, by the French revolutionary calendar. General Bonaparte had taken power as First Consul, which made him, at age thirty-three, sovereign ruler of France and much of Europe. The French Revolution was over, as declared Bonaparte himself.

Jefferson, who had pinned his highest hopes on the revolution, commented only that the situation was "painfully interesting." Clearly, American enchantment with France and the revolution were also at an end. Washington's death had seemed to mark the close of one era; the arrival of Napoleon Bonaparte ushered in another. Adams, who like Edmund Burke had predicted dictatorship as the inevitable outcome for the revolution, wisely kept silent.

"ELECTIONEERING" had already begun. A "stormy session" was forecast, and from the tone of their letters home—to Mary Cranch, Cotton Tufts, and others—both the Adamses seem to have concluded that there was to be no second term for them. That Jefferson would be the Republican choice to oppose him in the election was a foregone conclusion.

Congress was doing little. From the Vice President's chair upstairs at Congress Hall, Jefferson lamented the overbearing "dreariness" of the scene. As much as possible, he was associating with the "class of science," as he said, his friends and fellow members of the Philosophical Society, of which he had become president. He took time to have his portrait painted by young Rembrandt Peale, the gifted son of Charles Willson Peale, and of all the portraits done of him, it was perhaps the strongest—Jefferson in his prime at age fifty-seven, grey-haired, handsome, and confident.

Acutely conscious of the mistakes Adams had made as Vice President, Jefferson, when presiding in the Senate, never talked out of turn, or tried to impose his own opinion from the chair, conduct all in keeping with his nature. Moreover, he saw no necessity to be constantly present, as Adams had. There were better ways to spend his time, Jefferson felt. Seeing the need for a manual of parliamentary rules for the Senate, he wrote one, distinguished by its clarity, emphasis on decorum, and the degree to which he had drawn on the British model. Had it been Adams paying such tribute to English foundations and traditions, the uproar would have been immediate; he would have been denounced still again as "tainted" by his years in London and love for all things British. But among Jefferson's many contributions to the new republic, his *Senate Manual* would stand as one of the most useful and enduring.

In writing one rule, No. 17.9, under "Order in Debate," it was almost as though he had his predecessor as Vice President specifically in mind.

No one is to speak impertinently or beside the question, superfluously or tediously.

If Adams found any relief or pleasure in his duties, it was approving, on April 24, legislation that appropriated $5,900 to "purchase such books as may be necessary" for a new Library of Congress. It was one of the few measures upon which he and the Vice President could have heartily agreed.

IV

THAT THE CONTEST for the presidency in 1800 was to be unlike any of the three preceding presidential elections was clear at once. For the first (and last) time in history, the President was running against the Vice President. The two political parties had also come into their own with a vitality and vengeance exceeding anything in the country's experience.

Further, under the Sedition Act anyone openly criticizing the President ran the risk of being fined or sent to prison. Since the first sensational case against Congressman Matthew ("Spitting") Lyon of Vermont, eleven others had been charged and convicted under the law. In one instance, a New Jersey tavern loafer who had done no more than cast aspersions on the President's posterior was arrested, prosecuted, and fined $150.

That spring of 1800, the notorious James Callender reemerged, determined to defeat "the wretch" Adams, elect his patron Jefferson, and make himself a martyr. Matthew Lyon, after being sentenced to four months in a foul Vermont jail, had become a national hero and was overwhelmingly reelected to Congress.

Callender, who had quit Philadelphia, was now working as a Republican propagandist in Richmond, Virginia, with the encouragement and financial support of Jefferson, who, at the same time, was actively distributing a variety of campaign propaganda throughout the country, always careful to conceal his involvement. "Do not let my name be connected with the business," he advised James Monroe. That Adams was never known to be involved in such activity struck some as a sign of how naïve and behind the times he was.

In the *Richmond Examiner*, where he praised Jefferson as "an ornament to human nature," Callender assaulted Adams in a series of essays that would soon appear as a book titled *The Prospect Before Us*. It was the first salvo of the election and a clear sign of the sort of contest it would become.

Not satisfied that the old charges of monarchist and warmonger were sufficient, Callender called Adams a "repulsive pedant," a "gross hypocrite," and "in his private life, one of the most egregious fools upon the continent." Adams was "that strange compound of ignorance and ferocity, of deceit and weakness," a "hideous hermaphroditical character which has neither the force and firmness of a man, nor the gentleness and sensibility of a woman."

"The reign of Mr. Adams," said Callender, "has hitherto been one continued tempest of malignant passions." Once, according to Callender, Adams had become so enraged, he tore his wig off, threw it to the floor, and stomped on it. By what "species of madness" had America submitted to accept such a man as president?

> The historian will search for those *occult* causes that induced her to exalt an individual who has neither that innocence of sensibility which incites it to love, nor that omnipotence of intellect which commands us to admire. He will ask why the United States degrades themselves to the choice of a wretch whose soul came blasted from the hand of nature, of a wretch that has neither the science of a magistrate, the politeness of a courtier, nor the courage of a man?

Adams's sole objective was to make war on France, Callender asserted. The choice was clear—Adams and war, or Jefferson and peace.

To all this Jefferson gave his approval. Having seen the proof sheets of the new volume, he assured Callender, "Such papers cannot fail to produce the best effects."

To no one's surprise Callender was promptly arrested for inciting the American people against their President. In May he went on trial in a federal court in Richmond where the jury returned a verdict of guilty and he was sentenced to nine months in jail. But as he and Jefferson expected, it was another victory for the Republicans, just as Matthew Lyon's conviction had been.

Adams's far greater concern, meanwhile, was his cabinet. Particularly in his dealings with Pickering and McHenry, tension had been building for months, Adams feeling ever more isolated and certain that their first loyalty was to Hamilton, not him. Reports of ill will within the executive departments appeared in the papers. Adams and Pickering were said to "hate each other with the utmost cordiality."

The long-overdue showdown came after the Republicans defeated the Federalists in the election of the New York legislature, a crucial election in that it would determine New York's electoral vote for President. It was as if all Adams's troubles, all the pent-up anger and frustration he had had in his dealings with the cabinet, let go in a furious outburst at James McHenry, an incompetent but affable man whom Adams rather liked.

On the evening of May 5, Adams summoned McHenry to the presidential mansion to discuss the appointment of a minor federal official. The discussion was quickly concluded and McHenry was about to leave when something he said, or the way he said it, started Adams on the subject of Hamilton and the loss of the New York election. Adams charged McHenry with working secretly with Hamilton to undercut the administration. When McHenry protested, Adams cut him off, saying, "I know it, sir, to be so." Hamilton, said Adams, seething with anger, was an "intrigant . . . a man devoid of every moral principle, a bastard . . . a foreigner." Then Adams let fly with what to any faithful Hamiltonian was the ultimate insult. Jefferson, Adams declared, was a better man, "a wiser one," than Hamilton, and, furthermore, Jefferson would make a better president.

How could McHenry and Pickering presume to know what to do in matters of foreign affairs, Adams went on. How dare they try to suspend the mission to France! And why had he been given no warning that Hamilton would turn up at Trenton? Adams charged McHenry with inept management, of failing to clothe the troops adequately. "You cannot, sir, remain longer in office," Adams declared at last.

But then, when McHenry agreed to resign, Adams, his fury spent, said almost in apology he had always considered McHenry a man of understanding and integrity.

McHenry immediately wrote his own account of the scene, copies of which he sent to both Adams and Hamilton. Writing to explain his dismissal to a nephew, McHenry portrayed Adams as "actually insane."

While Adams's outbursts of temper could be explosive, they never happened in public, always in private confrontations. It was then that "he would give to his language the full impress of his vehement will." But never until now was he known to have berated a subordinate, and his regret over the outburst was considerable.

Still, nothing he had said was untrue, nor was his anger without justification. In firing McHenry he had done what he should have done well before this. After a pause of a few days—possibly to cool down—he fired Pickering.

This time there was no unpleasant confrontation. On May 10, in customary fashion, Adams asked for Pickering's resignation by letter. Almost inconceivably, Pickering refused to comply. In a written response of May 12, he said he did not feel it his duty to resign, and implied that he needed the government salary to subsist. Adams discharged him at once and the same day named as his new Secretary of War, Senator Samuel Dexter of Massachusetts, and as Secretary of State, John Marshall, who was now a member of the House of Representatives.

Why Adams failed to discharge Oliver Wolcott while cleaning house was never adequately explained. Though Wolcott had been quite as duplicitous and disloyal to Adams as either McHenry or Pickering, he somehow succeeded in winning Adams's trust and would continue as Secretary of the Treasury.

Hearing of the dismissals, Alexander Hamilton quickly asked Pickering to search the files at the Department of State for "copies of extracts of all such documents as will enable you to *explain* both *Jefferson and Adams.*" The time had come, Hamilton said, when "men of real integrity" must unite against all charlatans.

THE REMOVAL of the government from Philadelphia to the new Federal City by the Potomac was scheduled to take place in June. The President was to go there himself for a first look as soon as he could get away. But two critical issues required decisions in the weeks that remained—what to do about the temporary army and what to do about three Pennsylvania German farmers who had been sentenced to hang for treason.

The fate of the now useless and unpopular army was settled with remarkably little fuss, showing how greatly times had changed. Adams declared that were it left to him the army "should not exist a fortnight." Both Federalists and Republicans in Congress, seeing no reason why Adams should get the credit, voted to disband the army by summer. Had Hamilton been given free reign with the army, Adams would remark, it would have required a second army to disband the first one.

The fate of the condemned men, however, was left to Adams alone.

In southeastern Pennsylvania the previous year there had been an armed uprising by German (Pennsylvania Dutch) farmers angry over the federal tax on land and the high-handed ways of the federal tax collectors. The "rebellion" had died down by the time state and federal troops arrived, but its leader, John Fries, and two others were taken captive and tried in federal court. Found guilty of treason and sentenced to hang, they had appealed to the President for a pardon.

Adams had been initially incensed at the news of the rebellion—it was he who had ordered the federal troops to the scene—but had since insisted on making his own study of the case. "The issue of this investigation," he wrote, "has opened a train of very serious contemplations to me, which will require the closest attention of my best understanding, and will prove a severe trial to my heart." Again he asked for the opinions of his cabinet officers, all of whom recommended that, to set an example, the sentence should be carried out.

Capital punishment was part of life. Nor was Adams opposed to it. As President, he had signed death warrants for military deserters. Secretary of State Pickering, in giving his opinion, was, like the others, only expressing what he viewed as a duty of office. "Painful as is the idea of taking the life of a man," Pickering wrote, "I feel a calm and solid satisfaction that an opportunity is now presented in executing the justice of the law, to crush that spirit, which, if not overthrown and destroyed, may proceed in its career and overturn the government."

It was what Adams himself might have written earlier. But with his review completed, Adams saw that he had been mistaken. Fries, it was his judgment, had led a riot, not an insurrection, and was therefore not guilty of treason. Rejecting the verdict of the jury and the unanimous opinion of his cabinet, Adams pardoned Fries and the two others, never doubting he had done the right thing. And though the decision aggravated still further the already infuriated Hamiltonians, who saw it as still one more example of Adams's weakness and capriciousness, much of the electorate approved, and especially in Pennsylvania.

IF THE PRESIDENT and his wife had misgivings about vacating Philadelphia and the great brick mansion on Market Street, if they were at all saddened by the prospect, such feelings went unrecorded. In her last letters to Mary Cranch before leaving, Abigail wrote mainly of the lovely spring weather—"as luxuriant a season as I ever knew"—and the arrangements to be made for a final dinner party.

She started for Quincy on May 19. The President departed for Washington on May 27, heading southwest in his coach-and-four accompanied by Billy Shaw, and escorted by the ever-faithful John Briesler on horseback. For miles through Pennsylvania's Lancaster County, where well-tended farms were burgeoning with crops in the "luxuriant" season, Adams delighted in the scenery. At Lancaster and later at Frederick, Maryland, he spoke before public gatherings, and was warmly received, as he was at other towns along the way, enjoying what, in that day and age, passed for campaigning. Such were the tributes and entertainments in his honor en route, it was not until June 3 that he reached the boundary line of the ten-mile square of the District of Columbia.

GIVEN WHAT there was to see, Adams might have been terribly disappointed by the Federal City. He could rightfully have fumed over the heat, the mosquitoes, the squalid shacks of the work crews; or the projected cost of the project; or the questionable real estate ventures that had failed year after year, despite so many grand promises. Another nephew, William Cranch, had become involved in one such scheme and gone bankrupt. Being that it was his first foray into the South, Adams might have been disturbed by the sight of slaves at work.

For all the talk, there was no city as yet, only a rather shabby village and great stretches of tree stumps, stubble, and swamp. There were no schools, not a single church. Capitol Hill comprised a few stores, a few nondescript hotels and boardinghouses clustered near a half-finished sandstone Capitol. To accommodate the different departments of the government, only one structure had been completed, the Treasury, a plain two-story brick building a mile to the west of the Capitol, next door to the new President's House, which was still a long way from being ready.

Oliver Wolcott, in a letter to his wife, described the Capitol and the President's House as "magnificent," yet was astounded at how much had still to be done.

> I cannot but consider our Presidents as very unfortunate men if they must live in this dwelling. It must be cold and damp in winter. . . . It was built to be looked at by visitors and strangers, and will render its occupants an object of ridicule with some and pity with others.

Dr. William Thornton, a commissioner of the District and architect of the Capitol, spoke confidently of a population in Washington of 160,000 people within a few years. To Wolcott, as to many, it seemed no one in Washington knew what he was talking about. In fact, it would be nearly eighty years before the city had such a population.

Adams, with his memories of Paris and London, with his fondness for Philadelphia and his belief that the capital of a great nation ought to be a great city, could have been appalled by the whole place and seen it as a colossal blunder. He could have dismissed it as Jefferson's city, Jefferson having devoted more time and thought to the project than anyone in government. Everything considered, there was almost no reason for Adams to have liked anything about it.

Yet by all signs he was quite pleased. "I like the seat of government very well," he wrote Abigail. He stayed ten days, lodging at Tunnicliffe's City Hotel, near the Capitol. He was joined by his new appointments, Secretary of State Marshall and Secretary of War Dexter, who with the rest of the executive branch had made the move from Philadelphia, along with the complete files of the President and the departments shipped in eight packing cases.

Adams made a brief inspection of the new President's House. Once, when asked by Washington how he thought a President ought to live—in what manner and style—Adams had said it should be in a fairly grand way. And though he had said nothing specific about the sort of house a President should have, this under construction seems to have met his approval. He imagined himself asleep there, or lying awake, he told Abigail, but referred only to the coming winter, not the next four years.

He enjoyed most of all his visits to Mount Vernon to call on Martha Washington, and to Alexandria, where he was acclaimed by the townspeople and given a dinner in his honor at the home of Attorney General Lee, the net effect of which was to make him extremely homesick.

"Oh! That I could have a home!" He felt he had been forever on the move, on the road. "Rolling, rolling, rolling, till I am very nearly rolling into the bosom of Mother Earth."

By first light, June 14, he was rolling north to Quincy, leaving John Marshall to manage in his absence.

V

IN THE SUMMER and fall of 1800 the question of who was to lead the nation rapidly became a contest of personal vilification surpassing any presidential election in American history. The spirit of party had taken hold with a vengeance, and whether Adams or Jefferson was the most abused would be hard to say. In Federalist pamphlets and newspapers, Jefferson was decried as a hopeless visionary, a weakling, an intriguer intoxicated with French philosophy, more a Frenchman than an American, and therefore a bad man. He was accused of favoring states' rights over the Union, charged with infidelity to the Constitution, called a spendthrift and libertine.

One New York paper assured its readers that a Jefferson victory would mean civil war. Hordes of Frenchmen and Irishmen, "the refuse of Europe," would flood the country and threaten the life of "all who love order, peace, virtue, and religion." It was said Jefferson had swindled clients as a young lawyer. The old smear of cowardice during his time as governor of Virginia was revived. But most amplified were charges of atheism. Not only was Jefferson a godless man, but one who mocked the Christian faith. In New England word went out that family Bibles would have to be hidden away for safekeeping, were he elected. So widespread and pervasive was such propaganda that even Martha Washington, who may have been smarting still from the "Mazzei Letter," remarked to a visiting clergyman that she thought Jefferson "one of the most detestable of mankind."

Stories were spread of personal immorality. It was now that a whispering campaign began to the effect that all southern slave masters were known to cohabit with slave women and that the Sage of Monticello was no exception.

Adams was inevitably excoriated as a monarchist, more British than American, and therefore a bad man. He was ridiculed as old, addled, and toothless. Timothy Pickering spread the rumor that to secure his reelection Adams had struck a corrupt bargain with the Republicans. According to another story, this secret arrangement was with Jefferson himself—Adams was to throw the election Jefferson's way and serve as Jefferson's vice president.

If Jefferson carried on with slave women, Adams, according to one story in circulation, had ordered Charles Cotesworth Pinckney to London to procure four pretty mistresses to divide between them. When the story reached Adams, he was highly amused. "I do declare upon my honor," he wrote William Tudor, "if this is true General Pinckney has kept them all for himself and cheated me out of my two."

Most vicious were the charges that Adams was insane. Thus, if Jefferson was a Jacobin, a shameless southern libertine, and a "howling" atheist, Adams was a Tory, a vain Yankee scold, and, if truth be known, "quite mad."

But the great difference in the attacks on Adams in this election was that they came from Republicans and High Federalists alike. While the Republicans assaulted him as a warmonger, he was berated by the High Federalists as fainthearted in the face of the French. While one side belittled him as a creature of the Hamiltonians, the other scorned him as a friend of Elbridge Gerry.

Jefferson in his four years as Vice President had so effectively separated himself from Adams and the administration that he could be held accountable for nothing that had disappointed, displeased, or infuriated anyone, whereas Adams was held forever accountable for the new taxes, the Alien and Sedition Acts, the standing army, and a host of other "menaces," as said Philadelphia's *Aurora*.

There were, as well, striking ironies. Jefferson, the Virginia aristocrat and slave master who lived in a style fit for a prince, as removed from his fellow citizens and their lives as it was possible to be, was hailed as the apostle of liberty, the "Man of the People." Adams, the farmer's son who despised slavery and practiced the kind of personal economy and plain living commonly upheld as the American way, was scorned as an aristocrat who, if he could, would enslave the common people. "My countrymen!" exclaimed William Duane in the *Aurora* in his crusade for Jefferson, "If you have not virtue enough to stem the current, determine to be slaves at once."

For Adams, abuse from the Jefferson Republicans was an old story. It was to be expected. Far more hurtful were the personal attacks from the Hamilton Federalists.

When Oliver Wolcott wrote from his office in Washington to tell Fisher Ames of Massachusetts that he would work to defeat Adams and that between Adams and Jefferson there was scarcely a difference, that one would be as disastrous as the other, he was only expressing what many Hamilton Federalists had concluded, taking their cue from their leader. For again as in 1788 and 1796, Hamilton was throwing his weight into the contest to tip the balance against Adams, except this time there was no pretense of secrecy.

As early as May, Hamilton had launched a letter campaign to his High Federalist coterie declaring Adams unfit and incapable as President, a man whose defects of character were guaranteed to bring certain ruin to the party. "If we must have an enemy at the head of the government, let it be one whom we can oppose . . . who will not involve our party in the disgrace of his foolish and bad measures."

On a tour of New England, ostensibly to bid farewell to his army before it disbanded, Hamilton spent as much time as possible among local Federalist leaders to whom he spread the same charge against Adams. Hamilton's scheme was to make Charles Cotesworth Pinckney President.

Reports of Hamilton's activities inevitably reached Quincy. "It was soon understood that . . . his visit was merely an electioneering business, to feel the pulse of the New England states, and impress those upon whom he could have any influence to vote for Pinckney," Abigail wrote. But by such intrigues, she was sure, "the little cock sparrow general" would lose more votes for Pinckney than he would gain.

When such an old friend as Francis Dana turned his back on Adams, it was extremely painful for him. Yet he himself and his efforts for peace were widely approved in New England, as Hamilton discovered to his dismay. While "strong-minded men" stood ready to support Pinckney, Hamilton wrote in his analysis of the political climate, there was still "in the body of that people . . . a strong attachment" to Adams.

As Abigail observed in mid-August, not a public event or levee took place "without being attended by many persons who never before came and never were they so full, and so crowded as they have been this season." Meanwhile, local Republicans were noticeably uncritical.

As handsome a tribute as any to Adams appeared in the *Washington Federalist*. In answer to "late attempts to undervalue" the President, readers were reminded that Adams stood "among the few surviving, steady, tried patriots" whose services to the country were of a kind almost beyond compare:

> Bred in the old school of politics, his principles are founded on the experience of ages, and bid defiance to French flippancies and modern crudities. . . . Always great, and though sometimes alone, all weak and personal motives were forgotten in public energy and the security of the sacred liberties of his country. . . . Deeply versed in legal lore, profoundly skilled in political science; joined to the advantage of forty years' unceasing engagement in the turbulent and triumphant scenes, both at home and in Europe, which have marked our history; learned in the language and arts of diplomacy; more conversant with the views, jealousies, resources, and intrigues of Great Britain, France and Holland than any other American; alike aloof to flattery and vulgar ambition, as above all undue control [he has as] . . . his sole object . . . the present freedom and independence of his country and its future glory. On this solid basis he has attempted to raise a monument of his honest fame.

With reports from the peace commission maddeningly thin and long delayed, the issue of peace and war remained foremost, almost to the end. What the *Aurora* would proclaim at the close of the campaign was no different from what James Callender had written in early spring. "With Jefferson we shall have peace . . . the friends of war will vote for *Adams*."

The two candidates conveyed the customary air of indifference, neither saying anything publicly or appearing to lift a finger in his own behalf. Jefferson remained at Monticello, Adams at his farm, which he had lately taken to calling Stoneyfield, instead of Peacefield, perhaps feeling the new name was more in keeping with New England candor, or that it better defined the look of the political landscape at the moment.

He devoted himself almost entirely to official duties, maintaining steady correspondence with Secretary Marshall in particular. Nothing mattered more—over nothing did Adams fret more—than the state of negotiations in France. And still there was no word.

The great imponderable was Napoleon Bonaparte. "I cannot account for the long delay of our envoys," wrote Marshall, who had begun to have doubts and reminded the President that there must be no sacrifice of American honor to please the First Consul. "We ought not be surprised if we see our envoys without a treaty," he warned, and this could produce "a critical state of things."

But Adams needed no reminding. In reply, he advised prudent preparations for war, in the event of another rebuff. "I am much of your opinion that we ought not to be surprised," he told Marshall on September 4.

... the government ought to be prepared to take a decided part. Questions of consequence will arise, and among others, whether the President ought not at the opening session to recommend an immediate and general declaration of war against the French Republic. ... We have had wonderful proofs that the public mind cannot be held in a state of suspense. The public opinion, it seems, must always be a decided one, whether in the right or not. ... I wish the heads of departments to turn their thoughts to the subject, and view it in all its lights.

For his part, Jefferson appeared to be devoting his time at Monticello to rural interests only.

BOTH ABIGAIL and John enjoyed comparatively good health, and Adams's love of home, his everyday delight in his farm, were as constant as ever—no less than what Washington had felt for Mount Vernon or Jefferson for Monticello.

But as Abigail confided in family correspondence, her own and the President's private days and frequent sleepless nights were deeply troubled by the sad fate of their alcoholic son. On her way home from Philadelphia in early November, Abigail had stopped again at East Chester, where this time she saw Charles himself. "The whole man [is] so changed that ruin and destruction have swallowed him up," Abigail confided to John Quincy. "Poor, poor unhappy, wretched man," she wrote, her heart breaking. Charles's wife had gone with her younger child to stay with her mother, while Abigail had brought the other child, four-year-old Susanna, home to Quincy. So with Nabby and her daughter Caroline again spending the summer, it was a full house.

Nothing she had been able to say to Charles had had any effect, Abigail wrote. She had tried "remonstrances." She had reminded him of all that was dear in life—honor, reputation, family, friends. "But all is lost on him."

She and the President would provide for his family. "Yet I am wounded to the soul by the consideration of what is to become of him. What will be his fate embitters every moment of my life." At age thirty, Charles seemed beyond saving.

ON MONDAY, October 13, Adams set off by coach from Quincy on the journey back to Washington. His own heartbreak over Charles was no less than what Abigail suffered, as his later writings disclose, but he had not softened in his decision to renounce his son. Passing through East Chester, Adams did not stop to see him, as Abigail would, he knew, when she followed later, resolved to be with John in Washington whatever lay in store.

The greetings he received along the way were of a kind to help his sagging spirits. Clearly he stood well with the large majority of the Federalist party and a great many more besides who saw him as a staunch, old patriot carrying on in the tradition of Washington. John Adams, it was said, was "a good husband, a good father, a good citizen, and a good man." He was a peacemaker, whatever the Hamiltonians might say, and the American people did not hold that against him.

Republicans, too, were expressing new regard, even affection for Adams. "The Jacobins profess to admire and respect the independence of

Mr. Adams's character," Thomas reported from Philadelphia to his mother, "and several of them have *told me* that *next* to their idol Jefferson they would definitely prefer him to any man in the country." But this did not mean they would vote for him, and Thomas was pessimistic. "I am glad you are to be with my father this winter," he told her. "The prospect is dreary enough, not for him, but for the country."

Then, without warning, while Adams was on the road to Washington, a "thunderbolt" struck.

Since summer Alexander Hamilton had been working on a "letter" intended initially for a select few Federalists in several states. Timothy Pickering, James McHenry, and Oliver Wolcott had all been recruited to help. Pickering and McHenry had supplied what confidential information they could from past experience in Adams's cabinet, while Wolcott, still a member of the cabinet, continued to have access to confidential files. But when asked for their views on Hamilton's initial draft of the letter, most of them were astonished, and urged Hamilton not to put his name on it. Wolcott suggested that it not be released at all, because, he wrote, "the poor old man" was quite capable of doing himself in without help from anyone else. But Hamilton paid no attention.

Not long past, Abigail had warned Adams to "beware of that spare Cassius." Now, in the eleventh hour of the election, Hamilton lashed out in a desperate effort to destroy Adams, the leading candidate of his own party.

A Letter from Alexander Hamilton, Concerning the Public Conduct and Character of John Adams, Esq., President of the United States, a fifty-four-page pamphlet, was published in New York at the end of October. Nothing that Hamilton ever wrote about Jefferson was half so contemptuous. He berated Adams in nearly every way possible—for his "great intrinsic defects of character," his "disgusting egotism," weaknesses, vacillation, his "eccentric tendencies," his "bitter animosity" toward his own cabinet. He deplored Adams's handling of relations with France, the "precipitate nomination" of William Vans Murray, the firing of Timothy Pickering, the pardoning of John Fries. Though Hamilton did not go so far as to call Adams insane, he cited his "ungovernable temper" as evidence of a man out of control. "It is a fact that he is often liable to paroxisms of anger which deprive him of self-command and produce very outrageous behavior."

Yet Hamilton made no charges of corruption or misconduct on Adams's part. He even acknowledged Adams's patriotism and integrity, and conceded, without getting specific, that Adams had "talents of a certain kind." And finally, most strangely, having spent fifty pages tearing Adams to pieces, Hamilton concluded by saying Adams must be supported equally with General Pinckney in the election.

Republicans were euphoric. Whatever crazed notions had taken hold of Hamilton, he had surely dealt Adams a blow and "rent the Federal party in twain." In a high-spirited letter to Jefferson, James Madison said Hamilton's "thunderbolt" meant certain victory for Jefferson. "I rejoice with you that Republicanism is likely to be so *completely* triumphant."

Federalists everywhere were aghast, disbelieving, or seething with anger. In Connecticut, Noah Webster produced a pamphlet accusing Hamilton of extreme disloyalty and ambition to become the American Caesar. By contrast to Hamilton, Webster wrote, Adams was "a man of pure morals, of firm attachment to republican government, of sound and inflexible patriotism." Were Jefferson to be elected, Webster wrote to Hamilton, "the fault will lie at your door and . . . your conduct on this occasion will be discerned little short of insanity."

In fact, Hamilton had amply demonstrated that it was he who had become a burden to the party, he, if anyone, who seemed to have departed from his senses.

Speculation as to why he had done it, what possible purpose he might have had, would go on for years. Possibly, as John Quincy surmised, it was because Adams had denied him his chance for military glory, humiliated him at Trenton, and made his army superfluous. Perhaps he believed he was improving Pinckney's chances. Or he wanted to bring down the Federalist party, so that in the aftermath of a Jefferson victory he could raise it up again as his own creation.

Probably not even Hamilton knew the answer. But by his own hand he had ruined whatever chance he ever had for the power and glory he so desperately desired.

FOR SEVERAL DAYS toward the end of October, plasterers and painters at work on the President's House in Washington, as well as the Commissioners of the District of Columbia, had been keeping an eye out for the

President, not knowing just when he might appear. With the imponderables of travel, no one's arrival could be predetermined or planned for precisely, not even a President's.

The immense house was still unfinished. It reeked of wet plaster and wet paint. Fires had to be kept blazing in every fireplace on the main floor to speed up the drying process. Only a twisting back stair had been built between floors. Closet doors were missing. There were no bells to ring for service. And though the furniture had arrived from Philadelphia, it looked lost in such enormous rooms. Just one painting had been hung, a full-length portrait of Washington in his black velvet suit, by Gilbert Stuart, which had also been sent from Philadelphia.

The house stood in a weedy, wagon-rutted field with piles of stone and rubble about. It all looked very raw and unkempt. Yet the great white-washed stone building, the largest house in America—as large as the half of the Capitol that had been erected—was truly a grand edifice, noble even in its present state.

At midday, Saturday, November 1, Commissioners William Thornton and Alexander White were inspecting the main floor, when, at one o'clock, the President was seen rolling up to the south entrance in his coach-and-four. He was accompanied still by Billy Shaw and Briesler following on horseback. There was no one else, no honor guard, no band playing, no entourage of any kind.

The two commissioners and a few workers at hand comprised the welcoming committee for the arrival of John Adams, the first President to occupy what only much later would become known as the White House.

An office was made ready in an ample room with a southern exposure on the second floor, next door to what was to be Adams's bedroom. Secretaries Marshall and Stoddert, the two in the cabinet Adams counted on, came to pay their respects. Later, supper finished, he climbed the back stairs candle in hand and retired for the night.

At his desk the next morning, on a plain sheet of paper, which he headed, "President's House, Washington City, Nov. 2, 1800," he wrote to Abigail a letter in which he offered a simple benediction:

I pray heaven to bestow the best of blessings on this house and all that shall hereafter inhabit. May none but honest and wise men ever rule under this roof.

But for Adams the house was to be the setting of great disappointment and much sorrow. By the time he wrote to Abigail again, he had
seen the Hamilton pamphlet and concluded as Madison had that it
meant his certain defeat. "The ancients thought a great book a great
evil," he told her. "Mr. H. will find a little book an evil great enough for
him . . . for [it] will insure the choice of the man he dreads or pretends to
dread more than me."

To judge by what he said privately in a letter to a friend, he took the
blow with notable equanimity. Like others, he thought Hamilton had
succeeded mainly in damaging himself. He was not Hamilton's enemy,
Adams wrote, and Hamilton was not without talent. "There is more bur-
nish, however, on the outside than sterling silver in substance." But this
was as much as he would say, at least while President.

AT THE END of the first week in November, Adams's long wait for news
from France ended. The mission had succeeded. A treaty with France,
the Convention of Mortefontaine, had been signed on October 3, 1800, at
a château north of Paris. At a grand fete celebrating the event, Bonaparte declared that the differences between France and the United States
had been no more than a family quarrel. Gifts were presented to the
American envoys, toasts raised to perpetual peace between the two
nations.

The first report appeared in a Baltimore paper on November 7.
Another month would pass before the official copy of the Convention
arrived in Washington, at which point it would be submitted to the Senate for approval.

The news had come too late to affect the election, but peace had truly
been achieved. Though Adams could say nothing of it yet, the Quasi-War
was over, and for Adams it was an immense victory.

ABIGAIL REACHED Washington on November 16, at the end of an
extremely arduous journey. Stopping to see Charles at East Chester, she
was stunned to find him desperately ill in the care of Nabby. Abigail had
had no forewarning; no one had been told, because his condition had

come on so rapidly. Sitting by his bedside, she sensed she was seeing him for the last time. When she left, she again took Susanna with her for the rest of the journey.

In Maryland, as she later described it to Mary Cranch, there was only forest, the roads so rough and uncertain that she and her party were lost for two hours. "But woods are all you see from Baltimore until you reach *the city*, which is only so in name." She thought the President's House beautifully situated by the Potomac, the country around "romantic but wild." Nearby Georgetown, however, was "the very dirtiest hole I ever saw."

The house, she told Mary in a letter of November 21, was twice as large as the meetinghouse at home. "It is habitable by fires in every part, thirteen of which we are obliged to keep daily, or sleep in wet and damp places." The great, unplastered "audience room" at the east end of the main floor, she made her "drying room" to hang out the laundry.

There were many who would have refused to live in the house in the state it was in, but the Adamses made do without complaint. The "great castle," Abigail knew, had been built for ages to come. She judged it would require thirty servants to run it properly. As it was, she had six, including John and Mary Briesler.

She had not liked what little she had seen of the South thus far. The presence of slaves working about the house left her feeling depressed. The whole system struck her as woefully slow and wasteful, not to say morally wrong. She watched twelve slaves clothed in rags at work outside her window, hauling away dirt and rubble with horses and wagons, while their owners stood by doing nothing. "Two of our hardy New England men would do as much work in a day as the whole 12," she told Cotton Tufts. "But it is *true Republicanism* that drive the slaves half fed, and destitute of clothing . . . whilst an owner walks about idle, though one slave is all the property he can boast."

With the weather turning colder, she found it maddening that with woods everywhere it was impossible to find a woodcutter to keep the fires going. She despaired that anything could ever be accomplished in such a society. "The lower class of whites," she wrote, "are a grade below the Negroes in point of intelligence, and ten below them in point of civility." But she wrote, "I shall bear and forebear."

· · ·

ON SATURDAY, November 22, Congress convened for the first time in joint session in the unfinished Capitol, and John Adams delivered what he knew to be his last speech as President.

"I congratulate the people of the United States on the assembling of Congress at the permanent seat of their government," he began, "and I congratulate you, gentlemen, on the prospect of a residence not to be changed." As he had privately for the President's House, he now publicly offered a benediction for the Capitol, the Federal District, and the City of Washington:

> It would be unbecoming the representatives of this nation to assemble for the first time in this solemn temple without looking up to the Supreme Ruler of the universe, and imploring his blessing.
>
> May this territory be the residence of virtue and happiness! In this city may that piety and virtue, that wisdom and magnanimity, that constancy and self-government, which adorned the great character whose name it bears, be forever held in veneration! Here, and throughout our country, may simple manners, pure morals, and true religion flourish forever!

The speech that followed was a brief, gracious summation of the state of the union, notable for its clarity and absence of exaggeration. He praised the officers and men of the discharged temporary army, both for their patriotism and their readiness to return to the "station of private citizens." He praised the navy and recommended further measures for a defensive naval force.

> While our best endeavors for the preservation of harmony with all nations will continue to be used, the experience of the world and our own experience admonish us of the insecurity of trusting too confidently to their success. We cannot, without committing a dangerous imprudence, abandon those measures of self-protection which are adapted to our situation, and to which, notwithstanding our pacific policy, the violence of injustice of others may again compel us to resort.

Because he had still to receive official word of the negotiations with France, he said only that it was hoped that American efforts for an accommodation would "meet with a success proportioned to the sincerity with which they have so often been repeated"—which was as close as he came to speaking of his own persistent efforts.

He spoke of the need for amending the judiciary system, and congratulated the Congress for the revenue that year, the largest of any year thus far.

"We find reason to rejoice at the prospect which presents itself," he said at the last. The country was "prosperous, free, and happy, . . . thanks to the protection of laws emanating only from the general will," and "the fruits of our own labor."

Shortly after, in reply to the then customary answer to his speech from the Senate, Adams said of the new Capitol, "Here may the youth of this extensive country forever look up without disappointment, not only to the monuments and memorials of the dead, but to the examples of the living."

LESS THAN two weeks later, on or about December 3, the same day the electors convened, a postrider arrived at the President's House with a letter from East Chester. Charles was dead. He had died on November 30— of dropsy, it was said, but most likely of cirrhosis as well.

> His constitution was so shaken [Abigail wrote to her sister Mary], that his disease was rapid, and through the last part of his life, dreadfully painful and distressing. He bore with patience and submission his sufferings and heard the prayers for him with composure. His mind at times was much deranged. . . . He was no man's enemy but his own. He was beloved in spite of his errors.

To Charles's widow, Abigail wrote, "[I] would to God I could administer to you that comfort which [I] stand in need of myself." In his early life, she recalled, no child was ever so tender and amiable. "The President sends his love to you and mourns, as he has for a long time, with you."

In another few days the outcome of the election was known. Adams had lost. "My little bark has been overset in a squall of thunder and lightning and hail attended by a strong smell of sulfur," he wrote to Thomas. However crushed, disappointed, saddened, however difficult it was for him to bear up, he expressed no bitterness or envy, and no anger. Nor was anyone to feel sorry for him. "Be not concerned about me," he told Thomas. "I feel my shoulders relieved from the burden."

As always, both Adamses were entirely candid with their children. To Thomas, Abigail wrote, "For myself and family I have few regrets . . . I shall be happier at Quincy." Only her private grief and public ingratitude could at times bear her down. "I lose my sleep often, and I find my spirits flag," she wrote to Cotton Tufts. "My mind and heart have been severely tried."

The election had been closer than expected. Adams carried all of New England, but lost in New York, the South, and the West. The Republican victory in New York had been all-important and was due largely to extraordinary efforts by Aaron Burr in New York City. But it was not until Federalist strength in South Carolina proved insufficient to carry the state, and its 8 electoral votes, that the outcome was settled.

In the final electoral count of all sixteen states, Jefferson had 73 votes to Adams's 65; Pinckney had 63. But Burr had also wound up with 73 votes, and so was tied with Jefferson. The outcome, according to the Constitution, would have to be decided in the House of Representatives.

What was surprising—and would largely be forgotten as time went on—was how well Adams had done. Despite the malicious attacks on him, the furor over the Alien and Sedition Acts, unpopular taxes, betrayals by his own cabinet, the disarray of the Federalists, and the final treachery of Hamilton, he had, in fact, come very close to winning in the electoral count. With a difference of only 250 votes in New York City, Adams would have won with an electoral count of 71 to 61. So another of the ironies of 1800 was that Jefferson, the apostle of agrarian America who loathed cities, owed his ultimate political triumph to New York.

Had the news of the peace agreement at Mortefontaine arrived a few weeks sooner, it, too, could very well have been decisive for Adams. Also, were it not for the fact that in the South three-fifths of the slaves were counted in apportioning the electoral votes, Adams would have been reelected.

To Adams the outcome was proof of how potent party spirit and party organization had become, and the most prominent was Burr's campaign in New York. Washington, in his Farewell Address, had warned against disunion, permanent alliances with other nations, and "the baneful effects of the spirit of party." Adams could rightly claim to have held to the ideals of union and neutrality, but his unrelenting independence—his desire to be a President above party—had cost him dearly.

"How mighty is the spirit of party," he wrote to Elbridge Gerry. There was nothing unexpected about Jefferson's success, Adams thought, but Burr's good fortunes surpassed "all ordinary rules." All too plainly, times had changed:

> All the old patriots, all the splendid talents, the long experience, both Federalists and Anti-Federalists must be subjected to the humiliation of seeing this dextrous gentleman [Burr] rise like a balloon, filled with uninflammable air over the heads. . . . What an encouragement to party intrigue and corruption!

In the last analysis, however, it was not Jefferson or the "dextrous" Burr who defeated Adams so much as the Federalist war faction and the rampaging Hamilton. And none of this would have happened but for Adams's decision to send the second peace mission to France. It was his determination to find peace and check Hamilton that cost him the full support of the party and thus the election.

VI

TENSION AND UNCERTAINTY over the Jefferson-Burr deadlock increased by the day. Burr refused to step aside in deference to Jefferson and was said to be secretly bargaining with the Federalists in return for support when the issue went to the House. Hamilton, in an effort to play kingmaker at the last, was again in the thick of things. Given his intense dislike and distrust of both men, the choice was painful, but after consideration he had decided on Jefferson.

> Mr. Jefferson, though too revolutionary in his notions, is yet a lover of liberty and will be desirous of something like orderly government [Hamilton wrote in explanation]. Mr. Burr loves nothing but

himself; thinks of nothing but his own aggrandizement. . . . In the choice of evils, let them [the Federalists in Congress] take the least. Jefferson is in my view less dangerous than Burr.

Adams, who could have applied influence behind the scenes, refused to say or do anything. Firm in his belief in the separation of powers, he saw it as a question for the legislature in which he, as President, had no business and he would stay far from it.

It was said Adams so bitterly resented that Jefferson had bested him in the election that he refused to come to his aid, and that if the truth were known he preferred Burr. But Adams expressed no enmity toward Jefferson; and in private correspondence, he and Abigail both said they preferred—and expected—Jefferson to be the one chosen. It was not that they had recovered their former affection for Jefferson, but they knew his ability, "all the splendid talents, the long experience," in Adams's words. Like Hamilton, they saw Jefferson as the less "dangerous" man. To Abigail, Burr was a figure "risen upon stilts," with no thought to the good of the country.

If there was a gleam of justice to the crisis, it was the dreadful pass Hamilton had come to. "Mr. Hamilton has carried his eggs to a fine market," Adams told William Tudor, using the old farmer's expression. "The very man—the very two men of all [in] the world that he was most jealous of are now placed above him."

On January 1, 1801, the Adamses held the first New Year's Day reception at the President's House. Several days later, they invited Jefferson to dine, one of several events that belie claims made then and later that Adams and Jefferson refused to speak. "Mr. Jefferson dines with us and in a card reply to the President's invitation, he begs him to be assured of his homage and his high consideration," Abigail wrote Thomas in a letter dated January 3, 1801. Adams having made the overture, Jefferson had responded graciously. Whatever private feelings either harbored, civility prevailed.

Other guests were included and Abigail left an undated account of a conversation with Jefferson, who was seated beside her and professed not to know several members of Congress at the table. She said she knew them all. When he asked what she thought "they mean to do" about the election in the House, she said she did not know, that it was a subject she did not "choose to converse upon," and then demonstrated that she could make him laugh.

> I replied . . . I have heard of a clergyman who upon some difficulty amongst his people, took a text from these words: "And they knew not what to do," from whence he drew this inference, that when a people were in such a situation, they do not know what to do, they should take great care that they do not do they know not what.
> At this he laughed out, and here ended the conversation.

A month later, shortly before she planned to leave for Quincy ahead of the President, Jefferson would come to tea. He "made me a visit . . . in order to take leave and wish me a good journey. It was more than I expected," she wrote. Were it ever in his power to serve her or her family, he said, nothing would give him more pleasure.

Abigail had come to Washington with a "heavy heart," as she told John Quincy in a long letter, and events since had provided little relief. "My residence in this city has not served to endear the world to me. To private and domestic sorrow is added a prospect of public calamity for our country. . . . What is before us Heaven only knows."

"The President," she was pleased to report, "retains his health and his spirits beyond what you could imagine."

They had no plans for the future, except to return to Quincy and take up the life they had both professed so often to want more than anything else, except that this time it would be to stay. To a suggestion from William Tudor that he and Tudor reunite as law partners, Adams replied in a letter of January 20, "I must be farmer John of Stoneyfield and nothing more (I hope nothing less) for the rest of my life."

That evening, when fire broke out next door in the Treasury Building, Adams was immediately out the door and across the way to lend a hand. A newspaper described the event the next day: "The fire for some time threatened the most destructive effects—but through the exertions of the citizens, animated by the example of the President of the United States (who on this occasion fell into the ranks and aided in passing the buckets) was at length subdued."

. . .

WITH LITTLE MORE than a month left to his term in office, Adams made one of the most important decisions of his presidency. Oliver Ellsworth had resigned as Chief Justice. To replace him Adams first turned to his old friend John Jay, but when Jay declined, he chose John Marshall.

According to Marshall's account, Adams and he were conversing in Adams's office at the President's House. "Who shall I nominate now?" Adams asked. When Marshall said he did not know, Adams turned and declared, "I believe I must nominate you."

But it is probable that Adams knew exactly whom he would choose before Marshall ever entered the room. In many ways the nomination was inevitable. Few men had so impressed Adams as Marshall, with his good sense and ability. Nor had anyone shown greater loyalty. He was Adams's kind of Federalist and one who at forty-five—"in the full vigor of middle age," as Adams said—could be expected to serve on the Court for years to come. On January 31, 1801, at the President's House, Adams signed Marshall's commission as Chief Justice, which the Senate confirmed without delay. In its far-reaching importance to the country, Adams's appointment of Marshall was second only to his nomination of George Washington to command the Continental Army twenty-five years before. Possibly the greatest Chief Justice in history, Marshall would serve on the Court for another thirty-four years.

As time ticked away in the "castle house," as he called it, Adams kept steadily at work, awaiting decisions in Congress on a judiciary bill that mattered greatly to him, the fate of the peace treaty, which mattered above all, and ultimately February 11, when the electoral vote would be officially declared and the House would go into special session to resolve the Jefferson-Burr tie.

On February 3, the Senate at last approved the Convention of Mortefontaine. No one was overly enthusiastic. As was once said of the Jay Treaty, it was thought to be about as good as could be expected under the circumstances. What was not known, or even suspected, was that Bonaparte, at the very time he had been dealing with the American commission, was secretly negotiating a transfer of Louisiana from Spain to France.

This portrait of George Washington by Edward Savage was painted at John Adams's request in 1790 and still hangs in the Adams homestead in Quincy. Though at times critical of Washington, Adams admired especially his capacity for self-command.

In a contemporary print, George Washington takes the oath of
office on the balcony of Federal Hall, New York, the first Capitol of
the United States, April 30, 1789. The handsome building was the
work of the French architect Pierre L'Enfant. Not shown are
the tremendous crowds of the day.

40

Vice President John Adams in a
portrait by Charles Willson Peale.

"Never did I live in so delightful a spot," wrote John Adams of
Richmond Hill, the Adams's rented house overlooking the Hudson River.

42

43

Unlike Washington and Adams, Secretary of State Jefferson gloried in the French Revolution.

The first envoy from Jacobin France was the audacious young Citizen Genêt, the son of an old friend of John Adams.

44

The execution by guillotine of King Louis XVI in Paris, January 21, 1793. In America, Adams was among the very few who foresaw the coming bloodbath of the Terror.

The President's House, Philadelphia. Moving in after his inauguration
in 1797, Adams found the furniture in "deplorable condition,"
beds and bedding in a "woeful pickle," the house unbearably
lonely without Abigail.

Crayon portrait of President John Adams made about 1800 by the French artist C. B. J. Fevret de Saint-Memin, by means of a "physionotrace," a device that traced the subject's profile.

47

Benjamin Rush, physician, reformer,
and John Adams's steadfast friend.

Political independent Elbridge Gerry
in whom Adams put his entire trust.

49

High Federalist Timothy Pickering, who as
Secretary of State opposed or secretly undercut
Adams at almost every chance.

Alexander Hamilton of New York in a portrait by John Trumbull. As Washington's brilliant Secretary of the Treasury, Hamilton had at first greatly impressed Adams but later betrayed him. To Abigail Adams, Hamilton was a dangerous man, "another Bonaparte."

A cartoon version of Republican Matthew Lyon and Federalist Roger Griswold battling with fire tongs and cane on the floor of Congress, 1798.

Building the "wooden walls" of a new navy—the 36-gun frigate *Philadelphia* under construction in Philadelphia, 1799.

America and France—*Constellation* and *L'Insurgente*—clash in the most famous encounter of the undeclared war at sea, February 9, 1799.

XYZ Affair—in an American cartoon three U.S. envoys refuse the demands of a five-headed "Paris Monster," the Directory.

John Marshall, Chief Justice of the United States for thirty-five
years, was John Adams's proudest appointment as President.
Adams described Marshall as "plain . . . sensible . . . cautious,
and learned in the law of nations."

Before I end my Letter I pray Heaven to bestow the best of Blessings on this House and all that shall hereafter inhabit it. May none but honest and wise Men ever rule under this roof.

I shall not attempt a description of it. You will form the best Idea of it from Inspection.

Mr Brisler is very anxious for the arrival of the Man and Women and I am much more so for that of the Ladies. I am with unabated confidence and affection yours

John Adams

In his first letter to Abigail from the President's House, November 2, 1800, Adams wrote: "I pray Heaven to bestow the best of Blessings on this House and all that shall hereafter inhabit it. May none but honest and wise men ever rule under this roof." Below: the lines as carved in the mantlepiece of the State Dining Room at the White House.

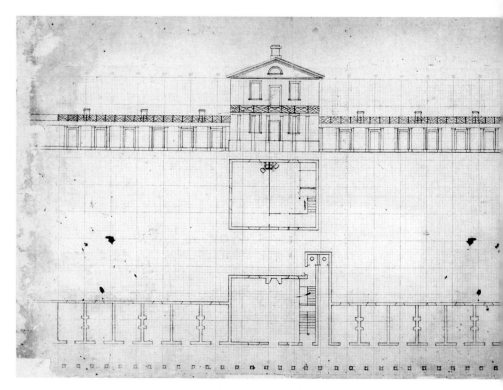

Jefferson's plan for a pavilion at the new University of Virginia, the creation of which Adams called "noble employment."

Thomas Jefferson at seventy-eight, in a life-portrait painted by Thomas Sully at Monticello in 1821.

The Adams House in Quincy, where John and Abigail spent the last years of their lives, remained the family homestead for three more generations.

John Quincy Adams, the sixth President of the United States, in a portrait begun by Gilbert Stuart in 1825 and finished by Thomas Sully in 1830.

The John Adams bust by J. B. Binon, 1819, was thought
remarkably true to life. Jefferson kept a plaster copy of
the original beside his desk at Monticello.

Dreading her long trip home, with "so many horrid rivers to cross and such roads to traverse," Abigail put off her departure until after February 11. "Today," she recorded on February 7, "the judges and many others with the heads of departments dine with me for the last time."

At the Capitol, Wednesday, February 11, the Congress met in joint session. The certificates of the electors were duly opened by the Vice President, who declared the result, and the House went immediately into session to start balloting. But days passed with the House deadlocked, unable to reach a decision. As crowds gathered outside the Capitol, the tension grew extreme. "The crisis is momentous," reported the *Washington Federalist*. There was talk of desperate schemes to prevent the election, talk of civil war.

Abigail decided she should wait no longer. Early in the morning of Friday, February 13, she bid Adams goodbye and with her granddaughter, Susanna, set off by public stage through the "wilderness" to Baltimore, the first leg of the journey home. Her stay in the President's House was over, and she was to have little to say about it ever again.

YEARS LATER, recalling the suspense of waiting for the House decision on the election, Jefferson would describe meeting with Adams on or about February 12 or 14.

"When the election between Burr and myself was kept in suspense by the Federalists," Jefferson would write to Benjamin Rush, "and they were mediating to place the President [pro tempore] of the Senate at the head of government, I called on Mr. Adams with a view to have this desperate measure prevented by his negative." According to Jefferson, Adams acted extremely displeased.

He grew warm in an instant, and said with a vehemence he had not used towards me before, "Sir, the event of the election is within your own power. You have only to say you will do justice to the public creditors, maintain the navy, and not disturb those holding office, and the government will instantly be put into your hands. We know it is the wish of the people it should be so."

"Mr. Adams," said I, "I know not what part of my conduct, in either public or private life, can have authorized a doubt of my fidelity to the public engagements. I say, however, I will not come into the government by capitulation. I will not enter on it, but in perfect freedom to follow the dictates of my own judgment."

"Then," said he, "things must take their course." I turned the conversation to something else, and soon took my leave. It was the first time in our lives we had ever parted with anything like dissatisfaction.

There is nothing to contradict Jefferson's account, or anything to verify it. Neither Adams nor his secretary Billy Shaw made note of a visit by Jefferson, or said anything of such an exchange in later years. Nor is there evidence that Adams ever discussed such terms with the Federalists in the House or took an interest in Federalist strategy. But it was also understandable that the Federalists wanted some assurance on where Jefferson stood, since he had made no statements on public issues.

The suspense ended on Tuesday, February 17, when, on the thirty-sixth ballot in the House, Jefferson was chosen President. One Federalist representative, James A. Bayard of Delaware, decided at last to switch his vote.

Later, Bayard would say Jefferson had agreed to the three Federalist terms, but this Jefferson vehemently denied. The question of what actually happened would remain unresolved.

"The Revolution of 1776 is now, and for the first time, arrived at its completion," proclaimed the *Aurora*.

Till now the Republicans have indeed beaten the slaves of monarchy in the field of battle, and driven the troops of the King of Great Britain from the shores of our country; but the secret enemies of the American Revolution—her internal, insidious, and indefatigable foes, have never till now been completely discomfitted. This is the true period of the triumph of Republican principle.

IN THE LAME-DUCK Federalist Senate, meanwhile, an act expanding the Federal judiciary, something that Adams had proposed more than a year earlier, was passed into law. The number of circuit courts was doubled to six. Twenty-three new judges were added. For Adams, who had so long championed a strong, independent judiciary as proper balance to the other two branches, it was a major improvement and he proceeded at once to fill the new positions.

For weeks Adams had been exercising his presidential prerogative to fill government positions of all kinds, including some for friends and needy relatives. Scruples of the kind he had once preached to Mercy Warren concerning such appointments were considered no more. Colonel Smith was named surveyor of the Port of New York. Joshua Johnson, the father-in-law of John Quincy, who had fled England to avoid his creditors, after his reputed wealth turned out to be a fiction, was made postmaster of the District of Columbia.

But Adams's court appointments particularly were given careful consideration. There was no frenzied rush to name "midnight judges," as portrayed by Jefferson and the Republican press. Most of the nominations for judges were made on February 20, the rest completed by February 24, more than a week in advance of the inauguration. That nearly all those selected were Federalists was no more surprising than the indignation of the President-elect. In fact, most all of the nominees were perfectly good choices and the Republicans opposed hardly any of them. Abigail's nephew, William Cranch, who was nominated and approved for the circuit court of the District of Columbia, went on to have a distinguished fifty-year career, both as a judge and a court reporter.

Without any prompting or pressure, Adams also named Oliver Wolcott for the Second Circuit Court. Incredibly, Adams still trusted and liked Wolcott, never suspecting him of the treachery of others in the cabinet. (Wolcott, for his part, often privately ridiculed the President for being abnormally suspicious.) "I wish you much pleasure and more honor . . . and I doubt not you will contribute your full share to make justice run down our streets as a stream," Adams wrote. "My family joins in friendly regards to you and yours." Wolcott, for all he had done secretly to destroy Adams, was happy to accept the appointment.

Abigail was not to expect much in the way of correspondence from him, Adams told her. "My time will be all taken up. I pray you to continue to write me." He would be entertaining a delegation of Indians that evening, February 16, 1801, his last official dinner—and was glad to say he was sleeping better "for having the shutters open."

Among Adams's final acts as President, and undoubtedly with strong encouragement from Abigail, was to recall John Quincy from his diplomatic service abroad.

Among the last letters he wrote as time ran out was a considerate reminder to Jefferson that he need not purchase horses or carriages, since those in the stable at the President's House were the property of the United States and would therefore remain behind.

ON INAUGURATION DAY, Wednesday, March 4, John Adams made his exit from the President's House and the capital at four in the morning, traveling by public stage under clear skies lit by a quarter moon. He departed eight hours before Thomas Jefferson took the oath of office at the Capitol, and even more inconspicuously than he had arrived, rolling through empty streets past darkened houses, and again with Billy Shaw and John Briesler as his companions.

To his political rivals and enemies Adams's predawn departure was another ill-advised act of a petulant old man. But admirers, too, expressed disappointment. A correspondent for the *Massachusetts Spy* observed in a letter from Washington that numbers of Adams's friends wished he had not departed so abruptly. "Sensible, moderate men of both parties would have been pleased had he tarried until after the installation of his successor. It certainly would have had good effect."

By his presence at the ceremony Adams could have set an example of grace in defeat, while at the same time paying homage to a system whereby power, according to a written constitution, is transferred peacefully. After so vicious a contest for the highest office, with party hatreds so near to igniting in violence, a peaceful transfer of power seemed little short of a miracle. If ever a system was proven to work under extremely adverse circumstances, it was at this inauguration of 1801, and it is regrettable that Adams was not present.

It would also have been more politic to have expressed confidence in his successor, but, such expressions were not Adams's way if he did not mean them.

No President having ever been defeated for reelection until then, there was no tradition of a defeated president appearing at the installation of the winner. It is also quite possible that Adams was not invited to attend, or made to feel he would be welcome. When it was rumored, for example, that Adams might deliver a valedictory to Congress, the *Aurora* had questioned how possibly the "Duke of Braintree" could ever consider appearing before "a body in which his former friends are his enemies, and his former opponents the only persons who pity him." Adams, said the *Aurora*, was a man who had been cast out by God like "polluted water out at the back door." "May he return in safety to Braintree, that Mrs. Adams may wash his befuddled brains clear."

Perhaps, given what Adams had been through at the hands of the Republicans and a number of Federalists still in Congress, those who had done all they could to overthrow him, he simply could not face being made a spectacle of their triumph.

Also, Adams's departure was no sudden, dark-of-the-night impulse. It had been planned more than a week in advance, as is clear from the correspondence of Billy Shaw, and there was no secret about it. To get to Baltimore in a day, one had to take the early stage, and the early stage departed at four in the morning.

Adams himself never explained why he did not stay for Jefferson's inauguration, but then it seems he was never asked.

"We are all Republicans, we are all Federalists," Jefferson said famously in his inaugural address before a full Senate Chamber, his voice so soft many had difficulty hearing him. A passing tribute to Washington was made before he finished, but of Adams he said nothing.

To the victorious Republicans, and to generations of historians, the thought of the tall Jefferson, with his air of youth at fifty-seven, assuming the presidency in the new Capitol at the start of a new century, his eye on the future, would stand in vivid contrast to a downcast, bitter John Adams, old and "toothless" at sixty-five, on his "morning flight" to Baltimore.

Downcast, bitter, Adams may have been, but there is no evidence to support such a description. Adams loved the start of a new day, loved being on the move. Conceivably he felt immense relief to be homeward-bound, free finally of his burdens, his conscience "neat and easy," as he would say. No one will ever know, but it is perfectly possible that as the sun rose higher that cloudless morning, Adams felt contentment of a kind he had not known for years—once he got over the fact that traveling with him on the same stage, as chance would have it, was Theodore Sedgwick. Like two warring boys who are made to sit in the same room until they get along, they would ride together all the way to Massachusetts.

VII

WHATEVER ADAMS'S state of mind, he was leaving his successor a nation "with its coffers full," as he wrote, and with "fair prospects of peace with all the world smiling in its face, its commerce flourishing, its navy glorious, its agriculture uncommonly productive and lucrative."

In turbulent, dangerous times he had held to a remarkably steady course. He had shown that a strong defense and a desire for peace were not mutually exclusive, but compatible and greatly in the national interest. The new navy was an outstanding achievement. In less than two years, it had grown from almost nothing to 50 ships, including the frigates *United States*, *Constitution*, and *Constellation*, and over 5,000 officers and seamen, and this bore heavily on the outcome of the negotiations with France. Indeed, Adams's insistence on American naval strength proved decisive in achieving peace with France in 1800. Further, by undercutting Hamilton and making his army useless, he may have saved the country from militarism.

In his four years as President, there had been no scandal or corruption. If he was less than outstanding as an administrator, if he had too readily gone along with the Alien and Sedition Acts, and was slow to see deceit within his own cabinet, he had managed nonetheless to cope with a divided country and a divided party, and in the end achieved a rare level of statesmanship. To his everlasting credit, at the risk of his career, reputation, and his hold on the presidency, he chose not to go to war when that would have been highly popular and politically advantageous in the short run. As a result, the country was spared what would almost certainly have been a disastrous mistake.

In much the way he had rushed out in the night to help fight fires in Philadelphia and Washington, he had done his all to put out the fire of war—to the immeasurable benefit of the American people, and with no loss of honor or prestige to the nation. It was a brave, heroic performance.

Adams understood clearly the importance of what he had accomplished. To his dying day he would be proudest of all of having achieved peace. As he would write to a friend, "I desire no other inscription over my gravestone than: 'Here lies John Adams, who took upon himself the responsibility of peace with France in the year 1800.' "

In the brief spell of goodwill that followed Adams's inaugural address in 1797, Benjamin Bache had reminded the country that the new President was a "man of incorruptible integrity," "dignity," exceptional "resources of mind," and high purpose. "He declares himself the friend of France and of peace, the admirer of republicanism, the enemy of party. . . . How characteristic of a patriot." The same could have been said at the conclusion of Adams's presidency no less than at the beginning.

Subjected to some of the most malicious attacks ever endured by a president, beset by personal disloyalty and political betrayal, suffering the loss of his mother, the near death of his wife, the death of a son, tormented by physical ailments, he had more than weathered the storm. His bedrock integrity, his spirit of independence, his devotion to country, his marriage, his humor, and a great underlying love of life were all still very much intact.

CHAPTER ELEVEN

REJOICE EVER MORE

This phrase "rejoice ever more" shall never be out of
my heart, memory, or mouth again as long as I live,
if I can help it.

— John Adams

———————————————

I

"THE ONLY QUESTION remaining with me is what shall I do with myself?" Adams had written earlier to Cotton Tufts. "Something I must do, or ennui will rain upon me in buckets."

He could go each morning and evening to fodder his cattle, he supposed. Or take noontime walks to Penn's Hill. Or "potter" among his fruit trees and cucumbers. But what then? If he had money enough to spend on his farms, he might keep busier. But where was the money to come from? Talk of himself as Farmer John of Stoneyfield came easily. The reality would require adjustments.

He worried about the effect on mind and body of slowing to a standstill. His constitution, he was sure, would be put to a severe test after "a life of journeys and distant voyages." Stillness "may shake my old frame," he observed to another friend. "Rapid motion ought not be succeeded by sudden rest."

He sensed he had little time left. "The day is far spent with us all," he would tell Mercy Warren. "It cannot be long before we must exchange this theater for some other." He only hoped it would be one with no politics. He and Abigail both had had enough of politics. "No more elective office for me," she had written with absolute certainty. But neither would ever lose interest in politics.

For Abigail it was not just that the long journey of public life was ended, but that their capacity to "do good" was to be "so greatly curtailed," as she had written before leaving Washington.

As it was, she and Adams had ten days of forced seclusion in which to ponder such concerns, starting almost the moment Adams arrived at Quincy on the evening of March 18, 1801. He was no sooner in the door than a wild northeaster struck, a storm of a kind such as they had not seen in years. Black skies, violent winds, and a flood of rain kept on day after day, no one budging from the house.

Somehow the mail got through, bringing a pointedly formal note of one sentence from the President dated March 8:

> Th. Jefferson presents his respects to Mr. Adams and incloses him a letter which came to his hands last night; on reading what is written within the cover, he concluded it to be a private letter, and without opening a single paper within it, folded it up and now has the honor to inclose it to Mr. Adams, with the homage of his high consideration and respect.

Adams's reply, written on March 24, the fifth day of the storm, was one of the few times he ever acknowledged his suffering over the death of Charles, but suggests also that Jefferson may never have offered a word of sympathy to him.

> Had you read the papers inclosed [Adams wrote] they might have given you a moment of melancholy or at least of sympathy with a mourning father. They relate wholly to the funeral of a son who was once the delight of my eyes and a darling of my heart, cut off in the flower of his days, amidst very flattering prospects by causes which have been the greatest grief of my heart and the deepest affliction of my life.

In closing, Adams said he saw "nothing to obscure your prospect of a quiet and prosperous administration, which I heartily wish you."

Jefferson did not respond, however. Adams's letter was the last there would be between them for eleven years.

The violence and duration of the storm appears to have left Adams in better spirits once it passed. It was, he wrote to Benjamin Stoddert, "so old fashioned a storm that I begin to hope that nature is returning to her old good nature and good humor, and is substituting fermentations in the elements for revolutions in the moral, intellectual, and political world."

Complaining was not the Adamses' mode. The adjustments were more difficult than they would concede. The humiliation that defeat and popular rejection had inflicted on them, the death of Charles, and now sudden, total seclusion took a heavy toll. In some circles, they knew, they were openly despised. In others they were now considered irrelevant. Worst perhaps was the sense that no one any longer cared about them one way or the other.

In the year prior to March 4, letters to President Adams numbered in the thousands; in the year that followed, citizen Adams received fewer than a hundred. Once, while president, he had written to Abigail, "We cannot go back. We must stand our ground as long as we can." In the years following the presidency, it was resolve of a kind they had to summon more often than they admitted.

When members of the Massachusetts legislature came to Quincy to present Adams with a tribute to his devoted service to his country, he was moved to tears.

Feelings of dejection and bitterness would come and go for a long time. Nearly six months after the return to Quincy, in a letter to Billy Shaw, Adams would allow that if he had it to do over again he would have been a shoemaker. His own father, the man he admired above all, had been a shoemaker. Joseph Bass, the young neighbor who had ridden with Adams to Philadelphia the winter of 1776, was a shoemaker and a familiar figure still in Quincy, as well liked and respected as ever.

Long before, on his rounds of Boston as a young lawyer, Adams had often heard a man with a fine voice singing behind the door of an obscure house. One day, curious to know who "this cheerful mortal" might be, he had knocked at the door, to find a poor shoemaker with a large family living in a single room. Did he find it hard getting by, Adams had asked. "Sometimes," the man said. Adams ordered a pair of shoes. "I had scarcely got out the door before he began to sing again like a nightingale,"

Adams remembered. "Which was the greatest philosopher? Epictetus or this shoemaker?" he would ask when telling the story.

Epictetus, the Greek Stoic philosopher, had said, among other things, "It is difficulties that show what men are."

WITH THE REVIVAL of spring on the farm, with fruit trees in flower and warmer days steadily lengthening, familiar roles and routines resumed. Abigail, in a letter to Colonel Smith, asked that he tell Nabby, "I have commenced my operation of dairy woman, and she might see me at five o'clock in the morning skimming my milk." To Catherine Johnson, John Quincy's mother-in-law, she described how the beauties of her garden, "from the window at which I write . . . the full bloom of the pear, the apple, the plum and peach," helped her forget the past and rejoice. "Envy nips not their buds, calumny destroys not their fruits, nor does ingratitude tarnish their colors."

"Your father," she told Thomas, "appears to enjoy tranquility and a freedom of care which he has never before experienced. His books and farm occupy his attention."

Adams professed to be perfectly content in his new "employment," but how long this tranquility would continue, he could not honestly say. "Men are weak," he added in a letter to William Cranch. "No man can answer for himself."

He wrote but few letters, and these mostly to friends who had written to wish him well in retirement. But then, as he said, he did not have a great deal to write about, except for how his corn was growing or "how much wall I lay up every day."

Only occasionally in what he wrote did he reflect on the national or world scene. There was no use trying to predict what Bonaparte might do, because Bonaparte was not like any conqueror of the past, he offered at one point in a letter to Thomas. "Everything I read only serves to confirm me in the opinion of the absolute necessity of our keeping aloof from all European powers and influences, and that a navy is the only arm by which it can be accomplished." Jefferson, he noted, had lately said some "very strong things" about the navy and Adams felt "irresistibly inclined to agree with him." But there was a problem with Jefferson, he told Thomas.

The only misfortune of it is that Mr. Jefferson's sayings are never well digested, often extravagant, and never consistently pursued. He has not a clear head, and never pursues any question through. His ambition and his cunning are the only steady qualities in him. His imagination and ambition are too strong for his reason.

In mid-June came welcome news from John Quincy. After several miscarriages and a difficult pregnancy, Louisa Catherine had given birth to a baby boy on April 12 in Berlin. They would be departing for home as soon as mother and child were strong enough.

Abigail worried about how well John Quincy might cope with his added burdens. "I pray God send him a safe and fortunate passage to his native land, with his poor, weak and feeble wife and baby," she wrote to Thomas. When, a few weeks later, she learned that the baby had been named George Washington Adams, rather than John, she was not pleased. "I am sure your brother had not any intention of wounding the feelings of his father, but I see he has done it."

After seven years abroad, John Quincy would have to begin all over again in the law in Boston, in "a profession he never loved, in a place which promises him no great harvest," Abigail wrote sympathetically. It was "a humiliating prospect." Yet she saw no other choice for him. So long as the Republicans were in power, "the post of honor" would be in private pursuits.

Adams, meantime, was busy in his hayfields, bringing in the biggest crop ever. Where once the yield had been six tons on the same acreage, it was now thirty, to his immense delight.

The Adams domain comprised in all three farms. In addition to the main house, there were the two old houses by Penn's Hill where Adams had been born and where he and Abigail had raised their family. In total, by now, there were more than 600 acres of fields, woods, and salt marsh, and as usual in summer the work required hired help.

Adams loved joining in the work as much as ever—for the exercise and "pure air," the companionship of men he had known and worked with for years, and the pride he took in seeing things done just so. But it all had to be taken with utmost seriousness. Stoneyfield was no gentleman's farm and he no gentleman farmer. The farm that had sustained the Adamses and their family through the lean years of the Revolution would have to sustain them again. They could expect no additional income. And while the farm had expanded over the years, so had the family. The Adams household was more crowded now than it had ever been and would remain so.

John and Abigail had taken Charles's wife Sally and her two daughters in to live with them, and this, in addition to Louisa Smith, made six. Nabby and her four children also moved in for the summer, which brought the total to eleven, not counting servants or visiting cousins or friends, of which there were often two or three. At times, there were twenty people or more beneath their roof. In addition, since the return from Washington, Abigail had acquired a Newfoundland puppy, which she named Juno.

JOHN QUINCY, Louisa Catherine, and their infant son arrived at Philadelphia on the ship *America* on September 4, 1801. "Her health, though yet very infirm, is better than we could have expected," John Quincy said of Louisa Catherine in a letter to his father, "and your grandson is as hearty as any sailor of his age that ever crossed the ocean." They were staying with Thomas and had so much to talk about, there was little time for anything else.

The day the letter reached Quincy, Adams wrote, was one of the happiest of his life.

> I hope you will consider my house as your home, for yourself, your lady, and son, as well as your servants. . . . We can accommodate you all as well as destiny intends that you and I ought to be accommodated, at least until you have time to deliberate on your future arrangements.

After a rest in Philadelphia, Louisa Catherine and the baby traveled to Washington to see her parents, while John Quincy set off for Massachusetts. The only difference he saw in his brother, Thomas reported to his parents, was a "sort of fatherly look." Also, Thomas informed them, "He has no propensity to engage in a political career."

John Quincy wrote of his reunion with his parents as a moment of "inexpressible delight." Arriving on September 21, he found his father in "good health and spirits." His mother, though "very ill," was fast on the mend. Both mother and father, he assured Louisa Catherine, were waiting to receive her with "most cordial affection." In a few weeks, having purchased a house in Boston, he left for Washington to bring her and the baby home. Any apprehensions he may have had about Louisa Catherine's first meeting with his family, he kept to himself.

According to what she wrote long afterward, Louisa Catherine arrived at Quincy and almost immediately decided she liked nothing about it or its quaint ways. It was the Thanksgiving season, the days chill, and she was feeling miserably ill and depressed. Family and friends were gathered to look her over.

Raised in France and London, well read, well mannered, and well spoken with an English accent, she found herself being "gazed" at as a curiosity, "a *fine* lady." Only "the old gentleman took a fancy to me," she would write, remembering Adams's warmth and interest in her. Otherwise, she felt hopelessly out of place.

> Quincy! What shall I say of my impressions of Quincy! Had I stepped into Noah's Ark I do not think I could have been more utterly astonished—Dr Tufts!... Mr Cranch! Old Uncle Peter!... It was lucky for me that I was so much depressed, and so ill, or I should certainly have given mortal offense. Even the church, its form, its snuffling through the nose, the singers, the dressing and dinner hours, were all novelties to me; and the ceremonious parties, the manners, and the hours of meeting half past four were equally astonishing to me.

Thomas, who had been quite taken with Louisa Catherine, wrote to his mother of her "sprightliness and vivacity." Even when "in only tolerable health," Thomas said, "her spirits are abundant." But she was not in tolerable health at Quincy, and her spirits were far from abundant. As she herself recalled, she was "cold and reserved, and seldom spoke which was deemed pride." Everyone wanted to please her and at meals particularly, but the more she was fussed over, the more she resented it.

> I had a separate dish set by me of which no one was to partake; and every delicate preserve was brought out to treat me with in the kind-

est manner ... and though I felt very grateful, it appeared so strongly to stamp me with unfitness that often I would not eat my delicacy, and thus gave offense. Mrs. Adams was too kind.... Louisa Smith was jealous to excess, and the first day that I arrived, left the table crying and sobbing, and could not be induced to eat any dinner.

Abigail's impressions, written at the time, express concern rather than disapproval. The young woman seemed so terribly frail and suffered such a racking cough that Abigail feared for her life. "Her frame is so slender and her constitution so delicate that I have many fears that she will be of short duration."

Except for "the old gentleman's" obvious approval of Louisa Catherine, it was not an auspicious beginning. Abigail found it impossible to ignore the "weight of worry" that had been added to John Quincy's brow.

Louisa Catherine was twenty-six years old, John Quincy thirty-four. In the time he had been away, his hair had greatly thinned, which made him look older, and he did indeed have a serious expression most of the time. With age he was looking more like his father than he had, and there was no mistaking his extraordinary intelligence. But he was less ardent, less spontaneous than his father. He had little of Adams's passion for life or his humor.

By Christmas the young family had moved into their new home in Boston. John Quincy worried over expenses, worried that his parents might find themselves with too little money. Finding it difficult to get started again in the law, feeling like a stranger, and bored with what work he had, he toyed with the thought of giving it up and striking out for a life of "rustic independence" in the wilds of upstate New York, an idea encouraged by his brother-in-law Colonel Smith and that appealed at once to brother Thomas. "I am your man for a new country," Thomas affirmed, convinced that his own legal career in Philadelphia was going nowhere. That neither of them was the least prepared or suited for such a venture seems not to have occurred to them.

But the impulse passed as John Quincy began to feel more at home in Boston and acquired a circle of friends. And whatever prior aversion to politics he had had, or that his parents may have expressed, he was very soon involved. "Walked in the mall just before night," he recorded in his diary on January 28, 1802. "I feel a strong temptation and have great provocation to plunge into political controversy." Then he wrote, "A politician in this country must be the man of a party. I would fain be the man of my whole country."

In April 1802, less than four months after settling in the city, John Quincy was elected to the Massachusetts Senate. The following November, he ran as a Federalist candidate for Congress and lost, but by less than 100 votes. He had become a rising star. In February 1803, at age thirty-five, John Quincy Adams was elected a United States senator, a victory made all the sweeter by the fact that his opponent was Timothy Pickering.

In the meantime, he could not have been a more dutiful son, riding out to Quincy to be with his parents nearly every weekend. He kept his father supplied with books and encouraged him to undertake an autobiography, which Adams, with some reluctance, began in October 1802, with Part I, titled "John Adams."

But it was the following spring, in 1803, just after he had been elected to the Senate, that John Quincy came to the rescue of his father and mother as no one else could have.

Partly on his advice, most of what John and Abigail had managed to save over the years—some $13,000—had been invested with the London banking house of Bird, Savage & Bird, bankers for the United States Treasury. It had seemed an entirely prudent step. But in 1803, the house of Bird, Savage & Bird collapsed, leaving the Adamses on the brink of ruin.

At once, John Quincy stepped in to save them. "The error of judgment was mine," he wrote, "and therefore I shall not refuse to share in the suffering." By selling his house in Boston, drawing on his own savings, and borrowing, he was able to proceed slowly to buy up his parents' property, ultimately paying them what they had lost, while they retained title to the land for life.

To their joy, he also announced that he would move to Quincy with his family, which by the summer of 1803 included a newborn second son, this one named John Adams. The plan was to live in the house where John Quincy had been born. But by September he and his family were off to Washington.

II

To the great surprise of those who had predicted nothing but dire consequences should Thomas Jefferson ever rise to the presidency, the advent of Jefferson in the President's House turned out to be far from a radical upheaval, or a second Revolution, as he claimed.

Not surprisingly, Jefferson made Madison the Secretary of State and chose Albert Gallatin as Secretary of the Treasury. He did away with presidential levees, something Adams had wanted to do but felt obliged to continue. Under the new system, Jefferson received the public only twice a year at the President's House, New Year's Day and the Fourth of July. He entertained frequently, but preferred small, elegant dinners, which were part of his way of carrying on the process of government. Rather than going to the Capitol to speak before Congress, he submitted his annual message in writing.

Among his first decisions after taking office was to release from jail those sentenced for violating the Sedition Act, and with the avid support of the Republican majority in Congress, he did away with Adams's Judiciary Act and the new circuit courts. Further, Jefferson abolished the old whiskey tax and began cutting back on the navy, halting shipbuilding and selling off ships already built, while at the same time, ironically, starting to deal effectively with the Barbary pirates.

Yet the first year and more passed with surprisingly little commotion or sensation, until the first weeks of September 1802, shortly before John Quincy declared himself a candidate for Congress. It was then, in the second year of Jefferson's new administration, that the rumor hitherto only whispered, of a liaison between Jefferson and a slave woman, broke into print. What made it especially sensational was that the source of the allegation was his own former ally and unrelenting scourge of John Adams, the notorious James Callender. As Abigail would later tell Jefferson bluntly, it was as though the serpent he had "cherished and warmed" had turned and "bit the hand that nourished him."

The slave woman, as the Adamses and the country learned, was Sally Hemings, who fifteen years before, at age fourteen, had arrived with little Polly Jefferson at the house on Grosvenor Square in London, and Abigail had judged her too immature to look after the child.

Callender, having served his sentence for violating the Sedition Act, was out of jail by the time Jefferson took office. But unable to pay the fine imposed by the court, he had appealed to Jefferson for help, asking also that he be made postmaster in Richmond. Feeling that Jefferson owed him as much and more, Callender went to Washington to see Madison and in the course of the meeting implied that if denied his requests he might have things to say. Madison warned Jefferson, who immediately, on May 28, 1801, had his secretary, Meriwether Lewis, give Callender $50.

Furious at Jefferson's parsimony, Callender switched sides to become the editor of a new Federalist paper, in Richmond, the *Recorder*. In the summer that followed, writing in the *Recorder*, Callender revealed that Jefferson, while Vice President, had secretly subsidized and encouraged him as he broke the Hamilton-Reynolds scandal and did all he could to defame John Adams. For proof Callender quoted several of Jefferson's letters to him.

"I am really mortified at the base ingratitude of Callender," Jefferson wrote to James Monroe on July 14. His concern, Jefferson said, was that his own "mere motives of charity" might be misunderstood.

When the Republican press attacked Callender for his "apostasy, ingratitude, cowardice, lies, venality, and constitutional malignity," Callender struck back in the *Recorder* on September 1, 1802, under the title "The President Again":

> It is well known that the man *whom it delighteth the people to honor*, keeps and for many years has kept, a concubine, one of his slaves. Her name is Sally. . . .
>
> By this wench Sally, our President has had several children. There is not an individual in the neighborhood of Charlottesville who does not believe the story, and not a few who know it. . . . The AFRICAN VENUS is said to officiate as housekeeper at Monticello.

In subsequent articles Callender reported that Sally Hemings had five children, that she had been in France with Jefferson, and claimed that now, with the truth out, Jefferson could expect certain defeat in the next election. The stories spread rapidly, appearing in the Federalist press— the *New York Evening Post*, the *Washington Federalist*, the *Gazette of the*

United States, and in Boston in the *Gazette* and the *Columbian Centinel*, papers read by the Adamses. A cartoon published at Newburyport, titled "A Philosophic Cock," pictured Jefferson as a rooster strutting with his dark hen Sally. In October the *Boston Gazette* ran the words to a song of several stanzas, supposed to have been written by the sage of Monticello to be sung to the tune of "Yankee Doodle":

> *Of all the damsels on the green*
> *On mountain, or in valley*
> *A lass so luscious ne'er was seen,*
> *As Monticellian Sally.*
> *Yankee Doodle, who's the noodle?*
> *What wife were half so handy?*
> *To breed a flock of slaves for stock,*
> *A blackamoor's a dandy.*

The *Aurora* and the rest of the Republican press remained conspicuously silent on the subject, taking their lead from the President. Jefferson, who made it a "rule of life" not to respond to newspaper attacks, neither denounced Callender nor denied or admitted a connection with Sally Hemings.

That Callender was a malicious scoundrel was undeniable and more than enough for many people to dismiss his charges out of hand. There was no evidence, and further, the story seemed preposterously out of character for a man of such refinement and intellect, not to say for the President of the United States. To Republicans it was but one more act of Federalist villainy.

What was actually known of "Monticellian Sally" amounted to little, and for all the rumors, all that was written then and later, relatively little would ever be known. She was the daughter of a slave woman named Betty Hemings, who had belonged to Jefferson's father-in-law, John Wayles, who reputedly was Sally's father. If true, this made her the half-sister of Jefferson's wife Martha, and it was said that she resembled Martha Jefferson and was fair-skinned and "decidedly good looking." An aged former Monticello slave, Isaac Jefferson, would later remember Sally as "very handsome, long straight hair down her back." To what degree she had benefited from her years in France, whether she could read

or write, or anything about her disposition or abilities are matters of speculation.

It was true, as Callender reported, that by 1802 Sally had given birth
to five children, but two had died in infancy. According to surviving
records, she had seven children, all born at Monticello, two of whom
came later, Madison in 1805 and Easton in 1808. From Jefferson's own
records, it is clear that he was at home at Monticello at least nine months
before the birth of each of her children, and that she never conceived
when he was not there. Her children were all light-skinned and several, as
gossiped then, looked astonishingly like Jefferson.

More than half a century later, Jefferson's grandson, Thomas Jefferson Randolph, the son of Jefferson's daughter Martha, would declare
that the real father of Sally Hemings's children was Jefferson's nephew,
Peter Carr, which was said to explain the striking Jefferson resemblance
in the Hemings children.

Sally Hemings's son Madison would say his mother told him that his
father was Jefferson. According to Madison's account, given long afterward, her relationship with Jefferson began in Paris, and she was pregnant with her first child when she returned to Monticello.

How the Adamses felt about the Callender accusations would not
come to light until much later and in private correspondence only. Of the
two, Adams would have less to say, and unlike Abigail, he did not confront Jefferson with his ire.

Considering all that Adams had suffered at the hand of Callender, it
would have been quite understandable had he lashed out at Jefferson for
his hypocrisy and immorality. Adams could well have gloated over the
spectacle of Jefferson under fire. But he did not.

It was not until 1810—not until Jefferson's presidency was over—
that Adams, in a letter to a friend, took up the subject of Callender, Jefferson, and Sally Hemings, privately offering several opinions and
suggesting at the close of the letter, "You may burn it if you please."

For Callender, Adams had no use whatever. "I believe nothing that
Callender said any more than if it had been said by an infernal spirit. I
would not convict a dog of killing a sheep upon the testimony of two such
witnesses," Adams wrote with characteristic verve, indicating that he
did not believe Callender's accusations about Jefferson. Jefferson's

"charities" to Callender, however, were a "disgrace." "I give him up to censure for this and I have a better right to do so, because my conscience bears me witness that I never wrote a line against my enemies nor contributed one farthing to any writer for vindicating me or accusing my enemies." But continuing on, Adams clearly implied that, in fact, he did believe Callender. An unnamed "great lady" who knew the South, he wrote, had said "she did not believe there was a planter in Virginia who could not reckon among his slaves a number of children."

Then Adams put the issue squarely where it belonged, saying, in essence, that all such stories of slave masters and their slave women were metaphors for the overriding sin of slavery itself.

Callender and Sally will be remembered as long as Jefferson as blots on his character. The story of the latter is a natural and almost unavoidable consequence of that foul contagion in the human character, Negro slavery.

ABIGAIL, to judge by her correspondence, had no wish to say anything on the subject, or to have any contact with Jefferson. She did not consider him a great man, she had told Thomas earlier. She pitied his "weakness" and took much that he professed to be "hollow." Still, she wrote, there was "a little corner of my heart where once he sat . . . [and] from whence I find it hard wholly to discard him."

But in the spring of 1804, nearly two years after the Callender accusations, Abigail learned of the death of Jefferson's daughter, Mary Jefferson Eppes, the Polly for whom she had felt such affection during the child's stay with her in London. Deeply touched, Abigail wrote Jefferson to express her heartache and sympathy. Until then, she had not written a word to him in seventeen years, not since London. Reasons of "various kinds" had withheld her pen, she explained, "until the powerful feelings of my heart have burst through the restraint. . . . The attachment which I formed for her, when you committed her to my care, has remained with me to this hour." Yet she signed herself not in friendship, or as his friend, but as one "who once took pleasure in subscribing herself your friend."

Her letter profoundly moved him, Jefferson wrote from the President's House. He would ever remember her kindness to Polly, he said, at the same time expressing regret that "circumstances should have arisen which seemed to draw a line between us." He wished to be friends still:

> The friendship with which you honored me has ever been valued and fully reciprocated; and although events have been passing which might be trying to some minds, I never believed yours to be of that kind, nor felt that my own was. Neither my estimate of your character, nor the esteem founded in that, have ever been lessened for a single moment.

Reflecting on his friendship with Adams, he recalled how it had accompanied them "through long and important scenes," and that while their differences of opinion, resulting from "honest conviction," might make them seem rivals in the minds of their fellow citizens, they were not in their own minds. "We never stood in one another's way."

There Jefferson might well have ended the letter, and the extraordinary exchange that followed with Abigail would never have happened. But he had a wound to air.

> I can say with truth that one act of Mr. Adams's life, and only one ever gave me a moment's personal displeasure. I did consider his last appointments to office as personally unkind. . . . It seemed but common justice to leave a successor free to act by instruments of his own choice.

Affirming his "high respect" for her husband, he closed saying, "I have thus, my dear madam, opened myself to you without reserve, which I have long wished an opportunity of doing; and, without knowing how it will be received, I feel relief from being unbosomed."

Abigail left little doubt of her anger in what she wrote in reply. He had no right to complain of his predecessor's appointments, she lectured Jefferson. The Constitution empowered the president to fill offices when they were vacant and "Mr. Adams" had chosen well. Besides, she argued inaccurately, he made his choices before it was known whether he, Jefferson, or Burr would be President, and so Jefferson had no cause to take personal offense.

Then, mincing no words, she got to what for her was the heart of the matter. However smoothly he wrote of past differences being only those resulting from "honest conviction," she refused to let him slide by. "And now, sir, I will freely disclose to you what has severed the bonds of former friendship and placed you in a light very different from what I once viewed you in."

She was outraged by his dealings with Callender, and particularly as revealed in the letters Callender had published. Of the accusations concerning Sally Hemings she said nothing. The issue to her was Callender, who by then was dead. He had been found on a Sunday in June 1803, in Richmond, floating by the shore of the James River in three feet of water. He had been seen earlier wandering the town in a drunken state, but the circumstances of his death were unknown.

Abigail mistakenly understood that Jefferson had liberated the "wretch" Callender from jail, and this to her was totally unacceptable, after the attacks Callender had made on Adams, a man, she reminded Jefferson, "for whom you professed the highest esteem and friendship." Was he not, as President, she asked, answerable for the influence of his example upon the manners and morals of the nation? She had tried, she said, to believe him innocent of any part in Callender's slanderous attacks.

Until I read Callender's seventh letter, containing your compliment to him as a writer and your reward of 50 dollars, I could not be made to believe that such measures could have been resorted to: to stab the fair fame and upright intentions of one who, to use your language, "was acting from an honest conviction in his own mind that he was right." This, sir, I considered as a personal injury. This was the sword that cut asunder the Gordian knot which could not be untied by all the efforts of party spirit, by rivalship, by jealousy, or any other malignant fiend.

The serpent you cherished and warmed, bit the hand that nourished him, and gave you sufficient specimens of his talents, his gratitude, his justice, and his truth. When such vipers are let loose upon society, all distinction between virtue and vice are leveled, all respect for character is lost.

Her letter, she assured him, was written in confidence. She had shown it to no one. "Faithful are the wounds of a friend," she concluded, quoting *Proverbs*. "I bear no malice, I cherish no enmity. I would not retaliate if I could—nay more in the true spirit of Christian charity, I would forgive, as I hope to be forgiven."

Jefferson protested. He was being falsely accused. "My charities to him [Callender] were no more meant as encouragements to his scurrilities than those I give to the beggar at my door are meant as rewards for the vices of his life, and to make them chargeable to myself." He had never suspected Adams of being party to the "atrocities" committed against him by Fenno and Porcupine, so why should he be suspected? He himself had "ever borne testimony to Mr. Adams's personal wrath," he assured her.

It was all quite disingenuous, as doubtless Abigail knew. Jefferson had indeed encouraged and paid Callender for his efforts, and he had spoken of Adams in quite unflattering terms on a number of occasions.

Altogether seven letters passed between Abigail and the President, in the course of which she brought up one further matter that, to her mind, had put great strain on the past friendship. A district judge had earlier appointed John Quincy a commissioner of bankruptcy in Boston, a petty federal office involving petty fees, but that had made a difference to him in his first lean year in Boston. When, under Jefferson, John Quincy was suddenly replaced, Abigail had taken it as an act of personal reprisal by Jefferson himself, which it was not, as he managed now to convince her.

"I conclude with sincere prayers for your health and happiness, that yourself and Mr. Adams may long enjoy the tranquility you desire and merit," Jefferson wrote, bringing to a conclusion his part in the exchange.

Abigail wished him well in his responsibilities and promised to intrude on his time no more. But his part as a "rewarder and encourager" of Callender, "a libeler whom you could not but detest and despise," she could not and would not forget. Once she had felt both affection and esteem for him, she wrote. "Affection still lingers in the bosom, even after esteem has taken flight."

This, her last letter, was written on October 25, 1804. On November 19, Adams wrote the following at the bottom of her letter-book copy:

The whole of this correspondence was begun and conducted without my knowledge or suspicion. Last evening and this morning at the desire of Mrs. Adams, I read them whole. I have no remarks to make upon it at this time and in this place.

III

THE PROSPECT OF WRITING an autobiography had never really appealed to Adams. Writing history was difficult at best, he knew, and if personal history, it could be most discomforting. "It is a delicate thing to write from memory," he told John Quincy. "To me the undertaking would be too painful. I cannot but reflect upon scenes I have beheld." So having barely begun his projected memoir in the fall of 1802, he let it drop.

For more than a year he wrote little at all, devoting the greater part of his time to the farm. As always, he read much of every day—old favorites in Latin, Greek, and French, English poetry and history, journals such as the *Edinburgh Review*, and newspapers to the point he feared he might become a newspaper (as "button-maker becomes button at last"). He saw a few old friends, went on long walks with Richard Cranch, attended church, and hugely enjoyed the company of his grandchildren.

But his days on the move, on the road, were truly over. Only on rare occasions did he go even to Boston or Cambridge, to attend a Harvard commencement or a dinner of the American Academy of Sciences. At Fourth of July celebrations in Boston he would join Robert Treat Paine and Elbridge Gerry "in the place of honor" as surviving signers of the Declaration of Independence. But at the most now, the radius of his world was about fifteen miles.

Like Abigail, he worried about Thomas, who seemed incapable of taking hold in Philadelphia and suffered spells of gloom and loneliness, his "blue devils," and with Abigail he rejoiced when Thomas quit Philadelphia and moved back to Quincy to try a fresh start. Thomas's presence, the pleasure of his company in the evenings, helped compensate for the large vacant place in the Adamses' life since the departure of John Quincy for Washington. For her part, Abigail told John Quincy to eat well, not work too hard, and mind his appearance.

I do not wish a Senator to dress like a beau, but I want him to conform so far as to the fashion as not to incur the character of singularity, nor give occasion to the world to ask what kind of mother he had or to charge upon a wife negligence and inattention when she is guiltless. The neatest man, observed a lady the other day, wants his wife to pull up his collar and mind that his coat is brushed.

John Quincy took his seat in the Senate in time to give Jefferson support in the biggest accomplishment of his presidency, the purchase of the Louisiana Territory. With the acquisition of Louisiana from Spain, Napoleon Bonaparte had begun planning a French empire in North America. But when the army he sent to crush the slave revolt in San Domingo was wiped out by war and yellow fever, Bonaparte abandoned his plans and suddenly, in 1803, offered to sell the United States all of the vast, unexplored territory of Louisiana. It was an astounding turn of events and one that probably would not have come to pass had the Quasi-War burst into something larger. Were it not for John Adams making peace with France, there might never have been a Louisiana Purchase.

Federalists in Congress argued that under the Constitution the powers of the President did not include buying foreign territory. Jefferson, who had for so long advocated less, not more, power in the executive, chose to take a larger view now, given the opportunity he had to double the size of the nation at a stroke. John Quincy crossed party lines to support the purchase, which his father, too, strongly favored. " 'Curse the stripling, how he apes his sire,' " declared one irate Massachusetts Federalist.

When John Quincy joined in an unsuccessful attempt to stop the spread of slavery into Louisiana, he found it harder than pulling a "jaw tooth," he told his father. "This is now in general the great art of legislation at this place," he continued, venting his frustration. "To *do* a thing by assuming the appearance of *preventing* it. To *prevent* a thing by assuming that of *doing* it."

In the summer of 1804, on the banks of the Hudson River at Weehawken, New Jersey, Alexander Hamilton was fatally wounded in a duel with Vice President Aaron Burr. Carried back across the river to New York, Hamilton died the next day, July 12.

When the Vice President returned to Washington to preside over the Senate, he was looked upon by many, including young Senator Adams, as no better than a murderer. John Adams would write that though he had forgiven his "arch enemy," Hamilton, Hamilton's "villainy" was not forgotten. Nor did he feel obliged "to suffer my character to lie under infamous calumnies because the author of them with a pistol bullet in his spinal marrow, died a penitent."

In the election of 1804, Jefferson and George Clinton of New York, the vice-presidential candidate for the Republicans, won by an overwhelming margin. Even Massachusetts went for Jefferson.

Much that John Quincy wrote to his parents from the Capitol had a familiar ring. "Hitherto my conduct has given satisfaction to neither side," he observed, "and both are offended at what they consider a vain and foolish presumption of singularity, or an ambition of taking a lead different from the views of either. All this I cannot help."

John Quincy and Louisa Catherine had dined at the President's House, and would again several times, finding Jefferson no less engaging than ever, but overly fond of extravagant claims and "large stories." One evening, John Quincy listened in amazement as Jefferson described how, during one of his winters in Paris, the temperature had dropped to twenty below zero for six weeks. It was a preposterous claim. Nothing of the sort had ever happened, as John Quincy knew from having been there. "He knows better than all this, but loves to excite wonder." At another point, commenting on the French Revolution, Jefferson said it seemed all to have been a dream. John Quincy, as he reported to his father, could hardly believe his ears.

Jefferson had installed a French chef in the presidential mansion. His wine bill alone exceeded $2,500 a year. "There was, as usual, the dissertation upon wines, not very edifying," John Quincy recorded after another dinner. "Mr. Jefferson said that the *Epicurean* philosophy came nearest to the truth, in his opinion, of any ancient system of philosophy."

In addition to serving in the Senate, John Quincy also accepted a new professorial chair of rhetoric and oratory at Harvard. Adams's pride in his brilliant son could not have been greater, as he let him know when at times John Quincy grew discouraged with the pettiness and hypocrisies of politics.

Patience and perseverance will carry you with honor through all difficulties. Virtuous and studious from your youth, beyond any other instance I know, I have great confidence in your success in the service of your country, however dark your prospects may be at present. Such talents and such learning as you possess, with a character so perfectly fair and a good humor so universally acknowledged, it is impossible for you to fail.

Reminding him of their ordeal on the *Boston*, when "you and I . . . clasped each other together in our arms, and braced our feet against the bedboards and bedsteads to prevent us from having our brains dashed out," Adams said he himself had since weathered worse political storms, "and here I am alive and hearty yet."

Alive and hearty he was, and remarkably so, all things considered. He was a picture of health, as visitors and family members would attest. He still nursed wounds of defeat; he could brood over past insults; he longed for vindication, and for gratitude for so much that he had done and the sacrifices he had made. And he dwelled often on death. Dear old friends were passing from the scene—Parson Wibird, Samuel Adams. He was "never more to see anything but my plow between me and the grave," Adams told a correspondent, sounding more than a little sorry for himself. Yet in the same letter he claimed to be happier than he had ever been, which if said partly for effect—as a matter of pride—was also fundamentally true, once the initial years of retirement had passed and particularly after he began writing again.

In early 1805, after four years at Quincy, during which he had made little effort to contact others, Adams decided to send a letter of greetings to his old friend Benjamin Rush.

"Dear Sir," Adams began on February 6, "It seemed to me that you and I ought not to die without saying goodbye, or bidding each other adieu. Pray how do you do? How does that excellent lady, Mrs. R?

Is the present state of the national republic enough? Is virtue the principle of our government? Is honor? Or is ambition and avarice, adulation, baseness, covetousness, the thirst for riches, indifference concerning the means of rising and enriching, the contempt of principle, the spirit of party and of faction the motive and principle that governs?

"My much respected and dear friend," Rush answered. "Your letter of the 6th instant revived a great many pleasant ideas in my mind. I have not forgotten—I cannot forget you."

You and your excellent Mrs. Adams often compose a conversation by my fireside. We now and then meet with a traveler who has been at Quincy, from whom we hear with great pleasure not only that you enjoy good health, but retain your usual good spirits.

And so began an extended, vivid correspondence between the two men that was to occupy much of their time and bring each continuing enjoyment. For Adams it was as if he had found a vocation again. His letters to Rush became a great outpouring of ideas, innermost feelings, pungent asides, and opinions on all manner of things and mutual acquaintances—so much that he had kept within for too long. He wrote of his worries about the future and the sham of the political scene. "My friend! Our country is a masquerade! No party, no man dares to avow his real sentiments. All is disguise, vizard, cloak."

Much of his strength and capacity for study were gone, Adams professed. "But such is the constitution of my mind that I cannot avoid forming an opinion."

[Samuel] Johnson said when he sat upon his throne in a tavern, there he dogmatized and was contradicted, and in this he found delight. My throne is not in a tavern but at my fireside. There I dogmatize, there I laugh and there the newspapers sometimes make me scold; and in dogmatizing, laughing, and scolding I find delight, and why should not I enjoy it, since no one is the worse for it and I am the better.

He had by now resumed work on his autobiography as well, Part II, "Travels and Negotiations," though it was still labor he did not relish. "To rummage trunks, letter books, bits of journals and great heaps of bundles of old papers is a dreadful bondage to old age, and an extinguisher of old eyes." And how, after all, did one write about one's self, he asked Rush. What must he say of his own vanity and levity? How was he to account for so many impulsive, tactless, ill-considered things he had said down the years?

There have been very many times when I have been so agitated in
my own mind as to have no consideration at all of the light in which
my words, actions, and even writings would be considered by others.
Indeed, I never could bring myself seriously to consider that I was a
great man, or of much importance or consideration in the world. The
few traces that remain of me must, I believe, go down to posterity in
much confusion and distraction, as my life has passed. Enough
surely of egotism!

He wrote of how greatly friendship mattered to him. "There is something in my composition which restrains me from rancour against any
man with whom I have once lived in friendship." He wrote of his sense of
duty to his country. "Our obligations to our country never cease but with
our lives." And the threats he saw to the country: "The internal intrigues
of our monied and landed and slaved aristocracies are and will be our
ruin." He reported to the learned physician of his own health and disposition, assuring him "my spirits have been as cheerful as they ever were
since some sin, to me unknown, involved me in politics." And he
described his physical activities, which began at five or six in the morning
with work on his stone walls.

I call for my leavers and iron bars, for my chisels, drills, and wedges
to split rocks, and for my wagons to cart seaweed for manure upon
my farm. I mount my horse and ride on the seashore, and I walk
upon Mount Wollaston and Stonyfield Hill.

For a healthful diet, he told the abstemious Rush, he believed, like the
doctors of his youth, in milk and vegetables, "with very little animal food
and still less spiritous liquors." In his autobiography, however, Adams
told how his "excellent father" had encouraged him to partake of more
meat as well as more "comforting" drink than milk.

He wrote of his renewed enjoyment of Shakespeare—Adams would
read Shakespeare twice through again in 1805—and in his continued
devotion to Cicero and the Bible. And he dwelt much on ideas. The ideal
of the perfectibility of man as expounded by eighteenth-century philosophers—perfectibility "abstracted from all divine authority"—was unacceptable, he declared.

It is an idea of the Christian religion, and ever has been of all believers of the immortality of the soul, that the intellectual part of man is capable of progressive improvement for ever. Where then is the sense of calling the perfectibility of man an original idea or modern discovery. . . . I consider the perfectibility of man as used by modern philosophers to be mere words without a meaning, that is mere nonsense.

He had himself, he told Rush, "an immense load of errors, weaknesses, follies and sins to mourn over and repent of." These were "the only affliction" of his present life. But St. Paul had taught him to rejoice ever more and be content. "This phrase 'rejoice ever more' shall never be out of my heart, memory or mouth again as long as I live, if I can help it. This is my perfectibility of man."

The letters sparkled with aphorisms—on the virtue of America standing free from binding involvement with other nations: "We stand well, let us stand still"; on the perils of majority rule: "Absolute power in a majority is as drunk as it is in one"; on lawyers: "No civilized society can do without lawyers." Of kings and presidents, Adams said he saw little to distinguish them from other men. "If worthless men are sometimes at the head of affairs, it is, I believe, because worthless men are at the tail and the middle." In a spirited appraisal of the overall folderol of an election year, he wrote:

Our electioneering racers have started for the prize. Such a whipping and spurring and huzzaing! Oh what rare sport it will be! Through thick and thin, through mire and dirt, through bogs and fens and sloughs, dashing and splashing and crying out, the devil take the hindmost.

How long will it be possible that honor, truth or virtue should be respected among a people who are engaged in such a quick and perpetual succession of such profligate collisions and conflicts?

Rush, a champion of reform in education, thought Greek and Latin were outmoded and should be replaced with the study of modern languages, which Adams considered thoroughly wrongheaded. "Your labors will be as useless as those of Tom Paine against the Bible," Adams declared, but wrote also, "Mrs. Adams says she is willing [for] you [to] discredit Greek and Latin, because it will destroy the foundation of all pretensions of the gentlemen to superiority over the ladies, and restore liberty, equality, and fraternity between the sexes."

Adams made frequent mention of his high regard for physicians as professional men and as friends. Benjamin Waterhouse was "a jewel of a man"; Cotton Tufts was "one of the best men in the world." And the respect and affection he felt for Rush were abundantly apparent, even in the ways Adams would address him: "Honored and Learned Sir," "My dear Philosopher and Friend," "My Sensible and Humorous Friend," "Learned, Ingenious, Benevolent, Beneficient Old Friend of 1774," "My Dear Old Friend." "I am not subject to low spirits," Adams would tell Rush, "but if I was, one of your letters would cure me at any time for a month."

For all their differences in political views, neither man had ever abandoned the other. When, in the aftermath of the yellow fever epidemics of 1793 and 1797, Rush had been publicly attacked for his bloodletting treatment, both by Philadelphia physicians and the press, and his practice dwindled to the point that he could barely survive, Adams, who was then President and struggling with troubles of his own, had appointed him treasurer of the United States Mint. It had been a generous act of friendship that Rush and his family never forgot. Though bound by political philosophy to Jefferson, Rush felt a closer personal tie to Adams.

Rush proved an eager and engaging correspondent, his letters brimming with opinion and vitality, and quite as candid as Adams's own. "You see," Rush wrote, "I think *aloud* in my letters to you as I did in those written near 30 years ago, and as I have often done in your company."

But then they were both thinking aloud, both writing the way they spoke, each keeping the other company with common interest and shared miseries. If Adams had been rejected by the vote of the people, Rush had been made an outcast by much of his own profession. Each was lonely except for friends and family. "I live like a stranger in my native state," Rush confided. "My patients are my only acquaintances, my books my only companions, and the members of my family nearly my only friends." If Adams thought he might have been better off as a shoemaker, Rush would tell him, "I often look back upon the hours I spent serving my country (so unproductive of the objects to which they were devoted) with deep regret." But much that Rush wrote was exactly the medicine Adams needed, as if the old physician in Philadelphia understood his distant patient perfectly.

Mr. Madison and his lady are now in our city [he reported to Adams]. It gave me great pleasure to hear him mention your name in the most respectful terms a few days ago. He dwelt upon your "genius and integrity," and acquitted you of ever having had the least friendly designs in your administration upon the present forms of our American governments. [Madison did not consider Adams a monarchist, in other words.] He gave you credit likewise for your correct opinion of banks and standing armies in our country.

To Adams, Rush was a true cohort, in the original meaning of the word—one belonging to the same division of a Roman legion and united in the same struggle. With Rush, Adams felt free to say things not possible with just anyone, as for example in appraising those they had known in the struggle.

When considering George Washington, said Adams, one must always bear in mind that he was a Virginian, which was worth at least five talents, in that "Virginian geese are all swans." Washington, furthermore, was a great actor who had "the gift of silence," which, wrote Adams, "I esteem as one of the most precious talents." Washington was too "unlearned" and had seen too little of the world for someone in his "station." Still, Washington was a "thoughtful man," and had great self-command, a quality Adams admired in the extreme.

Dabbling in medical theory, Adams suggested that all Hamilton's overheated ambitions and impulses might be attributed to "a superabundance of secretions which he could not find whores enough to draw off!" and that "the same vapors produced his lies and slanders by which he totally destroyed his party forever and finally lost his life in the field of honor."

Knowing how much Rush admired Jefferson, Adams was nonetheless equally candid on the subject. Hamilton was a great "intriguer," but so, too, was Jefferson, Adams wrote. "Jefferson has succeeded, and multitudes are made to believe that he is pure benevolence. . . . But you and I know him to be an intriguer."

He held no resentment against Jefferson, "though he has honored and salaried almost every villain he could find who had been an enemy to me." Nor would he publicly criticize Jefferson's handling of the presidency. "I think instead of opposing systematically any administration, running down their characters and opposing all their measures, right or wrong, we ought to support every administration as far as we can in justice."

THE RESUMPTION of correspondence with Benjamin Rush was one of the happiest events of Adams's life in retirement. Rush's wife remarked that the two elderly gentlemen were behaving like a couple of schoolgirls. And though they were never to see one another, the friendship grew stronger than ever.

But while Rush substantiated so much that Adams liked to believe about the meaning of friendship, another old friend, Mercy Otis Warren, hurt and provoked him as no one had in years, and without warning.

In 1806, Mercy Warren published her *History of the Rise, Progress, and Termination of the American Revolution* in which she singled out Adams as one of those who had betrayed the Revolution. Adams, she declared, reviving the old charge, had been "corrupted" by his time in England. The man who had "appeared to be actuated by the principles of integrity" became "beclouded by a partiality for monarchy . . . by living long near the splendor of courts and courtiers," and came home enamored by rank, titles, and "all the insignia of arbitrary sway." The most prominent features of his character, she further charged, were "pride of talents and much ambition." "Mr. Adams's passions and prejudices were sometimes too strong for his sagacity and judgment," she observed.

With Bache, Callender, and Alexander Hamilton all in their graves, Adams could only have assumed that such accusations were things of the past. Like nearly everyone who ever played a large part in public life and helped make history, Adams wondered how history would portray him, and worried not a little that he might be unfairly treated, misunderstood, or his contributions made to look insignificant compared to those of others. He had no great expectation of being celebrated. No statues or monuments would be erected in his memory, he told Rush, adding, "I wish them not," which was hardly so. It was an understandable desire to make his own case before the bar of history that propelled him in his labors at autobiography. But to have such a blow as this fall now in his old age, and inflicted by a friend, was infuriating.

In his years in office Adams had felt obliged to say nothing when subjected to ridicule and abuse. But now he felt no such restraint, and in a series of letters he unleashed his wrath as he seldom had, demonstrating, just as Mercy Warren had said, that his passions could at times overcome his sagacity, but also how deeply she had hurt him.

"What have I done, Mrs. Warren," he wrote, "to merit so much malevolence from a lady concerning whom I never in my life uttered an unkind word or disrespectful insinuation?"

"Corrupted!" he exploded. "Madam!... Corruption is a charge that I cannot and will not bear. I challenge the whole human race, and angels and devils, too, to produce an instance of it from my cradle to this hour!"

He denied still again any "partiality for monarchy" and implied that she was getting even with him for once refusing to give her husband a federal job.

To be charged with a surfeit of ambition cut deepest, it would appear. An overweening ambition was the flaw Adams so often attributed to others, that he warned his sons against, and that privately he recognized in himself. But to see it brought against him in print was another matter. "Ambition ... is the most lively in the most intelligent and most generous minds," he asserted. However:

> If by ambition you mean love of power or a desire of public offices, I answer I never solicited a vote in my life for any public office. I never swerved from any principle, I never professed any opinion—I never concealed even any speculative opinion—to obtain a vote. I never sacrificed a friend or betrayed a trust. I never hired scribblers to defame my rivals. I never wrote a line of slander against my bitterest enemy, nor encouraged it in any other.

In reply, Mercy Warren protested the "rambling manner in which your angry and undigested letters are written." When the letters kept coming, she accused him of "vulgarisms" and worse: "There is a mean-ness as well as malignancy in striving to blast a work that many of the best judges of literary merit . . . have spoken of [as] very flattering to the author."

The letters finally stopped, and by all signs the lifelong friendship between the Adamses and the Warrens had ended, which was deeply troubling on both sides. In time, however, the break would heal, and cor-respondence between them would resume.

In the meanwhile, the episode had shown that Adams was quite as capable as ever of furious indignation. The old lion could still roar.

Never wholeheartedly devoted to the task of writing his autobiogra-phy, he now abandoned the project altogether and launched into a lengthy—some thought interminable—spate of letters to the *Boston Patriot*, his last passionate exercise in self-justification. At the start he concentrated on answering the charges leveled by Hamilton in the heat of the 1800 election, then continued on to review his role in foreign affairs, from his difficulties with Franklin in Paris to the dismissal of Timothy Pickering to the XYZ Affair and the missions to France. He became the attorney for the accused—fierce and vivid in defense, writing with excep-tional vigor and not a little self-admiration, even occasional wonderment at his own virtuous tenacity in the face of opposition and intrigue.

The letters appeared almost weekly for three years, until Adams, too, it appears, realized how tiresome he had become and called a halt. "Voltaire boasted that he made four presses groan for sixty years, but I have to repent that I made the *Patriot* groan for three," he later wrote to a friend, aware that his efforts had been largely in vain.

THE DAILY ROUNDS and established patterns of domestic life contin-ued within the Adams homestead, which had come to be called the Big House—to distinguish it from the other houses by Penn's Hill—and an eyewitness account written years afterward by a kinsman is notable not only for its portraits of the elderly Abigail and John at home in or about the year 1808, but as evidence that "domestic economy," too, pertained no less than ever.

Josiah Quincy, a cousin of Abigail's, was six or seven years old when he began attending Sunday dinners at the Big House, which would have been an ordeal for a boy, he wrote, except for "the genuine kindness of the President, who had not a chip of an iceberg in his composition."

> With Mrs. Adams there was a shade more formality. A conscious-ness of age and dignity, which was often somewhat oppressive, was customary with old people of that day in the presence of the young. Something of this Mrs. Adams certainly had, though it wore off or came to be disregarded by me, for in the end I was strongly attached to her.

It was with certain pride, too, that he, as a Quincy, saw her as one of the last of the true, old-style New England ladies of another era:

> She was always dressed handsomely, and her rich silks and laces seemed appropriate to a lady of her dignified position in the town. If there was a little savor of patronage in the generous hospitality she exercised among her simple neighbors, it was never regarded as more than a natural emphasis of her undoubted claims to precedence. The aristocratic colonial families were still recognized, for the tide of democracy had not risen high enough to cover all its distinctions. The parentage and descent of Mrs. Adams were undoubtedly of weight establishing her position; though, as we now look at things, the strong personal claims of herself and husband would seem to have been all sufficient.

Sunday dinners, served at one o'clock, he remembered as sufficiently plentiful but modest, and beginning invariably with a pudding of corn-meal, molasses, and butter.

> This was the custom of the time—it being thought desirable to take the edge off of one's hunger before reaching the joint [of veal or mut-ton]. Indeed, it was considered wise to stimulate the young to fill themselves with pudding, by the assurance that the boys who man-aged to eat the most of it should be helped most abundantly to the meat, which was to follow. It need not be said that neither the win-

ner nor his competitors found much room for meat at the close of
their contest; and so the domestic economy of the arrangement was
very apparent.

When the time came for the meat course, Louisa Smith did the carv-
ing while the President made his contribution in the form of "good-
humored, easy banter." What Adams talked about, his young guest was
unable to recall in later years, though he remembered distinctly "a certain iron spoon which the old gentleman once fished up from the depths of
a pudding in which it had been unwittingly cooked."

With dinner ended, nearly all at the table went a second time to
church. At tea following church, another guest would recount, topics of
conversation could range from religion, politics, and literature, to Mrs.
Siddons, Shakespeare, and Benedict Arnold.

Like countless grandparents in all times, Abigail worried that she
might be spoiling the grandchildren under her charge. "I begin to think
grandparents not so well qualified to educate grandchildren as parents,"
she wrote to Nabby. "They are apt to relax in their spirit of government,
and be too indulgent." It was a thought that appears never to have concerned John Adams.

BY THE TIME Jefferson's second term was under way, Bonaparte had
crowned himself the Emperor Napoleon and with his victorious armies
had become master of Europe. France and Britain were still at war, and
on the high seas both the French and the British were again attacking
American commerce, seizing American ships, and impressing American
seamen. More than a thousand ships and millions of dollars in goods had
been lost, and everywhere in the country debate raged over what to do.

Determined to avoid war, Jefferson called for an embargo on all
American shipping, which John Adams, like most New Englanders, saw
as a catastrophe for New England, if not the nation. But alone of the Federalists in Congress, John Quincy supported and voted for the embargo
as a worthy "experiment," the same term used by Jefferson.

"If ever a nation was guilty of imprudence, ours has been so in making
a naval force and marine preparations unpopular," Adams wrote to
Rush. He thought the embargo "a cowardly measure." He had always

been against embargoes, but he would "raise no clamor" now, "being determined to support the government in whatever hands as far as I can in conscience and honor."

When Massachusetts Federalists denounced John Quincy as no longer one of the party, Adams wrote to him to say he wished they would denounce him the same way, for he had long since "abdicated and disclaimed the name and character and attributes of that sect, as it now appears."

The embargo proved a colossal mistake for the country, and a catastrophe for New England. For John Quincy, it meant the end of his Senate career. In 1808 the Massachusetts legislature elected a successor even earlier than they had to, which prompted John Quincy to resign before his term ended. If he or his father ever entertained any thought that Jefferson, before leaving office, might reward John Quincy for the support he had given, they were greatly disappointed, for this was not to happen. It was Jefferson's successor, James Madison, who after taking office as President, rescued John Quincy from practicing law in Boston by appointing him minister to Russia.

Abigail was crestfallen. She thought the appointment unsuitable and urged John Quincy not to accept. "The period is not yet arrived when your country demands you," she wrote. Adams differed, as much as he dreaded the thought of John Quincy in St. Petersburg. "As to my son, I would not advise him to refuse to serve his country when fairly called to it," he told Rush, "but as to myself, I would not exchange the pleasure I have in his society once a week for any office in or under the United States."

By midsummer of 1809, John Quincy and Louisa Catherine had departed for Russia, taking with them the most recent addition to their family, two-year-old Charles Francis Adams, while eight-year-old George and five-year-old John remained behind in Quincy.

"It was like taking our last leave," Abigail wrote. The separation, Adams told Rush, tore him to pieces. How long it might be until they saw them again, if ever, there was no telling.

TWO MONTHS LATER, feeling the time was ripe, Rush sent Adams a memorable letter, dated October 17, 1809. With Jefferson also in retirement now, Rush thought it time for a renewal of the old friendship between Adams and Jefferson, and that he, Rush, as the friend of both, could help bring it about. He had been corresponding with Jefferson all along, and thus felt he knew the hearts of both men.

As part of his medical investigations, Rush had a long-standing interest in dreams. Dreams, he told his students, should be allowed to "sport themselves idly" in their brains. Observed, dreams could provide useful inferences. In the course of his correspondence with Adams, Rush had already related several dreams of his own. Now he had another to report. He had a dream of reading a history of America written at some point in the future, and of a particular page saying that among the "most extraordinary events" of the year 1809 was the renewal of friendship and correspondence between the two former presidents, Mr. John Adams and Mr. Thomas Jefferson. And it was Adams, according to Rush's dream history, who rekindled the old friendship.

> Mr. Adams addressed a short letter to his friend Mr. Jefferson in which he congratulated him upon his escape to the shades of retirement and domestic happiness, and concluded it with assurances of his regard and good wishes for his welfare. This letter did great honor to Mr. Adams. It discovered a magnanimity known only to great minds. Mr. Jefferson replied to this letter and reciprocated expressions of regard and esteem. These letters were followed by a correspondence of several years.

Delighted by Rush's good-natured performance, Adams replied: "A dream again! I wish you would dream all day and all night, for one of your dreams puts me in spirits for a month. I have no other objections to your dream, but that it is not history. It may be prophecy."

But then Adams did nothing, and no more was said of the matter. Silence between Stoneyfield and Monticello continued.

"OUR READING has been all about Russia," Adams wrote to John Quincy that winter, when it looked for all the world like Russia outside Adams's window and the palsy in his hands was "rather increased" by the severe cold. He wrote of the pleasure he was taking in John Quincy's two sons and of their progress in their studies. He reported on his own son Thomas, who was by now married to Ann Harrod of Haverhill and with his growing family had settled in the old house by Penn's Hill where Adams had been born; and on Elbridge Gerry, who had lately been elected governor of Massachusetts. In October of 1810, Adams celebrated his seventy-fifth birthday.

He had taken up reading modern epic poems and novels, "romances," he reported to Rush—Walter Scott's *Lady of the Lake*, Jane Porter's *Scottish Chiefs*—and was finding great enjoyment in them.

"My days glide smoothly away," he wrote early in the new year of 1811. Snow fell for twelve consecutive days, leaving drifts ten feet high.

"I am well, my appetite as good as ever," he reported after another six months had passed. "I sleep well nights. My natural vision is not bad, but I use glasses for ease to my eyes. . . . My hearing . . . is as good as ever." His only difficulties were the "quiveration" in his hands and a loss of voice. "It would divert you to witness conversation between my ancient friend and colleague Robert T. Paine and me. He is above eighty. I cannot speak and he cannot hear. Yet we converse."

But 1811 was to be an almost unbearably difficult and painful year for the Adamses, indeed, "the most afflictive" year they had known. In April, when his horse reared and threw him, Thomas was so badly injured it was feared he would be crippled for life. By early summer Mary Cranch, who suffered from what was probably tuberculosis, appeared to be dying. Then, Sally, Charles's widow, began spitting up blood, which as Adams later reported to Benjamin Rush, confined her under the constant care of physicians for three or four months.

One night in September, going out in the dark to view a comet, Adams tripped over a stake in the ground and ripped his leg open to the bone, so that for months he too was confined to the house, a doctor "daily hovering" to bathe and dress the wound.

Abigail, who almost alone of the household remained on her feet, went back and forth across town to the Cranches, nursing her sister as well as those at home. "Neither the morals of Epictetus or the stoic philosophy of the ancients could avail to allay the tumult of grief excited by such a succession of distress," she wrote to John Quincy.

But greatest was the anguish over Nabby, about whom Abigail said nothing yet to John Quincy, probably to spare him the worry.

Nabby had discovered a "hardness" in her right breast, and had come on to Quincy from the farm in upstate New York where she and Colonel Smith had been living for some while in near poverty. She consulted with Cotton Tufts and several physicians in Boston and wrote to Benjamin Rush for his advice. The Boston doctors all advised the surgical removal of her breast, as did Rush in a thoughtful letter to her father. He preferred giving his opinion this way, Rush told Adams, so that he and Abigail could "communicate it gradually."

From the experience of more than fifty years in such cases, Rush said, he knew but one remedy, "the knife." "From her account of the *moving* state of the tumor, it is now in a proper situation for the operation. Should she wait till it superates or even inflames much, it may be too late. . . . I repeat again, let there be no delay. . . . Her time of life calls for expedition in this business, for tumors such as hers tend much more rapidly to cancer after 45 than in more early life." Nabby was forty-six.

A mastectomy was performed on Nabby in the bedroom beside that of her mother and father on October 8. As Adams wrote to Rush, the operation took twenty-five minutes, the dressing an hour longer. The agony she endured in that day before anesthetics is unimaginable. The four surgeons who performed the operation told Adams afterward that they had never known a patient to show such fortitude.

Two days later, on October 10, the beloved Richard Cranch died of heart failure at age eighty-five, and the day following, Mary Cranch died at age seventy. For Abigail it was the greatest loss since the death of Charles.

The horror of Nabby's ordeal brought a marked change in Adams. The old shows of temper were not to be seen again. He became more mellow, more accepting of life, and forgiving. He had felt during Nabby's agony, he said, as if he were living in the Book of Job.

JUST BEFORE CHRISTMAS, Adams heard again from Benjamin Rush, who wished to remind him of a visit Adams had had the summer before from two young men from Virginia. They were brothers named Coles, Albemarle County neighbors of Jefferson's, and in the course of conversation Adams had at length exclaimed, "I always loved Jefferson and I still love him." This had been carried back to Monticello, and was all Jefferson needed to hear. To Rush he wrote, "I only needed this knowledge to revive towards him all the affections of the most cordial moments of our lives."

"And now, my dear friend," declared Rush to Adams "permit me again to suggest to you to receive the olive branch offered to you by the hand of a man who still loves you."

On New Year's Day 1812, seated at his desk in the second-floor library, Adams took up his pen to write a short letter to Jefferson very like the one Rush had prophesied in his dream.

I V

It was a brief, cordial note to wish Jefferson many happy new years, and to say he could expect to receive a bit of "homespun lately produced in this quarter by one who was honored in his youth with some of your attention and much of your kindness." Posted separately, the "homespun" was a copy of John Quincy's *Lectures on Rhetoric and Oratory*, but before it could arrive, Jefferson had concluded that it must be some article of home-produced clothing, and so in reply to Adams wrote at length about the virtues of the spinning jenny and loom, and of the thriftiness of household manufactures.

If, as stage-managed by Rush, it had been left to Adams to make the first move, Jefferson more than fulfilled his part. "A letter from you calls up recollections very dear to my mind," he continued. "It carried me back to the times when, beset with difficulties and dangers, we were fellow laborers in the same cause, struggling for what is most valuable to man, his right of self-government."

Jefferson was fond of images of storm-tossed seas and employed them often, as he did now, though in his own travels at sea he himself had known only smooth sailing.

> Laboring always at the same oar, with some wave ever ahead threatening to overwhelm us and yet passing harmless under our bark, we knew not how we rode through the storm with heart and hand, and made a happy port.

Like Adams, he claimed to be out of touch with politics, which was hardly so. He was kept abreast regularly by Madison and Monroe, among others. "I have given up newspapers in exchange for Tacitus and Thucydides, for Newton and Euclid," he wrote, which was also an over-statement, but one certain to please his fellow classical scholar at Quincy.

Adams answered in high spirits and at greater length than Jefferson had written to him. "What an exchange have you made? Of newspapers for Newton!" he wrote. "Rising from the lower deep of the lowest deep of dullness and bathos to the contemplation of the heavens and the heavens of the heavens." Responding to Jefferson's figurative storm at sea, Adams recalled again his own real voyage on the *Boston*, chased by British frigates, struck by "a hideous tempest of thunder and lightning," the mainmast split, twenty men down, one dead. It was the story of his life, he said.

"I walk every fair day," he told Jefferson, "sometimes three and four miles. Ride now and then, but very rarely more than ten or fifteen miles." The tremble in his hands made it difficult to write at all and impossible to write well, as Jefferson could readily see.

Adams wrote to Rush to report the new state of affairs. "Your dream is out. . . . You have wrought wonders! You have made peace between powers that never were at war," he said, happy about the news but choosing to make light of it, as if no one was supposed ever to think there had been any serious differences between him and the man he had earlier told Rush was a consummate intriguer. Apparently, Adams was ready now both to forgive and to forget.

Rush was exultant. Nothing could have pleased him more, as he wrote immediately to Adams.

> I rejoice in the correspondence which has taken place between you and your old friend Mr. Jefferson. I consider you and him as the North and South Poles of the American Revolution. Some talked, some wrote, and some fought to promote and establish it, but you and Mr. Jefferson *thought* for us all. . . .
>
> I admire, as do all my family, the wonderful vivacity and imagery of your letters. Some men's minds wear well, but yours doesn't appear to wear at all! "Oh! King, live forever," said the east-ern nations to their monarchs! Live—live, my venerable friend.

Rush wrote to Jefferson to assure him that posterity would acclaim the reconciliation and that Jefferson was certain to find Adams a refreshing correspondent. "I view him as a mountain with its head clear and reflecting beams of the sun, while below it is frost and snow."

Within months a half dozen letters had traveled the roads between Quincy and Monticello, and one of the most extraordinary correspondences in American history—indeed, in the English language—was under way. In two years' time fifty letters went back and forth, and this was but the beginning. They wrote of old friends and their own friendship, of great causes past, common memories, books, politics, education, philosophy, religion, the French, the British, the French Revolution, American Indians, the American navy, their families, their health, slavery—eventually—and their considered views on life, society, and always, repeatedly, the American Revolution.

"Who shall write the history of the American Revolution?" Adams asked. "Who can write it? Who will ever be able to write it?"

"Nobody," Jefferson answered, "except perhaps its external facts."

The level and range of their discourse were always above and beyond the ordinary. At times memory failed; often hyperbole entered in. Often each was writing as much for posterity as for the other. They were two of the leading statesmen of their time, but also two of the finest writers, and they were showing what they could do.

In fundamental ways each proved consistently true to his nature—they were in what they wrote as they had been through life. Jefferson was far more guarded and circumspect, better organized, dispassionate, more mannered, and refused ever to argue. Adams was warm, loquacious, more personal and opinionated, often humorous and willing to poke fun at himself. When Jefferson wrote of various self-appointed seers and mystics who had taken up his time as president, Adams claimed to have had no problem with such people. "They all assumed the character of ambassadors extraordinary from the Almighty, but as I required miracles in proof of their credentials, and they did not perform any, I never gave public audience to any of them."

Jefferson wrote as an elegant stylist performing for a select audience, as Adams fully appreciated, telling him his letters should be published for the delight of future generations. Adams wrote as he talked, bouncing subjects about with no thought to organization. Adams later told a friend he had no more thought of publishing a letter as he wrote it than he had of giving an account to the press of his going to bed that night. "I considered when I wrote to Mr. J. that I was not writing psalms . . . nor sermons, nor prayers. It was only, as if one sailor had met a brother sailor, after 25 years absence, and had accosted him, 'How fare you, Jack?' "

By late spring of 1812, the year the correspondence began, the country was again at war with Great Britain, twenty-nine years after the Paris Peace Treaty of 1783. Continuing British impressment of American seamen was the principal issue—"injuries and indignities heaped upon our country," in the words of President Madison. And though the country was ill prepared to fight, war was declared on June 19. Five days later Napoleon and his Grande Armée invaded Russia, which, with John Quincy and his family in St. Petersburg, was to the Adamses a matter of extreme interest.

If only a few more frigates had been built, Adams wrote to Jefferson, who had cut the navy drastically. "Without this our Union will be a brittle china vase." But then in August the *Constitution* defeated the British ship *Guerriere* off Nova Scotia, and later sank the British frigate *Java*, near Brazil. The *Wasp*, an American sloop of war, defeated the *Frolic*, the *Hornet* sank the *Peacock*, and in a letter to Adams, Jefferson generously gave credit where credit was due. "I sincerely congratulate you on the success of our little navy, which must be more gratifying to you than to most men, as having been the early and constant advocate of wooden walls."

As the War of 1812 went on, as Madison was elected for a second term with Elbridge Gerry his Vice President, as the seasons came and went at Quincy and Monticello, the letters continued on. It was not an even exchange. Adams wrote at greater length than Jefferson, and he wrote more often. On average Adams wrote two letters for every one from Jefferson, but this was of no matter to him. During one stretch of several months, Adams wrote twelve times before he had an answer from Jefferson. "Never mind . . . if I write four letters to your one," Adams told him, "your one is worth more than my four."

For a while, when addressing letters to Jefferson, Adams would even refer to his farm as "Montezillo." "Mr. Jefferson lives at Monticello, the lofty mountain. I live at *Montezillo*, a little hill," Adams would explain, apparently unaware that both words mean "little mountain."

At first, Adams tried to draw Jefferson out on a variety of matters important to him. "Whether you or I were right posterity must judge," Adams would observe equably, then launch headlong into what he thought. "I never have approved and never can approve the repeal of taxes, the repeal of the judiciary system, or the neglect of the navy." He brought up the Alien Law, claiming absurdly that since Jefferson had signed it, too, as Vice President, he therefore shared in the responsibility for it. "Checks and balances, Jefferson, however you and your party may have ridiculed them, are our only security," he wrote in another letter.

The patriots of the French Revolution, Adams declared, knowing perfectly well how it would provoke Jefferson, were like drunken sailors on wild horses, "lashing and speering till they would kill the horses and break their own necks." Recalling the Jacobin threat to America, he accused Jefferson of having been "fast asleep in philosophical tranquility." "What think you of terrorism, Mr. Jefferson?" Adams demanded, as if he were back in court and Jefferson on the witness stand.

"My friend! You and I have passed our lives in serious times," he reminded Jefferson, and, as an example, pointed to the all-too-serious perils of sedition contained in the Kentucky Resolutions, unaware that Jefferson had been their author.

"You and I ought not to die before we have explained ourselves to each other," Adams wrote, still trying to draw Jefferson out.

But Jefferson, who must have wondered what he had gotten himself into, refused to engage in wrangling or dispute. "The *summum bonum* with me is now truly Epicurean, ease of body and tranquility of mind," he wrote, "and to these I wish to consign my remaining days."

> My mind has been long fixed to bow to the judgment of the world, who will judge me by my acts and will never take counsel from me as to what the judgment will be. If your objects and opinions have been misunderstood, if the measures and principles of others have wrongly been imputed to you, as I believe thay have been, that you should leave an explanation of them would be an act of justice to yourself. I will add that it has been hoped you would leave such explanations as would place every saddle on its right horse, and replace on the shoulders of others the burdens they shifted on yours.

But all this, my friend, is offered merely for your consideration and judgment, without presuming to anticipate what you alone are qualified to decide for yourself. I mean to express my own purpose only, and the reflections which have led to it. To me then it appears that there have been differences of opinion, and party differences, from the establishment of governments to the present day, and on the same question which now divides our country, that these will continue through all future times: that everyone takes his side in favor of the many, or of the few, according to his constitution and the circumstances in which he is placed, that opinions, which are equally honest on both sides, should not effect personal esteem or social intercourse . . . nothing new can be added by you or me to what has been said by others, and will be said in every age.

Jefferson refused to be drawn out, refused to explain himself, and Adams, accepting this, shifted his focus to other matters much on his mind or dear to his heart.

HAD ADAMS at this time in his life done nothing else but produce the letters he wrote to Jefferson, it would have been remarkable. But he was also actively corresponding with others, including an old Dutch friend from the years in Amsterdam, the Reverend Francis van der Kemp, who had lately settled in upstate New York, and Benjamin Waterhouse, who had become a leading figure at the Harvard Medical School. If a grandchild wrote to him, Adams responded at once, always affectionately and very often with a measure of guiding philosophy drawn from experience.

"Your letter touches my heart," he wrote to Nabby's second son, John, who was by now in his twenties. "Oh, that I may always be able to say to my grandsons, 'You have learned much and behave well, my lads. Go on and improve in everything worthy.'

Have you considered the meaning of that word "worthy"? Weigh it well. . . . I had rather you should be worthy possessors of one thousand pounds honestly acquired by your own labor and industry, than of ten millions by banks and tricks. I should rather you be worthy shoemakers than secretaries of states or treasury acquired by libels in newspapers. I had rather you should be worthy makers of brooms and baskets than unworthy presidents of the United States procured by intrigue, factious slander and corruption.

Nor was there any easing off in the exchange with Rush.

Why was it that a nation without wars to fight seemed to lose its honor and integrity, Adams pondered in one letter to Rush. "War necessarily brings with it some virtues, and great and heroic virtues, too," he wrote. "What horrid creatures we men are, that we cannot be virtuous without murdering one another?"

Thousands upon thousands were being killed at sea and on the steppes of Russia. An infant grandchild, a son of Thomas, died. "I have been called lately to weep in the chamber of my birth over the remains of a beautiful babe of your brother's, less than a year old," he wrote to John Quincy. "Why have I been preserved at more than three quarters of a century, and why was that fair flower blasted so soon, are questions we are not permitted to ask."

In November of 1812, Rush sent Adams a first copy of what he considered his most important work, *Medical Inquiries and Observations upon the Diseases of the Mind.* For years Rush had been investigating the causes of and remedies for madness and other "diseases" of the mind. "The subjects of them have hitherto been enveloped in mystery," he wrote to Adams. "I have endeavored to bring them down to the level of all other diseases of the human body, and to show that the mind and body are moved by the same causes and subject to the same laws." He expected to be chastised by his fellow physicians. "But time I hope will do my opinions justice. I believe them to be true and calculated to lessen some of the greatest evils of human life. If they are not, I shall console myself of having aimed well and erred honestly."

The book was to become the standard American guide for mental illnesses, and in later years Rush would become known as the father of American psychiatry.

Writing to thank Rush for the volume, Adams assured him it would put mankind still deeper in his debt. "You apprehend 'attacks.' I say, the more the better," Adams declared, speculating that what Rush had written would surpass the writings of Franklin in the good it would do.

Shortly after, in another letter to Rush, Adams described a dreamlike incident in his life, the chance purchase of a young horse that reminded him of America. Lest Rush take it to be the account of a dream, Adams assured him it was the literal truth.

"On horseback on my way to Weymouth on a visit to my friend Dr. Tufts, I met a man leading a horse, who asked if I wanted to buy a horse.

> Examining the animal in the eyes, ears, head, neck, shoulders, legs, feet and tail, and inquiring of his master, his age, his history, temper, habits, etc., I found he was a colt of three years old that month of November. His sucking teeth were not shed, he was seventeen or eighteen hands high, bones like massy timbers, ribbed quite to his hips, every way broad, strong, and well filled in proportion; as tame, gentle, good natured and good humored as a cosset lamb. Thinks I to my self, this noble creature is the exact emblem of my dear country. I will have him and call him Hobby. He may carry me five-and-twenty or thirty years if I should live. I ride him every day when the weather suits, but I should shudder if he should ever discover or feel his own power.

Rush was delighted by the story, and in his next letter addressed himself to the horse:

> Tread gently and safely, high favored beast, while your master bestrides your back. Shake well every blood vessel of his body, and gently agitate every portion of his brain. Keep up the circulation of his blood for years to come, and excite aphorism and anecdotes and dreams for the instruction and amusements by the action of his brain upon his mind.

But confined to the house in the bitter cold of January 1813, Adams portrayed himself as a case study worthy of Rush's attention and pity. How much longer could an ancient specimen of seventy-seven years be expected to continue? How many aches and pains and low spirits had he still to endure? How many more of his family must he lose? How many friends must disappear?

The mystery to this ancient creature, Adams continued, was where his life had all gone—stage-by-stage, "away like the morning cloud." The last twelve years "in solitude" had been the pleasantest of all. "Yet where are they?"

Picturing the "withered, faded, wrinkled, tottering, trembling" stage to come, Adams wrote, "Oh! I have some scruples of conscience whether I ought to preserve him, whether it would not be charity to stumble, and relieve him from such a futurity."

Weeks later the Adamses learned of the death of another grandchild, Louisa Catherine Adams, who had been born in Russia little more than a year before. Trying to console John Quincy and Louisa Catherine, not to say himself, Adams wrote one letter after another at his desk by the library fire. The universe, he told John Quincy, was "inscrutable and incomprehensible."

> While you and I believe that the whole system is under the constant and vigilant direction of a wisdom infinitely more discerning than ours and a benevolence to the whole and to us in particular greater even than our own self love, we have the highest consolation that reason can suggest or imagination conceive. The same general laws that at times afflict us are in your neighborhood bereaving millions of their fathers, brothers, and sons and millions more of their food and their shelter. In our own country of how many deprivations do we read, and how many savage cruelties. What grounds have we to expect or to hope to be excepted from the general lot. . . . Sorrow can make no alternative, afford no relief to the departed, to survivors or to ourselves.

Another evening, watching granddaughters Susanna and Abigail blowing soap bubbles with one of his clay pipes, he wondered about the "allegorical lesson" of the scene.

> They fill the air of the room with their bubbles, their air balloons, which roll and shine reflecting the light of the fire and candles, and are very beautiful. There can be no more perfect emblem of the physical and political and theological scenes of human life.
>
> Morality only is eternal. All the rest is balloon and bubble from the cradle to the grave.

John Quincy wrote from St. Petersburg that on the day his child had died, Moscow was in flames set by its inhabitants as the city was surrendered to Napoleon, and that within less than three months Napoleon's disastrous retreat had begun—"the invader himself was a wretched fugitive and his numberless host was perishing by frosts, famine, and sword." Yet none of this, John Quincy told his father, could comfort him in the loss of his own child. "I mourned over the fallen city, and even its fallen conquerors, because I was a man and a Christian, but their fate would neither sharpen nor mitigate my private woe."

A MONTH into that spring of 1813, word reached Quincy from Philadelphia that Benjamin Rush had died suddenly on April 19, apparently from typhus. "Another of our friends of '76 is gone, my dear sir, another of the co-signers of the Independence of our country," Jefferson wrote to Adams.

"I know of no character living or dead who has done more real good for his country," Adams answered, borne down with grief. To Rush's widow he wrote that there was no one outside his own family whose friendship was so essential to his happiness. At sixty-eight Rush had still been seeing patients until a few days before his death. Adams's last letter to him was written only the day before Rush died. The loss of such a friend, Abigail told Nabby, was a "heavy stroke to your father."

THE FULL GLORY of spring comes late along coastal Massachusetts, but by the last week of May, Quincy was green and blooming, the air fragrant, and Adams's outlook greatly revived. In a letter to Francis van der Kemp, urging him to come for a visit, Adams promised to show him "a pretty hill" and "a friendly heart."

> I damn nobody [he wrote]. I am an atom of intellect with millions of solar systems over my head, under my feet, on my right hand, on my left, before me, and my adoration of the intelligence that contrived and the power that rules the stupendous fabric is too profound to believe them capable of anything unjust or cruel.

Callers came and went, one of whom warmed his "friendly heart" as perhaps no one else could have—Captain Samuel Tucker of Marblehead, commander of the *Boston* on the voyage of 1778, who was now in his sixties and retired from the sea, but robust still and as salty a talker as ever.

Earlier, Adams had vowed to Rush that the admonition "rejoice ever more" would "never be out of my heart, memory, or mouth again as long as I live, if I can help it." This, he had said, was his "perfectibility of man." Now to John Quincy he wrote, "Rejoice always in all events, be thankful always for all things is a hard precept for human nature, though in my philosophy and in my religion a perfect duty." In the ensuing months his philosophy and religion were, as Adams said, "brought to trial."

On July 26, after a journey of fifteen days and three hundred miles from upstate New York, Nabby arrived at Quincy in such weakened condition that she had to be carried inside the house. Her cancer had returned and was spreading, but despite terrible pain, she had insisted on coming home, accompanied by her son John and daughter Caroline, to be with her mother and father in the little time left to her. Colonel Smith was in Washington. Having failed at nearly everything he ever tried, he had lately been elected to Congress.

Upstairs in the house, Sally Adams was critically ill with tuberculosis. Abigail was suffering from rheumatism and physical and emotional exhaustion. "My dear, my only daughter lies in the next chamber, consumed with cancer," Adams wrote to Francis van der Kemp, "my daughter-in-law, Charles's widow, lies in the next chamber extremely weak and low. . . . My wife, a valetudinarian through a whole life of 69 years, is worn down with care. In the midst of all this my own eyes are awakened by a venom that threatens to put them out." Nabby was so emaciated as to be almost unrecognizable; her suffering was extreme. Opium provided her only relief.

The family gathered. Colonel Smith arrived from Washington. "She told her physician that she was perfectly sensible of her situation and reconciled to it," Abigail later wrote. "Although she was bolstered up in her bed and could neither walk or stand, she was always calm."

Nabby died before dawn on Sunday, August 15, 1813. She was forty-nine and for most of her life, as Adams would tell Jefferson, she had enjoyed the best health of anyone in the family.

Abigail was shattered. It would be a month before she could write to anyone. "The loss is irreparable," she said at last in a letter to John Quincy. "Heaven be praised your father and I have been supported through all this solemn scene with fortitude and I hope Christian resignation."

Death was no stranger to him, Adams wrote. He had lost children and grandchildren and could never think of any of them without pain. His dear Nabby had shown extraordinary courage, he told John Quincy. Her death was a release, the most "magnanimous" he ever witnessed. "I am grateful and resigned."

Jefferson had earlier sent Adams a "Syllabus" he had prepared on the merit of the doctrines of Jesus, and a discussion of religion had since filled much of their correspondence. Now Adams wrote to Jefferson, "The love of God and His creation, delight, joy, triumph, exultation in my own existence . . . are my religion."

By October, emerging from her grief, Abigail was writing to John Quincy of the blessings still left to her. High on the list, she said, was "the life, health and cheerfulness of your father. Bowed down as he has been . . . he has not sunk under it."

CHAPTER TWELVE

JOURNEY'S END

But weak as was his material frame, his mind was
still enthroned.

—Dr. Benjamin Waterhouse

I

CONCERNING SUCH MATTERS as who was to be the next governor
of Massachusetts or the next President of the United States, Adams professed to take increasingly less interest. Adverse comments about his own
role in public life that appeared occasionally in print, or the "strange" letters he occasionally received, were no longer of any matter to him. They
were like insects buzzing about, he told John Quincy. "Their bite in former times tingled, but I am grown almost as insensible as a Boston dray
horse in September."

"I assure you in the sincerity of a father," he wrote to John Quincy in
1815, "the last fourteen years have been the happiest of my life." The
noticeable improvements he had brought to the farm were highly gratifying. The small, everyday pleasures, the calm, the reassuring sameness of
life in and about Quincy had proven as beneficial as the pastoral ideal portrayed by the poets he loved and that he himself had so long pictured as
his salvation.

But there was no indifference to the larger world. In a time of tu-
multuous history unfolding, as war raged at home and abroad and
Napoleon's armies suffered continuing defeat, little escaped Adams's
attention or a goodly measure of his opinion. Reading all they could lay
hands on, he and Abigail remained informed as always, and not the least

of their reasons was the part John Quincy had been delegated to play in events.

On April 1, 1814, at St. Petersburg, John Quincy received word that he had been appointed a peace envoy to negotiate an end to the War of 1812, and was to proceed at once to Ghent in Flanders (Belgium). It seemed as though history was repeating itself, with John Quincy taking up the same role his father had played at Paris in 1782.

Events were moving fast. On April 11, after further defeat on the battlefield, Napoleon abdicated his throne and went into exile on the island of Elba. The French monarchy was restored under the Comte de Provence, Louis XVIII. In America, on August 24, British troops made a successful assault on Washington, scattered the government, and set fire to the Capitol and the President's House. American warships had been driven from the sea. The Treasury was empty, the outlook grim.

In December, Federalists from the five New England States, led by Timothy Pickering, met at Hartford to denounce the "ruinous war." There was even talk of New England seceding from the union. At Ghent the same month, the American commissioners led by John Quincy Adams signed a peace treaty with Britain, news that would not reach the United States until February, by which time Americans under General Andrew Jackson had won a decisive victory, on January 15, at the battle of New Orleans.

Then, on March 1, 1815, Napoleon escaped from Elba, landed at Cannes, and with 1,500 men marched on Paris, thus beginning the fateful "100 days" that ended with Napoleon's ultimate defeat at Waterloo on June 18. Within days he was on his way to the British island of St. Helena for the remainder of his life.

The Napoleonic Wars were over, and John Quincy, after a brief sojourn in Paris, moved on to London to serve, again like his father, as minister to the Court of St. James's.

As dark as prospects had appeared during the war at home, Adams never lost confidence, even as the British advanced on Washington. He had known worse times, he said. He had seen Congress "chased like a covey of partridges" from Philadelphia, and "we had ropes about our necks then." The very thought of New England leaving the Union, he found outrageous. As always, he took a national, not sectional, view of the country, and strongly supported President Madison.

That the likes of Napoleon came to bad ends was among the lessons of history. Concerning America's place in the world, Adams wrote to Benjamin Rush's son Richard, who had lately become Attorney General of the United States, "We must learn to know ourselves, to esteem ourselves, to respect ourselves."

"At this time we are very anxious to hear every day, if we could, what is passing abroad," Abigail wrote John Quincy, still having no idea where he was. "Never was there a period when curiosity was more alive, or expectation more eager, or anxiety more active."

Letters from John Quincy written in Paris months before began arriving at last on May 6, one of the most joyful days of her life, Abigail exclaimed. And more followed through the summer, recounting the ups and downs of Napoleon and the changing moods of Paris. "I seem to be rambling with you to the Hôtel de Valois, the Hôtel du Roi," Adams wrote in reply. Had John Quincy been to Passy yet? Or Auteuil or Versailles?

As requested, the Adamses parted with grandsons George and John, who sailed for London to join their parents and brother Charles Francis, from whom they had been separated for nearly six years. The departure of the two boys left both grandparents feeling desolate. They must keep diaries, Adams told them as once he had told their father. Without a diary, their travels would "be no better than a flight of birds through the air," leaving no trace.

To John Quincy he kept up a steady flow of private ruminations, advice, and the suggestion that he take time for a tour of the English country gardens. He must purchase Whatley's book on modern gardening, bring his sons "and your lady, too, if she chooses," Adams wrote, "and visit the gentlemen's country seats."

Abigail sent John Quincy her own approving evaluation of each of the "dear boys," and the wish that his and Louisa Catherine's joy in seeing them again would equal the pain she felt at parting with them.

"DEATH IS SWEEPING his scythe all around us, cutting down our old friends and brandishing it over us," Adams wrote a year later, in the summer of 1816. Abigail's sister Elizabeth, the last of her family, had died. Robert Treat Paine and Vice President Elbridge Gerry were gone, Gerry dying of a heart attack while riding in his carriage to the Senate. The death of Cotton Tufts, in December 1815, was another heavy blow. "Winter in this country is still winter, and carries off a few hundred of our oldest people," observed Adams, who had turned eighty.

Abigail prepared her will, parceling out among children, grandchildren, and her niece, Louisa Smith, her silk gowns and jewelry, a white lace shawl, beds, blankets, and some $4,000. In addition, to her two sons she left two equal parcels of land she had inherited.

Six months later, in June of 1816, came word that Colonel Smith, too, was no longer among the living.

Jefferson, in his continuing correspondence with Adams, had observed that old and worn as they were they must expect that "here a pivot, there a wheel, now a pinion, next a spring will give way." There was nothing to be done about it. Meanwhile, he wrote, "I steer my bark with hope in the head, leaving fear astern."

Their exchange of views remained a sustaining exercise for both men. Whatever the state of their physical "pinions and springs," there was nothing whatever wrong with their minds, nor any decline in the respect each had for the other's talents and learning. Having run on for several pages about Cicero, Socrates, and the contradictions in Plato, Jefferson asked, "But why am I dosing you with these antediluvian topics? Because I am glad to have someone to whom they are familiar, and who will not receive them as if dropped from the moon."

Jefferson had offered to sell his private library to the government in Washington to replace the collection of the Library of Congress destroyed by the British when they burned the Capitol. It was both a magnanimous gesture and something of a necessity, as he was hard-pressed to meet his mounting debts. After prolonged debate in Congress, a figure of $23,950 was agreed to, and in April 1815 ten wagons carrying 6,707 volumes packed in pine cases departed from Monticello. When Adams learned what Jefferson had done, he wrote, "I envy you that immortal honor."

Jefferson immediately commenced to collect anew. He could "not live without books," he told Adams, who understood perfectly. They remained two of the greatest book lovers of their bookish generation. Adams's library numbered 3,200 volumes. People sent him books, "overwhelm me with books from all quarters," as he wrote to Jefferson. Yet he wished he had 100,000. He longed particularly, he said, for a work in Latin available only in Europe, titled *Acta Sanctorum*, in forty-seven volumes, on the lives of the saints compiled in the sixteenth century. "What would I give to possess in one immense mass, one stupendous draught, all the legends, true and false."

Unable to sleep as long as Abigail, he would be out of bed and reading by candlelight at five in the morning, and later would read well into the night. When his eyes grew weary, she would read aloud to him.

Unlike Jefferson, who seldom ever marked a book, and then only faintly in pencil, Adams, pen in hand, loved to add his comments in the margins. It was part of the joy of reading for him, to have something to say himself, to talk back to, agree or take issue with, Rousseau, Condorcet, Turgot, Mary Wollstonecraft, Adam Smith, or Joseph Priestley. *"There is no doubt that people are in the long run what the government make out of them . . . ,"* Adams read in Rousseau. "The government ought to be what the people make it," he wrote in response.

At times his marginal observations nearly equaled what was printed on the page, as in Mary Wollstonecraft's *French Revolution*, which Adams read at least twice and with delight, since he disagreed with nearly everything she said. To her claim that government must be simple, for example, he answered, "The clock would be simple if you destroyed all the wheels . . . but it would not tell the time of day." On a blank page beside the contents, he wrote, in part:

If [the] empire of superstition and hypocrisy should be overthrown, happy indeed will it be for the world; but if all religion and all morality should be over-thrown with it, what advantage will be gained? The doctrine of human equality is founded entirely in the Christian doctrine that we are all children of the same Father, all accountable to Him for our conduct to one another, all equally bound to respect each other's self love.

In all, in this one book, Adams's marginal notes and comments ran to some 12,000 words.

To the pronouncements of the French philosophes in particular, he would respond with an indignant "Nonsense" or "Fool! Fool!" But he could also scratch in an approving "Good" or "Very Good" or an emphatic "Excellent!"

"Your father's zeal for books will be one of the last desires which will quit him," Abigail observed to John Quincy in the spring of 1816, as Adams eagerly embarked on a sixteen-volume French history.

TWO PORTRAITS of the Adamses by Gilbert Stuart, painted when Adams was President but never delivered, were added to the walls at Quincy after Adams decided to go himself to Stuart's Boston studio and bring them home. The portrait of Adams, Abigail thought quite admirable. But hers, she told John Quincy, would be recognizable only to those who had known her twenty years before. Her hair had since turned entirely white and she had so "fallen away" as to be "but a spectre" of what she once was.

At the July 4 celebration in Boston that summer of 1816, Adams looked about and realized he was nearly the last of the generation of 1776, and the only "signer" present.

He and Abigail lived for John Quincy's return, as they made plain. When during that autumn of 1816 it appeared that James Monroe was to be the next President and newspapers were reporting John Quincy the choice for Secretary of State, Adams sent off a letter to London saying he hoped it was true and that John Quincy would accept the office and come home. If not true, Adams hoped he would come home anyway. Later, with still no word from London, Abigail was more emphatic. "The voice of the nation calls you home," she wrote. "The government calls you home—and your parents unite in the call. To this summons you must not, you cannot, refuse your assent."

By the summer of 1817, when President Monroe, on a tour of New England, came to Quincy to dine with the Adamses on the evening of July 7, they entertained forty guests for dinner but could report nothing of their son's intentions, as there was still no word from him. It was not until July 15 that they learned from Richard Rush that the appointment had been accepted, and not until the second week of August that a letter arrived from John Quincy himself, saying he and his family were safely landed at New York.

"Yesterday was one of the most uniformly happy days of my whole

long life," Adams wrote his son. "A thousand occasions exalted delight
. . . a succession of warm showers all day, my threshers, my gardeners,
and my farmers all behaved better than usual, and altogether kept me in
a kind of trance of delight the whole day."

"God be thanked," Abigail wrote. "Come then all of you."

IN THE HISTORY of the Adams family there was probably no more joy-
ous homecoming than took place in the heat of midmorning on August
18, 1817, when John Quincy, Louisa Catherine, and their three sons came
over the hill from Milton in a coach-and-four trailing a cloud of dust.

As Abigail recorded, Louisa Smith was the first to see them coming
and begin shouting. Abigail hurried to the door. First out of the coach
was young John, who ran to her, followed by George calling, "Oh, Grandmother, oh, Grandmother." Ten-year-old Charles Francis, with no memory of his grandparents, approached with caution. "By this time father
and mother were both out, and mutually rejoicing with us," Abigail
wrote. John Quincy had been away for eight years.

At a party given by Abigail that evening, her long drawing room was
crowded with neighbors and relatives, one of whom, young Eliza Susan
Quincy, described John Quincy as the focus of attention, seated at the
end of the room, everyone "rather in awe of him." At age fifty, he had
already served as minister to the Netherlands and Prussia, as United
States senator, Harvard professor, minister to Russia and Great Britain,
and was soon to assume the second-most-important office in the government. In view of the fact that the past three Presidents in a row—Jefferson, Madison, and Monroe—had earlier served as Secretary of State, it
was already being said that the presidency was his destiny, too.

II

THE MONTHS that followed, despite another severe winter and the
increasing aggravations of old age, were as happy a time for the Adamses
as any in their years of retirement. While John Quincy and Louisa
Catherine had departed for Washington, the three grandsons remained
nearby—George at Harvard, John and Charles Francis in school in

Boston. After dining at Quincy in mid-January 1818, Benjamin Water-house reported to John Quincy that his parents seemed in splendid health, but his father in particular. "I never saw your father in better spirits. I really believe that your return to America with all its honorable consequences has not only brightened his chain of life, but added links to it."

It was "very cold and the snow falling fast," Abigail wrote to Louisa Catherine, delighted by the spectacle. "It is now a foot or more deep. Winter appears to have set in, with all its beauties." No President, she was sure, had ever had such a fine or harder-working Secretary of State as her son, Abigail continued in another letter to Louisa Catherine, written in May as her plum trees were blooming and the first peas "looking up newly arrived to daylight." His father lived for John Quincy's letters and to write to him in return, difficult as that had become for him.

Through the summer Abigail maintained strength and pleasure in life, by all accounts. John Quincy and Louisa Catherine returned for a much-needed vacation, and several of those who came to call at about this time would remember Abigail seated on a couch sorting a basket of laundry or shelling beans as she talked. "I found a freedom in conversation [with her]. . . . She was possessed of the history of our country and the great occurrences in it," wrote the noted Salem clergyman William Bently. "She had a distinct view of our public men and measures and had her own opinions."

But in October, Abigail was taken seriously ill. The diagnosis was typhoid fever, and she was told to remain perfectly still and try not to speak.

"The dear partner of my life for fifty-four years as a wife, and for many years more as a lover, now lies in extremis, forbidden to speak or be spoken to," Adams wrote in anguish to Jefferson on October 20. The day following, Benjamin Waterhouse sent off a letter to John Quincy advising him to be prepared for the worst. "She has recovered from a similar state once before, and she may again, but *typhoid* . . . at 74 years of age is enough to create alarm."

Friends and neighbors took turns with Adams, son Thomas, and niece Louisa Smith at Abigail's bedside. She was dosed with quinine and Madeira by her physician, Amos Holbrook, and for a day or so she seemed to improve. "Your mother was pronounced so much better this morning that your father has resumed his book," wrote a friend, Harriet Welsh, to John Quincy and Louisa Catherine. But in another day Abigail had taken a turn for the worse.

On Monday morning, October 26, as Adams sat with her, she spoke for the first time. She told him she was dying and that if it was the will of Heaven, she was ready. She had no wish to live except for his sake.

"He came down," wrote Harriet Welsh, who was waiting on the first floor, "and said in his energetic manner, 'I wish I could lie down beside her and die, too.' " "The whole of her life has been filled up doing good," Adams told the others who were gathered. "I cannot bear to see her in this state."

Returning to her room later, Adams was trembling so much that he could not stand and had to take a chair, but then seeing that Louisa Smith was in worse distress, he got up and went to her side to tell her they must be strong.

Abigail died at approximately one o'clock in the afternoon, Wednesday, October 28, 1818. She was, according to her son Thomas, "seemingly conscious until her last breath."

She was buried on November 1. Adams insisted on walking in the procession to the meetinghouse, and except for a momentary dizziness due to the unseasonable heat of the day, he went through "all the rest," as Thomas wrote, "with great composure and serenity."

BENJAMIN WATERHOUSE's letter warning John Quincy to be prepared for the worst had not reached Washington until the day before his mother's death, and it was not until the day after her funeral that he learned she was gone, "the tenderest and most affectionate of mothers," as he wrote to his father. "How shall I offer consolation for your loss, when I feel that my own is irreparable?"

"Gracious God! Support my father in this deep and irreparable affliction!" he wrote in his diary.

My mother . . . was a minister of blessing to all human beings within her sphere of action. . . . She had no feelings but of kindness and beneficence. Yet her mind was as firm as her temper was mild and gentle. She . . . has been to me more than a mother. She has been a spirit from above watching over me for good, and contributing by my mere consciousness of her existence, to the comfort of my life. . . . Never have I known another human being, the perpetual object of whose life, was so unremittingly to do good.

"My ever dear, ever affectionate, ever dutiful and deserving son," Adams wrote, in the first letter he could manage:

The bitterness of death is past. The grim spider so terrible to human nature has no sting left for me.

My consolations are more than I can number. The separation cannot be so long as twenty separations heretofore. The pangs and the anguish have not been so great as when you and I embarked for France in 1778.

All Quincy was in mourning. "The tidings of her illness were heard with grief in every house, and her death is felt as a common loss," the Reverend Peter Whitney had said without exaggeration at the funeral service.

Madame Adams possessed a mind elevated in its views and capable of attainments above the common order of intellects. . . . But though her attainments were great, and she had lived in the highest walks of society and was fitted for the lofty departments in which she acted, her elevation had never filled her soul with pride, or led her for a moment to forget the feelings and the claims of others.

The obituary notice in Boston's *Columbian Centinel* emphasized her importance to her husband's career in public service and thus to the nation:

Possessing at every period of life, the unlimited confidence, as well as affection of her husband, she was admitted at all times to share largely of his thoughts. While, on the one hand, the activity of her mind, and its thorough knowledge of all branches of domestic economy, enabled her almost wholly to relieve him from the cares incident to the concerns of private life; on the other, she was a friend whom it was his delight to consult in every perplexity of public affairs; and whose counsels never failed to partake of that happy harmony which prevailed in her character; in which intuitive judgment was blended with consummate prudence; the spirit of conciliation, with the spirit of her station, and the refinement of her sex. In the storm, as well as the smooth sea of life, her virtues were ever the object of his trust and veneration.

Letters of condolence arrived for Adams, including one from Jefferson, who had himself been gravely ill. Time and silence were the only medicines, he counseled Adams. "God bless you and support you under your heavy affliction."

"While you live," Adams answered, "I seem to have a bank at Monticello on which I can draw for a letter of friendship and entertainment when I please.

I believe in God and in his wisdom and benevolence [he continued], and I cannot conceive that such a Being could make such a species as the human merely to live and die on this earth. If I did not believe in a future state, I should believe in no God. This universe, this all, this το παν ["totality"] would appear with all its swelling pomp, a boyish firework.

That he had been blessed in a partnership with one of the most exceptional women of her time, Adams never doubted. Her letters, he was sure, would be read for generations to come, and with this others strongly agreed. Years later Louisa Catherine, who had not always enjoyed a close or easy relationship with her mother-in-law, would say that it was especially in the letters of Abigail Adams that "the full benevolence of an exceptional heart and the strength of her reasoning capacity" were to be found. "We see her ever as the guiding planet around which all revolved performing their separate duties only by the impulse of her magnetic power."

To his granddaughter Caroline, Adams would write of Abigail's "virtues of the heart." Never "by word or look" had she discouraged him from "running all hazards" for their country's liberties. Willingly, bravely, she had shared with him "in all the dangerous consequences we had to hazard."

For years afterward, whenever complimented about John Quincy and his role in national life, and the part he had played as father, Adams would say with emphasis, "My son had a mother!"

III

TWO WEEKS after Abigail's death, the painter John Trumbull, as well as several of the Quincy family, insisted that Adams go with them to Boston—"carried me off by storm," he reported to John Quincy—to view Trumbull's enormous new painting of the signing of the Declaration of Independence. Commissioned by Congress for the rotunda at the Capitol, it was on tour through several cities and was now on display at Faneuil Hall.

In preparation for an earlier, much smaller version of the scene, Trumbull had painted studies from life of thirty-six of the signers, including Adams, whom Trumbull sketched in London. If there was anyone who ought to see the colossal new rendition, measuring twelve by eighteen feet, it was surely Adams. Also, it was hoped the excursion to town would do him good.

The arrival of Adams at Faneuil Hall was described that night in her journal by Eliza Susan Quincy, herself an artist, who was among those riding with him. "Colonel Trumbull came to the carriage door . . . assisted Mr. Adams to alight and offered his arm to descend the steps. But Mr. Adams pushed him aside and insisted in handing Mrs. Quincy up the stairs and into Faneuil Hall, in which many persons had assembled." The aged Adams standing before the painting, gazing silently at "the great scene in which he had borne a conspicuous place," was a sight long remembered.

In composing the picture, Trumbull had placed Adams at the exact center foreground, as if to leave no doubt about his importance. Hand on hip, Adams looked stout but erect, the expression on his face, one of bold confidence and determination. Beside him, facing the desk where John Hancock sat in the president's chair, were Roger Sherman, Robert Livingston, Jefferson, and Franklin, all dead now except Jefferson, who in the painting held the Declaration in his hands.

Ranged behind were forty-seven of the fifty-six delegates who had signed the Declaration, each quite recognizable, including Adams's favorite, Stephen Hopkins of Rhode Island, standing at the rear with his Quaker hat on.

What Adams thought as he looked at the painting will never be known. A few years earlier, hearing that Trumbull was to undertake such a commission, Adams had lectured him on the importance of accuracy. "Truth, nature, fact, should be your sole guide," Adams had said. "Let not our posterity be deluded with fictions under the pretense of poetical or graphical license." Further, he had expressed concern over the projected size of the painting. "The dimensions, 18 by 12, appear vast. . . . I have been informed that one of the greatest talents of a painter is a capacity to comprehend a large space, and to proportion all his figures in it." During his years in Europe, Adams recalled, he had never passed through Antwerp without stopping to see the paintings of Rubens. "I cannot depend upon my memory to say that even his *Descent from the Cross* or his *Apotheosis of the Virgin* exceeded these measures."

Clearly, Trumbull was no Rubens, and concern for accuracy had not been a major consideration. No such scene, with all the delegates present, had ever occurred at Philadelphia.

His audience in Faneuil Hall waited for Adams's response. Then, pointing to a door in the background, on the right side of the painting, he said only, "When I nominated George Washington of Virginia for Commander-in-Chief of the Continental Army, he took his hat and rushed out that door."

Possibly it was Adams's old vanity that prompted the remark—to remind those gathered of how much else he had done of importance in that room in Philadelphia—or perhaps, confronted all at once with so many faces from the past, he was reminded of the all-important man whose face was not to be seen. Afterward, in a note to John Quincy, Adams remarked only on how cold it had been in the hall and that he had "caught the pip [a sore throat] as a result."

John Quincy was vexed—"forgive me my dear father for saying it"— that Adams had not paid greater homage to the "mighty consequences" of July 4, 1776. "It was not merely the birthday of a powerful nation. It was the opening of a new era in the history of mankind." As for the painting, which he had already seen, John Quincy thought it highly disappointing, no more than a collection of interesting portraits, "cold and unmeaning." But then in capturing so sublime a scene, even a Raphael or a Michelangelo would have been inadequate, he was sure.

"All is now still and tranquil," Adams wrote to Jefferson as the year ended. "There is nothing to try men's souls. . . . And I say, God speed the plough, and prosper stone wall."

To THE GREAT DELIGHT of everyone around him, Adams remained remarkably healthy and good-spirited. In the exchange of correspondence with Jefferson he continued to be by far the more productive, sending off thirteen letters to Monticello in the year 1819, for example, or more than two for every one from Jefferson.

To his immense pleasure, his Dutch friend, Francis van der Kemp, came for a visit of several days. Writing to Jefferson, Adams described Van der Kemp as "a mountain of salt of the earth."

With Nabby and Abigail gone, Louisa Catherine filled a great need in his life, writing to him steadily and with affection, and welcoming what he wrote in return. Concerned about the trials she would face as the wife of so prominent a public man, Adams cautioned her to study stoicism. But who was he to preach stoicism, she responded warmly. "You, my dear sir, have ever possessed a nature too ardent, too full of benevolent feelings . . . to sink into the cold and thankless state of stoicism. Your heart is too full of all the generous and kindly affections for you ever to acquire such a cold and selfish doctrine."

John Quincy's achievements as Secretary of State were proving all that a proud father could hope for. When the Adams-Onis Treaty of 1819 added Spanish Florida to the United States, the old President in Quincy proclaimed it a blessing "beyond all calculation," largely for the ways it might serve American naval operations.

His enjoyment of his family never diminished. He kept close watch on how George, John, and Charles Francis were progressing in their education. To help his son Thomas, who was having a difficult time supporting his wife and five children—but also for his own pleasure—Adams insisted they move in with him. When it was said he deserved to be known as the father of the American navy, Adams answered that he was father of enough as it was, with two sons, fourteen grandchildren, and five great grandchildren, all of whom required his attention and support.

He loved company, the house full. He was rarely without aches and pains and suffered spells of poor health. Some days were extremely difficult. But he could still ride horseback, at nearly eighty-five, and on "rambles" over the farm or his walks about town he sometimes covered three miles.

He never tired of the farm. He loved every wall and field, loved its order and productiveness, the very look of it. "My crops are more abundant than I expected," he would write one September. "I have the most beautiful cornfield I ever saw. It is drawn up like an army in array, in a long line before my house."

His appetite strong, he delighted in the plain, substantial fare of the family table. As he wrote to Louisa Catherine, "We go on . . . eating fat turkeys, roast beef—and Indian pudding—and more than that, mince pies and plum pudding in abundance, besides cranberry tarts."

In the hours he spent alone, reading, thinking, or just looking out the window by his desk, he found an inner peace, even a sense of exhilaration such as he had seldom known. Old poems, ballads, books he had read many times over, gave greater pleasure than ever. "The Psalms of David, in sublimity, beauty, pathos, and originality, or in one word poetry, are superior to all the odes, hymns, and songs in any language," he told Jefferson. He had read Cicero's essay on growing old gracefully, *De Senectute*, for seventy years, to the point of nearly knowing it by heart, but never had it given such joy as on his most recent reading, he told another correspondent.

> *For as I like a young man in whom there is something of the old* [ran a famous passage], *so I like an old man in whom there is something of the young; and he who follows this maxim, in body will possibly be an old man but he will never be an old man in mind.*

The simplest, most ordinary things, that in other times had seemed incidentals, could lift his heart and set his mind soaring. The philosophy that with sufficient knowledge all could be explained held no appeal. All could not be explained, Adams had come to understand. Mystery was essential. "Admire and adore the Author of the telescopic universe, love and esteem the work, do all in your power to lessen ill, and increase good," he wrote in the margin of one of his books, "but never assume to comprehend."

Even the punctuation of a page, or the spelling of an individual word, could seem infinitely beautiful to him as part of what he had come to see as "this wonderful whole.

> I never delighted much in contemplating commas and colons, or in spelling or measuring syllables; but now . . . if I attempt to look at these little objects, I find my imagination, in spite of all my exertions, roaming in the Milky Way, among the nebulae, those mighty orbs, and stupendous orbits of suns, planets, satellites, and comets, which compose the incomprehensible universe; and if I do not sink into nothing in my own estimation, I feel an irresistible impulse to fall on my knees, in adoration of the power that moves, the wisdom that directs, and the benevolence that sanctifies this wonderful whole.

The view from his window the morning after one of the worst March storms on record filled him with ecstasy, despite the damage done to his trees. It was "the most splendid winter scene ever beheld," Adams wrote.

> A rain had fallen from some warmer region in the skies when the cold here below was intense to an extreme. Every drop was frozen wherever it fell in the trees, and clung to the limbs and sprigs as if it had been fastened by hooks of steel. The earth was never more universally covered with snow, and the rain had frozen upon a crust on the surface which shone with the brightness of burnished silver. The icicles on every sprig glowed in all the luster of diamonds. Every tree was a chandelier of cut glass. I have seen a Queen of France with eighteen millions of livres of diamonds upon her person and I declare that all the charms of her face and figure added to all the glitter of her jewels did not make an impression on me equal to that presented by every shrub. The whole world was glittering with precious stones.

• • •

IN LATE 1820, at age eighty-five, Adams found himself chosen as a delegate to a state convention called to revise the Massachusetts constitution that he had drafted some forty years before.

"The town of Quincy has been pleased to elect me a member of the Convention—and wonderful to relate—the election is said to be unanimous. . . . I am sufficiently advanced in my dotage to have accepted the choice," he reported to Louisa Catherine. "I feel not much like a maker or mender of constitutions, in my present state of imbecility. . . . But I presume we shall not be obliged to carry windmills by assault." But in what was to be his last public effort, in a speech considered "very remarkable" for its energy and conviction, Adams boldly offered an amendment guaranteeing complete religious freedom in the commonwealth. As he believed that all were equal before God, so he believed that all should be free to worship God as they pleased. In particular, he wanted religious freedom for Jews, as he had written earlier to a noted New York editor, Mordecai Noah, who had sent him a discourse delivered at the consecration of a synagogue in New York.

"You have not extended your ideas of the right of private judgment and the liberty of conscience both in religion and philosophy farther than I do," Adams wrote in appreciation.

> I have had occasion to be acquainted with several gentlemen of your nation and to transact business with some of them, whom I found to be men of as liberal minds, as much as honor, probity, generosity, and good breeding as any I have known in any seat of religion or philosophy.
>
> I wish your nation to be admitted to all the privileges of citizens in every country in the world. This country has done much, I wish it may do more, and annul every narrow idea in religion, government, and commerce.

Jefferson wrote to tell Adams he "rejoiced" at the news that Adams had "health and spirits enough" to take part in such an effort in the "advance of liberalism." On arrival at the convention, Adams had received a standing ovation. But his amendment failed to pass. Blaming himself, he told Jefferson, "I boggled and blundered more than a young fellow just rising to speak at the bar." But to young Josiah Quincy, who came by frequently to visit, Adams spoke with regret of the intolerance of Christians.

Josiah, a student at Harvard, was to keep Adams company over several years, spending summers as Adams's secretary, and in his diary he devoted frequent entries to "the President" and his observations on life. "Visited the President as usual," he wrote at the end of one session. "He was quite amusing, and gave us anecdotes of his life. He was particularly funny in an account of an interview he had with the Turkish ambassador [the envoy from Tripoli] in England." Another time Adams stressed the need for "commotion" in life, to keep it from going stagnant. "For my own part," he exclaimed, "I should not like to live to the Millennium. It would be the most sickish life imaginable."

One June evening, when Adams came to call on the Quincys and brought along a letter from Jefferson to read aloud, he was asked to explain how he could possibly be on such good terms with Jefferson, after all the abuse he had suffered from him. According to Josiah's diary, Adams replied as follows:

> I do not believe that Mr. Jefferson ever hated me. On the contrary, I believe he always liked *me:* but he detested Hamilton and my whole administration. Then he wished to be President of the United States, and I stood in his way. So he did everything that he could to pull me down. But if I should quarrel with him for that, I might quarrel with every man I have had anything to do with in life. This is human nature. . . . I forgive all my enemies and hope they may find mercy in Heaven. Mr. Jefferson and I have grown old and retired from public life. So we are upon our ancient terms of goodwill.

Indeed, Adams had become sufficiently confident in their "ancient goodwill" to broach the subject of slavery. In 1819, with Congress in debate over whether to admit Missouri into the union as a slave state, Adams had expressed the hope to Jefferson that the issue might "follow the other waves under the ship and do no harm." Yet he worried. "I know it is high treason to express a doubt of the perpetual duration of our vast American empire," but a struggle between the states over slavery "might rend this mighty fabric in twain."

The Missouri Compromise of 1820—whereby Missouri was admitted as a slave state, Maine (until then part of Massachusetts) as a free state, and slavery excluded in the Louisiana Territory north of latitude 36° 30'—left Adams in torment over the future. She would think him mad were he to describe "the calamities that slavery was likely to produce in the country," he wrote to Louisa Catherine. He imagined horrible massacres of blacks killing whites, and in their turn, whites slaughtering blacks until "at last the whites exasperated to madness shall be wicked enough to exterminate the Negroes."

All possible humanity should be shown the blacks, he told another correspondent. And while he did not know what the solution to the presence of slavery should be, he was certain it should not be allowed to expand. He was "utterly adverse" to the admission of slavery into Missouri, which was in exact opposition to Jefferson, who favored it. Slavery, he now told Jefferson, was the black cloud over the nation. He had a vision of "armies of Negroes marching and countermarching in the air, shining in armor." Yet he knew not what to do.

> I have been so terrified with this phenomenon that I constantly said in former times to the southern gentlemen, I cannot comprehend this object; I must leave it to you. I will vote for forcing no measure against your judgments. What we are to see God knows, and I leave it to him and his agents in posterity. I have none of the genius of Franklin, to invent a rod to draw from the cloud its thunder and lightning.

Jefferson, who believed that slavery was a "moral and political depravity," nonetheless refused to free his own slaves and gave no public support to emancipation. "This enterprise is for the young," he wrote to a young Albemarle County neighbor who was freeing his slaves and urged Jefferson to "become a Hercules against slavery."

In response to Adams's impassioned letter of foreboding, Jefferson said nothing. To others, however, he wrote privately at some length. He favored gradual emancipation and eventual colonization for the slaves. Should they ever be set free all at once, Jefferson wrote to Albert Gallatin, "all whites south of the Potomac and the Ohio must evacuate their states, and most fortunate those who can do it first." But with Adams he avoided any discussion of the subject.

When, in his next letter, Adams suggested that in addition to the military academy at West Point, which had been established during Jefferson's presidency, there ought to be a naval academy, Jefferson replied at once in agreement.

Jefferson's own great preoccupation, his all-consuming interest for several years now, was the establishment of a new university for Virginia at Charlottesville. It was one of the proudest efforts of his life, and he was involved in every aspect, organizing the curriculum, choosing the site, and designing the buildings. Once construction was under way, he kept watch from his mountaintop by telescope. The full complex, when finished, would be his architectural masterpiece. The faculty, as he told Adams proudly, would be drawn from the great seats of learning in Europe.

Adams, who had no project to keep him occupied, said Jefferson's university was surely "noble employment." He did not, however, approve of sending abroad for professors when, as he told Jefferson, there were a sufficient number of American scholars with more active, independent minds than to be found in Europe.

The two old correspondents continued to write of their declining health and persistent ailments, of old memories and the death of friends, but the letters grew fewer in number, and there was much about each of their lives that they kept to themselves.

Jefferson told Adams nothing of the new house he had built at his other plantation, Poplar Forest, or that Monticello, as visitors noted, was going to decay. He made no mention of his worsening financial straits and said not a word ever on the subject of Sally Hemings and her children. Indeed, he never referred to his slaves or the fact that his entire way of life was no less dependent on them than ever. Nor did he say anything of the dreadful turmoil within his own household—of the erratic behavior of his son-in-law, Martha's husband, Thomas Mann Randolph, or of the grandson-in-law, Charles Bankhead, who was subject to violent alcoholic rages.

But then neither did Adams write of his own increasing worry and sorrow over his son Thomas, who, having failed in the law, was drinking heavily and employed now primarily as a caretaker for his father and the farm. John Quincy's son Charles Francis, writing of his uncle Thomas, described him as "one of the most unpleasant characters in this world . . . a brute in manners and a bully in his family."

The question of how two of his sons, Charles and Thomas, could have so sadly fallen by the wayside, while John Quincy so conspicuously excelled could only have weighed heavily on Adams's mind. But of this, for all that he wrote on nearly everything else, he wrote nothing. The closest he seems to have come in blaming himself was in a letter to John Quincy admonishing him that "children must not be wholly forgotten in the midst of public duties."

VISITORS CONTINUED to call out of curiosity or genuine friendship, and Adams took pleasure in nearly all. Only occasionally would some leave him feeling low and more alone than before. Of one couple he wrote to Louisa Catherine, "They had eyes and ears to perceive the external person, but not feelings to sympathize with the internal griefs, pains, anxieties, solitudes, and inquietudes within." But he refused to complain.

The morning of August 14, 1821, 200 West Point cadets, an entire corps, who were touring New England, marched out from Boston to parade past the Adams house, colors flying and band playing. Half the town turned out for the excitement. Adams, who stood watching from the porch, had provided breakfast for the cadets at his own expense. Tables were set up under an open tent. When they had stacked their arms and lined up before him, Adams made a brief speech, his voice faint at first but growing stronger as he went on. It was the example of the character of George Washington that they should keep before them, he said.

His remarks finished, the band played a tune called "Adams and Liberty," while he beat time to the music. At the last, when all 200 cadets came up onto the porch one by one, Adams shook hands with each. "President Adams seemed highly gratified," recorded Eliza Susan Quincy.

IV

IF ADAMS'S LIFE—indeed, Adams himself—could be defined by what was left to him that he loved, there was still a great deal to the life and to the man, and he was extremely grateful. "No man has more cause for gratitude," he assured Louisa Catherine.

He had his library room, where he slept now among his treasured books. On the table beside his reading chair were the latest novels of Walter Scott and James Fenimore Cooper, the sermons of Bishop Joseph Butler, along with Pascal's *Provincial Letters*.

He had almost continuous company and thrived on it. "In the evening I . . . [went] to the President's and found the old gentleman well and lively," reads one entry in Josiah Quincy's diary. "I scarcely ever saw him look better or converse with more spirit," reads another. One June evening at the Quincys', having talked more than anyone, Adams declared happily, "If I was to come here once a day, I should live half a year longer," to which the family said he must therefore come twice a day and live a year longer. The next day he was back again.

His pride in John Quincy knew no bounds. If he was writing to him less frequently, Adams explained, it was for good reason. "I know that you would answer every scratch of a pen from me, but I know the importance of your occupations and your indefatigable attentions to them, and no trifling letter from me should divert your mind." The weeks in summer when John Quincy and Louisa Catherine returned home were invariably the summit of the year for the old man.

He wrote regularly to his grandsons on all manner of subjects, from books to the therapeutic benefits of riding horseback to the importance of maintaining one's independence through life. To Charles Francis he issued a summons to make of himself all that was possible. "Arouse your courage, be determined to be something in the world," Adams wrote. "You have a fine capacity, my dear boy, if you will exert it. You are responsible to God and man for a fine genius, a talent which is not to be buried in the earth."

In the spring of 1823, when John was expelled from Harvard, along with fifty others of the senior class for taking part in a student riot, Adams, in an effort to intercede in his behalf, explained to his mother that he could not find it in his own heart to reproach the boy, since he "did no more than all the rest, nor so much as many," and urged Louisa Catherine to "receive him tenderly, and forgive him kindly."

The affection Adams felt for Jefferson was expressed repeatedly and often with touching candor. When an old private letter of Adams's attacking Jefferson turned up in print, to Adams's extreme embarrassment, Jefferson proved that the friendship meant no less to him. "It would be strange indeed," Jefferson wrote, "if, at our years, we were to go an age back to hunt up imaginary, or forgotten facts, to disturb the repose of affections so sweetening to the evening of our lives."

Physically, Adams was declining rapidly. He suffered severe pains in his back. In cold weather his rheumatism was such that he could get about only with a cane. His teeth were gone. His hearing was going. Sadly, he had to admit he could mount a horse no longer. Yet he insisted, "I am not weary of life. I still enjoy it."

IN 1824, with James Monroe due to retire from the presidency, Secretary of State John Quincy Adams was nominated as a candidate to replace him, exactly as long predicted. With three others also nominated, and all, like John Quincy, avowed Republicans—William Crawford of Georgia, Henry Clay of Kentucky, and General Andrew Jackson of Tennessee—it became a crowded contest of "increasing heat." John Adams was a great admirer of Andrew Jackson, but the prospect of his adored son winning the highest office was thrilling and a strong reason to stay alive.

To compound the excitement of the summer of 1824, the Marquis de Lafayette returned for a triumphal tour of America, causing a sensation. Landing at New York, he proceeded northward to Boston, accompanied by his son George Washington Lafayette, and on August 29 arrived at Quincy to pay an afternoon call on Adams.

As a crowd gathered outside the Adams house, numbers of the family filled the room where the two old heroes sat reminiscing, Adams hugely enjoying the occasion. "Grandfather exerted himself more than usual, and as to conversation, appeared exactly as he ever was," recorded Charles Francis. "I think he is rather more striking now than ever, certainly more agreeable, as his asperity of temper is worn away."

Afterward, Adams is said to have remarked, "That was not the Lafayette I knew," while Lafayette, saddened by the visit, reportedly remarked, "That was not the John Adams I knew."

John Quincy, when he arrived in September for a holiday of several weeks, was shocked by his father's drastically deteriorating condition.

His sight is so dim that he can neither write nor read. He cannot walk without aid. . . . He bears his condition with fortitude, but is sensible to all its helplessness. . . . He receives some letters, and dictates answers to them. In general the most remarkable circumstance of his present state is the total prostration of his physical powers, leaving his mental faculties scarcely impaired at all.

Such was the change in his father that John Quincy decided that one last portrait must be done and persuaded Gilbert Stuart, who was himself nearly seventy and seriously ill, "to paint a picture of affection, and of curiosity for future times."

Adams agreed to sit, but only because of his regard for Stuart. Adams had little faith in portraits of himself. "Speaking generally," he said, "no penance is like having one's picture done." When a French sculptor, J. B. Binon, had been commissioned a few years earlier to render a marble bust for Faneuil Hall, Adams had posed most reluctantly—"I let them do what they please with my old head," he had told Jefferson. Stuart, however, was a famously entertaining talker, and thus another matter. "I should like to sit to Stuart from the first of January to the thirty-first of December," Adams said, "for he lets me do just as I please, and keeps me constantly amused by his conversation."

Wearing a best black suit, Adams posed on a red velvet settee in the parlor. As anticipated, he and Stuart had a thoroughly fine time during several sittings, and the finished portrait was one of Stuart's finest. Had it been done by an inferior hand, as Josiah Quincy observed, it might have been painful to look at. But Stuart had caught "a glimpse of the living spirit shining through the feeble and decrepit body. He saw the old man at one of those happy moments when the intelligence lights up the wasted envelope."

EVER SINCE Abigail's death, the last days of October had become the most difficult time of the year for Adams. As his grandson George reminded Louisa Catherine, "He was married on the 27th, Grandmother died on the 28th, his birthday [was] the 30th, her funeral, the 31st." These days, and their memories, as Adams had told George, brought overwhelming sorrow. The "encroaching melancholy" made everything else seem uninteresting and insignificant.

But among the family and friends who gathered at the Big House on October 30, 1824, to celebrate Adams's eighty-ninth birthday, it was thought that because of the forthcoming election he looked better and "conversed with more spirit" than he had in years. When, after election day, it became known that in Quincy, Braintree, and Weymouth, John Quincy had received every vote cast for the presidency, Adams declared it one of the most gratifying events of his life.

The outcome of the contest nationally, however, was not to be resolved until February. For though Andrew Jackson received more popular votes, no candidate had a majority in the electoral count. So again the decision was left to the House of Representatives, where Speaker of the House Henry Clay used his influence to make John Quincy Adams president. The deciding vote took place in Washington on February 9, 1825. Five days later the news reached Quincy, and again family and friends crowded about "the old President" to wish him congratulations.

> He ... was considerably affected by the fulfillment of his highest wishes [wrote Josiah Quincy]. In the course of conversation, my mother compared him to that old man who was pronounced by Solon to be the highest of mortals when he expired on hearing of his son's success at the Olympic games. The similarity of their situations visibly moved the old gentleman, and tears of joy rolled down his cheek.

Later, however, Adams told those gathered, "No man who ever held the office of President would congratulate a friend on obtaining it."

From Monticello came warm congratulations. "It must excite ineffable feelings in the breast of a father to have lived to see a son to whose educ[atio]n and happiness his life has been so devoted so eminently distinguished by the voice of his country," Jefferson wrote. Nor should Adams worry about how the country would respond to the outcome.

> So deeply are the principles of order, and of obedience to law impressed on the minds of our citizens generally, that I am per-

suaded there will be an immediate acquiescence in the will of the majority as if Mr. Adams had been the choice of every man.

"Every line from you exhilarates my spirits and gives me a glow of pleasure, but your kind congratulations are solid comfort to my heart," Adams wrote. "The little strength of mind and the considerable strength of body that I once possessed appear to be all gone, but while I breathe I shall be your friend."

ON FRIDAY, March 4, 1825, inside the Hall of the House of Representatives at the Capitol in Washington, John Quincy Adams took the oath of office as the sixth President of the United States, administered by Chief Justice John Marshall; and as the year proceeded in Quincy, Massachusetts, the health and physical strength of his aged father, the second President of the United States, seemed to improve rather than decline. Benjamin Waterhouse, who had thought Adams very near death, was amazed by the change, as he wrote to the President. "But physicians do not always consider how much the powers of the mind, and what is called good spirits, can recover the lost energies of the body. I really believe that your father's revival is mainly owing to the demonstration that his son has not served an ungrateful public."

Adams, reported Waterhouse, could still tell stories and laugh heartily, "and what is more, eats heartily, more than any other at table. We stayed until he smoked out his cigar after dinner."

A stream of visitors continued through the seasons and among them was young Ralph Waldo Emerson, who a few years earlier had graduated from Harvard as class poet. He found Adams upstairs in his library seated in a large overstuffed armchair, dressed in a blue coat, a cotton cap covering his bald head. Recounting the interview, Emerson wrote, "He talks very distinctly for so old a man—enters bravely into long sentences which are interrupted by want of breath but carries them invariably to a conclusion without ever correcting a word."

Speaking of the mood of the times, Adams exclaimed with vehemence, "I would to God there were more ambition in the country," by which he meant, "ambition of that laudable kind, to excel."

Asked when he expected to see his son the President, he said,

"Never," meaning presumably that the press of John Quincy's duties would keep him in Washington. But John Quincy did return, in the early fall of 1825, and spent several days with his father, though what conversation passed between them is unknown. Probably they both knew it was the last time they would spend with one another, and possibly they reviewed the will Adams had drawn up some years before, whereby he left to John Quincy the house, an estimated 103 acres, his French writing desk, "all my manuscript letter-books and account books, letters, journals, and manuscript books, together with the trunks in which they are contained," as well as his library, on "the condition that he pays to my son, Thomas Boylston Adams, the value of one half of the said library." The remainder of the estate was to be divided among his two sons, grandchildren, and Louisa Smith.

"My debts, which I hope will not be large," Adams had stipulated, "and my funeral charges, which I hope will be very small, must be paid by my executors."

On the day of his departure, Monday, October 13, John Quincy wrote only, "Took leave of my father."

ANOTHER OF THE visitors who climbed the stairs to the library, a writer named Anne Royall, found Adams nearly blind, his hair "perfectly white," but was struck by the "sunshine of his countenance," which, when he spoke, became "extremely animated."

As Emerson had been told, Adams was always better for having visitors from morning until night, and never was this quite so evident as an evening in the fall of 1825, when Josiah Quincy was assigned to escort his great-aunt Hannah on a visit to the old President.

Hannah Quincy Lincoln Storer was the flirtatious "Orlinda" of Adams's early diaries, to whom he had once nearly proposed. She had since buried two husbands—Dr. Bela Lincoln of Hingham and Ebenezer Storer, the treasurer of Harvard—and as Josiah noted, she and Adams were now both verging on their ninety-first year.

As his visitor entered, Adams's face lighted up. "What! Madam," he greeted her, "shall we not go walk in Cupid's Grove together?" "Ah, sir," she said after an embarrassed pause, "it would not be the first time we have walked there!"

Perhaps the incident is not worth recording [Josiah wrote], as there is really no way of getting upon paper the suggestiveness it had to a witness. . . . The flash of old sentiment was startling from its utter unexpectedness. It is the sort of thing which sets a young fellow to thinking. It is a surprise to find a great personage so simple, so perfectly natural, so thoroughly human.

Late in November, Adams submitted to one further ordeal for the sake of posterity, when an itinerant sculptor named John Henry Browere appeared at Quincy to make a life mask by a secret process of his own invention. It was known that the experience could be extremely disagreeable for the subject, as the entire head had to be covered with successive layers of thin grout and these given time to dry. When, earlier in October, Browere had gone to Monticello to do Jefferson, the mask had dried so hard it had to be chopped off with a mallet, Jefferson suffering, as he said, a "severe trial." But John Quincy and young Charles Francis had also been done by Browere, and so Adams consented, even though Charles Francis, worried about his grandfather, warned how unpleasant, even dangerous, the experience could be.

The life mask that resulted was not the aged John Adams of the Gilbert Stuart portrait, with a "glimpse of the living spirit shining through." It was instead the face of a glowering old man at odds with life and the world. But then the expression was doubtless greatly affected by the ordeal he had been put through. "He did not tear my face to pieces," Adams wrote good-naturedly to Charles Francis afterward, "though I sometimes thought he would beat my brains out with his hammer."

Then, at the year's end, a granddaughter of Jefferson's, Ellen Wayles Randolph, who had recently married a Massachusetts man, Joseph Coolidge, Jr., came to call accompanied by her husband. Adams was extremely pleased. All the high praises he had heard about her were true, he told Jefferson, aware no doubt that she was Jefferson's favorite.

"She entertained me with accounts of your sentiments of human life, which accorded so perfectly with mine that it gave me great delight." Only on one point did he differ, Adams said. She had told him that Jefferson would like to repeat his life over again. "In this I could not agree; I had rather go forward and meet whatever is to come."

. . .

WITH 1826 marking the fiftieth anniversary of the Declaration of Independence, it was not long into the new year when Adams and Jefferson were being asked to attend a variety of celebrations planned to commemorate the historic event on the Fourth of July. Invitations poured into Quincy and Charlottesville from Washington, Philadelphia, New York, and Boston. The two former presidents were, with eighty-eight-year-old Charles Carroll of Maryland, the last signers of the Declaration still alive. Further, as everyone knew, Jefferson was its author and Adams had been its chief advocate on the floor of Congress. One was "the pen," the other "the voice," of independence, and the presence of either at any Independence Day celebration, large or small, would give it significance as nothing else could.

But the time was past when either Adams or Jefferson could leave home. Adams was ninety, Jefferson would be eighty-three in April, and each grew steadily more feeble. After calling on Adams that spring, Benjamin Waterhouse wrote to John Quincy, "To the eyes of a physician your father appeared to me much nearer to the bottom of the hill."

Still, the old mind prevailed, the brave old heart hung on. As once he had been determined to drive a declaration of independence through Congress, or to cross the Pyrenees in winter, so Adams was determined now to live to see one last Fourth of July.

In March, knowing he had little time left, Jefferson drew his last will. Suffering from bouts of diarrhea and a chronic disorder of the urinary tract, caused apparently by an enlargement of the prostate gland, he depended for relief on large doses of laudanum. Besides, he was beset by troubles at his university—disappointing enrollment, unruly students— and by now suffered such personal financial distress that, in desperation, he had agreed to a proposal that the Virginia legislature create a special lottery to save him from ruin.

But then Jefferson, too, was resolved to hang on until the Fourth.

Jefferson's last letter to Adams, dated Monticello, March 25, 1826, was written at the desk in his office, or "cabinet," where a recently acquired plaster copy of the Adams bust by Binon, a gift of a friend, looked on from a near shelf. He was writing to say that his grandson,

Thomas Jefferson Randolph, was on his way to New England, and that if the young man did not see Adams, it would be as though he had "seen nothing."

> Like other young people [Jefferson wrote] he wished to be able, in the winter nights of old age, to recount to those around him what he has heard and learned of the heroic age preceding his birth, and which of the argonauts particularly he was in time to have seen.

Thus, it was the future generation and the Revolution that occupied Jefferson's thoughts at the last. The world their grandchildren knew could give no adequate idea of the times he and Adams had known. "Theirs are the halcyon calms succeeding the storm which our argosy had so stoutly weathered," Jefferson reminded his old friend in Massachusetts.

Adams, in the letter that would close their long correspondence, wrote on April 17, 1826, to remark on how tall young Randolph was, and how greatly he enjoyed his visit. Also, characteristically Adams was thinking of his son John Quincy, and the rough treatment he was receiving from an uncivil Congress. "Our American chivalry is the worst in all the world. It has no laws, no bounds, no definitions; it seems to be a caprice."

Several days later the young Reverend George Whitney, son of the Reverend Peter Whitney, who had preached at Abigail's funeral, called on Adams and came away doubtful that he could last much longer.

ON JUNE 24 at Monticello, after considerable labor, Jefferson completed a letter to the mayor of Washington declining an invitation to the Fourth of July celebration at Washington. It was his farewell public offering and one of his most eloquent, a tribute to the "worthies" of 1776 and the jubilee that was to take place in their honor. Within days it was reprinted all over the country.

> May it be to the world, what I believe it will be (to some parts sooner, to others later, but finally to all) the signal of arousing men to burst the chains under which monkish ignorance and superstition had persuaded them to bind themselves, and to assume the blessings and

security of self-government. . . . All eyes are opened or opening to the rights of man. The general spread of the light of science has already laid open to every view the palpable truth, that the mass of mankind has not been born with saddles on their backs, nor a favored few, booted and spurred, ready to ride them legitimately by the grace of God. These are the grounds of hope for others; for ourselves, let the annual return to this day forever refresh our recollections of these rights, and an undiminished devotion to them.

As he had often before—and as was considered perfectly acceptable—Jefferson had done some borrowing for effect. In this case it was imagery from a famous speech of the seventeenth century by one of Cromwell's soldiers, Richard Rumbold, who, from the scaffold as he was about to be executed, declared, "I never could believe that Providence had sent a few men into the world, ready booted and spurred to ride, and millions ready saddled and bridled to be ridden."

Adams attempted to write nothing so ambitious, and probably, given his condition, it would have proved impossible for him. "The old man fails fast," the Reverend George Whitney recorded after another visit on June 27.

But when on Friday, June 30, Whitney and a small delegation of town leaders made a formal call on Adams, he received them in his upstairs library seated in his favorite armchair. They had come, they told the old patriot, to ask for a toast that they might read aloud at Quincy's celebration on the Fourth.

"I will give you," Adams said, "Independence forever!" Asked if he would like to add something more, he replied, "Not a word."

The day following, July 1, Adams was so weak he could barely speak. The family physician, Amos Holbrook, the ever faithful Louisa Smith, and one or another of the family remained at his bedside around the clock.

When a townsman and frequent visitor named John Marston called at the house on the afternoon of July 3, Adams was able to utter only a few words. "When I parted from him, he pressed my hand, and said something which was inaudible," Marston wrote, "but his *countenance* expressed all that I could desire."

Early on the morning of Tuesday, July 4, as the first cannon of the day commenced firing in the distance, the Reverend George Whitney arrived at the house to find "the old gentleman was drawing to his end. Dr. Holbrook was there and declared to us that he could not live more than through the day." Adams lay in bed with his eyes closed, breathing with great difficulty. Thomas sent off an urgent letter to John Quincy to say their father was "sinking rapidly."

As efforts were made to give Adams more comfort, by changing his position, he awakened. Told that it was the Fourth, he answered clearly, "It is a great day. It is a *good* day."

AT MONTICELLO, Thomas Jefferson had been unconscious since the night of July 2, his daughter Martha, his physician Robley Dunglison, and others keeping watch. At about seven o'clock the evening of July 3, Jefferson awakened and uttered a declaration, "This is the Fourth," or, "This is the Fourth of July." Told that it would be soon, he slept again. Two hours later, at about nine, he was roused to be given a dose of laudanum, which he refused, saying, "No, doctor, nothing more."

Sometime near four in the morning Jefferson spoke his last words, calling in the servants "with a strong clear voice," according to the account of his grandson, Thomas Jefferson Randolph, but which servants he called or what he said to them are unknown.

Jefferson died at approximately one o'clock in the afternoon on July 4, as bells in Charlottesville could be faintly heard ringing in celebration in the valley below.

AT QUINCY the roar of cannon grew louder as the hours passed, and in midafternoon a thunderstorm struck—"The artillery of Heaven," as would be said—to be followed by a gentle rain.

Adams lay peacefully, his mind clear, by all signs. Then late in the afternoon, according to several who were present in the room, he stirred and whispered clearly enough to be understood, "Thomas Jefferson survives."

Somewhat later, struggling for breath, he whispered to his granddaughter Susanna, "Help me, child! Help me!" then lapsed into a final silence.

At about six-twenty his heart stopped. John Adams was dead.

As those present would remember ever after, there was a final clap of thunder that shook the house; the rain stopped and the last sun of the day broke through dark, low hanging clouds—"bursting forth . . . with uncommon splendor at the moment of his exit . . . with a sky beautiful and grand beyond description," John Marston would write to John Quincy.

By nightfall the whole town knew.

V

AN ESTIMATED 4,000 people crowded silently about the First Congregational Church on July 7. A suggestion that the funeral of John Adams be held at public expense at the State House in Boston had been rejected by the family, who wished no appearance of "forcing" public tribute and asked that the service be kept as simple as possible, as Adams had wanted. But throngs came from Boston and surrounding towns. Cannon boomed from Mount Wollaston, bells rang, and the procession that carried the casket from the Adams house to the church included the governor, the president of Harvard, members of the state legislature, and Congressman Daniel Webster. Pastor Peter Whitney officiated, taking his text from 1 Chronicles: "He died in good old age, full of days . . . and honor." With the service ended, the body of John Adams was laid to rest beside that of his wife, in the graveyard across the road from the church.

The funeral could not have been "conducted in a more solemn or affecting manner," Josiah Quincy wrote to President Adams, who still did not know of his father's death.

The news of Jefferson's death on July 4 had only reached Washington from Charlottesville on July 6. Not until Sunday, July 9, after receiving several urgent messages from home, did John Quincy start north by coach, accompanied by young John, and it was later that day, near Baltimore, that he learned of his father's death.

That John Adams and Thomas Jefferson had died on the same day, and that it was, of all days, the Fourth of July, could not be seen as a mere coincidence: it was a "visible and palpable" manifestation of "Divine favor," wrote John Quincy in his diary that night, expressing what was felt and would be said again and again everywhere the news spread.

Arriving at Quincy on July 13, the President went directly to his father's house, where suddenly the gravity of his loss hit him for the first time.

> Everything about the house is the same [he wrote]. I was not fully sensible of the change till I entered his bedchamber.... That moment was inexpressibly painful, and struck me as if it had been an arrow to my heart. My father and mother have departed. The charm which has always made this house to me an abode of enchantment is dissolved; and yet my attachment to it, and to the whole region around, is stronger than I ever felt it before.

In the weeks and months that followed, eulogies to Adams and Jefferson were delivered in all parts of the country, and largely in the spirit that their departure should not be seen as a mournful event. They had lived to see "the expanded greatness and consolidated strength of a pure republic." They had died "amid the hosannas and grateful benedictions of a numerous, happy, and joyful people," and on the nation's fiftieth birthday, which, said Daniel Webster in a speech in Boston, was "proof" from on high "that our country, and its benefactors, are objects of His care." Webster's eulogy, delivered at Faneuil Hall on August 2, lasted two hours.

Never a rich man, always worried about making ends meet, John Adams in his long life had accumulated comparatively little in the way of material wealth. Still, as he had hoped, he died considerably more than just solvent. The household possessions, put on auction in September, and largely bought by John Quincy, brought $28,000. Several parcels of land and Adams's pew at the meetinghouse—these also purchased by John Quincy—added another $31,000. All told, once the estate was settled, John Adams's net worth at death was approximately $100,000.

John Quincy would insist on keeping the house, and thus it was to remain in the family for another century.

Jefferson, by sad contrast, had died with debts exceeding $100,000, more than the value of Monticello, its land, and all his possessions, including his slaves. He apparently went to his grave believing the state lottery established in his behalf would resolve his financial crisis and provide for his family, but the lottery proved unsuccessful.

By his will Jefferson had freed just five of his slaves, all of whom were members of the Hemings family, but Sally Hemings was not one of them. She was given "her time," unofficial freedom, by his daughter Martha Randolph after his death.

In January 1827 on the front lawn of Monticello, 130 of Jefferson's slaves were sold at auction, along with furniture and farm equipment. Finally, in 1831, after years of standing idle, Monticello, too, was sold for a fraction of what it had cost.

Unlike Jefferson, Adams had not composed his own epitaph. Jefferson, characteristically, had both designed the stone obelisk that was to mark his grave at Monticello and specified what was to be inscribed upon it, conspicuously making no mention of the fact that he had been governor of Virginia, minister to France, Secretary of State, Vice President of the United States, or President of the United States. It was his creative work that he wished most to be remembered for:

> *Here Was Buried*
> *THOMAS JEFFERSON*
> *Author of the Declaration of American Independence,*
> *Of the Statute of Virginia for Religious Freedom,*
> *And Father of the University of Virginia*

Adams had, however, composed an inscription to be carved into the sarcophagus lid of Henry Adams, the first Adams to arrive in Massachusetts, in 1638.

> This stone and several others [it read] have been placed in this yard by a great, great, grandson from a veneration of the piety, humility, simplicity, prudence, frugality, industry and perseverance of his ancestors in hopes of recommending an affirmation of their virtues to their posterity.

Adams had chosen to say nothing of any of his own attainments, but rather to place himself as part of a continuum, and to evoke those qualities of character that he had been raised on and that he had strived for so long to uphold.

The last of the ringing eulogies to Adams and Jefferson was not delivered until October of 1826, when Attorney General William Wirt addressed Congress in Washington, speaking longer even than Webster had. Recounting Adams's career, he cited Adams's defense of the British soldiers after the Boston Massacre, his break with his old friend Jonathan Sewall, the crucial role he had played at Philadelphia in 1776 and Jefferson's line "he moved his hearers from their seats." Describing the friendly correspondence between the two old patriots in their last years, Wirt said that "it reads a lesson of wisdom on the bitterness of party spirit, by which the wise and the good will not fail to profit."

But the accomplished orators who celebrated the two "idols of the hour" had all drawn on the historic record, or what could be gathered from secondhand accounts. They had not known Adams or Jefferson, or their "heroic times," from firsthand experience. Those who had were all but vanished.

It was among the children of his children that Adams and his words to the wise would live longest in memory. "The Lord deliver us from all family pride," he had written to John Quincy's son John, for example. "No pride, John, no pride."

"You are not singular in your suspicions that you know but little," he had told Caroline, in response to her quandary over the riddles of life. "The longer I live, the more I read, the more patiently I think, and the more anxiously I inquire, the less I seem to know. . . . Do justly. Love mercy. Walk humbly. This is enough. . . . So questions and so answers your affectionate grandfather."

Adams had, however, arrived at certain bedrock conclusions before the end came. He believed, with all his heart, as he had written to Jefferson, that no effort in favor of virtue was lost.

He felt he had lived in the greatest of times, that the eighteenth century, as he also told Jefferson, was for all its errors and vices "the most honorable" to human nature. "Knowledge and virtues were increased and diffused; arts, sciences useful to man, ameliorating their condition, were improved, more than in any period."

His faith in God and the hereafter remained unshaken. His fundamental creed, he had reduced to a single sentence: "He who loves the Workman and his work, and does what he can to preserve and improve it, shall be accepted of Him."

His confidence in the future of the country he had served so long and dutifully was, in the final years of his life, greater than ever.

Human nature had not changed, however, for all the improvements. Nor would it, he was sure. Nor did he love life any the less for its pain and terrible uncertainties. He remained as he had been, clear-eyed about the paradoxes of life and in his own nature. Once, in a letter to his old friend Francis van der Kemp, he had written, "Griefs upon griefs! Disappointments upon disappointments. What then? This is a gay, merry world notwithstanding."

It could have been his epitaph.

Acknowledgments

The Adams Papers, from which much of this book has been drawn, may be rightly described as a national treasure. There is no comparable written record of a prominent American family. Housed in the Massachusetts Historical Society in Boston, the full collection of letters, diaries, and family papers of all kinds, ranges from the year 1639 to 1889 and in volume alone is surpassing. On microfilm it takes up 608 reels, or more than five miles of microfilm. The letters of John and Abigail Adams number in the thousands, and because they both wrote with such consistent candor and in such vivid detail, it is possible to know them—to go beneath the surface of their lives—to an extent not possible with other protagonists of the time. Not Washington, not Jefferson or Madison or Hamilton, not even Franklin for all that he wrote, was so forthcoming on paper as was John Adams over a lifetime of writing about himself and his world. When his private correspondence and diaries are combined with the letters penned by Abigail, the value of the written record is compounded by geometric proportions. Their letters to each other number more than a thousand, and only about half have ever been published. But then the letters of Adams to Jefferson and Benjamin Rush number in the hundreds, as do those by Abigail to her sisters. And beyond all that is the remarkable body of correspondence between the Adamses and their offspring.

Publication of the Adams Papers began in 1961, with the first volume of the *Diary and Autobiography of John Adams,* under the editorial direction of Lyman Butterfield, to whom all Adams biographers and students of the Adams family are indebted. Mr. Butterfield brought to the immense project the high scholarly and literary standards that have distinguished it to this day, as publication of the Papers continues in one splendid volume after another.

For the help they have been in my work with the Papers, I wish to express my thanks to each of the present editorial staff, Richard Ryerson, Anne Decker Cecere, Jennifer A. Shea, and Gregg L. Lint, but especially to the gracious, dedicated Celeste Walker, whose knowledge of the subject, whose answers to innumerable questions, and whose suggestions and thoughtfulness have been invaluable.

Notes on the sources and a full bibliography follow. However, certain works have been mainstays. Of the few biographies ever written of John Adams, those by Gilbert Chinard, Page Smith, and John Ferling are first-rate, fair in judgment, and well written. Other particularly valuable studies are Zoltan Haraszti's *John Adams and the Prophets of Progress*, *The Character of John Adams* by Peter Shaw, and two works on the Adams presidency by Ralph A. Brown and Stephen G. Kurtz. And to Joseph Ellis I owe a special word of gratitude, for it was his excellent *Passionate Sage*, on Adams in his last years, that started me on the path that led to this book.

I am greatly indebted also to three major works upon which I have relied: Dumas Malone's distinguished six-volume biography of Thomas Jefferson, *The Adams-Jefferson Letters* in two volumes edited by Lester J. Cappon, and *The Age of Federalism* by Stanley Elkins and Eric McKitrick, a landmark work in American history if ever there was.

But how does one properly acknowledge the pleasure one finds in such books? Or in the works of those front-rank historians who have written with such extraordinary insight on the nation's founding time—Edmund Morgan, Gordon Wood, Bernard Bailyn, Pauline Maier, Richard Ketchum, David Hackett Fischer, to name only a few? Or how to describe adequately the delight of immersing oneself, as I have tried to do, in the writing of the eighteenth century—to read again after long years, or for the first time, the writers John Adams read and loved—Swift, Pope, Defoe, Addison, Fielding, Richardson, Sterne, Smollett, Johnson, and Voltaire? I so enjoyed Tobias Smollett's *The Expedition of Humphrey Clinker*, a book I knew little about, that I read it twice.

The research has been done in libraries, archives, museums, and historic sites in Massachusetts, Virginia, Philadelphia, Washington, Amsterdam, Paris, and London, and I thank all those who were so very helpful: Len Tucker, William Fowler, Nicholas Graham, Anne Bentley, Brenda Lawson, Oona E. Beauchard, Jennifer Smith, and the remarkably knowledgeable Peter Drummey of the Massachusetts Historical Society; the staff of the Boston Athenaeum; Brian Sullivan of the Harvard University Archives; Ellen Dunlap, Georgia Barnhill, Joanne Chaison, and Russell Martin of the American Antiquarian Society; Susan Godlewski, Gunars Rutkovskis, and Jamie McGlone of the Boston Public Library, repository of John Adams's own library; Marianne Peake, Caroline Keinath, Kelly Cobble, and John Stanwich of the National Park Service staff at the Adams National Historical Park, Quincy; Will LaMoy of the Peabody Essex Museum, Salem; Paula Faust Newcomb, Peter J. Hatch, Lucia Stanton, Susan Stein, William L. Beiswanger, Ann Lucas, Fraser Neiman, Zanne MacDonald, Rebecca Bowman, Michael B. Merriam, and my friend and wise counselor Daniel P. Jordan of the Jefferson Memorial Foundation, Charlottesville; Karin Wittenborg, Michael Plunkett, Bryson Clevenger Jr., Margaret Hrabe, Christina Deane, Alice Parra, Irene Norvelle, Anne Benham, Terry Belanger, Kendon Stubbs, and Roger Munsick of the Alderman Library at the University of Virginia; Dorothy Twohig and Philander Chase of the Washington Papers, also at the University of Virginia; Roy Strohl, Jack Bales, Douglas Sanford, and Beth Perkins of the Simpson Library at Mary Washington College; Charles Bryan and the staff of the Virginia Historical Society; Robert C. Wilburn of Colonial Williamsburg; Edward C. Carter III, Bruce Laverty, and Roy Goodman of the American Philosophical Society, Philadelphia; Martha Wolfe of Bartram's Garden; Jennifer Esler of "Clivedon"; Martha Aikens, Ann Coxe Toogood, and Frances Delmar of the National Park Service staff at Independence Park; John Carter and Michael Angelo of the Independence Seaport Museum; the staff of the Pennsylvania Historical Society; the staff of the Free Library of Philadelphia; James Billington, Jeffrey Flannery, David Wigdor, Gerald Gawalt, James Hutson, Staley Hitchcock, Larry E. Sullivan, and Mary Wolfskill of the Library of Congress; the staff of the White House Historical Association; Wagner Loderwyck of the Amsterdam Historical Museum; the staffs of the Rijksmuseum, the Van Loon Museum, and the Maritime Museum, Amsterdam; Michael Crump of the British Museum; and the staffs of Blenheim Palace and the Stowe Landscape Gardens.

In Philadelphia Bruce Gill helped me duplicate John Adams's climb up the bell tower of historic Christ's Church. With the help of Captain Samuel Tucker's log of the 1778 voyage of the *Boston*, Nat Benjamin of Martha's Vineyard plotted the ship's exact course across the North Atlantic to Bordeaux and explained the perils of a winter voyage on the North Atlantic; and Daniel and Alice Jouve were expert guides to the eighteenth-century American landmarks of Paris.

For their favors, interest, advice, and encouragement, I thank Mr. and Mrs. Charles F. Adams, Merrill D. Peterson, Lee and George Cochran, Sandy Fisher, Jane and David Acton, Anne Sibbald, John Gable, Dr. C. A. Van Minnen, Douglas L. Wilson, Charles Fagan III, Daniel J. Boorstin, Theodore K. Rabb, Richard D. Brown, Ian Macpherson, Vincent Scully, Suzy Valentine, Ann Nelson, Noel Bagnall, Deborah DeBettencourt, Chip Stokes and Bud Leeds, Curtis Tucker, Rebecca Purdy, Michelle Krowl, Richard Moe, Arthur

Sack, Josiah Bunting III, Steve Spear, Bonnie Hurd Smith, Royall D. O'Brien, Mary Beth Norton, Paul and Cathy Rancourt, Robert Wilson, Roger Kennedy, Richard Gilder, the Reverend Sheldon W. Bennett, Joan Paterson Kerr, and Margaret Goodhue.

Richard Ketchum, Susan Stein, Celeste Walker, William Fowler, Richard Ryerson, Daniel P. Jordan, Lucia Stanton, Dorie McCullough Lawson, John Zentay, Nat Benjamin, Richard Craven, Patrick J. Walsh, Richard A. Baker, Donald Ritchie, and Thomas J. McGuire each read parts or all of the manuscript, and for their thoughtful comments and criticism I am very grateful. They have made it a better book than it would have been without their contributions. Any errors of fact or interpretation it may contain are mine alone.

Patrick J. Walsh and Thomas J. McGuire also contributed to the research. But I am indebted above all to the tireless, ever resourceful efforts of my research assistant Michael Hill, who has been unfailingly involved from start to finish.

My friend and literary agent Morton L. Janklow has been an enthusiastic believer in the book all along. My editor, Michael Korda, has provided encouragement and expert guidance, as well as frequent kindnesses. Nor can I say enough for copy editors Gypsy da Silva and Fred Wiemer; the gifted designer of the book, Amy Hill; Wendell Minor, who designed the jacket; Sydney Wolfe Cohen, who did the index; and my son William B. McCullough, who took the jacket photograph.

For her help in dozens of ways, I thank my daughter Dorie Lawson, and for their sustained interest in my work, their patience and good cheer, I thank all of my family—children and spouses, grandchildren numerous and spirited, and foremost and always, my wife Rosalee.

—David McCullough
West Tisbury, Massachusetts
January 10, 2001

Source Notes

———————————

Abbreviations Used

AFC   *Adams Family Correspondence*, L. H. Butterfield, ed.

AP   Adams Papers, Massachusetts Historical Society (MHS). Numbers correspond to MHS microfilm reel number.

DJA   *Diary and Autobiography of John Adams*, L. H. Butterfield, ed.

DJQA   *Diary of John Quincy Adams*, David Grayson Allen, Allan Nevins, eds.

EDJA   *Earliest Diary of John Adams*, L. H. Butterfield, ed.

LOC   Library of Congress

LOD   *Letters of Delegates to Congress*, Paul H. Smith, ed.

MHS   Massachusetts Historical Society, Boston, Massachusetts

PBF   *The Papers of Benjamin Franklin*, Leonard W. Labaree, Claude A. Lopez, Barbara B. Oberg, eds.

PGW   *The Papers of George Washington*, W. W. Abbott, Philander D. Chase, Dorothy Twohig, eds.

PJA   *Papers of John Adams*, Robert J. Taylor, ed.

PMHB   *Pennsylvania Magazine of History and Biography*

PTJ   *The Papers of Thomas Jefferson*, Julian P. Boyd, John Catanzariti, Charles Cullen, eds.

Works   *The Works of John Adams*, Charles Francis Adams, ed.

1. The Road to Philadelphia

Page

17 *a New England winter:* Meteorological Journal of Professor John Winthrop, January 1776, HUG 1879.207.5 mfp, Harvard University Archives.

18 *five feet seven: Works*, IX, 612.
18 *Archbishop of Canterbury:* JA to Benjamin Waterhouse, March 19, 1817, AP, #436, MHS.
18 *"the animal spirits": DJA*, I, 27.
18 *"old acquaintances":* Ibid., II, 9.
19 *"an habitual contempt": AFC*, I, 317.
19 *"like a faint meteor":* Ibid., V, 391.
19 *the "labyrinth" of human nature: DJA*, I, 61.
19 *"You will never be alone": AFC*, IV, 114.
19 *"my farm, my family":* Ibid., II, 100.
20 *"I have a zeal":* Ibid., I, 135.
20 *"possessed of another species":* Corner, ed., *Autobiography of Benjamin Rush*, 140.
20 *"He saw the whole of a subject":* Ibid., 140–42.
21 *"Winter makes its approaches": AFC*, I, 324.
21 *"like a nun":* Ibid., 325.
21 *"arduous task":* Ibid., 222.
21 *"You cannot be":* Ibid., 172.
21 *"The cry for pins":* Ibid., 219.
21 *"The alarm flew":* Ibid., 204.
22 *"Sometimes refugees":* Ibid., 205.
22 *"Pray don't let Bass":* Ibid., 240.
22 *"How many have fallen":* Ibid., 222.
22 *Joseph Warren:* Ibid.
23 *"I wander alone": DJA*, II, 97.
24 *I think it will be necessary: AFC*, I, 129.
24 *"It is to be a school": PJA*, II, 99–100.
24 *grandest, most important assembly: DJA*, II, 98.
24 *"as if to see a coronation":* Ibid., 100.
25 *"They talk very loud":* Ibid., 109.
25 *"theater of action": AFC*, I, 144.
25 *"Such is the distress":* Ibid., 277.
25 *"Mrs. Randall has lost":* Ibid., 278.
26 *"Woe follows woe":* Ibid., 284.
26 *"You often expressed":* Ibid., 289.
26 *"the most shocking":* Ibid., 296.
26 *" 'Tis only in my night visions":* Ibid., 305.
26 *"befall a city":* Ibid., 313.
27 *"entirely continental":* Twohig, ed., *PGW, Revolutionary War Series*, III, 1.
27 *"It is not in the pages":* Ibid., 19.
27 *"The reflection on":* Ibid., 89.
27 *"I am exceedingly desirous":* Ibid., 93.
27 *"Your commission constitutes":* Ibid., 37.
27 *"the gentleman from Virginia": DJA*, III, 323.
28 *"one of the most": AFC*, I, 216.

28 *enough in praise:* Ibid., 246.

28 *"Oh that I was a soldier!":* Ibid., 207.

29 *Henry Adams of Barton St. David: DJA,* III, 254, n. 4.

29 *a second Joseph:* Ibid., 255, n. 6.

30 *first Henry Adams:* Ibid., 254, n. 4.

30 *"What has preserved":* JA to Benjamin Rush, July 19, 1812, AP, MHS.

31 *"of making and sailing boats": DJA,* III, 257.

33 *"Let frugality": AFC,* I, 114.

33 *"the honestest man": DJA,* III, 256.

33 *Joseph Adams:* Shipton, *Sibley's Harvard Graduates,* V, 502.

33 *Taught to read at home: DJA,* III, 257.

33 *"churl": Works,* IX, 613.

33 *He cared not for books: DJA,* III, 257.

33 *to be a farmer:* Ibid., 257.

34 *which meant Harvard:* Ibid., 259; *EDJA,* 43.

34 *admitted to Harvard:* Shipton, *Sibley's Harvard Graduates,* XIII, 513.

35 *class of 1755:* Ibid., XIII, 512.

35 *"Total and complete misery":* Ibid., XIII, 514.

35 *"I read forever": DJA,* III, 262.

35 *"lowermost northwest chamber": EDJA,* 43, n. 2.

35 *Thomas Sparhawk:* Shipton, *Sibley's Harvard Graduates,* XIII, 645.

35 *Joseph Stockbridge:* Ibid., XIII, 647.

35 *evening prayers:* Morison, *Three Centuries of Harvard,* 27–28.

36 *wiped clean on the table cloth:* Timothy Pickering Papers, Reel #53, MHS.

36 *"I shall never forget":* Shipton, *Sibley's Harvard Graduates,* III, 514.

36 *"All scholars":* Pierce, *History of Harvard,* 169.

36 *Adams was fined:* March 15, 1755, Harvard Archives.

36 *"amorous disposition": DJA,* III, 260.

36 *I shall draw no characters: DJA,* III, 260, 261.

37 *Adams was listed fourteenth:* Shipton, *Sibley's Harvard Graduates,* XIII, 512.

37 *"Is civil government":* Ibid., 515.

37 *unsuited for the life: DJA,* III, 263.

37 *"I saw such a spirit":* Ibid., 262.

38 *"But we must be cautious":* Ibid., I, 9.

38 *One student remembered:* Shipton, *Sibley's Harvard Graduates,* XIII, 514.

38 *I sometimes: DJA,* I, 13.

38 *Upon common theaters: PJA,* I, 12.

39 *becoming a doctor: DJA,* III, 264.

39 *"reveries": PJA,* I, 5.

39 *"All that part of Creation":* Ibid., 4–6.

40 *"soft vernal showers": DJA,* I, 27.

41 *"Oh! that I could":* Ibid., 7.

41 *"I have no books":* Ibid., 22.

41 *"I can as easily":* Ibid., 21.

41 *Actual thunderstorms:* Ibid., 136.

42 *"Honesty, sincerity":* Ibid., 12.

42 *"Vanity, I am sensible":* JA to Christopher Gadsen, April 16, 1801, AP, MHS.

42 *"A puffy, vain":* DJA, I, 37.

42 *"glorious shows":* Ibid., 43.

42 *"the amazing concave":* PJA, I, 15.

42 *But all the provisions:* DJA, I, 43.

42 *"It will be hard work":* PJA, I, 17.

43 *"Can you imagine":* JA to Richard Rush, February 16, 1814, AP, #95, MHS.

43 *King's troops:* DJA, III, 266.

43 *"I am not without":* PJA, I, 19.

43 *"I am beginning":* EDJA, 65.

44 *"I have read Gilbert's":* DJA, I, 45.

44 *"Rose about sun rise":* Ibid., 46.

44 *I had the pleasure:* EDJA, 99.

44 *"pursue the study of the law":* DJA, I, 55.

45 Lambert v. Field: See editorial note in *EDJA* beginning on p. 82.

45 *He blamed his mother:* DJA, I, 64.

46 *terrible family row:* Ibid., 65.

46 *soul to the law:* Ibid., 72.

46 *"Reputation":* Ibid., 78.

46 *My eyes are so diverted:* Ibid., 80–81.

47 *"I never shall shine":* Ibid., 133.

47 *"Why have I not genius":* Ibid., 95.

47 *"Ballast is what I want":* EDJA, 73.

47 *"a heart formed":* Ellis, *Passionate Sage*, 182.

47 *not by John Adams:* Shipton, *Sibley's Harvard Graduates*, XIII, 627.

47 *"distinguishing glorys":* PJA, I, 5.

48 *"gallanting":* DJA, I, 57.

48 *"in future ages":* PJA, I, 40.

48 *"Let me search":* DJA, I, 61.

49 *"grandeur":* Ibid., 83.

49 *"imitating Otis":* Ibid., 84.

49 *"squaddy, masculine creature":* Ibid., 75.

49 *Zab Hayward:* Ibid., 172.

50 *P[arson] W[ibird]:* Ibid., 92–93.

51 *If I look:* EDJA, 70.

51 *"there laughed and screamed":* DJA, I, 77.

51 *"Let no trifling diversion":* Ibid., 72.

52 *"Let love and vanity":* Ibid., 87.

52 *"fond, nor frank":* Ibid., 109.

52 *"crafty, designing man":* Ibid., 108.

52 *The testator:* PJA, I, 35.

53 *forty acres:* DJA, III, 277.

53 *Now to what:* Ibid., I, 124.

54 *"I grow more expert":* Ibid., 193.

54 *The story of B. Biknal's wife:* Ibid., 231–32.

55 *Di was a constant:* Ibid., 234.

56 *"Candor is my characteristic":* AFC, I, 49.

56 *"a gentleman has no business":* Ibid., 47.

56 *"smoked":* Ibid., 29.

56 *Also, two black slaves:* Withey, *Dearest Friend*, 6; Akers, *Abigail Adams*, 3.

57 *Oh, my dear girl:* AFC, I, 49.

58 *"I never shall shine":* DJA, I, 133.

59 *news of the Stamp Act:* Boston Gazette, May 27, 1765.

59 *immediate uproar:* Ibid., June 24, 1765.

59 *"utmost consternation":* Ibid., July 22, 1765.

59 *"like devils let loose":* Ibid., Sept. 2, 1765.

59 *A Dissertation on the Canon and the Feudal Law:* See the *Boston Gazette*, Aug. 12, 1765; Aug. 19, 1765; Sept. 30, 1765; Oct. 2, 1765.

61 *"the most thorough understanding":* DJA, I, 271.

61 *"liable to great inequities":* Ibid., 271.

62 *"The year 1765":* Ibid., 263.

63 *He handled every kind of case:* See, generally, Wroth and Zobel, *Legal Papers of John Adams*, I, xxv–lx.

63 *as "honest[a] lawyer":* Works, I, 58.

63 *"What shall I do":* DJA, I, 338.

64 *"My good man":* AFC, I, 56.

64 *"I want to see my wife":* Ibid., 83.

64 *"My biographer":* DJA, I, 355.

64 *"To what object":* Ibid., 337.

65 *no difficulty saying no:* Ibid., III, 288.

65 *"He always called me John":* Peabody, ed., *John Adams*, 130.

65 *soldiers suddenly opened fire:* Zobel, *Boston Massacre*, 198–99.

66 *John Adams was asked to defend:* DJA, III, 292.

66 *"incurring a clamor":* Ibid., 294.

66 *a retainer of eighteen guineas:* Ibid., 293.

66 *"The only way to compose myself":* Ibid., I, 352.

67 *If, by supporting the rights:* Legal Papers of John Adams, III, 242.

67 *two conspicuously fair trials:* See ibid., Cases #63 and #64, 266.

67 *"electrical":* Legal Papers of John Adams, III, 28. Comment of John Quincy Adams.

67 *"I am for the prisoners":* Ibid., III, 242.

67 *We have entertained:* Ibid., 266.

68 *"Do you expect":* Ibid., 268.

68 *"The reason is":* Ibid., 242.

68 *"Facts are stubborn":* Ibid., 269.

68 *branded on their thumbs:* Ibid., 31.

68 *"one of the most gallant"*: Ibid., 33.
69 *"she thought I had done"*: *DJA*, III, 294.
69 *"Especially the constant"*: Ibid., 296.
69 *five hours:* JA to John Adams Smith, June 15, 1812, AP, #118, MHS.
69 *Government is nothing: DJA*, II, 57.
70 *"Above all things"*: Ibid., 67.
70 *"I cannot but reflect"*: Ibid., 76.
70 *the destruction of the tea:* Ibid., 86.
70 *"We live, my dear soul"*: *AFC*, I, 107.
71 *"in the dumps"*: Ibid.
71 *During a break:* Peabody, ed., *John Adams*, 133–34.
71 *"Swim or sink"*: *Works*, IV, 8.
71 *"It is not despair"*: Shipton, *Sibley's Harvard Graduates*, XII, 317.
71 *"Novangelus"*: See, generally, *PJA*, II, 216–387.
72 *dine with General Washington: AFC*, I, 343.
72 *Caughnawaga Indians:* Ibid., 343.
73 *"It was a savage feast": DJA*, II, 227.
73 *decidedly pleased: AFC*, I, 343.
73 *Henry Knox: DJA*, II, 227; Diary of Henry Knox, MHS.
73 *Fort Ticonderoga: DJA*, II, 227.
73 *making careful note of the inventory:* Ibid., 227.
74 *"cold journey"*: *AFC*, I, 345.
74 *"for the amusement of Swift"*: *DJA*, III, 268.
74 *. . . as I was cold: Old Family Letters*, 140.
75 *"I could not join"*: *AFC*, I, 324.
75 *the title* Common Sense: Ibid., 348.
76 *"My God, these fellows"*: Ibid., 358.
77 *"marvelous in our eyes"*: Ibid., 360.

2 .   T R U E   B L U E

Page

78 *largest, wealthiest city:* See, generally, Weigley, *Philadelphia: A 300 Year History*, 109–54.
78 *Shipbuilding was a:* Cresswell, *Journal of Nicholas Cresswell*, 156.
79 *Franklin arrived from Boston:* LeMay and Zall, eds., *Autobiography of Benjamin Franklin*, 24.
79 *population was approaching 30,000:* Bridenbaugh, *Cities in Revolt*, 216.
79 *"I like it": DJA*, II, 136.
79 *Front Street is near:* Ibid., 116.
80 *"All this is done"*: *LOD*, I, 56.
80 *prince's palace:* Ibid., III, 360.
80 *"for the promoting of useful knowledge"*: *Pennsylvania Gazette*, May 20, 1776.
80 *all philosophical:* Van Doren, *Benjamin Franklin*, 139.

81 *twenty-three printing establishments:* Stevens, *Birthplace of a Nation,* 95.

81 *John Sparhawk: Pennsylvania Gazette,* April 29, 1776.

81 *thirty bookshops:* Carl Bridenbaugh, "The Press and the Book in 18th Century Philadelphia," *PMHB,* LXV (Jan. 1941): 13.

81 *"dirty, dusty, and fatigued":* *DJA,* II, 114.

81 *Adams had first met George Washington:* Ibid., 141.

82 *"I drink no cider":* *AFC,* I, 164.

82 *"thundering of coaches":* *PMHB,* XLVIII (1924): 237.

82 *most recent outbreak, in 1773:* Hopkins, *Princes and Peasants,* 243.

82 *new hospital: DJA,* II, 116.

83 *"Philadelphia Salute":* Albertz, *Benjamin West,* 22–23.

83 *Christ Church: DJA,* II, 127.

83 *"My time is too totally":* *AFC,* I, 155.

83 *The Reverend Thomas Coombe: DJA,* II, 122.

84 *"He reaches the imagination":* Ibid., 156.

84 *mass at St. Mary's:* Ibid., 150.

84 *"awful": AFC,* I, 167.

84 *at the State House: DJA,* II, 134.

85 *"I shall be killed": AFC,* I, 164.

85 *"A most sinful feast": DJA,* II, 127.

85 *"Dined with Mr. [Benjamin] Chew":* Ibid., 136.

85 *"tall, spare":* Ibid., 120.

85 *Roger Sherman:* Ibid., 150.

86 *"sly, surveying eye":* Ibid., 106.

86 *"design and cunning":* Ibid., 121.

86 *John Dickinson:* Ibid., 117.

86 *Caesar Rodney:* Ibid., 121.

86 *"The art and address": AFC,* I, 163.

86 *This assembly:* Ibid., 166.

87 *"happy, peaceful": DJA,* II, 157.

87 *"There are in this city": AFC,* I, 212.

88 *in strictest secrecy:* Ibid., 157.

88 *"wasting, exhausting":* Ibid., 251.

88 *"a great, unwieldy body":* Ibid., 216.

88 *"I will not despond":* Ibid., 213.

89 *"minds and hearts":* Ibid., 295.

89 *"An alliance": DJA,* II, 231.

90 *There is a tide: AFC,* I, 354. Quote from *Julius Caesar,* Act IV, Scene 3.

90 *"The plot thickens":* "Diary of James Allen," *PMHB,* IX (1895): 186.

90 *"The malignant air":* Christopher Marshall diary, February 15, 1776, Pennsylvania Historical Society.

91 *"There is a deep anxiety": AFC,* I, 345.

91 *the stoves were removed: LOD,* III, 299.

91 *Thomas Lynch of South Carolina:* Ibid., 292.

91 *Samuel Ward of Rhode Island:* Ibid., 460.

92 *"He has not assumed":* AFC, I, 252–53.

93 *profane and pious:* DJA, III, 371.

93 *"Young Ned Rutledge":* Ibid., II, 156.

93 *warning advice:* Works, II, 512.

93 *"avow their opinions":* DJA, I, 12.

94 *"has an excellent heart":* Ibid., II, 133.

94 *Olive Branch Petition:* Ibid., 162.

95 *"Powder and artillery":* JA to John Gill, June 10, 1775, AP, MHS.

95 *"blood . . . on their heads":* LOD, I, 373.

95 *"What is the reason":* DJA, III, 318.

95 *"piddling genius":* JA to James Warren, July 24, 1775, AP, MHS.

95 *He passed without moving:* DJA, II, 173.

95 *"The Quakers and many others":* Seed, "A British Spy in Philadelphia," PMHB, LXXXV (Jan. 1961): 22.

96 *"an object of nearly universal":* Corner, ed., *The Autobiography of Benjamin Rush,* 142.

96 *"Who is the author":* Philadelphia Evening Post, March 26, 1776.

97 *"what they call the American flag":* Seed, "A British Spy in Philadelphia," PMHB, LXXXV (Jan. 1961): 28–29.

97 *"common faith":* AFC, I, 348.

97 *"has a better hand":* Ibid., 363.

97 *"this American contest":* Ibid., II, 2.

98 *On February 26:* LOD, III, 306.

98 *Silas Deane:* Ibid., 320.

98 *"decide the fate":* Ibid., 325.

98 *Adams busily jotted notes:* DJA, II, 236.

99 *"clear and sonorous":* Works, I, 31.

99 *On March 14:* DJA, III, 370.

99 *On March 23:* Ibid., 374.

99 *"the maddest idea":* Calkins, "The American Navy and the Opinions of One of its Founders," 457.

100 *the pleasantest part of his labors:* DJA, III, 350.

100 *"dull as beetles":* AFC, II, 170.

100 *His custom:* DJA, III, 350.

100 *"Fortify, fortify":* LOD, III, 473.

100 *"The middle way":* Ibid., 429.

101 *"This story of [peace]":* AFC, I, 383.

101 *"I am more and more":* Ibid., IV, 329.

102 *"It has been the will of Heaven":* Thoughts on Government, in Works, IV, 203ff.

102 *"'an empire of laws' ":* Credited by Adams to James Harrington.

103 *"Men of experience":* Works, IV, 207.

103 *"Frugality, industry":* AFC, I, 377.

103 *"I have," she wrote:* Ibid., 369.

104 *"I wish most sincerely"*: Ibid., 162.

104 *"I think the sun"*: Ibid., 370.

104 *"Remember all men"*: Ibid., 329. Quote from Daniel Defoe, *The Kentish Petition,* in *Bartlett's Quotations.*

105 *"I cannot but laugh"*: Ibid., 382.

105 *"People can't account"*: *PJA,* IV, 45.

105 *"Have you seen the privateering"*: *LOD,* III, 536.

105 *"All great changes"*: Ibid., 570.

106 *"I miss my partner"*: *AFC,* I, 375.

106 *On April 18:* Ibid., 387.

106 *on April 23:* Ibid., 392.

107 *Is there no way:* Ibid., 400.

107 *"a people may let a King"*: Ibid., 402.

107 *"I think you shine"*: Ibid., 420.

108 *"true saying of a wit"*: *LOD,* III, 523.

108 *"a most interesting spectacle"*: *Pennsylvania Gazette,* May 15, 1776.

108 *"the happiness and safety"*: *DJA,* III, 383.

109 *"Why all this haste?"*: Ibid., II, 238.

109 *"I wonder the people"*: Ibid., 239.

109 *"Before we are prepared"*: Ibid., 240.

109 *"a machine for the fabrication of"*: Ibid., III, 386.

109 *"passed the most important"*: *LOD,* III, 676.

109 *"the* cool considerate men": Ibid., IV, 30.

110 *When I consider the great events: AFC,* I, 410.

110 *"Fine sunshine"*: Christopher Marshall diary, May 23, 1776, Pennsylvania Historical Society.

110 *"Uncommonly hot"*: *LOD,* III, 33.

110 *"as the excessive heats"*: Boyd, ed., *PTJ,* I, 292.

110 *Bob Hemings:* Malone, *Jefferson the Virginian,* 216.

111 *"I've been so long"*: Boyd, ed., *PTJ,* I, 293.

112 *"Nothing was too small"*: Bear, *Jefferson at Monticello,* 78.

112 *"man of science"*: William Plumer, *Memorandum,* 454.

113 *"Never contradict"*: Randolph, *The Domestic Life of Thomas Jefferson,* 318.

113 *"utter three sentences"*: *DJA,* III, 335–36.

113 *shall I become a Don Quixote:* Ibid.

113 *You rose:* Schutz and Adair, eds., *Spur of Fame,* 227.

114 *"only impatience of temper"*: Randall, *Life of Thomas Jefferson,* I, 78.

114 *"rubber off of dust"*: *DJA,* II, 218.

115 *5,000 acres:* Betts, ed., *Thomas Jefferson's Farm Book,* xv.

115 *window frames:* McLaughlin, *Jefferson and Monticello,* 163.

115 *indentured servant:* Ibid., 69.

115 *a hundred black slaves:* Monticello Research Center, Charlottesville, Virginia.

116 *earliest childhood memory:* Randall, *Life of Thomas Jefferson,* I, 11.

116 *substantial debts:* Malone, *Jefferson the Virginian,* 162.

116 *"all geese are swans"*: JA to Frances Vanderkemp, November 24, 1814, AP, MHS.

116 *"looking with fondness"*: Boyd, ed., *PTJ*, I, 241.

116 *"return of the happy period"*: Ibid., 241.

116 *"rather than submit"*: Ibid., 242.

117 *"Every post"*: LOD, IV, 40.

117 *"natural course"*: Ibid., 122.

117 *Richard Henry Lee:* Fehrenbach, *Greatness to Spare*, 201.

118 *That these United Colonies:* Boyd, ed., *PTJ*, I, 298.

118 *notes kept by Jefferson:* Ibid., 309.

118 *"The sensible part"*: LOD, IV, 174.

119 *"Great things"*: AFC, II, 13.

119 *According to Adams: Works*, II, 514.

119 *"I consented"*: Lipscomb, ed., *Writings of Thomas Jefferson*, XV, 461.

120 *wrote disparagingly of John Adams: DJA*, III, 396.

120 *Windsor chair:* See Bedini, *Declaration of Independence Desk*, 6–7.

120 *"to place before mankind"*: TJ to Henry Lee, May 8, 1825, in Lipscomb, ed., *Writings of Thomas Jefferson*, VII, 407.

121 *I was delighted: Works*, II, 514.

122 *transcribed the full text: AFC*, II, 35, n. 3.

122 *copy to Abigail:* Ibid., 48–49, n. 8.

122 *ravages of smallpox:* Shurkin, *Invisible Fire*, 173–77.

123 *"I have not been idle"*: LOD, IV, 304, n. 1.

123 *"What in the name"*: Works, II, 291.

123 *"The only question"*: LOD, IV, 290.

124 *"the bloody conflict"*: Commager, *Spirit of Seventy-six*, 308.

124 *"You see therefore"*: LOD, IV, 304.

3. COLOSSUS OF INDEPENDENCE

Page

125 *"This morning is assigned"*: LOD, IV, 345.

125 *The object is great:* Ibid., 345–46.

126 *John Dickinson had resolved: DJA*, III, 396.

126 *"He had prepared himself"*: Ibid., 396.

126 *"My conduct this day"*: LOD, IV, 352.

126 *"determined to speak"*: DJA, III, 396.

127 *Objects of the most stupendous:* LOD, IV, 178.

127 *"not graceful"*: Hazelton, *Declaration of Independence*, 162.

127 *" 'carried out in spirit' "*: Shaw, *Character of John Adams*, 99.

127 *"the Atlas"*: Works, III, 56.

127 *not an actor: DJA*, III, 397.

128 *"started suddenly"*: Hazelton, *Declaration of Independence*, 119.

128 *Caesar Rodney:* Ibid., 193.

129 *another cloudburst:* P. H. Smith, *Time and Temperature,* 4.

130 *The second day of July 1776: AFC,* II, 30.

130 *"transported":* Ibid., 31.

130 *"You will see in a few days":* Ibid., 28.

130 *"This day":* Miller, ed., *Selected Papers of Charles Willson Peale,* I, 189.

130 *well known in the taverns: LOD,* IV, 370.

130 *mercifully the temperature:* See P. H. Smith, *Time and Temperature,* 4.

131 *"the ceaseless action":* Hazelton, *Declaration of Independence,* 145.

131 *JOHN THOMPSON:* Ibid.

131 *nearly 2,500,000:* Wood, *Radicalism of the American Revolution,* 125.

131 *some 500,000 men:* Harley, *Timetables of African-American History,* 42.

131 *more than 200,000 slaves:* John Miller, *Wolf by the Ears,* 2.

131 *was about 200:* Estimate by Lucia Stanton of the Jefferson Memorial Foundation, Charlottesville, Virginia.

132 *John Dickinson:* Nash, "Slaves and Slaveowners in Colonial Philadelphia," 250.

132 *Even Benjamin Franklin:* Campbell, *Recovering Franklin,* 243.

132 *buying and selling:* Van Doren, *Benjamin Franklin,* 129.

132 *"a likely wench":* Ibid.

133 *When Samuel Adams:* Lewis, *Grand Incendiary,* 150.

133 *pamphlet attacking slavery:* Corner, ed., *Autobiography of Benjamin Rush,* 83.

133 *Yet he himself:* Hawke, *Benjamin Rush: Revolutionary Gadfly,* 84.

133 *"a sprightly, pretty fellow": DJA,* II, 182.

134 *"equally strong": AFC,* I, 369.

134 *"foul contagion":* JA to Colonel Ward, January 8, 1810, AP, #118, MHS.

134 *several slave cases:* See Wroth and Zobel, *Legal Papers of John Adams,* II, 48–52.

134 *"repeated" rather than "unremitting": LOD,* IV, 360.

134 *"suffered the administration":* Ibid., 361.

135 *"our British brethren":* Ibid., 363.

135 *"fighting fearlessly":* Hazelton, *Declaration of Independence,* 145.

135 *for the support of this Declaration: LOD,* IV, 364.

136 *pleasantly cool:* P. H. Smith, *Time and Temperature,* 3.

136 *Of Jefferson's Day:* Malone, *Jefferson the Virginian,* 229.

137 *"on the common":* Hazelton, *Declaration of Independence,* 242.

137 *"Fine starlight":* Christopher Marshall diary, Pennsylvania Historical Society.

137 *"very few respectable":* Hazelton, *Declaration of Independence,* 555.

137 *Savannah:* Ibid., 280.

138 *black flies:* Randolph, *Domestic Life of Thomas Jefferson,* 49.

138 *"We must all hang together":* Fehrenbach, *Greatness to Spare,* 19.

138 *"My hand trembles":* Ibid.

138 *produced a new era: LOD,* IV, 527.

139 *"gallant spirit": AFC,* II, 49.

139 *"I think an individual": LOD,* IV, 512.

139 *"Mr. Dickinson's alacrity"*: *AFC*, I, 347.

140 *Nathanael Greene*: *PJA*, IV, 382.

140 *"unsoldierly conduct"*: Twohig, ed., *PGW*, *Revolutionary War Series*, V, 290.

140 *"vastly unequal"*: *AFC*, II, 24.

140 *"We are all inexperienced"*: *PJA*, IV, 325.

140 *"very exactly and minutely"*: Ibid., 388.

141 *Continental currency*: Ibid., 375.

141 *"Jefferson in those days"*: *Works*, III, 68–69.

141 *"Smallpox!"*: *AFC*, II, 24.

141 *dispatch of July 11*: Twohig, ed., *PGW*, *Revolutionary War Series*, V, 277.

142 *"Never—never"*: *AFC*, II, 50.

142 *Her letter of explanation*: Ibid., 45.

142 *Dr. Zabdiel Boylston*: Shurkin, *Invisible Fire*, 152.

142 *Onesimus*: Ibid., 155.

142 *"pus from the ripe pustules"*: Ibid., 162.

143 *"Such a spirit of inoculation"*: *AFC*, II, 45.

143 *"Nabby has enough of the smallpox"*: Ibid., 93.

143 *"in honor and duty"*: Ibid., 52.

144 *"Not one word"*: Ibid., 56.

145 *Jefferson checked his thermometer*: Bear and Stanton, eds. *Jefferson's Memorandum Books*, I, 433.

145 *"For God's sake"*: Boyd, ed., *PTJ*, I, 482–83.

145 *"My mother"*: Randolph, *Domestic Life of Thomas Jefferson*, 30.

145 *"great pain"*: Boyd, ed., *PTJ*, I, 483.

146 *"the whole subject"*: Corner, ed., *Autobiography of Benjamin Rush*, 140.

146 *"minutia"*: Boyd, ed., *PTJ*, I, 477.

146 *"a great deal of difference"*: *LOD*, IV, 527.

146 *If a confederation*: *AFC*, II, 68.

147 *"a mere sound"*: Boyd, ed., *PTJ*, I, 325.

147 *Hopkins of Rhode Island*: Ibid., 326.

147 *"The more a man"*: *DJA*, II, 247–48.

147 *Jefferson did speak up*: *LOD*, IV, 603–4.

148 *"suspense, uncertainty"*: *AFC*, II, 83.

148 *"as a bridegroom"*: Ibid., 76.

148 *"If Bass is in the land"*: Ibid., 84.

148 *"This country knows not"*: Ibid., 99.

148 *"I know not how"*: *AFC*, II, 73.

148 *"I am really astonished"*: Ibid., 78.

148 *Henry Popple*: Ibid., 91–92.

149 *My countrymen want art*: Ibid., 76.

149 *Benjamin Rush*: Ibid., 59.

149 *Charles Willson Peale*: Ibid., 103–4.

150 *Here, I say*: Ibid., 112.

151 *"of above 300 ships"*: Tatum, ed., *American Journal of Ambrose Serle*, 72.

152 *"The Hessians"*: Commager, *Spirit of Seventy-six*, 443.

152 *"Good God!"*: Flexner, *George Washington*, II, 111.

152 *"peculiar providential"*: Commager, *Spirit of Seventy-six*, 445.

153 *"Our situation"*: Sept. 3, 1776.

153 *"Have we not"*: *PJA*, V, 3.

153 *"In general"*: *AFC*, II, 140.

153 *letter of September 4:* Ibid., 117.

154 *"The panic may seize"*: Ibid., 120.

154 *Adams remarked under his breath:* Corner, ed., *Autobiography of Benjamin Rush*, 140.

154 *"satisfy some disturbed minds"*: *LOD*, V, 120.

154 *"Machiavellian maneuvers"*: *DJA*, III, 430.

154 *"The staunch and intrepid"*: Ibid., 425.

154 *His Lordship on Staten Island:* Ibid., 417.

156 *The Billopp House: AFC*, II, viii.

156 *"good claret"*: *DJA*, III, 420.

156 *Lord Richard Howe:* Ibid., 422.

157 *"changed the ground"*: *LOD*, V, 138.

157 *"Your Lordship"*: *DJA*, III, 422.

157 *"warmly"*: *LOD*, V, 140.

158 *"Mr. Adams is a decided character"*: *DJA*, III, 423.

158 *He was to hang:* Ibid., 423.

158 *Howe had no authority: AFC*, II, 124.

158 *"They met, they talked"*: Tatum, *American Journal of Ambrose Serle*, 101.

158 *"So terrible"*: Ibid., 104.

159 *began cursing:* See account in Freeman, *Leader of the Revolution*, 153–75.

159 *"Our affairs"*: *LOD*, V, 212.

159 *September 25:* Twohig, ed., *PGW*, Revolutionary War Series, VI, 394.

159 *To place any dependence:* Ibid., 396.

160 *$20 and 100 acres of land: AFC*, II, 131.

160 *Articles of War: DJA*, III, 434.

160 *a military academy:* Ibid., 437.

160 *"Unfaithfulness": AFC*, II, 131.

160 *"if we fear God"*: Corner, ed., *Autobiography of Benjamin Rush*, 142.

161 *"great abilities"*: Boyd, ed., *PTJ*, I, 522.

162 *"circumstances very peculiar"*: Ibid., 524.

162 *"tedious time of it": AFC*, II, 107.

162 *"I am stupefied"*: Ibid., 139.

162 *"your Ladyship"*: Ibid., 141.

163 *"This illustrious patriot": LOD*, V, 183.

163 *"Every member of Congress"*: Corner, ed., *Autobiography of Benjamin Rush*, 140.

4. APPOINTMENT TO FRANCE

Page

167 *"When do you expect"*: *AFC*, II, 142.

168 *"I had it in my heart"*: Ibid., 150.

168 *"I am apt to think"*: Ibid., 151.

169 *From her window*: Ibid., 171.

169 *"I want a bird of passage"*: Ibid.

169 *" 'Tis a constant remembrancer"*: Ibid., 173.

169 *"not an hour in the day"*: Ibid., 241.

169 *"We want your industry"*: Cappon, ed., *Adams-Jefferson Letters*, 6.

169 *"They worry one another"*: *AFC*, II, 245.

170 *"I begin to suspect"*: Ibid., 176.

170 *You have discovered*: Ibid., 179.

170 *"A taste for literature"*: Ibid., 177.

170 *"the arts of peace"*: Ibid., 180.

170 *Smollet's* History of England: Ibid., 254.

170 *"solid instruction"*: Ibid., 307.

171 *"Our money"*: Ibid., 340.

171 *"like to outshine"*: Ibid., 238.

171 *"still more painful one"*: Ibid., 258.

171 *"shaking fit"*: Ibid., 277.

172 *"It appeared to be a very fine babe"*: Ibid., 282.

172 *"The corn looks well"*: Ibid., 288.

172 *"The loss of this sweet little girl"*: Ibid., 292.

172 *" 'Tis almost 14 years"*: Ibid., 301.

173 *"Oh, Heaven!"*: *DJA*, II, 265.

173 *"spirited exertions"*: *AFC*, II, 351.

173 *"Great advantages"*: Ibid., 376.

174 *It was my intention*: *DJA*, IV, 1.

174 *told by Elbridge Gerry*: Ibid., 3.

174 *named Adams a commissioner*: *LOD*, VIII, 335.

174 *a formal letter of notification*: *PJA*, V, 333.

174 *"We are by no means"*: *LOD*, VIII, 372.

175 *"one man of inflexible integrity"*: Ibid., 338.

175 *expert on cryptology*: See Kahn, *Codebreakers*, 181ff.

175 *"This knowledge is only part"*: *AFC*, II, 333.

175 *And can I, sir*: Ibid., 371.

176 *acceptance to Henry Laurens*: *PJA*, V, 367.

176 *"I should have wanted"*: Ibid., 369.

176 *"My desire was"*: *AFC*, II, 390.

176 *You are in possession*: Ibid., III, 37.

177 *They were to sail*: *DJA*, II, 269.

177 *I am aware*: Butterfield, ed., *Letters of Benjamin Rush*, I, 190–92.

178 *"The heavens frown"*: *DJA*, IV, 7.

179 *"The wind was very high"*: Ibid., 7.

179 *14 degrees:* Journal of Professor John Winthrop, Feb. 15, 1778, Harvard University Archives.

180 *"This morning weighed the last anchor"*: *DJA*, II, 271.

180 *Nicholas Noel:* Ibid., IV, 7.

180 *lacking in erudition:* Ibid., 10.

180 You are to afford: Tucker Papers, I, 26–27.

180 *"detestable"*: *DJA*, IV, 17.

181 *Potter's Field: AFC*, II, 209.

181 *"rolling and rocking"*: *DJA*, II, 274.

181 *When night approached:* Ibid., 274.

182 ship *"shuddered"*: Ibid., IV, 12.

182 *"raving mad"*: Ibid., II, 276, see n. 1.

182 *"The sea being very cross"*: Sheppard, *Life of Samuel Tucker*, 266.

182 *No man could keep: DJA*, II, 275–76.

183 *[His] behavior:* Ibid., IV, 15–16.

183 *"perfectly calm"*: Ibid., II, 276.

183 *"I am constantly"*: Ibid., 278.

183 *"I did not say"*: Ibid., 368.

184 *"What is this Gulf Stream?"*: Ibid., 279.

184 *"The wind is fresh"*: Ibid., 280.

184 *John Quincy had undertaken:* Ibid., IV, 21.

184 *"our infant navy"*: Ibid., 25.

185 *"We see nothing"*: Ibid., II, 281.

185 *"Nothing very remarkable"*: Sheppard, *Life of Samuel Tucker*, 269.

185 *"We spied a sail"*: *DJA*, IV, 24.

186 *over the head of John Adams:* Ibid., II, 285.

186 *"among my marines"*: Ibid., 286–87.

186 *Lieutenant Barron:* Ibid., 288.

187 *"Europe, thou great theater"*: Ibid., 292.

187 *"as clean as in any gentleman's"*: Ibid.

188 *"I hope I shall never forget"*: *AFC*, III, 11.

188 *symbolic of his whole life:* Cappon, ed., *Adams-Jefferson Letters*, II, 294, Feb. 3, 1812.

189 *warned Adams of bad blood: DJA*, IV, 39.

189 "le fameux Adams": Ibid., II, 351.

189 *"I believe at first"*: *DJA*, IV, 37.

190 *"accoutered"*: Ibid., 41.

190 *"bold, masculine"*: Ibid., 42.

191 *"I was astonished"*: Ibid., 47.

191 *"hard study"*: Ibid., 67.

191 *"The reception I have met"*: *AFC*, III, 9.

192 *"I cannot help suspecting"*: Ibid., 10.

192 *"If human nature"*: Ibid., 17.

193   *To tell you the truth:* Ibid.

193   *His name was familiar: Works,* I, 660.

195   *"Although he was very advanced": DJA,* IV, 78.

195   *Voltaire and Franklin:* Ibid., 80–81.

195   *"Nature and art": AFC,* III, 31–32.

195   *"coolness": DJA,* IV, 43.

196   *"mercurial temperament":* Shipton, *Sibley's Harvard Graduates,* XIII, 245.

196   *"I am old":* Lopez, ed., *PBF,* XXVI, 223.

196   *"the most corrupt":* Shipton, *Sibley's Harvard Graduates,* XIII, 252.

196   *"He believes all men selfish": DJA,* II, 347.

197   *Franklin's character: PJA,* IV, 26–27.

197   *"great and good man": AFC,* I, 253.

197   *He had wit at will: Works,* I, 663.

198   *"It was impossible": DJA,* IV, 87.

199   *Franklin spoke the language poorly:* Ibid., II, 302.

200   *John Adams is a man:* Tolles, "Franklin and the Pulteney Mission," 54.

200   *"I suppose": DJA,* IV, 65.

201   *I have long observed:* Lopez, ed., *PBF,* XXIII, 211.

201   *Dr. Edward Bancroft:* A. R. Riggs, *The Nine Lives of Arthur Lee, Virginia Patriot* (Williamsburg, Va.: Virginia Independence Bicentennial Commission, 1976), 52.

202   *"The longer I live": PJA,* VI, 348.

202   *writing to Samuel Adams: DJA,* IV, 106–8.

202   *"Pas un mot!":* Ibid., 92.

203   *"becoming the station I held":* Ibid., 132.

203   *"a royal supper":* Ibid., 133.

204   *"I found that the business":* Ibid., 118–19.

205   *"My countrymen":* Ibid., 67–68.

206   *Between you and me: PJA,* VI, 354.

206   *"joy of my heart": AFC,* III, 125.

206   *Marie Grand:* Ibid., 91.

207   *"I am very sincere": PJA,* Ibid., 126–27.

207   *The longer I live:* Ibid., 244.

209   *"observed much":* Hale, *Benjamin Franklin in France,* 141.

209   *"There is [a] danger": PJA,* VI, 254.

209   *"Are we to be beholden":* Ibid., V, 174.

210   *Adams drafted a letter:* See ibid., VI, 294–304.

210   *all three commissioners: Works,* VII, 72–77.

210   *"restored to the character": PJA,* VI, 416.

211   *"I shall therefore": AFC,* III, 169.

211   *"best becomes me": PJA,* VI, 407.

211   *he vowed never again:* Ibid., 429.

211   *"All things look gloomy": AFC,* III, 95.

211   *"changed hearts":* Ibid., 111.

211   *"some infernal":* Ibid., 173.

211 *"You know not"*: *AFC*, III, 174.

212 *"But my soul is wounded"*: Ibid., 119.

212 *"write but very little"*: Ibid., 176.

212 *"If ever I had any wit"*: Ibid., 182.

212 *"The climate is more favorable"*: Ibid., 178.

213 *"the wise conduct"*: *PJA*, VI, 424.

213 *translating Cicero*: *DJA*, II, 362.

213 *Franklin gave instructions:* Oberg, ed., *PBF*, XXIX, 370.

213 *John Paul Jones*: *DJA*, II, 370.

214 *"the old conjurer"*: Ibid., 369.

214 *Do I see that these people:* Ibid., 369.

214 *Eccentricities:* Ibid., 371.

214 *"By my physical constitution"*: Ibid., 362.

215 *"The language is nowhere"*: Ibid., 370.

215 *"Nobody seems to have"*: *AFC*, III, 209.

215 *"Known only to my own heart"*: Ibid., II, 407.

216 *"If I ever had any"*: Ibid., III, 120.

216 *"This is a painful"*: Ibid., 148.

217 *"delight"*: Ibid., 1.

217 *"a very dangerous man"*: Ibid., 48.

217 if *"ye were mine"*: Ibid., 83.

220 *chose him as a delegate:* Ibid., 226.

220 *a sub-sub committee of one:* Ibid., 228.

221 *"A Constitution or Form of Government"*: See, generally, *Works*, IV, 219–67.

223 *a dinner at Harvard:* *AFC*, III, 225.

224 *"flowing" from his pen:* Ibid., 226.

224 *"I take vast satisfaction"*: *Works*, IX, 509.

225 *"None of us"*: Ibid., 484.

225 *"Be assured you have"*: Hutson, *John Adams and the Diplomacy of the American Revolution*, 44.

225 *"Upon the whole"*: *Works*, IX, 493.

226 *"dismissed without censure"*: Ibid., 497.

226 *an offer of return passage:* *DJA*, IV, 174.

226 *"It will be expected"*: *AFC*, III, 268.

226 *"Alas! When I reflect"*: *DJA*, IV, 175.

227 *The wind was favorable:* Ibid., 235.

227 *"My habitation"*: *AFC*, III, 233.

5 . Unalterably Determined

Page

228 *the* Sensible: *DJA*, IV, 192, *AFC* III, 237.

229 *"We have had"*: *AFC*, III, 243.

229 *proceeding overland:* *DJA*, IV, 193.

229   *"The season":* Ibid., 205.

229   *a scene from* Don Quixote: *AFC,* III, 251.

229   *"enemies of all repose":* DJA, IV, 213.

230   *We carried:* Ibid., 217.

230   *"There is the grandest profusion":* Ibid., II, 419.

230   *"We had nothing":* D. G. Allen, ed., *DJQA,* I, 21.

230   *"almost perpendicular":* Ibid., 30.

230   *"Smoke filled every part":* DJA, II, 416.

230   *"We go along barking":* Ibid., 426–27.

230   *a mistake coming overland: AFC,* III, 258.

231   *part with his mule: DJA,* IV, 238.

231   *"had the honor":* Ibid., 241.

231   *"so frank": Works,* VII, 121.

232   *a letter of explanation: DJA,* IV, 244.

232   *"It is the part of prudence":* Ibid., 245.

233   *"Always keep in mind":* Shepherd, *Adams Chronicles,* 92.

233   *"The delicacies": Works,* VII, 138.

235   *Although I am convinced:* Ibid., 151.

235   *"I have written more":* JA to Elbridge Gerry, May 23, 1780, AP, MHS.

235   *"I am so taken up": AFC,* III, 320.

236   *"Can't you keep":* Ibid., 309.

236   *"Ornaments of this kind":* Ibid., 316.

236   *How long would it be:* Ibid., 332.

236   *"There is everything here":* Ibid., 333.

236   *I must study politics:* Ibid., 342.

237   *You tell me, sir: PJA,* IX, 256–57.

237   *"delicate" Charles:* Ibid., 305.

238   *May Heaven permit you:* Ibid., 367.

238   *"Keep us weak": DJA,* II, 446.

239   *official letter of June 21: Works,* VII, 190–92.

239   *"retrace its steps":* Ibid., 192.

240   *"Foreigners, when they come":* Ibid., 198.

240   *Whatever the size:* Ibid., 220.

240   *"the best policy":* Ibid., 226.

241   *"determined to omit":* Ibid., 241–42.

241   *But Vergennes had had enough:* Ibid., 243.

241   *"The King expects":* Smyth, ed., *Writings of Benjamin Franklin,* VIII, 117.

241   *August 9, 1780:* Lopez, ed., *PBF,* XXIII, 160–66.

243   *"a virgin state":* Ibid., 511.

243   *"The wheat": DJA,* II, 442.

243   *"We passed by Mons":* D. G. Allen, ed., *DJQA,* I, 37.

244   *"a certain king":* Nordholt, *Dutch Republic and American Independence,* 107.

244   *"The whole is an astonishing":* Francis Dana Journal, MHS.

245 *liberal atmosphere:* Boxer, *Dutch Seaborne Empire,* xxvi.

245 *"Wherever the eye ranges":* Owen, *Travels into Different Parts of Europe in the Years 1791–1792,* I, 90–91.

245 *"The verdure":* Nordholt, *Dutch Republic and American Independence,* 5.

246 *"so laden with filth":* Radcliffe, *Journey Made in the Summer of 1794,* 106.

246 *James Boswell of London:* Pottle, ed., *Boswell in Holland,* 236.

246 *One says America: Works,* VII, 247.

247 *"Madame La Veuve du Henry": DJA,* II, 451.

247 *"Papa went out to dinner":* D. G. Allen, ed., *DJQA,* I, 53.

247 *A "considerable" loan: Works,* VII, 245.

247 *"the greatest curiosity": AFC,* III, 413–14.

247 *Adams notified John Thaxter:* Ibid., 423.

247 *enrolled in Amsterdam's:* Ibid., 424.

248 *"If I could have my will":* Ryerson, ed., *PJA,* X, 165.

248 *"A navy is our natural":* Ibid., 270.

249 *"I think I see very clearly":* Wharton, ed., *Revolutionary Diplomatic Correspondence of the United States,* IV, 97.

249 *This country:* Ibid., 98.

249 *"people of the first character": Works,* VIII, 342.

250 *"The burgomasters of Amsterdam": Works,* VIII, 329.

251 *"littleness of soul": AFC,* IV, 35.

252 *A woman who sang:* Wharton, ed., *Revolutionary Diplomatic Correspondence of the United States,* IV, 197.

252 *"War is to a Dutchman":* Ibid., 209.

252 *"obscure":* John Adams, Correspondence of the Late President Adams, Letter XLIII.

253 *"the best house":* JA to Messrs. Sigourney, Ingraham & Bromfield, April 9, 1781, AP, #102, MHS.

253 *In lengthy correspondence:* JA to Messrs. Sigourney, Ingraham & Bromfield, April 11 and 13, 1781, AP, #102, MHS.

253 *"a thousand unfortunate incidents":* Gianta, ed., *The Emerging Nation,* I, 152.

253 *"America . . . has been too long": Works,* VIII, 393.

253 *"Mr. Adams could not refrain":* Watson, *Tour in Holland,* 104.

254 *On April 19, 1781: Works,* VII, 396–404.

255 *I never shall forget:* Benjamin Waterhouse to Levi Woodbury, February 20, 1835, Levi Woodbury Papers, DLG, vol. XVI, MHS.

255 *"What!" said the Duke:* John Adams, *Correspondence of the Late President Adams,* Letter LI.

256 *On Friday, May 4, 1781: Works,* VII, 413.

256 *"desires her tenderest": AFC,* IV, 3.

256 *"Handkerchiefs will turn":* Ibid., III, 321.

257 *"a country so damp":* Ibid., IV, 14.

257 *"I am wholly unconscious":* Ibid., 13.

257 *On Christmas Day, 1780:* Ibid., 50–52.

258 *Keizersgracht:* Ibid., 108.

258 *"Oh! Oh!":* Ibid., 116.

259 *"with a constancy":* Ibid., 121.

259 *"You are now at a university":* Ibid., 38.

259 *"It is not simple velocity":* Ibid., 55.

259 *"Terence is remarkable":* Ibid., 80.

259 *"I absolutely":* Ibid., 144.

260 *Read somewhat in the English poets:* Ibid., 114.

260 *"You will ever remember":* Ibid., 117.

261 *"without [the] knowledge":* Richard Morris, *Peacemakers,* 215.

261 *"I think it must convince":* LOD, XVII, 325.

262 *"You will send me":* AFC, IV, 165.

262 *"I consented [to the departure]":* John Adams, *Correspondence of the Late President Adams,* Letter LXIII.

263 *"long journey":* AFC, IV, 170.

263 *"fit for the Hôtel":* JA to Messrs. Sigourney, Ingraham & Bromfield, April 13, 1781, AP, #102, MHS.

263 *"Congress may have done":* Works, VII, 460.

264 *Adams fell ill:* AFC, IV, 224.

264 *"all powerful [Peruvian] bark":* JA to Thomas McKean, October 15, 1781, AP, #104, MHS.

264 *"wondrous virtue":* JA to M. Dumas, October 15, 1781, AP, #102, MHS.

265 *This is always:* Huxham, *Essay on Fevers,* 62–63.

265 *typhus:* editorial note, Greg L. Lint, AP, MHS.

265 *"unwholesome damps":* AFC, IV, 225, n. 3.

265 *his "fever":* JA to Edmund Jenings, April 28, 1782, AP, #356, MHS.

266 *on October 4:* Works, VII, 465–66.

266 *In reply, Franklin:* Smyth, ed., *Writings of Benjamin Franklin,* VIII, 317.

266 *In mid-October:* Works, VII, 471–75.

266 *"Don't distress yourself":* AFC, IV, 249–51.

267 *"Ah my dear John":* Ibid., 256.

267 *"God willing":* Works, IX, 513.

267 *"Oh, God!":* Richard Morris, *Peacemakers,* 251.

267 *"the glorious news":* Works, VII, 481.

268 *"Cornwallization":* Ibid., 498.

268 *"categorical answer":* Ibid., 515.

269 *"The charge of vanity":* Ibid., 528.

269 *"'What dust we raise'":* Ibid., 527.

270 *"Friesland is said to be":* Ibid., 539.

270 *"Your humble servant":* AFC, IV, 300.

270 *On Monday, April 22:* Works, VII, 571.

271 *"made an entertainment":* Ibid., 573–74.

271 *"liveliest transports"*: Nordholt, *Dutch Republic and American Independence*, 218.

271 *"The resolution"*: JA to Edmund Jenings, April 28, 1782, AP, #356, MHS.

272 *"If this had been"*: *AFC*, IV, 338–39.

272 *"I have rendered"*: Ibid., 370.

272 *"I must be an independent man"*: Ibid., 337.

272 *a letter to Edmund Jenings:* JA to Edmund Jenings, September 27, 1782, AP, #358, MHS.

273 *If they avoid:* Robert Livingston to JA, March 5, 1782, AP, #356, MHS.

273 *Heer Adams: Pennsylvania Journal*, Sept. 14, 1782.

273 *a treaty of commerce: AFC*, V, 15.

273 *"say nothing of this": Works*, VII, 641.

274 *"troublesome business": AFC*, V, 15.

274 *he started for Paris: DJA*, III, 29, 30.

274 *Rubens altarpiece at Antwerp:* Ibid., 31.

274 *While we were viewing:* Ibid., 35–36.

275 *"[Mr. Adams] is much pleased"*: Klingelhofer, "Matthew Ridley's Diary," *William and Mary Quarterly*, XX, Jan. 1963, 123.

276 *I cannot express: Works*, VII, 652–54.

276 *After what Franklin:* Klingelhofer, "Matthew Ridley's Diary," *William and Mary Quarterly*, XX, Jan., 1963, 123.

276 *"with much persuasion"*: Ibid.

276 *His base jealousy:* JA to Edmund Jenings, July 20, 1782, AP, #107, MHS.

277 *to "speak or hear": AFC*, V, 28.

277 *to praise Jay: DJA*, III, 38.

279 *"In the air"*: Ibid., 45.

280 *"took it amiss"*: Ibid., 47.

280 *"hear an expostulation?"*: Ibid., 47, n. 2.

280 *"The Comte"*: Ibid., 49.

280 *"French gentlemen"*: Ibid., 50.

280 *included with a report:* Ibid., 50, n. 2.

281 *"What powers?"*: Ibid., 61.

281 *France does not feel obliged:* Morris, *The Peacemakers*, 330.

281 *"vast deal"*: Ibid., 75.

282 *"carrying away any Negroes"*: Ibid., 82.

282 *Gentlemen, is there:* Ibid., 79.

283 *"a pretty good meal"*: Klingelhofer, "Matthew Ridley's Diary," *William and Mary Quarterly*, XX, Jan., 1963, 132.

283 *performed "nobly": DJA*, III, 81.

284 *"I am at a loss"*: Smyth, ed., *Writings of Benjamin Franklin*, VIII, 641.

284 *"English buy peace"*: Morris, *The Peacemakers*, 383.

285 *"Sharp fiery humors": AFC*, V, 170.

285 *"My friend, you and I"*: Cappon, ed., *Adams-Jefferson Letters*, 349.

286 *"You may depend": AFC*, V, 60.

6. ABIGAIL IN PARIS

Page

287 *terrified of the sea: AFC*, V, 271.

287 *"I know not"*: Ibid., 277.

287 *Reverend William Smith, had died:* Ibid., 253.

287 *"I cannot consent"*: Ibid., 271.

288 *"fine majestic girl"*: Ibid., 57.

288 *She has stateliness:* Ibid., 7.

288 *"If he is steady"*: Ibid., 62.

288 *"dissipation"*: *EDJA*, 23, n. 50.

289 *Daughter!:* JA to AA, April 8, 1783, Shaw Family Papers, LOC.

289 *"courting mothers"*: *AFC*, V, 74–75.

290 *"attachment"*: Ibid., 260.

290 *I recollect the untitled:* C. F. Adams, *Letters of Mrs. Adams*, I, 169.

290 *"parade and nonsense"*: *AFC*, V, 259.

290 *Her health was poor:* Ibid., 270.

290 *even by balloon:* Ibid., 236.

291 *"The lady comes"*: Ibid., 256.

291 *You invite me:* Ibid., 303.

291 *"I can scarcely think it"*: Ibid., 302.

291 *"Sir, you and the"*: Ibid., 317.

291 *by two servants:* Ibid., 305, n. 4.

292 *named Phoebe:* Ibid., 303.

292 *Phoebe is to be allowed:* Ibid., 345.

293 *"But let no"*: Ibid., 331.

293 *"not of unmeaning complimenters"*: *DJA*, III, 154.

293 *"I thanked him for his politeness"*: *AFC*, V, 398.

294 *the* Active: *DJA*, III, 155.

294 *"We crawled"*: *AFC*, V, 359.

294 *"We can only live"*: Ibid., 361.

294 *"as some gentlemen sat"*: Ibid.

294 *rheumatism:* Ibid., 365.

295 *"lazy, dirty"*: Ibid., 364.

295 *"make a bustle"*: Ibid., 359.

295 *she mastered the names:* Ibid., 364.

295 *"Great and marvelous"*: Ibid.

295 *reading on medicine: DJA*, III, 158.

295 *"haughty Scotchman"*: *AFC*, V, 366.

296 *One of the crew: DJA*, III, 162.

296 *"No matter where"*: Ibid., 162.

296 *"Man was made"*: *AFC*, V, 365.

296 *We set off from the vessel:* Ibid., 368.

297 *seventy-two miles:* Ibid., 369.

297 *Black Heath:* Ibid., 370.

297 *"as quiet as at any place"*: Ibid., 373.

297 *"Heaven give us"*: Ibid., 399

297 *portrait done by Copley*: *DJA*, III, 31.

298 *"walk a vast deal"*: Ibid., 40.

298 *"Young Mr. Adams"*: Ibid., 43.

298 *"You can imagine"*: *AFC*, VI, 32.

299 *Everything around appeared*: Butterfield et al., ed., *Book of Abigail and John*, 397–98.

299 *"You know my dear sister"*: *AFC*, VI, 17.

300 *"I was chilled to the heart"*: *DJA*, III, 153.

301 *"The house, the garden"*: Ibid., 171.

301 *"I make a little America"*: Shaw, *Character of John Adams*, 195.

301 *"Why, my dear"*: *AFC*, V, 434.

301 *"delightful"*: Ibid., 433.

302 *"One [servant]"*: Ibid., 441.

302 *"business is to purchase"*: C. F. Adams, *Letters of Mrs. Adams*, II, 49.

302 *"a sprat in a whale's belly"*: JA to Cotton Tufts, Dec. 15, 1784, AP, #363, MHS.

302 *"We spend no evenings"*: C. F. Adams, *Letters of Mrs. Adams*, II, 50.

302 *"The inquiry is not whether"*: *AFC*, VI, 136.

303 *"dancing here and there"*: Ibid., V, 440.

303 *"To be out of fashion"*: C. F. Adams, *Letters of Mrs. Adams*, II, 69.

303 *"smelt it"*: Ibid., 54.

303 *"What idea, my dear madame"*: *AFC*, V, 447.

303 *a Paris orphanage*: Ibid., VI, 57.

304 *John Paul Jones*: Ibid., 5.

304 *"Less money"*: Ibid., 6.

305 *She entered the room*: Ibid., V, 436–37.

306 *"I have been here"*: Ibid., 446.

307 *Fancy, my dear Betsy*: Ibid., VI, 39.

307 *The dresses*: C. F. Adams, *Letters of Mrs. Adams*, II, 82.

308 *"And oh!"*: Ibid., 83.

308 *They are easy*: Ibid., 76.

308 *Adrienne François de Noailles*: *AFC*, VI, 15–16.

309 *"You would have supposed"*: Ibid., 16.

309 *"I have often complained"*: Smith, *Journal and Correspondence of Miss Adams*, 34.

309 *"I have got their profiles"*: Ibid., 30.

310 *"Aya, I had rather"*: Ibid., V, 468.

310 *"I shall always"*: Ibid., VI, 102.

310 *"May Heaven reward him"*: Ibid., V, 471.

310 *"I wish I could give you"*: Ibid., 465.

311 *"Dined at Mr. Jefferson's"*: D. G. Allen, ed., *DJQA*, I, 216.

312 *"eight or ten thousand"*: A. A. Smith, *Journal and Correspondence of Miss Adams*, II, 18.

312 *"My new partner"*: JA to Arthur Lee, Jan. 31, 1785, AP, #364, MHS.

312 *"He professes"*: C. F. Adams, *Letters of Mrs. Adams*, II, 68.

312 *"perfect freedom and unreserve"*: *AFC*, VI, 169.

312 *"one of the choice ones"*: Ibid., 119.

313 *Martha had died*: Malone, *Jefferson the Virginian*, 396.

313 *"confined himself from the world"*: A. A. Smith, *Journal and Correspondence of Miss Adams*, II, 45.

313 *"rode out"*: Randolph, *Domestic Life of Thomas Jefferson*, 63.

314 *90,000 bricks*: Malone, *Jefferson the Virginian*, 287.

314 *"You will find"*: Ibid., 296.

315 *"so excessive"*: Boyd, ed., *PTJ*, III, 643.

315 *Captain Jack Jouett*: See Malone, *Jefferson the Virginian*, 355–58.

315 *"I ordered a carriage"*: Mayo, ed., *Jefferson Himself*, 104.

316 *thirty slaves*: Ibid., 105.

316 *George Nicholas called*: Malone, *Jefferson the Virginian*, 361.

316 *"a wound in my spirit"*: Boyd, ed., *PTJ*, VI, 185.

316 *"[I] have retired"*: Ibid., 118.

317 *"stupor of mind"*: Ibid., 203.

317 *"venom"*: Ibid., 235.

318 *He hates Franklin*: Ibid., 241.

318 *"Jefferson is an excellent hand"*: JA to Elbridge Gerry, April 25, 1785, AP, #107, MHS.

318 *"You can scarcely"*: Boyd, ed., *PTJ*, VII, 383.

319 *"seasoning"*: Ibid., VIII, 43.

319 *he did not expect to live*: *AFC*, V, 458.

319 *"never buying anything"*: Betts and Bear, eds., *Family Letters of Thomas Jefferson*, 43.

319 *fifty-nine bottles of Bordeaux*: Bear and Stanton, eds. *Jefferson's Memorandum Books*, I, 564.

320 *he turned to Adams*: *AFC*, VI, 43.

321 *"small laughing busts"*: Bear and Stanton, eds., *Jefferson's Memorandum Books*, I, 565.

321 *Devoted to chess*: Ellen Coolidge Correspondence, University of Virginia Special Collections.

322 *"affecting sight"*: A. A. Smith, *Journal and Correspondence of Miss Adams*, II, 25.

322 *"She is a sweet girl"*: Ibid., 45.

322 *Lucy, had died*: Ibid.

324 *"an excellent man"*: *AFC*, VI, 78.

324 *"If you were to examine him"*: Ford, ed., *Statesman and Friend*, 6.

325 *"The table is covered"*: *AFC*, VI, 47.

325 *"We see but little"*: Ibid., 25.

325 *"I feel very loath"*: Ibid., 20.

326 *You must know*: C. F. Adams, *Letters of Mrs. Adams*, II, 78.

326 *a Te Deum was sung*: D. G. Allen, ed., *DJQA*, I, 242.

328 *There are perhaps*: Ibid., 239.

328 *My father:* Ibid., 256.

328 *Elbridge Gerry: AFC,* VI, 109.

329 *"I shall find":* Ibid., 111.

329 *He said that Lord Carmarthen: DJA,* III, 176.

329 *"I have not one":* Ibid.

329 *"and such shall I live":* MHS, *Warren-Adams Letters,* II, 40.

330 *"great thing": DJA,* III, 176.

330 *"We journeyed":* Boyd, ed., *PTJ,* VIII, 178.

330 *"our meditation":* Ibid., 160.

331 *The whole commerce:* Peden, ed., *Thomas Jefferson: Notes on the State of Virginia,* 162, 139, 141, 143.

331 *"The departure":* Boyd, ed., *PTJ,* VI, 164.

7 . London

333 *the greatest talker:* JA to John Langdon, February 24, 1812, AP, #118, MHS.

334 *If at times:* JA to Elbridge Gerry, May 2, 1785, AP, #364, MHS.

335 *as instructed:* May 27, 1785, AP, #111, MHS.

335 *audience with the King:* JA to John Jay, May 29, 1785, AP, #111, MHS.

335 *a brief speech before the King: Works,* VIII, 255.

335 *"I felt more":* Ibid., 257.

336 *The circumstances:* Ibid., 257.

337 *I retreated:* Ibid., 258.

337 *"character": AFC,* VI, 17.

338 *"I cannot bear":* Ibid., 187.

338 *Handel's* Messiah: Ibid., 329.

338 *"elegant but plain":* Ibid., 189.

338 *"A very dress cap":* C. F. Adams, *Letters of Mrs. Adams,* II, 101.

339 *"Thus equipped":* Ibid.

339 *"master of the human heart": AFC,* VI, 313.

339 *Only think of the task:* Ibid., 102–4.

340 *"well shaped":* C. F. Adams, *Letters of Mrs. Adams,* II, 104.

341 *northeast corner:* Memorandum of JA's rental agreement for the house on Grosvenor Square, AP, June 19, 1785, MHS.

341 *"We shall live": AFC,* VI, 205.

341 *"tumult and hurry":* Smollett, *Humphrey Clinker,* 88

342 *"sacrificed upon the gallows":* Ibid., 329.

342 *Royal Bell Ringers:* June 1785, AP, #364, MHS.

343 *"learned pig": AFC,* VI, 331.

343 *"enchanted palace":* Smollett, *Humphrey Clinker,* 92.

343 *Sir William Herschel:* A. A. Smith, *Journal and Correspondence of Miss Adams,* I, 84.

343 *"The English may call": AFC,* VI, 213.

343 *"not the pleasantest":* Ibid., 347.

344 *"tasty":* Ibid., xiii.

344 *"candor, probity":* Ibid., xiv.

344 *"a good likeness":* Ibid., 216.

345 *cut Adams's salary:* JA to William Tudor, Sept. 18, 1785, AP, #115, MHS.

345 *"I am driven":* JA to Mercy Warren, May 24, 1785, AP, MHS.

345 *she won four games:* AA to Mrs. Cranch, April 6, 1786, in C. F. Adams, *Letters of Mrs. Adams,* II, 135.

346 *"Othello [played by John Kemble]":* *AFC,* VI, 366.

346 *"a man must be of rock":* Boyd, ed., *PTJ,* VIII, 548.

346 *It would have:* Ibid.

347 *French dessert: AFC,* VI, 264–65.

347 *"But when writing":* Boyd, ed., *PTJ,* VIII, 549.

348 *There is a strong:* JA to President Lee, Aug. 26, 1785, AP, #111, MHS.

348 *"a new order of things":* JA to Matthew Robinson, March 4, 1786, AP, #113, MHS.

348 *"They hate us":* JA to Charles Storer, May 22, 1786, AP, #368, MHS.

348 *"I had rather":* JA to Elbridge Gerry, July 15, 1785, AP, #107, MHS.

348 *John Adams hanged: AFC,* VI, 196.

348 *"When Mr. Adams came in":* Ibid., I, 136.

349 *"those sanctified hypocrites":* Berkin, *Jonathan Sewall,* 124.

350 *a broken heart:* Peabody, ed., *John Adams,* 134.

351 *"We must not":* Cappon, ed., *Adams-Jefferson Letters,* 61.

351 *Portugal's need:* Ibid., 90.

352 *sculptor Houdon:* Boyd, ed., *PTJ,* VIII, 267, 302, 340, 577, 663.

353 *It is long since:* Ibid., IX, 285.

353 *His Excellency appeared:* Abigail Adams Smith to JQA, Feb. 8–27, 1786, AP, #367, MHS.

354 *"aversion to have anything":* Lipscomb, ed., *Writings of Thomas Jefferson,* I, 95.

355 *"They require":* Boyd, ed., *PTJ,* XII, 193.

356 *"This people": Works,* III, 393.

356 *"their little journey":* AA to Cotton Tufts, April 8, 1786, AP, #367, MHS.

356 *the longest time they had had:* AA to Mrs. Cranch, in C. F. Adams, *Letters of Mrs. Adams,* II, 135–36.

356 Observations on Modern Gardening: Boyd, ed., *PTJ,* IX, 374.

358 *"Four people":* Ibid., 370.

358 *"I mounted": DJA,* III, 186.

358 *"no pretension":* Boyd, ed., *PTJ,* IX, 371.

358 *Venus and Bacchus unnecessary: DJA,* III, 184.

359 *"according to the custom":* Ibid., 185.

359 *"There is nothing":* Ibid.

359 *"kissed the ground":* AA to George Adams, Aug. 7, 1815, AP, #426, MHS.

359 *"ground where liberty was fought for": DJA,* III, 185.

359 *farm known as Leasowes:* Boyd, ed., *PTJ,* IX, 371.

360 *"the simplest and plainest"*: *DJA*, III, 186.

361 *You know the opinion*: Boyd, ed., *PTJ*, XI, 94.

362 *"He possesses"*: AA to Cotton Tufts, Jan. 10, 1786, AP, #367, MHS.

362 *"like to become your brother"*: AA to JQA, Feb. 16, 1786, AP, #367, MHS.

363 *"this unhappy connection"*: *AFC*, VI, 486.

363 *"I cannot, however"*: AA to Mary Cranch, Feb. 10, 1788, AP, MHS.

363 *"The young couple"*: JA to James Warren, July 4, 1786, AP, MHS.

363 *dreamed of Royall Tyler*: AA to Mary Cranch, June 13, 1786, AP, MHS.

364 *"Suppose you give"*: Boyd, ed., *PTJ*, X, 162.

364 *"smell of the midnight lamp"*: JA to JQA, April 2, 1786, AP, #367, MHS.

364 *a "memorable change"*: JA to Matthew Robinson, March 23, 1786, AP, MHS.

365 *"Watchfulness over yourself"*: AA to JQA, July 21, 1786, AP, #368, MHS.

365 *"You have in your nature"*: JA to Charles Adams, June 2, 1786, AP, #113, MHS.

365 *"I flatter myself"*: Lord Carmarthen to JA, Feb. 28, 1786, AP, #367, MHS.

366 *"too long trifled"*: JA to Cotton Tufts, May 26, 1786, AP, #368, MHS.

366 *"I will go"*: Boyd, ed., *PTJ*, X, 177.

367 *"everyone fled"*: AA to Cotton Tufts, Aug. 1, 1786, AP, #368, MHS.

367 *"miserable"*: Abigail Adams Smith to JQA, July 27–Aug. 22, 1786, AP, #368, MHS.

367 *"As this presents"*: AA to Cotton Tufts, Aug. 1, 1786, AP, #368, MHS.

367 *"Not a hill to be seen"*: AA to Mrs. Cranch, in C. F. Adams, *Letters of Mrs. Adams*, II, 146.

368 *"Don't be alarmed"*: Boyd, ed., *PTJ*, X, 557.

369 *proposed trade of her son*: Ibid., 202.

369 *"An unfortunate dislocation"*: Ibid., 621.

369 *Maria Cosway*: See, generally, Malone, *Jefferson and the Rights of Man*, II, chap. 5. *AA and Cosways*: Abigail Adams Smith to JQA, Jan. 22, 1786, AP, MHS.

370 *"Head" and "Heart"*: Boyd, ed., *PTJ*, X, 443-53.

370 *"tyranny of Britain"*: AA to Mary Cranch, Feb. 25, 1787, AAS.

370 *"Ignorant, restless"*: Cappon, ed., *Adams-Jefferson Letters*, 168.

371 *he hoped the captured rebels*: Boyd, ed., *PTJ*, XI, 174.

371 *"a little rebellion"*: Ibid.

371 *"workhouse of nature"*: Boyd, ed., *PTJ*, X, 447.

371 *daughter had safely arrived*: Ibid., II, 50.

371 *"The tree of liberty"*: Ibid., XII, 356.

371 *"a fine boy"*: AA to Lucy Cranch, April 26, 1787, American Antiquarian Society.

372 *"I show her your picture"*: Cappon, ed., *Adams-Jefferson Letters*, 178.

372 *"The old nurse"*: Ibid.

372 *"as rough as a little sailor"*: Ibid., 183.

373 *"Popularity"*: JA to James Warren, Jan. 9, 1787, AP, MHS.

374 *"philosophic solitude"*: JA to AA, Dec. 25, 1786, AP, #369, MHS.

374 *"He is so much swallowed"*: AA to JQA, Nov. 22, 1786, AP, #369, MHS.

374 *"setting up a king"*: AA to JQA, March 20, 1787, AP, #369, MHS.

374 A Defence of the Constitutions: See, generally, *Works*, IV–VI.

378 *"I have read"*: Boyd, ed., *PTJ*, XI, 177.

379 *"a powerful engine"*: Ibid., 402.

379 *"secret design"*: Rutland, ed., *Papers of James Madison*, X, 44.

379 *"What think you"*: Cappon, ed., *Adams-Jefferson Letters*, 210.

379 *"things" in the Constitution*: Boyd, ed., *PTJ*, XII, 350.

380 *"You are afraid"*: Cappon, ed., *Adams-Jefferson Letters*, 213.

380 *The public mind*: *Works*, VIII, 467.

381 *"and how we say at sea"*: Cappon, ed., *Adams-Jefferson Letters*, 214.

381 *"the Vassall-Borland place"*: AA to Mary Cranch, Oct. 1787, American Antiquarian Society.

382 *William had died*: AA to Mary Cranch, Feb. 10, 1788, American Antiquarian Society.

382 *Esther Field*: Ibid.

382 *emergency trip*: AA to Cotton Tufts, Feb. 20, 1788, AP, #371, MHS.

382 *"I have considered"*: Boyd, ed., *PTJ*, XII, 553.

383 *"in the midst of the bustle"*: Cappon, ed., *Adams-Jefferson Letters*, 226.

383 *By his opinions*: Nabby to JQA, Feb. 10, 1788, AP, #371, MHS.

8. HEIR APPARENT

Page

389 *Boston lighthouse*: *Two-Hundredth Anniversary of Boston Light*, 70–71.

389 *"My coach"*: John Hancock to JA, May 7, 1788, AP, MHS.

390 *"The bells in the several churches"*: *Massachusetts Centinel*, June 18, 1788.

390 *The oldest has given*: JA to Abigail Adams Smith, July 16, 1788, AP, MHS.

391 *"Busy unpacking"*: *DJQA*, II, 420.

391 *"Parson Wibird"*: Ibid., 419.

391 *"In height and breadth"*: AA to Abigail Adams Smith, July 7, 1788, AP, MHS.

391 *"It is not large"*: *Works*, IX, 557.

391 *Brissot de Warville*: Brissot de Warville, *New Travels in the United States of America, 1788*, 102.

391 *"no Paris lawyer"*: La Rochefoucauld-Liancourt, François. *Travels Through the United States of North America*, I, 407–8.

392 *"And who can object"*: *Massachusetts Centinel*, June 25, 1788.

392 *Benjamin Rush wrote*: Butterfield, ed., *Letters of Benjamin Rush*, II, 469.

393 *"I think of my poor"*: AA to Mary Cranch, Dec. 15, 1788, AP, MHS.

393 *"The new government"*: Cappon, ed., *Adams-Jefferson Letters*, 234.

393 *"Mr. A, to a sound understanding"*: Syrett, ed., *Papers of Alexander Hamilton*, V, 231.

394 *Merit must be*: *Massachusetts Centinel*, April 15, 1789.

394 *"Freedom of the City"*: Ibid., May 2, 1789.

395 *4 million by 1789*: See population figures in *New York Daily Gazette*, July 9, 1789.

396 *Virginia was still*: See population figures ibid.

396 *American Indians:* See, Purvis, *Revolutionary America, 1763–1800*, 24.

397 *"Aristotle and Plato":* JA to Arthur Lee, July 18, 1788, Princeton University.

397 *"people secretly wish":* Abbot, ed., *PGW*, II, 59–60.

397 *"fate of this government":* JA to William Tudor, May 9, 1789, Tudor Papers, MHS.

398 *nearly 700,000 men, women:* See population figures in *New York Daily Gazette*, July 9, 1789.

398 *fully 500,000:* See population figures ibid.

398 *"Patriotism is ridiculed":* MHS, *Warren-Adams Letters*, II, 249.

398 *"in a land of strangers":* Abigail Adams Smith to AA, Sept. 7, 1788, AP, MHS.

398 *"I find men and manners":* JA to Abigail Adams Smith, Nov. 11, 1788, AP, MHS.

399 *"Not wholly without experience":* Works, VIII, 487.

399 *"not quite adapted":* JA to JQA, July 9, 1789, AP, MHS.

400 *recompense for office holders:* Works, IX, 533.

400 *"May Heaven assist me":* Freeman, *George Washington.* Vol. VI, 155.

400 *Federal Hall:* See, generally, Christman, *First Federal Congress*, 104–10.

401 *"I wish the business":* Ibid., 108.

401 *"cheerfully and readily":* Works, VIII, 486.

402 *But if from inexperience:* Ibid., 487.

402 *"Gentlemen, I feel":* Maclay, *Journal of William Maclay*, 2.

402 *"I find, sir":* Ibid., 3.

402 *Richard Henry Lee offered:* Ibid., 7.

403 *"Many persons in the crowd":* Gazette of the United States, April 25, 1789.

403 *"Long live George Washington":* New York Gazette, May 1, 1789.

404 *With the crowd in raptures:* Gazette of the United States, May 2, 1789.

404 *"a confidence as pure":* O'Dwyer, "A French Diplomat's View of Congress, 1790," *William and Mary Quarterly*, July 1964.

404 *"with great cordiality":* JA to AA, May 1, 1789, AP, MHS.

404 *"No man on earth":* Cappon, ed., *Adams-Jefferson Letters*, 238.

405 *There were presidents of fire companies:* Maclay, *Journal of William McClay*, 23.

405 *how to address Washington:* Works, VIII, 513.

406 *The Contrast:* Tyler, *The Contrast*, 20.

407 *"The more simple":* Hobson, ed., *Papers of James Madison*, XII, 155.

407 *"For forty minutes":* Maclay, *Journal of William Maclay*, 26.

407 *"I cannot help thinking":* Ibid., 29.

408 *"His Rotundity":* Ibid.

409 *"Is not my election":* Old Family Letters, 36.

409 *"corruption of ambition":* JA to William Tudor, June 14, 1789, AP, #115, MHS.

409 *"anything at any rate":* JA to AA, May 14, 1789, AP, MHS.

409 *Hume, Johnson:* JA to AA, May 24, 1789, AP, MHS.

409 *"My sincere thanks":* JA to AA, May 19, 1789, AP, MHS.

410 *"dear friend":* Butterfield, ed., *Letters of Benjamin Rush*, I, 522–23.

410 *"the most superlatively":* Boyd, ed., *PTJ*, XV, 315.

410 *preserve the laws:* Old Family Letters, 37.

410 *"I am a mortal":* Ibid., 60.

410 *I deny an "attachment"*: Ibid.

410 *"A hundred years hence"*: Butterfield, ed., *Letters of Benjamin Rush*, I, 522.

411 *"familiar and unaffected"*: Corner, ed., *Autobiography of Benjamin Rush*, 143.

411 *"anxious hours"*: AA to JA, May 30, 1789, AP, MHS.

411 *"What shall I do"*: JA to Cotton Tufts, June 12, 1789, AP, MHS.

411 *Charles's difficulties:* Harvard Archives, Faculty Records, 5:272; 6:29-30.

412 *"We are all very happy"*: JA to Cotton Tufts, June 28, 1789, AP, MHS.

412 *"We are delightfully situated"*: AA to Mary Cranch, June 28, 1789, AP, MHS.

412 *"At Richmond Hill"*: AA to Mary Cranch, Aug. 9, 1789, AP, MHS.

413 *"She is plain in dress"*: AA to Mary Cranch, June 28, 1789, AP, MHS.

413 *He is polite:* AA to Mary Cranch, Jan. 5, 1790, AP, MHS.

414 *"busy indeed"*: Maclay, *Journal of William Maclay*, 112.

414 *"advantages from pride"*: John Trumbull to JA, Feb. 6, 1790, AP, #373, MHS.

414 *"You talk of my enemies"*: JA to John Trumbull, March 9, 1790, AP, #115, MHS.

415 *Public business, my son:* JA to Thomas Boylston Adams, Sept. 2, 1789, AP, MHS.

416 *young Charles to clerk:* Hecht, *Odd Destiny*, 176.

416 *dripping head: New York Daily Gazette*, Sept. 23, 1789.

416 A COMPLETE REVOLUTION: *New York Daily Gazette*, Sept. 23, 1789.

416 *France seems travailing:* Maclay, *Journal of William Maclay*, 151.

419 *"It seemed impossible"*: Gardner, ed., *Thomas Jefferson*, 210.

420 *"The essence of the whole"*: *Old Family Letters*, 55.

420 *"Jefferson is here"*: AA to Mary Cranch, April 3, 1790, AP, MHS.

420 *It rests now with ourselves:* Malone, *Jefferson and the Rights of Man*, 247.

421 *"Discourses on Davila"*: See *Works*, VI, 227-403.

422 *"division of sentiments"*: JA to William Smith, May 20, 1790, AP, MHS.

422 *Washington was suddenly taken so ill:* See, generally, *Gazette of the United States*, May 8 and May 19, 1790.

422 *"every eye full of tears"*: Maclay, *Journal of William Maclay*, 259.

423 *"At this early day"*: AA to Mary Cranch, May 30, 1790, AP, MHS.

423 *"I hate to complain"*: AA to Mary Cranch, March 21, 1790, AP, MHS.

425 *"most adjacent"*: Hobson, ed., *Papers of James Madison*, XII, 375.

425 *"John Adams has neither judgment"*: Maclay, *Journal of William Maclay*, 278.

426 *New Yorkers were outraged:* See *New York Journal and Patriotic Register, July 2, July 9, July 20, 1790; New York Daily Gazette*, July 3, 1790.

427 *"the dazzling Mrs. Bingham"*: AA to Abigail Adams Smith, Dec. 26, 1790, AP, MHS.

427 *"fine ladies show"*: AA to Cotton Tufts, Feb. 6, 1791, AP, MHS.

428 *"this young man"*: AA to JA, Jan. 5, 1794, AP, MHS.

428 *"We all preach patience"*: AA to Mary Cranch, March 12, 1791, AP, MHS.

428 *her greater worry:* AA to Mary Cranch, Dec. 12, 1790, AP, MHS.

429 *"the political heresies"*: Boyd, ed., *PTJ*, XX, 290.

429 *"mortified"*: Ibid., 292.

431 *Adams answered Jefferson:* Cappon, ed., *Adams-Jefferson Letters*, 247-50.

432 *"Indeed, it was impossible"*: Ibid., 250-52.

433 *"a clever, sober"*: AA to Mary Cranch, Dec. 18, 1791, AP, MHS.

434 *"I firmly believe"*: AA to Mary Cranch, April 20, 1792, AP, MHS.

436 *"not only a monarchist"*: J. C. Miller, *Alexander Hamilton*, 317.

436 *"pretenders to profound knowledge"*: Malone, *Jefferson and the Rights of Man*, 459.

436 *"mutual forebearances"*: Catanzariti, ed., *PTJ*, XXIV, 317.

436 *"North and South"*: Ibid., XXIII, 538–39.

437 *"a real friend"*: Syrett, ed., *Papers of Alexander Hamilton*, XII, 568.

437 *"I am persuaded"*: Ibid., 342.

438 *6,000 to 7000 people*: *Massachusetts Centinel*, Oct. 3, 1792.

438 *"too dreadful to relate"*: Abigail Adams Smith to AA, Sept. 13, 1792, AP, MHS.

438 *a stinging confidential reply*: Catanzariti, ed., *PTJ*, XXV, 14.

439 *"he had been long"*: JA to AA, Nov. 24, 1792, AP, MHS.

440 *"I am with all the ardor"*: JA to AA, Jan. 27, 1793, AP, MHS.

441 *"You apologize for the length"*: JA to AA, Feb. 4, 1794, AP, MHS.

441 *"newspaper warfare"*: AA to JA, Dec. 23, 1792, AP, MHS.

441 *"hell hounds"*: JA to AA, Jan. 24, 1793, AP, MHS.

441 *"His skin is thinner"*: JA to AA, Jan. 31, 1793, AP, MHS.

442 *"For God's sake"*: Mason, ed., *Papers of James Madison*, XV, 43.

442 *"polite enough to accompany"*: JA to AA, Feb. 3, 1793, AP, MHS.

442 *"the whole man"*: Ibid.

442 *"blind spirit of party"*: JA to AA, Dec. 28, 1792, AP, MHS.

443 *"Danton, Robespierre"*: JA to AA, Jan. 14, 1793, AP, MHS.

443 *"The whole drama"*: JA to AA, Feb. 27, 1793, AP, MHS.

443 *"his head was severed"*: *New York Daily Gazette*, April 3, 1789.

444 *Mankind are now enlightened*: *New York Journal and Patriotic Register*, April 6, 1793.

445 *"All the old spirit"*: Catanzariti, ed., *PTJ*, XXV, 661.

447 *"pretty short of cash"*: Thomas Adams to JA, Oct. 9, 1793, AP, MHS.

447 *"Would to Heaven"*: AA to Abigail Adams Smith, Feb. 3, 1794, AP, MHS.

447 *"I go to the Senate"*: JA to AA, Jan. 21, 1794, AP, MHS.

447 *"My country in its wisdom"*: JA to AA, Dec. 19, 1793, AP, MHS.

448 *"But his want of candor"*: JA to AA, Dec. 26, 1793, AP, MHS.

448 *"Jefferson went off"*: JA to AA, Jan. 6, 1794, AP, MHS.

448 *Jefferson thinks he shall*: JA to JQA, Jan. 3, 1793, AP, MHS.

449 *"din of politics"*: Cappon, ed., *Adams-Jefferson Letters*, 253–54.

449 *"find a way to reconcile"*: Ibid., 255.

449 *"tranquility becomes daily"*: Ibid., 257.

450 *This has injured*: Ibid., 258.

450 *"paper transactions"*: Ibid., 254.

450 *"The rights of one generation"*: Ibid., 255.

450 *Reasoning has been all lost*: Ibid., 259.

451 *"My health is entirely"*: Stagg, ed., *Papers of James Madison*, XVI, 1.

452 *"nail manufactory"*: Cappon, ed., *Adams-Jefferson Letters*, 258.

452 *"Move or die"*: JA to Charles Adams, Feb. 7, 1795, AP, MHS.

452 *red, watery eyes:* Adams's eye troubles through much of his life may have been caused by a disease known as thyrotoxicosis. See John Ferling and Lewis E. Braverman, "John Adams's Health Reconsidered," *William and Mary Quarterly*, Jan. 1998.

452 *"painful to the vanity":* JA to JQA, April 26, 1795, AP, MHS.

453 *"Much more depends":* JA to JQA, April 3, 1794, AP, MHS.

453 *"How the present age":* JA to Charles Adams, Jan. 9, 1794, AP, MHS.

453 *"I know not what":* JA to AA, Jan. 21, 1794, AP, MHS.

454 *"My aged and venerable mother":* JA to Abigail Adams Smith, Jan. 7, 1794, AP, MHS.

454 *"I have often thought":* JA to AA, May 19, 1794, AP, MHS.

455 *"superior to all sense":* Twining, *Travels in America a Hundred Years Ago*, 37–39.

458 *"Were I to declare":* Charles Adams to JA, March 12, 1794, AP, MHS.

458 *"After all the hairbreadth":* Abigail Adams Smith to JQA, Oct. 26, 1795, AP, MHS.

458 *"I am heir apparent":* JA to AA, Jan. 20, 1796, AP, MHS.

458 *"I will be second":* AA to JA, Jan. 21, 1796, AP, MHS.

459 *"I am weary":* JA to AA, Feb. 10, 1796, AP, MHS.

459 *"You know what is before you":* AA to JA, Feb. 20, 1796, AP, MHS.

459 *"I have looked into myself":* JA to AA, March 1, 1796, AP, MHS.

459 *"If I were near":* JA to AA, March 11, 1796, AP, MHS.

459 *"teeth and . . . nails":* Ibid.

460 *"He detained me there":* JA to AA, March 25, 1796, AP, MHS.

460 *"and good humor":* JA to AA, May 5, 1796, AP, MHS.

460 *"This day my new barn":* D*JA*, III, 227.

461 *"a soft, fine":* Ibid., 228.

461 *"mosquitoes numerous":* Ibid., 238.

462 *"Of all the summers":* Ibid., 238.

462 *"venomous as Macbeth's":* AA to TA, Aug. 16, 1796, AP, MHS.

462 AN ALARM: *Aurora*, Oct. 29, 1796.

463 *"Poor Jefferson":* JA to JQA, Nov. 11, 1796, AP, MHS.

463 *"as great a hypocrite":* Smith, *John Adams*, II, 908.

463 *"Take his character":* AA to JA, Nov. 8, 1796, AP, MHS.

465 *"The old man":* *Works*, I, 495.

465 *"he had always been":* Lipscomb, ed., Writings of Thomas Jefferson, IX, 351.

466 *"open for your perusal":* Cappon, ed., *Adams-Jefferson Letters*, 262.

466 *The letter was never sent:* Ibid., n. 254.

9. OLD OAK

Page

467 *"like marks of approbation":* Boston *Gazette*, March 16, 1797.

467 *"the most affecting":* JA to AA, March 17, 1797, AP, MHS.

468 *"simple but elegant":* JA to AA, March 5, 1797, AP, MHS.

468 *Quincy coat of arms:* JA to AA, Feb. 2, 1797, AP, MHS.

468 *"They shall have a republican":* JA to AA, Jan. 31, 1797, AP, MHS.

469 *"I have been so strangely":* JA to AA, March 9, 1797, AP, MHS.

469 *Adams energetically repeating:* Washington (D.C.) *Gazette,* March 8–11, 1797.

469 *"A solemn scene":* JA to AA, March 5, 1797, AP, MHS.

469 *"Thus ended":* Boston *Gazette,* March 16, 1797.

470 *"Republican plainness":* Aurora, March 20, 1797.

470 *It is universally admitted:* Ibid., March 15, 1797.

470 *"an old fielder":* JA to AA, Jan. 16, 1797, AP, MHS.

470 *a ship ballasted with iron:* Elbridge Gerry to AA, Jan. 7, 1797, AP, MHS.

470 *"I will not":* Cotton Tufts to JA, Jan. 23, 1797, AP, MHS.

470 *"I congratulate you":* Cushing, ed., *Writings of Samuel Adams,* IV, 408.

471 *"between the rising":* William and Mary Quarterly, Oct. 1954, 608.

471 *Andrew Brown fire:* Gazette of the United States, Jan. 30, 1797.

471 *"I am not alarmed":* JA to Abigail Adams Smith, Feb. 21, 1797, AP, MHS.

471 *"The die is cast":* JA to AA, Feb. 9, 1797, AP, MHS.

473 *"Pickering and all his colleagues":* Works, VIII, 523.

473 *"I may say":* JA to Tristram Dalton, Jan. 19, 1797, AP, MHS.

473 *"which is and shall be":* JA to Elbridge Gerry, Feb. 20, 1797, AP, #117, MHS.

473 *"speak with pleasure":* Butterfield, ed., *Letters of Benjamin Rush,* II, 785.

473 *"entered immediately":* "The Anas," Lipscomb, ed., *Writings of Thomas Jefferson,* I, 414.

474 *"first wish of his heart":* Ibid.

474 *certain Madison would not accept:* Ibid.

474 *"eminent character":* Malone, *Jefferson and the Ordeal of Liberty,* 297.

475 *"steer impartially":* "The Anas," Lipscomb, ed., *Writings of Thomas Jefferson,* I, 415.

476 *"I give it as my* decided opinion": *Works,* VIII, 530.

476 *"The President":* Stagg, ed., *Papers of James Madison,* XVI, 448.

476 *"He is as he was":* JA to AA, March 13, 1797, AP, MHS.

476 *"My entrance into office":* JA to JQA, March 31, 1797, AP, MHS.

477 *"I have a great cold":* JA to AA, March 13, 1797, AP, MHS.

477 *"From the situation":* JA to AA, March 17, 1797, AP, MHS.

477 *The furniture:* JA to AA, March 22, 1797, AP, MHS.

478 *"very dry, dull":* JA to AA, April 13, 1797, AP, MHS.

478 *"certain ex-Secretary":* Aurora, April 15, 1797.

478 MR. PINCKNEY: *Porcupine's Gazette,* April 4, 1797.

479 *It is manifestly:* Ibid., April 25, 1797.

479 *"I must entreat you":* JA to AA, April 11, 1797, AP, MHS.

479 *"The times are critical":* JA to AA, April 6, 1797, AP, MHS.

479 *"My pen runs riot":* AA to JA, Jan. 29, 1797, AP, MHS.

480 *"Beware that spare Cassius":* AA to JA, Jan. 28, 1797, AP, MHS.

480 *James Prince:* AA to JA, Feb. 13, 1797, AP, MHS.

481 *"matrimonial prospects":* JQA to AA, Feb. 18, 1797, AP, MHS.

481 *"a man wholly devoid"*: AA to JA, Jan. 28, 1797, AP, MHS.

481 *"The good old lady"*: AA to JA, April 17, 1797, AP, MHS.

482 *"My reflections"*: AA to Mary Cranch, May 16, 1797, AP, MHS.

482 *I quitted my own carriage*: AA to Mary Cranch, May 16, 1797, AP, MHS.

484 *"inflicted a wound"*: *Works*, IX, 114-15.

484 *"emblems of defense"*: *Columbian Centinel*, May 24, 1797.

485 *It may be justly called*: *Gazette of the United States*, May 20, 1797.

485 *"placed matters upon their true ground"*: Fitzpatrick, ed., *Writings of George Washington*, XXXV, 456.

485 *"The President by Three Votes"*: *Aurora*, May 19, 1797.

486 *"he is a plain man"*: *Works*, VIII, 549.

487 *"The task of the President"*: AA to Mary Cranch, June 23, 1797, AP, MHS.

487 *"such close application"*: Stewart Mitchell, *New Letters of Abigail Adams*, 96.

487 *The day is past*: Ibid., 91.

488 *"Mrs. Tufts"*: Ibid., 90.

488 *"closet politician"*: William Plummer, *Memorandum*, 454.

490 *"The President really suffers"*: Stewart Mitchell, *New Letters of Abigail Adams*, 98.

490 *"steady and resolute"*: *William and Mary Quarterly*, Oct. 1954, 613.

490 *"The hot weather"*: AA to Mary Cranch, July 19, 1797, AP, MHS.

491 *"absconded"*: *Aurora*, July 28, 1797.

491 *"I have now the happiness"*: JQA and Louisa Catherine Adams to AA and JA, July 28, 1797, AP, MHS.

492 *"I cannot leave her"*: AA to Mary Cranch, Oct. 22, 1797, AP, MHS.

493 *"My real crime"*: Syrett, ed., *Papers of Alexander Hamilton*, XXI, 122.

493 *"Alas, alas"*: AA to Thomas Adams, Jan. 3, 1798, AP, MHS.

494 *"We are yet all"*: AA to William Smith, Feb. 22, 1798, AP, MHS.

494 *"It is an undoubted"*: Syrett, ed., *Papers of Alexander Hamilton*, XXI, 342.

495 *"you do not speak to the point"*: DeConde, *Quasi-War*, 49.

496 *"insane"*: Mattern, ed., *Papers of James Madison*, XVII, 99.

496 *"Beds of roses"*: AA to Mary Cranch, March 20, 1798, AP, MHS.

497 *"He has no ambition"*: AA to Mary Cranch, March 27, 1798, AP, MHS.

497 *"Gallatin . . . stood to propose"*: Walters, *Albert Gallatin*, 106.

497 *"struck dumb"*: AA to Cotton Tufts, May 25, 1798, AP, MHS.

498 *"unhinged"*: *Aurora*, May 23, 1798.

498 *"malice and falsehood"*: AA to Mary Cranch, April 21, 1798, AP, MHS.

498 *"Such lies"*: Stewart Mitchell, *New Letters of Abigail Adams*, 154.

500 *"In short, we are now"*: AA to Mary Cranch, April 28, 1798, AP, MHS.

500 *"The theater"*: AA to Thomas Adams, May 1, 1798, AP, MHS.

501 *"reign of witches"*: Malone, *Jefferson and the Ordeal of Liberty*, 382.

501 *"Politics and party hatreds"*: Betts and Bear, *Family Letters of Thomas Jefferson*, 162.

502 *"he falls away"*: AA to Mary Cranch, May 20, 1798, AP, MHS.

502 *"I dare not say"*: AA to Cotton Tufts, June 8, 1798, AP, MHS.

502 *"I think sometimes"*: Stewart Mitchell, *New Letters of Abigail Adams*, 178.

502 *"Poor wretches"*: Ibid., 190.

503 *Can it be possible*: Ibid., 192.

503 *"among the wolves"*: Mary Cranch to AA, June 22, 1798, AP, MHS.

503 *"I will never send"*: R. A. Brown, *Presidency of John Adams*, 57.

504 *"This city"*: AA to JQA, June 12, 1798, AP, MHS.

504 *"Why, when we have"*: AA to Mary Cranch, June 9, 1798, AP, MHS.

504 *"the weather so hot"*: AA to Mary Cranch, June 25, 1798, AP, MHS.

507 *"I wish the laws"*: Stewart Mitchell, *New Letters of Abigail Adams*, 179.

507 *"It was one of those strokes"*: AA to Mary Cranch, July 9, 1798, AP, MHS.

508 *"I meant to have it"*: AA to Mary Cranch, April 28, 1798, AP, MHS.

509 *"The illness"*: Abigail Adams Smith to JQA, Sept. 28, 1798, AP, MHS.

509 *"the most gloomy"*: *Works*, VIII, 613.

509 *"and mine in consequence"*: Ibid., 601.

509 *lighthouse at Cape Hatteras*: Oliver Wolcott to JA, Sept. 21, 1798, AP, #391, MHS.

509 *$5,000,000*: JA to Oliver Wolcott, Oct. 1, 1798, AP, #391, MHS.

509 *"I have supposed"*: James McHenry to JA, Sept. 3, 1798, AP, #391, MHS.

509 *"Wooden walls"*: JA to Boston Marine Society, Sept. 7, 1798, AP, #391, MHS.

510 *"The arrangement"*: Syrett, ed., *Papers of Alexander Hamilton*, XXI, 535.

510 *"Do not, I pray"*: Ibid., XXII, 176.

511 *letter to Oliver Wolcott*: JA to Oliver Wolcott, Sept. 24, 1798, AP, #391, MHS.

513 *"dying bed"*: AA to JQA, Nov. 15, 1798, AP, MHS.

513 *"The best skill"*: *Aurora*, Sept. 6, 1798.

514 *"I have not enjoyed"*: AA to JQA, Dec. 2, 1798, AP, MHS.

514 *"He is not at peace"*: AA to JQA, Nov. 15, 1798, AP, MHS.

10. Statesman

Page

515 *"Our horses"*: JA to AA, Nov. 14, 1798, AP, MHS.

515 *"We glided along"*: JA to AA, Nov. 15, 1798, AP, MHS.

515 *"fretful nor peevish"*: JA to AA, Nov. 13, 1798, AP, MHS.

515 *"Nelson's victory"*: JA to AA, Nov. 13, 1798, AP, MHS.

516 *"Almost the whole"*: *Aurora*, Nov. 12, 1798.

516 *received Logan*: *Works*, IX, 244.

517 *"But I'll do no such thing"*: DeConde, *Quasi-War*, 166.

517 *"I had no reason"*: *Works*, IX, 244.

518 *"We are friends"*: *Works*, I, 532.

518 *"This you perceive"*: Syrett, ed., *Papers of Alexander Hamilton*, XXII, 389.

518 *"The man is stark mad"*: DeConde, *Quasi-War*, 171.

518 *"That man would ... become"*: Ibid., 97.

519 *Joseph Bunel*: Ibid. 135–36.

519 *"with the greatest part"*: Ibid., 135.

519 *"Toussaint's clause"*: Ibid., 136.

519 *"good health and spirits"*: *Aurora*, Nov. 12, 1798.

519 *"If you come"*: JA to AA, Dec. 4, 1798, AP, MHS.

520 *"A peck of troubles"*: JA to AA, Dec. 13, 1798, AP, MHS.

520 *"warm opposition"*: JA to AA, Jan. 5, 1799, AP, MHS.

520 *"My daughter and son"*: JA to AA, Dec. 17, 1798, AP, MHS.

520 *"I am old"*: JA to AA, Dec. 25, 1798, AP, MHS.

521 *"natural right"*: Malone, *Jefferson and the Ordeal of Liberty*, 405.

521 *"Firmness on our part"*: Lipscomb, ed., *Writings of Thomas Jefferson*, X, 94.

521 *"We may expect"*: Ford, ed., *Writings of Thomas Jefferson*, VII, 349.

522 *"The circle of our nearest"*: Betts and Bear, *Family Letters of Thomas Jefferson*, 170.

522 *"[Adams] thought Hamilton"*: "Meeting of March 26, 1799 with John Adams." Papers of Elbridge Gerry, LOC.

522 *"I write to you nothing"*: JA to AA, Dec. 25, 1798, AP, MHS.

522 *"Thomas is my delight"*: JA to AA, Jan. 25, 1799, AP, MHS.

523 *February 18, 1799:* DeConde, *Quasi-War*, 178.

523 *"honor of the country"*: Twohig, ed., *PGW*, *III*, 389.

524 *"I beg you"*: Syrett, ed., *Papers of Alexander Hamilton*, XXII, 500.

524 *"event of events"*: Mattern, ed., *Papers of James Madison*, XVII, 233.

523 *"hoping that his friends"*: Ibid., 244.

524 *"fair applause"*: *Aurora*, Feb. 27, 1799.

525 *"This was pretty saucy"*: AA to JA, Feb. 27, 1799, AP, MHS.

525 *"I wish all other officers"*: *Works*, VIII, 636.

525 *Nor do I think:* Ibid., 651.

526 *"The public sentiment"*: Ibid., 637–38.

527 *"It always gives me pain"*: Ibid., 669.

527 *"genius in the command"*: Ibid., 662.

527 *"Genius in a general"*: Ibid.

528 *"It is far below"*: Ibid., IX, 10.

529 *"considerable difference"*: Ibid., 20.

529 *"that artful designing"*: Ibid., 28.

529 *"I have only one favor"*: Ibid., 34.

529 *"I pitied her"*: JA to AA, Oct. 12, 1799, AP, MHS.

529 *"I renounce him"*: JA to AA, Oct. 12, 1799, AP, MHS.

530 *"Any calamity"*: Stewart Mitchell, *New Letters of Abigail Adams*, 211.

530 *"loaded with sorrow"*: JA to AA, Oct. 12, 1799, AP, MHS.

531 *"His eloquence and vehemence"*: *Works*, IX, 255.

531 *"The President has resolved"*: Syrett, ed., *Papers of Alexander Hamilton*, XXIII, 545.

532 *"It has been received"*: Stewart Mitchell, *New Letters of Abigail Adams*, 220.

532 *"brightest, best and most peaceful"*: Ibid., 218.

532 *"I have heard of"*: Ibid., 215.

534 *"Wise and judicious"*: Ibid., 229.

534 *"I congratulate you"*: JA to Cotton Tufts, Jan. 1, 1800, AP, MHS.

535 *"Electioneering"*: Stewart Mitchell, *New Letters of Abigail Adams*, 217.

537 *"in his private life"*: Walt Brown, *John Adams and the American Press*, 126.

537 *"Such papers cannot"*: Malone, *Jefferson and the Ordeal of Liberty*, 470.

538 *"hate each other"*: *Aurora*, March 6, 1800.

538 *"I know it"*: Syrett, ed., *Papers of Alexander Hamilton*, XXIV, 555.

538 *"You cannot, sir"*: Ibid., 564.

539 *"copies of extracts"*: Ibid., XXIV, 487.

540 *"The issue of this investigation"*: *Works*, I, 572.

541 *"as luxuriant"*: Stewart Mitchell, *New Letters of Abigail Adams*, 250.

542 *nearly eighty years*: Waring, *Report of the Social Statistics of Cities*, 27.

542 *"I like the seat"*: JA to AA, June 13, 1800, AP, MHS.

543 *"Oh! That I could"*: JA to AA, June 13, 1800, AP, MHS.

544 *"most detestable"*: Brodie, *Thomas Jefferson*, 325.

544 *"I do declare"*: JA to William Tudor, Dec. 13, 1800, AP, #399, MHS.

544 *"menaces"*: *Aurora*, March 29, 1800.

545 *"My countrymen!"*: Ibid.

546 *"without being attended"*: AA to Thomas Adams, Aug. 15, 1800, AP, MHS.

546 *Bred in the old school*: *Washington Federalist*, Oct. 7, 1800.

547 *"I cannot account"*: Cullen, ed., *Papers of John Marshall*, IV, 240.

547 *... the government*: Ibid., 256.

548 *"The whole man"*: AA to JA, Sept. 1, 1800, AP, MHS.

548 *"But all is lost"*: AA to William Smith, Sept. 6, 1800, AP, MHS.

549 *"I am glad you are"*: Thomas Adams to AA, Oct. 19, 1800, AP, MHS.

549 A Letter from Alexander Hamilton: See Syrett, ed., *Papers of Alexander Hamilton*, XXV, 169–234.

553 *"But woods are all"*: AA to Abigail Adams Smith, Nov. 21, 1800, AP, MHS.

553 *"very dirtiest hole"*: Stewart Mitchell, *New Letters of Abigail Adams*, 257.

553 *"Two of our hardy"*: AA to Cotton Tufts, Nov. 28, 1800, AP, MHS.

553 *"The lower class of whites"*: Ibid.

555 *His constitution*: Stewart Mitchell, *New Letters of Abigail Adams*, 261.

555 *"[I] would to God"*: AA to Sarah Smith Adams, Dec. 8, 1800, AP, MHS.

555 *"My little bark"*: JA to Thomas Adams, Dec. 17, 1800, AP, MHS.

556 *"For myself and family"*: AA to Thomas Adams, Dec. 13, 1800, AP, MHS.

556 *"I lose my sleep"*: AA to Cotton Tufts, Jan. 15, 1801, AP, MHS.

557 *"How mighty"*: *Works*, IX, 577.

558 *"carried his eggs"*: JA to William Tudor, Dec. 13, 1800, AP, #399, MHS.

558 *undated account*: Notes of Conversation Between AA and Thomas Jefferson, January, 1801. Note handwritten comment: "This conversation must have taken place in last days of January, 1801. CSA," AP, #400, MHS.

559 *"made me a visit"*: AA to Thomas Adams, Feb. 3, 1801, AP, MHS.

559 *"heavy heart"*: AA to JQA, Jan. 29, 1801, AP, MHS.

559 *"The President"*: AA to JQA, Jan. 29, 1801, AP, MHS.

559 *"farmer John of Stoneyfield"*: JA to William Tudor, Jan, 20, 1801, AP, #400, MHS.

559 *"The fire for some time"*: *Washington Federalist*, Jan. 21, 1801.

560 *"Who shall I nominate now?"*: J. E. Smith, *John Marshall*, 14.

561 *"The crisis is momentous"*: *Washington Federalist*, Feb. 12, 1801.

561 *"When the election"*: Ford, ed., *Writings of Thomas Jefferson*, IX, 297.

562 *"The Revolution of 1776"*: *Aurora*, Feb. 20, 1801.

564 *"Sensible, moderate men"*: *Massachusetts Spy*, March 18, 1801.

565 *"Duke of Braintree"*: *Aurora*, March 11, 1801.

566 *The new navy*: Hagan, *This People's Navy*, 39, 43.

567 *"I desire no other"*: R. A. Brown, *Presidency of John Adams*, 174.

11. Rejoice Ever More

Page

568 *"The only question"*: JA to Cotton Tufts, Dec. 26, 1800, AP, MHS.

568 *"a life of journeys"*: JA to Colonel Joseph Ward, Feb. 4, 1801, AP, #120, MHS.

568 *"The day is far spent"*: MHS, *Warren-Adams Letters*, II, 344.

568 *"No more elective office"*: AA to JA, Jan. 25, 1801, AP, MHS.

570 *"so old fashioned"*: *Works*, IX, 582.

570 *Massachusetts legislature*: *Works*, I, 601.

570 *been a shoemaker*: JA to Thomas Adams, Sept. 9, 1801, AP, MHS.

570 *"this cheerful mortal"*: JA to Francis van der Kemp, Feb. 23, 1815, AP, MHS.

571 *"I have commenced"*: AA to William Smith, May 3, 1801, AP, MHS.

571 *"from the window"*: AA to Catherine Johnson, May 8, 1801, AP, MHS.

571 *"Your father"*: AA to Thomas Adams, June 12, 1801, AP, MHS.

571 *"Men are weak"*: JA to William Cranch, May 23, 1801, AP, MHS.

571 *"how much wall"*: JA to Thomas Adams, June 29, 1801, AP, MHS.

571 *"Everything I read"*: JA to Thomas Adams, July 11, 1801, AP, MHS.

571 *"very strong things"*: Ibid.

572 *The only misfortune*: Ibid.

572 *"I pray God"*: AA to Thomas Adams, July 5, 1801, AP, MHS.

572 *"I am sure your brother"*: AA to Thomas Adams, July 12, 1801, AP, MHS.

572 *"a profession he never loved"*: AA to Thomas Adams, July 5, 1801, AP, MHS.

573 *"Her health"*: JQA to JA, Sept. 4, 1801, AP, MHS.

573 *I hope you will consider*: JA to JQA, Sept. 12, 1801, AP, MHS.

573 *"sort of fatherly look"*: Thomas Adams to AA, Sept. 20, 1801, AP, MHS.

573 *"He has no propensity"*: Ibid.

574 *"very ill"*: JQA to Louisa Catherine Adams, Sept. 23, 1801, AP, MHS.

574 *Quincy!*: "Adventures of a Nobody," AP, #269, MHS.

575 *"Her frame is so slender"*: AA to Thomas Adams, Dec. 27, 1801, AP, MHS.

575 *"weight of worry"*: Ibid.

575 *"I am your man"*: Thomas Adams to JQA, Dec. 7, 1801, AP, MHS.

576 *Bird, Savage*: AA to Thomas Adams, April 26, 1803, AP, MHS.

576 *selling his house*: AA to Thomas Adams, May 8, 1803, AP, MHS.

577 *release from jail*: Malone, *Jefferson the President*, 35.

577 *"cherished and warmed"*: Cappon, ed., *Adams-Jefferson Letters*, 271.

577 *Sally Hemings:* See Malone, *Jefferson the President*, 206–23; Lewis and Onuf, eds., *Sally Hemings and Thomas Jefferson;* Gordon-Reed, *Thomas Jefferson and Sally Hemings.*

578 *Meriwether Lewis:* Malone, *Jefferson the President*, 210.

578 *Federalist press:* See *New York Evening Post*, Sept. 2, 7, 10, 13, 1802; *Boston Gazette*, Sept. 16, 1802; *Gazette of the United States*, Sept. 22, 1802; *Columbian Centinel*, Oct. 9, 1802.

579 *"decidedly good looking"*: Dabney, *The Jefferson Scandals*, 23.

579 *"very handsome"*: Ibid.

580 *Jefferson paternity of Hemings children:* The results of a DNA study released in November 1998, together with other available evidence, indicate a high probability that Jefferson was the father of at least one of Sally Hemings's children, Easton Hemings, and was most likely the father of all her children. See Eugene A. Foster, et al., "Jefferson Fathered Slave's Last Child," *Nature*, November 5, 1998; also, "Report on Thomas Jefferson and Sally Hemings," Thomas Jefferson Memorial Foundation, January 2000.

580 *"I believe nothing"*: JA to Colonel Joseph Ward, Jan. 8, 1810, AP, #118, MHS.

581 *"I give him up"*: Ibid.

581 *Callender and Sally:* Ibid.

581 *"a little corner of my heart"*: AA to Thomas Adams, May 23, 1802, AP, MHS.

581 *Mary Jefferson Eppes:* Cappon, ed., *Adams-Jefferson Letters*, 268.

582 *The friendship with which you honored:* Ibid., 270.

583 *"And now, sir"*: Ibid., 273.

583 *Until I read Callender's:* Ibid.

584 *"My charities"*: Ibid., 274.

584 *John Quincy was suddenly replaced:* Ibid., 277.

584 *"I conclude with sincere prayers"*: Ibid., 280.

585 *"It is a delicate"*: JA to Thomas Adams, April 2, 1803, AP, MHS.

585 *"blue devils"*: Thomas Adams to JQA, Dec. 15, 1803, AP, MHS.

586 *"This is now in general"*: JQA to JA, Jan. 31, 1804, AP, MHS.

587 *"arch enemy"*: *DJA*, III, 434.

587 *"Hitherto my conduct"*: JQA to AA, Dec. 22, 1803, AP, MHS.

587 *Patience and perseverance:* JA to JQA, Nov. 9, 1804, AP, MHS.

588 *Is the present state:* Old Family Letters, 62.

589 *You and your excellent:* Butterfield, ed., *Letters of Benjamin Rush*, II, 890.

589 *"My friend!"*: Old Family Letters, 185.

589 *[Samuel] Johnson:* Ibid., 99.

589 *"To rummage trunks"*: Ibid., 106.

590 *What must he say:* Ibid.

590 *There have been very many times:* Ibid.

590 *"There is something in my composition"*: Ibid., 69.

590 *"Our obligations"*: Ibid., 182.

590 *"The internal intrigues"*: Ibid.

590 *I call for my leavers:* Ibid., 64.

590 *"with very little animal food"*: Ibid., 341.

591 *It is an idea:* Ibid., 111.

591 *"an immense load"*: Ibid., 137.

591 *"This phrase 'rejoice' "*: Ibid.

591 *"We stand well"*: Ibid., 103.

591 *"No civilized society"*: Ibid., 63.

591 *"If worthless men"*: Ibid., 108.

592 *"a jewel of a man"*: Ibid., 294.

592 *"one of the best men"*: Ibid., 276.

592 *"I am not subject"*: Ibid., 235.

592 *"I think aloud"*: Butterfield, ed., *Letters of Benjamin Rush*, II, 903.

592 *"I live like a stranger"*: Ibid., 891.

593 *Mr. Madison and his lady:* Ibid., 903.

593 *"a superabundance"*: *Old Family Letters*, 118.

593 *"intriguer"*: Ibid., 163.

594 *"Jefferson has succeeded"*: Ibid.

594 *"Mr. Adams's passions"*: Warren, *History*, II, 675.

595 *"I wish them not"*: *Old Family Letters*, 226.

596 *Josiah Quincy:* Quincy, *Figures of the Past*, 61–62.

598 *"If ever a nation"*: *Old Family Letters*, 175.

599 *"The period is not yet arrived"*: AA to JQA, Feb. 1809, AP, #407, MHS.

599 *"As to my son"*: *Old Family Letters*, 225.

599 *tore him to pieces:* Ibid., 237.

601 *"My days glide smoothly away"*: JA to JQA, Jan. 15, 1811, AP, #411, MHS.

601 *"I am well"*: *Old Family Letters*, 285.

601 *"It would divert"*: Ibid., 285.

601 *"the most afflictive"*: Ibid., 288.

601 *confined her under:* Ibid., 289.

601 *dark to view a comet:* AA to JQA, Sept. 24, 1811, AP, #412, MHS.

601 *"Neither the morals"*: AA to JQA, Dec. 8, 1811, AP, #412, MHS.

602 *"communicate it gradually"*: Butterfield, ed., *Letters of Benjamin Rush*, II, 1104.

602 *"the knife"*: Ibid.

602 *"From her account"*: Ibid.

602 *brothers named Coles:* Cappon, ed., *Adams-Jefferson Letters*, 284.

602 *"I always loved Jefferson"*: Ibid.

603 *"I only needed this knowledge"*: Butterfield, ed., *Letters of Benjamin Rush*, II, 1110.

603 *"And now, my dear friend"*: Ibid.

603 *"A letter from you calls up"*: Cappon, ed., *Adams-Jefferson Letters*, 291.

603 *Laboring always at the same oar:* Ibid., 291.

604 *"I have given up newspapers"*: Ibid.

604 *"What an exchange"*: Ibid., 294.

604 *"a hideous tempest"*: Ibid.

604 *"I walk every fair day"*: Ibid., 199.

604 *"Your dream is out"*: *Old Family Letters*, 453.

604 *I rejoice in the correspondence:* Butterfield, ed., *Letters of Benjamin Rush*, II, 1127.

605 *"Who shall write"*: Cappon, ed., *Adams-Jefferson Letters*, 451.

605 *"Nobody, except perhaps"*: Ibid., 452.

606 *"not writing psalms"*: John Pierce Memoirs, MHS.

606 *"Without this our Union"*: Cappon, *Adams-Jefferson Letters*, 311.

606 *"I sincerely congratulate"*: Ibid., 324.

606 *"Never mind"*: Ibid., 357.

606 *"Montezillo"*: JA to Francis Van der Kemp, Sept. 23, 1814, AP, #122, MHS.

607 *"Whether you or I"*: Ibid., 301.

607 *"Checks and balances"*: Ibid., 334.

607 *"lashing and speering"*: Ibid., 358.

607 *"fast asleep"*: Ibid., 347.

607 *"You and I have passed"*: Ibid., 358.

607 *"You and I ought"*: Ibid.

607 *"The* summum bonum*"*: Ibid., 335.

607 *My mind:* Ibid., 337.

608 *"Your letter touches"*: JA to John Adams (grandson), Feb. 2, 1812, AP, #413, MHS.

609 *"War necessarily"*: *Old Family Letters*, 224.

609 *"I have been called"*: JA to JQA, April 7, 1812, AP, #413, MHS.

609 *The subjects of them:* Butterfield, ed., *Letters of Benjamin Rush*, 1164.

609 *"But time I hope"*: Ibid.

609 *"You apprehend 'attacks' "*: *Old Family Letters*, 317.

610 *Examining the animal:* Ibid., 322.

610 *Tread gently:* Butterfield, ed., *Letters of Benjamin Rush*, II, 1171.

611 *"away like the morning cloud"*: *Old Family Letters*, 332.

611 *"withered, faded"*: Ibid., 333.

611 *"inscrutable and incomprehensible"*: JA to JQA, March 11, 1813, AP, #415, MHS.

611 *They fill the air:* JA to JQA, March 13, 1813, AP, #415, MHS.

612 *"the invader himself"*: JQA to JA, Aug. 10, 1813, AP, #416, MHS.

612 *"I mourned over the fallen"*: Ibid.

612 *"Another of our friends"*: Cappon, ed., *Adams-Jefferson Letters*, 323.

612 *"I know of no character"*: Ibid., 328.

612 *I damn nobody:* JA to Francis Van der Kemp, May 28, 1813, AP, #95, MHS.

613 *Samuel Tucker:* JA to Matthew Carey, June 1, 1813, AP, #95, MHS.

613 *"rejoice ever more"*: *Old Family Letters*, 137.

613 *"Rejoice always"*: JA to JQA, June 18, 1813, AP, #95, MHS.

613 *"My dear, my only daughter"*: JA to Francis Van der Kemp, Aug. 9, 1813, AP, #95, MHS.

613 *"She told her physician"*: AA to JQA, Aug. 30, 1813, AP, MHS.

614   *"The loss is irreparable"*: AA to JQA, Sept. 13, 1813, AP, #416, MHS.

614   *"Syllabus"*: Cappon, ed., *Adams-Jefferson Letters*, 369.

614   *"The love of God"*: Ibid., 374.

12. Journey's End

615   *"I assure you"*: JA to JQA, March 18, 1815, AP, #422, MHS.

617   *"We must learn to know"*: JA to Richard Rush, May 30, 1814, AP, #122, MHS.

617   *"very anxious"*: AA to JQA, May 30, 1815, AP, #423, MHS.

617   *"I seem to be rambling"*: JA to JQA, May 14, 1815, AP, #423, MHS.

617   *"be no better"*: JA to George Adams and John Adams, Jr., May 3, 1815, AP, MHS.

617   *"and your lady, too"*: Ibid.

617   *"dear boys"*: AA to JQA, April 11, 1815, AP, #423, MHS.

617   *"Death is sweeping"*: JA to JQA, June 10, 1816, AP, #432, MHS.

618   *"Winter in this country"*: JA to JQA, Feb. 22, 1816, AP, #429, MHS.

618   *Abigail prepared her will*: Will of Abigail Adams, Jan. 18, 1816, AP, #429, MHS.

618   *Colonel Smith*: AA to JQA, June 10, 1816, AP, #432, MHS.

618   *"here a pivot"*: Cappon, ed., *Adams-Jefferson Letters*, 43.

618   *"I steer my bark"*: Ibid., 467.

618   *"But why am I dosing"*: Ibid., 434.

618   *$23,950 was agreed to*: Malone, *The Sage of Monticello*, 176.

618   *"I envy you"*: Cappon, ed., *Adams-Jefferson Letters*, 440.

618   *He could "not live without books"*: Ibid., 443.

618   *"overwhelm me with books"*: Ibid., 515.

619   *"What would I give"*: Ibid., 429.

619   "There is no doubt": Haraszti, *John Adams and the Prophets of Progress*, 94.

619   *"The clock would be simple"*: Ibid., 214.

619   *"Fool! Fool!"*: Ibid., 263.

620   *"Your father's zeal"*: AA to JQA, March 22, 1816, AP, #430, MHS.

620   *"The voice of the nation"*: AA to JQA, March 12, 1817, AP, #436, MHS.

620   *"Yesterday was one of the most uniformly"*: JA to JQA, Aug. 10, 1817, AP, #438, MHS.

621   *"Oh, Grandmother"*: AA to Harriet Welsh, Aug. 18, 1817, AP, #438, MHS.

621   *"rather in awe"*: Eliza Susan Quincy Journal, MHS.

622   *"I never saw your father"*: Benjamin Waterhouse to JQA, Jan. 12, 1818, AP, #442, MHS.

622   *"very cold and the snow falling"*: AA to Louisa Catherine Adams, Jan. 24, 1818, AP, #442, MHS.

622   *"looking up newly"*: AA to Louisa Catherine Adams, May 20, 1818, AP, #443, MHS.

622   *"The dear partner"*: Cappon, ed., *Adams-Jefferson Letters*, 529.

622   *"She has recovered"*: Benjamin Waterhouse to JQA, Oct. 21, 1818, AP, #444, MHS.

622 *"Your mother was pronounced"*: Note of Harriet Welsh, Oct. 23, 1818, AP, #444, MHS.

623 *"He came down"*: Harriet Welsh to Louisa C. A. DeWint, ca. Nov. 1818, AP, #445, MHS.

623 *"I cannot bear"*: Ibid.

623 *"seemingly conscious"*: Thomas Adams to JQA, Nov. 1, 1818, AP, #445, MHS.

623 *"with great composure"*: Ibid.

623 *"the tenderest and most affectionate"*: JQA to JA, Nov. 2, 1818, AP, #445, MHS.

624 *"My ever dear"*: JA to JQA, Nov. 10, 1818, AP, #445, MHS.

624 *"The tidings of her illness"*: Funeral Sermon for AA, Nov. 1, 1818, AP, #445, MHS.

624 *Possessing at every period of life:* Whitney, *Sermon*, 16.

625 *"God bless you"*: Cappon, ed., *Adams-Jefferson Letters*, 529.

625 *"While you live"*: Ibid., 530.

626 *to view Trumbull's painting:* JA to JQA, Dec. 7, 1818, AP, #445, MHS.

626 *"Colonel Trumbull came"*: Eliza Susan Quincy Journal, Dec. 5, 1818, MHS.

627 *"Truth, nature"*: JA to John Trumbull, March 13, 1817, AP, #123, MHS.

627 *"When I nominated"*: Elza Susan Quincy, Dec. 5, 1818, MHS.

627 *"caught the pip"*: JA to JQA, Dec. 7, 1818, AP, #445, MHS.

627 *"It was not merely"*: JQA to JA, Dec. 14, 1818, AP, #445, MHS.

628 *"All is now still"*: Cappon, ed., *Adams-Jefferson Letters*, 531.

628 *"You, my dear sir"*: Louisa Catherine Adams to JA, April 16, 1819, AP, #447, MHS.

629 *"I have the most"*: JA to Ward Nicholas Boylston, Sept. 2, 1820, AP, #124, MHS.

629 *"We go on"*: JA to Louisa Catherine Adams, Jan. 1, 1820, AP, #449, MHS.

629 *"The Psalms of David"*: Cappon, ed., *Adams-Jefferson Letters*, 394.

630 *A rain had fallen:* JA to Mr. DeWint, March 3, 1820, AP, #124, MHS.

631 *"The town of Quincy"*: JA to Louisa Catherine Adams, Oct. 21, 1820, AP, #450, MHS.

631 *"You have not extended"*: JA to Mordecai Noah, July 31, 1818, AP, #123, MHS.

631 *"health and spirits"*: Cappon, ed., *Adams-Jefferson Letters*, 569.

631 *"I boggled"*: Ibid., 571.

632 *"Visited the President"*: Quincy, *Figures of the Past*, 69.

632 *I do not believe:* Ibid., 80.

632 *"I know it is high treason"*: Cappon, ed., *Adams-Jefferson Letters*, 551.

633 *"at last the whites"*: JA to Louisa Catherine Adams, Jan. 13, 1820, AP, #449, MHS.

633 *black cloud:* Cappon, ed., *Adams-Jefferson Letters*, 571.

633 *"armies of Negroes"*: Ibid.

633 *I have been so terrified:* Ibid.

633 *"This enterprise"*: Peterson, *Thomas Jefferson and the New Nation*, 999.

633 *"become a Hercules"*: Ibid.

633 *"all whites south of the Potomac"*: Malone, *Sage of Monticello*, 340.

634 *military academy:* Ibid., 573-74.

634 *"noble employment"*: Ibid., 607.

634 *"one of the most unpleasant"*: Donald and Donald, eds., *Diary of Charles Francis Adams*, I, 64.

635 *"They had eyes"*: JA to Louisa Catherine Adams, June 3, 1821, AP, #452, MHS.

635 *"President Adams seemed"*: Eliza Susan Quincy Journal, MHS.

635 *"No man has more cause"*: JA to Louisa Catherine Adams, June 3, 1821, AP, #452, MHS.

636 *"In the evening"*: Quincy, *Figures of the Past*, 73.

636 *"You have a fine capacity"*: JA to Charles Francis Adams, Dec. 19, 1825, AP, #473, MHS.

636 *"did no more than all the rest"*: JA to Louisa Catherine Adams, May 10, 1823, AP, #460, MHS.

637 *"It would be strange indeed"*: Cappon, ed., *Adams-Jefferson Letters*, 601.

637 *"not the Lafayette I knew"*: Quincy, *Life of Josiah Quincy*, 406–7.

638 *His sight is so dim:* Nevins, ed., *Diary of John Quincy Adams*, 329.

638 *"I let them do what they please"*: Cappon. ed., *Adams-Jefferson Letters*, 526.

638 *"He was married"*: George Washington Adams to Louisa Catherine Adams, Nov. 20, 1824, AP, #466, MHS.

639 *He . . . was considerably:* Quincy, *Figures of the Past*, 74.

639 *"It must excite"*: Cappon, ed., *Adams-Jefferson Letters*, 609.

639 *So deeply are the principles:* Ibid.

640 *"Every line from you"*: Ibid.

640 *"But physicians do not"*: Benjamin Waterhouse to JQA, July 4, 1825, AP, #471, MHS.

640 *Ralph Waldo Emerson: Adamses at Home*, 29–32.

641 *Anne Royall:* Ibid., 32–34.

642 *"He did not tear my face"*: JA to Charles Francis Adams, Dec. 3, 1825, AP, #473, MHS.

642 *"She entertained me"*: Cappon, ed., *Adams-Jefferson Letters*, 611.

642 *"In this I could not"*: Ibid.

643 *"To the eyes of a physician"*: Benjamin Waterhouse to JQA, May 12, 1826, AP, #475, MHS.

644 *Like other young people:* Cappon, ed., *Adams-Jefferson Letters*, 614.

644 *"Theirs are the halcyon"*: Ibid.

644 *May it be to the world:* Lipscomb, ed., *Writings of Thomas Jefferson*, XVI, 181–82.

645 *"The old man fails fast"*: "The Diary of George Whitney," AP, #475, MHS.

645 *"I will give you"*: Ibid.

645 *"When I parted from him"*: John Marston to JQA, July 8, 1826, AP, #476, MHS.

646 *"the old gentleman"*: "The Diary of George Whitney," AP, #475, MHS.

646 *"This is the Fourth"*: Randolph, *The Domestic Life of Thomas Jefferson*, 428.

646 *"The artillery of Heaven"*: John Marston to JQA, July 8, 1826, AP, #476, MHS.

646 *"Thomas Jefferson survives"*: Susan Boylston Adams Clark to Abigail Louisa Smith Adams Johnson, July 9, 1826, A. B. Johnson Papers, MHS.

646 *"Help me, child!"*: Ibid.

647 *"bursting forth"*: John Marston to JQA, July 8, 1826, AP, #476, MHS.

647 *4,000 people:* Josiah Quincy to JQA, July 8, 1826, AP, #476, MHS.

647 *held at public expense:* Ibid.

647 *"conducted in a more solemn"*: Ibid.

647 *"visible and palpable"*: Nevins, ed., *Diary of John Quincy Adams*, 360.

648 *"expanded greatness"*: *Selection of Eulogies*, 156.

648 Webster speech: Ibid.

651 *"Griefs upon griefs!"*: JA to Francis Van der Kemp, Aug. 14, 1816, AP, #122, MHS.

ILLUSTRATION CREDITS

Numbers in roman type refer to illustration numbers in the inserts; numbers in *italics* refer to book pages.

The illustrations appear courtesy of the following sources:

Adams National Historic Park: 25, 33, 38, 60.

American Antiquarian Society: 21.

American Philosophical Society: 59.

Boston Athenaeum: 28, 55, 62.

Boston Public Library: 2, 15.

Culver Pictures: 22, 44, 54.

Free Library of Philadelphia: 52.

Harvard University: 3, 23, 34, 61.

Historical Society of Pennsylvania: 9, 45.

Independence National Historic Park: 40.

Library of Congress: 1, 39, 41, 42, 47, 48, 49, 50, 51.

Maryland Historical Society: 43.

Massachusetts Historical Society: front endpaper; *15; 165;* back endpaper; 4, 5, 7, 8, 10, 11, 12, 14, 16, 17, 19, 20, 24, 26, 27, 31, 32, 56.

Metropolitan Museum of Art: *4,* 46.

Museum of Fine Arts: 30.

National Archives: 13, 53.

National Gallery of Art: 35, 36.

National Portrait Gallery: 29, 37.

New York Public Library: 6.

University of Virginia: 58.

White House Collection, copyright White House Historical Association: *387;* 57.

Henry Francis Du Pont Winterthur Museum: 18.

Bibliography

MANUSCRIPT COLLECTIONS

Abigail Adams Papers, American Antiquarian Society
Abigail Adams Papers, Carl Roach Library, Cornell University
Abigail Adams Papers, Massachusetts Historical Society
John Adams Papers, Massachusetts Historical Society
John Quincy Adams Papers, Massachusetts Historical Society
Ellen Randolph Coolidge Papers, University of Virginia, Alderman Library, Special
    Collections
Cranch Family Papers, Library of Congress
William Cushing Collection, Massachusetts Historical Society
Francis Dana Papers, Massachusetts Historical Society
Papers of Elbridge Gerry, Library of Congress
Lafayette Papers, Library of Congress
Robert Treat Paine Papers, Massachusetts Historical Society
Timothy Pickering Papers, Massachusetts Historical Society
Shaw Family Papers, Library of Congress
Margaret Bayard Smith Papers, Library of Congress
Ezra Stiles Papers, Yale University
Samuel Tucker Papers, Harvard University
John Winthrop Papers, Harvard University
Levi Woodbury Papers, Massachusetts Historical Society

BOOKS

Adams, Charles Francis, ed., *Familiar Letters of John Adams and His Wife Abigail Adams During the Revolution*. New York: Hurd & Houghton, 1876.

———. *Letters of Mrs. Adams*. Vols. I–II. Boston: Little, Brown, 1840.

———. *The Works of John Adams*. Vols. I–X. Boston: Little, Brown, 1856.

Adams, Charles Francis, Jr. "Quincy," 1884.

Adams, Henry. *History of the United States of America During the Administration of Thomas Jefferson*. New York: Library of America, 1986.

Adams, James Truslow. *The Adams Family*. Boston: Little, Brown, 1930.

———. *New England in the Republic, 1776–1850*. Boston: Little, Brown, 1926.

———. *Revolutionary New England, 1691–1776*. Boston: Atlantic Monthly Press, 1923.

Adams, John. *Correspondence of the Late President Adams, Originally Published in the Boston Patriot in a Series of Letters*. Boston: Everett & Munroe, 1809.

Adams, William Howard. *The Eye of Thomas Jefferson*. Washington, D.C.: National Gallery of Art, 1976.

———. *Jefferson and the Arts: An Extended View*. Washington, D.C.: National Gallery of Art, 1976.

———. *Jefferson's Monticello*. New York: Abbeville Press, 1983.

———. *The Paris Years of Thomas Jefferson*. New Haven, Conn.: Yale University Press, 1997.

The Adamses at Home: Accounts by Visitors to the Old House in Quincy, 1788–1886. Portland, Maine: Anthoensen Press, 1970.

Akers, Charles W. *Abigail Adams: An American Woman*. Boston: Little, Brown, 1980.

———. *The Divine Politician: Samuel Cooper and the American Revolution in Boston*. Boston: Northeastern University Press, 1982.

Alberts, Robert C. *Benjamin West: A Biography*. Boston: Houghton Mifflin, 1978.

Albion, Robert Greenlaugh, and Jennie Barnes Pope. *Sea Lanes in Wartime: The American Experience, 1775–1942*. New York: Norton, 1942.

Alden, John R. *A History of the American Revolution*. New York: Knopf, 1969.

Allen, David Grayson, ed. *The Diary of John Quincy Adams*. Vols. I–II. Cambridge, Mass.: Belknap Press of Harvard University Press, 1981.

Allen, Gardner W. *Our Naval War with France*. Hamden, Conn.: Archon Books, 1967.

———. *Our Navy and the Barbary Corsairs*. Hamden, Conn.: Archon Books, 1965.

Allison, John Murray. *Adams and Jefferson: The Story of a Friendship*. Norman: University of Oklahoma Press, 1966.

Alsop, Susan Mary. *Yankees at the Court: The First Americans in Paris*. Garden City, N.Y.: Doubleday, 1982.

Ammon, Harry. *The Genet Mission*. New York: Norton, 1973.

———. *James Monroe: The Quest for National Identity*. Charlottesville: University Press of Virginia, 1990.

Andrist, Ralph K., ed. *George Washington: A Biography in His Own Words*. The Founding Fathers. New York: Newsweek/Harper & Row, 1972.

Austin, James T. *The Life of Elbridge Gerry*. Vols. I–II. New York: Da Capo Press, 1970.

Bailyn, Bernard. *Faces of Revolution: Personalities and Themes in the Struggle for American Independence*. New York: Knopf, 1990.

———. *The Ideological Origins of the American Revolution*. Cambridge, Mass.: Belknap Press of Harvard University Press, 1967.

———. *The Ordeal of Thomas Hutchinson*. Cambridge, Mass.: Belknap Press of Harvard University Press, 1974.

———. *The People of British North America*. New York: Vintage, 1986.

Bakeless, John, and Katherine Bakeless. *Signers of the Declaration of Independence*. Boston: Houghton Mifflin, 1969.

Ballagh, James Curtin, ed. *The Letters of Richard Henry Lee*. Vols. I–II. New York: Da Capo Press, 1970.

Bate, W. J. ed., *Samuel Johnson: Essays from the Rambler, Adventurer, and Idler*. New Haven, Conn.: Yale University Press, 1968.

Bear, James A., Jr. *Jefferson at Monticello*. Charlottesville: University Press of Virginia, 1985.

Bear, James A., Jr., and Lucia C. Stanton, eds. *Jefferson's Memorandum Books: Accounts, with Legal Records and Miscellany, 1767–1826*. The Papers of Thomas Jefferson. 2nd Series. Princeton, N.J.: Princeton University Press, 1997.

Becker, Carl L. *The Declaration of Independence: A Study in the History of Political Ideas*. New York: Vintage, 1970.

Bedini, Silvio A. *Declaration of Independence Desk*. Washington, D.C.: Smithsonian Institution Press, 1981.

———. *Thomas Jefferson: Statesman of Science*. New York: Macmillan, 1990.

Bemis, Samuel Flagg. *John Quincy Adams and the Foundations of American Foreign Policy*. New York: Knopf, 1949.

Berkin, Carol. *Jonathan Sewall: Odyssey of an American Loyalist*. New York: Columbia University Press, 1974.

Bernard, J. F. *Talleyrand: A Biography*. New York: Putnam, 1973.

Bernhard, Winfred E. A. *Fisher Ames: Federalist and Statesman, 1758–1808*. Chapel Hill: University of North Carolina Press, 1965.

Bernier, Olivier. *Lafayette: Hero of Two Worlds*. New York: Dutton, 1983.

Betts, Edwin M., ed. *Thomas Jefferson's Farm Book*. Princeton, N.J.: American Philosophical Society/Princeton University Press, 1953.

———. *Thomas Jefferson's Garden Book, 1766–1824*. Philadelphia: American Philosophical Society, 1944.

Betts, Edwin M., and James Adam Bear, Jr., eds. *The Family Letters of Thomas Jefferson*. Charlottesville: University Press of Virginia, 1986.

Billias, George Athan. *Elbridge Gerry: Founding Father and Republican Statesman*. New York: McGraw-Hill, 1976.

———. *General John Glover and His Marblehead Mariners.* New York: Holt, 1960.

Blake, John B. *Public Health in the Town of Boston, 1630–1822.* Cambridge, Mass.: Harvard University Press, 1959.

Bobrick, Benson. *Angel in the Whirlwind: The Triumph of the American Revolution.* New York: Simon & Schuster, 1997.

Boorstin, Daniel J. *The Americans: The Colonial Experience.* New York: Random House, 1993.

———. *The Lost World of Thomas Jefferson.* Chicago: University of Chicago Press, 1948.

Bowen, Catherine Drinker. *John Adams and the American Revolution.* Boston: Little, Brown, 1950.

———. *Miracle at Philadelphia.* Boston: Little, Brown, 1966.

Boxer, C. R. *The Dutch Seaborne Empire, 1600–1800.* London: Penguin, 1965.

Boyd, Julian, ed. *The Papers of Thomas Jefferson.* Vols. I–XX. Princeton, N.J.: Princeton University Press, 1950.

Bridenbaugh, Carl. *Cities in Revolt: Urban Life in America, 1743–1776.* New York: Knopf, 1955.

Brissot de Warville, J. P. *New Travels in the United States of America, 1788.* Cambridge, Mass.: Belknap Press of Harvard University Press, 1964.

Brodie, Fawn M. *Thomas Jefferson: An Intimate History.* New York: Norton, 1974.

Brogan, D. W., ed. *The Education of Henry Adams: An Autobiography.* Boston: Houghton Mifflin, 1961.

Brooke, John. *King George III.* London: Constable, 1972.

Brookhiser, Richard. *Alexander Hamilton.* New York: Free Press, 1999.

———. *Founding Father.* New York: Free Press, 1996.

Brown, Everett Somerville. *William Plumer's Memorandum of Proceedings in the United States Senate, 1803–1807.* London: Macmillan, 1923.

Brown, Ralph Adams. *The Presidency of John Adams.* Lawrence: University Press of Kansas, 1975.

Brown, Richard D. *Knowledge Is Power: The Diffusion of Information in Early America, 1700–1865.* New York: Oxford University Press, 1989.

———. *Revolutionary Politics in Massachusetts: The Boston Committee of Correspondence and The Towns, 1772–1774.* Cambridge, Mass.: Harvard University Press, 1970.

———. *The Strength of a People: The Idea of an Informed Citizenry in America, 1650–1870.* Chapel Hill: University of North Carolina Press, 1996.

Brown, Walt. *John Adams and the American Press.* Jefferson, N.C.: McFarland & Co., 1995.

Brugger, Robert J., ed. *The Papers of James Madison: Secretary of State Series.* Vol. I. Charlottesville: University Press of Virginia, 1986.

Burke, Edmund. *Reflections on the Revolution in France.* London: Penguin, 1986.

Burstein, Andrew. *The Inner Jefferson: Portrait of a Grieving Optimist.* Charlottesville: University Press of Virginia, 1995.

Burt, Struthers. *Philadelphia Holy Experiment.* Garden City, N.Y.: Doubleday, 1945.

Bush, Alfred L. *The Life Portraits of Thomas Jefferson*. Charlottesville, Va.: Thomas Jefferson Memorial Foundation, 1987.

Butterfield, L. H., ed. *Adams Family Correspondence*. Vols. I–VI. The Adams Papers. Cambridge, Mass.: Harvard University Press, 1963.

———, ed. *Diary and Autobiography of John Adams*. Vols. I–IV. The Adams Papers. Cambridge, Mass.: Harvard University Press, 1961.

———, ed. *Diary of Charles Francis Adams*. The Adams Papers. Cambridge, Mass.: Harvard University Press, 1964.

———. *The Earliest Diary of John Adams*. The Adams Papers. Cambridge, Mass.: Harvard University Press, 1966.

———. *Butterfield in Holland*. Cambridge, Mass.: Harvard University Press, 1961.

———. *Letters of Benjamin Rush*. Vols. I–II. Princeton, N.J.: American Philosophical Society, 1951.

Butterfield, L. H., Marc Friedlaender and Mary Jo Kline, eds. *The Book of Abigail and John: Selected Letters of the Adams Family, 1762–1784*. Cambridge, Mass.: Harvard University Press, 1975.

Campbell, James. *Recovering Franklin*. Chicago: Open Court, 1999.

Cappon, Lester J., ed. *The Adams-Jefferson Letters*. Chapel Hill: University of North Carolina Press, 1959.

Cary, John. *Joseph Warren: Physician, Politician, Patriot*. Urbana: University of Illinois Press, 1961.

Catalogue of the John Adams Library in the Public Library of the City of Boston. Boston, Mass.: Boston Trustees, 1917.

Catanzariti, John, ed. *The Papers of Thomas Jefferson*. Vols. XXIV–XXVII. Princeton, N.J.: Princeton University Press, 1990–97.

Cervantes, Miguel. *Don Quixote*. New York: Modern Library, 1930.

Chambers, S. Allen, Jr. *Poplar Forest and Thomas Jefferson*. Poplar Forest, Va.: Corporation for Jefferson's Poplar Forest, 1993.

Chambers, William Nisbet. *Political Parties in a New Nation: The American Experience, 1776–1809*. New York: Oxford University Press, 1963.

Chastellux, Marquis de. *Travels in North America in the Years 1780, 1781, and 1782*. Vols. I and II. Howard C. Rice, Jr., ed. Chapel Hill: University of North Carolina Press, 1963.

Chinard, Gilbert. *Honest John Adams*. Boston: Little, Brown, 1933.

Chitwood, Oliver Perry. *Richard Henry Lee: Statesman of the Revolution*. Morgantown: West Virginia University Library, 1967.

Christman, Margaret C. S. *The First Federal Congress, 1789–1791*. Washington, D.C.: Smithsonian Institution Press, 1989.

Cicero. *On the Good Life*. Harmondsworth, England: Penguin Classics, 1984.

Clarfield, Gerald H. *Timothy Pickering and American Diplomacy, 1795–1800*. Columbia: University of Missouri Press, 1969.

———. *Timothy Pickering and the American Republic*. Pittsburgh: University of Pittsburgh Press, 1980.

Cohen, I. Bernard. *Science and the Founding Fathers*. New York: Norton, 1995.

Collier, Christopher. *Connecticut in the Continental Congress*. Chester, Conn.: Pequot Press, 1973.

Commager, Henry Steele. *The Empire of Reason: How Europe Imagined and America Realized the Enlightenment*. Garden City, N.Y.: Doubleday, 1977.

Commager, Henry Steele, and Richard B. Morris. *The Spirit of Seventy-Six*. Vols. I–II. Indianapolis: Bobbs-Merrill, 1958.

Constitution of the Commonwealth of Massachusetts. William Francis Galvin, Secretary of the Commonwealth of Massachusetts. February 1996.

Cook, Don. *The Long Fuse: How England Lost the American Colonies, 1760–1785*. New York: Atlantic Monthly Press, 1995.

Cooke, Jacob Ernest. *Alexander Hamilton*. New York: Scribner, 1982.

Cooper, Duff. *Talleyrand*. Stockholm: Forlag, 1946.

Corner, George W., ed. *The Autobiography of Benjamin Rush*. Westport, Conn.: Greenwood Press, 1948.

Cresswell, Nicholas. *The Journal of Nicholas Cresswell, 1774–1777*. New York: Dial Press, 1924.

Cronin, Vincent. *Napoleon Bonaparte: An Intimate Biography*. New York: Morrow, 1972.

Cruttwell, Patrick, ed. *Samuel Johnson Writings*. London: Penguin, 1968.

Cullen, Charles, ed. *The Papers of John Marshall*. Chapel Hill: University of North Carolina Press, 1984.

———. *The Papers of Thomas Jefferson*. Vols. XXI–XXIII. Princeton, N.J.: Princeton University Press, 1983.

Cunningham, Noble E., Jr. *In Pursuit of Reason: The Life of Thomas Jefferson*. Baton Rouge: Louisiana State University Press, 1987.

———. *The Jeffersonian Republicans in Power: Party Operations, 1801–1809*. Chapel Hill: University of North Carolina Press, 1963.

Cushing, Harry Alonzo, ed. *The Writings of Samuel Adams*. New York: Putnam, 1908.

Dabney, Virginius. *The Jefferson Scandals: A Rebuttal*. New York: Dodd, Mead, 1981.

Dangerfield, George. *Chancellor Robert Livingston of New York, 1746–1813*. New York: Harcourt Brace, 1960.

Davenport, Beatrix Cary, ed. *A Diary of the French Revolution, by Gouverneur Morris*. Vols. I–II. Boston: Houghton Mifflin, 1939.

Davis, Richard Beale. *Intellectual Life in Jefferson's Virginia, 1790–1830*. Chapel Hill: University of North Carolina Press, 1964.

DeConde, Alexander. *The Quasi-War*. New York: Scribner, 1966.

Donald, Aïda DiPace, and David Donald. *Diary of Charles Francis Adams*. The Adams Papers. Vols. VII–VIII. Cambridge, Mass.: Harvard University Press, 1964.

Donaldson, Thomas. *The House in Which Thomas Jefferson Wrote the Declaration of Independence*. Philadelphia: Avil Printing Co., 1898.

Dorsey, John M., ed. *The Jefferson-Dunglison Letters*. Charlottesville: University Press of Virginia, 1960.

Draper, Theodore. *A Struggle for Power*. New York: Times Books, 1996.

Dunn, Susan. *Sister Revolution: French Lightning, American Light*. New York: Faber & Faber, 1999.

Durey, Michael. *"With the Hammer of Truth": James Thomson Callender and America's Early National Heroes*. Charlottesville: University Press of Virginia, 1990.

Eberlein, Harold Donaldson, and Cortland Van Dyke Hubbard. *Diary of Independence Hall*. Philadelphia: Lippincott, 1948.

Einstein, Lewis. *Divided Loyalties: Americans in England During the War of Independence*. Boston: Houghton Mifflin, 1933.

Eisenhart, Luther P., ed. *Historic Philadelphia*. Philadelphia: American Philosophical Society, 1953.

Elkins, Stanley, and Eric McKitrick. *The Age of Federalism*. New York: Oxford University Press, 1993.

Ellis, Joseph J. *After the Revolution*. New York: Norton, 1979.

——. *American Sphinx: The Character of Thomas Jefferson*. New York: Knopf, 1997.

——. *Passionate Sage*. New York: Norton, 1993.

Fehrenbach, T. R. *Greatness to Spare*. Princeton, N.J.: Van Nostrand, 1968.

Ferling, John. *John Adams: A Bibliography*. Westport, Conn.: Greenwood Press, 1994.

——. *John Adams: A Life*. New York: Holt, 1992.

Ferris, Robert G., and Richard E. Morris. *The Signers of the Declaration of Independence*. Flagstaff, Ariz.: Interpretive Publications, 1960.

Fischer, David Hackett. *Albion's Seed*. New York: Oxford University Press, 1989.

——. *Paul Revere's Ride*. New York: Oxford University Press, 1994.

Fiske, John. *The Critical Period of American History, 1783–1789*. Boston: Houghton Mifflin, 1888.

Fitzpatrick, John C., ed. *The Writings of George Washington*. Washington, D.C.: Government Printing Office, 1940.

Fleming, Thomas. *Benjamin Franklin: A Biography in His Own Words*. The Founding Fathers. New York: Newsweek, 1972.

——. *1776: Year of Illusions*. New York: Norton, 1975.

Flexner, James Thomas. *America's Old Masters*. New York: Dover Publications, 1967.

——. *George Washington. Vol. I, The Forge of Experience, 1732–1775*. Boston: Little, Brown, 1965.

——. *George Washington. Vol. II, In the American Revolution, 1775–1783*. Boston: Little, Brown, 1967.

——. *George Washington. Vol. III, Anguish and Farewell, 1793–1799*. Boston: Little, Brown, 1969.

Fliegelman, Jay. *Declaring Independence*. Stanford, Calif.: Stanford University Press, 1993.

Flower, Milton E. *John Dickinson: Conservative Revolutionary*. Charlottesville: University Press of Virginia, 1983.

Foner, Eric, ed. *Paine: Collected Writings*. New York: Library of America, 1995.

———. *The Story of American Freedom*. New York: Norton, 1998.

———. *Tom Paine and Revolutionary America*. New York: Oxford University Press, 1976.

Ford, Paul, ed. *The Writings of Thomas Jefferson*. Vol. III. New York: Putnam, 1894.

Ford, Worthington Chauncey. *Statesman and Friend: Correspondence of John Adams with Benjamin Waterhouse, 1784–1822*. Boston: Little, Brown, 1927.

———, ed. *Thomas Jefferson and James Thomson Callender, 1798–1802*. Brooklyn: History Print Club, 1897.

Fowler, William M., Jr. *The Baron of Beacon Hill: A Biography of John Hancock*. Boston: Houghton Mifflin, 1980.

———. *Poor Richard's Almanack*. New York: Spencer Press, 1936.

———. *Rebels Under Sail: The American Navy During the Revolution*. New York: Scribner, 1976.

Franklin, John Hope, and Alfred A. Moss, Jr. *From Slavery to Freedom: A History of Negro Americans*. 6th ed. New York: McGraw-Hill, 1988.

Freeman, Douglas Southall. *George Washington: Vol. I–II, Young Washington*. New York: Scribner, 1948.

———. *George Washington. Vol. III, Planter and Patriot*. New York: Scribner, 1948.

———. *George Washington. Vol. IV, Leader of the Revolution*. New York: Scribner, 1951.

———. *George Washington. Vol. V, Victory with the Help of France*. New York: Scribner, 1952.

———. *George Washington. Vol. VI, Patriot and President*. New York: Scribner, 1954.

Friedel, Frank, and William Pencak. *The White House: The First Two Hundred Years*. Boston: Northeastern University Press, 1994.

Fruchtman, Jack, Jr. *Thomas Paine: Apostle of Freedom*. New York: Four Walls Eight Windows, 1994.

Furnishings Plan for the Graff House. Philadelphia: Independence National Historical Park, 1988.

Gaines, William H., Jr. *Thomas Mann Randolph*. Baton Rouge: Louisiana State University Press, 1966.

Gardner, Joseph L., ed. *Thomas Jefferson: A Biography in His Own Words*. The Founding Fathers. New York: Newsweek, 1974.

Gelles, Edith. *Portia: The World of Abigail Adams*. Bloomington: Indiana University Press, 1992.

George, M. Dorothy. *London Life in the Eighteenth Century*. London: Penguin, 1965.

Gianta, Mary A. *The Emerging Nation: A Documentary History of the U.S. under the Articles of Confederation*, Washington, D.C., 1996.

Gibbs, George. *Memoirs of the Administrations of Washington and John Adams. Edited from the Papers of Oliver Wolcott*. New York, 1846.

Goldsmith, William M. *The Growth of Presidential Power: A Documented History*. Vols. I–III. New York: Chelsea House, 1974.

Goodman, Dena. *The Republic of Letters*. Ithaca: Cornell University Press, 1994.

Goodman, Nathan. *Benjamin Rush: Physician and Citizen, 1746–1813*. Philadelphia: University of Pennsylvania Press, 1934.

Gordon-Reed, Annette. *Thomas Jefferson and Sally Hemings: An American Controversy*. Charlottesville: University Press of Virginia, 1997.

Gough, Deborah Matias. *Christ Church, Philadelphia*. Philadelphia: University of Pennsylvania Press, 1995.

Gross, Robert A. *The Minutemen and Their World*. New York: Hill & Wang, 1995.

Hagan, Kenneth J. *This People's Navy*. New York: Free Press, 1991.

Hale, Edward, and Edward Hale, Jr. *Benjamin Franklin in France*. Boston: Roberts Brothers, 1887.

Haliday, F. E. *A Concise History of England: From Stonehenge to the Atomic Age*. New York: Thames & Hudson, 1983.

Handler, Edward. *America and Europe in the Political Thought of John Adams*. Cambridge, Mass.: Harvard University Press, 1964.

Handlin, Oscar, and Lilian Handlin. *A Restless People: Americans in Rebellion, 1770–1787*. Garden City, N.Y.: Doubleday, 1982.

Hanley, Thomas O'Brien. *Revolutionary Statesman: Charles Carroll and the War*. Chicago: Loyola University Press, 1983.

Haraszti, Zoltan. *John Adams and the Prophets of Progress*. Cambridge, Mass.: Harvard University Press, 1952.

Harbert, Earl N., ed. *Henry Adams: History of the United States of America During the Administrations of Thomas Jefferson*. Washington, D.C.: Library of America, 1980.

Harris, John. *Historical Walks in Old Boston*. 3rd ed. Old Saybrook, Conn.: Globe Pequot, 1993.

Hawke, David Freeman. *Benjamin Rush: Revolutionary Gadfly*. Indianapolis: Bobbs-Merrill, 1971.

———. *Everyday Life in Early America*. New York: Harper & Row, 1988.

———. *In the Midst of a Revolution*. Philadelphia: University of Pennsylvania Press, 1961.

———. *Paine*. New York: Harper & Row, 1974.

———. *A Transaction of Free Men: The Birth and Course of the Declaration of Independence*. New York: Da Capo Press, 1964.

Hazelton, John H. *Declaration of Independence: Its History*. New York: Dodd-Mead, 1906.

Hecht, Marie B. *Odd Destiny: The Life of Alexander Hamilton*. New York: Macmillan, 1982.

Hibbert, Christopher. *The Days of the French Revolution*. New York: Morrow Quill, 1981.

———. *George III: A Personal History*. New York: Viking Press, 1998.

———. *Redcoats and Rebels*. New York: Avon, 1990.

Higginbotham, Don. *The War of American Independence: Military Attitudes, Policies, and Practice, 1763–1789*. New York: Macmillan, 1971.

Hobson, Charles F., ed. *The Papers of James Madison.* Vols XII–XIII. Chapel Hill: University of North Carolina Press, 1990.

Hofstadter, Richard. *The American Political Tradition and the Men Who Made It.* New York: Knopf, 1948.

Hopkins, Donald R. *Princes and Peasants: Smallpox in History.* Chicago: University of Chicago Press, 1983.

Howe, John R., Jr. *The Changing Political Thought of John Adams.* Princeton, N.J.: Princeton University Press, 1966.

Hutchinson, William T., ed. *The Papers of James Madison.* Vol. VI. Chapel Hill: University of North Carolina Press, 1990.

Hutson, James H. *John Adams and the Diplomacy of the American Revolution.* Lexington: University Press of Kentucky, 1980.

Huxam, Dr. John. *An Essay on Fever.* 8th ed. Edinburgh: Donaldson, 1779.

Hyams, Edward. *Capability Brown and Humphrey Repton.* New York: Scribner, 1971.

Irwin, Ray W. *The Diplomatic Relations of the United States with the Barbary Powers, 1776–1816.* Chapel Hill: University of North Carolina Press, 1931.

Jackson, Donald. *A Year at Monticello: 1795.* Golden, Colo.: Fulcrum, 1989.

Thomas Jefferson. *The Jefferson Bible.* Boston: Beacon Press, 1989.

Johnson, Nicholas. *Eighteenth-Century London.* London: Museum of London, 1991.

Jordan, Daniel P. *Political Leadership in Jefferson's Virginia.* Charlottesville: University Press of Virginia, 1983.

Jordan, Winthrop. *White over Black.* Chapel Hill: University of North Carolina Press, 1968.

Josephy, Alvin, Jr. *On the Hill: A History of the American Congress.* New York: Simon & Schuster, 1979.

Jouve, Daniel and Alice. *Paris: Birthplace of the U.S.A.* Paris: Gründ, 1995.

Kahn, David. *The Codebreakers.* London: Weidenfeld & Nicholson, 1974.

Kaminski, John P., ed. *Citizen Jefferson: The Wit and Wisdom of an American Sage.* Madison, Wisc.: Madison House Publishing, 1994.

Kammen, Michael. *A Season of Youth.* New York: Knopf, 1978.

Kennedy, Roger. *Burr, Hamilton, and Jefferson.* New York: Oxford University Press, 2000.

Ketcham, Ralph. *James Madison: A Biography.* Charlottesville: University Press of Virginia, 1990.

Ketchum, Richard M. *Decisive Day: The Battle for Bunker Hill.* Garden City, N.Y.: Doubleday, 1974.

———. *The Winter Soldiers.* Garden City, N.Y.: Doubleday, 1973.

Kimball, Marie. *Jefferson: The Road to Glory, 1743–1776.* New York: Coward-McCann, 1943.

———. *Jefferson: The Scene of Europe, 1784–1789.* New York: Coward-McCann, 1950.

———. *Jefferson: War and Peace, 1776–1784.* New York: Coward-McCann, 1947.

King, Dean, et al. *A Sea of Words: A Lexicon and Companion for Patrick O'Brien's Seafaring Tales.* New York: Holt, 1995.

Kline, Mary-Jo, ed. *Alexander Hamilton: A Biography in His Own Words.* The Founding Fathers. New York: Newsweek/Harper & Row, 1973.

Knollenberg, Bernhard. *Growth of the American Revolution, 1766–1775.* New York: Free Press, 1975.

Kramnick, Isaac. *James Madison, Alexander Hamilton, and John Jay: The Federalist Papers.* London: Penguin, 1987.

——, ed. *The Portable Enlightenment Reader.* New York: Penguin, 1995.

Kurtz, Stephen G. *The Presidency of John Adams: The Collapse of Federalism, 1795–1800.* New York: A. S. Barnes, 1961.

Langguth, A. J. *Patriots: The Men Who Started the American Revolution.* New York: Simon & Schuster, 1988.

Langhorne, Elizabeth. *Monticello: A Family Story.* Chapel Hill, N.C.: Algonquin Books of Chapel Hill, 1989.

La Rochefoucauld-Liancourt, François. *Travels in the United States of North America.* Vol. I. London: R. Phillips, 1799.

Laver, James. *The Age of Illusion: Manners and Morals, 1750–1848.* New York: David McKay, 1972.

Leder, Lawrence H., ed. *The Meaning of the American Revolution.* Chicago: Quadrangle Books, 1969.

Leiner, Frederick. *Millions for Defense: The Subscription of Warships, 1798.* Annapolis, Md.: Naval Institute Press, 2000.

Lemay, J. A. Leo, ed. *Benjamin Franklin/Writings.* New York: Library of America, 1987.

Lemay, J. A. Leo, and P. M. Zall, eds. *Autobiography of Benjamin Franklin.* Knoxville: University of Tennessee Press, 1981.

Levin, Phyllis Lee. *Abigail Adams.* New York: St. Martin's, 1987.

Levy, Leonard W. *Freedom of Speech and Press in Early American History: Legacy of Suppression.* New York: Harper Torchbooks, 1963.

——. *Jefferson and Civil Liberties: The Darker Side.* Chicago: Elephant Paperbacks, 1989.

Lewis, Jan Ellen, and Peter S. Onuf, eds. *Sally Hemings and Thomas Jefferson.* Charlottesville: University Press of Virginia, 1999.

Lewis, Paul. *The Grand Incendiary.* New York: Dial Press, 1973.

Lincoln, William. *History of Worcester, Massachusetts.* Worcester, Mass.: Charles Hersey/Henry Howland, 1862.

Lipscomb, Andrew A., ed. *The Writings of Thomas Jefferson.* Washington, D.C.: Jefferson Memorial Association, 1903.

Lloyd, Stephen. *Richard and Maria Cosway: Regency Artists of Taste and Fashion.* Edinburgh: Scottish National Portrait Galleries, 1995.

Lodge, Henry Cabot. *Memorial Address Delivered November 17, 1915. In Charles Francis Adams 1835–1915: An Autobiography.* Boston: Houghton Mifflin, 1916.

Lonsdale, Roger. *The New Oxford Book of Eighteenth Century Verse.* Oxford: Oxford University Press, 1989.

Lopez, Claude-Anne. *Mon Cher Papa: Franklin and the Ladies of Paris.* New Haven, Conn.: Yale University Press, 1966.

Lutnick, Solomon. *The American Revolution and the British Press, 1775–1783.* Columbia: University of Missouri Press, 1967.

Maclay, William. *The Journal of William Maclay.* New York: F. Ungar Publishing Co., 1965.

MacVeagh, Lincoln, ed. *The Journal of Nicholas Cresswell, 1774–1777.* New York: Dial Press, 1924.

Maier, Pauline. *American Scripture: Making the Declaration of Independence.* New York: Knopf, 1997.

Malone, Dumas. *Jefferson and His Time.* Vol. 1, *Jefferson the Virginian.* Boston: Little, Brown, 1948.

———. *Jefferson and His Time.* Vol. II, *Jefferson and the Rights of Man.* Boston: Little, Brown, 1951.

———. *Jefferson and His Time.* Vol. III, *Jefferson and the Ordeal of Liberty.* Boston: Little, Brown, 1962.

———. *Jefferson and His Time.* Vol. IV, *Jefferson the President: First Term, 1801–1805.* Boston: Little, Brown, 1970.

———. *Jefferson and His Time.* Vol. V, *Jefferson the President: Second Term, 1805–1809.* Boston: Little, Brown, 1974.

———. *Jefferson and His Time.* Vol. VI, *The Sage of Monticello.* Boston: Little, Brown, 1970.

———. *Thomas Jefferson: A Brief Biography.* Woodlawn, Md.: Wolk Press, 1933.

Marsh, Philip M. *Philip Freneau: Poet and Journalist.* Minneapolis: Dillon Press, 1967.

Martin, Wendy, ed. *Colonial American Travel Narratives.* New York: Penguin, 1994.

Mason, Joseph, ed. *The Papers of James Madison.* Charlottesville: University Press of Virginia, 1985.

Massachusetts: A Guide to Its Places and People. American Guide Series. Boston: Houghton Mifflin, 1937.

Massachusetts Historical Society. *The Metropolis of New England: Colonial Boston, 1630–1776.* Boston, 1976.

———. *A Pride of Quincys.* Boston, 1969.

———. *Some Early Massachusetts Broadsides.* Boston, 1964.

———. *Thomas Hutchinson and His Contemporaries.* Boston, 1974.

———. *The War of 1812.* Boston, 1962.

———. *Warren-Adams Letters.* Vol. II, 1925.

Mattern, David B., ed. *The Papers of James Madison.* Vol. XVII. Charlottesville: University Press of Virginia, 1991.

Matthews, Richard K. *The Radical Politics of Thomas Jefferson: A Revisionist View.* Lawrence: University Press of Kansas, 1984.

Mayo, Bernard, ed. *Jefferson Himself.* Charlottesville: University Press of Virginia, 1942.

McDonald, Forest. *The Presidency of George Washington*. Lawrence: University Press of Kansas, 1974.

——. *The Presidency of Thomas Jefferson*. Lawrence: University Press of Kansas, 1976.

McEwan, Barbara. *Thomas Jefferson: Farmer*. Jefferson, N.C.: McFarland & Co., 1991.

McLaughlin, Jack. *Jefferson and Monticello*. New York: Holt, 1988.

McNeill, William H. *Plagues and Peoples*. New York: Anchor Books/Doubleday, 1976.

Mead, William Edward. *The Grand Tour in the Eighteenth Century*. Boston: Houghton Mifflin, 1914.

Middlekauf, Robert. *Benjamin Franklin and His Enemies*. Berkeley: University of California Press, 1996.

——. *The Glorious Cause: The American Revolution, 1763–1789*. New York: Oxford University Press, 1982.

Miller, John C. *Alexander Hamilton: Portrait in Paradox*. New York: Harper & Brothers, 1959.

——. *Crisis in Freedom: The Alien and Sedition Acts*. Boston: Little, Brown, 1951.

——. *The Wolf by the Ears: Thomas Jefferson and Slavery*. Charlottesville: University Press of Virginia, 1991.

Miller, Lillian, ed. *The Selected Papers of Charles Willson Peale and His Family*. Vol. 1. New Haven, Conn.: Yale University Press, 1983.

Miller, Perry. *The New England Mind in the Seventeenth Century*. Cambridge, Mass.: Harvard University Press, 1939.

Mitchell, Broadus. *Alexander Hamilton*. *Vol. I, Youth to Maturity*. New York: Macmillan, 1957.

——. *Alexander Hamilton*. *Vol. II, The National Adventure*. New York: Macmillan, 1962.

Mitchell, Stewart, ed. *New Letters of Abigail Adams, 1788–1801*. Boston: Houghton Mifflin, 1947.

Mollo, John. *Uniforms of the American Revolution in Color*. New York: Macmillan, 1975.

Montross, Lynn. *The Reluctant Rebels: The Story of the Continental Congress, 1774–1789*. New York: Barnes & Noble, 1950.

Morgan, Edmund S. *The Birth of the Republic, 1763–1789*. Chicago: University of Chicago Press, 1992.

——. *The Meaning of Independence*. New York: Norton, 1976.

——. *The Puritan Family*. New York: Harper Torch Books, 1966.

Morison, Samuel Eliot. *John Paul Jones: A Sailor's Biography*. Boston: Little, Brown, 1959.

——. *Those Misunderstood Puritans*. North Brookfield, Mass.: Sun Hill Press, 1931.

——. *Three Centuries of Harvard, 1636–1936*. Cambridge, Mass.: Harvard University Press, 1946.

Morris, James McGrath, and Persephone Weene, eds. *Thomas Jefferson's European Travel Diaries*. Ithaca, N.Y.: Isodore Stephanus Sons, 1987.

Morris, Richard B. *The Forging of the Union, 1781–1789*. New York: Harper & Row, 1987.

———. *The Peacemakers: The Great Powers and American Independence*. New York: Harper & Row, 1965.

———. *Seven Who Shaped Our Destiny*. New York: Harper & Row, 1973.

———, ed. *John Jay: The Making of a Revolutionary*. New York: Harper & Row, 1975.

Murphy, Orville T. *Charles Gravier, Comte de Vergennes*. Albany: State University of New York Press, 1982.

Nagel, Paul C. *The Adams Women: Abigail and Louisa Adams, Their Sisters and Daughters*. New York: Oxford University Press, 1987.

———. *John Quincy Adams: A Public Life, A Private Life*. New York: Knopf, 1997.

Nash, Gary B. *Race and Revolution*. Madison, Wis.: Madison House, 1990.

Nevins, Allan, ed. *The American States During and After the Revolution, 1775–1789*. New York: Macmillan, 1924.

———. *The Diary of John Quincy Adams, 1794–1845*. New York: Scribner, 1951.

Nichols, Frederick Doveton. *Thomas Jefferson's Architectural Drawings*. Charlottesville: Thomas Jefferson Memorial Foundation, 1995.

Nordholt, J. W. Schulte. *The Dutch Republic and American Independence*. Chapel Hill: University of North Carolina Press, 1982.

———. *Till I Knew John Adams*. Holland: Esso Companies, 1982.

Norton, Mary Beth. *Liberty's Daughters*. Boston: Little, Brown, 1980.

Oberg, Barbara B., ed. *The Papers of Benjamin Franklin*. New Haven, Conn.: Yale University Press, 1997.

O'Brien, Conor Cruise. *The Long Affair*. Chicago: University of Chicago Press, 1996.

O'Connor, Thomas H. *Bibles, Brahmins, and Bosses: A Short History of Boston*. Boston: Boston Trustees of the Public Library, 1991.

Old Family Letters Copied from the Originals for Alexander Biddle. Philadelphia: Lippincott, 1892.

Onuf, Peter, ed. *Jefferson Legacies*. Charlottesville: University Press of Virginia, 1993.

Osborne, Angela. *Abigail Adams*. New York: Chelsea House, 1989.

Ousterhout, Anne M. *A State Divided*. New York: Greenwood Press, 1987.

Owen, John. *Travels into Different Parts of Europe in the Years 1791–1792*. London: Cadell, 1796.

Padelford, Philip, ed. *Colonial Panorama: Dr. Robert Honyman's Journal for March and April*. San Marino, Calif.: Huntington Library, 1939.

Padover, Saul K. *A Jefferson Profile*. New York: John Day, 1956.

———. *Thomas Jefferson and the National Capital*. Washington, D.C.: Government Printing Office, 1946.

Paine, Thomas. *Rights of Man; and, Common Sense*. New York: Knopf, 1994.

Palmer, Michael A. *Stoddert's War*. Columbia: University of South Carolina Press, 1987.

Peabody, James Bishop, ed. *John Adams: A Biography in His Own Words*. The Founding Fathers. New York: Newsweek, 1973.

Peden, William, ed. *Thomas Jefferson: Notes on the State of Virginia*. New York: Norton, 1982.

Peterson, Merrill D. *Adams and Jefferson: A Revolutionary Dialogue*. Oxford: Oxford University Press, 1976.

——. *The Jefferson Image in the American Mind*. New York: Oxford University Press, 1960.

——. *Jefferson's Writings*. Washington, D.C.: Library of America, 1984.

——. *Thomas Jefferson and the New Nation*. London: Oxford University Press, 1970.

——, ed. *James Madison: A Biography in His Own Words*. The Founding Fathers. New York: Newsweek/Harper & Row, 1974.

——, ed. *The Political Writings of Thomas Jefferson*. Woodlawn, Md.: Wolk Press, 1993.

——, ed. *The Portable Thomas Jefferson*. New York: Penguin, 1983.

——, ed. *Visitors to Monticello*. Charlottesville: University Press of Virginia, 1989.

Pickering, Timothy. *A Review of the Correspondence Between John Adams and William Cunningham*. Salem, Mass.: Cushing & Appleton, 1824.

Pierce, Benjamin. *A History of Harvard University*. Cambridge, Mass., 1833.

Phillips, James Duncan. *Salem in the Eighteenth Century*. Boston: Houghton Mifflin, 1937.

Plumb, J. H. *England in the Eighteenth Century*. New York: Penguin, 1983.

Porter, Roy. *English Society in the Eighteenth Century*. New York: Penguin, 1990.

——. *London: A Social History*. London: Penguin, 1994.

Pottle, Frederick A., ed. *Boswell in Holland, 1763–1764*. New York: McGraw-Hill, 1952.

——. *Boswell's London Journal, 1762–1763*. New York: McGraw-Hill, 1950.

Potts, Louis. *Arthur Lee: A Virtuous Revolutionary*. Baton Rouge: Louisiana State University Press, 1981.

Powell, J. M. *Bring Out Your Dead*. Philadelphia: University of Pennsylvania Press, 1993.

Prince, Munro. *Preserving the Monarchy*. Cambridge: Cambridge University Press, 1995.

Quincy, Edmund. Life of *Josiah Quincy*, 6th ed. Boston: Little, Brown, 1874.

Quincy, Josiah. *Figures of the Past*. Boston: Little, Brown, 1819.

Radcliffe, Ann. *A Journey Made in the Summer of 1794 Through Holland and the Western Frontier of Germany*. London: G. G. & J. Robinson, 1794.

Randall, Henry S. *The Life of Thomas Jefferson*. Vols. I–III. New York: Derby & Jackson, 1858.

Randall, Willard Sterne. *Thomas Jefferson: A Life*. New York: Holt, 1993.

Randolph, Sarah N. *The Domestic Life of Thomas Jefferson*. Charlottesville: University Press of Virginia, 1978.

Reardon, John J. *Edmund Randolph: A Biography*. New York: Macmillan, 1974.

Reborg, Carrie, et al. *John Singleton Copley in America*. New York: Abrams, 1995.

Redman, Ben Ray, ed. *The Portable Voltaire*. New York: Penguin, 1977.

Ribeiro, Aileen. *The Art of Dress: Fashion in England and France, 1750–1820*. New Haven, Conn.: Yale University Press, 1995.

Rice, Howard C., Jr. *The Adams Family in Auteuil, 1784–1785: As Told in the Letters of Abigail Adams*. Boston: Massachusetts Historical Society, 1956.

———. *Thomas Jefferson's Paris*. Princeton, N.J.: Princeton University Press, 1976.

Richardson, Edgar P., Brooke Hindel, and Lillian B. Miller. *Charles Willson Peale and His World*. New York: Abrams, 1982.

Richardson, Samuel. *Clarissa*. London: Penguin, 1985.

Ritcheson, Charles R. *Aftermath of Revolution: British Policy Towards the United States, 1783–1795*. New York: Norton, 1969.

Roberts, Kenneth, and Anna M. Roberts, eds. *Moreau de St.-Méry's American Journal, 1793–1798*. Garden City, N.Y.: Doubleday, 1947.

Robinson, John Martin. *Temples of Delight*. London: National Trust/Pitkin, 1990.

Roof, Katherine Metcalf. *Colonel William Smith and His Lady*. Boston: Houghton Mifflin, 1929.

Rosenfeld, Richard N. *American Aurora*. New York: St. Martin's, 1997.

Rutland, Robert A. *The Papers of James Madison*. vols. 8–11, 14. Chicago: University of Chicago Press, 1977.

St. John de Crèvecoeur, J. Hector. *Letters from an American Farmer and Sketches of Eighteenth-Century America*. New York: Penguin, 1981.

Sanders, Frederick K. *John Adams Speaking: Pound's Sources for the Adams Cantos*. Orono: University of Maine Press, 1975.

Sandoz, Ellis, ed. *Political Sermons of the American Founding Era*. Indianapolis: Liberty Fund, 1991.

Sanford, Douglas Walker. "The Archaeology of Plantation Slavery at Thomas Jefferson's Monticello: Context and Process in an American Slave Society." Ph.D. diss. University of Virginia, 1995.

Schama, Simon. *Citizens: A Chronicle of the French Revolution*. New York: Knopf, 1989.

———. *The Embarrassment of Riches*. New York: Vintage, 1987.

Scheer, George F., and Hugh F. Rankin. *Rebels and Redcoats*. New York: Da Capo Press, 1957.

Schoenbrun, David. *Triumph in Paris: The Exploits of Benjamin Franklin*. New York: Harper & Row, 1976.

Schutz, John A., and Douglass Adair, eds. *The Spur of Fame: Dialogues of John Adams and Benjamin Rush, 1805–1913*. San Marino, Calif.: Huntington Library, 1966.

Seale, William. *The President's House*. Vols. I–II. Washington, D.C.: White House Historical Association, 1986.

Selby, John E. *The Revolution in Virginia, 1775–1783*. Williamsburg, Va.: Colonial Williamsburg Foundation, 1988.

Selection of Eulogies, Pronounced in the Several States in Honor of Those Illustrious Patriots and Statesmen, John Adams and Thomas Jefferson. Hartford, Conn.: D. F. Robinson, 1826.

Shackelford, George Green. *Thomas Jefferson's Travels in Europe, 1784–1789*. Baltimore: Johns Hopkins University Press, 1995.

Sharp, James Roger. *American Politics in the Early Republic: The New Nation in Crisis*. New Haven, Conn.: Yale University Press, 1993.

Shaw, Peter. *The Character of John Adams*. New York: Norton, 1976.

Shephard, Jack. *The Adams Chronicles: Four Generations of Greatness*. Boston: Little, Brown, 1976.

Sheppard, John H. *The Life of Samuel Tucker*. Boston: Alfred Mudge & Son, 1868.

Shipton, Clifford K. *New England Life in the Eighteenth Century*. Cambridge, Mass.: Belknap Press of Harvard University Press, 1995.

———. *Sibley's Harvard Graduates: Biographical Sketches of Those Who Attended Harvard College*. Boston: Massachusetts Historical Society, 1965.

Shuffelton, Frank. *Thomas Jefferson: A Comprehensive, Annotated Bibliography of Writings About Him (1826–1980)*. New York: Garland Publishing Co., 1983.

———. *Thomas Jefferson, 1981–1990: An Annotated Bibliography*. New York: Garland Publishing Co., 1992.

Shurkin, Joel N. *The Invisible Fire*. New York: Putnam, 1979.

Shy, John. *A People Numerous and Armed: Reflections on the Military Struggle for American Independence*. Ann Arbor: University of Michigan Press, 1990.

Sloan, Herbert E. *Principle and Interest: Thomas Jefferson and the Problem of Debt*. New York: Oxford University Press, 1995.

Smith, Abigail Adams. *Journal and Correspondence of Miss Adams*. New York: Wiley & Putnam, 1841.

Smith, Billy, ed. *Life in Early Philadelphia*. University Park: Pennsylvania State University Press, 1995.

Smith, James Morton. *Freedom's Fetters: The Alien and Sedition Laws and American Civil Liberties*. Ithaca, N.Y.: Cornell University Press, 1956.

———, ed. *The Republic of Letters: Correspondence Between Thomas Jefferson and James Madison, 1776–1826*. Vols. I–III. New York: Norton, 1995.

Smith, Jean Edward. *John Marshall: Definer of a Nation*. New York: Holt, 1996.

Smith, Page. *John Adams*. Vols. I–II. Garden City, N.Y.: Doubleday, 1962.

———. *The New Age Now Begins: A People's History of the American Revolution*. Vol. I. New York: Penguin, 1976.

———. *The Shaping of America*. New York: McGraw-Hill, 1980.

Smith, Paul H., ed. *Letters of Delegates to Congress, 1774–1789*. Vols. I–VIII. Washington, D.C.: Library of Congress, 1976–81.

———. *Time and Temperature: Philadelphia, July 4, 1776*. Washington, D.C.: Library of Congress, 1977.

Smith, Peter. *The Diary of William Bently*. Vols. I–IV. Salem, Mass.: Essex Institute, 1962.

Smith, Philip Chadwick Foster. *Captain Samuel Tucker*. Salem, Mass.: Essex Institute, 1976.

———. *Philadelphia on the River*. Philadelphia: Philadelphia Maritime Museum, 1986.

Smith, Richard Norton. *Patriarch*. Boston: Houghton Mifflin, 1993.

Smollett, Tobias. *The Expedition of Humphrey Clinker*. Oxford: Oxford University Press, 1984.

———. *Roderick Random*. London: Penguin, 1995.

Smyth, Albert Henry, ed. *The Writings of Benjamin Franklin*. London: Macmillan, 1907.

Snyder, Martin P. *City of Independence*. New York: Praeger, 1975.

Sobel, Mechal. *The World They Made Together*. Princeton, N.J.: Princeton University Press, 1987.

Stagg, J. C. A., ed. *The Papers of James Madison*. Charlottesville: University Press of Virginia, 1989.

Stanton, Lucia. *Slavery at Monticello*. Richmond, Va.: Spencer, 1993.

Stein, Susan R. *The Worlds of Thomas Jefferson at Monticello*. New York: Abrams, 1993.

Steiner, Bernard C. *The Life and Correspondence of James McHenry*. Cleveland: Burrows Bros., 1907.

Sterne, Laurence. *A Sentimental Journey*. London: Penguin, 1986.

Stevens, Sylvester. *Birthplace of a Nation*. New York: Random House, 1964.

Stinchcombe, William C. *The American Revolution and the French Alliance*. Syracuse, N.Y.: Syracuse University Press, 1969.

———. *The XYZ Affair*. Westport, Conn.: Greenwood Press, 1980.

Stowe Landscape Gardens. London: National Trust, 1997.

Strickland, Thomas, M.D. *Hunter's Tropical Medicine*. 7th ed. Philadelphia: W. B. Saunders Co., 1991.

Stroud, Dorothy. *Capability Brown*. London: Country Life, 1950.

Summerson, John. *The Architecture of the Eighteenth Century*. New York: Thames & Hudson, 1994.

Symonds, Craig. *A Battlefield Atlas of the American Revolution*. Baltimore: Nautical & Aviation Publication Co. of America, 1986.

Syrett, Harold C., ed. *Papers of Alexander Hamilton*. Vols. XXI–XXVII. New York: Columbia University Press, 1974.

Szatmary, David P. *Shay's Rebellion*. Amherst: University of Massachusetts Press, 1980.

Tames, Richard. *American Walks in London*. New York: Interlink Books, 1997.

Tanselle, G. Thomas. *Royall Tyler*. Cambridge, Mass.: Harvard University Press, 1967.

Tatum, Edward H., Jr., ed. *The American Journal of Ambrose Serle*. San Marino, Calif.: Huntington Library, 1940.

Taylor, Patrick. *The Daily Telegraph Gardener's Guide to Britain*. London: Pavilion Books, 1996.

Taylor, Robert J., ed. *Diary of John Quincy Adams*. Vols. I–II. Cambridge, Mass.: Belknap Press of Harvard University Press, 1981.

———. *Papers of John Adams*. Vols. I–X. Cambridge, Mass.: Belknap Press of Harvard University Press, 1983.

Thacker, Christopher. *The Genius of Gardening: A History of Gardens in Britain and Ireland.* London: Weidenfeld & Nicolson, 1994.

Thompson, C. Bradley. *John Adams and the Spirit of Liberty.* Lawrence: University Press of Kansas, 1998.

Trevelyan, G. M. *English Social History.* London: Penguin, 1986.

Tuchman, Barbara. *The First Salute.* New York: Knopf, 1988.

Tucker, Glenn. *Dawn Like Thunder: The Barbary Wars and the Birth of the U.S. Navy.* Indianapolis: Bobbs-Merrill, 1963.

Turner, Roger. *Capability Brown and the Eighteenth-Century English Landscape.* New York: Rizzoli, 1985.

Twining, Thomas. *Travels in America a Hundred Years Ago.* New York: Harper Bros., 1894.

Two-Hundredth Anniversary of Boston Light, September 25, 1916. Washington, D.C.: Government Printing Office, 1916.

Tyler, Royall. *The Contrast.* New York: AMS Press, 1970.

Unger, Harlow Giles. *The Life and Times of Noah Webster: An American Patriot.* New York: Wiley, 1998.

Van Doren, Carl. *Benjamin Franklin.* New York: Viking Press, 1938.

———. *Secret History of the American Revolution.* Garden City, N.Y.: Garden City Publishing Co., 1941.

Walters, Raymond, Jr. *Albert Gallatin: Jeffersonian Financier and Diplomat.* New York: Macmillan, 1957.

Walther, Daniel. *Gouverneur Morris: Witness of Two Revolutions.* New York: Funk & Wagnalls, 1970.

Ward, Christopher. *The War of the Revolution.* Vols. I–II. New York: Macmillan, 1952.

Waring, George E., Jr. *Report on the Social Statistics of Cities.* Washington, D.C.: Government Printing Office, 1887.

Warren, Mercy Otis. *History of the Rise, Progress, and Termination of the American Revolution.* Vols. I–II. Edited by Lester H. Cohen. Indianapolis: Liberty Foundation, 1989.

Watson, Elkanah. *Tour in Holland in MDCCLXXXIV.* Worcester, Mass.: Isaiah Thomas, 1790.

Watson, Winslow. *Men and Times of the Revolution.* New York: Dana & Co., 1856.

Weigley, Russell F., ed. *Philadelphia: A 300 Year History.* New York: Norton, 1982.

Wernsdorfer, Walter H., and Sir Ian McGregor, C.B.E., eds. *Malaria: Principles and Practice of Malariology.* Edinburgh: Churchill Livingstone, 1988.

Weston, George F., Jr. *Boston Ways.* Boston: Beacon Press, 1974.

Wharton, Francis, ed. *The Revolutionary Diplomatic Correspondence of the United States.* Washington, D.C.: Government Printing Office, 1889.

Whitney, The Rev. Peter. *A Sermon Delivered on the Lord's Day Succeeding the Interment of Madam Abigail Adams.* Boston: 1819.

Wieder, Lois. *A Pleasant Land—A Goodly Heritage: First Church of Christ in Wethersfield, Connecticut, 1635-1985.* Wethersfield, Conn.: The Church, 1986.

Wills, Garry. *Cincinnatus: George Washington and the Enlightenment.* Garden City, N.Y.: Doubleday, 1984.

———. *Inventing America.* Garden City, N.Y.: Doubleday, 1978.

Wilson, L. Douglas, ed. *Jefferson's Books.* Lynchburg, Va.: Progress Printing, 1986.

———. *Jefferson's Literary Commonplace Book.* Princeton, N.J.: Princeton University Press, 1989.

Withey, Lynne. *Dearest Friend: A Life of Abigail Adams.* New York: Free Press, 1981.

Wolf, Stephanie Grauman. *As Various as Their Land.* New York: HarperCollins, 1993.

Wood, Gordon S. *The Creation of the American Republic, 1776–1787.* Chapel Hill: University of North Carolina Press, 1969.

———. *The Radicalism of the American Revolution.* New York: Knopf, 1992.

Wright, Conrad Edick, ed. *Massachusetts and the New Nation.* Boston: Massachusetts Historical Society, 1992.

Wright, Esmond. *Fabric of Freedom, 1763–1800.* New York: Hill & Wang, 1978.

———. *Franklin of Philadelphia.* Cambridge, Mass.: Harvard University Press, 1986.

Wroth, L. Kinvin, and Hiller B. Zobel, eds. *Legal Papers of John Adams.* Cambridge, Mass.: Harvard University Press, 1965.

Young, James Sterling. *The Washington Community, 1800–1828.* New York: Columbia University Press, 1966.

Zerbe, Jerome, and Cyril Connolly. *Les Pavillons: French Pavilions of the Eighteenth Century.* New York: Norton, 1979.

Ziegler, Philip, and Desmond Seward, eds. *Brooks's: A Social History.* London: Constable, 1991.

Zobel, Hiller B. *The Boston Massacre.* New York: Norton, 1970.

ARTICLES

Anderson, William G. "John Adams: The Navy and the Quasi-War with France." *American Neptune* XXX, no. 2 (April 1970).

Appleby, Joyce. "The New Republican Synthesis and the Changed Political Ideas of John Adams." *American Quarterly* XXV, no. 5 (Dec. 1973).

Bailyn, Bernard. "Butterfield's Adams: Notes for a Sketch." *William and Mary Quarterly* XIX, no. 2 (April, 1962).

Balinky, Alexander S. "Gallatin's Theory of War Finance." *William and Mary Quarterly* XVI, 3rd series, no. 1 (Jan. 1959).

Bowling, Kenneth R. "Dinner at Jefferson's: A Note on Jacob Cooke's 'The Compromise of 1790.'" *William and Mary Quarterly* XXVIII, 3rd series, no. 4 (Oct. 1971).

Boyd, Julian P. "Silas Deane: Death by a Kindly Teacher of Treason?" *William and Mary Quarterly* XVI, 3rd series (April 1959).

Brown, Richard D. "Shay's Rebellion and Its Aftermath: A View from Springfield, Massachusetts 1787." *William and Mary Quarterly* XI, 3rd series, no. 4 (Oct. 1983).

Bruchey, Stuart. "Alexander Hamilton and the State Banks." *William and Mary Quarterly* XXVII, 3rd series, no. 3 (July 1970).

Calkins, Carlos G. "The American Navy and the Opinions of One of Its Founders: John Adams, 1735–1826." *U.S. Naval Institute* XXXVII, no. 2 (June 1911): 457.

Charles, Joseph. "Adams and Jefferson: The Origins of the American Party System." *William and Mary Quarterly* XII, 3rd series, no. 3 (July 1955).

———. "Hamilton and Washington: The Origins of the American Party System." *William and Mary Quarterly* XII, 3rd series, no. 2 (April 1955).

———. "The Jay Treaty." *William and Mary Quarterly* XII, 3rd series, no. 4 (Oct. 1955).

"Diary of James Allen, Esq., of Philadelphia." *Pennsylvania Magazine of History and Biography* IX (1885).

"Dr. Solomon Drowne." *Pennsylvania Magazine of History and Biography* 48 (1924).

"Extracts from the Diary of Dr. James Clitherall, 1776." *Pennsylvania Magazine of History and Biography* 22 (1898).

Farrell, James M. "John Adams's *Autobiography:* The Ciceroian Paradigm and the Quest for Fame." *New England Quarterly* LXII, no. 4 (Dec. 1989).

Ferling, John, and Lewis E. Braverman. "John Adams: Diplomat." *William and Mary Quarterly* LI, 3rd series, no. 2 (April 1994).

———. "John Adams's Health Reconsidered." *William and Mary Quarterly* LV, 3rd series, no. 1 (Jan. 1998).

Foster, Eugene A., et al. "Jefferson Fathered Slave's Last Child." *Nature*, Nov. 5, 1998.

Gelles, Edith. "Abigail Adams: Domesticity and the American Revolution." *New England Quarterly* LII, no. 4 (Dec. 1979).

———. "The Abigail Industry." *William and Mary Quarterly* XIL, 3rd series, no. 4 (Oct. 1988).

———. "A Virtuous Affair: The Correspondence Between Abigail Adams and James Lovell." *American Quarterly* XXXIX (Summer 1987).

Gummere, Richard M. "The Classical Politics of John Adams." *Boston Public Library Quarterly*, Oct. 1957.

Heinlein, Jay C. "Albert Gallatin: A Pioneer in Public Administration." *William and Mary Quarterly* VII, 3rd series, no. 1 (Jan. 1950).

Henderson, H. James. "Congressional Factionalism and the Attempt to Recall Benjamin Franklin." *William and Mary Quarterly* XXVII, 3rd series, no. 2 (April 1970).

Hutson, James H. "John Adams's Title Campaign." *New England Quarterly* XLI, no. 1 (March 1968).

———. "Letters from a Distinguished American: The American Revolution in Foreign Newspapers." *Quarterly Journal of the Library of Congress* XXXIV, no. 4 (Oct. 1977).

Klingelhofer, Herbert E. "Matthew Ridley's Diary During the Peace Negotiations of 1782." *William and Mary Quarterly* XX, 3rd series, no. 1 (Jan. 1963).

Kurtz, Stephen G. "The French Mission of 1799–1800: Concluding Chapter in the Statecraft of John Adams." *Political Science Quarterly* LXXX (Dec. 1965).

Larson, Harold. "Alexander Hamilton: The Fact and Fiction of His Early Years." *William and Mary Quarterly* IX, 3rd series, no. 2 (April 1952).

Lerche, Charles O., Jr. "Jefferson and the Election of 1800: A Case Study in the Political Smear." *William and Mary Quarterly* V, 3rd series, no. 4 (Oct. 1948).

Lewis, Anthony M. "Jefferson's *Summary View* as a Chart of Political Union." *William and Mary Quarterly* V, 3rd series, no. 1 (Jan. 1948).

Meschutt, David. "The Adams-Jefferson Portrait Exchange." *American Art Journal* XIV, no. 2 (Spring 1982).

Morison, Samuel Eliot. "Elbridge Gerry: Gentleman-Democrat." *New England Quarterly* II (Jan. 1929).

Nash, Gary B. "Slaves and Slaveowners in Colonial Philadelphia." *William and Mary Quarterly* XXX, no. 2 (April 1973).

Perkins, Bradford. "A Diplomat's Wife in Philadelphia: Letters of Henrietta Liston, 1796–1800." *William and Mary Quarterly* XI, 3rd series, no. 4 (Oct. 1954).

Prelinger, Catherine M. "Benjamin Franklin and the American Prisoners of War in England During the American Revolution." *William and Mary Quarterly* XXXII, 3rd series, no. 2 (April 1975).

"Report on Thomas Jefferson and Sally Hemings." Thomas Jefferson Memorial Foundation, January 2000.

Risjord, Norman K. "The Compromise of 1790: New Evidence on the Dinner Table Bargain." *William and Mary Quarterly* XXXIII, 3rd series, no. 2 (April 1976).

Ritcheson, Charles R. "The Fragile Memory: Thomas Jefferson at the Court of George III." *Eighteenth-Century Life* VI (Jan. and May 1981).

Schachner, Nathan. "Alexander Hamilton Viewed by His Friends: The Narratives of Robert Troop and Hercules Mulligan." *William and Mary Quarterly* IV, 3rd series, no. 2 (April 1947).

Seed, Geoffrey. "A British Spy in Philadelphia, 1775–1777. *Pennsylvania Magazine of History and Biography* LXXXV (January 1961).

Stinchcombe, William. "The Diplomacy of the WXYZ Affair." *William and Mary Quarterly* XXXIV, 3rd series, no. 4 (Oct. 1977).

Tolle, Frederick B. "Franklin and the Pulteney Mission: An Episode in the Secret History of the American Revolution." *Huntington Library Quarterly*, Nov. 1953.

Turner, Kathryn. "The Appointment of Chief Justice John Marshall." *William and Mary Quarterly* XVII, 3rd series, no. 2 (April 1960).

Wilson, Douglas L. "Thomas Jefferson and the Character Issue." *Atlantic* 27, no. 5 (November 1992).

———. "Thomas Jefferson's Early Notebooks." *William and Mary Quarterly* XLII, 3rd series, no. 4 (Oct. 1985).

REFERENCE SOURCES

American Guide Series: Massachusetts: A Guide to Its Places and People. Boston: Houghton Mifflin, 1937.

Baedeker's France. Englewood Cliffs, N.J.: Prentice Hall, 1986.

Boatner, Mark Mayo, III. *Encyclopedia of the American Revolution.* New York: David McKay, 1966.

Branyon, Richard A. *Latin Phrases and Quotations*. New York: Hippocrene Books, 1994.

Byrd, Robert C. *The Senate, 1789–1989: Historical Statistics, 1789–1992*. Vol. 4. Washington, D.C.: Government Printing Office, 1993.

Commager, Henry Steele. *Documents of American History*. 5th ed. New York: Appleton-Century-Crofts, 1949.

Dictionary of American Biography. New York: Scribner, 1932.

France: Eyewitness Travel Guides. London: Dorling Kindersley, 1994.

Harley, Sharon. *Timetables of African-American History*. New York: Touchstone, 1995.

Kennedy, Lawrence F. *Biographical Directory of the American Congress 1774–1971*. Washington, D.C.: Government Printing Office, 1971.

London Michelin Guide. 1st ed. London, 1977.

Morison, Samuel Eliot; Henry Steele Commager; and William Leuchtenburg, eds. *A Concise History of the American Republic*. New York: Oxford University Press, 1977.

The Negro Almanac: A Reference Work on the African American. 5th ed. Edited by Harry A. Ploski and James Williams. New York: Gale Research, 1989.

Olmert, Michael. *Official Guide to Colonial Williamsburg*. Williamsburg, Va.: Colonial Williamsburg Foundation, 1985.

Paris Michelin Guide. 6th ed. London, 1986.

Purvis, Thomas L. *Almanacs of American Life: Revolutionary America, 1763–1800*. New York: Facts on File, 1995.

Scott, Samuel F., and Barry Rothaus, eds. *Historical Dictionary of the French Revolution, 1789–1799*. Westport, Conn.: Greenwood Press, 1985.

Weinreb, Ben, and Christopher Hibbert, eds. *The London Encyclopedia*. London: Macmillan, 1993.

Wren, R. C. *Potter's New Cyclopaedia of Botanical Drugs and Preparations*. Holsworthy, England: Health Science Press, 1975.

NEWSPAPERS AND JOURNALS

Amherst (Massachusetts) *Farmers' Cabinet*
Boston Evening Post
Boston Gazette
Boston Independent Chronicle
Charleston (South Carolina) *City Gazette and Daily Advertiser*
Claypoole's America Daily Advertiser (Philadelphia, Pennsylvania)
Columbian Centinel (Boston, Massachusetts)
Dunlap's Pennsylvania Packet and General Advertiser
Gazette of the United States (Philadelphia)
Gentleman's Magazine (London, England)
Haverhill (Massachusetts) *Gazette and Essex Patriot*
Le Journal des Scavans (Paris, France)

London Chronicle

London Gazette

London General Evening Post

London Public Advertiser

Massachusetts Centinel (Boston)

Massachusetts Spy (Worcester)

New England Palladium

New York Commercial Advertiser

New York Daily Advertiser

New York Evening Post

Newburyport (Massachusetts) *Herald*

Pennsylvania Evening Post (Philadelphia)

Philadelphia Aurora

Philadelphia General Advertiser

Philadelphia Journal

Philadelphia Ledger

Porcupine's Gazette and United States Daily Advertiser

Savannah (Georgia) *Republican*

St. James's Chronicle (London, England)

Vermont Gazette (Bennington)

Virginia Gazette (Williamsburg)

Washington (D.C.) *Federalist*

Washington (D.C.) *Gazette*

Washington (D.C.) *National Intelligencer*

Index